UNIVERSITY COLLEGE
Brescia

THE DAWN OF CANADA'S CENTURY

THE DAWN OF CANADA'S CENTURY

Hidden Histories

Edited by Gordon Darroch

McGill-Queen's University Press
Montreal & Kingston | London | Ithaca

ISBN 978-0-7735-4252-5 (cloth)
ISBN 978-0-7735-8939-1 (ePUB)
ISBN 978-0-7735-8940-7 (ePDF)

Legal deposit first quarter 2014
Bibliothèque nationale du Québec

Printed in Canada on acid-free paper that is 100% ancient forest free (100% post-consumer recycled), processed chlorine free

McGill-Queen's University Press acknowledges the support of the Canada Council for the Arts for our publishing program. We also acknowledge the financial support of the Government of Canada through the Canada Book Fund for our publishing activities.

LIBRARY AND ARCHIVES CANADA CATALOGUING IN PUBLICATION

The dawn of Canada's century : hidden histories / edited by Gordon Darroch.

Includes bibliographical references and index.
Issued in print and electronic formats.
ISBN 978-0-7735-4252-5 (bound). –
ISBN 978-0-7735-8939-1 (ePDF) –
ISBN 978-0-7735-8940-7 (ePUB)

1. Canada – Census, 1911. 2. Canada – History – 1867–1914.
3. Canada – Social conditions – 1867–1918 – Statistics.
4. Canada – Economic conditions – 1867–1918 – Statistics.
I. Darroch, Gordon, editor of compilation

FC550.D39 2014 971.05'6 C2013-906826-0
C2013-906827-9

Set in 10/13 Warnock Pro with Futura
Book design & typesetting by Garet Markvoort, zijn digital

CONTENTS

PART V · MARKETS AND MOBILITY: CLASS, ETHNICITY, GENDER

TABLES

FIGURES

ACKNOWLEDGMENTS

This book is the first based on the *Canadian Century Research Infrastructure* (CCRI). The CCRI is one of the most ambitious interuniversity projects ever undertaken in the humanities and social sciences in Canada, providing an unparalleled series of national, historical microdata for current and future researchers. Most of the authors of the following chapters are my academic colleagues in the project. They are Peter Baskerville, Claude Bellevance, Sean Cadigan, Chad Gaffield, Adam Green, Charles Jones, France Normand, Evelyn Ruppert, Eric Sager, and Marc St-Hilaire. I thank them for rare collegial engagement over the years, despite other commitments, and, believe it or not, lives lived beyond their teaching and research. The other authors and coauthors include several project coordinators and other close associates of the endeavour. Byron Moldofsky, one of the project coordinators and manager of the GIS and Cartography Office, Department of Geography, University of Toronto, contributed maps to chapters seven and eight, as well as to the chapters he authored and coauthored.

Chad Gaffield initiated and led the project. He was our composer and conductor until September 2006, when he took up his current position as President of the Social Sciences and Humanities Research Council of Canada. Thereafter he remained an active team leader. I and my colleagues deeply appreciate his vision, his unwavering commitment to the promotion of interdisciplinary historical scholarship, and his friendship.

This book is dedicated to the CCRI coordinators, Carmen Bauer (University of Ottawa), Nicola Farnworth (York University), Bryon Moldofsky (University of Toronto), Laurent Richard (Université Laval), Douglas Thompson (University of Victoria), Martine Tremblay (Université du Québec à Trois Rivières), and Terry Quinlan (Memorial University). Angela Mattiacci, the first University of Ottawa coordinator, tragically died in 2003, just as the vision she shared with us was beginning to materialize. Day-by-day, over seven years, these coordinators dedicated themselves to the fulfilment of this initial vision.

The other participants in this enterprise are too many to name, although I wish I could do so. A few were full-time employees, but most were part-time student assistants. Undertaking the essential tasks of programming, data entry and processing, checking and coding, many came to share the principal investigators' intellectual commitment to the project. We thank them sincerely.

Principal funding for the CCRI came from the Canada Foundation for Innovation. The provinces of British Columbia, Ontario, Quebec, and Newfoundland and Labrador provided matching funds for the work in their provinces. The eight participating universities (those named above and the University of Alberta) provided vital additional support, as did our partners, Statistics Canada, IBM, Mitel, the Harold Crabtree Foundation, the Newfoundland and Labrador Statistics agency, L'Institut de la Statistique du Québec, and Library and Archives Canada. Without their support the CCRI could only have been imagined. The universities and the Newfoundland and Labrador Statistics Agency made singular contributions of space and other facilities. In 2009 the infrastructure was transferred from the University of Ottawa to the University of Alberta, Université Laval, and Université du Québec à Trois Rivières. These three will maintain the infrastructure into the immediate future and the University of Alberta has committed itself to the longer term. This service to the research community fills an unfortunate void in Canada, the absence of a national institution providing for long-term maintenance and dissemination of digital databases, a vital resource for the future of the digital humanities and social sciences in this country. These universities are to be congratulated for their commitment and foresight.

Collections are not readily published, even if they are unified, as this one is, by topics, periodization, and a primary data source. I have had the privilege from my first proposal through publication of the strong support of Donald Akenson and Philip Cercone of McGill-Queen's University Press. I have also appreciated the collaboration of the Press's staff, Joan Harcourt, Dorothy Beavan, and especially Jessica Howarth, who coached me through the long process. It is customary for authors to make some gesture of appreciation to copyeditors, if one is lucky enough to have their assistance in the increasingly poorly edited world of print and digital publication. But there is nothing perfunctory about our collective admiration for the professional copyediting provided by Kate Baltais and Harold Otto, and for Celia Braves' indexing. A number of the experienced authors of this volume pointedly noted the quality of their work. We sincerely thank them.

I also thank Stan Shapson, Vice-president, Research and Innovation, and Bob Drummond, Dean of the Faculty of Arts at York University, for providing generous research support for the CCRI at York. Their support helped make the York Centre an exemplary research facility and facilitated its transformation into a Statistics Canada Research Data Centre. Other York staff, especially Donna Smith, and members of York's Office of Research Accounting provided indispensable support.

I could take responsibility for the interpretations that follow, but in the spirit of our collegial work, the authors of the chapters will have to bear their share. I accept responsibility for inviting the authors to participate in a book based on the initial 1911 national sample. The CCRI series, 1911 through 1951, is available in Statistic Canada's Research Data Centres (RDCs), but for reasons of confidentiality, 1911 is currently the only publicly available sample, so most readily accessed for a collaborative effort. More important, our collective focus on the varied experiences of those who lived through the first decade of Canada's twentieth century sheds new light on lives that have remained largely in the historical shadows.

Ann has been by turns tolerant and encouraging of my self-absorption in undertaking this work, as she has been of other projects. She and our sons and their families are responsible for more of the work than they know, but mainly for my enduring happiness.

PART I

Introductions

— · 1 · —

New Sources: New Social Histories

GORDON DARROCH

This multi-authored book is a contribution to a rapidly expanding international scholarly endeavour based on systematic historical sources inquiring into the still-hidden histories of many peoples, places, and times. The varieties of social histories are now myriad, although all are grounded on some form of collective biography constructed from one, a few, or many sources that describe aspects of the lives of historical individuals. The following chapters tilt towards one end of the continuum of social histories, those concerned with connecting the circumstances and experiences of ordinary individuals with larger structural changes, although they also attend to questions of reconstituting these experiences in their own terms. Charles Tilly identified this difference between the aims of "connecting" the local to larger structural changes and "reconstituting" the local as the apparently competing goals of social history, although he, sensibly, argued that the differences were more matters of the choice of conceptual lens, focus, topic, and intellectual tradition than of division in practice or principle.[1]

The studies included here all undertake new analyses of the opening decades of Canada's twentieth century. The topics and style of analyses are diverse, unified by the focus on these still relatively uncharted decades and by employing new Canadian historical census "microdata," that is, individual-level, census manuscript data. The unifying source of these studies is the new national microdata sample for 1911, although a number of chapters enlist other nominative and documentary sources. The 1911 sample was created as the first in a series of comparable samples for each of the decennial censuses from 1911 to 1951 by the Canadian Century Research Infrastructure (CCRI). The origins, auspices, conduct, and funding of the project have been fully described elsewhere, but a brief account of the main features of the infrastructure and of the character of the samples will serve as background for the following chapters.[2] These are the first studies to be based on the 1911 national sample of census manuscript records, although others are in progress.

The CCRI emerged from the legacy of Canadian historical microdata projects ranging from the pioneering community-level studies to the creation of the 1871 and 1901 national census samples and encouraged by parallel international developments of national historical databases, such as those of the University of Minnesota's *Integrated Public Use Microdata Series* (IPUMS-USA) and North Atlantic Population Project (NAPP), as well as a number of European projects.[3]

The project began as a vision of Chad Gaffield, then University Research Chair in History at the University of Ottawa, and currently president of the Social Sciences and Humanities Research Council of Canada. It was Gaffield who first imagined the prospect of a uniquely collaborative, pan-Canadian project and the possibilities of its multi-agency, multi-institutional support. Recent years have seen the growth in a number of impressive, large cooperative historical projects in Canada and internationally, but from its inception, the CCRI demanded unusual collaboration among its lead researchers and institutions.[4] The research team was also Chad Gaffield's invention. The concept of the project met considerable scepticism in some circles. Following Gaffield's lead, the principal investigators thought differently. The completion of the data collection, documentation, and deposit for research purposes are also a credit to the partnerships formed and sustained with other institutions and agencies, in particular, our colleagues at Statistics Canada and Library and Archives Canada. For funding, we are indebted to the Canadian Foundation for Innovation, several provincial funding agencies. and the eight universities involved with this project.[5] The project could not have been completed without the support of each.

The CCRI is a harmonized and fully documented series of national samples drawn from the decennial censuses of 1911, 1921, 1931, 1941, and 1951. Historical census samples are, by now, a quite familiar source, and perhaps need little or no justification, but as context for the following studies it is worth reiterating their unique value. No other single historical source compares to a census in providing such a rich array of evidence about the attributes and experiences of individuals and about the character of their households and dwellings. This evidence is nominally provided for the entire population of the country, spanning its full geographical expanse. Not least, and obvious as it may seem, decennial census data provide a uniquely consistent chronological sequence of cross-sectional portraits of populations, a feature that a number of the chapters here make central to their analysis.

Other parallel projects have already made available or soon will make available databases for the complete 1881 Canadian census and for systematic dwelling and individual samples of the 1891 and 1851–52 censuses.[6] So, with the addition to the existing 1871 and 1901 national samples and the five CCRI samples, we have a full series of decennial databases from the colonial era to after the Second World War. This is a remarkable historical resource. Although not yet integrated or fully matched in their coding of variables, this mid-nineteenth-through mid-twentieth-century series opens up research vistas that could be barely imagined only a few years ago. This collection marks, we hope, the beginning of a flood of new studies. Moreover, once the series is more fully integrated, it can potentially be used in conjunction with Statistics Canada's Public Use Microdata Files now available from 1971 to 2006.[7]

As with all historical records, census manuscripts require attention to the peculiarities of their initial construction, their preservation, and their interpretation. Even as the taking of the census became more systematic with time, the ambitions of its administrators were often frustrated, in some measure, by their own limited or flawed designs, eliciting unintended responses, by the limited competence or carelessness of some enumerators, and not insignificantly, by the occasional recalcitrance of the respondents or, more interestingly, by their insistence on being differently recorded than was intended. Recent critical scholarship has illuminated the historical context of census taking as a state enterprise. Reflecting on this scholarship helps contextualize not only the character of the records as historical traces, but of our own efforts in transcribing and documenting them as a public research resource.

From the late eighteenth century onwards, national censuses were part of a virtual "avalanche of numbers," as Ian Hacking neatly phrased it,[8] in which counting and classifying became dominant ways of knowing and administering populations. Census taking was hardly unique. The nineteenth and twentieth centuries witnessed a deluge of enumeration and cataloguing – of mortality and births, suicides, illness, criminal convictions and recidivism, agricultural and industrial production, poverty, and life risks. Many enumerations were conducted by state agencies, but some were carried out under the aegis of other public and private initiatives, for example, as part of the great sanitary and moral reform movements, in the origins of systematic social surveys, and as the basis of actuarial assessment and new forms of insurance. Some of the recent history and sociology of this naming and numbering raises basic questions about the character of our knowledge of the social, particularly, regarding the normalization and regulation of social identities and their complex mediation and negotiation. Evelyn Ruppert most explicitly addresses such questions in chapter 3.[9]

One of the commitments of the CCRI was to draw on scholarship in social and in cultural history and to facilitate both the exploration of the historical census microdata and of relevant documentary sources, with key documents built into the infrastructure itself in order to encourage an integrated approach. The essential documentary sources include enumerator instructions, census schedules, digitized published tables, and uniquely, an extensive collective of the rich contemporary commentary about the making and taking of each census from 1911 through 1951. Nearly 170 newspapers as well as Canadian parliamentary debates and some provincial debates were systematically searched during the months preceding and following each census. The newspaper articles were drawn from purposive samples of existing runs of newspapers, including all national papers and a wide selection of local and regional ones, depending on archival resources, but with an effort to be representative of varied regional and local opinion. This collection is a complementary, stand-alone, publicly accessible database, described in more detail elsewhere, and explored in the chapters by Ruppert, Adam Green, and Chad Gaffield, Byron Moldofsky, and Katharine Rollwagen in this volume.[10]

The members of the CCRI shared an explicit working assumption that censuses are multi-authored sources, with authors ranging from senior census officials and clerks to enumerators and respondents, but including, as well, a range of state and public agencies and interest groups which, in declaring a stake in the conduct and results of each census, influenced its design and interpretation, including its published form.[11] This layered authorship presents an interpretive challenge in which one can only partially separate the authorial voices, but still invites us to strive to make sense of the originating encounter between enumerators and the enumerated.[12] Benedict Anderson, notably, has argued that, despite the ambition of administrators and census officials to design recording instruments intended to fix and homogenize identities, a census enumeration is perforce an act of cultural translation, reflecting local social and cultural practices.[13] It is revealing to pursue the notion of historical censuses as the outcome of successive acts of translation. Recent translation theory provides a number of useful lenses through which we may re-evaluate the social historian's interpretive task.[14] Translation theory points to the curious, powerful presumption in which translators tend to be invisible: a translation is conventionally taken to be a transparent and largely equivalent representation of a source text. But the presumption mistakes an unavoidably complex, hybrid representation for a simple conversion from one context to another.[15] It illuminates the complexity of census manuscript records to recognize them as polyphonic, linguistic constructions, translations of translations. Census manuscript records originated in the structured encounter between enumerators and respondents, first translated into an abbreviated, written record, and then reinterpreted by administrators and clerks who edited and standardized the texts according to their own protocols. And, they are *again* translated by us, as researchers attempting to make sense of the historical traces in our own social and cultural context. In this sense, our interpretations mimic the interpretive work of those we seek to understand.

The Census Samples

Despite the dramatic, formative changes to the character of the country in the opening decade of the twentieth century, much of Canada's social history remains unexplored. Although the 1911 national sample is only the first of the five created by the Canadian Century Research Infrastructure, it is the only one currently available to the public and, thus, the one most readily accessed by interested researchers at this time. The others are available to researchers within one of Statistics Canada's Research Data Centres (STC's RDCs). The release of confidential manuscript returns is restricted for ninety-two years, and for this reason, analysis based on the 1921 to 1951 data strictly protects the anonymity of those who were enumerated. The availability of these historical data in the RDCs represents an unparalleled opportunity for new historical research on the first half of Canada's twentieth century, and a number of researchers have began to examine these systematically.[16]

The studies in this volume assume an elementary understanding of the character of the 1911 sample. We briefly review the sample design here. Full details are provided in the User Guides to the sample, as well as in prior publications.[17]

The CCRI sample designs are intentionally quite simple, in order to encourage wide use. They provide large, comparable representative samples of the dwellings, households, and individuals enumerated in the five decennial censuses from 1911 to 1951. The sampled units are census-defined dwellings, but the samples include all the responses provided on the population schedule (Schedule 1) for every individual recorded in those dwellings. One can undertake analysis at the level of individuals, households, and dwellings, as well as at a selected level of geography in which the dwellings were located; a multilevel geographical analysis is presented here by Danielle Gauvreau and Patricia Thornton in chapter 9.

The sample densities for each census vary due to the growth of the national population and the usual constraint on sample size, limited resources. Each is a very large sample in terms of the total numbers of records, permitting quite detailed analysis even for relatively small groups that may be of interest. The samples vary from 5 per cent of dwellings, households, and individuals in 1911, and 4 per cent in 1921, to 3 per cent in each of the subsequent decades. This yielded national samples sizes of over 372,000 individuals in 1911 and from about 320,000 in 1921 to 420,000 in 1951.[18]

These samples are unique among current international microdata. For each decade, they provide separate samples of the main population residing in dwellings housing thirty individuals or fewer and two "oversamples" of census-defined dwellings housing more than thirty residents. The first oversample is of individuals residing in dwellings that were mainly multi-unit, such as row housing or apartment buildings. The second is of dwellings that were mainly institutional, such as hospitals, jails, asylums, convents, or larger boarding houses, hotels, and work camps. The two oversamples represent small proportions of the national population in any decade, but allow analysis both of the places of residence and their residents that are very rarely studied systematically and are of particular historical interest. Our sampling strategy entailed a complete national inventory of the dwellings qualifying for the oversamples. The samples of multi-unit households and of the mainly unrelated individuals in institutions and work camps were then drawn within each qualifying large dwelling.[19]

Another unique feature of the CCRI is its samples of the population of Newfoundland and Labrador. In contrast to the legislated confidentiality that applies to other Canadian enumerations after 1911, no provision has ever been made regarding confidentiality prior to the province joining Canada in 1949, including the 1945 census. The Atlantic Centre of the CCRI entered into the database not only the 3 to 5 per cent samples for the Atlantic provinces, but *all* available records for the pre-Confederation Newfoundland censuses for 1911, 1921, 1935, and 1945. Such a complete record of twentieth-century nominative data is very rare; see Terry Quinlan and Sean Cadigan (chapter 11) for an innovative use of these rich data.

The Chapters

We have organized the chapters in this volume broadly into five parts, grouping them around common themes. They can be read independently or as related analyses or as a collection of new inquiries into the still largely "hidden histories" of early twentieth-century Canada. Although the studies range widely in focus, with the 1911 census microdata at their core, they hardly exhaust the prospects of new analyses, since access to individual-level records frees us from the confines of the published census tabulations following the census, which naturally reflect the concerns of census officials and their readings of the political, social, and economic issues of the day. Although the chapters cover diverse, previously unexamined topics, they also reveal the possibilities of other, previously unimagined, prospects for new inquiries using all three of the related resources, the microdata, its detailed geocoding, and the contextual documentary database. The studies also make clear that, without exception, the questions asked and answers offered far exceed any that could be based on the published census volumes alone.

This overview is followed by Byron Moldofsky's complementary introduction (chapter 2) that adds to the existing documentation of the integrated georeferencing of the CCRI data. CCRI data entry ensured that addresses were recorded for each sampled dwelling (at the census subdivision level, and not without considerable complication, as Moldofsky makes clear). He also illustrates the prospects for undertaking new ways of mapping and visualizing these historical census data and extending their analysis through applications of geographical information systems (GIS). As he reminds us, the lives of our forebears were enacted in specific geographical places.

Part II, "Canadian Diversities: Debates and Dimensions," begins with Evelyn Ruppert's interpretive account of the ways the complex administrative infrastructure of census taking configured the diversity of bodies and identities in social and geographical spaces in order to generate a knowable population. In so doing, Ruppert also introduces the CCRI contextual database, which is mainly comprised of newspaper articles and Hansard records of parliamentary debates published around the time of each of the decennial enumerations, 1911 to 1951.[20] These "data on the data," as Ruppert calls them, make possible, for the first time, a systematic exploration of the details of census-taking practices and processes as they were understood and debated in their time.

Adam Green (chapter 4) also draws on the contextual database, as well as some previously unexamined Dominion Bureau of Statistics archival sources unearthed during the project. He reconsiders the fraught question of asking about "racial or tribal origins" in 1911. Green finds striking parallels between the public debates about the origin question in 1911 and those that have followed decade upon decade. He provides new evidence that large numbers of citizens insisted that they be recorded as "Canadian" in "origin" as early as 1911, despite the effort of census officials to disallow and suppress such responses, which in their published "translations" of the original texts they did.

Chad Gaffield, Byron Moldofsky, and Katharine Rollwagen (chapter 5) pursue the issue of how the apparently straightforward language questions on the 1911 census enumeration collided with the complexity of language as it was understood by the speakers and the enumerators. As in the case of the meanings of "origins," census officials made concerted efforts to devise simple ways of recording the spoken language of Canadians, a grid that derived its meaning largely from their administrative and political contexts. But, the more complicated, nuanced, and variegated interpretations made by enumerators and respondents on the doorsteps of dwellings were sufficiently at odds with these politically sensitive meanings that, in the end, the officials were not prepared even to publish a version of them. Gaffield et al. mine the instructions to enumerators, the schedules, and contextual newspaper accounts of the census process in order to unravel the complex negotiations about individual and collective identities sparked by the language questions of 1911 and the complicated politics of the changes made for the 1921 census.

The 1911 census is a rare resource in another way, since a concerted effort was made to enumerate Aboriginal peoples, even in remote northern communities, a daring and naive effort that was not to be repeated for many decades. In the last chapter of Part II, Gustave Goldmann accepts the challenge of attempting to make sense of these records of First Nations communities across Canada, recognizing both the limitations and uncommon interpretive possibilities in such a venture. Carefully assessing and modifying the CCRI classifications of the recorded Aboriginal languages and origins, and critically reviewing the limits of the sample, Goldmann provides the first analysis of the sociodemography of these least visible of Canadian residents in the early twentieth century. His portrait also grants us a rare, systematic historical point of reference for interpreting subsequent Aboriginal experiences.

Part III, "Social Spaces, Historical Places," provides new explorations of the constraints and choices that fostered varieties of living arrangements from the late nineteenth century through the early twentieth century. Gordon Darroch (chapter 7) takes up the question of household and family experiences, which has been at the centre of much social history over the past half-century, employing comparable evidence from the 1901 and 1911 national samples. He examines the influence of basic demographic conditions on individual experiences in different household situations, as well as the consequences of recency of immigration, labour force sector, and class differences in a decade of unprecedented immigrant arrivals, economic change, and national territorial reconfiguration. Reporting strong and still puzzling regional variations, even considering the other demographic and economic conditions, Darroch concludes by illustrating the prospects of an interpretive dialogue between more intensive local studies of households and families and regional and national ones made possible by databases such as the CCRI.

Focusing on the living arrangements of the elderly, Lisa Dillon (chapter 8) pursues a comparative analysis of the 1901 and 1911 national samples, adding further evidence of strong regional variations at the beginning of the twentieth century. Addressing telling questions about the chances that elderly women were heads of their own households and that aged men lived with dependent children, Dillon indicates that demographic, social, and economic factors accounted for much of the regional variations, although the combination of conditioning circumstances varied between men and women, and some regional variations persisted. Like Darroch, Dillon employs the geocoded census data to map the main national patterns. She concludes with a number of questions for continued research, arguing that some key issues can only be addressed by large-scale linking of census-like records over time to establish residential pathways.

Danielle Gauvreau and Patricia Thornton (chapter 9) provide a new perspective on the question of social encounters between ethnoreligious communities in Quebec, drawing comparisons between the sample data for 1911 and complete-count census data for 1881. Their "geography of encounters" maps and interprets patterns of cultural mixing at several levels from residential segregation and intermingling within layers of geographical "milieu de vie," to within the most intimate contexts, households, and families. They present an innovative multilevel model that integrates the analysis of households and geographical milieux, revealing that the ethnoreligious diversity of Quebec was largely a matter of the interplay of opportunities and scale, although clearly influenced by both immigration and urbanization.

The studies of Part IV, "Locales in Transition," alter the scale and range of sources employed. Each chapter sheds new light on the history of specific communities, demonstrating not only the depth of analysis made possible by both sample data and complete-count census microdata at the local level, but the original research questions that can only be posed and addressed by linked individual microdata over time. The close study of Trois-Rivières by Claude Bellavance and France Normand (chapter 10) is unusual in revealing the dynamics of a relatively small, industrializing city, exploring its sociodemographic and labour force transitions in the context of the city's particular institutional and structural changes. Their microscopic lenses illuminate the implications of these changes for the lives of those who are often historically least visible, such as female teachers.

Terry Quinlan and Sean Cadigan (chapter 11) open a new inquiry into the geographical and religious differences distinguishing voters for and against Confederation by employing the remarkably complete CCRI database derived from the 1945 Newfoundland and Labrador census. In revisiting the consequences for the second, 1948, referendum of basic shifts in the nature of Newfoundland economy and society, Quinlan and Cadigan first correlate voter preferences with district-level data and then undertake a detailed local comparison of family names linked to other historical sources. Their unmatched, fine-grained evidence and careful analysis opens a new chapter in the socio-political history of the province.

Marc St-Hilaire, Laurent Richard, and Richard Marcoux (chapter 12) conclude Part IV with another close exploration of linked, longitudinal census analysis for Quebec City over the forty years from 1871 through 1911. Following two cohorts of young girls and boys from their original families in 1871, at ten-year intervals, allows them to examine in unusual detail the socio-economic conditions marking individual and family life courses as they were linked to out-migration or persistence within the city, during a period in which the city experienced deep economic restructuring and significant population turnover. An initial foray into these complicated microdata, the fine grain of the study newly illuminates the implications of intergenerational familial circumstances and membership in different cultural communities of the city, addressing the difficult questions of the play of choice and chance in the fates of those who left and those who stayed.

Each of these investigations employs combinations of different census microdata, developing different strategies for linking individual-level data across time and to other historical sources. In so doing, they demonstrate the continuity between the reconstitution of local historical experiences and broader interpretations of the relationships between individual lives and structural changes.

Part V, "Markets and Mobility: Class, Ethnicity, Gender," offers four studies that raise questions about conventional historical accounts of national patterns, demonstrating at least the need for greater nuance, if not thorough revision of current interpretations. Exploring features of the 1911 national sample, each chapter recasts key questions about the intersections of the new century's economic changes and ethnic, immigrant, class, and gender experiences. Addressing the dominant narrative about the Canadian economy at the turn of the century, Kris Inwood, Mary MacKinnon, and Chris Minns (chapter 13) compare the 1911 national sample with a newly available national sample for 1891, posing fresh questions about the changes in the locations, occupations, and earnings of Canadian and foreign-born cohorts between the late nineteenth and early twentieth centuries. Inwood et al. show that the growth of the labour market after 1900 was accompanied by a number of complex changes, including the intensification of labour, human capital development, and technological change. In turn, these changes both opened significant new opportunities for occupational mobility for members of the anglophone, francophone, and foreign-born communities, and simultaneously perpetuated inequalities among them.

A parallel inquiry by Charles Jones and Stella Park (chapter 14) examines the census evidence regarding ancestral origins – "Racial and Tribal Origins" – and socio-economic positions as they were recorded in the 1911 census. They focus particularly on the experiences of the enlarged communities from Eastern and Southern Europe and from Asia resulting from the mass immigration of the previous decades. Considering the economic fortunes of those whose origins were most visible, either because of their skin colour or modes of comportment or dress or speech, they also report that these visible minorities and the most recent immigrants experienced both opportunities for mobility and a demonstrable "glass ceiling" pattern of discrimination, even considering other influences, such as their levels of illiteracy and non-majority languages spoken. Only the Chinese had earnings that were very low at all job levels.

Eric Sager (chapter 15) presses further in asking about the dynamics of mutually reinforcing interactions between class and ethnicity in these years. Examining the 1901 and 1911 microdata samples, Sager makes use of their comparable, unique evidence on class positions (recorded as "status of employment"), demonstrating that immigrants were broadly dispersed among major social classes, but that the mass immigration of the opening decade of the twentieth century fostered more distinctly working-class immigrant communities. He argues that, despite persistent inequalities, one cannot speak of an ethnically determined class hierarchy among immigrants in Canada. He refines his national perspective with a case study of new, complete census data for Hamilton, Ontario, in 1911, mapping the relationship between class, immigrant status, and urban residential space. Sager ends with a detailed examination of income earning and its determinants, pursuing the notion that ethnic identity influenced economic fates only in its intersections with class and gender, while shaping and reinforcing their definitions and boundaries.

In the final chapter of this book, Peter Baskerville (chapter 16) makes innovative use of the 1911 census questions about insurance holdings, questions posed in this census year only. The questions were prompted by the growing demand for insurance and an insurance industry. Baskerville recognizes the opportunity to interpret the extensive insuring of the lives of women and children as a unique historical microscope through which to examine hitherto unrecognized forms of cultural and social change in the early twentieth century. Critically examining the census responses in the context of other information about insurance policies, he examines the holders in detail, finding that both cultural and economic differences within the working class prompted the decisions to purchase insurance in early twentieth-century Canada, including a distinct overrepresentation of French Catholic children among the insured. He marshalls evidence to take issue with a more conventional account of the diffusion of working-class insurance following middle-class values and practices; rather, he argues that the purchase of insurance for children, especially for girls and women, is better understood as a marker of broadly changing gendered behaviour in the public sphere.

The authors in this book appreciate that given the new, rich historical census sources now available to us, we are privileged to re-present features of the lives of those who left the records, both to recover through our own interpretive lenses their collective biographies and to connect them to perspectives on larger social processes and structures.[21] We hope that the diverse analyses presented here are invitations to others to make previously unimagined use of this recovered census legacy.

Notes

1 Charles Tilly, "Family History, Social History, and Social Change," *Journal of Family History* 12, nos 1–3 (1987): 319–30. Also see William Sewell, Jr's recent, similar reflections on the continuing (and one wonders, if often wilful) misunderstandings of the commonalities between "discursive and quantitative" historical evidence and between "interpretive and quantitative" research practices. See "Coda: Hermeneutical Quantification," in William Sewell, Jr, *Logics of History: Social Theory and Social Transformation* (Chicago: University of Chicago Press, 2005), 369–72.

2 See the special issue of *Historical Methods* 40, no. 2 (2007). The four articles describe the conception and construction of the infrastructure, the sample designs, data entry protocols and software, the geocoding and geographical component of the CCRI, and the associated "contextual database" of contemporary newspaper commentary and Hansard records of parliamentary debates about the taking and making of the twentieth-century censuses, 1911–1951.

3 For some of the major projects, see http://www.nappdata.org/napp/participants.shtml. The development of other census microdata databases continues to enlarge the geographical and temporal scope of possible analysis; see, e.g., Gruber and Szoltysek, http://www.demogr.mpg.de/papers/working/wp-2011-001.pdf.

4 The immediate precursor to the CCRI was the Canadian Families Project, a collaborative project conducted at the University of Victoria, which made available a 5 per cent sample of all census dwellings for 1901. This sample continues to facilitate a good deal of new scholarly investigation. Several of the studies in this book employ the 1901 national sample, and others use comparable microdata (e.g., a national sample for 1891) in conjunction with the 1911 sample. Studies in Parts III and IV of this book enlist complete counts of microdata for particular communities and linked samples of census data.

5 Principal funding support came from the Canada Foundation for Innovation. The provinces of British Columbia, Ontario, Quebec, and Newfoundland and Labrador provided essential matching funds for the work done in their respective provinces. The eight participating universities provided significant further assistance, as did our partners Statistics Canada, IBM, MITEL, the Harold Crabtree Foundation, the Newfoundland and Labrador Statistics Agency, L'Institut de la Statistique du Québec, and Library and Archives Canada. The university centres

that conducted the project were the University of Ottawa (the lead institution), Memorial University of Newfoundland, L'Université Laval, L'Université du Québec à Trois-Rivières, York University, the University of Toronto, and the University of Victoria. We wish to emphasize how essential university support is for the construction of research infrastructures: without the space and financial support provided by the partner universities and, for Atlantic Canada, by the Newfoundland and Labrador Statistics Agency, the CCRI could not have been undertaken. The database was housed initially at the University of Ottawa and Statistics Canada. The publicly available 1911 sample and the full documentation have been transferred to the University of Alberta and, along with L'Université Laval and L'Université du Québec à Trois-Rivières, the University of Alberta will maintain the databases into the future; see http://ccri.library.ualberta.ca/enindex.html. We, and future researchers, are indebted to the University of Alberta for its recognition of the importance of long-term institutional support for historical databases.

6 See http://www.prdh.umontreal.ca/census/en/uguide/1881work.aspx for the 1881 and 1852 databases and http://www.economics.uoguelph.ca/kinwood/1891/index.html for 1891.

7 For the 1971 through 2006 files, see http://datalib.chass.utoronto.ca/major/canpumf.htm. The CCRI was initiated in the knowledge that the 1961 census was the first to be converted to an electronic microdata file, but that the whereabouts of the file was uncertain. In the course of the partnership between Statistics Canada (STC) and the CCRI, some effort was devoted to locating the file and, subsequently, to reconstructing documentation of its contents. The future availability of the file for research purposes remains within the mandate of STC.

8 Ian Hacking, *The Taming of Chance* (Cambridge: Cambridge University Press, 1990), 2.

9 It has become almost perfunctory in Canadian census research to make reference to Bruce Curtis's *The Politics of Population: State Formation, Statistics, and the Census of Canada, 1840–1875* (Toronto: University of Toronto Press, 2001). The study deserves routine reference to it, whatever the divergent readings and deflections of its implications may be. In Canada, at least, the book and Curtis's prior writing clearly altered the discourse around manuscript census research. In my interpretation, the core of Curtis's work aims to have us understand census representations of the lives of those enumerated as constructed technologies of knowledge with deep implications for the governing of subjects in liberal social formations. His work contributes not only to the history of census statistics and interpretations of disciplinary regulation, but to historical epistemology.

10 Claude Bellevance, France Normand, and Evelyn Ruppert, "Census in Context: Documenting and Understanding the Making of Early Twentieth-Century Canadian Censuses," *Historical Methods* 40, no. 2 (2007): 92–103. For enumerators' instructions, schedules, and digitized tables, see the User Guides at http://ccri.library.ualberta.ca/enindex.html. This link also provides direct access to the bilingual, on-line contextual database and its documentation.

11 See Chad Gaffield, "Conceptualizing and Constructing the Canadian Century Research Infrastructure," *Historical Methods* 40, no. 2 (2007): 54–64. Also see Paul

Schor, *Compter et Classer: Histoire des recensements américains* (Paris: Editions de l'EHESS, 2009).

12 Census enumerations are not unique among historical documents in having multiple authors and translations. Other systematic microdata, like educational records, tax rolls, and city directories, are always composed by a series of such authors, in more or less complex ways, but particularly by the joint authorship of members of local communities and state or commercial recording officials. See, e.g., the interesting case examined by Rebecca Jean Emigh, "Numeracy or Enumeration? The Uses of Numbers by States and Societies," *Social Science History* 26, no. 4 (2002): 653–98.

13 Benedict Anderson, *Imagined Communities: Reflections on the Origins and Spread of Nationalism* (London: Verso, 1983; revised 1991, 2006).

14 Like all analogies, viewing census records as translated literary texts, the normal subject of translation theory, is partial in some respects, but shares other basic equivalences. All translations are interpretive acts in altered cultural and social circumstances, including those of oral accounts, life stories, or interviews. I am an interested reader of translation theory, neither a practitioner nor an informed theorist.

15 Theo Hermans provides the telling examples of statements among English speakers such as "President Yeltsin was speaking through an interpreter," and "I have read Dostoevsky." He notes how we unreflectively refer to speaking *through* an interpreter and as a consequence of this presumption the whole complicated process, say, of translating Dostoevsky's text, simply disappears. I am reminded in this context by Anderson's grim comment on how his discovery of Guerrero's "fascinatingly corrupt" translation of José Rizal's novel, *Noli Me Tangere*, helped prompt his revised edition of *Imagined Communities* (1991, xiii). See Theo Hermans, "Paradoxes and Aporias in Translation and Translation Studies," in Alessandra Riccardi (ed.), *Translation Studies: Perspectives on an Emerging Discipline* (Cambridge: Cambridge University Press, 2002), 10.

16 For a more complete account of the unique working partnership between the CCRI and Statistics Canada in the creation of the 1911 through 1951 national samples under conditions of confidentiality of the records, see Chad Gaffield, "Conceptualizing and Constructing." For access to the 1921 through 1951 CCRI national samples in the RDCs, see http://www.statcan.gc.ca/rdc-cdr/. Some current and much future work will draw on these samples, which unlike the 1911 and earlier census data are rendered completely anonymous in order to comply with the confidentiality requirements of the Statistics Act. Shortly, the 1911 publicly available file will be added to this series in the RDCs in order to facilitate analysis across the first half of the twentieth century.

A number of researchers are currently engaged in exploring new analyses using part of the CCRI series. At the time of writing (March 2012), none of the new work had progressed to publication, but a number of papers were to be reported in a roundtable of the Social Science History Association meetings in Vancouver, November 2012.

17 Gordon Darroch, Richard B. Smith, and Michel Gaudreault, "CCRI Sample Designs and Sample Point Identification, Data Entry, and Reporting (SPIDER) Software," *Historical Methods* 40, no. 2 (2007): 65–75. For the User Guides to the 1911 sample, see http://ccri.library.ualberta.ca/enindex.html.

18 Census definitions of dwellings varied somewhat over these years. We adapted the sampling design to take account of these changes while maintaining analytical comparability. Researchers using more than one sample should attend to the details as given in the CCRI User Guide.

19 We defined these "large dwellings" as places housing thirty-one or more individuals following a useful precedent set by some national samples in the IPUMS-USA. Potential users need to consult the CCRI User Guides regarding these samples, but they are relatively simple to employ and will immensely broaden the canvas on which the history of institutional and work camp life and of the built environment can be drawn.

The complete inventories of "large dwellings" should themselves provide opportunities for new research. One absence in the current collection is a focus on these subsamples. For example, the rapidly rising numbers of apartment and other multiple-household dwellers in the first half of the twentieth century remains almost wholly unexamined, nor do we have any systematic examinations of the institutional populations in these decades (or earlier). Of course, the national samples also provide for the appropriate comparisons with the non-apartment/row house–residing and non-institutional populations.

20 For a detailed description of the database, see Bellavance, Normand, and Ruppert, "Census in Context." The database can be accessed http://ccri-cd.cieq.ca/fmi/iwp/cgi?-db=IRCS_CONTEXTDATA_WEB&-loadframes or through http://ccri.library.ualberta.ca/en1911census/contextual/index.html.

21 Many features of the historical censuses that we rely on in these investigations are the equivalent of those that were included on the separate "long form census" from 1971 onwards for samples of 20 per cent of Canadian households. We would be remiss not to mention in this context that the recent, ill-informed political decision by the Government of Canada to cancel the long form census threatens to deny to future historical researchers a parallel opportunity to reflect systematically on the experiences of our time and for future Canadians to know themselves in social-historical context. Alternative sources will not prove to be adequate substitutes.

The decision also puts in jeopardy the contribution of the CCRI 1911 to 1951 national samples to the creation of an integrated series of Canadian census microdata beyond the extant databases from 1851–52 to 2006 (an 1861 census sample is incomplete because of lost data, and as noted, the 1961 census microdata, although recovered, remains with Statistics Canada pending consideration of its integrity and documentation).

Among many commentaries on this decision, see Lisa Dillon, "The Value of the Long Form Canadian Census for Long-Term National and International Research," *Canadian Public Policy* 36, no. 3 (2010): 389–93.

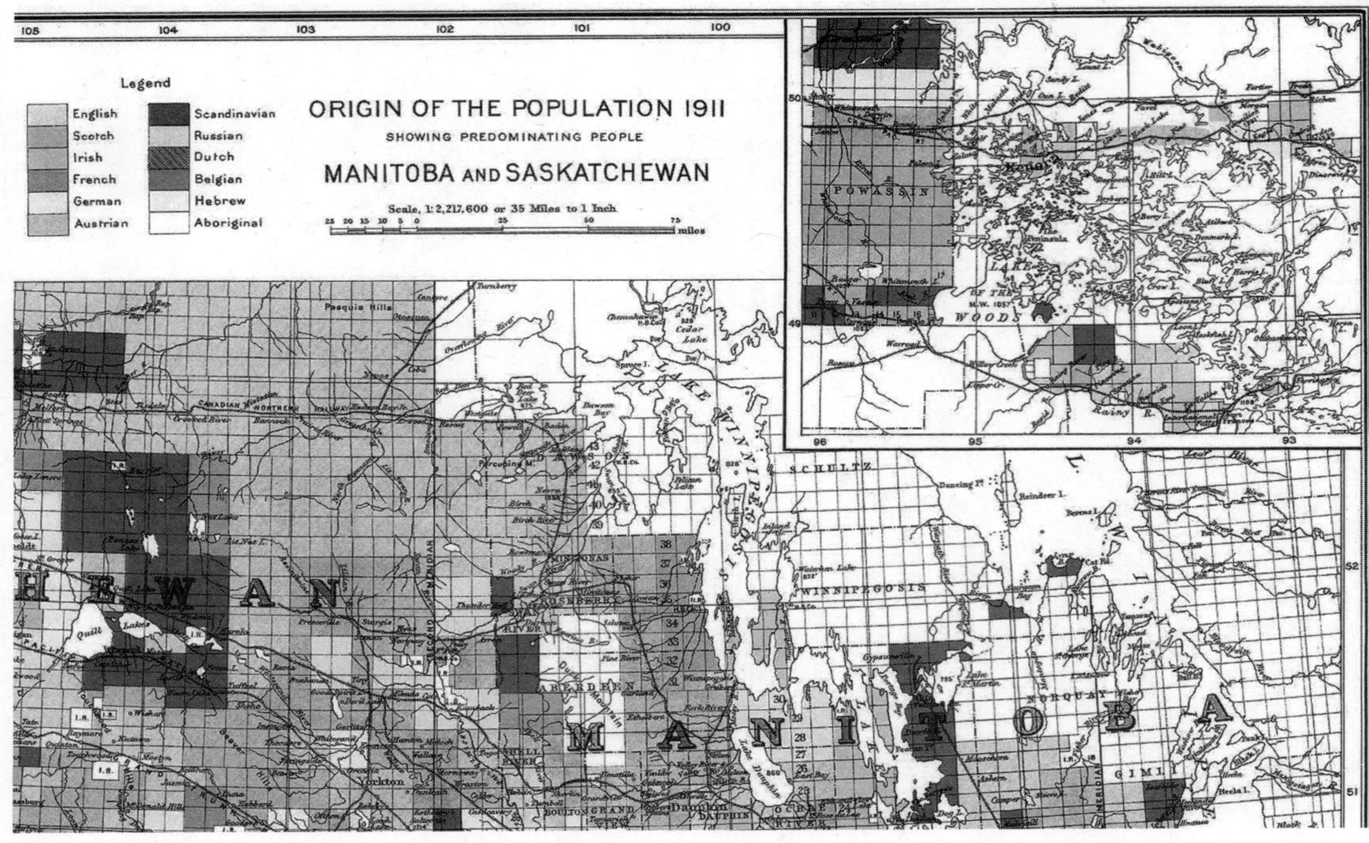
ORIGIN OF THE POPULATION 1911
SHOWING PREDOMINATING PEOPLE
MANITOBA AND SASKATCHEWAN
Scale, 1:2,217,600 or 35 Miles to 1 Inch
Legend
English
Scotch
Irish
French
German
Austrian
Scandinavian
Russian
Dutch
Belgian
Hebrew
Aboriginal
LAKE WINNIPEGOSIS
Lake Dauphin
Duck Mountain
Pasquia Hills
Yorkton
LAKE OF THE WOODS
Rainy R.

— · 2 · —

The CCRI Geographical Files: Introduction and Examples

BYRON MOLDOFSKY

CCRI Approach to a Geographical Perspective on the Census

In 1906, the first edition of the national *Atlas of Canada* was published. It included several maps of the country showing the results of the 1901 census, using the census subdistrict (CSD) as the basic unit of representation.[1] These full-colour maps of population density and of dominant ethnic origin of the population were the first comprehensive and widely seen graphic representations of the people of Canada to the outside world and to ourselves. In the second edition of the national atlas, published in 1915, the census of 1911 was similarly mapped, and the number of demographic maps expanded.[2] (See figure 2.1.) These maps were impressive in painting a picture of the breadth of the country, the spread of its population, and its diversity.[3]

Inspired by these cartographical efforts and by the potential of the censuses themselves, from its inception, one of the goals of the Canadian Century Research Infrastructure (CCRI) was to enable users to look at the census data from the perspective of geography. History takes place in a geographical context, and during the first half of the twentieth century, changes to political

Figure 2.1 (facing page) · Reproduction of detail from the *Atlas of Canada*, 1915: "Origin of the Population 1911, Showing Predominating People, Manitoba and Saskatchewan."

Source: *Atlas of Canada*, 1915, 2nd ed. (Ottawa: Department of the Interior, 1915), 25. http://geogratis.gc.ca/api/en/nrcan-rncan/ess-sst/ac64127a-d2c9-501f-93b4-0f4ba63b6b88.html.

boundaries, economic activities, social structures, and characteristics took place differently in different parts of the country, as trends of locational persistence or migration, fertility and mortality, industrialization and urbanization, and agricultural intensification or abandonment swept across the Canadian landscape. The census-taking process captures much of the information about where people live, as well as who they are and what they do.

The challenge to the geography team of the CCRI was to create a framework and system that would incorporate as much of this geographical information as feasible and allow researchers to use it effectively. Using geographical information system (GIS) technology, such a system can link to published aggregate data, sample data, and provide a consistent geographical basis for cross-census comparison. With the completion of the CCRI published tables in spreadsheet form linked to the CCRI geographical files, we can now utilize these data in an interactive GIS mapping environment. The greatest analytical benefit of mapping these tables using GIS lies in their potential for data exploration. Instead of a static map, users can classify, aggregate, and represent the data in whatever ways they wish, and they can dynamically change these parameters. Thus, the map becomes less a purveyor of pre-packaged "results" than a means for investigating the raw data and their spatial distribution. The scope for innovative teaching and research is wide.

The success of the geographical component of the CCRI will be measured by how well it enhances use of the published data, but even more so, by how well it promotes new visualizations and analyses based on the more granular sample data. The door is open to the geographical study of selected subpopulations, household types, or family characteristics. The geographical component allows automated selection and aggregation of sample data by geographical area or relationships. It will facilitate the study of user-defined regions and consistent cross-census comparison as never before.

The structure of the CCRI geographical framework has been described in detail elsewhere.[4] More details are available in the on-line User Guide to the CCRI data, as well as the documentation and metadata downloadable with the geographical files.[5] This introduction will only outline the main objectives of the geographical approach and its implementation. We will then look specifically at the 1911 CCRI census geography, for some examples of how it can be used to explore the CCRI sample and published census data and the prospects for comparison with previous and subsequent census years. The details of geographical coding are somewhat dry, but they are important in order to recognize how the maps in this and other chapters in this book were created, and the potential for their use with CCRI data for other census years.

The requirements of the geographical team's mission were twofold. The first was to decipher the geographical organization of the census: the geographical units such as enumeration areas (EAs), census districts (CDs), and census subdistricts (CSDs) used for collection and/or subsequent publication of the census and how these varied from year to year. The second was to locate the sampled dwellings within this census geography through the "place of residence" variable. These requirements led the subgroup to elaborate an overall strategy regarding the creation and use of the CCRI census geographical files. The goals of that strategy were the following:

1 To enable the CCRI project to geographically locate census data
2 To allow CCRI users to geographically select the data they need
3 To allow CCRI users to geographically process the data (aggregate data spatially, do spatial analysis, map the results) within the confidentiality restrictions of Statistics Canada (STC).[6]

The main decisions for implementation concerned what kind of GIS approach and technology to use; what base or reference geographical data layers to use; and what level of census geography would be practical and cost-effective to capture. The first two were essentially technical decisions: it was decided to use a database-structured GIS that could be integrated with the main CCRI database (ArcGIS); it was decided to use the STC 2001 geographical files as the standard reference upon which all subsequent geographical layers would be based.

The third decision, the level of geography to use for georeferencing, was more complex – made so by the lack of existing information about the census geography of our period. Historically, production and dissemination of census data use five spatial levels: the province, the CD, the CSD, the EA, and the address (street or cadastral). The decision of what level of geography to use was problematic because the answers to a number of questions, including the following, were unclear:

1 How much correspondence and persistence existed between each of these levels of geography from one census to the next between 1911 and 1951?
2 How much correspondence and persistence existed between the boundaries needed for these censuses and the STC 2001 reference geographical layers we were using as our base map?
3 How much correspondence existed between the EAs (used for census taking) and CSDs (used for publication of aggregate census data) –

Table 2.1 · Number of census districts (CDs), census subdistricts (CSDs), and enumeration areas (EAs) by province, 1901–21

	1901			*1911*			*1921*		
	CDs	*CSDs*	*EAs (enumerators)*	*CDs*	*CSDs*	*EAs*	*CDs*	*CSDs*	*EAs*
British Columbia	5	35	276	7	60	357	13	79	716
Alberta	1	134	139	7	2,256[a]	520	17	520[b]	700
Saskatchewan	1	68	64	10	3,194[a]	604	18	807[b]	932
Manitoba	7	94	574	10	1,165[a]	623	16	192[b]	633
Ontario	89	940	3,759	85	1,289	3,760	54	1,135	4,226
Quebec	65	1,019	2,592	65	1,168	2,553	64	1,363	2,820
New Brunswick	13	159	386	12	183	390	15	185	454
Nova Scotia	17	454	565	17	462	631	18	485	767
PEI	5	70	149	3	71	152	3	77	157
Yukon				1	100	32	1	3	18
Northwest Territories				1	56	81	1	1	2
Assiniboia	2	188	186						
Unorganized Territories	1	43	110						
Total	*206*	*3,204*	*8,800*	*218*	*10,004*	*9,703*	*220*	*4,847*	*11,425*
Source (published vol., table or p.)		1901 I, xii		1911 II, Tab. 2	1911 I, Tab. 1	1911 I, vi	1921 I, Tab. 27	1921 I, Tab. 27	1931 I, 52

Sources: Census of Canada, 1901, 1911, 1921, 1931. The full references for these censuses are found in the endnotes to this chapter.
[a] Each township on the prairies is listed as a separate CSD; [b] Townships combined into "Local Improvement Districts" are listed as CSDs.

that is, were EAs strictly nested subdivisions of CSDs? (Answer: "no," especially not in 1911.)

4 What cartographical and textual historical sources existed to document each of these levels of geography? (We knew some of this, of course, but much remained unknown.)

5 How much time and effort would it take to sort out these geographical relationships and redraw the appropriate census boundaries?

This last question about what was practically possible was key. There were simply too many EAs, and they were too inconsistent from one census year to the next to provide the basis for georeferencing (see table 2.1). The decision was made to use the CSD, as listed in the published census volumes, as the smallest level of geography for locating CCRI sample microdata.[7]

Given these conditions, the decision was also made to design the GIS framework to maintain the smallest size of geographical units in any year across all years. In 1911, there were many more CSDs than in any subsequent census year. This was mainly because of the listing of each township in the Prairie provinces, each First Nations reserve (called Indian reserves at the time), and many wards or other parts of major urban centres as separate CSDs in the most complete published census tables of 1911. The potential usefulness of these large numbers of small places in the CCRI geographical files will be outlined subsequently.

The system used for identification and geocoding census subdistricts for each census year was based on a "key" table, that is, the most complete CSD table published in each set of census volumes. For each census from 1911 to 1951, a series of published census volumes was produced (from six for 1911 to eleven for 1951), containing a variety of tables aggregated at different geographical levels. The table with the most complete basic population information at the CSD level was identified as the "key" table for each census year (in most cases, "most complete" meant total population numbers, male and female, and total number of dwellings, by CSD).[8] For the purposes of coding, each CSD was given a unique identifier based on the key table line number. A nested system of unique identification codes was created to capture the hierarchical geography of the census data. The CCRI User Guide provides the detailed information on the creation and use of these "CCRIUID" codes.[9]

In addition to the key table, it was decided to capture additional published tables of aggregate data containing the most consistent and significant variables at the CSD level.[10] The published tables of aggregate data contain a wealth of additional information that the project was able to link to the CCRI census geographical files (maps). On the one hand, these provide a statistical context for the CCRI sample data.[11] On the other hand, the published data are particularly valuable as a selection filter for areas of interest, or for aggregation of sample data, as well as for cross-census comparisons (between sample data of one year and published tabular data of a different year). Some of these uses will be illustrated later in this volume.

The Census Geography of 1911, a Period of Transition

Canada in 1911 was in a period of political transition. The central and Prairie provinces, as we know them today, became established during this period (see figure 2.2). In 1901, most of the territory of the Canadian west and north was part of the Northwest Territories. It was only in 1905 that Saskatchewan and

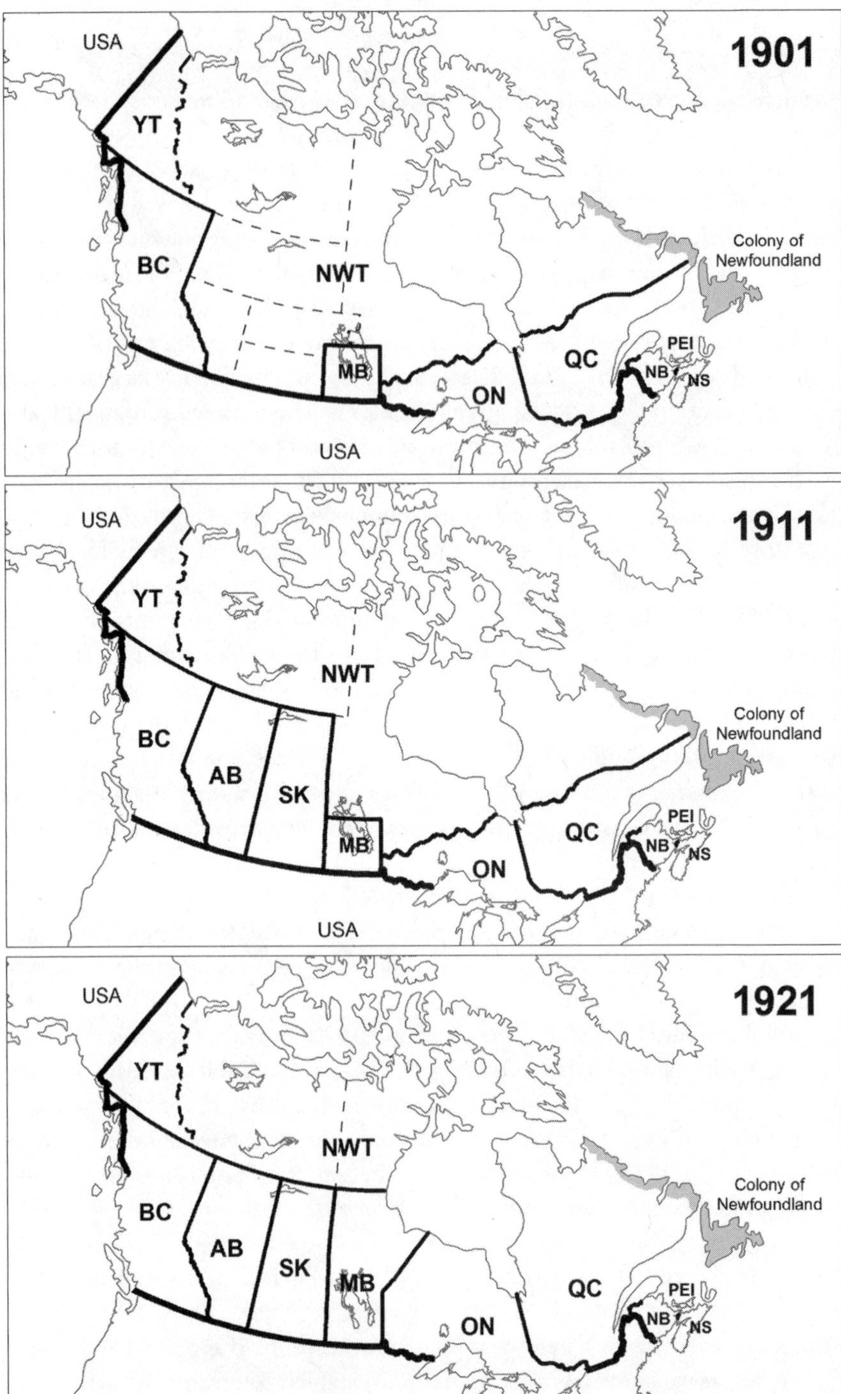

YT – Yukon Territory
NWT – Northwest Territories
BC – British Columbia
AB – Alberta
SK – Saskatchewan
MB – Manitoba
ON – Ontario
QC – Quebec
NB – New Brunswick
NS – Nova Scotia
PEI – Prince Edward Island

Alberta were carved out as provinces, and not until 1912 that Manitoba, Ontario, and Quebec were extended north to achieve their present boundaries.

In many places within the provinces and territories, internal boundaries were also in a state of flux. This was not an issue of land tenure or organization – the different regional survey systems across the country were well established. In the east, the county and parish or township systems were long-standing. Even in the west, the Dominion Land Survey Township-Range-Meridian system had been established since the 1870s, as the prairies were opened up for agricultural settlement.

In much of the country, however, especially in the west, municipal and territorial governance was still in a transitory stage of development. Manitoba, a province since 1870, enacted local (rural) municipal legislation between 1873 and 1900, which incorporated urban and rural municipalities. This was all before the major northern expansion in 1912. The Northwest Territories enacted municipal ordinances beginning in 1883, but many rearrangements of municipal organization occurred up until 1904. The creation of Saskatchewan and Alberta as provinces, in 1905, caused more reorganization. Saskatchewan, in 1909, enacted legislation to govern cities, towns, villages, and rural municipalities, with most of its rural municipalities incorporating between 1910 and 1913. Alberta's separate acts for towns, villages, rural municipalities, and improvement districts passed in 1912. In both provinces, rural municipalities (RMs) or (local) improvement districts (LIDs) generally came to consist of nine townships (three by three square), but this varied depending on local physical and historical geography. British Columbia, a province since 1871, allowed for both urban and rural municipalities (cities and districts), which ranged greatly in population size and area and were only incidentally tied to the land division or survey fabric.[12]

This meant that in 1911, in many parts of Canada, ad hoc combinations of surveyed entities were used for census purposes. This situation was exacerbated by the practical decision of the census organizers to make use of electoral divisions as much as possible for organizing the census enumeration.[13] CDs and CSDs are supposed to conform to existing, presumably federal, electoral divisions (FEDs) and subdivisions. Electoral divisions and subdivisions are not necessarily stable, frequently changing from one election to the next, and periodically being redrawn based on census results.[14] Federal electoral divisions are supposed to reflect provincial divisions; however, provincial elections take place at different times in different provinces (see table 2.2). Municipal

Figure 2.2 (opposite) · Changing boundaries of Canada's provinces, 1901, 1911, and 1921.

Source: CCRI geographical database. Unless otherwise noted, all subsequent figures in this chapter are from this source.

Table 2.2 · Federal and provincial elections, Canada, 1900–12

Federal	*1900*				*1904*				*1908*			*1911*	
PEI	1900				1904				1908				1912
NS		1901					1906					1911	
NB				1903					1908				1912
QC	1900				1904				1908				1912
ON			1902			1905			1908			1911	
MB				1903				1907			1910		
SK		PART OF NWT UNTIL 1905				1905			1908				1912
AB		PART OF NWT UNTIL 1905				1905				1909			
BC	1900			1903				1907		1909			1912
YT	1900			1903		1905		1907		1909			1912
NWT			1902			1905 AB AND SK SEPARATED; COUNCIL APPOINTED							

Note: The Sources are public records. See Parliament of Canada website, "History of federal ridings since 1867." http://www.parl.gc.ca/About/Parliament/FederalRidingsHistory/hfer.asp?Language=E&Search=G and individual provincial websites. The Electoral Atlas of 1906 recorded the Federal Electoral Districts (FEDs) of 1904; the Electoral Atlas of 1915 recorded the FEDs of 1914–15.

divisions are generally more stable than electoral ones, but especially in rural areas, may be inconvenient for census-taking purposes – for example, a rural municipality based on the regular, rectangular survey system may be split by water bodies or other physical features, making it easier to allocate portions to different enumerators rather than to one. So, the challenge of recreating census geography stems from inconsistencies in the definition of census geographical units themselves.

In practice, the most recent electoral divisions, from federal or from provincial elections, generally were the units used for enumeration purposes – drawing up the itineraries to be covered by each enumerator and recorded on the census schedules. Local municipal divisions – townships, parishes, and counties – were generally the units used for reporting purposes, that is, for the tables printed in the published census volumes. There is secondary evidence that massive recompilation tables were used at the Census and Statistics Office (CSO), later the Dominion Bureau of Statistics (DBS), after each census taking by which the collected data were reorganized into the published census tables, but these are no longer extant.[15]

Unfortunately, the relationship between electoral units and local municipal divisions is unclear and rather confusing in the available census documentation. The distinction is only made explicit from 1931 onwards, after which a table in the published volumes provides population by federal electoral district in addition to most other tables that provide results by census district. It is not until very recent times that there has been a concerted effort to standardize census geography for reporting purposes.[16]

During the initial planning of the CCRI project and through the detailed planning of the geocoding, it was impossible to fully appreciate the magnitude and impact of these differences. Only deep into the process of reconstructing the census geography did they become evident. To locate our sample population in the proper CSD, we could not just assume a one-to-one or many-to-one correspondence between enumeration areas and reporting districts. In many cases, EAs were split between more than one CSD, so it was necessary to analyze the contents of the "place of habitation" field in the original enumerations in order to locate dwellings correctly. The correspondence between the census-taking geography and the census-reporting geography does become more consistent as the census decades roll by, and as the documentation becomes clearer – but for the CCRI geography team, the reconstruction of 1911 was a rude awakening. For example, in retrospect, it can be seen that in Ontario the published CDs and CSDs followed the electoral atlas of 1906 fairly faithfully; in Quebec, the electoral atlas of 1915 is a more accurate rendition of the census geography.

Despite these challenges, the fact that the early twentieth century was a period of political and geographical transition led the chief of the CSO, Archibald Blue, and his colleagues to adopt a comprehensive approach to census reporting, which provides some unexpected fringe benefits in the census geography for 1911. The exhaustive detail of the published census for that year contains more unique CSDs than any other census before or since (see table 2.1.) This level of detail is a double-edged sword: it offers the potential for more fine-grained geographical analysis than any other census; at the same time, it poses challenges in using the data because of small sample sizes. Reaggregation may be required for what should be relatively simple analyses, as well as for comparative analyses over the 1911–51 CCRI data series. The major reasons for the large number of the 1911 CSDs are summarized below.

1 *Many small urban CSDs (towns and villages).* The definition of "urban" varies from one census to the next, including the size threshold for reported cities, towns, and villages. In the 1911 published key table, cities, towns, and villages of any size (not necessarily legally incorporated) were listed separately as CSDs, and shown with a "c," "t," or "v" after their names. There was no minimum population size requirement; the smallest two villages were Anthracite and Evarts, both in Alberta, with a population of twenty-five each. The CCRI team added a field to our geographical files called CCRI_URBAN_RURAL that coded all of these records URBAN, and all other records as RURAL. Obviously, in some cases, this is a somewhat dubious distinction. So, for the purposes of some of the chapters of this book, an urban reclassification scheme based on CSD population size was developed and used for selection and aggregation. See section on urban versus rural, below.

2 *Many CSDs within major urban areas (wards and part-wards) split between CDs.* As mentioned, the definition of "urban" varies between censuses. In our 1911 urban reclassification, we defined "major urban areas" as cities with a population over 20,000 as listed in the cities table.[17] In 1911, there are fifteen of these major urban areas. In 1911, the CDs followed electoral divisions in these areas, which did not always correspond to municipal boundaries. CSDs also generally followed municipal ward boundaries, but these did not always match the electoral districts.

As an example, the City of Toronto (see figure 2.3 top map, 1911 Toronto CDs and CSDs) comprises the entirety of five CDs (Toronto North, South, East, West, and Centre) and part of another CD (York

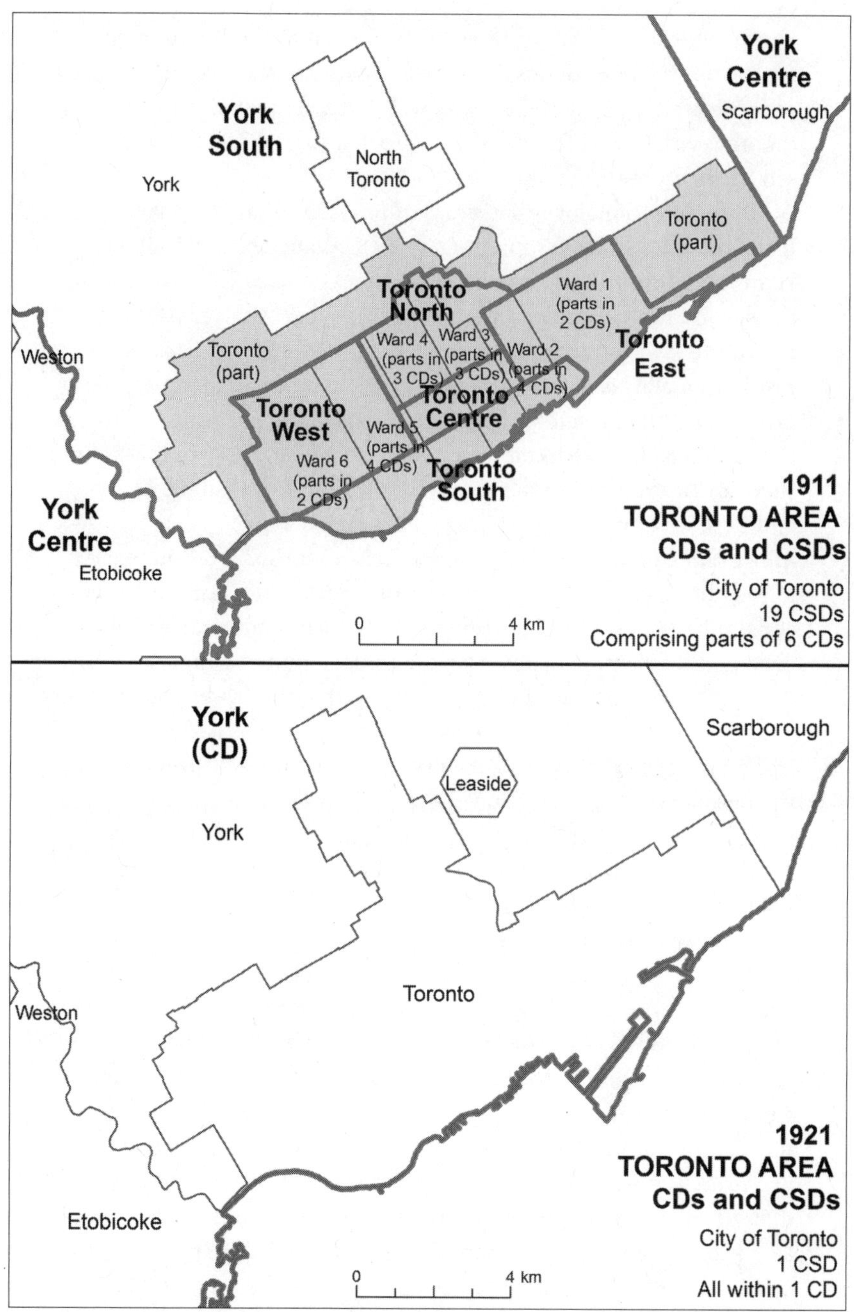

Figure 2.3 · Published census district (CD) and subdistrict (CSD) boundaries, Toronto area, 1911 and 1921.

South.) Within these CDs, the CSDs have been based on municipal wards, but the boundaries do not correspond to the electoral divisions, so these are split between CDs, as well. A total of nineteen CSDs, therefore, make up the City of Toronto. (In 1921, this is reduced to one; see figure 2.3 bottom map.)

Of the fifteen major urban areas in 1911, the following seven are made up of CSDs from more than one CD: Vancouver, Winnipeg, Hamilton, Toronto, Ottawa, Montreal, and Quebec City. Toronto is the second most complex situation of this type; Montreal is the most convoluted, with thirty-four CSDs from nine different CDs. As a result, to make basic comparisons between major urban areas, these groups of CSDs have to be aggregated. This has been done to simplify the analytical picture in many of the maps and analyses in this volume such as, for example, in the chapters by Gaffield et al. and by Jones and Park.

3 *Many and widely varying CDs in Ontario.* Ontario's CD boundaries follow the electoral divisions strictly in 1901 and 1911, and the numbers are similar (89 vs. 85). Unfortunately for census comparability, however, neither election kept very close to the county boundaries of the day, with township swapping rampant, so that the CD boundaries vary widely between 1901, 1911, and later years. (See maps in figures 2.4, 2.5, and 2.6.) By the 1921 census, county boundaries largely prevailed, as the number of CDs was reduced to fifty-four (and the numbers remain in that range through 1951). Fortunately, the underlying CSDs in southern Ontario, based on townships, towns, and villages, remained relatively consistent throughout the time periods.

4 *Many more CSDs on the Prairies (individual townships).* The most numerically significant feature of the 1911 census geography is the ballooning of the number of CSDs in the Prairie provinces, from 484 in 1901 (including Assiniboia) to 6,615 in 1911. This was the result of listing every prairie township as a separate CSD, as well as each small town or village (see table 2.1, point 1 above, and figure 2.7 for the example of southern Saskatchewan). This occurred despite the pre-existing amalgamations (rural municipalities or local improvement districts) that appear as named CSDs in the 1901 census, as well as on some contemporary maps.[18] The reason for this approach by the census makers is obscure, nor is it addressed in the reports included in the published volumes.[19] In 1921, as CSDs were redefined on the prairies according to the new and more stable organization of municipalities, the number of CSDs is reduced to a more manageable 1,519.

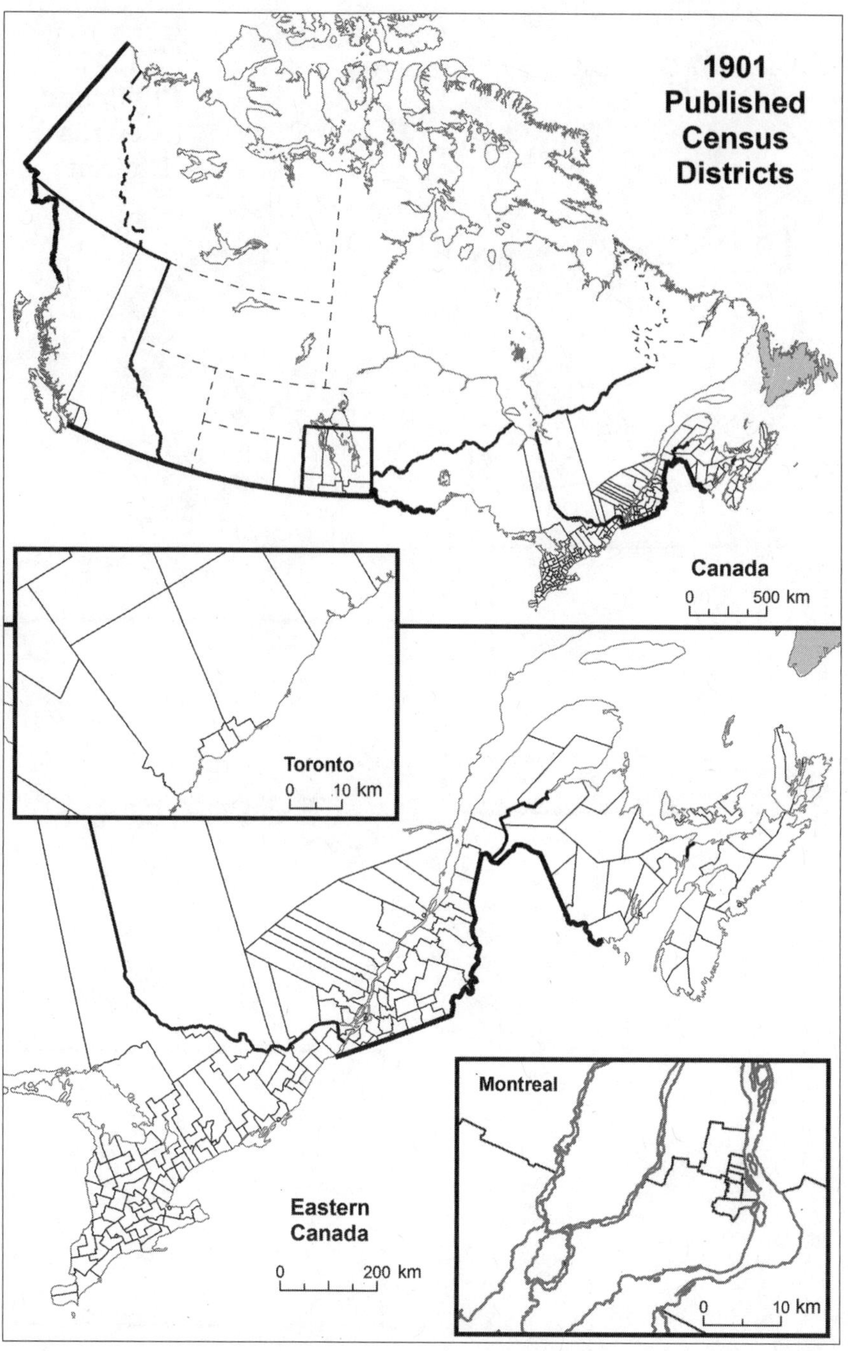

Figure 2.4 · Published census district boundaries: All Canada, Eastern Canada, Toronto, and Montreal, 1901.

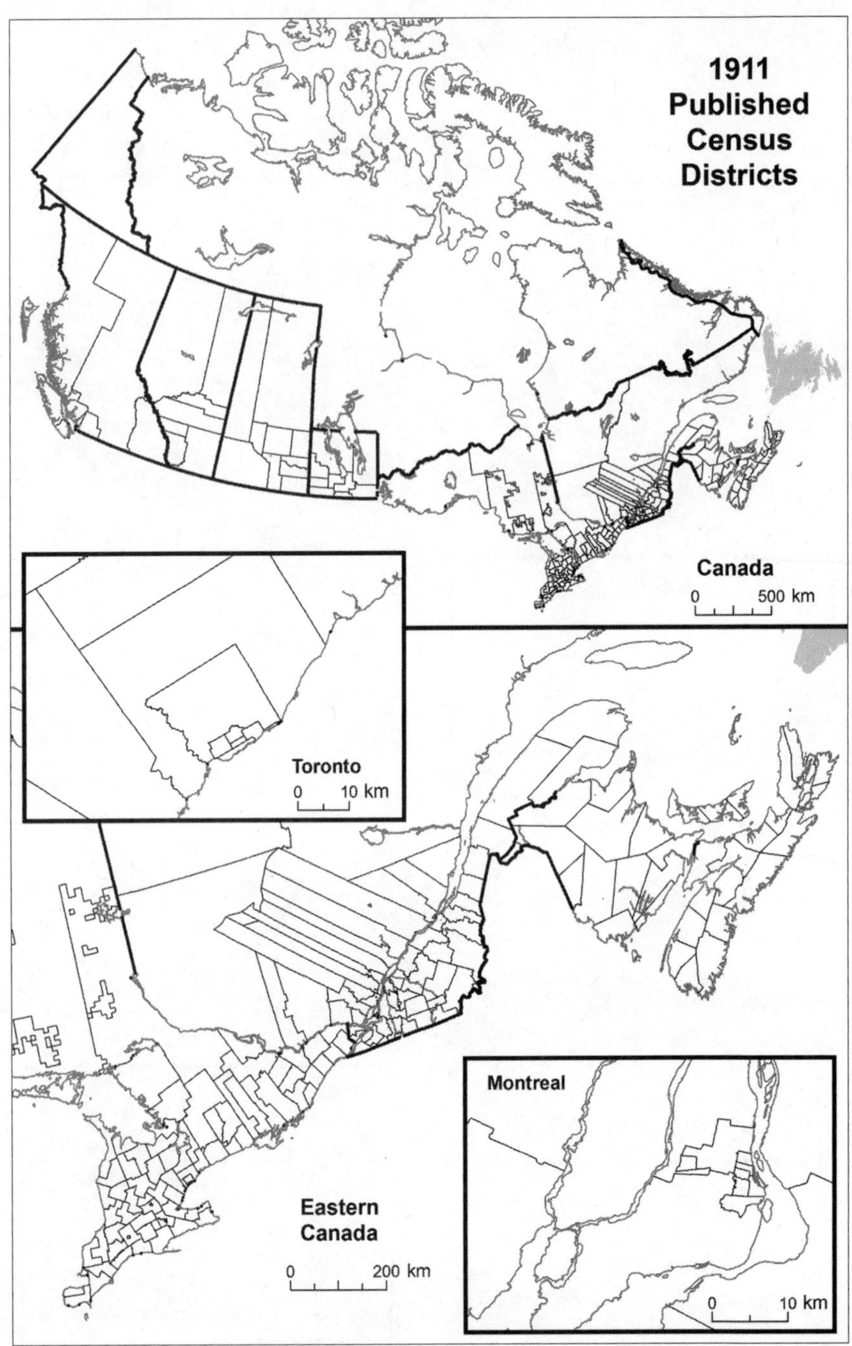

Figure 2.5 · Published census district boundaries: All Canada, Eastern Canada, Toronto, and Montreal, 1911.

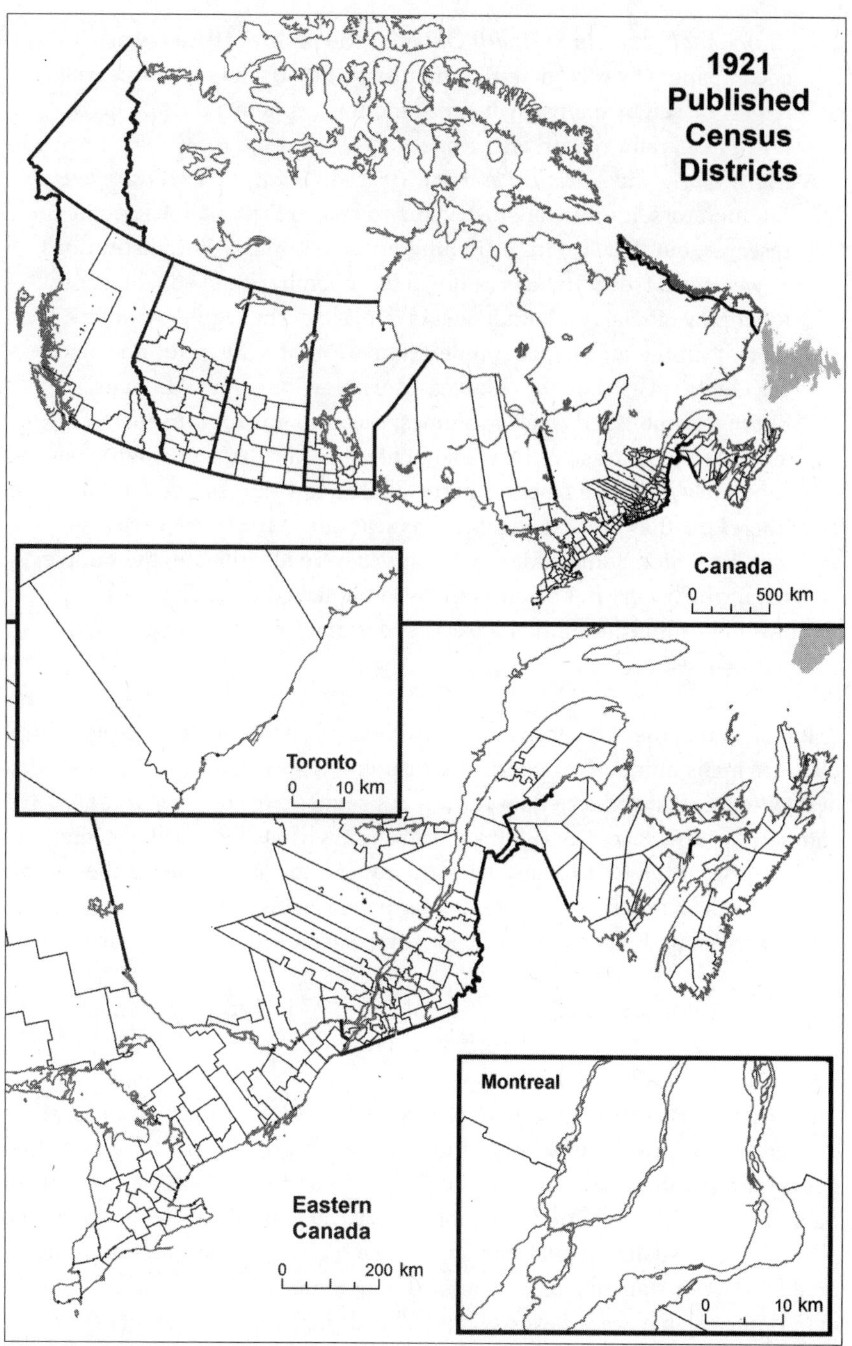

Figure 2.6 · Published census district boundaries: All Canada, Eastern Canada, Toronto, and Montreal, 1921.

5 *Many small CSDs in northern Ontario.* The prairie inflation was accompanied by record-setting numbers of CSDs in Ontario, as well, largely driven by many small and sometimes ephemeral CSDs in the north (e.g., railway workers camps).
6 *Many more First Nations Reserve CSDs than in any other census year.* Enumerators in 1901 were instructed to record First Nations people on reserves, but that "(9) In the enumeration of inmates of ... institutions, as well as of Treaty Indians ... it will be generally found advantageous to employ officials and other agents in place of the regular enumerators."[20] In the 1901 list of enumeration areas, at least thirty-one places are identified as "Indian" reserves, "Agencies," or simply, "Indians," but in the published census volumes, these do not appear separately as CSDs. In contrast, in 1911, a large number of CSDs were identified separately as Indian reserves in the published volumes, 151 in total. Therefore, they are also identified as separate CSDs in the CCRI geographical files. Some additional reserves were identified in the sample data, which were not listed as CSDs in published data. They were assigned an "Other Indian Reserves" designation, associated with the CD in question.[21]

It is clear that the 1911 census, the "base year" used for the CCRI geographical files, has many unique characteristics. Prominent among these is a higher level of geographical specificity than for any subsequent year – over 10,000 CSDs compared with 4,847 in 1921. This posed some serious logistical challenges to the creation of the CCRI census geography and the geocoding of the sample data. Yet, it also provides the potential for increased usefulness of the 1911 data, and enhanced usability as the basis for comparison with other census years.

Usefulness and Potential of the 1911 Geographical Coding and GIS Files

The 1911 census and geographical files can be used in a variety of ways, some exemplified in this volume, and others beyond its scope. We have seen that geographically the 1911 census was unique. It was also distinctive in terms of data content. As a microdata sample, the CCRI 1911 database provides the potential for visualizing relationships embedded within dwellings and households, between standard or customized geographical areas, as well as within data domains that were never compiled and published in the aggregate statistical volumes. The true potential of the CCRI geocoding and GIS files lies

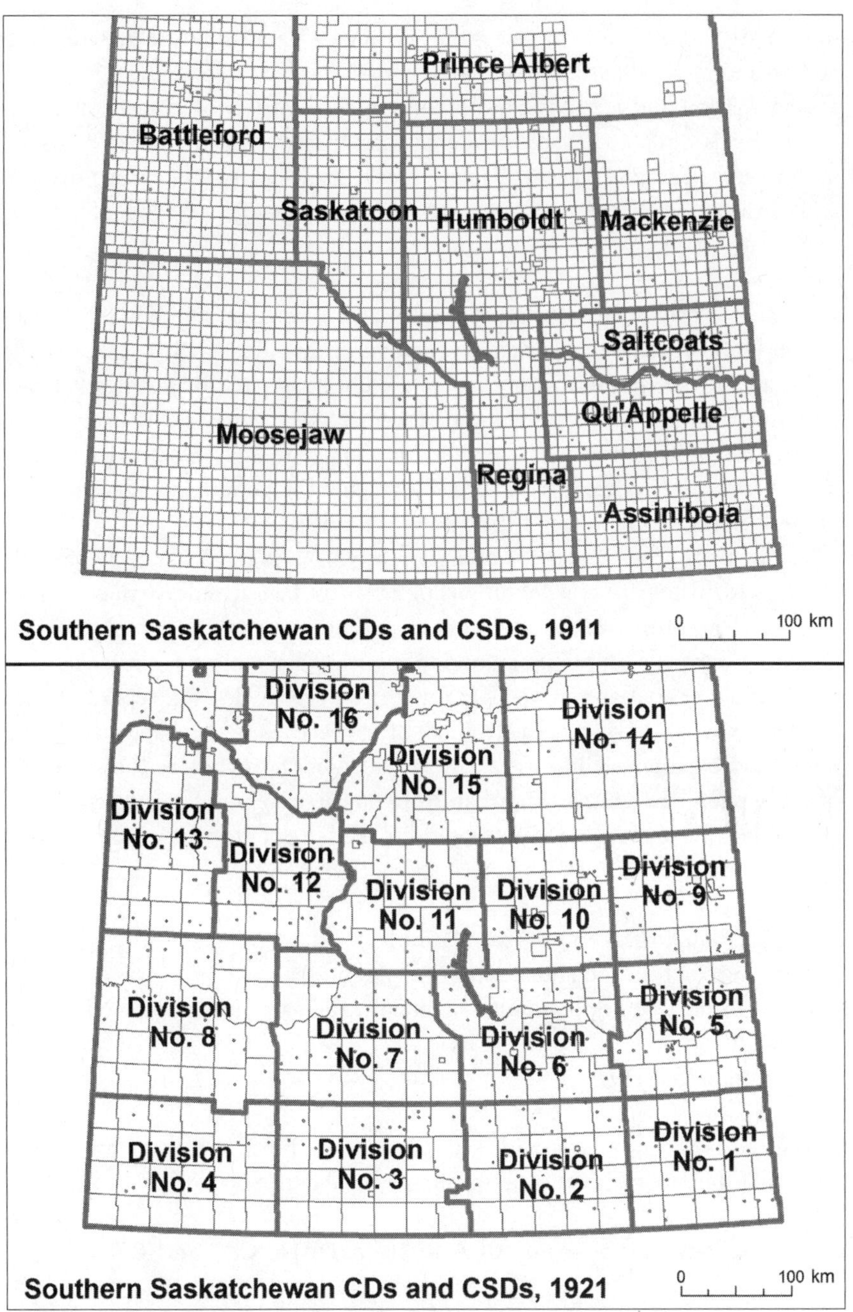

Figure 2.7 · Published census district (CD) and subdistrict (CSD) boundaries, Southern Saskatchewan, 1911 and 1921.

in two areas: being able to select and aggregate data using the geographical coding and being able to visualize and analyse these data spatially.

Aggregation and analysis can be done using a variety of criteria, at a variety of levels of detail. These can be categorized roughly into three types: (1) urban versus rural; (2) census geographical areas – province, census district, and census subdistrict; and (3) census subdistrict aggregation for analysis.

Urban versus Rural

Urban versus rural differentiation is critical to the understanding of the factors at work in shaping the country, and recommended by Statistics Canada for analysing the modern aggregate and Public Use Microdata files.[22] However, the definition of city or country varies between censuses, and even within them. The published census volumes for each year typically provide one or more tables with an urban/rural breakdown and the population of cities. Both of these change in definition from one year to the next.[23]

The 1911 published tables of population by CSD and the CSD-TYPE variable allow us to customize our definitions of urban and rural and use the criterion of city size according to the needs of any specific analysis. In this volume, Lisa Dillon uses the cut-off point of 3,000 to replicate her 1901 and previous analyses. Gaffield et al. map sample data for 1911 by census district, separating out residents of major urban areas from all other people. In his chapter analysing household experiences in 1901 and 1911, Gordon Darroch uses the threshold of 1,000 people to distinguish urban from quasi-rural populations. An urban/rural reclassification table was created for the latter purposes which categorizes the data records as follows:

Small urban (urban < 1,000 population)
Minor urban (> 1,000 and < 20,000 population)
Major urban (> 20,000 population, major urban area identified by name)
Rural unspecified
Rural Indian reserves

The reclassification is provided as a helpful convenience; users are free to construct their own classification from the database.

Census Geographical Areas: Province, CD, and CSD

Census geographical areas as defined in the published census tables are the standard units for mapping and analysing historical census data and, indeed, until now have been the only option available for 1911–51. Many examples of these analyses populate the literature, including historical atlases and studies at the national and provincial levels.[24] Using these predefined units, such as census districts, for mapping sample data also has its advantages, primarily, comparability with the published aggregate data tables and with previous studies of the same period. However, there are disadvantages, as well. Much of the data have only been published at the CD level; these cover very large geographical areas and so represent a very coarse filter for geographical analysis. Related to this is the well-known "modifiable areal unit problem" – the fact that the results and significance of statistical analyses based on geographically aggregated data can change depending on the areal unit used.[25] The basic approach to avoid potential errors of this type is to use the smallest geographical unit possible and, ideally, one that will faithfully reflect the scale of the underlying phenomena. Finally, an obvious issue is the changes in census geographical boundaries between censuses and the difficulty this raises for comparative analysis over time.

A main goal of the Canadian Century Research Infrastructure has been to permit the mapping of sample data. As with any data sample, this raises questions of sample size in detailed analysis. The strength of the CCRI geocoding is its fine-grained geographical mesh; nevertheless, care must be taken to ensure that small numbers in many CSDs do not yield sample sizes too small to be representative. Census districts, as defined in 1911, pose no problem for the usual statistical thresholds: the raw numbers of dwellings and people are always sufficient. Gaffield et al.'s maps showing CD populations broken down by dominant language or Gauvreau and Thornton's maps of mixed households by CD are examples of these. However, when subpopulations are extracted from CDs, these may be much smaller in size: for example, the cohort of the elderly analysed in Dillon's chapter had to be tested to ensure that minimum sample sizes of twenty were met, and selected CDs needed to be grouped to achieve this. When the unit of analysis is taken down to the CSD, the base numbers of dwellings and people shrink, so researchers have to exercise the usual judgment with respect to appropriate sample size, both with regard to numbers of dwellings and numbers of individuals within these cluster samples. For example, to study subpopulations of the elderly or of particular "origin" groups or of occupations, one is likely to need to amalgamate CSDs. In general, the issue of how CSDs should be regrouped should follow a few basic principles: geographical proximity, geographical contiguity, and data homogeneity. How these are defined and implemented depends on the context. However, this is not the only option – in addition to aggregation for reasons of minimum sample size, the CCRI census geography facilitates other forms of aggregation for the purposes of analysis.

CSD Aggregation for Analysis

Some aggregation of census subdistricts may be necessary or desirable for a number of reasons in addition to meeting minimum sample sizes: regrouping in order to pursue cross-census comparisons, to create a geographically defined regrouping, to create a statistically defined regrouping. The general issue has been discussed elsewhere.[26] Here, we briefly illustrate some applications of aggregation.

Operationally, the aggregation process normally occurs as a series of steps alternating between working with the geographical files in a GIS environment and working on the data files using statistical software. The aggregation of CSDs entails selecting a set of 1911 CCRIUIDs based on their locational relationship to some reference layer, defined by cross-census comparison, external geography, or statistically. The targeted CCRIUIDs are then recoded to reflect that relationship. From this, a correspondence table can be exported from the GIS and into the statistical software, where this new geographical attribute can be allocated to the sample. Sample data can then be cross-tabulated or statistically analysed, based on this new characteristic, and exported back out for analysis in the GIS.

Aggregation for analytical purposes may be best represented by examples. If we were interested in how the number of people in households in regular dwellings varied on the prairies in 1911, we might use the available data to aggregate CSDs and map average household size in 1911 in three different ways.

First, a cross-census comparison regrouping could be used to aggregate data linked to standard census geographical areas like CSDs in order to match standard census geographical areas in a different census. For example, the CSDs in 1911 could be reclassified to match the census districts of 1921. This would be useful for a comparison between 1911 and 1921, since the CSD and CD boundaries are very different in the two years. Figure 2.8 illustrates such a mapping for Saskatchewan.[27]

Second, one might geographically aggregate sample data based on other externally defined geographical boundaries or relationships.[28] For example, if one is interested in how settlement varied relative to climatic, soil, or other environmental conditions, given prior knowledge of one or more of these conditions, one could compare settlement patterns to them. In our Saskatchewan example, areas of poor agricultural capability, such as the southern short-grass prairie, were settled later and more slowly than the more fertile moist mixed

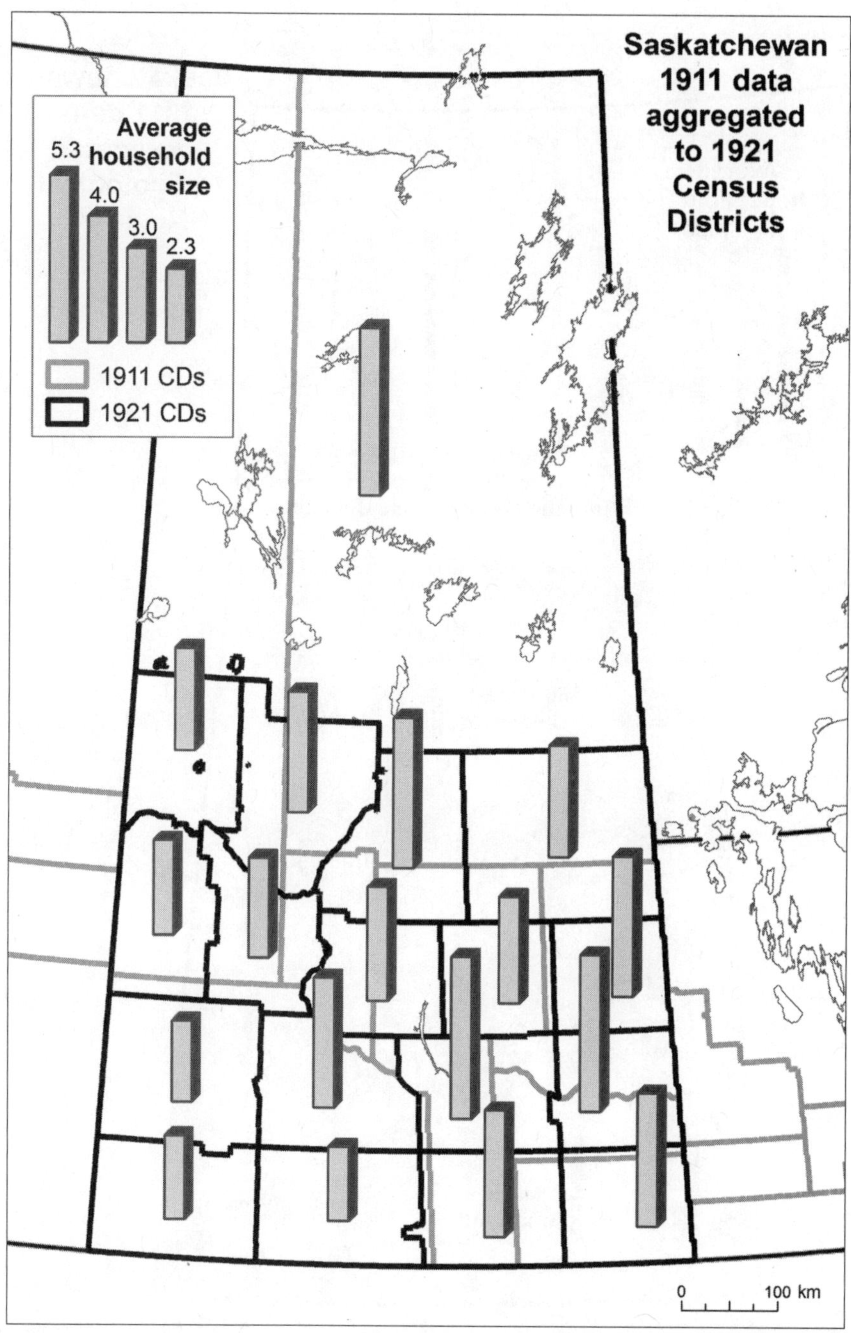

Figure 2.8 · Saskatchewan 1911 sample data aggregated to 1921 census districts (CDs), showing average household size by district.

Source: CCRI 1911 sample data and CCRI geographical database.

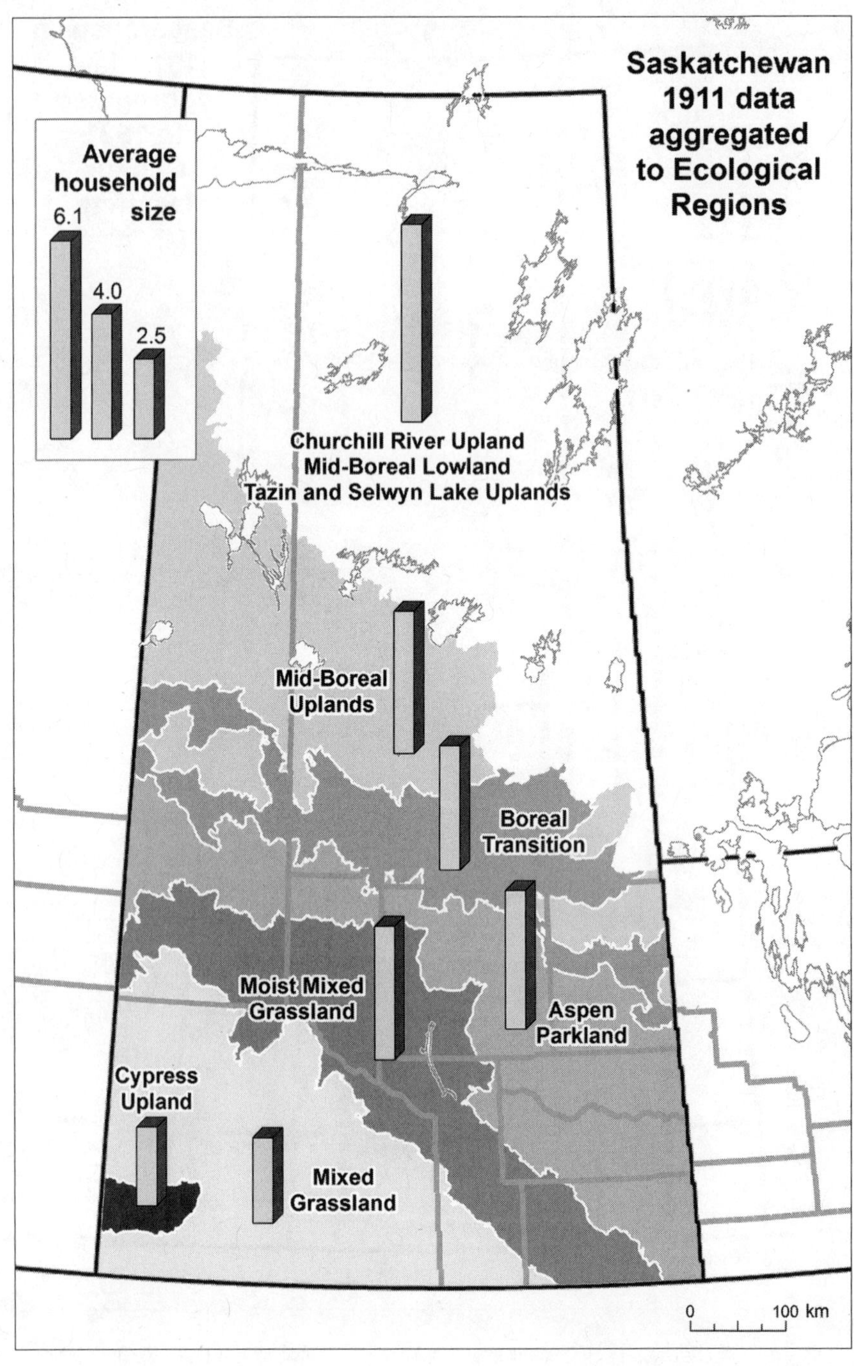
Saskatchewan
1911 data
aggregated
to Ecological
Regions
Average
household
size
6.1
4.0
2.5
Churchill River Upland
Mid-Boreal Lowland
Tazin and Selwyn Lake Uplands
Mid-Boreal
Uplands
Boreal
Transition
Moist Mixed
Grassland
Aspen
Parkland
Cypress
Upland
Mixed
Grassland
0
100 km

grassland region. In later years, these were subject to more farm abandonment as northern expansion into the parkland areas occurred.[29] How did these factors relate to household size, and how did this change over time? As an example, figure 2.9 illustrates the differences in average household size in 1911 between different ecological regions in Saskatchewan.[30]

Third, a statistically defined aggregation might be based on internal characteristics of the CSDs, such as their socio-economic or demographic circumstances. These could be generated from the sample data themselves, if sample sizes are sufficient, but they also may be obtained from the published aggregate data tables, if that suits the purpose.[31] One could define CSD groupings based on population density and region of the province, for example, and look at average household size within these aggregations. Figure 2.10 shows population density in 1911 by CSD – obviously, there is great variability around the province and abrupt local changes, as well. To generalize this into density regions, a smoothed surface representing varying population was developed and then broken into zones of comparable densities (sparse, low, medium, high, and urban) in three different regions of the province (southwest, central, and north). Figure 2.11 shows average household size as calculated for each of these subregion zones. A useful review of methods of geographical aggregation and spatial data processing for demographic analysis was published in 2007.[32]

Other potential avenues to pursue can readily be imagined. For example, the use of spatial statistical methods such as spatial autocorrelation to determine

Figure 2.9 (opposite) · Saskatchewan 1911 sample data aggregated to ecological regions, showing average household size by region.

Sources: CCRI 1911 sample database; CCRI geographical database; and Natural Resources Canada, Earth Sciences Sector, "The State of Canada's Ecosystems in Maps," GeoGratis (2002). http://geogratis.gc.ca/api/en/nrcan-rncan/ess-sst/9099a060-77ea-57f6-b1b9-50f9eeef435b.

Figure 2.10 (overleaf, left) · Saskatchewan 1911 published data showing population density in 1911 by census subdistrict (CSD).

Sources: CCRI geographical database; and CCRI digitized published tables, Census of Canada, 1911, vol. I, Table 1, the latter available from the CCRI website at http://ccri.library.ualberta.ca/endatabase/geography/digitizedpublictables/index.html.

Figure 2.11 (overleaf, right) · Saskatchewan 1911 sample data aggregated to subregions in the north, central, and southwest parts of the province, showing average household size in subregions of comparable population density.

Source: CCRI 1911 sample database; CCRI geographical database; and CCRI digitized published tables, Census of Canada, 1911, vol. I, Table 1, the latter available from the CCRI website at http://ccri.library.ualberta.ca/endatabase/geography/digitizedpublictables/index.html.

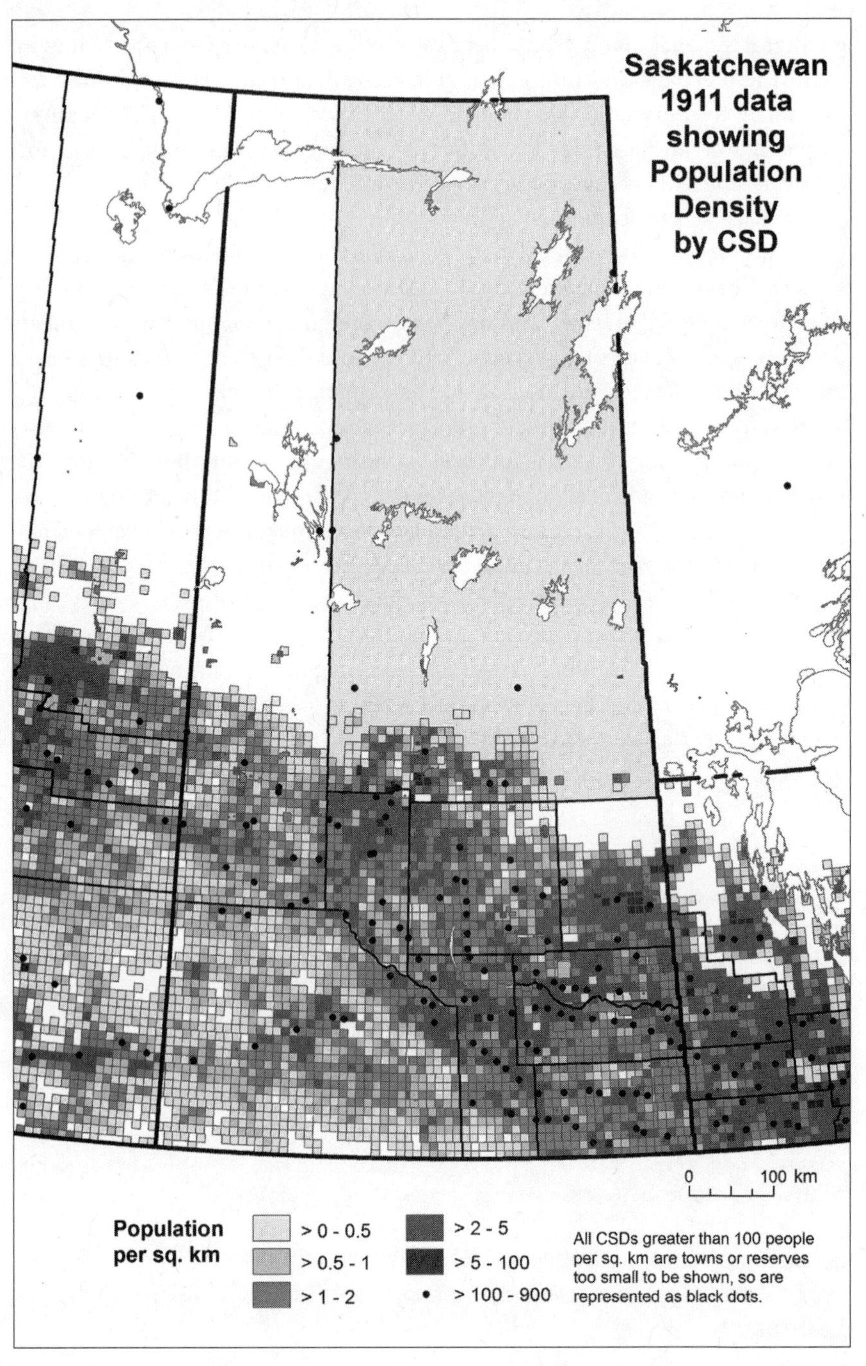
Saskatchewan
1911 data
showing
Population
Density
by CSD
0
100 km
Population
per sq. km
> 0 - 0.5
> 0.5 - 1
> 1 - 2
> 2 - 5
> 5 - 100
> 100 - 900
All CSDs greater than 100 people per sq. km are towns or reserves too small to be shown, so are represented as black dots.

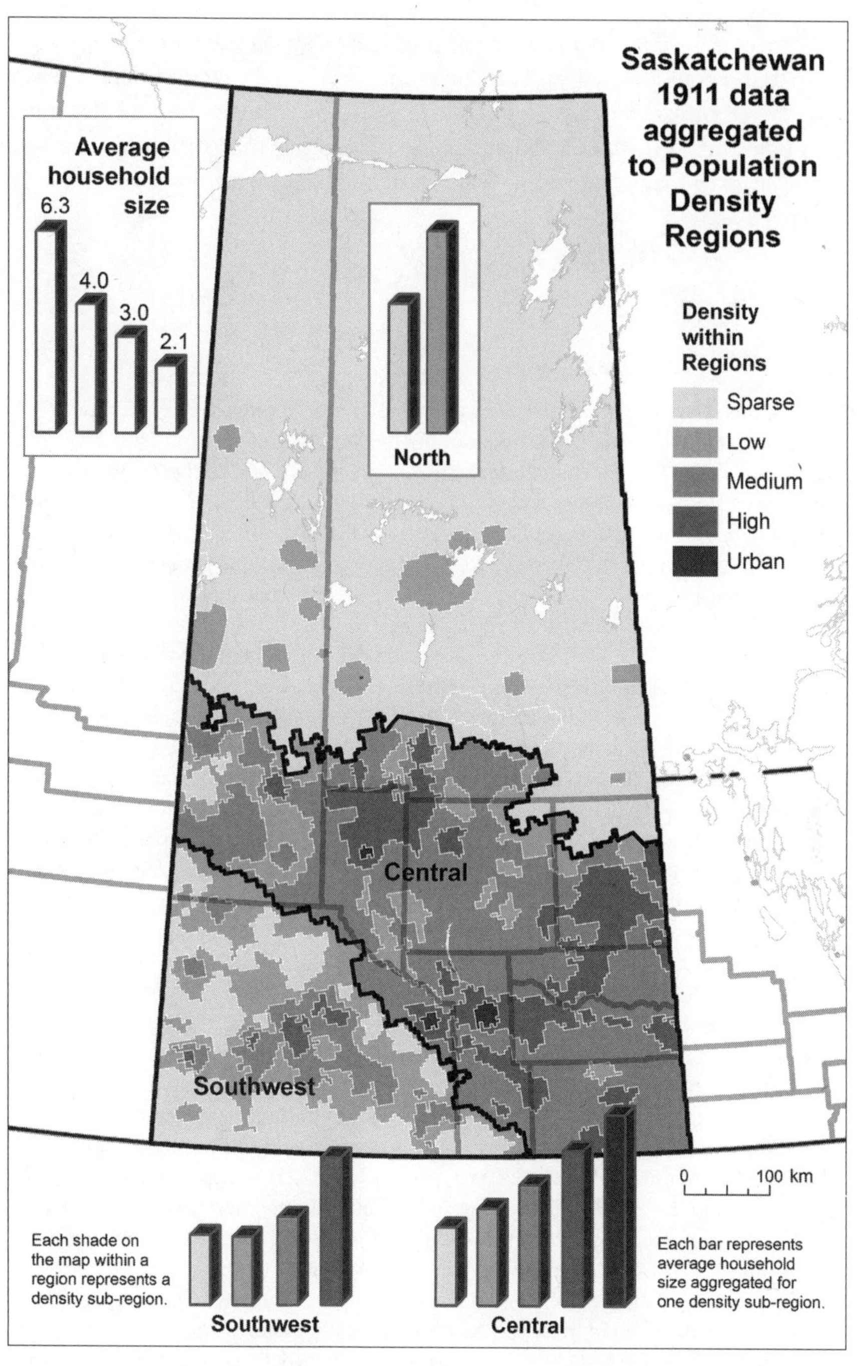
Saskatchewan 1911 data aggregated to Population Density Regions
Average household size
6.3
4.0
3.0
2.1
North
Density within Regions
Sparse
Low
Medium
High
Urban
Central
Southwest
0
100 km
Each shade on the map within a region represents a density sub-region.
Southwest
Central
Each bar represents average household size aggregated for one density sub-region.

clusters of geographical units in close proximity sharing similar characteristics, or spatial regression analysis to incorporate location as a factor in multivariate analysis, are promising areas for future research.[33] Depending on the question being studied, the Canadian Century Research Infrastructure data lend themselves to many alternative ways of being examined from a geographical perspective.

Notes

1 Canada, Department of the Interior, Railway Lands Branch, *Atlas of Canada, 1906*, 1st ed. (Ottawa: Department of the Interior, 1906).

2 Canada, Department of the Interior, *Atlas of Canada, 1915*, 2nd ed. (Ottawa: Department of the Interior, 1915).

3 Canada, Natural Resources Canada, "Atlas of Canada, 1915 – Origin of the Population, 1911 [Western Canada]," *Atlas of Canada, 1915*, http://geogratis.gc.ca/api/en/nrcan-rncan/ess-sst/ac64127a-d2c9-501f-93b4-0f4ba63b6b88.html.

4 M. St-Hilaire, B. Moldofsky, L. Richard, and M. Beaudry, "Geocoding and Mapping Historical Census Data: The Geographical Component of the Canadian Century Research Infrastructure," *Historical Methods* 40, no. 2 (2007): 76–91.

5 University of Alberta Library, *CCRI/IRCS – The Geographical Component*. 2011. http://ccri.library.ualberta.ca/enoverview/geography/index.html.

6 St-Hilaire et al., "Geocoding and Mapping Historical Census Data," 77.

7 For details, see ibid., 77–9.

8 Canada, Department of Trade and Commerce, Census and Statistics Office, *Fifth Census of Canada, 1911*, vol. I, *Areas and Population by Provinces, Districts and Sub-districts* (Ottawa: C.H. Parmalee, 1912), Table 1: 2–172.

9 For details, see User Guide to the CCRI: University of Alberta Library, *CCRI/IRCS – CCRIUID*, 2011, http://ccri.library.ualberta.ca/endatabase/geography/ccriud/index.html.

10 University of Alberta Library, *CCRI/IRCS – Digitized Public Tables*, 2011, http://ccri.library.ualberta.ca/enresources/digitizedtables/index.html. It should be noted, the additional tables, although purportedly by CSDs, in most cases do not correspond directly to the key tables; some additional aggregation was done at the compilation stage by the statistical agency. For example, in 1911 the CD of Brandon, Manitoba, had 88 CSDs in the key table; in the supplementary table of "Origins of the People," it was composed of only eleven lines: eight "Urban parts," two "Indian Reserves," and one line under "Rural parts" labelled "78 townships" (Canada, *Census of Canada, 1911*, vol. II, Table 7: 172, "Origins of the People by Sub-districts"). Therefore, the scheme linking the geography to the aggregate published data had to incorporate this variation in table organization, as well.

11 Referring back to the published tables is the way the CCRI project and Statistics Canada assessed the completeness and representativity of the sample data and the geocoding: weighted sampling numbers, by census district, were compared

with the published table totals and flagged if they differed by more than 10%. This was a check that caught a few errors introduced in the geocoding process, but also was necessary to assure Statistics Canada of the validity and accuracy of the georeferencing of the sample data. This assurance was required before Statistics Canada would allow the geocoded tables to be housed in their Research Data Centres (RDCs).

12 Sources for this section include the following: Government of Saskatchewan – Municipal Affairs, *Rural Municipality Incorporations*, http://www.municipal.gov.sk.ca/Municipal-History/RM-Incorporated-Dates-Alpha. Government of Alberta, Municipal Affairs, *About Municipalities*, 2011, http://municipalaffairs.gov.ab.ca/mc_about_municipalities.cfm. Alberta Government – HeRMIS, Provincial Archives of Alberta, *County of Minburn No. 27 Fonds*, https://hermis.alberta.ca/paa/Search.aspx?st=local+improvement+districts&cp=2. E.H. Oliver and S.D. Scott, "Local Government of Canada," in *Canada Year Book, 1915*, by Department of Trade and Commerce (Ottawa: J. de L. Taché, King's Printer, 1916), 14–26. E.H. Oliver and J. Hosie, "Provincial and Local Government in Canada," in *Canada Year Book, 1921*, by Dominion Bureau of Statistics Canada (Ottawa: F.A. Acland, King's Printer, 1922), 32–43. Canada Year Books accessed at Statistics Canada, *Canada Year Book (CYB) Historical Collection*, 1867–1967, http://www66.statcan.gc.ca/acyb_000-eng.htm.

13 According to the instructions to the Officers of the 1911 Census, and the Census Act (Revised Statutes of Canada, 1906, c. 68):

> 3(2). Census districts. The division of the country into Census districts and sub-districts shall correspond as nearly as may be with the existing electoral divisions and sub-divisions; and the said Census districts may be further divided into such sub-districts as the Minister of Agriculture may direct as units of enumeration for Census purposes; and in territories not so defined or situated as to admit of adhering to circumscriptions already established special divisions and sub-divisions shall be formed for Census purposes by authority of the Minister of Agriculture.
>
> 3(3). Census sub-districts. The sub-districts of a Census district shall ordinarily consist of townships, parishes, cities, towns and incorporated villages.

Canada, Department of Agriculture and Statistics, *Fifth Census of Canada, 1911: Instructions to Officers, Commissioners and Enumerators* (Ottawa: Government Printing Bureau, 1911).

14 Only two electoral atlases were published around this time, in 1906 and 1915. Canada, Department of the Interior, *Electoral Atlas of the Dominion of Canada as divided for the Tenth General Election held in the year 1904* (Ottawa: Government Printing Bureau, S.E. Dawson, King's Printer, 1906). J.E. Chalifour, *Electoral Atlas of the Dominion of Canada, according to the Redistribution act of 1914 and the Amending act of 1915* (Ottawa: Department of the Interior, 1915).

15 Tables of this type were saved as part of the uncatalogued collection of historical documents held at Statistics Canada which was systematically examined during CCRI research activities; selected key documents are now included in the archives of the CCRI.

16 Up until 1996, the census continued to be organized around the enumeration area (EA) as covered by a single enumerator, as the smallest statistical area polygon; see Statistics Canada, *1996 Census Handbook* (Ottawa: Industry Canada, 1997), 119–21. In 2001, a new geographical unit designed for reporting data and intended to be stable between censuses was established: the "dissemination area." See Statistics Canada, *Census 2011 – Publications – Illustrated Glossary – Dissemination Area – Detailed Definition*, 2011, http://www.statcan.gc.ca/pub/92-x/2011001/geo/da-ad/def-eng.htm.

17 *Fifth Census of Canada, 1911*, vol. I, Table 13 ("Population of Cities, Towns and Incorporated Villages in 1911 and 1901 by Provinces and Electoral Districts, and Increase in the Decade"), 535–53.

18 Scarborough Company, Map: "Survey of Western Part of the Dominion of Canada" (Hamilton, ON: Scarborough Company, 1904), Library and Archives Canada, record no. 19100.

19 It may well be explained by the administrative uncertainties of the day. With two new provinces just created (Alberta and Saskatchewan in 1905), three more in the process of expanding (Manitoba, Ontario, and Quebec in 1912), and most of these provinces introducing or amending municipal legislation, it may have seemed the only prudent course to reduce political aggregations to their lowest common denominator: the surveyed township. However volatile the rest of the political redistribution picture might be, at least those would stay constant. Or, it may be that the detailed collection of agricultural statistics for which Archibald Blue is credited meant that the infrastructure was in place to effectuate this level of detail, and so it was deemed prudent to do so. M.C. Urquhart, "Three Builders of Canada's Statistical System," *Canadian Historical Review* 68, no. 3 (1987): 423.

20 Canada, Census Office, *Fourth Census of Canada, 1901*, vol. I, *Population* (Ottawa: S.E. Dawson, 1902), xv.

21 No other published censuses, from 1921 and until 1951, list First Nations reserves separately in their CSD tables. Rather, the convention is to group all reserves together in one CSD per CD, generically named "Indian Reserves." These have been given a common CCRI CSD identifier for all the reserves in each CD. See published census volumes: Canada, Department of Trade and Commerce, Dominion Bureau of Statistics, *Sixth Census of Canada, 1921* (Ottawa: King's Printer 1924); Canada, Department of Trade and Commerce, Dominion Bureau of Statistics, *Seventh Census of Canada, 1931* (Ottawa: King's Printer 1933); Canada, Department of Trade and Commerce, Dominion Bureau of Statistics, *Eighth Census of Canada, 1941* (Ottawa: King's Printer 1950); Canada, Department of Trade and Commerce, Dominion Bureau of Statistics, *Ninth Census of Canada, 1951* (Ottawa: Queen's Printer 1953).

22 Robert Mendelson, "Geographic Structures as Census Variables: Using Geography to Analyse Social and Economic Processes," *Statistics Canada Geography Division: Geography Working Paper Series* (Ottawa: Statistics Canada, March 2001), p. 1 and throughout; see http://www.statcan.gc.ca/pub/92f0138m/92f0138m2001001-eng.pdf.

23 In the *Fourth Census of Canada, 1901*, vol. I, *Population*, urban is defined as any incorporated city, town, or village (Table 4), and cities are considered towns over 5,000 population (Table 5). In the *Fifth Census of Canada, 1911*, vol. I, *Areas and Population by Provinces, Districts and Sub-districts*, again, all incorporated places are listed (Table 13; and only those over 4,000 are shown in Table 14). In the *Sixth Census of Canada, 1921*, vol. I, *Population: Number, Sex and Distribution – Racial Origins – Religions*, there are separate tables for cities and towns (Table 10), villages (Table 11), places over 1,000 (Table 12), places over 5,000 (Table 13), places over 2,500 (Table 28, by racial origin), places over 10,000 (Table 17, by sex).

In 1901 and 1911, only total numbers are published for these defined units – cross-tabulations of other data are non-existent. The city total numbers are valuable as a cross-check for redefining major urban areas, which in 1911 are particularly complex, as explained above. This situation is not limited to 1911, however; it also applies in 1901. See *Fourth Census of Canada, 1901*, vol. I, xxii: "In Table 5 the whole population of incorporated towns and cities having over 5,000 inhabitants is given regardless of their position as parts of two or more Electoral districts."

24 Some examples are M. McInnis, "Elements of Population Change," Plate 28, in Donald Kerr and Deryck W. Holdsworth (eds.), *Historical Atlas of Canada*, vol. III, *Addressing the Twentieth Century, 1891–1961* (Toronto: University of Toronto Press, 1990). Also in the same volume, see C. Gaffield and L. Marks, "Schooling and Social Structure," Plate 33, and M. MacPherson and D. Campbell, "Religious Adherence," Plate 34. See also Canada, Department of the Interior, Plate 25, "Origins of the Population, 1911," in *Atlas of Canada, 1915*; Canada, Department of Mines and Technical Surveys, Geographical Branch, "Age and Sex Ratios, 1951," Plate 51, in *Atlas of Canada, 1957* (Ottawa: Queen's Printer, 1957); Canada, Dominion Bureau of Statistics, *Agriculture, Climate and Population of the Prairie Provinces of Canada: A Statistical Atlas Showing Past Development and Present Conditions* (Ottawa: F.A. Acland, King's Printer, 1932). Chester Martin, "'Dominion Lands' Policy," in Arthur S. Morton and Chester Martin, *History of Prairie Settlement and "Dominion Lands" Policy* (Toronto: Macmillan, 1938).

25 For a brief explanation of these issues, and further references, see Ian N. Gregory, "A Map Is Just a Bad Graph: Why Spatial Statistics Are Important in Historical GIS," in A.K. Knowles (ed.), *Placing History: How Maps, Spatial Data and GIS Are Changing Historical Scholarship* (Redlands, CA: ESRI Press, 2008), chapter 5.

26 St-Hilaire et al., "Geocoding and Mapping Historical Census Data," 90. The authors list a number of potential regroupings of CSDs according to socioeconomic or geographical characteristics, as well as "cross-census harmonization tools."

27 For a longer discussion of cross-census harmonization and mapping using the CCRI data, see B. Moldofsky, "Exploring Historical Geography Using Census Microdata: The Canadian Century Research Infrastructure Project," in M. Fortin and J. Bonnell (eds.), *Historical GIS Research in Canada* (Calgary: University of Calgary Press, 2013). See http://uofcpress.com/books/9781552387085.

28 For example, St-Hilaire et al. ("Geocoding and Mapping Historical Census Data," 90) suggest that "grouping will gather rural communities according to their

economy (agricultural, forest, fishing, or mining localities) or to a geographical characteristic (pioneer fringe, coastal, interior, mountain)."

29 J.G. McConnell and A.R. Turner, "Historical Geography," in J.H. Richards (ed.), *Atlas of Saskatchewan* (Saskatoon: University of Saskatchewan, 1969), 16–17. J.H. Richards, "The Prairie Region," in J. Warkentin (ed.), *Canada: A Geographical Interpretation* (Toronto: Methuen, 1967), 411–18. W.J. Carlyle and J.C. Lehr, "Peopling the Prairies," Plate 17, in Kerr and Holdsworth (eds.), *Historical Atlas of Canada*, vol. III. A.S. Morton, "History of Prairie Settlement," in Morton and Chester, *History of Prairie Settlement and "Dominion Lands" Policy*, 143–4.

30 Ecological regions have been derived from Natural Resources Canada's ECOMAP data sets. The four regions in the northern part of the province were combined to achieve a sample size larger than twenty dwellings. For details on ecological regions, see Natural Resources Canada, Earth Sciences Sector, "The State of Canada's Ecosystems in Maps," *GeoGratis*, 2002, http://geogratis.gc.ca/api/en/nrcan-rncan/ess-sst/9099a060-77ea-57f6-b1b9-50f9eeef435b.

31 The tables for 1911 showing complete CSD data are *Fourth Census of Canada, 1901*, vol. I, Table 1 ("Area and Population of Canada by Provinces, Districts and Subdistricts in 1911 and Population in 1901") and Table 2 ("Conjugal Condition of the People, classified as single, married, widowed, divorced, legally separated and not given, by districts and sub-districts").

32 Michael Reibel, "Geographic Information Systems and Spatial Data Processing in Demography: A Review," *Population Research and Policy Review* 26 (2007): 601–18.

33 One recent study using these techniques in a context with some similarities is Katherine J. Curtis White, "Population Change and Farm Dependence: Temporal and Spatial Variation in the U.S. Great Plains, 1900–2000," *Demography* 45, no. 2 (2008): 363–86.

PART II

Canadian Diversities: Debates and Dimensions

— · 3 · —

Infrastructures of Census Taking

EVELYN RUPPERT

On 2 June 1911, Thomas Vance, census commissioner for Centre Toronto, expressed delight with the way things had gone so far with the enumeration of his district. Based on his experience overseeing the same district in the 1901 census, things were proceeding ever more efficiently. Vance had accompanied three different enumerators the previous evening during their rounds of "The Ward" to ensure that counting the "foreign population" was going smoothly. And, leading up to census day, he had participated in meetings with the Ontario Special Commissioner Mr J.C. Macpherson and with the other four commissioners responsible for Toronto. He had also overseen the hiring of enumerators and their training based on instructions issued by Archibald Blue, the chief census commissioner for the Dominion of Canada.

Vance was part of a vast operation that included many actors beyond census officials. There were, of course, the politicians. At the top of the list was Minister of Agriculture Sydney Fisher, who was responsible for the "counting of noses." As part of Sir Wilfred Laurier's Liberal government, which had been in office since 1896, Fisher was well aware of the implications for parliamentary representation of this decennial enumeration. Since the last enumeration in 1901, two new provinces, Saskatchewan and Alberta, had become part of the Canadian federation, adding ever more numbers to an expanding western population. It was generally agreed that the count would result in the redistribution of seats in the House of Commons with the west making significant gains. In addition to the politicians, Vance was painfully aware of, yet also dependent on the interventions of civic officials, boards of trade and industrial bureaus, as well as the newspapermen. They began reporting on the pending enumeration well before June 1911 and proved very useful in educating the population, especially its "foreign element," about the process.

But, back in Toronto's Ward, Commissioner Vance encountered difficulties. There were many impressions in circulation about the practices of enumeration, which he and the other commissioners had to regularly counter or at least clarify. For example, enumerators had reported that some "foreigners" thought that information about their family size would be reported to the city's Water Department and lead to an increase in their water rates. In one account, a "foreigner" had reported his family as numbering two instead of nine, ostensibly because he had feared that a higher count would lead to an increase in his water rates. Yet others were hesitant to reveal details of their businesses as they were under the impression that this information would end up in the hands of the Tax Department. For Vance, however, these were minor difficulties; all that was required was to get the word out that answers would not be used for such purposes and would be kept strictly confidential.

Commissioner Archibald Blue was a veteran newspaperman, and this also proved to be beneficial in working with the fourth estate. Almost every newspaper across the country announced the coming date and the procedures, and most listed all forty-three questions on Schedule 1 verbatim, while others provided at least a summary. They were also very helpful in advertising the new date, for although previous enumerations had been taken on 1 April, legislation passed in 1905 had changed census day to 1 June. Furthermore, the newspapers were very thorough in pointing out that fines or imprisonment would result if questions were not answered or if false information were provided. But, on the other hand, their muckraking activities were a bother, sometimes fuelled by their political allegiance with the Conservative opposition. As June wore on, the most significant interventions involved claims that people were not counted or that whole districts or villages had been missed. In mid-July, R.L. Borden, leader of the Conservative party and Official Opposition, called attention to the fact that he had not been enumerated, while Hon. Sydney Fisher, minister of agriculture, admitted that he had been counted twice. Vance was thus pleased that the national daily papers published Commissioner Blue's notice that invited people to communicate with him by mail should they suspect they had been missed. Despite all these difficulties, as the end of July approached, Blue was able to report that almost 88 per cent of returns had been received in Ottawa.

On 18 October 1911, following the election of Borden's Conservative government, Blue sent his first tabulations to the new minister of agriculture, the Hon. Martin Burrell. The tabulations of the total population of the country, as well as of provinces and cities and towns, led to a great outcry, as the figures were lower than anticipated. Rather than the expected population of eight million, the first reports revealed a count of just over seven million. Western civic leaders complained the loudest that their cities were undercounted with Calgary, Edmonton, Saskatoon, and Moose Jaw announcing that they would undertake their own census to prove so.

The foregoing narrative on the intricacies and politics of census-taking practices was compiled from a few dozen newspaper articles published around the time of the 1911 enumeration. The articles can be found in the CCRI Context-Data database, which principally covers newspaper articles and parliamentary Hansard debates published around the time of each of the decennial enumerations (1911–51).[1] CCRI's objective in building the database was to provide additional "data on the data" to enable researchers to analyse the organization and taking of censuses. Despite extensive scholarly interest in nominal census returns as a source for much recent historical scholarship, there has been little scrutiny of these census-taking practices and processes. But, there are a few notable and recent exceptions, especially in relation to late nineteenth-century census taking, such as Bruce Curtis's book on the 1871 enumeration, *The Politics of Population* (2001), and Patrick Dunae's article, "Making the 1891 Census in British Columbia" (1998).[2] Yet, we still lack detailed understanding of the actual workings of census taking, which can inform interpretations of nominal census returns and critical analyses of the infrastructural work involved in making population data. Enumerator schedules, instructions, correspondence, and census reports provide important contextual data, and they have been the focus of the previously noted studies. CCRI's cross-country newspaper database complements these sources by providing data about other mediating actors and interveners and, especially, of popular understandings of census taking. How was census taking promoted and represented, and what criticisms, concerns, and interests did it inspire? Newspaper accounts provide us with insights into these questions as well as about some of the more mundane aspects of the practice such as how door-to-door canvassing was conducted and interpreted. They also reveal much about the immense social and technical infrastructure and relations between census officials, politicians, citizens, newspapermen, paper forms, and machines that were part of and mediated the taking of the 1911 census.[3]

It is the establishment of an elaborate infrastructure that Bruce Curtis has argued marked the 1871 enumeration as the first "scientific" and modern census of Canada.[4] That census marked the transformation from a loosely disciplined set of practices into a centrally organized practice of census taking that translated accounts of social relations into authoritative categories and statistical forms. Centrally, Curtis examines how the deputy minister of the Department of Agriculture and Statistics at the time, Joseph-Charles Taché (from 1864 to 1888) governed census taking "at a distance" through the deployment of inscription devices that translated observations into the two-dimensional surface of texts. Inscription devices are "immutable mobiles" in that they can transport social relations to distant sites where they can be worked up into administrative resources and come back again unchanged.[5] For Curtis, such devices consisted, principally, of the manuscript form with its categories that established classes of equivalence through which individuals could pass from their singularity to a generality.

But, census taking also involved many other people and things. In 1911, it included the often difficult negotiations of enumerators and commissioners with census subjects; the accoutrements that mediated the enumerators' translation of relations into categories: portfolios, instructions, paper forms, and pens; the mediations of hundreds of clerks, checkers, and counters, along with their adding machines, who translated manuscript forms into population subtotals and totals; and then the dozens of clerks, along with their card-punch machines and tabulators, who compiled tables on everything from origins and immigration to language spoken and wage earnings. It was through such relays and interactions between various technological, political, and cultural actors that the census population was known.[6] Thus, while centralized practices such as conventions of observing, reporting, and recording sought to "discipline" census taking, as Curtis has argued, they relied on the mobilization of dispersed and, sometimes, unruly technical and human mediators. How so can, in part, be elucidated from newspaper accounts, which in the early part of the twentieth century were especially attentive to census practices. In addition to interviews with enumerators, census commissioners, politicians, and citizens, verbatim transcripts of parliamentary debates were also published.[7] In short, these accounts provide additional insights into one of the hidden histories of Canada: the workings and mediations of a dispersed and heterogeneous administrative infrastructure of people and things that made it possible to know a population.

For 1911, there are some 3,538 records in the CCRI ContextData database. Rather than attempting a comprehensive survey and analysis, I focus on English-language articles principally published in Ontario newspapers that pertain to those records coded under the theme of "holding of the census": preparation and organization, the gathering of data, and reactions to and analyses of the results.[8] I supplement this with additional metadata, principally from the published reports and instructions to enumerators. Based on these sources, I identify two themes that encapsulate some of the people and things that made up the infrastructure of 1911 census taking: enumerators and devices. A third theme that I take up concerns other counting practices that also sought to know populations. The ContextData database includes newspaper accounts of some of these practices at the time of the 1911 enumeration. Municipal and provincial governments and religious, penal, charitable, and social service organizations all engaged in counting practices similar to census enumerations in regards to their classification systems and categories.[9] These reveal both a capacity and an investment in similar techniques and the new statistical thinking that was often invented and implemented outside of the state by different makers of population such as doctors and clergymen.[10] In other words, such practices were part and parcel of the infrastructure that formed and informed census-taking practices. In this last section – "Other Counting Practices" – I focus on a specific counting practice in the nineteenth and early twentieth centuries, that of the enumeration of populations living in city "slums."

Enumerators: Appointments and Responsibilities

> Archibald Blue, a quiet little gentleman, who sits in an office down on Slater Street, is the field marshal of a huge army that started out this morning to tag every living mother's son and daughter in Canada. If there is one job more than another that required careful and thorough organization and system it is the taking of the census [and its] chief controller must [be a] statistician extraordinary ... Such a task is enough to drive any ordinary man to drink. But the one man in a thousand grows fat and happy upon it. Archibald Blue just revels in figures. He dreams about mountains of them and he finds these mountains as rich and interesting as the hills into which he was wont to dig for precious metals when he was director of mines for Ontario ... When Archibald Blue is not twisting the figures of the census around like you and I might play a game of solitaire, he is analyzing the character of Mr. Pecksniff of Mr. Richard Swiveller or sympathizing with Little Nell ... By the way, Archibald Blue is an old newspaper man and has many good stories of Hon. George Brown, his chief.
>
> – *Ottawa Free Press*[11]

Archibald Blue, the chief census commissioner was head of the newly established permanent Census and Statistics Office (CSO) under the minister of agriculture. Established by legislation in 1905, the office was introduced to strengthen the Department of Agriculture's statistical mandate and enhance the knowledge and experience of staff responsible for census taking.[12] For all previous enumerations, the census was planned and conducted by staff assembled anew each time only to be disassembled just when competence had been assured. Although major personalities may have worked on several enumerations (Taché, for example), the lack of a continuous administrative infrastructure was a weakness that R.H. Coats, Blue's successor at the CSO, would later come to highlight in his judgment on the history of Canadian statistics.[13] So, while the 1871 enumeration under Taché was the first "scientific" enumeration, in that it put in place a national administrative infrastructure, its discontinuity significantly undermined the building of institutional capacity. According to Coats, that capacity included intercensal activities focused more generally on regular statistical activities.

Blue, who had previously held the position of special census commissioner, was confirmed as its chief officer, at a salary of $4,000 per annum. Prior to taking up this position, he had been a veteran journalist and latterly an Ontario bureaucrat for some sixteen years, first as assistant commissioner of agriculture and secretary of the Bureau of Industries, and then as head of the Bureau of Mines.[14]

Blue was described as "ruddy of face, white of hair, low and gentle of voice."[15] He was one of three permanent officers of the Census and Statistics Office assigned to meet with a team of 264 commissioners throughout the Dominion.[16] Approximately 9,703 enumerators completed the count of people between 1 June 1911 and the end of February 1912, with the majority of their returns (approximately 97%) submitted by the end of August 1911 (compared with 82% in 1901).

In the few weeks prior to census day, newspapers reported the names of all of the commissioners and, in smaller towns and cities, the names of all of the enumerators. For example, the *Owen Sound Sun* listed the names of all fifty-seven enumerators who were to cover the district of North Grey,[17] and *La Presse* published the names and photos of all thirteen commissioners responsible for Montreal.[18] Many newspapers also reproduced the instructions to enumerators and expectations about their conduct, in particular, that they should be courteous and expeditious and approach their work judiciously and with civility. In particular, newspapers highlighted that enumerators and commissioners had sworn a binding oath that they would undertake their duties as discharged, make no false declaration, and keep secret the information gathered.

The responsibilities of enumerators and how they were to conduct the count were also thoroughly documented, often by reproducing excerpts from their instructions: "The enumerator should start at one corner of the block and proceed around and through it, entering every house or building in regular order, and collecting all the information called for in the schedules, before proceed-

Figure 3.1 · Cartoon of a census enumerator in the home, from *La Presse*, 24 June 1911, 6. Heading: "LES JOYEUSETES DE RECENSEMENT NO. 7."

ing to the next block or square, and should so continue until the whole of his sub-district is finished."[19]

Enumerators conducted their canvass through interviews with the heads of families, households, and institutions (fathers, mothers, landlords, superintendents, keepers, administrators, wardens). Male heads of households were typically expected to be the qualified person to furnish the information. However, other individuals in a household could do so, and in apartment buildings, the janitor could be consulted or a neighbour.[20] Interviews were often conducted on the front doorstep, as many newspaper accounts confirm, but also possibly inside the dwelling. A series of humorous cartoon images of the interviewing practices were published in *La Presse* during the month of June[21] (see figure 3.1).

Most newspapers also reported on the consequences of refusing or wilfully supplying false information: "The penalty for refusing to answer questions asked by a census enumerator is a fine of $10 to $100; false answers $5 to $50; deception $10 to $100. For the benefit of ladies over sixteen years of age we may point out that the enumerators are sworn to secrecy under a $200 penalty."[22]

Census taking was not an easy occupation. Two of London's forty census takers quit, apparently because the "interrogations were too much for them."[23] But, rather than attempting to hire replacements, the census commissioner, Mr Scatherd, announced that the work would be allotted to those of the remaining thirty-eight enumerators who first finished their sections. With perhaps some exaggeration, an account was provided of a South Toronto enumerator who, after studying the instructions and attending a training meeting, complained of feeling unwell and lapsed into an epileptic fit.[24]

Notably, all enumerators were male, and little or no commentary attended to their occupations or social status. But, as one study of 1891 census enumerators in Ontario has shown, they were representative of the male population and typically "established men" who had "local knowledge and respectability."[25] The one characteristic of enumerators that received some attention in 1911 was that of their political connections. On 15 May 1911, the Conservative opposition tabled a motion in the House of Commons that stated, "In the selection and appointment of public officers the government is exercising a public trust and should be guided by consideration of the character and capacity of the person whom it is proposed to appoint. That the delegation of such a public trust to a local party committee or organizer is a public scandal and deserves the censure of this house."[26]

At issue was the claim that the appointment of census officials had been partisan, and several instances of party political influence were cited. H.E. Perry, the Liberal organizer for Manitoba, had been appointed enumerator and was found to have sent out letters signed with "Yours in the good cause, H.E. Perry." Opposition members from Ontario presented evidence to show that the enumerators in London and the surrounding districts were being appointed by a committee of three Liberals headed by G.M. Reid, who had been charged with conspiracy in a 1905 London by-election. Minister of Agriculture Fisher (who was responsible for the enumeration) refused to divulge the basis on which specific recommendations and appointments were made. This only fuelled speculation that Liberal appointments were being made in an effort to attain political advantage in the outcome.

Such claims are not novel. Census taking has often been seen to be influenced by politics, especially since the results determine the distribution of parliamentary seats and resources. Patrick Dunae, in his account of the taking of the 1891 census in British Columbia, found that nearly all census takers were political appointees, to some extent.[27] Bruce Curtis has also argued that the religious and political interests of Deputy Minister of the Department of Agriculture and Statistics Taché had influenced the shaping and making of the 1871 census.[28] Although, on the one hand, it was deemed the first "scientific" enumeration, Curtis's account suggests that it was also a feudal science guided by Taché's political strategy to construct and reinforce a Franco-Catholic nationality. His argument is that the science of census taking implemented through centralized and standardized administrative practices and statistical procedures did not completely banish local and political influences. Of course, the politics of census taking extend to the mediations and agencies of many actors beyond those of the central authority, of which the example of enumerator appointments is but one.

Yet, just as Taché was part of an administrative infrastructure, so, too, were the enumerators who were connected to a standardized set of practices consisting of tools and devices, which in 1911 were unique in that new machinery was introduced for tabulating the results.

Devices: Paper, Pens, Portfolios, and Machines

> The first batch of census schedules, weighing about eight tons, has just reached the Census Office. Something like 30 tons of returns are expected.
>
> – *Toronto Daily Star*[29]

> The troubles and trials of the enumerator are over; but this is by no means the end of it. Up in the census bureau in the Canadian building sits Mr. Archibald Blue, the man who thinks in figures. Around him are his cohorts, a staff of 31 regulars and 153 temporary clerks who will after three years' hard experience be second only to Mr. Archibald Blue in juggling with figures.
>
> – *Nelson Daily News*[30]

Census taking required a lot of paper. "Each enumerator was armed with his bundles of eight different forms, measuring 12 by 8 inches," reported one newspaper.[31] He was "furnished with a large canvas-covered folder, tied with the usual government red tape, and he might easily be taken for a large picture man, art calendar agent or book canvasser."[32] The bundles of forms consisted of some thirteen schedules and 549 questions, out of which two schedules and forty-three questions pertained to population.[33]

Enumerators were instructed "to make all entries on the schedules in ink of good quality," and so a pen was clearly a requirement. The "Canadian Census

Figure 3.2 · Advertisement for "Canadian Census Recording Pen."
Source: *Toronto Daily Star*, 20 May 1911, 22.

Recording Pen," a fountain pen designed by Waterman's in 1911, was advertised in the *Toronto Daily Star*, and perhaps was utilized by enumerators[34] (see figure 3.2). The description that it was "especially adapted for rapid recording and manifold work" suggests that it was functionally intended to be.

Given the mountains of paper that had to be counted and tabulated, ensuring clarity and legibility was not a trivial issue. The instructions to enumerators emphasized the importance of this both for the present and future uses of census returns: "Every name, word, figure or mark should be clear and legible. If a schedule cannot be read, or if the entries are made with a poor quality of ink, or in pencil, or if they are blurred or blotted, the work of the enumerator may be wholly wasted. The Census is intended to be a permanent record, and its schedules will be stored in the Archives of the Dominion."[35]

Unlike previous enumerations, each census book was sent to Ottawa as soon as it was completed, and only once the figures were verified and accepted would cheques be issued to the enumerators. When returns were received in Ottawa, a team of workers first registered them and then passed them on to a team of checkers who would go over the lists looking for errors and omissions and do revisions whenever possible.[36] If necessary, the returns would be sent back to local commissioners for correction and follow-up with the relevant enumerator. As the manuscript returns indicate, many corrections and changes were made, either by enumerators and local commissioners and/or by Ottawa checkers. One example of the latter is the numerous crossed-out entries of "Canadian" in the column pertaining to the question on "racial or tribal origins."[37] The category, which was not recognized or accepted at the time, was changed, in many instances, with handwriting different from the enumerator's and tended to indicate an ethnicity likely to correspond to a surname (e.g., O'Riordan as Irish).

The holding back of cheques until such time as verification had been completed was met with some consternation as enumerators often had to wait months before receiving their pay.[38] Enumerators were, thus, advised to get their books in early to avoid the inevitable volume that would eventually overwhelm the checking staff, thus delaying remuneration:

> "First come, first served," will be the manner in which the Government will treat the enumerators this time. Unlike previous occasions, it has been ordered that each census book shall be sent to Ottawa as soon as completed, and directly the figures have been verified and accepted by the Government, checks will be forwarded to the enumerators. Thus, those whose books go in early will be rushed through by the large checking staff which has been engaged, while those which do not arrive till the end will have to take their turn with the large number which will have accumulated, and in consequence late enumerators will not be paid for a month or more.[39]

Once a return passed the check, it then went through two independent tabulation processes conducted by "hand work"; one team of clerks tabulated the returns by "ordinary counting," while another used one of eighteen adding machines.[40] Finally, a third team compiled the totals on individual returns and grouped them into villages, towns, cities, parishes, townships, provinces, and electoral districts. While enumerators were all men, accounts of the census tabulation process indicate that the teams of clerks consisted mostly of women, a gendered division of labour that continued through to the mid-twentieth century. These compilations served the basis of the first release, on 18 October 1911, and the first volume of results on 30 April 1912 – population totals for provinces, census districts (CDs), and census subdistricts (CSDs), including sex, conjugal condition, and number of dwellings.[41] The returns were then "carefully stacked and preserved for the future historian," as Mr Blue remarked. *Le Temps* published an image (unfortunately of very poor quality) showing a long corridor lined with floor-to-ceiling shelves containing piles of paper returns called the "census archives."[42]

When Archibald Blue released the first volume of results, he noted that after the handwork was completed all other tables – of ages, origins, nativities, immigration, religions, occupations, literacy, language spoken, school attendance, wage earnings, etc. – were to be compiled mechanically using a punch-card system and electrical machines.[43] This process involved a temporary staff of 160 clerks working with seventy card-punching machines and twenty tabulators.[44] The 1911 census was the first enumeration processed by this method and machinery, modelled on that which had been successfully used in the 1910 census of the United States. The US machine was designed by the US Census Bureau to replace the first counting machine invented by Herman Hollerith in the late 1880s.[45] Hollerith, a former US Census Bureau employee, invented a machine that used specially encoded punch cards, where each card contained an individual's data: "The cards were fed into the counting machine, where the punched holes allowed metal pins to complete an electric circuit. When a circuit was completed, the dial for the corresponding trait would go up."[46] The US Census Office used the machine for the 1890 census. In 1896, Hollerith founded the Tabulating Machine Company, which eventually became the International Business Machines (IBM) Corporation. However, for the 1900 enumeration, Hollerith raised his rental prices to such a level that the US Census Bureau decided to build its own machines, led by an employee, James Legrand Powers. The new machine had an automatic feeder and card sorter, and it was considered an improvement over Hollerith's. It was first used for tabulating the 1910 census.

Given the successful use of the machine in tabulating the US census, the Canadian government bought the use of the patent and commissioned the manufacture of its own fleet of machines.[47] To supervise this undertaking, the Canadian bureau temporarily borrowed Charles W. Spicer of the US Census Bureau to oversee the manufacture of the machines in Toronto. Joseph P. Cleat was awarded the contract and, along with his mechanical engineer R.A. Scragg, set out to complete the machines by the middle of September 1911.

The seventy card-punching machines were used to condense the large manuscript forms into perforations on seven-by-three-inch census cards. The cards were then fed into the tabulator by an automatic feeder at the rate of two hundred per minute:

> When the machine is adjusted for the required information the cards are fed over a cylinder, and through the openings a magnetic contact is made which operates a series of chutes of the same thickness as the cards and stops and starts so that the card enters the proper chute. When the card is in its proper chute a series of fingers on an endless chain carries it from the chutes along two wires, which are about seven inches apart, to the proper compartment. When the card drops from the ends of the wires into the compartment the count is made by an electrical device.

> There are fourteen different compartments, and by running the cards through fourteen times all this information may be tabulated. By making other adjustments the information indicated by forty-two perforations may be tabulated.[48]

Two full-time specialists were employed to oversee the mechanical tabulating, A.E. Thornton and F. Bélisle, who continued working for the Dominion Bureau of Statistics for many years.[49] After all of these stages and relays, and even after final printed tables were checked and signed off by both the chief census commissioner and the minister of agriculture, and then printed and distributed in the published volumes, A.J. Pelletier, an employee of the Census Bureau, yet again made corrections.[50]

In sum, it was through such relays and interactions between various technological and political actors that the census was taken in 1911. It was an enumeration that introduced new procedures and devices that were intended to improve the administrative infrastructure such as the establishment of a continuous office and workforce and the introduction of punch-card technology and mechanical tabulators. But, such advancements occurred alongside a capacity and investment in similar techniques and counting practices conducted by municipal and provincial governments, and religious, penal, charitable, and social service organizations. Such practices can be considered part and parcel of the infrastructure that formed and informed census taking in Canada. One example from 1911 concerns population counts of an area of Toronto known as "The Ward."

Other Counting Practices: St John's Ward, Toronto

> "There is scarcely a one-family house in the district," said a man connected with the returns. "Every building is a hive of roomers, and the tenor of the whole district has changed during the last decade.
>
> – *Globe*[51]

These are some of the reflections of an enumerator concerning his canvassing of an area of Toronto, St John's Ward, which was later called "The Ward." By the mid-eighteenth century, The Ward, located in Toronto Centre, became the settlement area for different waves of immigrants.[52] Owing to its tenements and crowded conditions, the area was referred to as Toronto's version of the slums of the Lower East Side of New York. These references were, in part, a response to the rapid urban growth experienced in the late nineteenth and early twentieth centuries and the concomitant rise of urban poverty that was centred on the "slum."[53] By the time of the 1911 enumeration, The Ward was predominantly occupied by Eastern European Jews and was the centre of Jewish shops, cafes, theatres, and synagogues and the location of numerous tailoring factories such as those of the T. Eaton Company. Because of the addition of numerous factories and the clearance of several acres of the Ward for the building of the new Toronto General Hospital, there was some speculation that The Ward would show a decline in population. However, early results reported an increase[54] with estimates running from 50,000 to 60,000, up from the 43,000 reported in 1901.[55] This increase fuelled media discussions and accounts of the concentration and density of people and housing in the relatively small area of The Ward. Enumerators, for example, reported "dire conditions of congestion, finding as many as six families in six-roomed houses and, in others, a sufficient number of men to fill houses twice the size."[56]

But, the census was only one of many studies and surveys of The Ward, which was subject to many other counting practices and population studies. During the taking of the 1911 census, one such study was released by Dr Charles Hastings, medical officer of health for Toronto, which was variously summarized in newspaper articles and editorials: "The lodging-house evil. The foreign housing problem. Dark rooms. Back-to-back houses. Basement and cellar dwellings. Insanitary privy pits. Lack of drainage. Inadequate water supply. Exorbitant rents. Overcrowding of houses, rooms and lots. These are the conditions found by the medical health department in Toronto's slums."[57]

Hastings was a leader in Canadian public health reform as well as a key figure in Canadian urban reform. Between 1911 and 1913, his department published several reports on slum conditions in The Ward. Mariana Valverde argues that while Hastings sought to move away from the nineteenth-century moral discourses of social investigation, moralization continued to be an important undercurrent in his seemingly scientific approach. It was an approach that sought to move away from problematizing the population to that of the housing conditions, as evidenced in his 1911 study, which defined Toronto slums as follows: "Originally the term was applied to low, boggy back streets inhabited by a poor, criminal population. The term as used here, however, applies for the most part to poor, unsanitary housing, overcrowded, insufficiently lighted, badly ventilated, with unsanitary and in many cases, filthy yards."[58] However, as Valverde further argues, this shift did not result in shedding moralization but, instead, connected moral deviance to the physical environment and imbued slum conditions with the power to produce deviant people.[59] Thus, the slum was not only an economic and public health problem but also a moral one. This was evident in newspaper reports that took up the "problem" of inner city "slums" and the "foreign population":

> Toronto should make short work of her slums. They are a disgrace to the city and to Canadian civilization. Dr Hasting's report on housing in the congested area south of College and Carlton streets shows that over 26,000 people are living under conditions that are as bad for them morally as they are for the body ... The slum is a cancer that grows in the modern civic organism with terrible rapidity.[60]
>
> No city can be in any real sense beautiful or good in which many thousands of people live without the most vitally important requirements for health and morality.[61]

The Ward was, thus, subject to other counting practices that sought to enumerate and know the sanitary condition of its housing: baths, drains, water taps, windows, privy pits, water closets, rooms per dwelling, bathhouses, and so on. But, it was a moralization that was bound up with numbers – of bodies per square mile, per dwelling, and per room: "Over 26,000 people ... Of 4,696 houses inspected, no less than 2,137 of these houses had two families living in them. There were 198 one-roomed 'dwellings' occupied by families aggregating 472 persons."[62]

Moralization was also extended to include its racial composition as both the reports by Hastings and the census enumeration emphasized the ethnicity of The Ward's inhabitants: "The case of immigrants more or less recently arrived is always the more difficult. Born in some obscure province of Russia, Poland, or Italy, the newly-made Canadian really has very little idea of what is required of him. He knows that he was born 'In the Old Country,' but just when or where it is difficult to say. He knows that he came to Canada 'in a big ship,' but that was years ago, too."[63] In this light, moral and governmental concern was also extended to the problems encountered when enumerating the foreigner. Not only were housing densities and physical conditions at issue, but also the capacity of "slum dwellers" to participate and comprehend enumeration (as noted in the opening narrative to this chapter). An almost full-page article published in the *Toronto Daily Star* (and republished in several dailies across the country) focused on reports from enumerators about their difficulties in gaining the cooperation of the inhabitants of The Ward: "There is the most amazing ignorance of the things that everybody is supposed to know. They are a timid people, these brown-eyed, simple folk of 'The Ward,' and too great insistence, a quick word, or a display of impatience drives them into silence and secretiveness."[64]

In this regard, census taking introduced another problem of the slum: that of knowing or, as Valverde would say, "shedding light" on the population. But, it was a shedding of light that involved bringing this population into the same categories and knowledge as the rest of the city and country, a process of statistical normalization that established household and dwelling size and population density standards. To do so, the census required people with the capacities to respond and recognize themselves as members and parts of the population through the various classifications and categories circulated via the manuscript form.[65] Like other counting practices, census taking was a moral enterprise – its categories and standards normalized social relations, rendering problematic whether subjects could understand the process or answer questions regarding how their household size and density compared with a statistical norm.

Census classifications and categories as well as methods such as door-to-door canvassing were, thus, constituted alongside and in relation to many other counting practices and forms of expertise involved in constructing and knowing populations. Observing, interviewing, conducting surveys, recording information, and the like were all techniques developed earlier and, most significantly, in the nineteenth century through which cities and territories were administratively ordered, categorized, and known. From house-to-house visits and the detailed recordings of the character and characteristics of inhabitants, census-taking practices were connected to forms of expertise developed by historical urban researchers such as Sidney and Beatrice Webb, Charles Booth, and Seebohm Rowntree. As such, these practices were not disconnected but part of a general will to know populations, and it is in this regard that they can be considered part of the capacity and infrastructure of census taking.

Conclusion

I have argued that one of Canada's hidden histories is the working of the administrative infrastructure that made it possible to know a population. The standardization and normalization of categories, enumeration, training, and tabulation, as well as investments in an ongoing administration involved many relations between people and things. In 1911, such developments could be said to have extended the central government's authority and domination through "numbers." However, the expansion of the network of personnel and technologies, of hands and tabulators, served also to increase the number of mediators in the process such that the making of population knowledge was not simply improved or made more accurate. Rather, it was a process of social and statistical normalization that was mediated at every stage, by every hand and machine, and which extended across time and space even into the work of the Canadian Century Research Infrastructure in the twenty-first century.

Notes

1 For a detailed description of the methodology and database, see C. Bellavance, F. Normand, and E. Ruppert, "Census in Context: Documenting and Understanding the Making of 20th Century Canadian Censuses," *Historical Methods* 40, no. 2 (2007): 92–103. The database can be accessed at http://ccri.library.ualberta.ca/en1911census/contextual/index.html.

2 B. Curtis, *The Politics of Population: State Formation, Statistics, and the Census of Canada, 1840–1875* (Toronto: University of Toronto Press, 2001); P. Dunae, "Making the 1891 Census in British Columbia," *Histoire Social/Social History* 31, no. 62 (1998): 223–39. See Dunae for a summary of a few other studies (at n4).

3 For discussion and analysis of social and technical arrangements and their mediation of the taking of the 1911 census of the "far north," see E. Ruppert, "Becoming Peoples: 'Counting Heads in Northern Wilds,'" *Journal of Cultural Economy* 2, nos 1–2 (2009): 11–31.

4 Curtis, *Politics of Population.*

5 Curtis takes up this understanding of inscription devices from B. Latour, "Visualization and Cognition: Thinking with Eyes and Hands," *Knowledge and Society: Studies in the Sociology of Science Past and Present* 6, no. 1 (1986): 1–40.

6 Yet, even these were to be revised some 100 years later when the CCRI team incorporated Pelletier's corrections in their digitized versions of the 1911 published tables; see n46 below.

7 Some of these debates were also compiled in the *Ontario Newspaper Hansard*, a collection of articles from the *Globe* and the *Daily Mail and Empire* that were clipped by archivists in the 1960s, photographed, and turned into microfilm. Typically, articles were originally published on the day after the Legislature met and printed on the opening or editorial pages of either paper.

8 For an account of the criteria for the sample selection of Ontario newspapers, see H. Garrett, "Working Paper: Sampling Ontario Newspapers 1911–1951: Criteria, Coverage, Comparisons" (York University: Canadian Century Research Infrastructure, 2004). Available at http://www.ccri.uottawa.ca/CCRI/Images/Heather.Garret.pdf.

9 See, e.g., the various practices documented in J. Caplan and J. Torpey, Introduction, in J. Caplan and J. Torpey (eds.), *Documenting Individual Identity: The Development of State Practices in the Modern World* (Princeton, NJ: Princeton University Press, 2001).

10 P. Joyce, *Rule of Freedom: Liberalism and the Modern City* (London: Verso, 2003). See also the discussion in E. Ruppert. "Producing Population," *CRESC Working Paper Series*, Paper No. 37 (Milton Keynes: CRESC, 2007).

11 "The Census Man," *Evening Record*, 6 June 1911, 4.

12 D. Worton, *The Dominion Bureau of Statistics: A History of Canada's Central Statistical Agency* (Montreal and Kingston: McGill-Queen's University Press, 1998), 38. Blue died in office in 1914, and the 1911 census turned out to be his professional "swan song."

13 R.H. Coats, "Beginnings in Canadian Statistics" (1946), as cited in Worton, *Dominion Bureau of Statistics*, 44. The same issues were noted in relation to US census taking, which also involved little intercensal statistical activity.

14 "Taking the Census," *Daily British Whig*, 1 June, 4; Worton, *Dominion Bureau of Statistics*, 21.

15 "Taking the Census," *The Empire* (Morden, MB), 22 June 1911, 7.

16 Canada, Department of Trade and Commerce, Census and Statistics Office, *Fifth Census of Canada, 1911*, vol. I, *Areas and Population by Provinces, Districts and Sub-districts* (Ottawa: C.H. Parmalee, 1912). During the enumeration, newspapers reported 220 commissioners and 9,322 enumerators: e.g., "Taking the Census," *Daily British Whig*, 11 May 1911, 7; "Preparing to Take the Census," *Daily News*, 9 May 1911, 3; "Criticisms of Census Taking," *Ottawa Citizen*, 20 July 1911, 2.

17 "Census Takers Start Thursday," *Owen Sound Sun*, 30 May 1911, 1, 4.

18 "Les Commissaires du Recensement," *La Presse*, 3 June 1911, 31.

19 "Census Men Start at Work To-morrow," *Toronto Daily Star*, 31 May 1911, 6.

20 "Did the Census-Taker Miss You?" *London Free Press*, 11 July 1911, 1. Also see Canada, Department of Agriculture and Statistics, *Fifth Census of Canada, 1911: Instructions to Officers, Commissioners and Enumerators* (Ottawa: Government Printing Bureau, 1911).

21 Newspaper articles often contained photographs or artist renditions. However, because of the poor quality of historical newspaper images, only a small number of illustrative examples can be reproduced.

22 "News about Town," *St Mary's Journal*, 18 May 1911, 5.

23 "The Strain Is Too Great for These Enumerators," *London Free Press*, 7 June 1911, 1.

24 "The Lot of the Census Taker in The Ward Is Anything but an Easy One," *Toronto Daily Star*, 1 June 1911, 1, 3.

25 The CCRI microdata include the names of enumerators, so their socio-economic status and possibly political affiliations could be investigated. For an analysis of the socio-economic profiles of 1891 enumerators for Ontario, see G. Kennedy and K. Inwood, "A New Prosopography: The Enumerators of the 1891 Census in Ontario," *Historical Methods* 45, no. 2 (2012): 65–77. They conclude that enumerators "were broadly representative of the rest of 1891 Ontario, especially the large class of independent farmers and tradesmen in the countryside and the growing middle class in the towns and cities" (75).

26 "Warm Debate on Enumerators," *Ottawa Citizen*, 16 May 1911, 10.

27 Dunae, "Making the 1891 Census in British Columbia."

28 Curtis, *Politics of Population*.

29 "Heavy Census Returns," *Toronto Daily Star*, 22 May 1911, 3.

30 "Work of Census Only Just Begun," *Nelson Daily News*, 26 July 1911, 2.

31 "Counting Noses in the Capital," *Ottawa Citizen*, 1 June 1911, 1, 12.

32 "Census Takers Make Progress," *Daily News* (Port Arthur), 20 June 1911, 5. Many newspapers listed enumerators for every district and many included pictures of them. A photo in *La Presse* (17 June 1911, 11) illustrated a group of enumerators, each holding a large canvas folder, for the Montreal district of Maisonneuve along with the census commissioner for the district, Albert Gringas.

33 Worton, *Dominion Bureau of Statistics*, 42.

34 "Canadian Census Recording Pen," *Toronto Daily Star*, 20 May 1911, 22.

35 *Fifth Census of Canada, 1911: Instructions to Officers, Commissioners and Enumerators.*

36 This description of the handwork is summarized from the *Nelson Daily News* article: "Work of Census Only Just Begun." An image published in *La Presse* (23 Dec. 1911, 5) illustrated young women seated at rows of long tables poring over and checking manuscript forms.

37 As early as 1871, individuals were claiming their ancestral origins as "Canadian," and this continued throughout the twentieth century. It was not until 1986 that "Canadian" was accepted as a category. See the following for a full discussion: E. Ruppert, "Producing Population." Curtis (in *Politics of Population*) also notes that many corrections and changes were made to the 1871 returns by Ottawa compilers to ensure that the answers conformed to census standards. See Adam Green, chapter 4 in this volume, on this issue in the 1911 census.

38 "Cheques Are Issued," *Mail and Empire*, 5 Aug. 1911, 28.

39 "Congestion Grows in St John's Ward," *Globe*, 21 June 1911, 8.

40 An image in *La Presse* (23 Dec. 1911, 5) illustrated two woman clerks reading manuscript forms and typing entries into large adding machines described as "sophisticated."

41 Canada, *Fifth Census of Canada*, vol. 1; "Results Announced by New Minister of Agriculture," *Medicine Hat News*, 19 Oct. 1911, 8.

42 "Le travail du recensement," *Le Temps*, 16 May 1911, 8.

43 For an example of a punch-card machine used for the 1910 US census see http://www.census.gov/history/www/innovations/technology/tabulation_and_processing.html.

44 "Tabulating the Census Returns," *Evening Guide* (Port Hope), 28 June 1911, 4.

45 The description of the US-designed tabulation machine in this paragraph is summarized from "Tabulation and Processing," *U.S. Census Bureau History*. Available at http://www.census.gov/history/www/innovations/technology/tabulation_and_processing.html.

46 For an example of a Hollerith electric tabulator used in the 1901 US census see http://www.census.gov/history/www/innovations/technology/tabulation_and_processing.html.

47 The account is summarized from several newspaper reports, most notably, in the *Cobalt Daily Nugget*, 25 July 1911, 2; *Evening Guide* (Port Hope), 28 June 1911, 2, 4; *Toronto Daily Star*, 10 June 1911, 7; *Globe*, 18 Aug. 1911, 9.

48 "To Compile Census by Unique Device," *Globe*, 19 Aug. 1911, 9.

49 Worton, *Dominion Bureau of Statistics*, 42n12.

50 For Tables 1 and 2 of vol. I, the CCRI was given access to manuscript correction notes of A.J. Pelletier, and included these in the digitized published tables, which the CCRI has produced for 1911–51. For example, the CCRI notes changes to many of the totals for Battleford, Saskatchewan, as indicated in Pelletier's annotated correction volume. See http://bit.ly/CCRItables.

51 "Congestion Grows in St John's Ward," *Globe*, 21 June 1911, 8.

52 The following narrative is summarized from M. Kluckner, *Toronto the Way It Was* (Toronto: Whitecap Books, 1988), 135–42. The Ward was located roughly from Bathurst Street (west) to Sherbourne Street (east) and from College/Carlton Street (north) to Queen Street (south).

53 As discussed and argued in M. Valverde, *The Age of Light, Soap, and Water: Moral Reform in English Canada, 1885–1925* (Toronto: University of Toronto Press, 2008).

54 "Congestion Grows in St John's Ward," 8.

55 "Toronto Census," *Ottawa Citizen*, 22 June 1911, 5.

56 Ibid.

57 "Toronto's Slums the Real Thing," *Globe*, 5 July 1911, 9.

58 *Report of the Medical Health Officer on Slum Conditions in Toronto* (Toronto, 1911, 3), as cited in M. Valverde, *Age of Light, Soap, and Water*, 133.

59 A similar set of moralizing arguments about slum conditions in Montreal's inner city was published in the *Montreal Daily Star*, 15 July 1911, 7.

60 "Get Rid of the Slums," *Globe*, 6 July 1911, 6.

61 "Toronto the Good," *Daily British Whig*, 30 Sept. 1911, 3.

62 "Get Rid of the Slums."

63 "The Lot of the Census Taker in The Ward Is Anything but an Easy One," 1, 3.

64 Ibid.

65 See E. Ruppert. "Producing Population," for a discussion of the production of census subjects.

— · 4 · —

"Let Us Be Canadians!": The Debate Over Allowing "Canadian" as a Racial Origin in Early Twentieth-Century Canadian Censuses

ADAM J. GREEN

In 1944, the Dominion Bureau of Statistics (DBS) task force on how to solve the question of defining "race" threw up its hands. H.M. Marshall's "Committee on Suggested Alternative to Racial Origin Classification," which had been assembled to solve the ambiguities surrounding the slippery definitions of race, ethnicity, and origin, concluded after months of discussion, research, and heated debate, that "although the statistics on the origins of the Canadian people was subject to defects" – that is, that their value for objective, scientific purposes would be seriously impaired – political, economic, and social considerations in Canada made it "impossible for the Bureau to drop the question from the 1951 census schedule."[1]

The Committee's preoccupation with the public's sensitivities surrounding the question of origin was hardly given unanimous praise: one member suggested that DBS simply "draw up a list of racial origins, and when a man comes to register a birth, we can say to him 'This is the list; just pick out which one you are.'" Even the Committee's respected senior researcher Nathan Keyfitz suggested that they cease making the case of origin so complicated, given that "How people regard themselves seems indeed an unsuitable approach for a census question!"[2] And yet, the questions which had underscored the Committee's work – the problematization of one's "biological background," the emotional attachment to "heredity," and the impossibility of dissuading some stubborn respondents from selecting non-existent racial origins, especially "Canadian" – refused to comply with the desire to craft an elegant solution.

The frustrations expressed by that Committee in 1944 were, to some extent, representative of a larger discussion, which can be traced back to the nineteenth century, and which would continue to rear its head into the twenty-first century. The question on racial origin forced the DBS to be confronted with two incompatible pressures: the desire to collect useful information and the decreased relevance and linearity of the category it purported to measure. Indeed, this question points to what constitutes the tension at the centre of census taking itself: the requirement to quantify something that is not objective, static, or one-dimensional for its millions of respondents. It is, one might argue, one of the most palpable crossroads of the "quantitative" versus "qualitative" debates about data, one that is never quite solved.

This chapter examines the central tension of the Canadian census through the prism of the questions on racial origin. It suggests that the notion of "race" was never simply, clearly, or universally defined by census officials even though a working definition was always selected for use in census taking. In particular, the chapter focuses on this debate as it expressed itself through a very public discussion on whether or not "Canadian" constituted a "racial origin." Although the chapter centres on the 1911 census as well as its relationship to the 1921–41 censuses, its observations could easily be applied to many other censuses and, for that matter, to many other census variables.

Indeed, much has been written on the racial origins question of the Canadian census in regards to its purported reification of early twentieth-century notions of racial hierarchy. The critics' charge is that this linear categorization included the fabrication of social and political domination and subordination through explicit and favourable categorizations of race, and a biased and idealized vocabulary through which political and economic leaders maintained their elevated status in the shifting context of immigration, anti-colonialism, and anti-racism that threatened it. Moreover, several authors have suggested that the rough and biased categories employed by the Dominion Bureau of Statistics were part of a larger program whereby concepts of racial origin "played a certain role in early nation-building efforts, and in attempts to maintain the power of politically dominant groups."[3] As with so many of the census's stories, however, the reality was far more nuanced, far less linear, and we might even argue, far more interesting.

"Triangulating" Identity

Following the Confederation of Canada, one of the basic needs of the new government concerned gathering an accurate count of the population under its jurisdiction, along with some basic demographic information concerning its economic and social characteristics. Thus, having established a solid foundation for the gathering of statistics concerning the population of the Dominion of Canada beginning in 1871, by 1911 DBS went about ascertaining an individual's "origins" by asking a basket of five questions, all of which were meant to be utilized together and cross-referenced so as to "triangulate" a respondent's identity. These questions included: country of birth, year of immigration, naturalization, nationality, and origin. We might also add that, in the process of this triangulation, language sometimes came into play. For example, although enumerators were specifically instructed to recall that "the language spoken should not be relied upon to determine birthplace" (German as a spoken language was offered as an example of how a language could point to many different origins), the "mother tongue" question was also of great use here in squaring a respondent's immediate background (see chapter 5 by Chad Gaffield, Byron Moldofsky, and Katharine Rollwagen, in this volume). Questions concerning language spoken, although not considered as directly in 1911, would shortly thereafter come to be considered a critical part of the identity triangulation process.

The parameters for country of birth and year of immigration were fairly straightforward, although in the case of the former, enumerators had to be sensitized to a small range of contemporary political considerations. Such considerations included the temporary non-existence of Poland, the stated division of Turkey between its "European" and "Asiatic" components, and areas in which additional geographical information was desired, such as specific locations within the British Empire, or the province of the Austro-Hungarian Empire in question. The question on naturalization applied only to those 21 years of age and older, and only to those who were born anywhere other than the United Kingdom or its dependencies.

Addressing the question on nationality, however, was different, and granting that there are a number of ways in which the issue can be approached, there is at least one key difference between the responses accepted for questions on "national origin" rather than those based on "racial origin": nationality could be conceived as a specific, geopolitical reference, something that could be located on a map ("England") or referenced in a distinct political context ("Flemish"). Racial origin was much more an expression of personal identity, and it could include categories that defy geographical or political conventions (e.g., "German-Irish"), that employ alternate signifiers (e.g., "Celtic" or "Mulatto"), or that were not tied to any political or geographical context at all (e.g., "Jewish").[4]

Hence, the enumerators were instructed to be as inclusive as possible when filling out the nationality question. They were told, "It is proper to use Canadian in column 15 as descriptive of every person whose home is in the country and who has acquired rights of citizenship in it." Moreover, there was some personal flexibility built into this question when the answer was not Canadian; enumerators were told, "An alien person will be classed by nationality according to the country of birth, or the country to which he or she professes to owe allegiance."[5]

In more directly addressing the question that preoccupies the majority of this chapter, we can note a broad evolution: what had been a question asking a person's "origin" in the late nineteenth century became a question concerning one's "racial or tribal origin" for the 1901, 1911, and 1921 censuses. "Tribal" was dropped for 1931 and 1941, and following those years would be entirely repositioned as a question on a person's "ethnicity." As explained to the enumerators in 1911, the general rule was that racial/tribal origin was traced through the father, with his origin trumping the mother's. However, there were two exceptions given to enumerators: first, the origins of Aboriginals were to be traced through the mother, not the father. Second, the children of any mixed marriages (specifically labelled as between "white and black" races or "white and yellow" races) were to be recorded as the non-white ethnicity.[6]

This set of instructions would also be included with the 1921 census, and was essentially the same for both 1931 and 1941. However, the difference between the 1901 and 1911 censuses, as compared with the 1921–41 censuses, was that greater pains were taken – especially in the 1931 and 1941 cases – to explain to the enumerator what exactly racial origin was and why the information was being collected.

Moreover, as early as 1921, this group of questions would be expanded to seven, adding "birthplace of father" and "birthplace of mother" to the five already asked. Further refinements would follow by 1941, when the concept of citizenship was introduced, as was intra-Canadian mobility (taking note of years of residence within the same province and in the same municipality) and a specific question asked on the person's previous residence, wherever that was.

Census Data: Original and Revised

According to the DBS's official publications, the 1911 census determined that people of British origin – including English, Scottish, Irish, Welsh, and several smaller groups – represented just over half (54%) of the Canadian population. The second-largest group was made up of people of "French origin," mostly French Canadians, who represented 28.5 per cent of the population. Following these major groups, there was a substantial drop-off, as the next-largest group consisted of those with German origins, constituting 5.5 per cent of the popu-

Table 4.1 · Racial or tribal origin of persons (*n* and %) living in Canada, 1911: According to the CCRI 1911 weighted 5% sample (ranked from largest to smallest group) and the Census and Statistics Office (CSO) published tables

Origin	*CCRI sample*	*CSO published tables*	
	Frequency n *(%)*	*Origin*	*%*
French	103,041 (27.7)	French	28.5
English	91,235 (24.6)	British English	25.2
Irish	52,462 (14.1)	British Irish	14.6
Scottish	50,279 (13.5)	British Scottish	13.8
German	19,704 (5.3)	German	5.5
Canadian	7,710 (2.1)	—	—
Russian	3,208 (0.9)	Russian	0.6
Dutch	2,522 (0.7)	Dutch	0.7
American	2,484 (0.7)	—	—
Italian	2,457 (0.7)	Italian	0.5
Swedish	2,422 (0.7)	Swedish	
Norwegian	2,139 (0.6)	Norwegian	
Austrian	2,109 (0.6)	Austrian	
All others	29,601 (7.8)		
Complete Total	*371,373 (100)*		

Source: CCRI 1911 microdata database, http://ccri.library.ualberta.ca/en1911census/database/index.html. In all subsequent chapters, the references to the CCRI 1911 microdata database are from this source.

Note: In the Census of Canada published tables, "Swedish" and "Norwegian" were aggregated to the larger "Scandinavian" category, while "Austrian" was aggregated to "Austro-Hungarian."

lation; thereafter, there were no racial or tribal groups representing anything over 0.7 per cent of the population.[7]

According to the 5 per cent sample reanalysed by the Canadian Century Research Infrastructure (CCRI), in the original census returns, roughly 2.1 per cent of the respondents gave "Canadian" as their answer to the racial origins question. Although this number may seems small at first glance, had DBS officials not coded those responses to other choices, "Canadian" would have represented the sixth most popular answer in Canada to "What is your Racial Origin?" According to the 5 per cent sample, had "Canadian" been left in the final tables, only French, English, Scottish, Irish, and German would still stand as more popular answers; "Canadian" would have greatly surpassed Russian, Italian, Dutch, Austrian, Swedish, Norwegian, and Welsh. As an aside, "American" – which was also disallowed as a legitimate answer by the DBS, although drawing much less attention in doing so – figured in as the eighth most popular answer in the CCRI sample (see table 4.1).

What this sample suggests is that the 1911 census officials corrected over 2 per cent of the returns to remove the answers of "Canadian" and reposition them among other categories, most often under one of the British or French designations, depending on how respondents answered the other questions on identity. This large swath of answers, which together with the 2,500 answers of "American" accounted for nearly 4 per cent of the returns, undoubtedly contributed to the changes in wording that we find in the enumerators' instructions in subsequent censuses.[8] In 1921, those instructions specifically noted, "The words 'Canadian' or 'American' must not be used for this purpose, as they express 'Nationality' or 'Citizenship' but not a 'Race or people.'"[9]

Moreover, and unlike many other census questions, this experience of the 1911 data set prompted the need to include, on future censuses, a justification as to the meaning and need for the question itself, either as a piece of information for the enumerators or as an effort to equip those enumerators with the answers they would need when collecting the information among the population. For example, the 1931 instructions note, "The object of this question is to obtain a knowledge of the various constituent elements that have combined from the earliest times to make up the present population of Canada." Although providing lengthy instructions and sample responses, no such justification is offered, for example, as part of the text concerning religion or language. In fact, the only comparable instruction in 1931 comes under "nationality," which reads, "It is proper to use the term 'Canadian' in this column when the information furnished by the individual conforms to the foregoing definitions and explanations."[10]

By 1941, the instructions for answering the racial origins questions expanded significantly. In part, they read as the following:

(1) What is racial origin? The word "race" signifies descendants of a common ancestor.
  a It is imperative to understand that a person's racial origin and nationality very often are different, for instance the Canadian nationality comprises many different racial origins, e.g. English, French, Irish, Scottish, Welsh, Italian, German, etc.
  b The name of a country from which a person came to Canada gives no indication of that person's racial origin ...

c The word Canadian does not denote a racial origin, but a nationality; the same applies to the word American.
d It is therefore necessary for the Enumerator to ascertain a person's racial origin separately from his country of birth, or nationality.[11]

Why did the creators of the census go to so much pain to illustrate and enunciate not only the definition of "racial origin," but also the reasons why "Canadian" could not be included? Given the immense complications involved in defining religious categories, language use, and the concept of mother tongue, why was so much space spent on elucidating and clarifying the concept of "race"? What, beyond the statistical significance of the response rate of "Canadian" can guide our understanding of DBS's consternation on this topic and its continued insistence that it did not apply?

Public Discussion

One of the more fascinating exchanges concerning the place of and space for a "Canadian" race occurred across a range of Canadian newspapers in 1921 and early 1922, both before and shortly after the initial 1921 census results were published, a debate greatly influenced by the 1911 census results, and captured by the CCRI's Contextual Database. As the census of 1921 was being prepared, the enumerators' instructions – which specifically eliminated "Canadian" as a proper response – became known among segments of the general population, ultimately winding their way into the media and creating an aggressive public discussion, heightened during its actual enumeration period.

Touching off the controversy was a letter, which first appeared in the *Manitoba Free Press*, detailing some personal accounts of the restriction on racial origin answers, thereby prompting an editorial that railed against the inability of census respondents to give "Canadian" as their nationality: "Though a man's ancestors for six or seven generations have lived in Canada and helped to make this country what it is today, he cannot describe himself simply as a Canadian," wrote the *Free Press*.[12] Other newspapers chimed in. The *Sudbury Star* suggested, "If your ancestors have resided in Canada for ten generations, or even more, you will have to determine your racial origin by tracing the origin of your first great-grandfather who settled on this continent."[13] The *Kingston Whig-Standard* laid out the case more substantially for its readers:

> Think what it means to the new Canadian. Here, let us say, are a Swede and his wife who came to Canada fifteen years or so ago. They have a

> family who scarcely know the Scandinavian tongue or where Sweden is on the map. The census taker comes. Yes, he is a Swede and not ashamed of it, but his children, they are Canadians. No, says the Government of this Canada, they are Swedes. If in the course of a dozen of years more, one of the Swede's sons marries a young girl born in Canada of Scottish parents, their children are – what? Either Swedes or Scottish by choice – but not Canadians. About how long will it take to build up a healthy Canadian sentiment and patriotism under such absurd and grotesque methods?[14]

When several readers attempted to challenge the original *Manitoba Free Press*'s argument by carefully explaining the difference between "race" and "nationality," as well as reproducing the enumerator's instructions verbatim, the newspaper responded with a restatement of its core argument: "Our point is that there is now a Canadian people and that this should not be denied officially by our own government in its census returns. The average Canadian of three or four generations in Canada cannot accurately indicate his 'tribal' descent and the information collected by the census under this head is mostly incorrect. The *Free Press*'s contention is that it ought to be possible for a Canadian citizen to give his racial descent as Canadian if that is his desire."[15]

A tipping point, it seems, was reached when the Toronto *Globe* printed an editorial on 15 February 1922, entitled "Let Us Be Canadians!" Providing examples of Loyalists, new immigrants, and "Canadians of French origin who have been anchored on the soil of the New World for three centuries," the *Globe* lamented that none of these groups had "been able to earn the name Canadian." The paper, lambasting "the ridiculous system of classifying all persons according to their racial origin, however remote that may be," demanded that the Canadian government, "which is composed almost entirely of native Canadians ... should make an end at once of this farce."[16]

This *Globe* column was enough to draw a direct and printed response from Chief Dominion Statistician R.H. Coats, the man at the head of the DBS and, hence, in charge of the 1921 (as well as the 1931 and 1941) census. Suggesting that the census "should not be attacked in opprobrious forms by a newspaper having the influence of the *Globe* until the facts concerning it have been fully investigated," Coats addressed the concerns raised by various newspapers in the previous months by listing – with full detail – the seven questions which touch upon a person's national identity (discussed above) as well as the reason for collecting each one. On the specific question of "racial or tribal origin," Coats explained:

> The object of this question is to ascertain from what basic ethnic stocks the present Canadian population, more particularly the recently immigrated population, is derived. Both from a practical and from a scientific point of view, this is considered an important thing for a country in the position of Canada to know; in obtaining it, the Canadian census is usually regarded as in advance of rather than behind the censuses of other countries ... [The question] recognize[s] the fact that the Canadian race is still in the making, and that its constituent elements and the general process of making may conceivably be worthy of study.[17]

Coats's answer was, as we might imagine, insufficient in the eyes of the audience he was addressing. Despite admitting the imperfections of statistical inquiry, and despite raising a new possibility – that "the Canadian race is still in the making" (signalling that it could one day be added to the list of official races) – Coats, nevertheless, refused to accept the *Globe*'s argument. Indeed, the divergence of views between Coats and the readers and editors of the *Globe* went to the very centre of the meaning of the racial origin question, highlighting the assumptions that are built into the terms "race" and "origin." Coats's reasoning was that the identity of anyone who could be considered "Canadian" was already confirmed in a wealth of other questions: Canadians were accepted as citizens in the nationality question, pains were taken to record the birth of Canadian parents "for the express purpose of distinguishing Canadian families of more than one generation," and details concerning internal Canadian migration and language spoken were layered on top of that in order to add context, colour, and detail to the experience of entire swaths of Canadian society.

On the question of race itself, however, there was an intractable difference between Coats's stated point of view and the one expressed by the *Globe*. Essentially, Coats did not accept that "Canadian" was itself a "race," which was the very point the *Globe* was attempting to defend. For Coats and, hence, the decennial census, Canadians were all originally something else, and their "ethnic stock" found its roots in other places, mostly across the Atlantic. Although Coats suggested that the true point of the racial origins question was to ascertain the origins of *new* arrivals (not long-standing Canadian families) and, hence, was far less concerned with the latter (whose identity as "Canadians" was already triangulated via several other questions), he did not sufficiently address the underlying point that the *Globe* was making.

The gauntlet was, therefore, picked back up by the *Globe* two days later. Beginning dramatically ("Bewilderment is the uppermost sensation evoked by reading the letter of Mr R.H. Coats"), the *Globe* identified the key discrepancy:

> Mr Coats tells us that the question in the census schedules dealing with nationality provides for the entering as a Canadian of each and every person of Canadian citizenship, irrespective of race, language, place of birth, or other consideration. This is purely a formal question. Mr Coats is seeking to indicate citizenship. *The Globe* was discussing race. The answers to the question, standing alone, give not the remotest indication as to racial origin. Citizens who have come from the ends of the earth, and who in many cases do not even speak the English language, become "Canadians" under this classification equally with the descendants of the men who helped to build the first rude fort at Quebec in 1608.[18]

The *Globe* also underscored at least two fundamental, conceptual differences with Coats's starting point: first, that tracing the information based on a person's origin, no matter how far back it had to go, was of some value; and second, that the racial/ethnic environment of North America could be compared to the idealized version of that environment in Europe, whereby individuals could trace their French or German or English roots for hundreds of years. On the first point, the *Globe* asked, "What possible value to statisticians or ethnologists, or any else, can it be to learn that three hundred years ago when the remote ancestors of some of Toronto's well-known families arrived in America they were English or French?" On the second point, the *Globe*'s editors reconfigured their understanding of North America, which they suggested was a place of ethnic mixing, making the separation of individual races from generations past almost impossible:

> Perhaps in the very first generation an Englishman married a French woman or a Hollander – as in the case of some of the Pilgrims – and the "ethnic stock," thus disturbed, has been subjected to similar instructions for eight generations, so that the original English or French has become almost entirely submerged beneath a wave of Slavic or Germanic or even Turanian blood. Racial derivations ... are assuredly of no possible service in determining the actual race of people with several generations of American ancestors behind them.[19]

Imbued with both logic and emotion, the question would continue for some time, colouring even the election of the new (albeit short-lived) Progressive-controlled Parliament of 1922, which the *Toronto Daily Star* hoped would settle "the question as to whether Canadians are Canadians or merely visitors here from other and older lands," and finally, reverse the official view propagated by the census "that nobody is a Canadian."[20] But, of course, it was not settled; the very same debate, the very same objections, and the very same considerations at the DBS would continue through the 1931 census, through the 1941 census, and into the census of 1951. However, this exchange almost certainly influenced the care with which the DBS treated this question in subsequent years. With Coats still in charge, the 1931 census instructions to enumerators repeated almost word for word his explanation offered in the pages of the *Globe* in 1922, stating, "The purpose of the information sought in this column is to measure as accurately as possible the racial origins of the population of Canada, i.e. the original sources from which the present population has been derived." The instructions even rephrased this a second time in the same section of the instruction manual, stating, "The object of this question is to obtain knowledge of the various constituent elements that have combined from the earliest times to make up the present population of Canada."[21]

Origine in French Canada

It should be noted that this discussion was centred in English-speaking Canada; among French Canadians, both inside and outside Quebec, the emphasis was largely on ensuring reflection in the official numbers of the true scope of French-speakers across Canada. Canadian demographers have argued that there has always been a different, intensified preoccupation with the census numbers in Quebec, "with greater importance accorded in Quebec than elsewhere to the history, 'roots,' and survival of its people."[22] Although we should acknowledge that French Canadian communities outside Quebec were also quite preoccupied with the head count of French-speakers (such as in relation to French-language schooling in Ontario and Manitoba), and although we should expand this preoccupation to include communities of English-speakers in various provinces who were concerned with the erosion of their numbers resulting from both immigration to and out-migration from Quebec – thereby expanding the number of those groups with such an "intensified preoccupation" – French-language Quebec, nonetheless, anchored many of its social and political arguments directly to its proportion in Confederation.

Consistent with this emphasis explored by other authors, a range of articles in both Quebec and Ontario encouraged the French Canadian population around census time to answer as clearly as possible. In one case, L'Association canadienne-française d'éducation d'Ontario sent out a publication it then advertised in local newspapers to ask French Canadians "de bien faire inscrire leur origine au prochain recensement afin que la population canadienne-française ne soit pas méconnue par négligence, apathie ou autres causes."[23] In another case, the Quebec City–based *L'Action sociale catholique* broke out several specific questions to explain to its readers, including the question on racial origin, which, as it instructed, "Nos compatriotes doivent donc répondre à la question 14: origine canadienne-française pour marquer la différence des canadiens de langue française."[24]

This issue of properly and accurately enumerating the "French" population was also of interest in the House of Commons, as parliamentarians from several provinces kept an eye on how those numbers played themselves out in terms of national policy and political debate. Most often, this emerged in the form of ensuring that French-speaking enumerators would be deployed in the field. Naturally, in an era when the census was filled out by enumerators going door-to-door, the availability of a linguistically competent workforce was paramount to the integrity of the data and the accuracy of the count in French-speaking areas. As a result, and while this did not seem to be a problem in most of Quebec, MPs from Moncton, New Brunswick, the Ottawa region, and even from parts of Montreal, all consistently raised this issue each time the decennial census was about to be taken.[25]

The concern over accuracy went both ways, of course. As early as April 1911, a Conservative MP from Ontario stirred some debate in the House of Commons by offering rumours that census officials in Quebec had, going back to 1901, "stuffed" the results in order to inflate them. If true, the allegation was critical, given that the political representation of other provinces at the federal level was, in part, fixed in proportion to the population of Quebec.[26]

Discussion at the Dominion Bureau of Statistics

Returning the focus to the public back and forth on the racial origins question, as well as the seeming influence the public debate had on subsequent instructions to enumerators, the situation begs us to fill in the other side of the story, namely, the reasoning behind the decisions being made at the DBS. As mentioned above, the well-developed nexus of scholarship and analysis on the patently white, Eurocentric dominance of Canada's political establishment and budding civil service – the Dominion Bureau of Statistics included – is well established and does not need to be repeated here.[27] Moreover, such a bias was clearly at play: in the public exchanges noted above, the chief Dominion statistician himself defended the absence of the inclusion of the term "Canadian" in the racial origins question because "the racial inheritance of the individual, as must be evident to all who are acquainted with the Mendelian law, is not affected by terminology. To accept the answer 'Canadian' under this heading would, of course, defeat the purpose for which the question was inserted."[28]

However, and while not ignoring the obvious effect these larger dynamics had on the DBS (and more precisely on the men who governed the census distribution and processing), the scholarly conversation on the range of racial categorizations offered in the census has perhaps underplayed the level of awareness among DBS officials of the conceptual limits of the data they were collecting. They were, perhaps, more aware of the inherent faults of their limiting categorization of humanity by race, colour, and geography than is usually presumed, even if they were not as of yet willing to fully confront the ethnocentrism that helped formulate the characteristics they would highlight as constituting difference.

There is some evidence from the wider Canadian context to support the DBS's more nuanced position on the inevitability, universality, and rigidness of race categorization. For instance, the *Ottawa Citizen* noted, as it prepared its readers for the "Many Questions by Census Man" in the upcoming 1911 enumeration, that some questions, such as those surrounding nationality, would have "some room for interpretation."[29] Indeed, and while certainly remaining pejorative, the *Citizen*, in a contemporary article discussing an upcoming London conference on race in the British Empire, asked its readers more generally to consider the durability of the current order, given its biased imbalance: "Can we reasonably expect that ... native races will remain forever content (even supposing that they are so now) to be ruled and governed by a majority of white men?"

However, the census data collected in the early twentieth century pertaining to origins questions presented a number of challenges, not merely because of the shifting nature of the terms and conditions themselves over time, but because the DBS encountered a large range of "unexpected" responses. Leaving aside (for the moment) the stated origins of "Canadian," responses to the question of one's racial origin included at least four other challenges for those imputing the data: responses that the DBS classified as "nationalities" rather than "racial origins" (e.g., "American," "Mexican"); responses that were not related to a specific geographical place but were still considered a "race" (e.g., "Jewish," "Black"); hyphenated or dual-response answers[30] (e.g., "Scottish-Canadian," "French-Irish"); and an array of answers provided by various groups of Aboriginals, for which a comprehensive code set did not exist. To put such results succinctly: the actual Canadian population had a much more exhaustive impression of what constituted their "racial origins" than did the DBS.

The interplay between census questions and their interpretation "on the ground" is, to some extent, endemic to the census process. For example, when preparing for the 1921 census, the DBS deemed it important to acquire more accurate information on immigrants to Canada. In fact, it sought to address what it considered to be a major problem with the 1911 immigrant statistics: the number of short-term or transitory labour migrants had been more of a reasoned deduction than a known fact based on hard statistical evidence. To help transform those assumptions into fact, DBS official C.W. Cousins suggested making several adjustments to the collection of information in the schedule used for listing immigrants. Specifically, Cousins suggested that enumerators question immigrants on their ability to read and write English and/or another language. He also suggested that enumerators specify the respondent's birthplace and nationality or citizenship. Moreover, Cousins offered that individuals who were born in, but left Canada, should be asked why they left, and why they were returning. It is worth noting that these suggestions would ultimately exert influence on Canadian immigration procedures, and many of them were eventually applied to later censuses.

More broadly, however, the case of racial origin is an example of how the concerns of both the government of the day and the Canadian general public were actually intertwined; it should, perhaps, come as little surprise that there is evidence suggesting that the DBS was, behind the scenes, engaged in the very same debate as the public, and that some DBS officials made the very same points as did the *Globe*, a reality hinted at even in Coats's printed answer. To begin with, Coats, in his answer, attempted to implore the difficulty with which the census questions are first conceived when the census is crafted. Noting that generating the questions is "an exceedingly difficult problem on which a large literature exists," Coats adds that "the methods of the Dominion Bureau of Statistics were adopted only after the views of experts the world over had been considered, and in the light of half a century's experience in Canada," and that "several weeks during 1920 were spent in conference with the directors of the census of Great Britain and the several Dominions, in which these questions were discussed in the fullest detail." Finally, Coats rejected the rigidity with which his organization was charged, adding, "It is not claimed that our methods are final or incapable of improvement, demography being one of the most many-sided and elusive of studies."[31]

As time passed, the record of debate over these issues intensified. We know that by the late 1930s and early 1940s, the DBS had a much more established litany of reasons as to why the collection of racial origin was necessary, a list which, in many senses, was simply a much more developed version of the explanation hinted at by Coats during the 1921 discussion. Between the 1921 and 1941 censuses, the DBS would insist on at least four benefits that could be drawn from the data surrounding that question: First, the racial origins question helped the DBS to evaluate the rate of "assimilation" of immigrants into English and French populations, a question thought to be of value to provincial and federal governments. Figures on racial origin had an important bearing on the study of immigration for they helped measure the extent to which new arrivals mixed with the existing Canadian population and adapted to Canadian institutions, while maintaining their cultural identity.[32] The DBS also argued that racial origin data provided feedback for immigration policy by identifying "adaptable" and "fusible" cultural groups.

Second, and certainly by 1941, the DBS had recognized that most inquiries sent from the public – especially from the business community – regarding the census actually related to data on racial origin. A company wishing to market its product to a particular ethnic group or set of ethnic groups would request figures on racial origin for its target market. This information was considered by those in the private sector to be the most accurate portrait of a consumer audience available.[33]

Third, the DBS attempted to gather information on the racial composition of the population in specific areas of the country, where they were gathered, and whether they lived in scattered or close-knit groups. As quoted in a DBS text, "In a world where rumors and ignorance concerning the size and composition of minority groups feed suspicion and often persecution, even rough data bearing some relation to facts, can prove a useful counter."[34] It was argued that figures on birthplace, language spoken, religion, and origin taken together with questions on education and occupation, provided insight on the impact various groups had on the creation of culture in Canada and on its trajectory. Fourth, and as Coats affirmed in 1922, the collection of this data facilitated "academic" needs to study "ethnological and biological influences or conditions in the population" in order to develop new studies on diseases, which were suspected as occurring in elevated rates in certain segments of the population.[35] This included a supposed susceptibility to diabetes among the Jewish population, and the stated prevalence of tuberculosis among Chinese and Japanese immigrants as well as Canada's Aboriginals.

However, and despite this rich subsequent range of explanations, we are still left with the question of why, in 1922, R.H. Coats addressed the editors and readers of the *Globe* in the manner which he did. The answer is likely a combination of at least two factors. First, and following earlier work compiled on the prominence and tone of discussions surrounding "race" in the first half of the twentieth century, Coats was likely anxious to contribute to the major scholarly debates of his day by providing raw numbers that could animate them. As noted above, Coats's response to the *Globe* also stated, "The Canadian census is usually regarded as in advance of rather than behind the censuses of other countries. I believe that students of ethnology, eugenics, criminology, and the social 'biometric' sciences in general will agree to this."[36] Coats actively pursued a program that would raise the profile of the DBS internationally, and he was deeply involved in the emerging international debate around the standardization of statistics: he was the official Canadian representative to the

League of Nations Statistical Office, to the Imperial Statistical Conference of 1920, and to the International Labour Organization, and he played a key role in the subsequent organization of the yearly International Statistical Conference (which was hosted by Ottawa in 1963) and was asked, from 1920 to 1941, to contribute to the editorial direction of the *Journal of the American Statistical Association.*

What Is a "Race" Anyway?

Second, however, Coats was also likely presenting the public with a unified face from the DBS after having argued and disagreed, privately and within the confines of DBS board rooms, and he had come to a workable, if not ideal solution to the origins question. Indeed, part of the latitude given to the differing opinions on the racial origins question may have also emanated from the general lack of agreement on a definition – or even an acceptable, general understanding – of what exactly a "race" is. Although those involved in this debate, both among the public and in academic and government circles, were many years away from abandonment of the term "race" (the use of which became highly undesirable beginning just after the end of the Second World War), there was, nonetheless, a distinct lack of agreement on what constituted an acceptable range of answers.

As many authors have noted, the term, definition, and conception of "race," "racism," and "racial differentiation" have been unevenly evolving since at least the Victorian era, and often have included contemporary, contradictory categorizations based on everything from skin pigmentation to political ideology.[37] This ongoing and ever-changing conversation was, therefore, reflected in the range of understandings offered on what would constitute acceptable answers to the question of racial origin. For example, at several points – including in the 1922 remarks by DBS Chief R.H. Coats – the definition of "race" was said to both rest upon and be useful to those making "scientific" inquiries. Coats discussed the "students of ethnology, eugenics ... and the social 'biometric' sciences" who expressed strong support of the racial origins question, and for whom the census provided critical data. However, even these premises were far from clearly defined, as contemporary commentators soon suggested. In contemplating race, the *Saskatoon Star Phoenix* offered the following:

> Another phase of the subject covered by the census deals with the "origin" or source from which the Canadian population has been derived. The information sought under this heading is popularly described as

> involving the concept of "race," but this is not always the case. In a biological and ethnological sense, the term "race" signifies a physical differentiation (as in shape of head, stature, color of skin, etc.) between groups of human species, such as exists between the black and white races, or under the latter heading between the Nordic, Alpine and Mediterranean groups. Obviously the census cannot pursue inquiry to any length in a field of the latter character, the more so as ethnologists themselves are by no means agreed upon the principles of race classification.[38]

This version of what constituted "race" was not solely an academic issue, but shaped the much larger US census, also conducted every ten years. Indeed, given the proximity of the countries themselves and of their census (Canada's takes place in years ending in 11, the US's in years ending in 10), the differences between them on this question became glaring. In the words of the *Star Phoenix*, and echoed elsewhere, while the DBS asked Canadian respondents to reach back several generations to provide a distant origin, "the census bureau at Washington attempts no such classification: It asks: 'What is your race?' but the answer expected has to do with color of the skin, and the statistical product shows the population of the United States grouped into whites, negroes, Indians, Mexicans and Orientals. Those put down as white are not sub-divided on the Canadian plan."[39]

The *Winnipeg Free Press* went further, suggesting that Canadian and American statistics officials were of a very different mindset when it came to the ongoing relevance of ethnic origins:

> The assumption underlying the American practice clearly is that residence in the United States for three generations makes a family American, at least for statistical purposes. A native of the United States, born of parents who were also natives of the United States, may have had German, English or Polish, grandparents, but this fact does not interest the census bureau. In Canada, on the other hand, the census takers are concerned not only with grandparents, but perhaps with great-grandparents or even great-great-grandparents. In Canada a family can never become Canadian except in the political sense as signifying nationality. As the Canadian statistician sees it, the distinction between English, French, German and other European peoples persists for centuries after transplanting to the New World. The American statistician believes that, in three generations, these differences are either lost or too nebulous to be a subject of exact record.[40]

The solution, suggested the *Free Press*, was to "drop the attempt to sub-divide the people of European extraction, and rely on statistics about language and parentage as guides."[41]

Even the widely held view of academics and statisticians that race had to be traced through the father (at least, in the case of Caucasians/Europeans) was challenged. Criticizing the patrilineal nature of the question, the *Sudbury Star* facetiously wrote, "If a man's paternal grandfather is English and all three of his other grandparents are Irish, he is of English racial origin."[42] "Moreover," wrote the *Manitoba Free Press*, "the ignoring of maternal ancestors, while it may be justified from the strictly legal point of view and may be in line with the [principle] of naturalization, is a serious omission [in] any attempt to study the actual racial [illegible] of the people; and as our correspondent points out, it is paying scant honor to Canadian mothers."[43]

Although certainly not jettisoning our collective appreciation of the power that racial categories held in early twentieth-century Canada, the range of the debate over what constituted "race" – the lack of a "Canadian" option notwithstanding – adds yet another layer of nuance to the discussion. In addition, these questions most certainly underpin the public calls to alter the list of acceptable choices, and fuel speculation concerning the degree of difficulty with which DBS officials had to wrestle in order to measure the characteristics of the Canadian population, but in a way that would reveal useful, quantifiable results.

Of course, the challenges surrounding the "origin" questions are not linked only to the limitations and mindsets of the past, but continue today, and are, arguably, part and parcel of attempting to categorize such a subjective, malleable component of identity. When the CCRI grappled with the categorization of previous census responses, a few difficult decisions were inevitable: for example, when a response had multiple answers ("Austrian Jewish," "Russian Polish," "English and German," etc.), members of the Canadian Century Research Infrastructure had to decide whether this represented a novel category, whether one of the multiple identities took precedence, or whether the entire answer could be subsumed within an existing category. To some extent – and while the project's choices are well documented elsewhere – those choices could be challenged.

Conclusion: A Most Canadian Characteristic

Public, highly politicized debates surrounding the Canadian decennial census – and the utility of questions concerning origins – are, it would seem, part and parcel of its existence. In 1999, Statistics Canada and Canadian Heritage argued over whether or not the ethnicity question – the modern version of the questions studied here – should be kept on the Canadian census of 2001; as of January 2000, it actually seemed quite likely that the question would be dropped. In the lead-up to that decision, a number of inquiries were mounted so as to ascertain the best course of action: committees within Statistics Canada pondered the question and the various forms it could take (new definitions, with or without sample lists to choose from, etc.), a few alternate questions were field-tested over several months, and the possibility of replacing ethnicity with "other information about parental birthplace" was touted as a reasonable replacement. The ubiquitous place of the 1996 census's most common response to the ethnicity question – "Canadian" – was also specifically considered, as some suggested that it "skew[ed] the data, and makes it hard to determine true ethnic origins." In the end, however, the question was kept as-is for two reasons: the practical use of the information – federal institutions, medical researchers, ethnocultural groups, the media, and social scientists were all named as heavy users of the data – and the admission that "birthplace and ethnic origin are not precisely the equivalent."[44]

The parallels with the early twentieth century are so striking, it leads one to argue that rather than constituting some kind of exception, the discussion on "origin" – from the difficulty in defining the term to the intrusiveness of the "Canadian" response – has been so typical of the taking of the Canadian census over the past century as to almost constitute an official part of the process. Hardly a census has gone by without visceral public reaction to several of its assumptions and compromises, the place and definition of "Canadian" surviving as one of the more notable examples. Indeed, despite being a country so often portrayed as lacking the central definition or a sense of what "Canadian" even means, the right of the individual citizens to *call* themselves "Canadian" – whatever that is said to mean – is one of the longest-standing outgrowths of the taking of the decennial census.

Throughout the first half of the twentieth century, the Dominion Bureau of Statistics had already recognized that while the origins question was important, it also brought with it a number of problems for data collection. At the most basic level, it was appreciated that "racial origin" was not an objective classification; moreover, given the increasing complexity and specificity evident in the instructions to enumerators, as well as the range of public discourse presented in various newspapers, it was also clear that the population was finding it increasingly difficult to understand what exactly they were being asked. Over time, it would be admitted by DBS officials that while, for instance, religion was associated with a denominational "preference" that was specific (and for which the response "none" was an acceptable answer), in the case of racial origin, it was impossible to strike upon any single factor that would identify the origin of the person.[45] As a result, and as was later recognized, the birthplace – either one's own or, if born in Canada, one's most recent non–North American ancestors – predominated at least until 1941, after which language moved to the forefront of concepts of "origin."[46]

The documents left behind point to a concerted effort to maintain the integrity, consistency, and clarity of the decisions taken in advance of releasing the census design. To make sense of the data, one would expect no less. While not minimizing the latent role that ethnocentrism must have played, DBS officials, nonetheless, questioned and problematized their findings, aimed to make them as comprehensible as possible, and defended their decisions publicly once a consensus had been reached. Once the census was out, the Canadian government, Canadian commercial interests, and Canadian communities would all clamour to read the findings, and to understand the shifting picture that was Canada. From the perspective of those at the Dominion Bureau of Statistics, however, this would quickly become a time for reassessment, reviewing what was successful and what was problematic, followed by research and brainstorming on how to maximize the successes and deal with the shortcomings. In a sense, disagreements over the interpretation of results on, among others, the origins question, fed right back into the search for direct and applied solutions to solve the perceived problems of the previous census, beginning the whole process of review all over again, and continuing a cycle that has yet to cease.

Notes

1 *Memorandum for M.H. Marshall's Committee, Suggested Alternatives to Present Racial Origin Classification*, M. Flemming and J. Kelly, Box 8612308, 1944, Statistics Canada, uncatalogued holdings.

2 Ibid.

3 Sylvia T. Wargon does an excellent job of reviewing some of the major literature on the subject in *Demography in Canada in the Twentieth Century* (Vancouver: UBC Press, 2002), Appendix B.

4 It should, nonetheless, be noted that "nationality" is not identical to "country of birth." Even more so than nationality, "country of birth" is a geographical reference only. Nationality, while still grounded in geopolitical categories, can refer to a political entity that is not tied to or confined to a single political territory. "Basque," "Scandinavian," or "African" might be examples.

5 Canada, Department of Agriculture and Statistics, *Fifth Census of Canada, 1911: Instructions to Officers, Commissioners and Enumerators* (Ottawa: Government Printing Bureau, 1911), 29–30.

6 For a phenomenal bird's-eye view of the evolution of these categories over time, see table 3.2 in Monica Boyd, Gustave Goldmann, and Pamela White, "Race in

the Canadian Census," in Leo Driedger and Shiva S. Halli (eds.), *Race and Racism: Canada's Challenge* (Montreal and Kingston: McGill-Queen's University Press, 2000), 37.

7 Canada, Census and Statistics Office, *Fifth Census of Canada, 1911*, vol. II, *Religions, Origins, Birthplace, Citizenship, Literacy and Infirmities by Provinces, Districts and Sub-districts* (Ottawa: C.H. Parmelee, 1912).

8 There were also 260 cases of "Swiss," another category that would be singled out, from time to time, as not constituting a racial origin.

9 Canada, Department of Trade and Commerce, Dominion Bureau of Statistics (DBS), *Sixth Census of Canada, 1921: Instructions to Commissioners and Enumerators* (Ottawa: King's Printer, 1921), 26.

10 Canada, Department of Trade and Commerce, DBS, *Seventh Census of Canada, 1931: Instructions to Commissioners and Enumerators* (Ottawa: F.A. Ackland, 1931), 28–34.

11 Canada, Department of Trade and Commerce, DBS, *Eighth Census of Canada, 1941: Instructions to Commissioners and Enumerators* (Ottawa: Edmond Cloutier, 1941), 44.

12 Reprinted by the *Border Cities Star*, "Census Question," 4 July 1921, 4.

13 "Can't Say Race Is 'Canadian,'" *Sudbury Star*, 7 May 1921, 1.

14 Reprinted in "Why Not Canadians?" *Globe*, 28 Jan. 1922, 4.

15 Editor's Note affixed below "Canadian Descent," *Winnipeg Free Press*, 9 July 1921, 12.

16 "Let Us Be Canadians!" *Globe*, 15 Feb. 1922, 4.

17 R.H. Coats, "RE: 'Let Us Be Canadians!'" *Globe*, 20 Feb. 1922, 4.

18 "No Canadian Race," *Globe*, 22 Feb. 1922, 4.

19 Ibid.

20 "It's Time to Stop It," *Toronto Daily Star*, 13 April 1922, 8.

21 Canada, Department of Trade and Commerce, DBS, *Seventh Census of Canada, 1931: Instructions to Commissioners and Enumerators*, 28–34.

22 See Wargon, *Demography in Canada*, 28. A brief review of some of these issues is also offered by Jean-Pierre Beaud and Jean-Guy Prévost, "L'éxperience statistique canadienne," in Jean-Pierre Beaud and Jean-Guy Prévost (eds.), *L'ère du chiffre: Systèmes statistiques et traditions nationales* (Quebec: Presses de l'Université du Québec, 2000), 61–86.

23 *Le Temps*, 26 May 1911, 1.

24 *L'Action sociale catholique*, 30 May 1911, 4.

25 Examples include the following: Arthur B. Copp, MP for Westmoreland, New Brunswick (Canada, Parliament, House of Commons, *Debates* [hereafter *Debates*], 13th Parliament, 5th Session, vol. 146, 27 May 1921, col. 3792); Edgar-Rodolphe-Eugène Chevrier, MP for Ottawa (*Debates*, 17th Parliament, 2nd Session, 8 June 1931, col. 2370), and Pierre-François Casgrain, MP for Charlevoix-Saguenay, Quebec (*Debates*, 17th Parliament, 2nd Session, cols 2420–1).

26 Charles Lewis Owen, MP for Northumberland East, Ontario (*Debates*, 11th Parliament, 3rd Session, 12 April 1911, cols 7217–19).

27 See Wargon, *Demography in Canada*, Appendix B.

28 Coats, "RE: 'Let Us Be Canadians!'"
29 "Many Questions by Census Man," *Ottawa Citizen*, 29 May 1911, 2.
30 It would not be until the 1981 census that Statistics Canada would allow multiple answers to be given for a single question.
31 For all quotes in this paragraph, see Coats, "RE: 'Let Us Be Canadians!'"
32 *Problems of Questions such as Religion and Origin in the Canadian Census*, 7, found in M. Flemming and J. Kelly, Box 862066, Statistics Canada, uncatalogued holdings.
33 *Memorandum re the Purpose of the Question on Racial Origin in the Census*, found in M. Flemming and J. Kelly, Box 8612308, contains a breakdown of the types of inquiries received from the public.
34 *Problems of Questions such as Religion and Origin in the Canadian Census*, 7.
35 *Memorandum for M. H. Marshall's Committee*, 3.
36 Coats, "RE: 'Let Us Be Canadians!'"
37 For one excellent discussion on the evolution of academic and political thought on racism, see Alan J. Levine, "Redefining Racism," *American Outlook* (Washington, DC: Hudson Institute, Spring 2002), 38–43.
38 *Saskatoon Star Phoenix*, 4 June 1931, 11.
39 "Race Statistics in the U.S.," *Winnipeg Free Press*, 18 Aug. 1931, 11.
40 Ibid.
41 Ibid.
42 "Can't Say Race Is 'Canadian.'"
43 Reprinted by the *Border Cities Star*, "Census Question," 4.
44 Jim Bronskill, "Census Wants to Dump Ethnicity Question," *Ottawa Citizen*, 13 Jan. 2000. Author's note: It might be added here that, at the time of originally writing this piece, a very public discussion concerning the utility of the census was also taking place, leading to the cancellation of the long-form census, as elsewhere noted.
45 *Problems of Questions such as Religion and Origin in the Canadian Census*, 2. This study would also cite changing political boundaries and intermarriage as additional, complicating factors.
46 Ibid. This shift would not solve the problem, as it would be argued that many mother tongues could be spoken in most birthplaces and that, moreover, people could have different mother tongues and still retain cultural unity.

— · 5 · —

"Do Not Use for Comparison with Other Censuses": Identity, Politics, and Languages Commonly Spoken in 1911 Canada

CHAD GAFFIELD, BYRON MOLDOFSKY, AND KATHARINE ROLLWAGEN

Since the beginning of the twentieth century, the decennial census in Canada has posed questions about language. The 1901 enumeration asked three questions: "can speak English?"; "can speak French?"; and "Mother tongue (If spoken)?" Officials then used the completed census schedules to compile a summary table that was published in the official report of the enumeration. This table totalled the number of respondents in each census district across Canada who could, and could not, speak English or French, and those who could speak both English and French. Ten years later, the census included one question about language; residents in 1911 were asked to specify their "language commonly spoken." Surprisingly, no summary tables about language were included in the published volumes that reported on the enumeration; while the aggregate results for all the other questions were provided as expected, the official report on the 1911 census completely omitted any results from the language question.

Why were the results of the language question omitted from the official published report of the enumeration? Why were the three language questions of the 1901 census rejected in favour of a new single question in 1911? And, from the perspective of the early twenty-first century, what can the 1911 census enumeration of language tell us about the linguistic dynamics of the making of modern Canada?

These questions probe to the heart of our understanding of Canada in the rapidly changing geopolitical, economic, and cultural context of the period surrounding the First World War. In recent years, scholars have increasingly emphasized how Canada reached new heights of national confidence and international recognition during this period. Perhaps the most robust research has focused on the ways in which Canadian efforts on the battlefield played a key role not only in the Allied victory but also in domestic nation building; indeed, the battle of Vimy Ridge has been frequently depicted as a turning point in Canada's emergence as an important country on the world stage. But, scholars have also emphasized that, during the same decade, Canada descended to new lows of internal conflict as the two "founding peoples" fought each other not only about conscription in 1917 but also about other sensitive issues such as the language of instruction in public schools. The historian Robert Choquette has concluded that, in these years, "no solution seemed possible to the linguistic, cultural, racial and religious strife" between French and English; the two groups were quite literally "at each other's throats."[1] The domestic violence of this era is captured in the image of disenfranchised school trustees and parents – some armed with hatpins – asserting their determination to educate their children in French by forcefully barring police officers from entering an Ottawa school.[2]

Throughout the decade of the First World War, events in Europe and those in Canada were linked in public debate. In 1913, Henri Bourassa described the government of Ontario as "more Prussian than Prussia" for having issued Regulation 17, banning the use of French in schools after the first two grades. Bourassa depicted the enemies of French Canada as being located within Canada rather than on the other side of the Atlantic Ocean: "The enemies of the French language, of French civilization in Canada, are not the Boches on the shores of the Spree; but the English-Canadian anglicizers, the Orange intriguers, or Irish priests. Above all they are French Canadians weakened and degraded by the conquest and three centuries of colonial servitude. Let no mistake be made: if we let the Ontario minority be crushed, it will soon be the turn of other French groups in English Canada."[3] Taken together, the contrasting images of nation-building Canadian troops fighting shoulder-to-shoulder in Europe while armed francophone trustees faced off with anglophone school inspectors in a divided Canadian community illustrate the competing interpretations of national cohesion and conflict in the early twentieth century. In this context, the 1911 census enumeration of language provides a strategic window through which to view the interplay of official perspectives, public debate, and household dynamics at the beginning of a key decade.

The following discussion contributes to this effort by drawing upon the rich and diverse corpus of evidence contained within the Canadian Century Research Infrastructure (CCRI). By using each question of the decennial census enumerations between 1911 and 1951 as the core organizing source, the CCRI offers a digital archive based on the completed manuscript census schedules, government documentary records, political debate at the federal and provincial levels, and public discussion – especially as reported in newspapers.[4] As a first step in realizing the analytical potential of this research infrastructure for the study of language, the discussion begins with an analysis of the formulation of the 1911 question and then moves to an examination of contemporary public debate as the enumeration began on 1 June 1911. The focus then turns to what was actually written on the census schedules and to how this evidence was treated at the time by census officials. Surprisingly, it turns out that these officials did, indeed, tabulate the answers to the language question before deciding not to publish the prepared summary tables. Against this background, the CCRI data provide, for the first time, a way to explain this decision in the sociodemographic and political context of linguistic controversy during the period surrounding the First World War.[5]

Developing the 1911 Census

The results of the 1901 enumeration provide the point of departure for understanding the 1911 census question on language.[6] The mother tongue question proved to be especially problematic both for census officials and for respondents. The 1901 instructions to enumerators defined mother tongue as "one's native language, the language of his race" and noted specifically that, while the respondent should be able to speak the language, it might not be the language "in which he thinks, or which he speaks most fluently, or uses chiefly in conversation."[7] The focus of official attention was not those born in Canada – whether anglophone or francophone. Rather, the three questions were especially designed to triangulate on foreign-born residents. As census officials made clear in the published volumes of the census, they sought to measure the extent to which immigrants were being "absorbed and unified" in Canada by identifying and counting languages other than French and English that were still being spoken in Canada.[8] The assumption was that the ability to speak a mother tongue other than French or English would decline among those in the process of becoming true Canadians. In keeping with this view, the language questions were located on the 1901 census form with the education-related questions and, like questions about one's ability to read and write, were addressed to those 5 years of age and over. The implication was that those who spoke neither French nor English by this age but who still spoke some other mother tongue deserved official identification and counting, presumably with a view towards corrective public policy action.[9]

It quickly became clear, however, that the mother tongue question confused enumerators as well as respondents. The census returns show that a number of people gave answers to the mother tongue question that census officials were not expecting such as "Austrian," "Doukhobor," and "Canadian." Were certain people trying to assert a specific identity by giving these answers? A small percentage of those enumerated also gave multiple responses to the language question. Although census officials believed each person could only have one "mother tongue," some Canadians – whether enumerators or respondents – did not share this assumption. Overall, the total number of unexpected responses to the 1901 language question was not large. Nevertheless, these cases indicate that there was a difference between some individuals' assumptions about their own identity and officials' assumptions about how the census would be completed.[10]

Hoping to avoid these pitfalls the second time around, census officials modified – and, they hoped, clarified – how language was to be treated on the 1911 census schedule. At first glance, the three questions asked in 1901 appear to have been replaced by one question in 1911, "language commonly spoken." But, the instructions to enumerators for this question include the key components of the three language questions in 1901. In keeping with the earlier emphasis on English and French, enumerators were instructed to write an "E" in the column if the respondent "commonly spoke" English, and an "F" in the column if the respondent "commonly spoke" French. The instructions also readily anticipated that respondents might "commonly speak" both languages, and thus, enumerators were told to write both "E" and "F" in the column for those cases. Census officials did not define the criterion of "commonly spoken" but, rather, left that decision in the hands of enumerators and respondents – an omission that, as will be examined, became a central focus of public debate.[11] The language question in 1911, as in 1901, appeared on the same part of the census schedule as questions about the length of time spent at school and one's ability to read and write. It was asked of all Canadians 5 years of age and older. Also as in 1901, enumerators were instructed to pay special attention in posing the language question to those born outside of Canada. But, unlike the earlier enumeration, which asked for every person's "mother tongue," the instructions to enumerators in 1911 included this concept only in reference to those who had been born outside of Canada and who did not speak English or French as their "language of origin or race." Enumerators were to fill in the census schedule as follows: "For foreign-born persons whose mother tongue is neither English nor French and who have acquired either or both of these languages, the name of the language of origin or race, if spoken, will be written out in full on the line and the initial letter "E" for English or "F" for French, as the case may be, will be entered in the space above the line." For those born outside Canada who had not learned "either of the official languages of the Dominion, namely English and French," enumerators were told to enter the name of their language "commonly spoken." In this way, census officials tried to use the language question to triangulate on immigrants in 1911 just as they had in 1901. To correct some of the earlier results – such as when enumerators had written down "Canadian" as a mother tongue – the 1911 instructions included a list of languages "likely to be spoken in Canada," and enumerators were urged to "avoid giving other names when one given in this list can be applied to the language spoken."[12]

The instructions to enumerators reveal that the seemingly straightforward question of "language commonly spoken" included the ambition of census officials to measure the process of assimilation by counting how many foreign-born persons had learned English, French, or both. In pursuing this ambition, the enumeration assumed that only people born outside Canada could be expected to "commonly" speak a language other than French and English. In this way, for example, the instructions overlooked the importance of Aboriginal languages among Canadian-born respondents. Enumerators were cautioned not to assume that those born outside Canada spoke the dominant mother tongue associated with their birthplace; census officials did not want someone born in Poland, for example, recorded as speaking a "foreign" language simply because he or she was born in Poland. For example, census officials recognized that someone born in Poland might speak German or Russian as his or her mother tongue, and they wanted this information accurately documented. Enumerators were instructed to obtain the precise information "by diligent inquiry in every case."[13]

Carrying Out the 1911 Enumeration

Before, during, and after the enumeration began on 1 June, newspaper editorials and articles reported on, and expressed concern about, the language question on the 1911 census.[14] The political and cultural consequences of the enumeration for French-speakers were foremost in public discussion. In large part, these concerns sprang from an overarching fear that the French-speaking population of Canada would not be counted properly. Francophone newspapers and community leaders wanted to ensure that the census revealed a strong and vibrant French Canadian presence in as many communities as possible. An editorial in *La Presse* the day before census taking began reminded readers that the census offered an opportunity to show English Canadians that French Canadians were "toujours vivants, qu'en dépit de tous les obstacles, leur nombre augmente et qu'ils ne connaissent pas de défection."[15] The editorial reported that newspapers outside Quebec were arguing that assimilation was proceeding apace and that the French-speaking minority was being absorbed into the English majority. Why did Canada need two official languages, some English newspapers argued, if so many French Canadians were now speaking English?

The newspapers especially worried that it would be more difficult for French Canadians to obtain services and facilities such as schools in French if the number of French-speaking residents were reported to have decreased from the 1901 to the 1911 figures, or if it appeared that more French-speaking people were learning and "commonly speaking" in English. Jules Tremblay, secretary of L'Association canadienne-française d'éducation d'Ontario wrote a letter on the issue that was printed in both the *Ottawa Citizen* (in English) and *La Presse* (in French) in the week before the census enumeration began. Tremblay stressed that an accurate count of French-speakers was most important because it determined the "avantages et des privilèges que nous pourrons obtenir quant à l'enseignement du français dans les écoles, dans l'emploi de la langue française dans l'administration publique et dans tous les services d'utilisés publiques, comme les chemins de fer, les compagnies de navigation, d'électricité, de gaz, de tramway, et autres."[16] The secretary of the association also stressed that "the English-speaking population is trying to prove that the last census was not exact and that the French population of Ontario is not 200,000,"[17] as some French Canadian leaders had estimated.

For Tremblay and others, the primary concern was that French-speaking residents outside Quebec would be enumerated as speaking English. One reason for this possibility was the fact that those who lived among English-speakers were likely to speak some English; the French press worried that such residents would be enumerated as only English-speaking. This possibility would be made more likely by the fact that enumerators outside Quebec were characteristically anglophone. The result would be that an individual's "commonly spoken" language might be recorded as English when, in fact, the individual "commonly spoke" French. As *La Presse* explained in an editorial, "la langue communément parlée par [les francophones qui n'habitent pas au Québec] dans la plupart des circonstances extérieures de la vie, est naturellement anglais, bien que la langue parlée dans leur famille soit la langue maternelle, le français. S'ils respondent que la langue qu'ils parlent communément est l'anglais, c'est autant de perdu dans le recensement pour l'élément canadien-français."[18]

On 31 May, *L'Action sociale catholique* reiterated the danger for French communities outside Quebec, arguing that if these French-speakers reported that they most commonly spoke English, they would be "rangés parmi les anglophones, et l'influence de notre race baissera d'autant plus que se multipliera le nombre de ces naifs."[19] In other words, French Canadians were naive if they believed that enumerators would accurately record them as French-speakers if they lived outside of Quebec.

It appeared to some that the language question was designed to render French-speaking people outside Quebec statistically invisible, or at best, irrelevant. The press commented on the ambiguity of the language question repeatedly, trying to make sense of the instructions to enumerators and their ramifications. As the editorial quoted above noted, a "language commonly spoken" could be defined either as the language one spoke most often or as the language one spoke most fluently. Since census officials offered no official explanation in the instructions to enumerators, how would census takers interpret the question? For *L'Action sociale catholique,* the answer was simple – "language commonly spoken" had to be interpreted as "mother tongue"; "language commonly spoken" really meant the language learned at one's mother's knee, the one used with one's family, the one that came to one's lips at home, not the one used for "quelque banale relation d'affaires."[20]

Editorials and articles increasingly suggested that no matter what language people "commonly spoke" in their daily lives, census enumerators were, in practice, treating the question as if it asked for "mother tongue" – just like in 1901. The confusion was exacerbated when *La Presse* quoted the minister of agriculture himself, Sydney Fisher, who told the paper that in asking the language question, "recenseurs et recensés devaient entendre la langue maternelle."[21] As census officials attempted to move away from the "mother tongue" question used in 1901 by asking people what language they "commonly spoke," the minister responsible for the census undermined these efforts as the enumeration actually began by equating the two questions in public discussion.

As the enumeration continued in early June 1911, it became increasingly clear that the new language question was not able to account for the "mother tongue" of French- and English-speakers, despite Minister Fisher's interpretation. One ambiguity arose from the instructions that told enumerators to mark those who spoke only French or only English with an "F" or "E," and those who spoke both English and French with an "E" as well as an "F." Even before the enumeration began, newspaper commentators anticipated that census officials would be stymied about mother tongues when respondents were recorded with both an "E" and an "F." In an editorial on census day, *La Presse* informed readers that, according to an unnamed source, the order in which enumerators wrote "E" and "F" would indicate which language was a respondent's "mother tongue." Specifically, the newspaper explained that French-speakers who also spoke English would be enumerated with an "F" followed by an "E," and vice versa for English-speakers who also spoke French. *La Presse* judged that a method in which "tout dépend d'une lettre placée avant ou après"[22] was hazardous and complicated; nevertheless, the newspaper initially expressed confidence that French-speaking Canadians could be duly counted in this way. However, by the next day, *La Presse* told readers that it now realized that there was nothing in the actual instructions to guide enumerators on the proper ordering of responses to the language question. The editorial reported that the census commissioners in Montreal claimed that they had added these specific instructions for their enumerators but the newspaper was not reassured, since there was no way to know if all census takers had received special instructions in this regard. Moreover, *La Presse* predicted that enumerators were likely to stick to the letter of their written instructions, and there was a "grande risque de faire du recensement une belle bouillie."[23]

Because of the formulation of the question, and the chance that enumerators might not record respondents' answers in the appropriate order, the French-language press repeatedly advised French-speaking readers to answer "French" first and foremost in all cases when asked what language they "spoke commonly." *L'Action sociale catholique* stated, "Il est de nécessité absolue que tous les Canadiens-Français fassent inscrire la langue française comme langue communément parlée par eux. Et nous entendons par Canadiens-Français même les nombreuses familles de la province de Québec qui portent des noms anglais quoique canadiennes-françaises depuis plusieurs generations." Even if they spoke English as "commonly" as French, French Canadians were advised to say "French" first so that the letter "F" would be written first in the column, thereby implying French Canadian identity. This strategy was seen as especially important for French Canadians in minority-language communities such as those in Ontario. *La Presse* even argued that French Canadians should claim to speak only French, even if they could speak English, since the government had left French Canadians outside Quebec no other way to ensure that the census reflected "la place vraie qu'occupe la langue française en Canada."[24]

La Presse also advised readers to pay close attention to the way enumerators recorded their answers.[25] *Le Devoir* instructed readers in capital letters to "INDIQUENT LEUR LANGUE MATERNELLE EN LA NOMMANT LA PREMIÈRE."[26] *L'Action sociale catholique* urged French Canadians to ensure that they were enumerated as French-speaking first since so much was at stake: "pensons aux conséquences du recensement pour notre nationalité."[27]

As the enumeration proceeded, newspapers reported on myriad difficulties that the language question was said to be causing on Canadian doorsteps. In some areas, the language barrier between English-speaking enumerators and French-speaking respondents was reported to be especially problematic. On 10 June 1911, for example, *La Presse* reported several instances in which French Canadian families in Montreal were being undercounted by an English enumerator who had knocked on a door and found the household head – the father – absent. Being unable to understand the mother and children, who spoke only French, the enumerator had left only one form for the father to complete and submit to census officials, so the wife and children of the family were apparently not counted.[28] In other cases, the language of the form itself posed a problem even when French was the common language used on both sides of the front door. On 10 June 1911, *La Presse* reported that Montreal business owner Adélard Deslauriers had refused to complete the census form given to him because it was in English. When he asked the enumerator, J.L. Tremblay, for a French copy of the form, the enumerator replied that the government had not given him any French forms.[29] The Census Act did include provisions for enumeration in all languages, including the hiring of interpreters, with specific attention to those districts "populated by 'foreigners.'" However, the process to hire interpreters was complicated, and as one enumerator admitted, "We can't perform miracles ... if some people do not speak English and we can't speak their Babel of tongues, what are we to do?"[30] Although the CCRI contextual database does contain newspaper articles that refer to the need for interpreters in areas where foreigners live, there are no references to interpreters being used in French-speaking areas. The result was multiple reports during June and July in newspapers in Quebec and Ontario about the "improper" enumeration of French Canadians. One report, appearing in *Le Moniteur* of Hawkesbury, Ontario (and reprinted in *L'Action sociale catholique*), claimed that one enumerator in Ontario had systematically recorded French Canadian families in his district as speaking both English and French, writing "E" before "F" in the column. *Le Moniteur* was upset that nothing was being done to correct this injustice. An editorial in *La Presse* claimed that many such errors had occurred during the enumeration, and that it was impossible to correct them: "Si un énumérateur intervertit, délibérément ou non, l'ordre des initiales qui peut seul faire connaître la langue maternelle de la personne nommée, l'erreur est irremediable. Le commissaire ne peut pas deviner que cet ordre a été inexactement inscrite."[31] Although other misplaced or "incorrect" data could be corrected, such as claims that an infant could read, for example, the accuracy of answers to the language question depended on the enumerators. Newspapers made it clear that they doubted the enumerators' ability to do a proper and complete count.

This point was further underlined when several newspapers reported, in early July, that census officials had failed to enumerate an entire parish in Montreal. One newspaper reported that the area contained 135 families, 119 of whom were French Canadian Catholics.[32] Over the next few days, *La Presse* and the *Montreal Daily Star* investigated and reported on several similar incidents in parishes in and around Montreal.[33] These reports continued throughout the month of July. Census officials claimed that simple errors in communication and outdated enumeration maps were the cause, but people on the ground in the "missing" parish of St Alphonse d'Youville ascribed a more insidious motive. The parish priest, Father Simard, called the omission discrimination, "the result of which will be that the increase in our French-Canadian citizenship will not be shown." Simard continued, saying that he believed that "these tactics are intended to force us to reduce what some people call our pretensions and what we call our rights." [34] Rather than a simple oversight, the government was purposefully trying to undercount French Canadians in order to minimize their claims to language rights.

On 7 June, *L'Action sociale catholique* reprinted another report from *Le Temps*. The story was about a man in Russell, Ontario. When he told the enumerator he spoke French, he saw the enumerator write "F.E" in the language column. When the man explained that he had read in *L'Action sociale catholique* that the enumerator was supposed to write what he said, and asked him to change the entry, the enumerator refused to do so. The man also reported that he saw that those enumerated before him, who lived around him and were French-speaking, had been enumerated as speaking both French and English. "Voilà comment nous allons être traités," *Le Temps* continued, and asked that "les recenseurs qui font preuve de cette incompétence ou de cette mauvaise foi soient congédiés immédiatement." *Le Temps* implored enumerators to follow their instructions strictly, and to not use their own judgment or prejudice.[35] One problem, of course, was the fact that the instructions to enumerators said nothing about ordering the letters "F" and "E" to reflect the respondent's "mother tongue."

Examining the Completed Manuscript Census Schedules

Beyond what was reported at the time about the 1911 enumeration, there is the question of what was actually written on the completed census schedules. What did census officials in Ottawa discover on these schedules when they examined the results of the enumeration? Did they find that the newspaper reports about the difficulties of the language question were accurate? Was this the reason why the results were not published at the time?

To begin addressing these questions, examples from the enumeration in Russell and Hawkesbury, located just south of the Ottawa River on the border between Ontario and Quebec, allow comparison with those described in the newspapers during the enumeration. These communities are part of a geographical area that scholars have labelled "the bilingual belt."[36] The population along the Quebec-Ontario border, and in the Eastern Townships of Quebec, has contained a greater concentration of bilingual speakers since the earlier nineteenth century. Not surprisingly, residents in this area were often recorded in the 1911 census as commonly speaking French, English, or both languages, although there was considerable variation both within households and across census subdistricts. Moreover, enumerators did not always respect the age requirement. For example, Joseph Marion, his wife, Josephine, and their children were all listed as "French" in the "racial or tribal origin" column, while both parents and the two older of their five children were recorded as speaking both French and English. In contrast, their 8-year-old son was recorded as speaking only French. Surprisingly, no language was recorded for their 6-year-old while, as would be expected, the language question was also left blank for their youngest child who did not meet the 5-year-old age threshold stated in the instructions to enumerators. However, in other cases, young children were listed as having a language; in the Duford family, Lillian, aged 4, was recorded as "F E," as were her parents and eight other children in the family.

Some residents who were reported as of French origin were enumerated as speaking only English, which is noteworthy given the Village of Russell's reputation as being a predominantly French-speaking community. For example, Fabien and Anne L'evia, along with their 13-year-old granddaughter Leuella Wethington, were enumerated with an "E" only. The manuscript census schedules also raise questions about the ways in which enumerators ordered the letters "E" and "F" according to a respondent's "mother tongue." Differences within households are especially puzzling. For example, all four members of the Letour family of Russell were listed as "French" in the "racial or tribal origin" column. Dolore Letour and his wife Nora were listed as "F E" in the language column, but 7-year-old Evelyn and 4-year-old Lloyd were both recorded as "E F." Perhaps young Evelyn and Lloyd were attending school in English, and so were enumerated with an "E" before an "F." Another example is that of 2-year-old Arthur Deguerre, who was not only erroneously enumerated but also surprisingly recorded as commonly speaking only English, even though his four adolescent sisters and both his parents were recorded with an "F E."

In contrast to cases in which English was listed when French would have been the expected response, there are isolated examples of the opposite result. Moffat Stearns, born in 1907, was enumerated (in error given his age) as speaking both French (listed first) and English, despite the fact that his older sister and parents were listed as English-speaking Irish-origin Presbyterians. One explanation might be the family's hired help, enumerated directly after Moffat – a French Canadian named David Coussineau. Perhaps the enumerator inadvertently recorded "F E" for both Moffat and David, or maybe David was teaching young Moffat to speak French.

The 1911 manuscript census returns in these two neighbouring communities in the easternmost corner of Ontario also suggest that, beyond surprising differences within households, certain subdistricts reflected quite different approaches to the language question by enumerators. In Russell Township, for example, D. Cumming, Jr, recorded very few school-aged children or adults as speaking only French. The Laveau family was a typical example: the parents, the grandfather, and the three children aged 8 to 10 were listed as "F E," while the two younger children, aged 5 and one, were listed as speaking only French. In Cumming's district of 871 people, only one household was enumerated as speaking French only, while ten household heads were recorded as speaking French first, then English. In contrast, the enumerator in Embrun, Ontario (7 km east of Russell), was named Lionide Champagne. Almost all of the 622 people in his district listed "French" as their origin, and at least three-quarters were recorded with a single "F" in the language column. People of similar backgrounds in adjacent subdistricts could be enumerated differently, perhaps because of their own choice or perhaps because of the enumerator's perceptions or his interpretation of the language question.

Census Officials Confront the Completed Returns

Examples from the completed manuscript schedules illustrate that the concerns raised in newspaper articles about the enumeration of the language question were certainly not far-fetched; nevertheless, census officials were undoubtedly surprised that the preoccupation with French became predominant in public debate in 1911. The way that they had posed the question and carried out the enumeration reflected their own preoccupation with the English and French language ability of immigrants, not Canadian-born French- and English-speakers. But, as 1911 progressed, census officials must have realized that the language results would be publicly scrutinized with increasing interest in the status of francophones living outside Quebec, especially as events unfolded in Ontario, where the debate about the language of school instruction was heating up again after simmering for more than a decade.[37] Vocal leaders of the English-language majority were increasingly expressing concern that the children of French Canadian parents were not receiving an effective English-language education. In turn, French-speaking parents were pressing the government to establish bilingual normal schools so that their children could receive a better quality French-language education.

On the heels of the census enumeration, the provincial government, led by Conservative MPP Sir James Whitney, tasked Francis Walter Merchant, chief inspector of schools, to investigate and report on conditions in Ontario's bilingual schools. Merchant did not submit his report until 1912, but in the closing months of 1911, the *Toronto Daily Star* printed a series of articles based on its own investigations at schools in some of the province's more rural and

French-speaking districts. In late November 1911, the newspaper announced that "investigation by Star correspondents in Essex in the west, in Prescott and Russell in the east, and in the northern districts have already furnished ample demonstration that to thousands of Ontario children the schools of the Province are not furnishing a real knowledge of English."[38] The paper found the conditions of most bilingual schools to be deplorable, and the teachers, unilingual (unilingual meaning, uniformly, French-speaking). The paper strongly believed that English should be the only language of instruction in Ontario's schools. French children were ill-served by bilingual schools because "a French-Canadian child who does not understand English is seriously handicapped in the race for life, living on a continent of a hundred million English-speaking people."[39] Throughout November and December, the *Star*'s headlines raised the spectre of a French population growing at a more rapid rate than Anglo-Ontario (based on figures from an ecclesiastical census) and claimed that "over 50,000 French Now Know No English." This number was estimated – rather casually – from the 1901 census.[40] It was in this context that the results of the 1911 census held the potential to fuel the language controversy since population numbers played such a powerful role in the public debate; as Choquette has emphasized, a "battle of statistics marked [the] whole period" leading up to, and following, the institution of Regulation 17 in 1912.[41]

In this heated political context, it might be assumed that the reason why the language question was not reported on in the published volumes was that census officials realized, after reviewing the completed schedules, that the "language commonly spoken" question had not been enumerated successfully and, therefore, abandoned any effort to compile the results. In fact, however, officials at the Census and Statistics Office (CSO) prepared summary tables for the language question just as they did for the rest of the enumeration. When the first volume of the official census report was published in 1912, Archibald Blue informed readers that "all other tables of population are in process of compilation" including those of "language spoken" and that the tables would be "made ready for the press."[42] No results were ever published; however, the work was indeed completed and documented in the form of a handwritten pre-publication table entitled "Language Spoken by Sex, Canada and Provinces, 1911." The document includes a note, carefully printed in block letters, in the top right-hand corner of the first page: "DO NOT USE FOR COMPARISON WITH OTHER CENSUSES." As will be discussed, this brief note may further explain why the summary tables were never published.[43]

As promised by the title, the pre-publication table presented aggregate totals of the language responses for Canada, for each province, and for males and females. In addition, however, the table also provided summary totals by birthplace divided into three categories of Canadian-born, British-born, and foreign-born; within these categories, the totals were further divided into two age groups of under 10 years and 10 years and older. These age divisions are unexpected in light of the instructions to enumerators to collect responses for those older than 5 years. The responses were grouped into five language categories: English, French, German, other languages, and English and French. The separate categories for English, French, and German emphasize the three most commonly spoken languages in Canada, while the single "English and French" category is surprising given the debate over the careful ordering of the listing of languages for bilingual residents.

The decision to compare language by birthplace reflected the interest of census officials in tracking immigrants' language acquisition. The table shows how many "foreign-born persons" spoke English, French, or neither language, and how many of each category were under the age of 10 and how many were older; in turn, these figures can be compared with the figures for different areas of the country.

Overall, the table reports that 64 per cent of the nearly 753,000 foreign-born persons in Canada spoke English at the time of the 1911 census, while 24 per cent spoke a language other than English, French, or German.[44] The "other" category raises an important question – what happened to the multiple responses in the hands of census officials? The instructions to enumerators specified that people born outside Canada who still spoke their "mother tongue" could give such multiple responses. For example, a person who spoke English but still understood and spoke Russian as a mother tongue would be recorded with an "E." The enumerator would then draw a line and write "Russian" underneath it. Technically, this person could be categorized "English" or "other languages," or both. However, the numbers reveal that the response for each individual was only placed in one category by the census officials who compiled the summary tables. So, when the census forms were tabulated, were these people with multiple responses categorized as English-speakers or within the category of "other Languages"?

Preliminary tabulations of the CCRI data suggest that census officials placed some multiple responses in the "other" category, while they grouped some other responses with the English- or French-speakers; see discussion below of tables and figure 5.1 comparing unpublished Census and Statistics Office (CSO) compilations with those of the CCRI. It is not clear, however, what "rule" census officials applied to make this tabulation. Perhaps, when a language other than English, French, or German was listed first in the column, officials interpreted this as an indication that the person "commonly spoke" her or his mother tongue; even if she or he was able to speak English or French,

Table 5.1 · Speakers of English and French by province (*n* and %), Canada, 1911: According to the Census and Statistics Office

Province	*Speakers of English and French* n *(% of population)*
Alberta	10,003 (3)
British Columbia	5,632 (1)
Manitoba	14,168 (3)
New Brunswick	32,623 (9)
Northwest Territories	5 (0)
Nova Scotia	20,793 (4)
Ontario	76,219 (3)
Prince Edward Island	5,919 (6)
Quebec	277,670 (14)
Saskatchewan	9,343 (2)
Yukon	353 (4)
Canada	*452,728 (6)*

Source: Reproduced from unpublished Census and Statistics Office manuscript table.

these were not the languages she or he was most comfortable speaking. These cases highlight the way in which "language commonly spoken" certainly did not make counting Canadians' language use any easier.

In light of the concern in public discussion regarding the size of the French-speaking population, the "English and French" category appears especially relevant to the decision not to publish the language data. Although newspapers had repeatedly emphasized the special instructions that enumerators were to pay close attention to the order of the lettering of "E" and "F" in the language column, the census officials grouped together all bilingual responses when compiling the summary tables. The result was that, unless French Canadians had answered only "French," they would be included in the English and French total. It might be surmised that, despite their own instructions, census officials only wanted to know how many Canadians were bilingual and, thus, did not feel the need to compile totals within separate "English and French" and "French and English" categories. But, it seems more likely that they realized that these instructions had, in fact, failed to be implemented in consistent ways, especially in bilingual regions. As can be seen in table 5.1, nearly 453,000 people were classified as speaking English and French, 90 per cent of them Canadian-born. In total numbers, Quebec, Ontario, New Brunswick, and Nova

Table 5.2 · Speakers of English only and French only (%), by province and all of Canada, 1911: According to the Census and Statistics Office

Province	*Commonly spoken*	
	English only (%)	*French only (%)*
Alberta	82	2
British Columbia	85	0
Manitoba	78	4
New Brunswick	72	18
Northwest Territories	8	1
Nova Scotia	91	4
Ontario	90	4
Prince Edward Island	88	5
Quebec	15	69
Saskatchewan	78	3
Yukon	76	1
Canada	*66*	*22*

Source: Reproduced from unpublished Census and Statistics Office manuscript table.

Scotia had the largest bilingual populations, but as a percentage of each province's population Prince Edward Island had the greatest per capita number of English- and French-speakers, after Quebec. As would be expected, the higher percentage of bilingual residents in the Maritime provinces reflected the strong Acadian presence.

In the absence of other documentation related to the handwritten summary tables, the deliberations of census officials during their work remains unknown. In the heated political context of the time, however, census officials must have realized that the results of the 1911 language question related directly to the continuing debate about language of instruction in public schools. In late 1911, the *Toronto Daily Star* told readers that there were 38,000 French-speaking residents in Ontario at the time of the 1901 enumeration who could not speak English; the newspaper then asked, "How many are there today? Has the number increased or decreased? What have the bilingual schools been doing in the meantime?"[45] If published, the data in the French and English category could have been seen as justifying many of the fears expressed in the newspapers before and during the enumeration. The single "English and French" category would, inevitably, be seen as an attack on respondents who were – or should have been – enumerated as "F E." Moreover, the results for those counted as French-speaking would be seen as fulfilling the prediction made by Jules Tremblay, secretary of L'Association canadienne-française d'éducation d'Ontario, who had criticized the census on the eve of the enumeration, as an English-speaking effort to show that the French-language population of Ontario was under 200,000; if the French-speaking total were added to the bilingual total for the province, the summary table reported only a maximum of 173,620 for the French-language population. From the opposite point of view, these language results confirmed the suspicion of those who feared the continued strength of French outside Quebec not only in certain communities of Ontario but elsewhere, as well, especially in New Brunswick, where the French and bilingual categories reached a total of almost 100,000.

The CCRI Language Data for 1911

The CCRI evidence allows us to retabulate the 1911 results and, thereby, to enhance our understanding not only of public discussion and the work of census officials but also the patterns that emerge from charting and mapping the responses as freshly compiled a century after the enumeration itself. Figure 5.1 illustrates the differences between the approaches of the census officials and the CCRI. Overall, the proportions are very similar. It should be noted, however, that the CCRI data do not infer language for the approximately 7 per cent not entered or uncodable, most of whom were children under 5 years of age, so its total numbers equal 93 per cent of the official census totals. One would expect each language grouping to also be 93 per cent, but the census officials assigned a higher proportion to "English and French" (~97%) and a lesser proportion to "other languages" (~90%.) Therefore, the CSO table appears to have been based on assignment rules that went beyond the approach used by CCRI coding of reflecting verbatim data entry as much as possible.

The CCRI also enables research on the proportions and changing geography of bilingual speakers listed with English first and those listed with French first. Table 5.2 shows the percentages of each of these groups as they appeared on an unpublished Census and Statistics Office table. Table 5.3 indicates the percentages of each of these groups as derived from the CCRI 5 per cent sample weighted microdata. One feature is that the percentages of English-only and French-only are smaller using the CCRI data than in the unpublished CSO summary table. For example, the Ontario CCRI results diverge noticeably from the official summary table (English-only 90% vs 82%). Table 5.3 shows that, in the

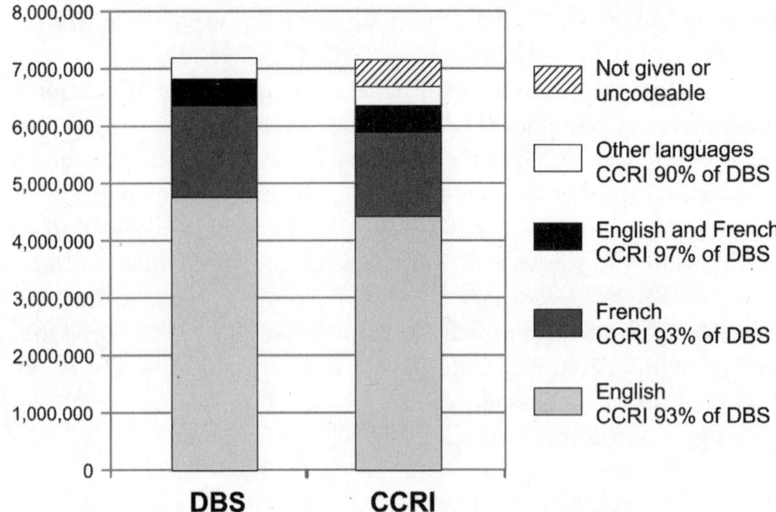

Figure 5.1 · Dominion Bureau of Statistics (DBS) and CCRI data compared regarding "language commonly spoken" in Canada in 1911.

Sources: Census and Statistics Office unpublished table; numbers derived from weighted microdata, CCRI 1911 microdata database, and CCRI geographical database.

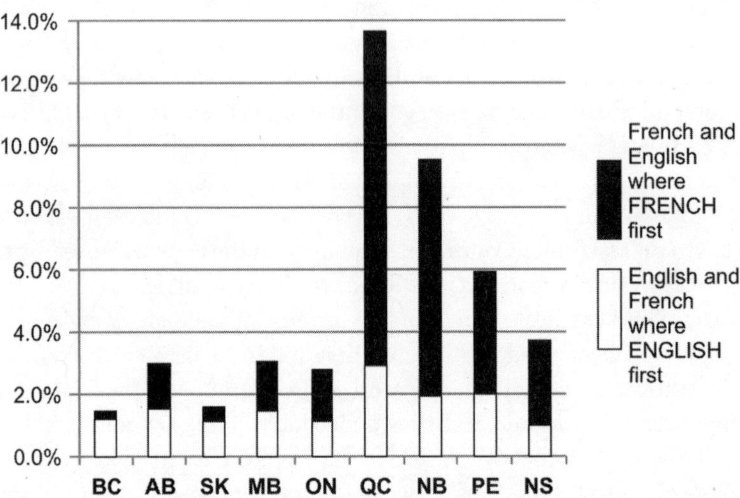

Figure 5.2 · Bilingual speakers of both English and French as percentage of total population, indicating proportions giving French first (F-E) and English first (E-F), by province, Canada, 1911.

Source: generated from weighted microdata, CCRI 1911 microdata database and CCRI geographical database.

Table 5.3 · Speakers of English only, French only, and English and French (%), by province and all of Canada, 1911: According to CCRI 1911 weighted 5% sample

Province	*Commonly Spoken*		
	English only (%)	*French only (%)*	*English and French (%)*
Alberta	66	2	3 (E 1.5, F 1.5)
British Columbia	72	0	1 (E 1, F 0)
Manitoba	63	3	3 (E 1.4, F 1.6)
New Brunswick	68	15	10 (E 2, F 8)
Northwest Territories	12	2	0 (N/A)
Nova Scotia	82	4	4 (E 1, F 3)
Ontario	82	3	3 (E 1, F 2)
Prince Edward Island	83	5	6 (E 2, F 4)
Quebec	14	65	14 (E 3, F 11)
Saskatchewan	62	2	2 (E 1, F 0.5)
Yukon	68	1	7 (E 6, F 1)
Canada	*58*	*21*	*6 (E 2, F 4)*

Source: weighted, CCRI 1911 microdata database.

eastern half of Canada, higher proportions of bilingual speakers listed French first, including in the Maritimes and Quebec, as well as, to a lesser extent, in Ontario. These proportions are then illustrated graphically in figure 5.2.

Mapping the French and English responses from the CCRI data allows us to see this geographical variation in more detail, thereby revealing a number of noteworthy trends. Each map is divided into census districts (modified to group urban areas together.) The colour of the district corresponds to the percentage of the population reported to be bilingual; the darker the shade of grey, the greater the proportion of people speaking both French and English.

Figure 5.3 shows the general picture across the country as well as a map enlarged for the eastern half, and the Montreal area. Western Canada included a few isolated enclaves of bilingual residents. In the east, the most bilingual areas were in the city of Montreal and south of the city in the Eastern Townships. There are also several census districts on both sides of the Ottawa River (the Quebec-Ontario boundary), where from 10 per cent to as much as 25 per cent of the population spoke both languages, thereby forming the "bilingual belt" mentioned above.[46] The map shows how census districts further east down the St Lawrence River contained fewer and fewer bilingual speakers. Proportions

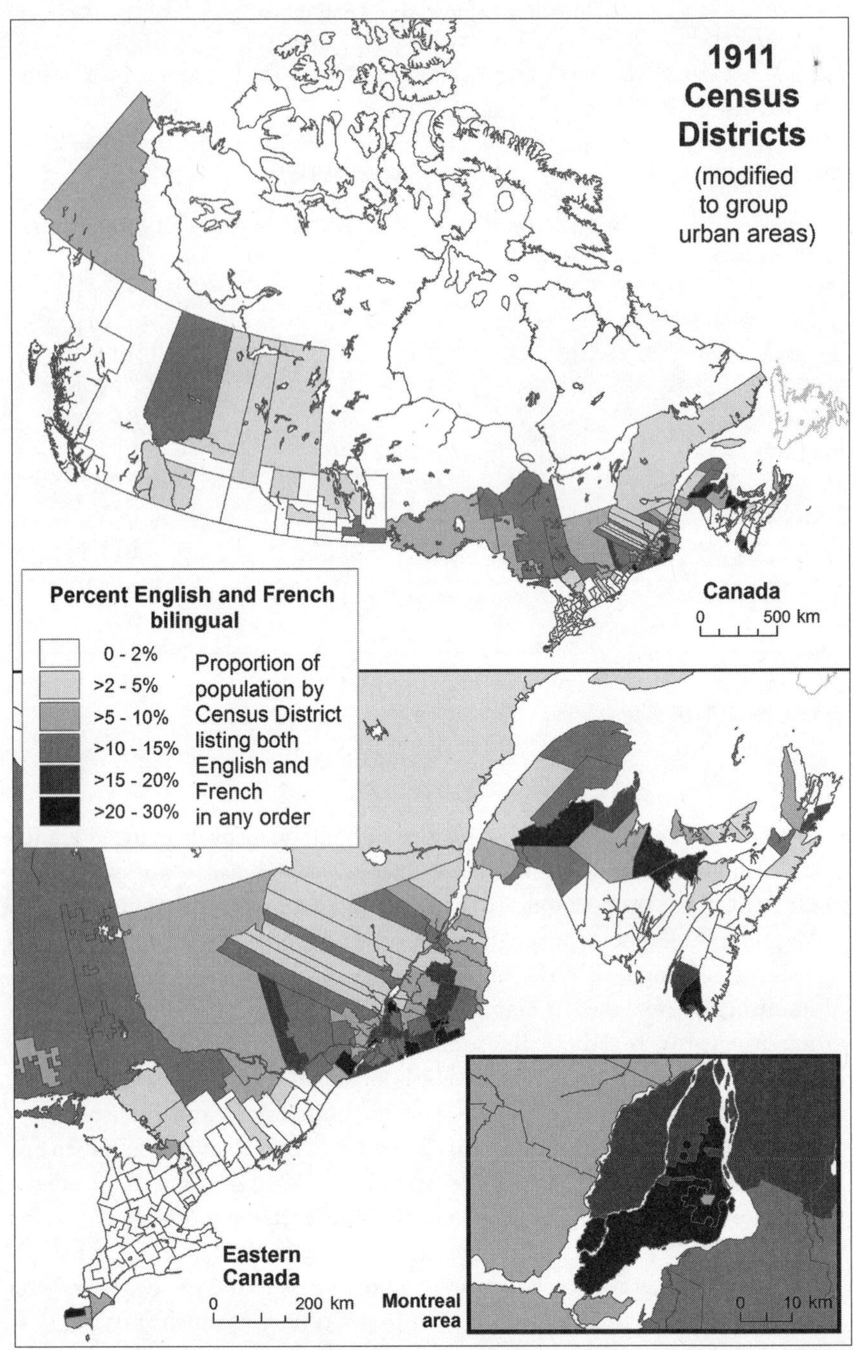

Figure 5.3 · Proportions of bilingual English and French speakers, in any order, by (modified) 1911 census district: Canada, Eastern Canada, and Montreal area.

Source: generated from weighted microdata, CCRI 1911 microdata database and CCRI geographical database.

in Quebec generally were still higher than those in southern Ontario, with the exception of a pocket in the extreme southwest near Windsor (Essex North district). In Northern Ontario, between 5 per cent and 15 per cent of the population was bilingual. The pattern in the Maritime provinces illustrates the distribution of bilingual speakers, generally corresponding to areas known to have a strong Acadian presence: the northern coast of New Brunswick, the Cape Breton Island area, the extreme southern reaches of Nova Scotia, and central and eastern Prince Edward Island.[47]

The maps in figure 5.4 are similar to those in figure 5.3, but proportional circles have been added to represent absolute numbers of bilingual speakers. These have been divided into pie segments for those who were listed as French first in the census (black) and those who were listed as English first (white). Mapping absolute numbers puts the relative magnitude of bilingual population into perspective. For example, the dominating size of Montreal (approximately 107,000 people) compared with the isolated circle in rural northern Alberta (Edmonton non-urban, about 3,400 people, a small but significant number considering its surroundings). The proportion of "French first" versus "English first" may reflect the underlying nature of the bilingual population – for example, the pies in the western half of the country generally show a predominance of white, "English first" responses. There are a few unexpected outliers that arise here, as well. There was, for example, a high proportion of "English first" responses in eastern Quebec's Gaspé census district.

The maps in figure 5.5 display these values in more detail for the "bilingual belt" area of eastern Ontario and western and southern Quebec. The top map duplicates the representation in figure 5.4 of pie charts for total bilingual speakers, segmented by "language first." The bottom map's bar charts show percentages of French only, English only, and bilingual with French or English first, which describe the linguistic relationships within the population more completely, especially the position of the bilingual population within the host environment. For example, Labelle in Quebec and Russell in Ontario have similar-looking pies, similar numbers and proportions of bilingual-speakers. Their bar charts, however, show a completely different profile, with Labelle having a host population dominated by unilingual French-speakers, but Russell containing a much more bifurcated population split between unilingual French-only and English-only groups. Among the "bilingual belt" census districts, Russell, Prescott, Wright, and Argenteuil show more of this split profile, while Labelle, Soulanges, Stormont, and Glengarry are more dominated by French only or English only.[48] Whether this split profile is truly indicative of "two solitudes," or whether it may be exaggerated by enumerators' methods or other inconsistencies in the census-taking process itself is open to future research.

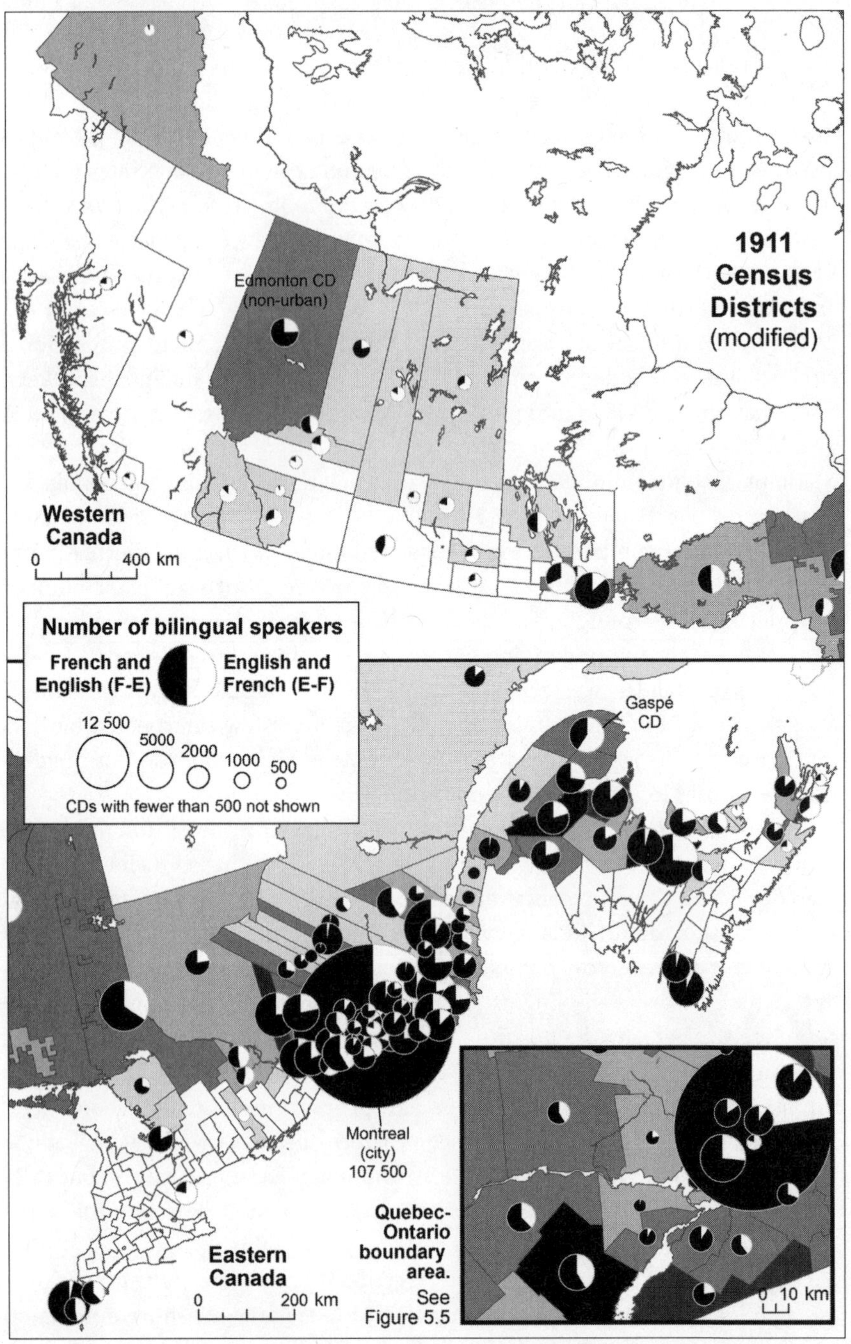

Figure 5.4 · Absolute numbers of bilingual English and French speakers, in any order, by (modified) 1911 census district: Western Canada, Eastern Canada, and Quebec-Ontario boundary area.

Source: generated from weighted microdata, CCRI 1911 microdata database and CCRI geographical database.

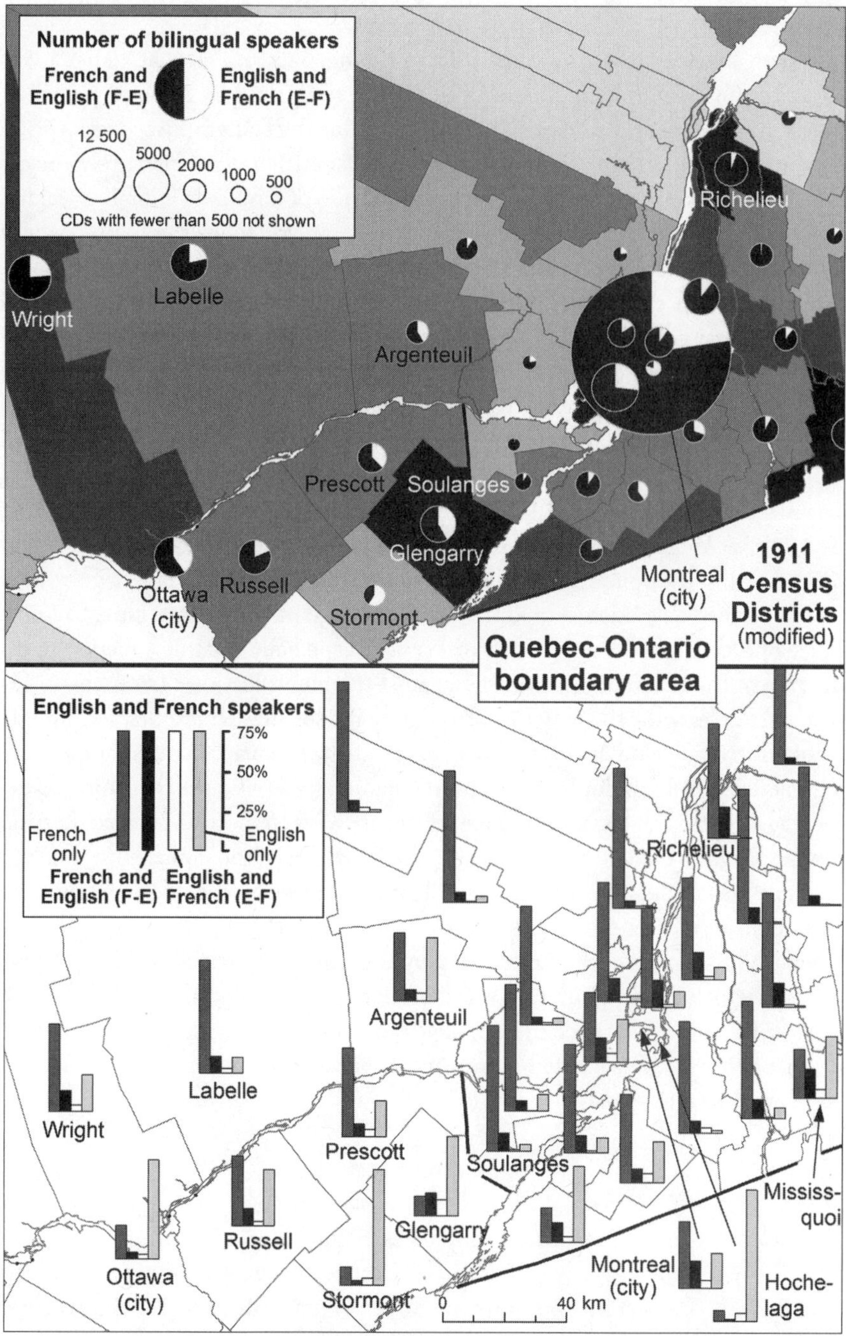

Figure 5.5 · Numbers and proportions of speakers of French only, English only, French and English (F-E), and English and French (E-F) in the Quebec-Ontario boundary area, by (modified) 1911 census district.

Source: generated from weighted microdata, CCRI 1911 microdata database and CCRI geographical database.

Taken together, the 1911 census data on language suggest that Canada was already composed of "linguistic regions," the term used by Richard Joy when he examined the 1961 census.[49] This fact explains the contemporary perception in Ontario that "there would be no bilingual problem were it merely one in ten, throughout the province. Were the quarter of a million French-speaking people in Ontario scattered throughout the country, there the matter would end. Instead, there are whole counties almost solidly French."[50] At the same time, the CCRI data do not support the claim that some counties in Ontario were "almost solidly French" since considerable diversity characterized even the counties in the bilingual belt, the most densely French-language region of Ontario. It should be emphasized, however, that the CCRI data do justify much of what newspapers perceived at the time: the official instructions to enumerators and the interactions at doorsteps all contributed to ambiguous results that could be used to confirm in contradictory ways the competing fears about language patterns expressed by both French Canadian leaders and English-only proponents. On the one hand, the 1911 census language results could be read as evidence of an English-language majority's attempts to minimize the continued importance of French, especially outside Quebec. Each feature of the enumeration worked against the identification of French-speakers, particularly for those in minority-language settings where the "commonly spoken" language outside the home was English, and where enumerators were characteristically anglophone. French Canadian leaders could, therefore, be expected to interpret summary tables of the answers to the 1911 census question on language as evidence that, despite official rhetoric, the demise of French in Canada was under way. On the other hand, those who expected the voluntary assimilation of French-speakers into the English-language majority could be similarly disappointed and disturbed by the same census results. Despite the ways in which the enumeration was conducted, the results showed that French was still a "commonly spoken" language outside Quebec – especially in specific areas of New Brunswick and easternmost Ontario, as the Merchant Commission would soon report.

Conclusion

The focus on Canada's official languages before, during, and after the 1911 census overshadowed any public discussion of languages other than French and English. The fact that no summary tables were published at the time further limited attention to the changing landscape of language in Canada. Although immigrants were the focus of official attention, and the size of the French-language population was a preoccupation of public discussion, the myriad other languages recorded by census enumerators in 1911 document an increasingly multilingual Canadian population. For this reason, the CCRI data related to language offer a particularly promising window to enhance our understanding of the making of modern Canada.

Further research on the importance of Aboriginal languages is especially warranted since census officials made a concerted effort in 1911 to enumerate all residents, even in northern communities (an effort not replicated for many decades[51]). The result is that more than 65,000 people were reported as speaking an Aboriginal language in 1911, and thus this enumeration offers a unique chance to improve our understanding of the complexity and diversity of First Nations communities across Canada (as Gustave Goldmann demonstrates in the next chapter in this volume). Further research opportunities are also offered by the evidence of significant language groups such as the 140,000 people reported speaking a Slavic, Celtic, or Scandinavian language or the more than 10,000 people reported as speaking multiple languages other than English and French.

For such future research, the CCRI census microdata are indispensable, but not sufficient as illustrated by the preceding analysis that demonstrated the value of the CCRI contextual data of official documents and contemporary newspaper coverage. The archival research at Statistics Canada that uncovered the manuscript Census and Statistics Office tabulations of the 1911 census question proved to be especially informative about the context within which the language question was meaningful for Canadians. In addition, our ability to compare the officials' tabulations with the CCRI sample census data helps provide an analytical framework for interpreting both sets of numbers. Similarly, our ability to examine the names of enumerators and what they recorded about respondents in various communities helps illuminate the spatial patterns of linguistic dynamics across Canada. Taken together, these features of CCRI enable analysis of the 1911 language responses as well as offering the prospect of comparison with other years; however, as with all historical evidence, the census data cannot be simply taken at face-value but rather must be understood in the larger context within which they were created.

In this context, the multifaceted CCRI evidence reveals how the apparently straightforward language question on the 1911 census enumeration collided with the complexity of language as a perceived and lived experience in early twentieth-century Canada. While devised to be an effective way to record the spoken language of Canadians, the language question on the 1911 census did not provide census officials with results that they were prepared to publish. Nonetheless, the events of the following decade continued to increase attention to questions of language and made imperative that census officials find ways to avoid the failure of 1911 in preparing for the 1921 enumeration. Their decision was to revert to the approach of 1901 but to revise the three questions and to move them on the census schedule from their previous position with the other education-related questions to a new grouping of questions entitled "race, language, and religion." In one sense, this grouping linked language to what were seen as enduring personal characteristics rather than to variable educational abilities. But, the instructions to enumerators redefined mother tongue as the "language of customary speech employed by the person," a completely different understanding from that used in 1901, when the mother tongue of a person was defined as "the language of his race." This must be kept in mind since, unlike the official decision not to publish the summary tables for the 1911 language question in order to avoid comparisons with the previous census results, the volumes that reported on the 1921 enumeration included the mother tongue question without even cautioning readers about the extent to which it was not comparable with its initial use in 1901.

Census officials did adopt for 1921 the decision in 1911 to only record a "language other than English or French spoken as Mother Tongue." And the instructions to enumerators specified that only those "whose racial or tribal origin is not described in column 21 as belonging to one of the British races ... or to persons of French origin" should be asked to answer the mother tongue question. Most importantly for public debate, the implication now was that the response to the racial or tribal origins question would identify a person as French Canadian. In this way, census officials downplayed the significance of language as a component of "origin" for French Canadians and British-origin residents while still maintaining the emphasis on language as an indicator of nation building. Along the way, census officials also began using the new expression "ethnic group," in keeping with the rapidly changing efforts to construct collective identities based on specific individual characteristics.

In these and other ways that will undoubtedly emerge as research continues on the twentieth-century census enumerations, the continuing changes to the language questions reflected deep conceptual shifts in the evolving debate about identity and behaviour that remained a preoccupation of public discussion. Indeed, if we glance forward to public debate about the 1921 enumeration, French-language newspapers now warned French Canadian respondents to respond with "French" to the question on racial or tribal origins. Commentators were worried, in 1921, that persons with English fathers and French mothers, or persons with English-sounding names, would be enumerated as belonging to the English "race."[52] Newspapers continued to interpret the census questions for readers; however, this time, instead of focusing on the importance of answering "French" to the language question, newspapers paid special attention to racial or tribal origins. *L'Évangéline*, an Acadian newspaper, told readers to "prendre bien soin de se dire de race française," to Question 21. About Question 24, the mother tongue question, the newspaper simply wrote, "Ne vous regarde pas."[53] *Le Droit*, a Franco-Ontarian newspaper founded in 1913 to oppose Regulation 17, did not even include Question 24 in its explanation of the census questions in May 1921. Like *L'Évangéline*, the paper told readers to respond with "French" to the racial and tribal origins question, and added that French Canadians should answer "no" to the "Speaks English" question only if they did not understand the language at all.[54] In other words, the new view towards the 1921 enumeration was that French Canadians had more to fear from not being classified appropriately in terms of racial or tribal origins than they did from how they answered the language questions.[55]

The changing ways that census officials, and federal, provincial, and community leaders, as well as individuals across Canada viewed the speaking of, and actually used, different languages reflected the complex interrelationships between the turbulent domestic and international forces that characterized the early twentieth century.[56] While Canada was attracting immigrants from diverse linguistic communities, the question of what language or languages would be seen and used as "Canadian" in different contexts was contested even with respect to the official languages of French and English. In 1911, the focus of census officials on immigrants was overwhelmed in public discussion by the provincial preoccupation with promoting the speaking of English, especially by students from French-speaking homes. Along the way, the emergence of new expressions like "mother tongue" and "language commonly spoken," as well as the changing definition of familiar words like "race," and for the first time in 1921, "ethnic group," produced ambiguous, competing, and often contradictory features of nation building during the decade of the First World War. As illustrated by the language question in the 1911 census, the Canadian Century Research Infrastructure enhances the possibility of developing interpretations of these features that do justice to the complex and changing character of policy and practice in the making of modern Canada.

Notes

1 Robert Choquette, *Language and Religion: A History of English-French Conflict in Ontario* (Ottawa: University of Ottawa Press, 1975), 193.

2 Ibid., 196.

3 Mason Wade, *The French Canadians, 1760–1967*, rev. ed., vol. 2 (Toronto: Macmillan, 1968), 671.

4 For an overall description of this interdisciplinary, multi-institutional, and internationally connected initiative, see Chad Gaffield, "Conceptualizing and Constructing the Canadian Century Research Infrastructure," *Historical Methods* 40, no. 2 (2007): 54–64. The CCRI built on previous projects on the nineteenth-century censuses as well as on the Canadian Families Project for the 1901 enumeration; see http://web.uvic.ca/hrd/cfp/index.html. For research assistance on the language question, the authors are indebted to Jo-Anne McCutcheon, Adam Green, and Barbara Lorenzkowski.

5 Until recently, very little attention was paid to the language questions on the Canadian census, especially those censuses taken before the later twentieth century. Among the small number of studies, see John De Vries and Frank G. Vallee, *Language Use in Canada* (Ottawa: Statistics Canada, 1980), and John Edwards (ed.), *Language in Canada* (Cambridge: Cambridge University Press, 1998). The increasing international attention to the census as a source for the study of language is illustrated by D.I. Kertzer and D. Arel (eds.), *Census and Identity: The Politics of Race, Ethnicity, and Language in National Censuses* (Cambridge: Cambridge University Press, 2002).

6 Although 1901 was the first census to pose language questions in Canada, the 1891 census did divide respondents into "native-born" and "born outside Canada," while further subdividing the "native-born" into "French-speaking" and "all others." In keeping with the approach of the CCRI and related projects, Kris Inwood and colleagues have constructed a public-use sample of the 1891 returns along with documentation on how to interpret the results of the enumeration; see http://www.census1891.ca/.

7 Canada, Census Office, *Fourth Census of Canada, 1901*, vol. I, *Population* (Ottawa: S.E. Dawson, 1902), xx.

8 Ibid., viii.

9 Canadian officials were certainly not alone in connecting language to nation building at this time. In the United States, as Jennifer Leeman has shown, "the census has historically used language as an index of race and as a means to racialize speakers of languages other than English, constructing them as essentially different and threatening to U.S. cultural and national identity." See Jennifer Leeman, "Racializing Language: A History of Linguistic Ideologies in the U.S. Census," *Journal of Language and Politics* 3, no. 3 (2004): 507–34.

10 For further discussion and analysis of the responses to the language question in the 1901 census, see Chad Gaffield, "Linearity, Nonlinearity, and the Competing Constructions of Social Hierarchy in Early Twentieth-Century Canada," *Historical Methods* 33, no. 4 (2000): 255–61, and Chad Gaffield "Language, Ancestry, and the Competing Constructions of Identity in Turn-of-the-Century Canada," in Eric W. Sager and Peter Baskerville (eds.), *Household Counts: Canadian Households and Families in 1901* (Toronto: University of Toronto, 2007), 423–40.

11 As Joshua Fishman has emphasized, the phrasing of this language question is highly unusual in census questions that do not characteristically focus on "current facilities" in this way; see "Language Maintenance," in Stephen Thernstrom (ed.), *Harvard Encyclopedia of American Ethnic Groups* (Cambridge, MA: Belknap

Press, 1980), 629. Fishman concludes that census data on language practices are notoriously “suspect.”

12 Canada, Department of Agriculture and Statistics, *Fifth Census of Canada, 1911: Instructions to Officers, Commissioners and Enumerators* (Ottawa: Government Printing Bureau, 1911), 38.

13 Ibid.

14 These editorials and articles were drawn from the CCRI's on-line contextual database, which contains more than 15,000 articles from nearly 170 publications, covering the 1911, 1921, 1931, 1941, and 1951 censuses.

15 “Les Canadiens-Français et le recensement,” *La Presse*, 30 May 1911, 4.

16 Jules Tremblay, “Le Recensement et Nos Compatriotes d'Ontario,” *La Presse*, 30 May 1911.

17 Ibid.

18 “Les Canadiens-Français et le recensement,” 4.

19 “Recensement III,” *L'Action sociale catholique*, 31 May 1911.

20 Ibid.

21 “Les Canadiens-Français et le recensement,” 4.

22 “La Langue Communément Parlée,” *La Presse*, 1 June 1911, 4.

23 “Les Problèmes du recensement,” *La Presse*, 2 June 1911, 4.

24 “Les Canadiens-Français et le recensement,” 4.

25 “La Langue Communément Parlée.”

26 “Le Recensement Est Commencé,” *Le Devoir*, 1 June 1911.

27 “Recensement,” *L'Action sociale catholique*, 3 June 1911, 11.

28 “Recensement Défectueux,” *La Presse*, 10 June 1911, 36.

29 “Les incidents du recensement,” *La Presse*, 10 June 1911, 36.

30 “The Interpreter Trouble,” *Toronto Daily Star*, 1 June 1911, 3; “The Lot of the Census Taker in the Ward Is Anything but an Easy One,” *Toronto Daily Star*, 1 June 1911, 2.

31 “Le Recensement,” *La Presse*, 15 June 1911, 4.

32 *Evening Guide*, 6 July 1911.

33 See, e.g., “Encore des oublis dans le recensement,” *La Presse*, 7 July 1911, 1–2; “Encore vingt-cinq familles victimes du recensement,” *La Presse*, 8 July 1911, 32; “Encore de plaints au sujet du recensement,” *La Presse*, 10 July 1911, 14; “Census Omissions,” *Montreal Daily Star*, 6 July 1911, 10; “More Complaints of Oversights by Census-Takers,” *Montreal Daily Star*, 7 July 1911, 17; “More Census Blunders,” *Montreal Daily Star*, 11 July 1911, 10.

34 “Overlooked by Enumerators: Parish in Quebec Claims that It Has Not Been Counted Yet,” *Globe*, 6 July 1911, 2.

35 “Le Recensement dans Russell,” *L'Action sociale catholique*, 7 June 1911, 8.

36 Donald Cartwright and Murdo MacPherson, “Population Composition,” in Donald Kerr and Deryck W. Holdsworth (eds.), *Historical Atlas of Canada*, vol. III, *Addressing the Twentieth Century, 1891–1961* (Toronto: University of Toronto Press, 1990), 36.

37 Debate during the previous decade about language of instruction in Ontario schools included the use of German, the third most important language in

Canada at the time; see the sophisticated and probing sociocultural analysis of language in Barbara Lorenzkowski, *Sounds of Ethnicity: Listening to German North America* (Winnipeg: University of Manitoba Press, 2010). The School Acts of Alberta and Saskatchewan designated English as the official language of instruction in 1905, limiting the use of French to the primary grades. English was made the sole language of instruction in Manitoba public schools in 1916.

38 "What One Little Blue-Eyed Irish Girl Is Able to Do," *Toronto Daily Star*, 28 Nov. 1911, 16.

39 *Toronto Daily Star*, 12 Dec. 1911.

40 "Ontario's French Population Grows from 158,000 to 250,000 in Ten Years," *Toronto Daily Star*, 6 Nov. 1911, 1.

41 Choquette, *Language and Religion*, 174.

42 Canada, Census and Statistics Office, *Fifth Census of Canada, 1911*, vol. I, *Areas and Population by Provinces, Districts and Sub-districts* (Ottawa: C.H. Parmelee, 1912), viii.

43 This document was saved as part of the uncatalogued collection of historical documents held at Statistics Canada which was systematically examined during CCRI research activities; along with other key documents, it is now included in the digital archive of the CCRI.

44 The decision by census officials to omit publication of summary tables of the 1911 language question even extended to the supplementary tabulations related to the foreign-born population. Despite the intent of census officials to use language to measure immigrant "absorption," no mention of language was made in the Census and Statistics Office, *Special Report of the Foreign-Born Population: Abstracted from the Records of the Fifth Census of Canada, 1911* (Ottawa: Government Printing Bureau, 1915).

45 *Toronto Daily Star*, 6 Nov. 1911, 1.

46 Cartwright and MacPherson, "Population Composition," Plate 4.

47 Jean Daigle and Robert LeBlanc, "Acadian Deportation and Return," in R. Cole Harris (ed.), *Historical Atlas of Canada*, vol. I, *From the Beginning to 1800* (Toronto: University of Toronto Press, 1987), Plate 30.

48 This linguistic profiling would help address the questions raised earlier regarding the suspicion that local political characteristics such as the attitude of enumerators may have affected the order of responses, or the recording of bilingual or unilingual responses. If this were the case, it may be possible to see these reflected in specific district profiles, or in geographical patterns. For example, the profile for Glengarry seems anomalous in the much higher proportions of bilingual "French first" responses compared with unilingual French. More detailed microdata analysis would help establish if the results were related to these potential causes rather than reflecting the actual proportion of English first- and French first-speakers.

49 Joy, *Languages in Canada*.

50 *Toronto Daily Star*, 6 Nov. 1911, 1.

51 Aboriginal languages are specifically excluded from the 1921 enumeration.

52 See "Encore le recensement – Fanatisme et incompétence," *Le Droit*, 17 June 1921, 10; "Le Recensement – Ce qu'il faut en penser," *Le Droit*, 29 June 1921, 3. And, in at least one case, a man complained that his children were recorded as being of the French race because they were born in Quebec, even though he himself was English. See "Letter: Taking the Census," *Montreal Daily Star*, 8 July 1921, 8.

53 "Le Recensement," *L'Évangéline*, 19 May 1921, 1.

54 "Préparez-vous au Recensement," *Le Droit*, 28 May 1921, 7.

55 Further research is also warranted on the 1916 census of the Prairie provinces which used the three language questions posed in the 1901 enumeration of Canada. The census report included multiple summary tabulations with a special focus on those listed as not being able to speak English.

56 One important example of the increasing scholarly interest in reinterpreting nation building in twentieth-century Canada is José E. Igartua, *The Other Quiet Revolution: National Identities in English Canada, 1945–71* (Vancouver: UBC Press, 2006). How research enabled by the CCRI can enrich such efforts is also suggested by the other chapters in this book.

— · 6 · —

Canada's Aboriginal Population: A Unique Historical Perspective

GUSTAVE GOLDMANN

In the Beginning ...

The dominant theory concerning the origins of the Aboriginal people in North America is based on the anthropological view that the land mass that is Canada today was first inhabited by people who migrated from Asia via a land bridge that spanned the Bering Strait.[1] This migration is considered to be the first settlement of Aboriginal people in North America. This chapter presents a sociodemographic profile of the first inhabitants of this territory based on data from Canada's 1911 census. While the data are an historical record of this particular population group, many of the concepts used in this chapter are based on contemporary theories and ideas concerning Aboriginal demography.

A number of expressions are used to designate the Aboriginal people of Canada in historical and contemporary sociological, demographic, and economic literature. For instance, terms such as "Aboriginal," "Native," "Indian," "Registered Indian," "Treaty Indian," and "First Nations" are often used to designate the indigenous population in Canada. Since some of these labels have taken on very specific meanings based on contemporary social, political, and legal interpretations, they will not necessarily be used in this chapter. However, the fundamental principle that, in Canada, the word "Aboriginal" includes many groups with unique heritages, languages, cultural practices, and spiritual beliefs, as well as distinct needs and aspirations will be retained. Furthermore, the analysis in this chapter will focus on the three distinct groups of Aboriginal people recognized in Section 35 of the 1982 Constitution Act of Canada: Indians (First Nations), Métis, and Inuit.

This chapter begins with a discussion of the data that were used for the analyses presented in subsequent sections. The challenges and opportunities in using historical census data will be highlighted as an instructional guide to future historical demographic analyses of Aboriginal people. The sections that follow will present an expanded demographic profile of the three Aboriginal groups (First Nations, Métis, and Inuit). This profile includes the standard demographic concepts of age and sex distributions as well as information on where the people lived. In addition, two sections will be devoted to language characteristics and literacy. The chapter concludes with a discussion of prospects for future research on this topic.

The 1911 Census and the Aboriginal Peoples

The 1911 census was the fifth census conducted by the Canadian government. Importantly, it was the first census conducted after the provinces of Saskatchewan and Alberta joined Confederation, in 1905. The scope and content of this census are described in detail elsewhere in this book, and therefore, will not be repeated here. This chapter focuses on the specific aspects of the 1911 census that pertain to the Aboriginal population of Canada.

The 1911 census is a valuable source of data on Canada's Aboriginal population because of its scope and coverage. Aboriginal people were living in all provinces and territories. They lived on reserves, in rural areas, and in urban centres, all of which were covered by the 1911 census.

Census data were generally collected directly from the respondents by enumerators working for the Department of Agriculture. However, this was not necessarily the case for the Aboriginal population living on reserves or in the Northwest Territories. Census documents indicate that in those areas data were to be collected "by officers, or employees of the Department of Indian Affairs, or by enumerators or agents appointed for the purpose; and the Census of the Northwest Territories and other unorganized regions in the northern parts of the Dominion by members of the Royal Northwest Mounted Police or by other persons or agents, as may in each case be deemed by the Minister of Agriculture advantageous and expedient."[2] As will be seen later in this chapter, it is possible that some of the specific responses were, in effect, interpretations made by the agents providing the information.

How the Population Was Defined

It has been argued in current research that identity rather than origin (or ancestry, as it is sometimes referred to) is the most appropriate method to designate Aboriginal people.[3] Identity tends to be a more subjective measure in which the respondent is asked with which cultural or ethnic group he or she

Table 6.1 · First language spoken by people enumerated as "Other Aboriginal" (*n* and %), Canada, 1911

First language spoken	*Weighted estimate*	*%*
First Nations language	4,270	24.6
Other Aboriginal language	5,030	28.9
English	2,820	16.2
French	140	0.8
Non-Aboriginal language	280	1.6
Missing values	4,850	27.9
Total	*17,390*	*100.0*

Source: weighted, CCRI 1911 microdata database.

Note: Percentages do not total 100 because of rounding.

identifies, whereas an origin question asks about the ethnic or cultural origins of the individual's parents or grandparents. No data on identity were collected in the Canadian census prior to 1986. Therefore, only origins-based analyses are presented in this chapter.

The primary means of identifying the Aboriginal population living in Canada in 1911 is through the data on racial or tribal origins derived from Question 14 on Schedule 1. Indians were generally identified by their tribal origins along matrilineal lines. Enumerators and other authorized collection personnel were instructed, "In the case of Indians the origin is traced through the mother."[4] All cases in which there was a valid tribal affiliation were coded as First Nations. However, the data included some instances that were listed as Aboriginal but were, in fact, other origins. Corrections were applied to the data to properly classify these cases.[5]

Although no specific instructions were given to the enumerators, the Métis population was derived from the following response categories to Question 14: "Metis," "Half-Breed," "Scots Half-Breed," "Other Breed," "French Half-Breed," and "English Metis."

The Inuit people were referred to either as "Eskimo," "Inuit," or "French Inuit." Extremely few people (only 16) were classified as having origins that could be attributed to belonging to the Inuit group. Since it is likely that the impact of sampling and estimation errors will be significant, this population group will be shown separately only in the descriptive tables.

The group labelled as "other Aboriginals" is a residual category in the CCRI coding scheme for racial and tribal origins. It includes all cases that are clearly

Table 6.2 · Province or region where people classified as "Other Aboriginal" lived (*n* and %), Canada, 1911

Province or region of residence	*Weighted estimate*	*%*
Atlantic provinces	410	2.4
Quebec	570	3.3
Ontario	2,690	15.5
Prairie provinces	3,440	19.8
British Columbia	8,300	47.7
Northwest Territories	1,980	11.4
Total	*17,390*	*100.0*

Source: weighted, CCRI 1911 microdata database.

Note: Percentages do not total 100 because of rounding.

Aboriginal but for whom no specific tribal affiliation was reported. Adjustments were applied to the data to exclude people from this group who were deemed not Aboriginal either by first language spoken or by place of residence. Table 6.1 shows the language distribution of the "other Aboriginals," using the weighted sample estimates of their distribution in the 1911 population. Table 6.2 shows their distribution based on region or province of residence.

Limitations due to Sample and Population Sizes

According to published sources for the 1911 census, the total population of Canada was 7,206,648 persons.[6] The estimated total population of Canada calculated from the sample with the appropriate weights applied to the main sample and oversamples is 7,295,065. This represents an estimation error of approximately 1.2 per cent. Estimates for aggregate populations can be assumed to be representative if one assumes a random distribution of the errors. However, the same does not apply when calculating estimates for smaller populations such as the Inuit, since the sampling error will have a much greater impact.[7]

Looking more specifically at the Aboriginal population, the 1911 census recorded 105,492 persons with Aboriginal origins.[8] The weighted estimate of the Aboriginal population derived from the CCRI file is 97,525 persons. The estimation error for the total Aboriginal population is approximately 7.5 per cent when comparing the CCRI sample and the published counts. Although it is difficult to attribute the error to either source (the 1911 census published counts or the CCRI sample file), it is reasonable to assume that the error is randomly distributed over the sample. Therefore, the calculated estimates and models presented in this chapter may be considered to be representative of the conditions for the Aboriginal people (in aggregate form) in Canada in 1911.

Estimating the characteristics for subgroups of the Aboriginal population was more challenging because of the increased impact of sampling and measurement error for any subgroup. For instance, the sample includes only sixteen respondents who are classified as Inuit. It is not possible to produce statistically significant estimates for a population this small. Therefore, they will be aggregated into the "other Aboriginals" category in some tables. Similarly, caution must be exercised in interpreting the results for the Métis group since they represent less than 10 per cent of the cases in the Aboriginal data set.

The Age Transition: An Historical and Aboriginal Perspective

Age is a characteristic of both individuals and of populations. However, the impact of age differs depending on whether we adopt a micro (individual) or macro (population) perspective. At the micro-level, it is a biological and chronological characteristic of individuals and it can have only one outcome: people grow older. At the macro-level, populations can age and can grow younger.[9] Consequently, it is important to consider the age composition of a population in demographic analyses since it has both a direct and an indirect impact on demographic processes such as birth, death, and migration.[10] Similar arguments may be made concerning the sex composition of a population in demographic analyses.

A population's age is generally indicated by the median age of its members. Table 6.3 compares the median ages of the Aboriginal groups and the non-Aboriginal population of Canada in 1911, again based on sample estimates of the respective populations.[11]

Both the Aboriginal and non-Aboriginal populations were relatively young based on the respective median ages. It is noteworthy that the median age for the Aboriginal peoples in 2006 was 24.7 years,[12] indicating that this population group has not aged at the same rate as the non-Aboriginal population.

The sex composition of the population can be represented through sex ratios and with population pyramids. The data show that there were 113 males per 100 females for the non-Aboriginal population and 99 males per 100 females for the Aboriginal groups.[13] It can be seen from the population pyramid (figure 6.1) that Aboriginal males outnumbered females between the ages of 35 and 49.[14] The wide base and generally uniform slopes also confirm that the Aboriginal population was relatively young in 1911. Furthermore, we see a small, but noticeable, representation of elderly people among the Aboriginal population, suggesting that the life expectancy for both population groups was comparable.

Table 6.3 · Median ages (in years) of the Aboriginal (First Nations, Métis, Inuit, Other) and non-Aboriginal population groups (*n*) living in Canada, 1911

Aboriginal group	*Median age (years)*	*Population size*
First Nations	20	70,080
Métis	18	7,015
Inuit	27	270
Other Aboriginal	21	16,280
Non-Aboriginal	23	7,129,065

Source: CCRI 1911 microdata database.

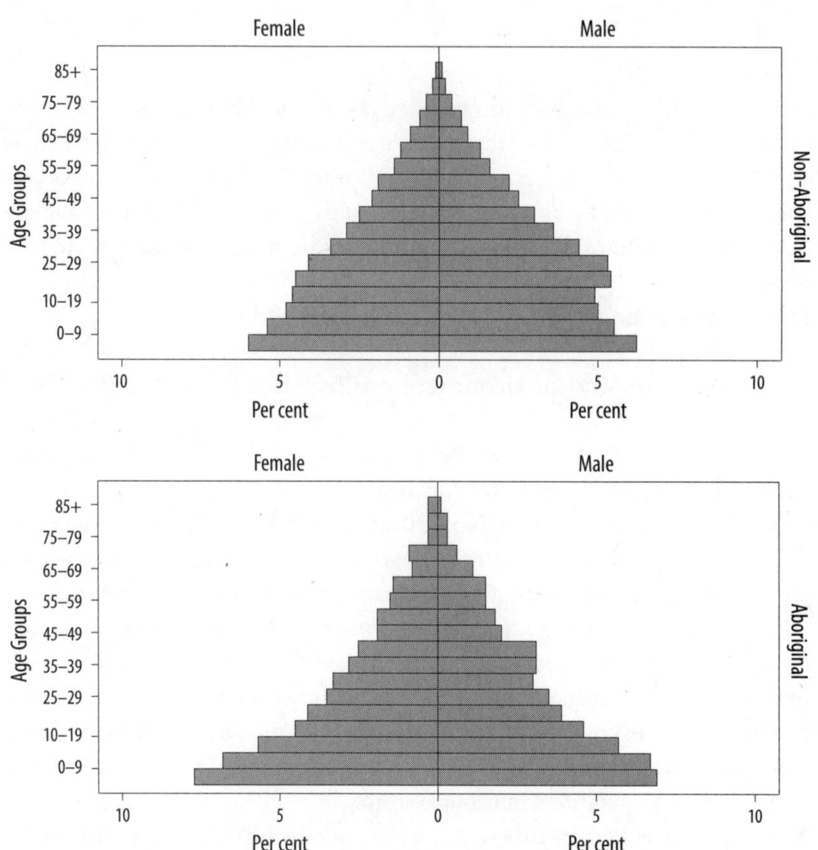

Figure 6.1 · Population pyramids for Aboriginal and non-Aboriginal populations, males and females by age group, Canada, 1911.

Source: CCRI 1911 microdata database.

Table 6.4 · Aboriginal (First Nations, Métis, Inuit, Other) and non-Aboriginal people living in urban and rural areas (*n* and %), Canada, 1911

Aboriginal group	*Urban*		*Rural*		*Total*	
	n	%	n	%	n	%
First Nations	1,950	2.7	70,820	97.3	72,770	100
Métis	750	10.6	6,350	89.4	7,100	100
Inuit		—	270	100.0	270	100
Other Aboriginal	720	4.2	16,260	95.8	16,980	100
Non-Aboriginal	3,278,720	46.1	3,826,300	53.9	7,105,020	100

Source: CCRI 1911 microdata database.

As noted earlier, the people classified as "other Aboriginals" were likely members of First Nations for whom the precise nation code was not available. Since the combination of First Nations and other Aboriginals represents over 90 per cent of the total Aboriginal population in the sample, it is reasonable to assume that the pyramid accurately represents their age and sex distribution as well.

We will now examine where the Aboriginal people lived.

The Beginning of Urbanization for Aboriginal People

Urban and rural environments differ socially, economically, and often demographically. Socially, urban living has been characterized as "impersonal and isolating" in a long-standing sociological account.[15] In contrast, rural living has been described as more communal in nature, encompassing the concept of a folk community.[16] Some form of urbanization existed in Canada since the time of the first European settlers.[17] Urbanization, in its broadest sense, was a feature that was limited to the settler groups in Canada. Aboriginal people lived in communities that were generally found in rural areas and that were consistent with the concept of folk community referred to earlier. This pattern is clearly evident when we examine the urban/rural distribution of the Aboriginal and non-Aboriginal populations in Canada in 1911.

Table 6.4 shows that in 1911 well over 90 per cent of the Aboriginal population lived in rural areas, compared with approximately 54 per cent of the non-Aboriginal population. Nevertheless, the data show the beginnings of urban settlement among the Aboriginal peoples. History has shown that this trend continued and accelerated, resulting in initiatives by the federal government (through, e.g., Aboriginal Affairs and Northern Development, and the Office of the Federal Interlocutor for Métis and Non-Status Indians, created in 1985) and Aboriginal groups (e.g., Network of Native Friendship Centres) to provide services and support to this segment of the Aboriginal population.[18]

In 1911, it is likely that the communities and neighbourhoods in which people lived had a bearing on their cultural environment since the concept of "cultural community" was often a function of proximity to others with common characteristics such as language, religion, and ethnic identity. We will now examine demo-linguistic characteristics of the Aboriginal people, in part, to assess the impact of urbanization on cultural retention.

An Introduction to the Demolinguistics of the Aboriginal People

Language is a fundamental and defining characteristic of the Aboriginal peoples of Canada. As well as territory, language is the foundation on which individual Aboriginal nations are defined. Also, it is the basis for the preservation of Aboriginal identity since Aboriginal people rely on oral tradition to pass their culture and history from one generation to the next. We know from contemporary demolinguistic research on Aboriginal peoples that the use and retention of Aboriginal languages is declining.[19] This section explores the extent to which the current trend with respect to Aboriginal language use and preservation was evident in 1911.

Education was viewed by successive federal governments as an instrument that could serve to assimilate the Aboriginal people into Canadian society.[20] Consequently, the government promoted the use of residential schools for the Aboriginal people who were under the administrative responsibilities of the Department of Indian and Northern Affairs. The use of Aboriginal languages was strongly discouraged in these schools, resulting in a gradual decline in their use among those generations who were obliged to attend. According to some estimates, more than 30,000 Aboriginal children were enrolled in such schools at the beginning of the twentieth century.[21] It would appear logical that the impact of this form of education on the use of Aboriginal languages would be evident in the 1911 census data. The analysis in this section confirms this hypothesis.

A brief history of the residential school program and system is presented at this stage in the analysis in order to place the results that will be presented below in their proper context. The newly formed Government of Canada adopted a policy of assimilation with respect to the indigenous population of its territory. Delegations were sent to examine the "industrial schools" that were established in the United States, and it was concluded by Nicholas Flood Davin that a system of residential schools that "teach the arts, crafts and industrial skills of a modern economy" should be established.[22] The schools began to accept students who were removed from their reserves and home communities during the 1880s. The schools were administered by Roman Catholic, Anglican, and Presbyterian clergy. All activities were conducted in either English or French. As stated in chapter 10 of the 1996 *Report of the Royal Commission on Aboriginal Peoples*, "Marching out from the schools, the children, effectively re-socialized, imbued with the values of European culture, would be the vanguard of a magnificent metamorphosis: the 'savage' was to be made 'civilized,' made fit to take up the privileges and responsibilities of citizenship."[23] In other words, language and cultural transformation were the major goals of these schools, which continued to operate until the 1960s. It is important to note that the impact of the residential schools on the Aboriginal peoples has been formally acknowledged by the federal government. Canada's Truth and Reconciliation Commission was formed in 2008 with "a mandate to learn the truth about what happened in the residential schools and to inform all Canadians about what happened in the schools."[24]

The preservation of any language requires that the incentive, the means, and the context exist to pass the language on from one generation to the next.[25] The context is defined as the places where people live and work, thereby defining the forum for interaction: "While it may be possible for Aboriginal people to function in their traditional languages within their own communities, assuming that the language is spoken by people living in the community, this is not the case when they deal with the remainder of Canadian society."[26] Any form of activity or interaction outside Aboriginal communities generally requires knowledge and competence in either English or French. It is assumed that those who lived in rural areas were most likely in communities in which there is a larger concentration of indigenous speakers. According to Beaujot and Kerr,[27] it is easier to retain a language if the individual lives in a community in which there is larger concentration of indigenous speakers. We have seen in the previous section that the process of urbanization was under way for the Aboriginal people in 1911. Therefore, where they lived will be included in the analysis.

The results in table 6.5 suggest strongly that the propensity to speak an Aboriginal language on a regular basis varies with Aboriginal group.[28] Almost 80 per cent of the members of First Nations commonly spoke an Aboriginal language, while approximately one-third of the Métis spoke an Aboriginal language. The results also confirm that context is important. There were marked differences in the proportions who spoke an Aboriginal language in urban and

Table 6.5 · Language (Aboriginal or non-Aboriginal) commonly spoken by all Aboriginal people (First Nations, Métis, Inuit, and Other), and according to urban or rural residence (*n* and %), Canada, 1911

Aboriginal group	*Aboriginal language*		*Non-Aboriginal language*		*Total*	
	Population size (estimate)	*%*	*Population size (estimate)*	*%*	*Population size (estimate)*	*%*
First Nations	55,900	76	17,200	24	73,100	100
Métis	2,680	38	4,435	62	7,115	100
Inuit and Other Aboriginal	10,240	59	7,070	41	17,310	100
Total	68,820	71	28,705	29	97,525	100
URBAN POPULATION						
First Nations	1,180	60	785	40	1,965	100
Métis	—	—	765	100	765	100
Inuit and Other Aboriginal	250	34	490	66	740	100
Total	1,430	41	2,040	59	3,470	100
RURAL POPULATION						
First Nations	54,720	77	16,415	23	71,135	100
Métis	2,680	42	3,670	58	6,350	100
Inuit and Other Aboriginal	9,990	60	6,580	40	16,570	100
Total	67,390	72	26,665	28	94,055	100

Source: CCRI 1911 microdata database.

rural settings. The relative importance of the impact of these two characteristics is explored in the multivariate analysis presented later in this section of the chapter.

Age is another characteristic of the individual that has a bearing on language use and retention.[29] It can be seen from the results in table 6.6 that the mean age of those who commonly spoke an Aboriginal language was less than 30 years.[30] Furthermore, we see that those who belonged to the First Nations and Métis groups and who commonly spoke an Aboriginal language tended to be younger than their counterparts belonging to the other two Aboriginal groups.

Given that we had access to detailed microdata (as opposed to published summary tables), two multivariate models were constructed to test the relative importance of the characteristics described above in determining whether or not an individual was likely to commonly speak an Aboriginal language. Both models consider the sex and age of the individual as well as the Aboriginal group to which he or she belonged. The first model used an urban/rural

Table 6.6 · Mean age (in years) of Aboriginal people (First Nations, Métis, Inuit, and Other) who spoke an Aboriginal language, Canada, 1911

Aboriginal group	*Mean age (years)*
First Nations	26.8
Métis	25.1
Inuit and Other Aboriginal	28.3

Source: CCRI 1911 microdata database.

indicator as a proxy for the context. The second model explored the regional differences.[31]

In 1911, men were more likely than women to be in regular contact with the non-Aboriginal members of Canadian society, either as part of the labour force or through regular social interactions. Therefore, it is reasonable to assume that men would be less likely than women to have commonly spoken an Aboriginal language. However, this assumption is not supported by the results shown in table 6.7. The sex of the individual was not a significant determinant of the likelihood that an Aboriginal person would speak an Aboriginal language.

The analysis of the impact of age on the likelihood to speak an Aboriginal language confirms two very important points. First, the older cohorts were more likely than the younger cohorts to speak an Aboriginal language. Second, the results show that those who were under 30 years of age were half as likely to speak an Aboriginal language as those in the oldest cohort. Many of the Aboriginal people in these cohorts were students in the residential schools referred to earlier, thereby confirming the likely impact of this form of education on the use of Aboriginal languages.

The First Nations people and the Inuit are the only two Aboriginal groups with distinct languages.[32] It can be seen that First Nations people were much more likely to speak an Aboriginal language than the other Aboriginal groups, controlling for the fact that many of the younger cohorts attended residential schools. It is also evident that the Métis were less likely than other Aboriginal peoples to speak an Aboriginal language.

Where the Aboriginal people lived definitely had an impact on whether or not they commonly spoke an Aboriginal language. Those living in urban areas (see model 1 in table 6.7) were much less likely to speak an Aboriginal language, indicating that language assimilation occurred in the cities. The results also show that the Aboriginal people living in the provinces (see model 2 in table

Table 6.7 · Contribution of sex, age (in years), Aboriginal group, urban/rural, and region to the likelihood that an Aboriginal person commonly spoke an Aboriginal language, Canada, 1911

		Model 1 *Odds ratio*		*Model 2* *Odds ratio*	
Sex	Male vs. female	0.917		0.909	
Age groups (years)	Under 15 vs. 60+	0.374	***	0.341	***
	15–19 vs. 60+	0.482	***	0.445	***
	20–29 vs. 60+	0.569	***	0.537	***
	30–39 vs. 60+	0.725	*	0.702	**
	40–49 vs. 60+	0.645	**	0.605	***
	50–59 vs. 60+	0.744		0.701	*
Aboriginal groups	First Nations vs. Inuit and Other Aboriginal	2.331	***	3.198	***
	Métis vs. Inuit and Other Aboriginal	0.459	***	0.481	***
Urban/rural	Urban vs. rural	0.349	***		
Region	Atlantic vs. Territories			0.082	***
	Quebec vs. Territories			0.438	***
	Ontario vs. Territories			0.296	***
	Prairies vs. Territories			0.432	***
	BC vs. Territories			0.704	**
Nagelkerke pseudo R^2		0.120		0.170	

Source: CCRI 1911 microdata database.

* $p < .1$; ** $p < .05$; *** $p < .01$.

6.7) were generally less likely to commonly speak an Aboriginal language than those living in the territories. This is to be expected given that no urban centres were located in the territories and that it was mostly the First Nations and Inuit who lived there. The previous point notwithstanding, the results show some interesting variations among the five major regions in Canada. Those who lived in British Columbia were more likely to speak an Aboriginal language, followed by those who lived in Quebec and the Prairie provinces. Again, this result is not surprising given the concentrations of First Nations people living in these provinces.

The preceding section examined the likelihood that Aboriginal people retained their own languages, thereby providing an important link to their cultures and communities. The next section focuses on the ability of Aboriginal people to interact with the non-Aboriginal community by exploring their ability to read and write.

Table 6.8 · Ability to read and write, by age group (in years), for the Aboriginal (First Nations, Métis, Other) and non-Aboriginal populations (*n* and %), Canada, 1911

Age (years)	*Were able to read*			*Were able to write*		
	n	%	*Total*	n	%	*Total*
FIRST NATIONS						
Under 15	7,390	32	22,920	7,330	32	23,080
15–19	3,830	61	6,230	3,830	62	6,210
20–29	5,250	54	9,730	5,310	54	9,770
30–39	3,650	45	8,100	3,630	45	8,100
40–49	2,200	34	6,380	2,160	34	6,360
50–59	1,310	28	4,720	1,310	28	4,720
60+	970	20	4,880	930	19	4,860
Total	*24,600*	*39*	*62,960*	*24,500*	*39*	*63,100*
MÉTIS						
Under 15	1,030	40	2,550	1,010	39	2,570
15–19	460	63	730	470	64	730
20–29	660	54	1,230	660	54	1,230
30–39	330	52	630	330	52	630
40–49	340	53	640	340	53	640
50–59	120	46	260	120	46	260
60+	120	30	400	100	25	400
Total	*3,060*	*48*	*6,440*	*3,030*	*47*	*6,460*
OTHER ABORIGINAL						
Under 15	1,380	25	5,560	1,380	25	5,560
15–19	590	50	1,190	570	48	1,190
20–29	980	42	2,320	960	41	2,320
30–39	440	23	1,900	440	23	1,900
40–49	440	28	1,550	440	28	1,550
50–59	140	16	880	140	16	880
60+	160	10	1,560	160	10	1,560
Total	*4,130*	*28*	*14,960*	*4,090*	*27*	*14,960*
NON-ABORIGINAL						
Under 15	1,204,210	63	1,897,670	1,190,920	63	1,895,770
15–19	637,050	96	660,520	636,290	96	660,700
20–29	1,270,820	95	1,334,980	1,268,760	95	1,335,120
30–39	940,070	95	993,800	937,800	94	993,890
40–49	653,270	93	701,310	650,190	93	701,240

/continued

Table 6.8 · continued

Age (years)	*Were able to read*			*Were able to write*		
	n	%	*Total*	n	%	*Total*
50–59	440,150	91	484,990	436,570	90	484,990
60+	424,710	87	489,840	415,520	85	489,380
Total	*5,570,280*	*85*	*6,563,110*	*5,536,050*	*84*	*6,561,090*

Source: CCRI 1911 microdata database.

Note: The totals for able to read and able to write are different due to non-responses. The same number of respondents did not necessarily complete both questions.

Literacy

Canadian society underwent important and far-reaching social, economic, demographic, and political changes at the turn of the twentieth century. The Prairie provinces joined Confederation in 1905. While agricultural development was growing in the Prairie provinces, primarily fuelled by immigrants from Central and Eastern Europe, the major urban centres in Canada were becoming more industrialized. These changes were bound to have an impact on the Aboriginal people since they were essentially hunter-gatherer societies at that time.[33] It was clear that they would have to adapt in order to function in the world that was changing around them.

Research has shown that education is an important driver of social and economic change for a society.[34] This observation applies to all members of a society, not just selected elites. The usual indicators of education are school attendance and qualifications attained. Unfortunately, neither of these basic measures is available in the 1911 census. Therefore, basic literacy skills are used as a proxy indicator of education. The analysis presented in this section will compare the outcomes for Aboriginal people living in rural and urban areas since, based on contemporary research, where people live is likely to have an impact on their level of education.[35]

The data show that literacy rates in 1911 were lower for the Aboriginal peoples when compared with the non-Aboriginal population (see table 6.8). Overall, slightly more than one-third of the First Nations people were able to read and write compared with over four-fifths of the non-Aboriginal population. The

Table 6.9 · Contribution of sex, age (in years), Aboriginal/non-Aboriginal, urban/rural location, and region to the likelihood of not being able to read or write, total population of Canada, 1911

		Reading		*Writing*	
		Model 1 *Odds ratio*	*Model 2* *Odds ratio*	*Model 3* *Odds ratio*	*Model 4* *Odds ratio*
Intercept		0.166 ***	0.238 ***	0.194 ***	0.266 ***
Sex	Male vs. female	1.138 ***	1.137 ***	1.125 ***	1.127 ***
Age groups (years)	Under 15 vs. 60+	3.661 ***	3.486 ***	3.258 ***	3.113 ***
	15–19 vs. 60+	0.243 ***	0.230 ***	0.219 ***	0.207 ***
	20–29 vs. 60+	0.336 ***	0.306 ***	0.302 ***	0.277 ***
	30–39 vs. 60+	0.386 ***	0.354 ***	0.350 ***	0.323 ***
	40–49 vs. 60+	0.492 ***	0.465 ***	0.454 ***	0.432 ***
	50–59 vs. 60+	0.671 ***	0.651 ***	0.631 ***	0.615 ***
Aboriginal person	Aboriginal vs. Non-Aboriginal	11.692 ***	12.051 ***	11.151 ***	11.752 ***
Urban/rural	Urban vs. rural	0.710 ***		0.702 ***	
Region	Atlantic vs. Territories		0.728 *		0.783
	Quebec vs. Territories		0.689 **		0.727 *
	Ontario vs. Territories		0.467 ***		0.473 ***
	Prairies vs. Territories		0.845		0.849
	BC vs. Territories		0.757		0.764
Nagelkerke pseudo R^2		0.247	0.251	0.245	0.249

Source: CCRI 1911 microdata database.

* $p < .1$; ** $p < .05$; *** $p < .01$.

data also show that literacy rates for the Aboriginal population declined with age cohort.[36]

Two series of multivariate logistic models were constructed to analyse the effect of age cohort, Aboriginal group, sex, and where the people were living on the likelihood that they were able to read and write. The first series of models (table 6.9) focuses on the total population, thereby making it possible to compare outcomes for Aboriginal and non-Aboriginal people. The second series of models (table 6.10) examines only the Aboriginal population and compares the outcomes between the three main Aboriginal groupings.[37]

The same demographic and identity characteristics of the populations are included in all models. Only the spatial characteristics differ between the models. Models 1 and 3 compare urban and rural populations. Models 2 and 4 explore regional differences.

The most striking result in this analysis is that Aboriginal people were about twelve times more likely than non-Aboriginal people to be unable to read, controlling for all the other characteristics included in the models. Although the instructions to the enumerators stated that the ability to read in any language was an acceptable response, it should be noted that many Aboriginal languages were predominantly oral – that is, they did not necessarily have a written component. Therefore, it is reasonable to expect that Aboriginal people who spoke those languages would not be able to read.

The multivariate analysis shows that men were more likely than women to be unable to read, controlling for all other characteristics. This outcome is not surprising since men were often called upon to enter the labour force before completing even the most rudimentary form of education. Furthermore, many of the manual occupations did not require reading skills.

The results also confirm that the age of the individual had an impact on his or her ability to read. Remembering that the youngest cohort included children as young as 5 years old, one can disregard the odds ratios for the first contrast. However, the remaining contrasts show very clearly that the inability to read increased monotonically with age, regardless of where people lived.

There is very little difference with respect to the precision between models 1 and 2.[38] This is likely because of the fact that the urban population was concentrated in Quebec and Ontario. The results show that people living in urban areas were more likely to be able to read (the odds ratio is less than 1) controlling for the other observed characteristics. This result reflects the access to education available in urban centres (when compared with rural areas). It also reflects the nature of social and economic interaction in urban centres.

The models that examine the characteristics of those who were not able to write show similar results to the models analysing reading ability since there is a strong correlation between the ability to read and the ability to write.

Let us now explore the differences between Aboriginal groups. Table 6.10 presents four models to assess the impact of individual characteristics on the ability of an Aboriginal person to read and to write. Once again, it should be noted that no distinction was made in the data with respect to the specific language in which the individual could read or write.

Both models 5 and 6 are statistically significant. Therefore, we know that the characteristics included contribute to determining whether or not an Aborig-

Table 6.10 · Contribution of sex, age (in years), Aboriginal group, urban/rural location, and region to the likelihood that an Aboriginal person was able to read or write, Canada, 1911

		Reading		Writing	
		Model 5 *Odds ratio*	*Model 6* *Odds ratio*	*Model 7* *Odds ratio*	*Model 8* *Odds ratio*
Intercept		0.130 ***	0.147 ***	0.123 ***	0.143 ***
Sex	Male vs. female	1.184 ***	1.161 **	1.163 ***	1.142 **
Age groups (years)	Under 15 vs. 60+	1.960 ***	2.097 ***	2.029 ***	2.166 ***
	15–19 vs. 60+	6.425 ***	6.903 ***	6.803 ***	7.346 ***
	20–29 vs. 60+	4.620 ***	4.808 ***	4.915 ***	5.120 ***
	30–39 vs. 60+	3.136 ***	3.436 ***	3.290 ***	3.615 ***
	40–49 vs. 60+	2.291 ***	2.373 ***	2.382 ***	2.480 ***
	50–59 vs. 60+	1.608 **	1.614 **	1.701 ***	1.712 ***
Aboriginal groups	First Nations vs. Other Aboriginal	1.697 ***	1.226	1.704 ***	1.211
	Métis vs. Other Aboriginal	2.138 ***	2.389 ***	2.111 ***	2.312 ***
	Inuit vs. Other Aboriginal	3.974 *	3.171	4.037 **	3.147
Urban/rural	Urban vs. rural	2.691 ***		2.776 ***	
Region	Atlantic vs. Territories		1.979 **		1.876 **
	Quebec vs. Territories		2.088 ***		2.042 ***
	Ontario vs. Territories		2.228 ***		2.246 ***
	Prairies vs. Territories		0.760		.763
	BC vs. Territories		0.527 ***		.501 ***
Nagelkerke pseudo R^2		0.102	0.168	0.105	0.172

Source: CCRI 1911 microdata database.

* $p < .1$; ** $p < .05$; *** $p < .01$.

inal person was able to read. However, we notice that model 6, the version that includes the region of residence as opposed to the simple dichotomous urban/rural distinction, appears to be stronger (based on the Nagelkerke pseudo R^2 statistic). Nevertheless, both models provide interesting outcomes.

According to both models, men were more likely than women to be able to read when we restrict the analysis only to Aboriginal people. This outcome may be due to two factors. First, Aboriginal men were more likely than Aboriginal women to be in the labour force. Second, these results may be indicating the impact of the residential school system. If this assumption is true, it is likely that the language the men spoke was either English or French.[39] As shown in the previous models, the ability to read declined with age cohort. We see from the results that individuals in the second youngest cohort (aged 15 to 19) were over six times as likely to be able to read when compared with those 60 years of age and older. The odds ratios remain high and significant for the other cohorts, although they decline monotonically from over four times as likely for the Aboriginal people aged 20 to 29 to just under twice as likely for those aged 50 to 59.

The analysis of the impact of Aboriginal group on the ability to read is complicated by the fact that it is not clear who is classified as being among "other Aboriginals."[40] Nevertheless, they form a constant reference category. Therefore, the respective odds ratios for the First Nations, Métis, and Inuit can be compared with one another.

The Métis appear to be more likely to have been able to read than the people belonging to the First Nations (odds ratio of over 2 compared with 1.7 – model 5 only). One can attribute this outcome to the fact that the Métis were more likely to be living outside of Aboriginal communities and that they were the product of a union between an Aboriginal and non-Aboriginal person (English- or French-speaking).

Where the Aboriginal people were living made a significant difference on their ability to read. Those living in urban areas were more than twice as likely as those living in rural areas to be able to read (model 5). The impact of the region in which they were living (model 6) indicates that those living in Ontario and Quebec were also twice as likely as those living in the territories to be able to read. A similar outcome is shown for those living in the Atlantic provinces, although the result is not as strong.

Once again, we see that the likelihood of being able to write for the Aboriginal people parallels their ability to read. The differences in the odds ratios in table 6.10 are very close to those in table 6.9. Therefore, the observations made with respect to the ability to read apply equally to the ability to write.

Conclusion

The analysis presented in this chapter provides an important historical context for the sociodemographic patterns that we see in the Aboriginal population in contemporary times. The Aboriginal people were a relatively young population in 1911, as was the non-Aboriginal population. However, more recently, the Aboriginal population remains younger than the non-Aboriginal population.

The beginnings of linguistic assimilation are evident in the analysis of the language characteristics of the Aboriginal population in 1911. When analysing the impact of selected individual characteristics on the likelihood that a person belonging to a First Nation spoke an Aboriginal language, we saw that the cohorts who were either in residential schools at the time of the census or who had been students in these schools were most likely to lose the ability, or lacked the opportunity, to speak an Aboriginal language. According to some authors, this pattern has become more acute in contemporary times.[41]

Demographers have been discussing the impact on contemporary societies of the urban transition in developing and in industrialized states.[42] The analysis presented in this chapter shows evidence that the urban transition was already under way for the Aboriginal people in Canada at the beginning of the twentieth century. It was also shown that there was a greater likelihood that Aboriginal people in urban areas had basic literacy skills (reading and writing).

Although it may appear that the analysis presented in this chapter was comprehensive in nature, many aspects of Aboriginal life in Canada in the first decade of the twentieth century remain to be explored. For instance, we know from other work on the topic that intermarriage (exogamy) can have far-reaching impact on the identity of subsequent generations and on cultural and linguistic continuity.[43] Further analysis of this aspect of family life in 1911 would yield interesting insights, and it would provide a foundation on which to analyse the effect of exogamy on subsequent generations. It would also be interesting to investigate migration patterns for Aboriginal people in Canada using the 1911 data, as well as data from other historical censuses. For instance, is it possible to attribute some measure of the migration to urban centres to the construction of the national railroad?

To conclude, this chapter augments the existing literature on the historical demography of Aboriginal peoples by adding a strong multivariate empirical analysis of national data collected by Canada's federal government in 1911. It has also shown the immense potential of historical census microdata for demographic and sociocultural analyses. The type of multivariate analysis used in this study can only be conducted from models constructed from detailed microdata files. This rich resource has opened interesting possibilities for future research.

Notes

1 Olive P. Dickason, *Canada's First Nations: A History of Founding Peoples from Earliest Times* (Don Mills, ON: Oxford University Press, 2002), 3–30.

2 Canada, Department of Agriculture and Statistics, *Fifth Census of Canada, 1911: Instructions to Officers, Commissioners and Enumerators* (Ottawa: Government Printing Bureau, 1911), 5.

3 See, e.g., the following articles from Joint Canada-United States Conference on the Measurement of Ethnicity and the US Department of Commerce, *Challenges of Measuring an Ethnic World: Science, Politics and Reality: Proceedings of the Joint Canada-United States Conference on the Measurement of Ethnicity, April 1–3, 1992* (Washington, DC: US Government Printing Office, 1993): R. Cohen, "Ethnicity, the State and Moral Order," 365–90; W.W. Isajiw, "Definition and Dimensions of Ethnicity: A Theoretical Framework," 407–30; and C. Goldscheider, "What Does Ethnic/Racial Differentiation Mean? Implications for Measurement and Analyses," 391–406. For additional examples, see G. Goldmann, "Shifts in Ethnic Origins among the Offspring of Immigrants: Is Ethnic Mobility a Measurable Phenomenon?" *Canadian Ethnic Studies* 30, no. 3 (1998): 121–48; E.T. Pryor, G.J. Goldmann, M. Sheridan, and P. White, "Measuring Ethnicity: Is 'Canadian' an Evolving Indigenous Category?" *Ethnic and Racial Studies* 15, no. 2 (1992): 214–35; and N.B. Ryder, "The Interpretation of Origin Statistics," *Estadistica: The Journal of the International American Statistical Institute* (1956): 651–65.

4 *Fifth Census of Canada, 1911: Instructions to Officers, Commissioners and Enumerators*, 29.

5 A small number of cases for which the following origins were originally classified as Aboriginal were Swedish, Italian, and Indian (from India). Data on language and country of birth were used to correctly reclassify these cases.

6 Canada, Census and Statistics Office (CSO), *Census of Canada, 1911*, vol. II, *Religions, Origins, Birthplace, Citizenship, Literacy and Infirmities by Provinces, Districts and Sub-districts* (Ottawa: C.H. Parmelee, 1912).

7 The use of complex weights that take into account the sampling structure that was used in creating the file may correct for these errors. However, the author was not successful in applying this methodology with SPSS.

8 *Census of Canada, 1911*, vol. II.

9 W.C. Sanderson and S. Scherbov, "Average Remaining Lifetimes Can Increase as Human Populations Age," *Nature* 435 (2005): 811–13.

10 F. Trovato, *Canada's Population in a Global Context: An Introduction to Social Demography* (Don Mills, ON: Oxford University Press, 2009).

11 The estimates of population size in table 6.6 exclude 72,355 weighted cases for which no age data were available.

12 Statistics Canada (2010), *CYB Overview 2006*, http://www41.statcan.gc.ca/2006/ceb_r000_2006-eng.htm.

13 The non-Aboriginal sex ratios and age distributions in 1911 were heavily influenced by the wave of immigrants arriving between 1896 and 1911. The majority of these immigrants were males between the ages of 20 and 40. This topic is discussed in detail in other chapters of this book.

14 The population pyramid was prepared with PYRAMIDE SYS developed by Stéphane Gilbert.

15 Trovato, *Canada's Population in a Global Context.*

16 Ibid.
17 Urbanization encompasses both the development of urban centres and the migration from rural to urban areas. As such, it describes both a state of a population and a flow.
18 The estimated values of the urban and rural populations are affected to a limited degree by instances of missing responses. Therefore, the total estimated population for this characteristic will not match exactly the estimated count of the total population.
19 R. Lachapelle and G. Goldmann, "Language and Demography," in Barry Edmonston and Eric Fong (eds.), *The Changing Canadian Population* (Montreal and Kingston: McGill-Queen's University Press, 2011), 347–66; M.J. Norris, "Canada's Aboriginal Languages," *Canadian Social Trends* (Dec. 1998): 8–16.
20 Dickason, *Canada's First Nations.*
21 Ibid.
22 Indian and Northern Affairs Canada, *Report of the Royal Commission on Aboriginal Peoples* (1996), http://www.collectionscanada.gc.ca/webarchives/20071115053257/http://www.ainc-inac.gc.ca/ch/rcap/sg/sgmm_e.html.
23 Ibid., vol. I, part 2, chapter 10. http://www.collectionscanada.gc.ca/webarchives/20071211055641/http://www.ainc-inac.gc.ca/ch/rcap/sg/sg28_e.html#100.
24 Truth and Reconciliation Commission Canada, http://www.trc.ca/websites/trcinstitution/index.php?p=4.
25 Lachapelle and Goldmann, "Language and Demography."
26 Ibid.
27 R. Beaujot and D. Kerr, *Population Change in Canada* (Toronto: Oxford University Press, 2004).
28 These results are derived from the language most commonly spoken. The author interprets "commonly spoken" to be an indicator that the language is used on a regular basis.
29 Beaujot and Kerr, *Population Change in Canada*; Norris, "Canada's Aboriginal Languages."
30 The mean age is used at this stage in the analysis since it is more sensitive to the extreme values in the distribution.
31 There is strong collinearity between the distribution of the population by urban/rural characteristics and by region. Therefore, it is not advised to include the two spatial characteristics in the same models.
32 The Inuit are aggregated with the "other Aboriginals" group since they represent a relatively small proportion of the Aboriginal population.
33 Dickason, *Canada's First Nations.*
34 J. Côté and A. Allahar, *Ivory Tower Blues: A University System in Crisis* (Toronto: University of Toronto Press, 2007). R. Ghosh and D. Ray, *Social Change and Education in Canada* (Toronto: Harcourt Brace Jovanonich, 1991).
35 N. Spence, J. White, and P.P. Maxim, "Modeling Success of First Nations Students in Canada: Community Level Perspectives," *Canadian Ethnic Studies* 39, nos 1 & 2 (2007): 145–67.

36 It should be noted that the data on ability to read and write were collected for the population aged 5 years and older. Therefore, the youngest cohort includes children who may not yet have learned to read and write.

37 The coding of the reference category of the dependent variables in these models was changed from the negative outcome to a positive outcome for ease of interpretation since the comparison in these models is restricted to within the Aboriginal population. The main concept of interest in these models is the ability to be able to read and write rather than illiteracy.

38 The pseudo R^2 measures, the Nagelkerke, are very close for the two models.

39 We cannot ignore the fact that this information was not necessarily obtained directly from the respondent. Therefore, the person who provided the information to the enumerators may not have been aware that the individual was able to read or write. It is possible that their contact with the Aboriginal women did not give them the opportunity to establish whether or not they were able to read or write.

40 See the discussion earlier in this chapter.

41 Norris, "Canada's Aboriginal Languages." Lachapelle and Goldmann, "Language and Demography."

42 Trovato, *Canada's Population in a Global Context.*

43 G. Goldmann and A. Siggner, "Statistical Concepts of Aboriginal People and Factors Affecting the Counts in the Census and the Aboriginal Peoples Survey," *Towards the XXIst Century: Socio-demographic Trends and Policy Issues in Canada* (Ottawa: Federation of Canadian Demographers, 1995), 265–79. Goldmann, "Shifts in Ethnic Origins among the Offspring of Immigrants."

PART III

Social Spaces, Historical Places

— · 7 · —

Household Experiences in Canada's Early Twentieth-Century Transformation

GORDON DARROCH

It is through their household and family experiences that most people in most times and places make sense of and respond to changes in the larger socio-economic and political formations that surround them. The household is the central historical site of the mediation between individual experience and structural change. The key debates in the history of households and families continue to focus on the question of the historical appearance and distribution of nuclear and more complex households, such as multigenerational ones or other forms of extension to kin. In the 1960s, pioneering English studies based on systematic historical listings of individuals challenged the orthodoxies of modernization theories, which had broadly asserted the progressive historical replacement of complex households by nuclear ones as a necessary accompaniment to early industrialization and concentrated urban life.[1] The initial revisionist work argued that, at least in Western Europe, nuclear co-residence had predominated over many centuries. The contention stimulated a stream of new historical research based on nominative sources. The 1970s and early 1980s saw British, US, and Canadian studies largely reverse the older view, arguing that in many cases the bleak conditions of early industrial capitalism fostered not nuclear, but complex households as a cushioning, adaptive response.[2]

Subsequent studies complicated both the earlier and revisionist accounts. In the past thirty years, as new evidence has become available and studies proliferated, providing a systematic account of the myriad historical and geographical patterns of household composition has become increasingly difficult, as it has in other realms of social historical inquiry, such as studies of migration, social mobility, or fertility.[3] Social history's challenge remains to go beyond the mere documentation of historical variety towards a larger interpretive perspective. The recent development of extensive interregional and international databases of household listings promises both fresh debates and new interpretations.[4]

This chapter presents a new analysis of co-residential households and families for Canada in 1901 and 1911 using the Canadian Century Research Infrastructure (CCRI) national sample of dwellings for 1911 and, for comparative purposes, the Canadian Families Project (CFP) 1901 5 per cent national sample.[5] The two census years bracket a decisive decade in the formation of twentieth-century Canada, given the massive immigration and territorial expansion of that short period. The study employs the wide aperture afforded by these census samples to illuminate the varieties of household experiences across the country, paying particular attention, first, to the implications of the decade's waves of immigration and attendant demographic shifts, and then, focusing on the clear and persistent regional variations. Were immigrants especially prone to sharing residential space? Did longer-resident immigrants adopt the household conventions of the Canadian-born? Were the immigrant/native-born differences largely a consequence of age and gender differentials? We approach the questions considering the implications of family and social networks. Then we turn to the question of how Canada's newly complicated regions varied in the types of household and family experiences. We find substantial, persistent differences in regional household complexity, and undertake a close analysis of the regional variations considering their differences in immigrant settlement, demographic and rural/urban patterns, and labour force distributions. We offer an initial account that draws on the evidence from local studies of the regionally varying character of family networks in Canada.

Canada Transformed

The census samples of 1901 and 1911 bracket a demographically, socially, and politically tumultuous decade. When Wilfrid Laurier proclaimed that "the twentieth century belongs to Canada," despite its rhetorical flare, the claim caught the new spirit of the times.[6] The long international trade recession from the 1870s had largely run its course, bringing in its wake renewed urban-industrial expansion and resource exports. Canadian staples – wheat, timber, and minerals – all found more ready markets in Britain, continental Europe, and in Canada's major trading partner, the United States. The "national policy" of high import tariffs inaugurated some twenty years earlier, along with the completion of transcontinental railways fostered national industrial growth and remarkably rapid settlement of the Canadian West.[7] The historical tides that had so often swept individuals and families south across the US border slowed and then turned by the closing of the American frontier after 1890 and in response to the bold national immigration policy after 1896 aimed at fostering both western Canadian prairie settlement and new supplies of urban industrial labour. The first decade of the twentieth century was the first decade of positive net migration in Canada since at least the 1860s.[8]

As a political project, the immigration policies were spectacularly successful. In barely fifteen years, 1896 to 1911, over two million immigrants joined a population in 1891 of just 5 million in British North America. As a point of comparison, Franca Iacovetta recently emphasized the huge scale of the post–Second World War influx of newcomers to Canada, an almost identical 2.1 million new arrivals in an equivalent sixteen years between 1946 and 1962.[9] But, transforming as this immigration was to be, the postwar newcomers joined a population that in 1941 was over twice as large as the receiving society in 1911. The earlier tide fully doubled the proportions of the foreign-born in Canada from approximately one in ten persons in 1901 to one in every five in 1911. By 1905, the west had expanded in both population and economic strength to such an extent that two new provinces, Alberta and Saskatchewan, were carved out of the Northwest Territories. The forty years from about the time of Confederation to the outbreak of the First World War represented the culmination for Canada of a first wave of "globalization," and in its wake radiating social transformations, including new adaptations of families and households.[10] For the first time, we explore in detail the character of these adaptations.

Households at the Dawn of Canada's Twentieth Century

National comparative studies of household formation and experience remain scarce, despite a large and growing literature on the history of the family.[11] The first studies based on national evidence suggest that the Canadian patterns largely paralleled those found for the United States, as first systematically set out by Steven Ruggles.[12] Census households included parents and their children, if any, plus other co-residing relatives, as well as boarders or lodgers or live-in domestic employees who were part of the "housekeeping community."[13] For comparative analysis, we examine a similarly defined portion of the census samples, the households in dwellings with thirty or fewer residents, as discussed in the introduction to this volume. This represents about 98 per cent of the population in 1901 and 97 per cent in 1911.

Figures 7.1a and 7.1b and table 7.1 offer a national portrait of the distribution of the household situations experienced by Canadians in 1901 and 1911, displaying the differences between the native-born and foreign-born populations.

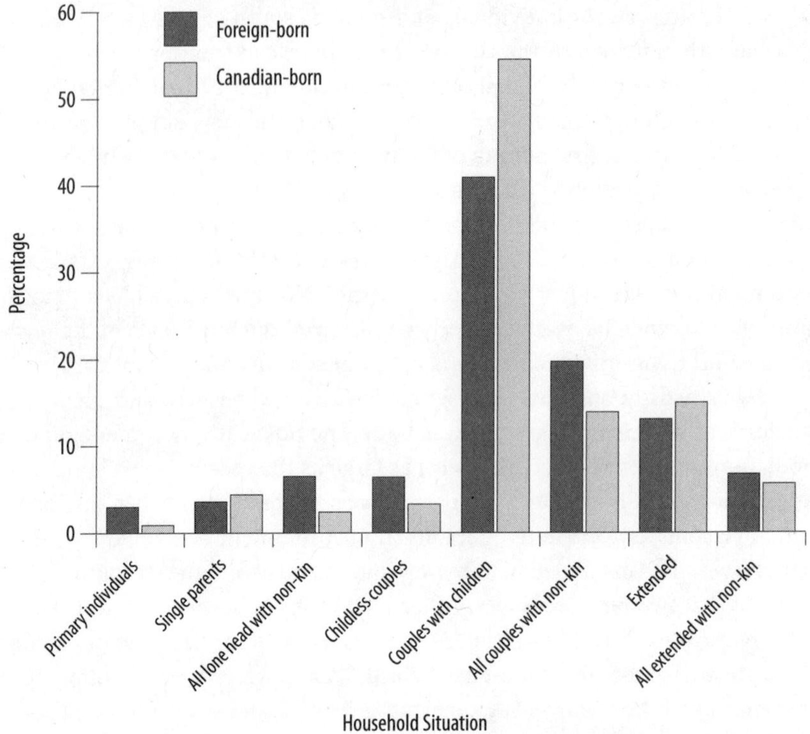

Figure 7.1a · Distribution of the population by nativity (Canada or elsewhere) and household situation, Canada, 1901.

Source: Canadian Families Project database, CFP 1901 (http://web.uvic.ca/hrd/CFP/data/index.html).

The table presents the distribution of *individuals* in terms of the types of households in which they lived, not a distribution or typology of households taken as units, although these are related measures. We focus on individual experiences in order to assess the effects on household membership of demographic and social conditions and constraints such as age, gender, or location in the labour force.[14]

We examine household situations in terms of eight categories, distinguishing three main ones: those headed by single persons including single parents (lone-headed households), those headed by married (intact) couples, and households extended to include other kin, parents, siblings, nieces and nephews, aunts and uncles, and so on. The classification follows the one first proposed by Ruggles and revised by Kenneth Sylvester, in his analysis of Canada in 1901.[15] Our two

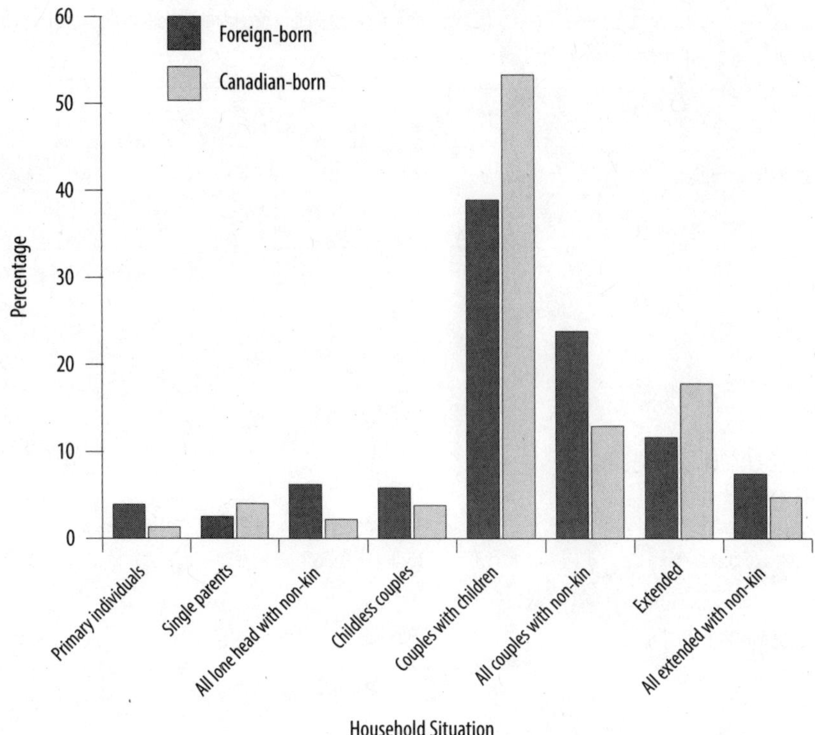

Figure 7.1b · Distribution of the population by nativity (Canada or elsewhere) and household situation, Canada, 1911.

Source: CCRI 1911 microdata database.

census sample snapshots freeze momentarily the social processes of household formation, reproduction, and dissolution, but provide a unique opportunity to interpret key implications of this transformative decade for family and individual lives.

Four main features of the distributions in table 7.1 are of interest. First, as Ruggles reported for the United States in about the same period, just about half the population resided in nuclear households, and the proportion appears to have declined very slightly over the decade. Small proportions were childless couples residing alone (3% or 4%).[16] The slightly reduced proportions in nuclear households hint at a longer-term decline that Ruggles documents between 1880 and 1980 in the United States. We know that by the 1980s and 1990s, in both Canada and the United States, the proportions of nuclear family

Table 7.1 · Actual and age-standardized (Stdiz) distribution of population according to household situation and whether foreign-born or born in Canada, 1901 and 1911

Household composition	1901 Census (%)				1911 Census (%)			
	Foreign-born		Native-born	Total	Foreign-born		Native-born	Total
	Actual	Stdiz			Actual	Stdiz		
LONE-HEAD HOUSEHOLDS								
Primary individuals	3.0	2.6	0.9	1.1	3.9	3.0	1.3	1.9
Single parents	3.6	3.0	4.4	4.3	2.5	2.5	4.0	3.6
All lone-head with non-kin	6.5	5.5	2.4	2.9	6.2	5.1	2.2	3.1
Total	*13.1*	*11.1*	*7.7*	*8.3*	*12.6*	*10.6*	*7.5*	*8.6*
MARRIED-COUPLE HOUSEHOLDS								
Childless couples	6.4	4.0	3.3	3.7	5.8	4.5	3.8	4.2
Couples with children	40.9	48.5	54.5	52.9	38.9	44.7	53.3	50.1
All married couples with non-kin	19.7	19.8	13.9	14.6	23.8	22.2	12.9	15.3
Total	*67.0*	*72.3*	*71.7*	*71.2*	*68.5*	*71.4*	*70.0*	*69.6*
EXTENDED HOUSEHOLDS								
Extended	13.1	11.5	15.0	14.8	11.6	11.4	17.8	16.4
All extended with non-kin	6.7	5.5	5.6	5.7	7.4	6.8	4.7	5.3
Total	*19.8*	*17.0*	*20.6*	*20.5*	*19.0*	*18.2*	*22.5*	*21.7*
N	31,952	31,470	228,482	260,434	77,023	75,718	271,766	348,789

Sources: Canadian Families Project database, CFP 1901, http://web.uvic.ca/hrd/CFP/data/index.html; CCRI 1911 microdata database.

Note: Includes all individuals residing in dwellings housing 30 or fewer people; this represents 98% of the 1901 sample and 94% of the 1911 sample. Larger dwellings, mainly institutions, group quarters, and work camps, are excluded. The age-standardized proportions are based on fewer records than the actuals due to illegible and missing age enumerations. Percentages do not always total 100 because of rounding.

households had fallen to around 35 per cent.[17] A more definitive account of the historical trends awaits analysis of the 1921 to 1951 CCRI census samples and later data.

Second, just less than a quarter of the population in both 1901 and 1911 shared their households with non-kin, mainly boarders and lodgers, continuing a well-known nineteenth-century practice. Among these, about 15 per cent resided in households headed by couples, 5 per cent or 6 per cent lived in households with both kin and non-kin, and 3 per cent in lone-headed households with only other unrelated persons. Third, throughout the decade, less than one person in ten resided in a "lone-headed household" (about 8%). As we shall see, these proportions varied quite widely by region. Fourth, living in kin-extended households was also a common experience even in cross-sectional snapshots of the first decade of the twentieth century, including about one in five individuals. Like in the United States, this proportion appears to have increased slightly over this decade.

Although interesting in their own right, national patterns mask very substantial differences between immigrants and the people born in Canada. Figures 7.1a and 7.1b and table 7.1 indicate that immigrants were distinctly more likely to be primary individuals, to be childless couples, and to share residential space with non-family members, and consequently, they were a good deal less likely to reside in nuclear family households. In 1901, the latter difference was between the 41 per cent of immigrants and 55 per cent of the Canadian-born, and in 1911, 39 per cent versus 53 per cent. Yet, we also observe that with virtually the same proportions, in 1901, immigrants (at 19.8%) had only slightly less tendency to reside in extended households than did the native-born (at 20.6%), with but a 3 per cent difference in 1911 (immigrants, 19.0% vs. native-born, 22.5%). The parallel requires some interpretation. Immigrants, surely, had fewer kin available than the native-born with whom to share a residence and less dense kin networks among those who were in Canada, but obviously, many immigrants had not come alone. Not only had they commonly arrived as families or were soon joined by them, as we know from a large literature, but also these data show that they immigrated within kin networks sufficiently intact to invent or to reinvent complex, presumably mutually aiding households on new soil.

Demographic conditions establish constraints and circumstances within which family histories are enacted, so some of the nativity differences in household experiences likely arose directly from the differences in demographic profiles. We first consider age differentials represented by the population pyramids given in figure 7.2.[18] The contrasts are expected, but are stark, nonetheless.

The median age of those who were born in Canada was just 20 years, in both 1901 and 1911; but the median age of the foreign-born was 38 years in 1901, declining with the influx of new immigrants to 29 years, in 1911. Figure 7.2 reveals the extent to which the foreign-born were a distinctly aged population. In 1901, fewer than one in five immigrants were under age 20 and just 7 per cent (6.6%) under age 10, while nearly half were over age 40, and over a third were over age 50. By contrast, the Canadian-born communities in the early twentieth century were awash with children and youth: in 1901, nearly half were under age 20 (48.9%) and a quarter under age 10, with barely a fifth over age 40 and 12 per cent over age 50. A decade later, while the Canadian-born distributions

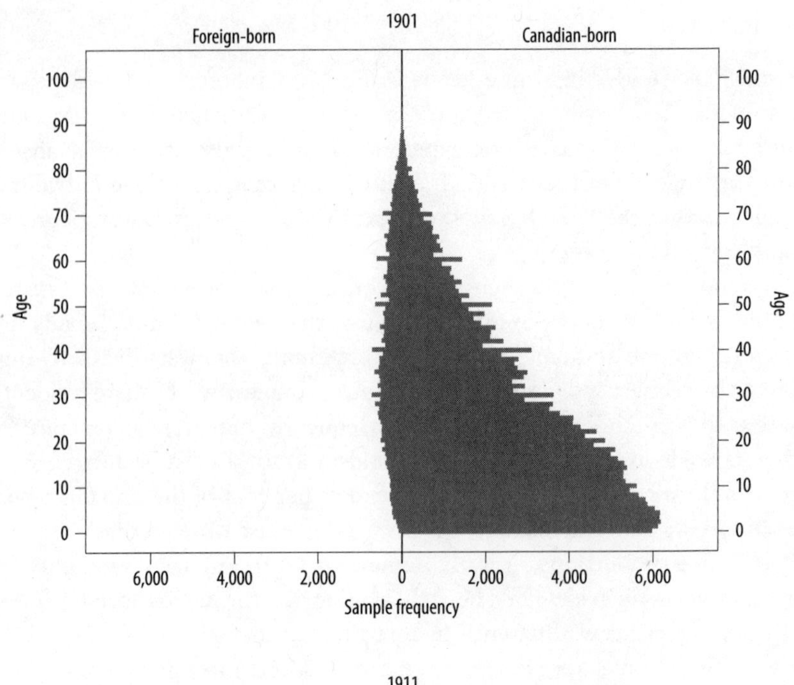

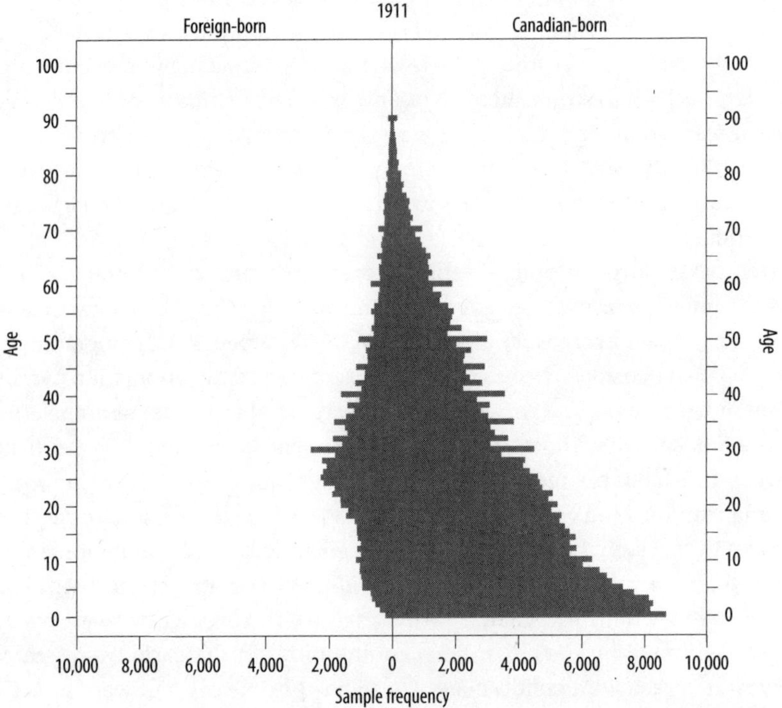

Figure 7.2 · Age-nativity pyramids, Canada, 1901 and 1911.

Sources: Canadian Families Project database, CFP 1901 (http://web.uvic.ca/hrd/CFP/data/index.html); CCRI 1911 microdata database.

remained more or less unchanged, the mass of immigrant newcomers had boosted the proportions of youth and children among all foreign-born to about a quarter under age 20 and reduced those over age 50 by about half (to 16%).

We incorporate these differences in age distributions more systematically in a first analysis of the effects of age on the patterns of household experiences. Table 7.1 provides age-standardized proportions in each household category for the foreign-born populations (columns 2 and 6). The standardized rates assess how much of the differences in household composition between immigrants and those who were born in Canada can be accounted for by the sharp differences in their age distributions alone. The hypothetical, age-standardized distributions are those that would have been the case if the foreign-born had shared the age distribution of the overall population.[19]

A comparison of the standardized and actual distributions reveals a mainly consistent pattern for both 1901 and 1911. The much older immigrant populations tended to depress the numbers of nuclear family households and raise the proportions of people who were in lone-headed households, living as childless couples, and residing in extended households. The first two of the non-nuclear household situations were mainly populated by people in their prime years, with extended households swollen mainly by the aged.

Historically, immigrant populations in Canada have been dominated by males. Such gender differentials between immigrant and native-born populations might be expected to influence household distributions. For the 1901 sample, the overall sex ratio, or the number of males per 100 females, was 104.7, and for the 1911 sample, it was 111.8 (these correspond closely to the ratios reported in the published volumes of the censuses). But, among immigrants in 1901, men outnumbered women by 1.3 to 1 (sex ratio of 129.7), and that ratio rose in 1911 to a remarkable 149.9. Observing a sex ratio this imbalanced is historically relatively rare. By contrast, the sex ratios for those who were born in Canada just barely favoured males (101.7 in 1901 and 103.1 in 1911). However, employing a similar standardization procedure to that for age, rather unexpectedly, indicates that the gender imbalances were much less influential than age in affecting nativity differences in the composition of households.[20]

Household Formation and the Timing of Immigration

Canada's rising fortunes at the opening of the twentieth century were fuelled by successively larger waves of immigrants after 1896, as international economic circumstances fortuitously favoured the country's reputation as a destination of choice. Most historical writing provides us with stories about the state immigration policies and their political and economic consequences. Here we ask about implications for the immigrant's everyday household and family experiences.

In both census years, enumerators were instructed to record year of immigration for the foreign-born.[21] Although more incomplete than some other census data, the questions still captured periods of immigration for a large majority. Nearly 60 per cent of immigrants in 1901 had arrived in the previous twenty years, and 35 per cent in the previous decade. But, if this population was dominated by relative newcomers, the new waves of immigrants in the first decade of the twentieth century completely swamped it. By 1911, fully seven in ten immigrants had arrived since the previous census, leaving only about one in ten arriving between 1891 and 1900 and fewer than one in five as earlier arrivals. How did this tsunami of immigrants affect the kinds of households in which they lived?

We can consider the distributions of household situations by decadal periods of immigration, in both 1901 and 1911, with those arriving prior to 1860 as the earliest group (data not displayed).

In overview, the patterns are strikingly similar in each year, despite the differences in the size of the immigrant populations and in how recently they had arrived in Canada. The combination of age and period of immigration strongly influenced household patterns. The passage of time clearly fostered the formation of nuclear families: fewer of the most recent immigrants by decade lived in nuclear households than those arriving in the prior three decades, although the age of earlier immigrants depressed the proportions. Those who had been in Canada for between ten and twenty years prior to each census were most likely to have formed couple-headed households with children (46% in 1901 and 44% in 1911).[22] The other side of this coin is that both in 1901 and in 1911 fewer than one in ten of the most recent immigrants resided in extended households, with steplike larger proportions of each prior decadal cohort of arrivals in such residences. In 1901, the proportion residing in extended households was 16 per cent among those arriving thirty to forty years previously, and nearly a quarter (23%) among the earliest, pre-1860 immigrants. In 1911, these proportions had risen to over a fifth of those arriving between forty and fifty years earlier (1861–70) and to nearly a third of the earliest surviving arrivals.

What about residence in households augmented by friends, former neighbours, or new acquaintances? Considering all three types of augmented households in our categories, we find that more than one in four among the recent arrivals shared their residential space with or as boarders, lodgers, or employees; of these, more than half lived in the augmented nuclear households. If shared space among immigrating families and non-kin was commonplace, it quickly declined. Household extension, however, increased systematically with time in Canada. Both period of immigration and age played a role on these patterns, and we will attempt shortly to disentangle their relative influences.

These patterns were not solely the consequence of shifting age and gender distributions. The association between the timing of immigration and variations in household experiences offer further hints about the kinds of social networks in which these households were embedded, although censuses, like other nominative historical sources, rarely provide direct knowledge about these connections, with some important exceptions.[23] Our observed patterns provide grounds for some inferences. For every individual, the censuses of 1901 and 1911 record the "relationship to the head" of each household. Examining these relationships in detail reveals a clear life-cycle pattern in which recent immigrants tended first to be lodgers themselves, then increasingly, with time, householders accommodating other more recent immigrants. Moreover, the evidence implies that even the most recent arrivals seldom were isolated sojourners, but were in some way connected to former neighbours, villagers, acquaintances, or friends of friends. A large migration literature documents how chain migration nourished family networks and networks of acquaintances through time and over regional, national, and international borders.[24] Such social webs also suggest the historical importance of the "strength of weak ties." Weakly tied, low-density social networks are more likely than concentrated, intimate ones to link a multiplicity of social groups, providing a wider range of sources of social and cultural information and basis of social integration.[25] Exactly such links would have assisted recent immigrants to find shelter and companionship as boarders and lodgers in others' homes. Peter Baskerville has neatly dubbed the latter as "familiar strangers," sharing religious and ethnic heritages, but not identifiable kinship with their hosts.[26] The households of longer-term immigrants paralleled the native-born in disproportionately housing extended family members. Moreover, our census data show that the extended members of households were commonly in late middle age or the aged: sharing residences with kin was often a means of housing the aging and aged by drawing on the more densely woven family networks among the native-born and immigrants who had been in Canada a longer time.

Demographic Models of Household Experience

Relatively straightforward multivariate models allow us to pose directly the question of the relative effects of age, gender, nativity, and period of immigration on household situations. We construct two initial models for 1901 and 1911. The first model considers the influence of age, gender, and nativity. The second model applies only to the foreign-born, including their period of immigration.

We treat household situations as the dependent variable. Since the variable is categorical and has more than two categories, an appropriate procedure is multinomial logistic regression. Using the eight categories of table 7.1 makes the interpretation quite complicated, since we must select one category as a reference group with the incidence of the other categories interpreted *relative* to it. It serves our purposes to consider only the three main household categories, that is, all lone-headed households, all couple-headed ones, and all extended households. Each independent variable in the model also has one reference category; in the first model, the reference categories are females, those age 70 and over, and the Canadian-born. In the second model, immigrants arriving prior to 1860 is the reference category. The results of the models are presented in table 7.2.

The coefficients in the table are relative odds ratios, that is, the odds are estimated for the likelihood of residing in either lone-headed or extended households and assessed relative to the odds of residence in a couple-headed household.[27] For example, for 1901 the coefficient (ExpB) given for gender differences in the odds of residing in lone-headed households is 1.086, meaning that males were about 8 or 9 per cent more likely than females to reside in such households, relative to the chances of residing in couple-headed households. A coefficient of exactly 1.0 implies no difference between the selected reference category and the one of interest. A coefficient greater than one indicates a greater relative likelihood; a coefficient of less than one, less relative likelihood compared with the reference category. In the following, when we refer to the relative odds, we mean relative to the chances of living in a couple-headed household.

The first models confirm that one's gender was a slight, although not a trivial condition of one's household experiences. In both years, 1901 and 1911, males were relatively more likely than females to be located in lone-headed households, and they were substantially more likely to do so in 1911 (some 38% more likely), no doubt due to the male preponderance among the most recent immigrants. In contrast, in both census years, males were less likely to reside in extended households independently of the age and nativity differentials. The difference was somewhat greater at the turn of the century than in 1911 (coefficients of 0.878 and 0.925, respectively).

The age effects are given in terms of ten-year categories for ease of interpretation. The effects are orderly and interesting. In both 1901 and 1911, the elderly were split between those who lived alone, or lived with non-kin only, or were older single parents (i.e., in lone-headed households) and those living in extended households, the majority of whom, our detailed data indicate, resided in households headed by their married children. The likelihood of residence in

Table 7.2 · Contribution of gender, age (in years), nativity (Canadian- or foreign-born), and year of immigration to the likelihood of residing in a lone-headed or extended household, relative to a couple-headed household, Canada, 1901 and 1911

Variable	*1901*				*1911*			
	Lone head		*Extended*		*Lone head*		*Extended*	
	Sample	*Foreign-born*	*Sample*	*Foreign-born*	*Sample*	*Foreign-born*	*Sample*	*Foreign-born*
	Exp(B)	*Exp(B)*	*Exp(B)*	*Exp(B)*	*Exp(B)*	*Exp(B)*	*Exp(B)*	*Exp(B)*
GENDER								
Female (Ref)								
Male	1.086 ***	1.401***	0.878***	0.747***	1.375***	2.315***	0.925***	0.977
AGE (years)								
5–9	0.105***	0.051***	0.162***	0.266***	0.091***	0.085***	0.144***	0.167***
10–19	0.328***	0.191***	0.187***	0.322***	0.270***	0.219***	0.160***	0.227***
20–29	0.541***	0.458***	0.270***	0.388***	0.495***	0.541***	0.229***	0.302***
30–39	0.392***	0.398***	0.257***	0.287***	0.343***	0.369***	0.206***	0.227***
40–49	0.348***	0.375***	0.224***	0.250***	0.328***	0.328***	0.195***	0.195***
50–59	0.436***	0.395***	0.268***	0.299***	0.382***	0.374***	0.233***	0.266***
60–69	0.644***	0.586***	0.471***	0.484***	0.578***	0.554***	0.386***	0.444***
≥ 70 (Ref)								
NATIVITY								
Canadian-born (Ref)								
Foreign-born	1.329***		0.775***		1.295***		0.761***	
YEAR OF IMMIGRATION								
1901–11						0.863		0.670***
1891–1900[a]		1.500***		0.603***		0.781**		0.633***
1881–90		0.910		0.660***		0.689***		0.774***
1871–80		0.895		0.753***		0.735***		0.725***
1861–70		0.913		0.893		0.794*		0.773***
1800–60 (Ref)								
N	259,446	28,481	259,446	28,481	345,346	67,650	345,346	67,650

Sources: CFP 1901 and CCRI 1911 microdata databases.

a This category for 1901 is 1891–1901; for 1911, it is 1891–1900.

Ref = reference category.

* $p < .05$; ** $p < .01$; *** $p < .001$.

either lone-headed or in extended households was lower at each age from 69 to 40, and lower still for adolescents and children under age 19 years, because both individuals in their prime years and youngsters and children are more likely to live in couple-headed households, as parents and children. For those aged 20 to 39, the relative chance of residence in either the simpler or more complex households was greater, although still lower than for those over age 60. So, we see the very different social dynamics that populated both the lone-headed and extended households. The first tended to house both older single parents and the isolated elderly and never-married young men and women who had struck out on their own to seek new livelihoods and new adventures. The second tended to house older men and women, often with their married children as the primary family, and young, never-married men and women, who had taken up residence with relatives in moving out of their natal family nests.

Finally, this analysis shows that age and gender differences between immigrants and those who were born in Canada were not sufficient to account for much of their dissimilar household situations. The coefficients for 1901 and 1911 (1.329 and 1.295 respectively) indicate that, independently of these demographic circumstances, immigrants were something like a third more likely to reside in the simpler, lone-headed households than were the native-born (relative to the odds of residing in couple-headed households) and about a quarter less likely to reside in the more complex, extended households (0.775 in 1901 and 0.761 in 1911). The similarity of the demographic patterns between the two censuses is also notable because it means that for the wave of newcomers arriving after 1901 simply being immigrant was not as salient as the other social, economic, and cultural factors that conditioned household formation and reproduction.

We noted above that the time of arrival and age were at least partially confounded in their effects on immigrants' household residence patterns. In the second models in table 7.2, for immigrants alone, we separate the effects statistically. Although these models are modestly complex, the key results can be readily summarized. For 1901 (column 3), unlike the slight gender differences in the population as a whole, male immigrants are relatively some 40 per cent more likely than female immigrants to reside in lone-headed households. Otherwise, the age differences among immigrants closely parallel those of the overall population. As for period of immigration, we find only one historically interesting effect in 1901 independently of gender and age: the most recent immigrants were relatively about 50 per cent more than any earlier immigrants to reside alone, without family, or as single parents. The result lends itself, again, to an interpretation in terms of the rapid expansion and deepening of familial and social networks for all but those most recently setting foot on Canadian soil.

With respect to extended household in 1901 (column 5), the effects of age and gender among immigrants largely parallel those for the population overall. Examining more closely the mix of age groups among those living in extended households (not shown), we find that the immigrant population differed notably from the native-born. Over a third of the immigrant residents in extended households were aged 60 or older, and fully a fifth were 70 and older, with only some 15 per cent under age 21. Moreover, it is striking that these older immigrants were disproportionately women. Among those born in Canada, only 11 per cent were aged 60 and older (5% 70 or older), and 40 per cent were aged 20 or younger. Household extension was a common strategy among both native-born and immigrants in turn of the century Canada, but these strategies entailed very different extended household experiences. Given the disproportionately large numbers of children and youth among the Canadian-born, extension often included them, whether residing with kin as apprentices or perhaps to attend school or simply as household help. Among immigrants, by contrast, household extension tended to house mature adults and the elderly.[28]

For immigrants, the timing of arrival mattered. Independently of gender and age, the more recent one's arrival prior to 1901 the less likely it was that one would share a residence with kin (or with kin and non-kin): each more recently arrived cohort was significantly less likely to have taken up extended household residence compared with the chances of residing in couple-headed households. The pattern is also reflected in the simple proportions of people residing in extended households, which were 32 per cent among those immigrating in 1860 or earlier, falling decade by decade of the timing of entry to 23 per cent (1861–70), 18 per cent (1871–80), 17 per cent (1881–90), and 14 per cent among those who arrived in the ten years before the taking of the 1901 census. Once again, we infer the historical significance of the widening over time in Canada of the social and familial networks in which households were embedded.

What change in these household dynamics followed the massive influx of immigrants between 1901 and 1911? The models for 1911 indicate that lone-headed households had become much more likely among males than females as a result of the swollen population of immigrants. Among immigrants, males had become more than two times as likely as females to reside alone, as a single parent, or unrelated person (coefficient, 2.315, relative to couple-headed ones). In contrast, the dramatic changes in population and its redistribution across the newly expanded country in 1911 more or less equalized the chances of men and women residing in extended households (coefficient, 0.977).

The analysis also reveals the quite different effects of period of immigration on lone-headed residence in 1911 from a decade earlier. On the one hand, the differences in the likelihood of lone-headed residence had become more pronounced, with immigrants arriving both earliest and most recently being most likely in lone-headed households, although not surprisingly, for quite different reasons. Digging further into the data, we find that the most recent immigrants in lone-headed households were largely in their prime working years, aged 20 to 40, while the earliest arrivals were almost exclusively over age 60. On the other hand, the relative chances that immigrants would reside in extended households more or less mirrored the period of immigration patterns of a decade earlier, the odds becoming distinctly less likely the more recent the arrival prior to 1911.

These changed patterns surely reflect the effects of the sheer numbers of new immigrants arriving in the first decade of the twentieth century, which not only shifted the context of household formation among the most recently arrived but also, and more broadly, provided wider opportunities for the formation of family-centred households within immigrant communities.[29] Moreover, these altered cultural and social conditions increased the relative chances that more recent immigrants would have the opportunity to share households with kin by comparison with 1901.[30]

Demographic regimes intersect with changing local and regional economies and shifting cultural formations in framing household strategies and experiences. The Canadian censuses of 1901 and 1911 provide an unusual array of data on which such analysis can be grounded.

Regional Household Formations

The regional character of Canada was recast during the first decade of the twentieth century. What changes in household experiences accompanied the transformation? Figures 7.3 and 7.4 map the variations in the household situations for five regions in 1901 and 1911.[31] For current purposes, we define the five regions as three provinces (BC, Ontario, and Quebec) and two aggregated areas (the Prairies and the Maritimes).[32] The patterns for rural and urban areas of each region are also displayed, with urban areas minimally defined for comparative purposes as all incorporated places with a population over 1,000. In 1901, this included about 35 per cent of the national population, increasing to 41 per cent by 1911.[33] As appendix to this chapter, table 7.A provides the detailed household distributions for the regions and rural and urban areas.

Couple-headed households dominated in every region, of course, but close examination reveals four distinctive regional patterns. First, nuclearity was

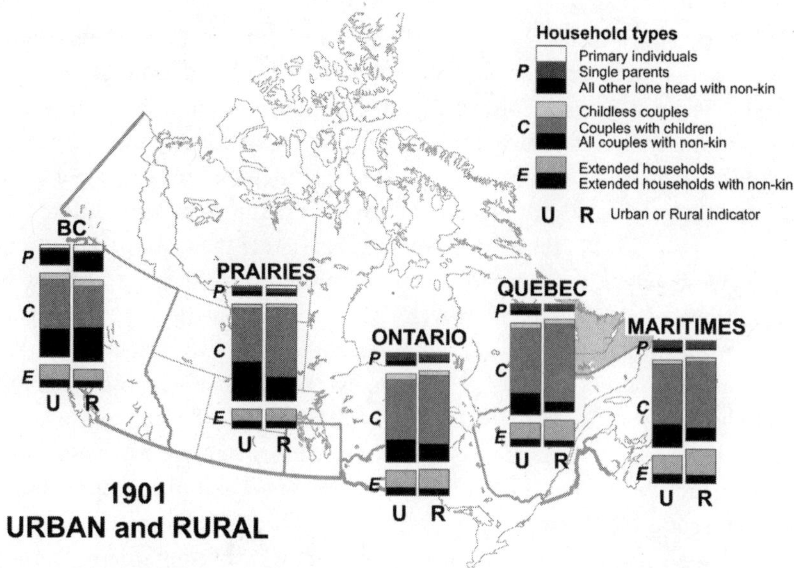

Figure 7.3 · Urban/rural distribution of household types: British Columbia, Prairies, Ontario, Quebec, Maritimes, 1901.

Sources: Canadian Families Project database, CFP 1901 (http://web.uvic.ca/hrd/CFP/data/index.html).

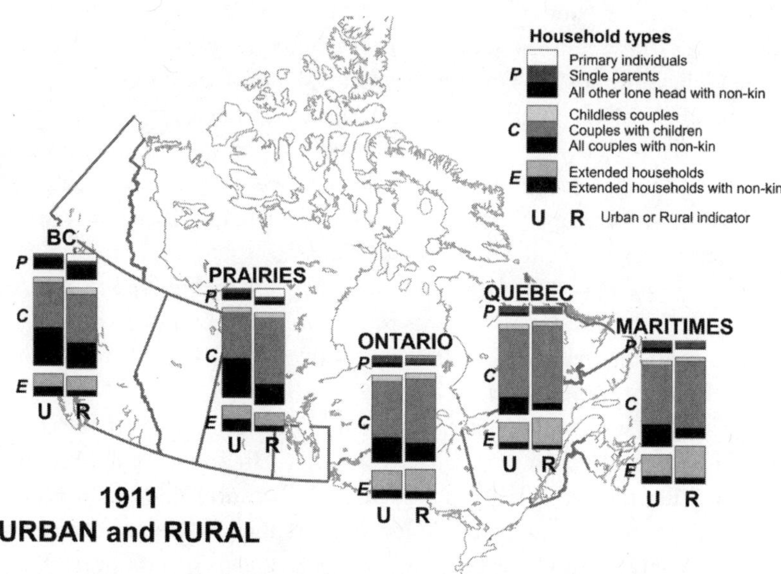

Figure 7.4 · Urban/rural distribution of household types: British Columbia, Prairies, Ontario, Quebec, Maritimes, 1911.

Source: CCRI geographical database.

a hallmark of life in Quebec: only there did over half of all urban residents and over six in ten rural residents live in nuclear family households across the decade. Second, British Columbia and the Prairies were marked by couple-headed households in which especially high proportions of individuals were boarders, lodgers, or employees; in both, this included 20 to 30 per cent of all regional residents, although their urban and rural patterns differed with smaller proportions in the prairie countryside (fewer than two persons in ten). On the west coast, this household augmentation resulted largely from the high proportions of single and often transient workers; on the Prairies, a partial explanation probably lies in the large numbers of hired, resident farm help. As John Herd Thompson has argued, many men (and some women) boarded and lodged in prairie cities while seeking to accumulate the wage-based capital needed to enter the promised land of western farm prosperity.[34] We will attempt to unravel further the relationship between household composition and regional economies below.

Third, we witness two strong west to east geographical gradients.[35] On the one hand, in each year, the further west one lived the greater the likelihood one would reside in lone-headed households and primarily with other unrelated persons, as shown by the bands labelled P in the figures (although the gradient is slightly variable for rural and urban areas; for exact proportions, see table 7.A). On the other hand, the further east one lived, the greater the chance of residing in extended households. Rural residents in British Columbia had by far the highest proportions of lone-headed residents (about one in five), again reflecting the region's unique fishing, mining, and lumbering frontiers to which many single men (as well as some widowed and married men without their families) had migrated since the late nineteenth century. In rural Quebec and the Maritimes, the proportions of people in lone-headed households were just 6 per cent and 7 per cent respectively, in both census years. In contrast, the chances of residing with kin were lowest in the west, and tended to rise as one moved east with Maritimes residents by far the most likely to be residing with kin. In the rural Maritimes, a quite remarkable nearly one in three residents lived with one or more relatives.

Fourth, these west to east patterns were more muted among urban residents, although the rural/urban differences are modest (see table 7.A). Apparently, living in cities, towns, or villages tended to homogenize household experiences, even in small places. Notably, living in households with boarders and lodgers appears only slightly more common in urban areas. This is not a difference that corresponds with conventional historical views in which boarding and lodging are often considered to be mainly urban experiences.[36]

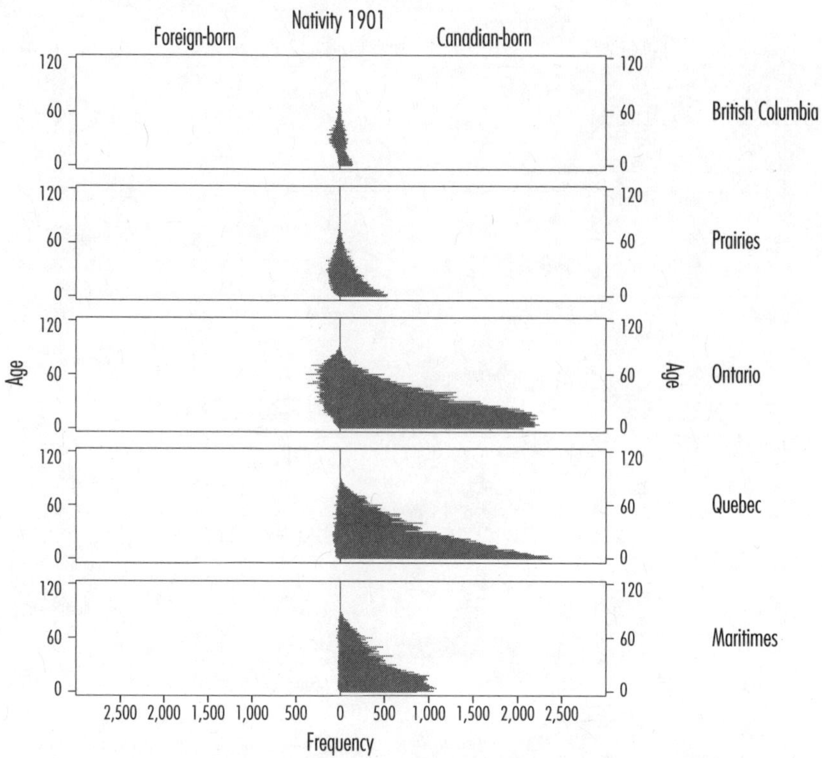

Figure 7.5 · Age-nativity pyramids: British Columbia, Prairies, Ontario, Quebec, Maritimes, 1901.
Source: Canadian Families Project database, CFP 1901 (http://web.uvic.ca/hrd/CFP/data/index.html).

How might we account for the regional patterns? Can they be largely explained with reference to the differences in the regional immigration and settlement patterns, and accompanying demographic variations? Figures 7.5 and 7.6 show the key regional differences in nativity and age in the form of population pyramids. The scale of these figures prevents detailed scrutiny, but the purpose of the comparisons is to highlight the wide regional variations.

Figures 7.5 and 7.6 underscore the widely varying regional concentrations of the Canadian population. Comparing them for 1901 and 1911 highlights the striking demographic changes wrought by the influx of immigrants in the decade. Ontario and Quebec held 41 per cent and 31 per cent respectively of the national population in 1901, but only 35 per cent and 28 per cent respectively in 1911, with the bulk of the change explained by the relative growth of the Prairies

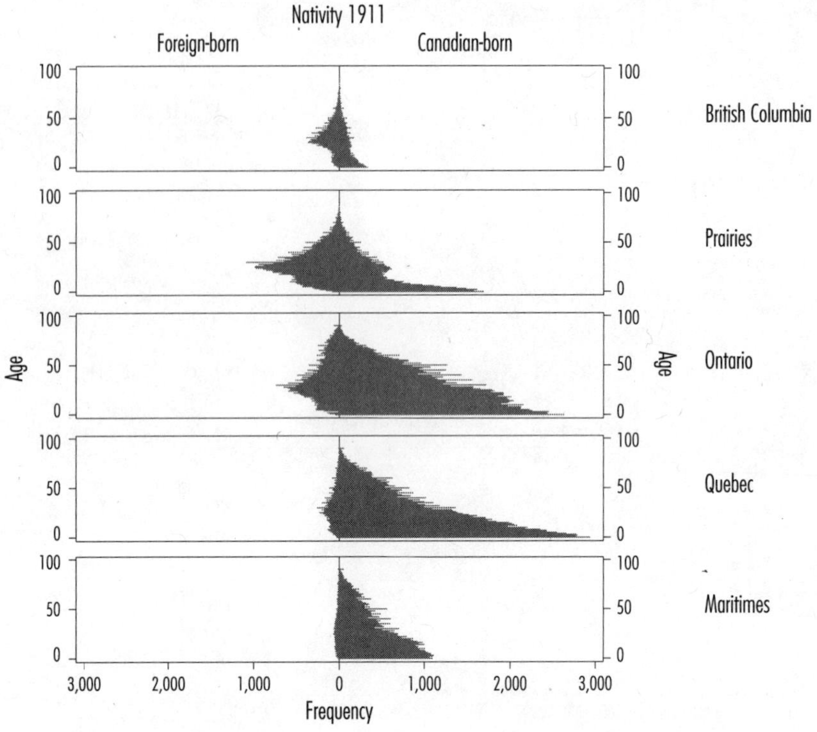

Figure 7.6 · Age-nativity pyramids: British Columbia, Prairies, Ontario, Quebec, Maritimes, 1911.
Source: CCRI 1911 microdata database.

and British Columbia. The Prairies, growing from about 8 per cent to over 18 per cent of the national population, overtook the Maritimes as the third largest of the regions in 1911, while BC's share grew from 3 per cent to 5 per cent. The contrast between the right and left sides of the pyramids in the figures puts into relief the steep west to east pattern of reduced immigrant presence becoming steeper in 1911. On the BC coast, nearly half (46%) of the population declared immigrant origins in 1901, but well over half did so in 1911 (56%). About a third of the Prairies population was immigrant in 1901, but this proportion had risen to half by 1911. Ontario held the middle ground, with 15 per cent immigrants in 1901 and one person in five being foreign-born by 1911. In Quebec and the Maritimes, immigrants remained but a minor presence throughout the decade, barely appearing on the left-hand side of the pyramids – 5 per cent in Quebec in 1901 rising to 8 per cent in 1911, and just 4 per cent and 6 per cent respectively in the Maritimes.

Finally, and most relevant to our household analysis, the pyramids in figure 7.5 and figure 7.6 reveal the marked variations in regional age distributions and especially the shifting age distributions of the immigrant populations. Although all the regional immigrant populations remained substantially older, on average, than the native-born, the older immigrant populations of 1901 were replaced by large numbers of new arrivals who were in their 20s and 30s. The oldest overall populations were in British Columbia and Ontario, with median ages of 27 years for British Columbia in both years and for Ontario of 24 years (1901) and 25 years (1911). The youngest regional populations were in the Prairies and Quebec, with median ages of 20 in 1901 and in 1911 of 23 (Prairies) and 20 (Quebec). The Maritimes were just slightly older, at 22 years in both censuses. Although regional differences in marriage and marital fertility may have been factors, these differing distributions mainly reflect the disparate regional balance of immigrant and native-born populations, and the varying regional rates of interregional migration, as evidenced by the long right-hand tail of the Prairies age pyramid among the native-born in 1911.[37]

We can extend our earlier multivariate analysis in order to address the implications for household experiences of these regional differences (we add their rural/urban variations).[38] Table 7.3 presents the relevant multinomial logistic regression.

The results of this exercise are readily summarized, if not readily explained: in neither 1901 nor 1911 did the effects of gender, age, and nativity much reduce the importance of region or of rural/urban residence in influencing the patterns of household experiences across Canada. The differences are strong and quite specific.

Comparing the models of table 7.3 with those for the full samples of table 7.2 indicates that gender and age remained important conditions of variations in household experiences. But, the enlarged models also indicate that the variations between immigrants and people who were born in Canada were significantly diminished taking into account the rural/urban and regional locations: in this enlarged analysis, whether one was native or foreign-born was of little if any consequence for the chances of residing in a lone-headed household, although immigrants were still some 15 per cent less likely to have resided in extended households than the native-born in both census years.

What were the main regional and rural/urban variations in household situations? Again, we find that rural/urban differences did not fully conform to conventional historical images. Although, in 1901, urban residents across Canada were over 25 per cent more likely than rural residents to live independently, relative to couple-headed residence, this urban propensity disappeared by 1911 once age, gender, and region of residence are considered. Moreover, we find

Table 7.3 · Contribution of gender, age (in years), nativity (Canadian- or foreign-born), urban/rural location, and region to the likelihood of residing in a lone-headed or extended household, relative to a couple-headed household, Canada, 1901 and 1911

	1901		*1911*	
Variable	*Lone head Exp(B)*	*Extended Exp(B)*	*Lone head Exp(B)*	*Extended Exp(B)*
GENDER				
Female (Ref)				
Male	1.054 ***	0.877 ***	1.338 ***	0.928 ***
AGE (years)				
0–9	0.094 ***	0.172 ***	0.080 ***	0.155 ***
10–19	0.297 ***	0.197 ***	0.248 ***	0.170 ***
20–29	0.470 ***	0.287 ***	0.445 ***	0.245 ***
30–39	0.330 ***	0.274 ***	0.306 ***	0.221 **
40–49	0.302 ***	0.236 ***	0.294 ***	0.206 ***
50–59	0.404 ***	0.279 ***	0.354 ***	0.244 ***
60–69	0.616 ***	0.480 ***	0.553 ***	0.396 ***
70 up (Ref)				
NATIVITY				
Canadian-born (Ref)				
Foreign-born	1.056	0.852 ***	1.039	0.867 ***
URBAN-RURAL LOCATION				
Rural (Ref)				
Urban	1.266 ***	0.928 **	1.015	0.946 **
REGION				
BC	2.242 ***	0.697 ***	1.977 ***	0.667 ***
Prairies	0.979	0.575 ***	1.396 ***	0.619 ***
Ontario	1.003	0.752 ***	0.990	0.788 ***
Quebec	0.836 ***	0.750 ***	0.888 **	0.817 ***
Maritimes (Ref)				
N	258,311		344,398	

Sources: CFP 1901 and CCRI 1911 microdata databases.

Ref = reference category.

* $p < .05$; ** $p < .01$; *** $p < .001$.

only very modest differences in the relative likelihood of residence in extended households, with urban residents just some 5 per cent (1901) or 7 per cent (1911) less likely to reside in them.

Most intriguing, the models indicate that the regional differences remain largely consistent with those observed in the simple, mapped patterns of figures 7.3 and 7.4. Specifically, in both census years, the relative odds of living in a lone-headed household in British Columbia, for example, were two or more times greater than in the Maritimes (the reference category), independently of any other variables in the model. Quebec residents still clearly favoured nuclear family residence considering the several other variables. Further, although in 1901, the relative likelihood of lone-headed residence was not measurably different among three regions (Ontario, the Prairies, or the Maritimes), by 1911, a substantial shift had taken place on the Prairies, where the relative chances of lone-headed residence had become about 40 per cent greater than in the Maritimes. But, this difference did not primarily result from the arrival of new immigrants to the region, since the influence of nativity is accounted for in the model. More likely, it was a consequence of a combination of strong westward migration of individuals from central Canada and the Maritimes and the unique settlement and farming conditions met on the Prairies. Many men moved west in this short period, aiming to establish families or to bring them from elsewhere in hopes of balancing the relative economic independence of family farming with a capacity to transform landed livelihoods into an inheritable legacy.[39]

As for extended households, the regional patterns also appear to be largely independent of the effects of gender, age, nativity, or rural/urban differences. Nor were these differences minor; in 1901, the relative chances of living in an extended household were about 25 per cent less in Quebec and in Ontario than in the Maritimes, over 40 per cent less on the Prairies, and 30 per cent less in British Columbia. Theses strong regional differences were somewhat reduced in 1911, with the exception of British Columbia, but remained in the same relative order. How might we further account for them?

Regional Economies and Household Strategies

The censuses of 1901 and 1911 provide two key variables that permit detailed examination of the character of the regional economies: occupational enumerations and a rare variable called "employment status," which distinguished employees from employers and the self-employed or those working on their own account. We consider these to be basic "class" distinctions.[40]

Our analysis focuses on the relationship between the regional economic patterns of these variables and household regimes. We classified the detailed occupational enumerations in the censuses in terms of five broad economic sectors for the sake of comparability both across censuses and across regions.[41] At the beginning of the twentieth century, over 44 per cent of those aged 15 years or over with a recorded occupation worked in agriculture; ten years later, this proportion was reduced to around 36 per cent. In the four other sectors, the proportions in 1901were non-agricultural primary work, 6 per cent; manufacturing and building, 22 per cent; service, 12 per cent; and professional, trade, and transportation, 17 per cent. These shifted only modestly by 1911 to 8 per cent for non-agricultural primary work, 22 per cent for manufacturing and building, 11 per cent for the service sector, and 23 per cent for professional, trade, and transportation. So, the primary, short-term changes were out of agriculture and into the broad group of professional, trade, and transportation, and mainly into the latter two. Regional patterns were quite variable, and the changes in these ten years were more dramatic than the national patterns would suggest.

Our working assumption is that local and regional economies encourage particular household formations. For example, Sylvester points to the tendency for large prairie farms at the turn of the century to have required extensive family or hired labour. Larry McCann documents the adaptive family economies of those practising plural occupations in the late nineteenth-century Maritimes. Gérard Bouchard links family reproduction strategies to migration, land settlement, fertility, and family size in the Saguenay region of Quebec.[42]

Looking at household experiences across the five regions of Canada in terms of their variations among the main labour force sectors reveals a very clear pattern in both 1901 and 1911, which does not require the full array of data to describe adequately. Despite some variations in household situations across the sectors within each region, the most striking feature is the consistency of the distinctive regional household patterns. For example, in British Columbia in 1901, all five main labour force sectors tended to display the region's relatively high proportions of residents in lone-headed households, ranging from 26 per cent in the professional, trade, and transportation sector to 46 per cent in the non-agricultural primary sector. No labour force sector in any other region in that year had as many individuals living in lone-headed households as did British Columbia; the proportions elsewhere never exceeded 20 per cent, and most were lower than that. Similarly, all five main labour force sectors in the Maritimes had relatively high proportions of their members living in extended households, varying from a low of about a fifth of those working in manufacturing and building to a high of nearly a third of those in agriculture. The highest rates of extended household residence in any sector in any other region (in the service sectors of Quebec and Ontario) only barely matched the lowest sectoral rate in the Maritimes. A quite similar pattern holds for 1911, although the regional variations in the household patterns were even more evident.

We extend the earlier multivariate models to include the independent effects of the labour force differences, and add the enumeration of the employment status/class situations of individuals. The two variables are related, but not so strongly as to compromise statistical estimates.[43] The results are presented in table 7.4.

Our primary interest in this model is the story it tells about regional variations in household situations once we explicitly take into account labour force and class circumstances of individuals as well as other factors. This analysis includes only those age 15 years and older and in the recorded labour force (in 1901, this was about 47%, and in 1911, 55%, of the population).

Regarding regional differences, the evidence strongly reinforces the previous conclusion: the inclusion of the labour force and employment status in the multivariate models somewhat modifies, but does not diminish the significance of regional variations in household experiences. We briefly consider the demographic and rural/urban patterns as a context for interpreting the economic and regional ones.

In sum, age and nativity patterns were very similar in the labour force and in the population as a whole; gender and rural/urban patterns were not. In contrast to the national population (table 7.3), the models of table 7.4 indicate that enumerated working women were relatively more likely than working men to have lived in lone-headed households as well as more likely to have lived in extended ones. Detailed census evidence makes the reasons for the difference clear. Almost one in four of the working women residing in the lone-headed households in 1901 were widows, and fully 60 per cent of these widows were single mothers; ten years later, about a third were widowed, and the same proportion were single parents. To put these gendered household tendencies in perspective, in the labour force as a whole, in 1901, about 13 per cent of women were widowed; in 1911, 10 per cent.

The age patterns of household circumstances largely replicated those of the population, although moderated, given the more restricted age groups. The very small proportion aged 70 years or older still reporting occupations remained most likely to live either in lone-headed or in extended households, followed by the 20- to 29-year-olds. The differences between native and foreign-born also paralleled those in the overall population.[44]

Like gender, the rural or urban location of one's work differed in its implications for living outside of couple-headed and nuclear households compared

Table 7.4 · Contribution of gender, age (in years), nativity (Canadian- or foreign-born), urban/rural location, region, labour force sector, and employment status (for the population aged 15 and over) to the likelihood of residing in a lone-headed or extended household, relative to a couple-headed household, Canada, 1901 and 1911

	1901		*1911*	
Variable	*Lone head Exp(B)*	*Extended Exp(B)*	*Lone head Exp(B)*	*Extended Exp(B)*
GENDER				
Female (Ref)				
Male	0.268 ***	0.583 ***	0.389 ***	0.642 ***
AGE (years)				
15–19	0.382 ***	0.544 ***	0.413 ***	0.524 ***
20–29	0.592 ***	0.753 ***	0.724 ***	0.743 ***
30–39	0.480 ***	0.694 ***	0.558 ***	0.685 ***
40–49	0.412 ***	0.557 ***	0.482 ***	0.598 ***
50–59	0.531 ***	0.555 ***	0.504 ***	0.578 ***
60–69	0.683 ***	0.692 ***	0.651 ***	0.708 ***
70 up (Ref)				
NATIVITY				
Canadian-born (Ref)				
Foreign-born	1.035	0.856 ***	1.091 **	0.858 ***
URBAN-RURAL LOCATION				
Rural (Ref)				
Urban	0.905	0.972	0.728 ***	1.000

/continued

with the population as a whole. At the outset of the century, the location did not differ in affecting the relative chances of living on lone-headed or extended households, whereas in the overall population, urban residents were more likely than rural residents to have lived independently and less likely to have shared households with their kinfolk. In 1911, the experiences of labour force members reversed those of the population as a whole, with the urban labour force significantly less likely (about 27% less) to reside in lone-headed households than the rural labour force, while they shared exactly the same relative odds of living with kin. The change, again, likely reflects the increased opportunities for the formation of nuclear, couple-headed, and extended households within the newly enlarged and younger immigrant communities by 1911.

Table 7.4 · continued

Variable	1901 Lone head Exp(B)	1901 Extended Exp(B)	1911 Lone head Exp(B)	1911 Extended Exp(B)
REGION				
BC	3.991 ***	0.533 ***	2.822 ***	0.725 ***
Prairies	1.308 **	0.628 ***	2.072 ***	0.663 ***
Ontario	1.044	0.765 ***	1.041	0.789 ***
Quebec	0.949	0.745 ***	0.937	0.790 ***
Maritimes (Ref)				
LABOUR FORCE SECTOR				
Agriculture	0.838 **	1.131 **	0.830 ***	1.087 *
Non-Agr. Primary	1.116	0.886	0.976	0.812 ***
Manuf & Building	0.787 ***	0.842 ***	0.751 ***	0.939 *
Dom & Civil Serv	0.783 ***	1.009	0.835 **	0.953
Prof-Trade-Transport (Ref)				
EMPLOYMENT STATUS				
Employer	0.997	1.066	0.770 ***	1.081 *
Employee	1.002	0.963	0.900 **	0.962
Own Account (Ref)				
N	63,293		121,201	

Sources: CFP 1901 and CCRI 1911 microdata databases.

Ref = reference category.

* $p < .05$; ** $p < .01$; *** $p < .001$.

Considering these and several other demographic, residential, and economic patterns, the most intriguing observation is that regional differences remained robust and, in some cases, were more sharply defined for the labour force than for the national population. Relative to couple-headed residence, the working populations of the west still had the greatest likelihood of lone-headed residence throughout the decade – in fact, the BC labour force in 1901 was nearly four times more likely than that in the Maritimes, and the Prairies labour force some 30 per cent more likely. Ten years later, those working in British Columbia were still about three times more likely to live in the more simple households than those in the Maritimes, while those in the expanded Prairies labour force were about two times more likely to do so. The two western regions contrasted throughout the decade with the labour forces of Ontario and Quebec and the Maritimes, which largely shared the tendency to avoid these simpler residential circumstances.

With regard to extended households, the regional labour force patterns largely parallel those of the population. Again, we witness the strong relative propensity in those at work in the Maritimes to have shared residences with kin or with kin and others. The Ontario and Quebec labour forces were significantly less likely to do so, and they were even less likely to do so on the Prairies and the west coast. Compared with the chances of residing in couple-headed households, those working on the Prairies in 1901 were, as a whole, 40 per cent less likely to share a residence with a relative than those working in the Maritimes, and about 30 per cent less likely to do so in 1911, independently of other variables in the model. At the turn of the century, a member of the BC labour force was relatively about half as likely as one in the Maritimes to reside with kin, a difference that was substantially diminished by 1911 (compared with the chances of living in a couple-headed household).

Although the persistent regional differences in household circumstances are most intriguing, the differences among the several labour force sectors and employment status groups are also of interest. The coefficients of table 7.4 reveal both the sector in which one earned a living and, especially, that one's class location had unexpectedly selective independent effects on household experiences.[45]

In 1901, working in one of two sectors, the non-agricultural primary sector or the professional, trade, and transportation sector, entailed the greatest relative likelihood of residing in a lone-headed household. Probably, this was so because single men tended to gravitate to the often temporary and migratory work in lumbering and mining as well as in the various trades and in transportation. The propensities were more or less duplicated in 1911. At both ends of the decade, residing in an extended household was relatively most likely for those working in agriculture, surely due to the labour requirements of family farming, although the relative odds were only marginally greater than those in other sectors. Living in an extended household was least likely among those working in manufacturing and building, where wage work and the nuclear household appeared to go hand in glove. In 1911, the non-agricultural primary group appear to have become least prone or able to live with kinfolk.[46] Moreover, the model for 1901 indicates that there were simply no detectable differences in household situations of individuals in the three main class circumstances identified in the analysis, given all the other variables in the models.[47] By 1911, some, mostly slight, but statistically significant independent differences had emerged: employers were a good deal less likely to reside in lone-headed residences than any others in the labour force, and they were very slightly more likely to occupy extended households, while employees were a little less likely than the self-employed to live independently.

In sum, we are struck by the fact that region of residence had a sustained influence on household formations and experiences whatever other demographic and economic influences we are able to assess. Working on the far west coast or on the Prairies significantly enhanced the relative chances that one would reside alone, as a single parent, or with unrelated others, while those working in the Maritimes remained distinctly more likely to live in kin-extended households. Central Canadians shared a proclivity for couple-headed and mainly nuclear households, and this was especially so in Quebec.

Observations and Speculations

Gender and age consistently and significantly conditioned one's household experiences in Canada in the first decade of the twentieth century, but in an era of unprecedented immigrant arrivals, economic change, and national territorial reconfiguration, foreign or native birth or timing of arrival among immigrants to Canada had more variable and more modest effects. More intriguing, we found that Canada's oft-cited regional diversity played a very formative role in shaping everyday household experiences, and it did so independently of the influence of both major demographic and economic conditions. What was it about regional locations in the first decade of the twentieth century that might have so strongly influenced who lived with whom? Such geographical puzzles have been a central topic throughout family and household history, beginning with Frédéric Le Play's influential writing in the 1870s, but no less so in the most recent international studies, although notably less prominently to date in North American than in the European literature.[48]

For future North American studies, one can imagine several possible approaches to the question. For example, one might consider the implications of the geography of the built environment and of housing markets. The census data do not allow us to address the question directly for the 1901–11 decade. Nevertheless, an initial assessment makes the approach less obvious, since in the longer-settled regions self-building and sweat equity were commonplace ways of providing housing in this era, and on the west coast, housing stock was readily supplied due to the availability and low cost of building material.[49] An alternative, cultural approach might consider the historical importance of common ancestry for family and household practices.[50] In this case, we have been able to employ the recorded "racial or tribal origins" for the 1901 and 1911 censuses in analysis. In brief, we found moderate direct relationships between household experiences and the main, large origin groups, but these differences virtually disappeared once origin was added to the multivariate models. This is not to suggest that such an assessment exhausts a range of cultural questions, but only that we find no interesting national patterns of association between ethnicity, in this sense, and household preferences or constraints.

A basic methodological issue in assessing household and family experiences with census data leads us to propose an alternative approach to the question. Although the co-residential units enumerated in a census are often our only extant historical evidence bearing on family systems, with few exceptions, census listings do not reveal how the compositions of households are related to the family and kinship systems in which they are embedded.[51] Throughout this study, we have interpreted the differences in the household experiences of immigrants and native-born Canadians, and of changing immigrant experiences, in terms of the clues they provide about the availability and density of family and social networks. We propose an approach to interpreting the deep, persistent regional differences we have documented that takes up a dialogue between the perspective afforded by national census samples and finer-grained studies of local communities, which sometimes provide evidence about the character of familial networks. We reflect on three illustrative cases for the Canadian patterns.

Consider, for example, the singular predominance of nuclear households in Quebec in the 1901–11 decade. A number of meticulous historical studies in Quebec provide accounts of the tendency for couples to establish and maintain independent households, usually immediately after marriage and certainly after the birth of a first child. The most complete account of this familial system is Bouchard's intensive study of the Saguenay region of mid-northern Quebec.[52] Tracking the movement of couples between 1842 and 1941, for example, he shows that the great majority of married sons established independent households within the same parishes as their parents.[53] Bouchard interprets these nuclear households as nodes of apparent independence tightly woven into a culture of family service and reproduction over space and through time.

Other studies in Quebec add weight to this interpretation. For the late nineteenth-century industrializing town of Saint Hyacinthe, in the plain of Montreal, Peter Gossage reports that newly married couples established nuclear households in close proximity to kin, indeed, "very often occupying distinct lodgings within the same building."[54] Studies of industrializing Montreal through the turn of the twentieth century add further support to the view. Sherry Olson and Jason Gilliland, for example, both show that, despite high rates of urban in-migration and unusually high rates of annual household circulation among dwellings, independent nuclear households were commonly maintained in close proximity to those of other family members, with frequent residential relocation of the related households a mode of family adaptation to changing life-cycle circumstances.[55] Although not unique to Quebec, our national perspective suggests that this system of nodal household nuclearity in the context of unusually dense familial and kinship networks was distinctively Québécois, at least through the early years of the twentieth century.[56]

How might we extend a family and social network perspective to interpret the unusually high proportions of extended households found in the Maritimes in this same era? We have a less rich lode of historical demographic and family studies on which to draw in this case, but one distinctive feature of the regional household economies – their cooperative labour pluralism – has been documented. These are shared households in which some members moved seasonally between farming, fishing, and lumbering as a means of sustaining a collective enterprise. Early historical census studies of some Maritime communities have provided evidence of the density of local kinship networks and the relative commonality of extended households and cooperative labour pluralism. The regional affinity for household extension seems likely to have been fostered by these elastic family networks and labour traditions.[57]

Finally, in the contrasting case of British Columbia, we have already suggested that the unusually large numbers living in lone-headed households can be understood in the context of the region's large numbers of transient, mainly male wage earners, whose relative household simplicity was engendered by the relatively weak kinship and social networks of the emerging resource economies. We hazard these preliminary interpretations of local studies of the character of households and families and our national perspective on them to illustrate their complementarity and the prospects of continuing integration. The Canadian Century Research Infrastructure data series will prove to be an invaluable resource in such an endeavour.

Notes

1 Among many accounts, the early influential one is Peter Laslett and Richard Wall (eds.), *Household and Family in Past Time* (Cambridge: Cambridge University Press, 1972).

2 Key contributions were Michael Anderson, *Family Structure in Nineteenth-Century Lancashire* (Cambridge: Cambridge University Press, 1971); Tamara Hareven, *Family Time and Industrial Time: The Relationship between the Family and Work in a New England Industrial Community* (Cambridge: Cambridge University Press, 1982); and for Canada, Michael Katz, *The People of Hamilton, Canada West: Family and Class in a Mid-nineteenth-Century City* (Cambridge,

Table 7.A · Distribution of the population (%) by household situation, regions, and rural/urban location, Canada, 1901 and 1911

Household composition	*Region*					
	BC	*Prairies*	*Ontario*	*Quebec*	*Maritimes*	*Total*
1901						
RURAL						
Lone-head households						
Primary individuals	5.0	2.7	1.2	1.0	0.8	1.3
Single parents	1.5	2.6	4.6	3.6	4.7	4.1
All lone-head with non-kin	14.7	2.8	2.0	1.2	1.7	2.1
Total	21.2	8.1	7.8	5.8	7.2	7.5
Married-couple households						
Childless couples	4.8	3.2	3.8	3.5	2.7	3.5
Couples with children	33.2	54.7	54.1	61.5	52.4	55.6
All married couples + non-kin	26.9	18.7	13.9	8.2	10.7	12.3
Total	64.9	76.6	71.8	73.2	65.8	71.4
Extended households						
Extended	8.7	9.5	15.0	16.2	20.5	15.8
All extended with non-kin	5.2	5.6	5.5	4.8	6.5	5.5
Total	13.9	15.1	20.5	21.0	27.0	21.3
N	4,051	15,404	65,185	51,872	32,465	168,976
URBAN						
Lone-head households						
Primary individuals	2..7	1.1	0.7	0.5	0.6	0.7
Single parents	1.6	2.8	5.5	4.3	4.8	4.7
All lone-head with non-kin	11.7	4.0	4.1	4.0	3.7	4.3
Total	16.0	7.9	10.2	8.8	9.1	9.8
Married-couple households						
Childless couples	4.9	3.0	4.3	4.0	3.0	4.0
Couples with children	39.3	42.7	47.5	51.2	47.4	48.1
All married couples + non-kin	22.3	31.0	18.2	17.3	18.7	18.7
Total	66.5	76.7	70.0	72.5	69.1	70.8
Extended households						
Extended	11.4	9.3	13.5	12.8	14.7	13.2
All extended with non-kin	6.1	6.1	6.2	5.9	7.2	6.2
Total	17.5	15.4	19.7	18.7	21.9	19.4
N	3,746	4,140	42,061	28,722	11,646	90,315

/continued

Table 7.A · continued

Household composition	*Region*					
	BC	*Prairies*	*Ontario*	*Quebec*	*Maritimes*	*Total*
1911						
RURAL						
Lone-head households						
Primary individuals	6.2	6.5	1.6	0.9	1.0	2.6
Single parents	2.0	2.4	3.7	4.0	4.2	3.5
All lone-head with non-kin	12.5	3.5	1.9	0.8	1.2	2.3
Total	20.6	12.5	7.2	5.8	6.5	8.5
Married-couple households						
Childless couples	5.5	4.2	4.7	3.4	3.3	4.1
Couples with children	37.8	51.8	50.6	60.8	52.8	53.4
All married couples + non-kin	20.5	16.6	14.7	5.6	8.0	11.9
Total	63.8	72.6	70.0	69.8	64.1	69.3
Extended households						
Extended	10.9	10.4	17.1	21.5	24.9	17.7
All extended with non-kin	4.6	4.6	5.7	2.9	4.5	4.4
Total	15.5	14.9	22.8	24.4	29.4	22.2
N	8,716	46,208	61,765	54,732	32,331	203,752
URBAN						
Lone-head households						
Primary individuals	1.0	0.9	0.7	0.6	0.6	0.7
Single parents	1.8	2.0	4.3	4.0	4.7	3.8
All lone-head with non-kin	9.4	5.7	3.9	3.1	3.9	4.2
Total	12.2	8.6	8.9	7.7	9.2	8.7
Married-couple households						
Childless couples	4.2	3.8	5.1	4.2	3.3	4.4
Couples with children	35.6	35.9	44.2	53.1	47.1	45.5
All married couples + non-kin	30.2	31.3	20.0	14.2	17.8	20.1
Total	70.0	71.0	69.3	71.5	68.2	70.0
Extended households						
Extended	10.1	10.6	15.1	15.7	16.7	14.5
All extended with non-kin	7.7	9.8	6.8	5.0	5.9	6.6
Total	17.8	20.4	21.9	20.7	22.6	21.1
N	8,859	18,119	60,823	42,177	14,041	144,019

Sources: CFP 1901 and CCRI 1911 microdata databases.

MA: Harvard University Press, 1975); and Michael Katz, Michael Doucet, and Mark Stern, *The Social Organization of Early Industrial Capitalism* (Cambridge, MA: Harvard University Press, 1982).

3 See, e.g., see Andrejs Plakans, "Interaction between Household and Kin Group in the Eastern European Past: Posing the Problem," *Journal of Family History* 12, no. 2 (1987): 163–78; Steven King, "The English Protoindustrial Family: Old and New Perspectives," *History of the Family* 8, no. 1 (2003): 21–43. Oris and Ochiai provide an overview of the variety of European family formations which were documented in the 1980s and 1990s, in "Family Crisis in the Context of Different Family Systems: Frameworks and Evidence on 'When Dad Died,'" in Renzo Derosas and Michel Oris (eds.), *When Dad Died: Individuals and Families Coping with Stress in Past Societies* (Bern: Peter Lang 2002), 27–89.

4 See, e.g., Mikolaj Szoltysek, "Three Kinds of Preindustrial Household Formation System in Historical Eastern Europe: A Challenge to Spatial Patterns of the European Family," *History of the Family* 13, no. 3 (2008): 223–57; Steven Ruggles, "Reconsidering the Northwest European Family System: Living Arrangements of the Aged in Comparative Historical Perspective," *Population and Development Review* 35, no. 2 (2009): 249–73.

5 An earlier exploration of the 1901 and 1911 household data was reported in the session "Démographie historique: nouvelles interrogations en histoire de la famille et en histoire de la population" of the Entretiens du Centre Jacques Cartier, Lyon, France, 30 Nov. and 1 Dec. 2009. I thank Bertrand Dejardins for the invitation and Michel Oris for subsequent interest in a revised version of the paper, "Canadian Households in Transition: New Perspectives on Household Experiences, Immigration, Regions and Class in Early Twentieth-Century Canada," in *Popolazione e Storia* 2 (2010): 133–67. The current analysis extends that initial work.

6 Among other references see Norman Hillmer, http://magazine.carleton.ca/2000_Spring/172.htm.

7 Douglas Francis, Richard Jones, and Donald Smith, *Destinies: Canadian History since Confederation* (Toronto: Holt, Rinehart, Winston, 1988), 46–63. Marvin McInnis, "Immigration and Emigration: Canada in the Late Nineteenth Century," in Timothy Hatton and Jeffrey Williamson (eds.), *Migration and the International Labor Market, 1850–1939* (London: Routledge, 1994), 139–282. Alvin Finkel and Margaret Conrad, eds., *History of the Canadian Peoples*, 3rd ed., vol. II (Toronto: Addison, Wesley, Longman, 2002), 112, Table 6.1.

8 See Warren Kalback and Wayne McVey, *The Demographic Basis of Canadian Society* (Toronto: McGraw-Hill, 1971), 41, Table 2.4.

9 Franca Iacovetta, *Gatekeepers: Reshaping Immigrant Lives in Cold War Canada* (Toronto: Between the Lines Press 2006), chapter 1.

10 See, e.g., Michael B. Katz and Mark J. Stern, *One Nation Divisible: What America Was and What It Is Becoming* (New York: Russell Sage Foundation, 2006), chapter 1; and Triadafilos Triadafilopoulos, "Building Walls, Bounding Nations: Migration and Exclusion in Canada and Germany, 1870–1939," *Journal of Historical Sociology* 17, no. 4 (2004): 385–427.

11 The history of the family in Canada has become a rich and diverse field of study, with Quebec still a leading focus. A full review cannot be undertaken here, but see the early collection by Bettina Bradbury (ed.), *Canadian Family History: Selected Readings* (Toronto: Copp Clark Pitman, 1992); and Cynthia Comacchio, *The Infinite Bonds of Family: Domesticity in Canada, 1850–1940* (Toronto: University of Toronto Press, 1999). Key regional and local studies of household formation are Chad Gaffield, *Language, Schooling and Cultural Conflict: The Origins of the French-Language Controversy in Ontario* (Montreal and Kingston: McGill-Queen's University Press, 1987); Gérard Bouchard, *Quelques arpents d'Amérique: Population,* économie, *famille au Saguenay, 1838–1971* (Montreal: Boréal 1996); Kenneth Sylvester, *The Limits of Rural Capitalism: Family, Culture and Markets in Montcalm, Manitoba, 1871–1940* (Toronto: University of Toronto Press, 2001).

12 Steven Ruggles, "The Transformation of American Family Structure," *American Historical Review* 99 (1994): 103–28. For related work, see Steven Ruggles, "The Demography of the Unrelated Individual, 1900–1950," *Demography* 25, no. 4 (1988): 521–36. These are the major patterns of household composition of the American white population; non-white patterns vary somewhat, see Ruggles, "The Transformation of the American Family Structure," Table 1. The earliest Canadian studies are Gordon Darroch and Michael Ornstein, "Family and Household in Nineteenth-Century Canada: Regional Patterns and Regional Economies," *Journal of Family History* 9, no. 2 (1984): 158–77; and Thomas Kausar and Thomas Burch, "Household Formation in Canada and the United States, 1900–1901 to 1970–1971: Trends and Regional Differentials," *Canadian Studies in Population* 12, no. 2 (1985): 159–82. The most recent relevant work is Stacie Burke, "Transitions in Household and Family Structure: Canada in 1901 and 1991," chapter 1, in Eric Sager and Peter Baskerville (eds.), *Household Counts: Canadian Households and Families in 1901* (Toronto: University of Toronto Press, 2007), 17–58; Eric Sager, "Canadian Families and Households in 1901: First Thoughts on a National Sample of the 1901 Census," unpublished paper presented to the Canadian Historical Association, Memorial University, June 1997; Kenneth Sylvester, "Rural to Urban Migration: Finding Household Complexity in a New World Environment," chapter 5, in Sager and Baskerville (eds.), *Household Counts*, 147–79.

13 The definitions of dwellings and households/families within them were almost identical in 1901 and 1911. See Canada, Department of Agriculture and Statistics, *Fifth Census of Canada, 1911: Instructions to Officers, Commissioners and Enumerators* (Ottawa: Government Printing Bureau, 1911), article nos 72, 77, and 78. For 1901, see Canada, Census Office, *Fourth Census of Canada, 1901: Instructions to Officers, Commissioners and Enumerators (*Ottawa: Department of Agriculture, 1901), article no. 42. Also see the CCRI and CFP User Guides, http://ccri.library.ualberta.ca/enindex.html and http://web.uvic.ca/hrd/cfp/. About 95% of dwellings and 98% of the households had a single head of household (a few dwellings contain more than one household).

14 A count, e.g., of the numbers of "nuclear" households is not the same as the numbers of individuals residing in them. Our classification is self-evident with

the possible exception of the meaning of "primary individuals." Primary individuals are heads of households without co-residing family, but potentially including *kin* as secondary individuals. In our samples, in 1901 and 1911, respectively, 88% and 95% were living alone; 59% and 68% were single; 13% and 15% were recorded as married without spouses; and 27% and 15% were widowed. In 1901 and 1911, respectively, 71% and 82% were male. Steven Ruggles and Susan Brower present the strongest rationale for using individual measures, since only individual measures allow one to undertake analyses of populations "at risk" and of the implications of individual attributes for household circumstances. See Ruggles and Brower, "Measurement of Household and Family Composition in the United States, 1850–2000," *Population and Development Review* 29, no. 1 (2003): 73–101. A demonstration of the relationship between household and individual measures is given by Miriam King and Samuel H. Preston, "Who Lives with Whom? Individual versus Household Measures," *Journal of Family History* 15, no. 2 (1990): 117–32.

15 Ruggles, "The Transformation of the American Family Structure," Table 1; Kenneth Sylvester, "Household Composition and Canada's Rural Capitalism: The Extent of Rural Labor Markets in 1901," *Journal of Family History* 26, no. 9 (2001): 289–309, Table 4. The revision includes the three separate categories of resident non-kin or augmenting household members, mainly boarders, lodgers, and domestic employees. The categories are based primarily on two census records, marital status of the head, and enumerated "relationship to the head" of all members of a given household. In cases where no head of household was identified, we substituted the first person listed. In cases where more than one head of household was recorded, we assigned the first listed head as the "primary" head for the purposes of classification. Selecting the first listed person as the head of household and relying mainly on the "relationship to head" variable in the classification risk misclassification of some households, e.g., youngsters who are the first listed persons. We did not attempt to undertake a reclassification of these few cases. Where there were large numbers of uncertain or confusing relationships to the head, such as "widow(er)," we reviewed all records and manually recoded them.

16 In both census years, the average size of the households in the sample of dwellings with 30 or fewer people was 6.4 (with SD of 3.1 and 3.4 in 1901 and 1911, respectively; dwellings were, on average, only slightly larger). The distributions of household size differ, however. In 1911, we find a larger proportion of smaller households. These proportions also varied by region.

17 In this initial work, Ruggles reported distributions of household types, not of the population by type. As noted, these are related measures. For the longer-term trends and contemporary proportions, see Ruggles, "The Transformation," Table 1, and Burke, "Transitions," Table 1.2.

18 Given the frequencies from the 5% national samples displayed here, estimates of the population distributions are simply 20 times the figures on the lower axis. One can also observe the well-known "heaping" of age reporting among historical populations, rounding ages to those ending in 5s or 0s.

19 The age-standardized rates of household composition in table 7.1 are based on the age distribution of the total national population and the age-specific rates of household composition for the foreign-born in each year. We used eight age categories 0–9, 10–19 ... 60–69, 70 and over.

20 We also generated expected distributions of household situations by gender, using the national gender distributions in each year as our standard and applying them to the household distributions of the foreign-born as given in table 7.1. The results are readily summarized and not reported. If the gender distributions of the foreign- and native-born had been identical, then in both 1901 and 1911 only slightly more of the former would have lived in nuclear and extended households and slightly fewer in lone-headed households than was actually the case.

21 For 1901, see *Fourth Census of Canada, 1901: Instructions to Officers, Commissioners and Enumerators*, xviii, no. 52. For 1911, see *Fifth Census of Canada, 1911: Instructions to Officers, Commissioners and Enumerators*, 29, no. 98. In 1901, about 11% of the 32,006 sample records of the foreign-born were missing recorded year of immigration; in 1911, of 77, 046 sampled immigrants, this was 12%. Most of these records were simply blank, but a few were numerical values that were out of conceivable range. In both years, the ages, marital statuses, and gender distributions for those reporting year of immigration are almost identical to those for all foreign-born. We assume no strong biases in the recorded samples.

22 In the slightly smaller populations for which year of immigration was recorded, the overall distributions in the eight main categories of our classification of household circumstances varies only slightly from those reported in table 7.1. The largest discrepancy is for the nuclear household category. In 1901, table 7.1 gives a sample estimate of 40.9% of the foreign-born in nuclear households, and for the year of immigration portion of the sample it is 41.2%. In 1911, the comparable figures are 38.9% and 39.1%.

23 For an exception, see Charles Wetherell, Andrejs Plakans, and Barry Wellman, "Social Networks, Kinship, and Community in Eastern Europe," *Journal of Interdisciplinary History* 24, no. 4 (1994): 639–63.

24 The literature is too vast to more than note here. For European and US examples, see Leslie Page Moch, *Moving Europeans: Migration in Western Europe since 1650* (Bloomington: Indiana University Press, 1992), esp. chapters 4 and 5; and Donna Gabaccia, *Women, Gender and Immigrant Life in the United States, 1920–1990* (Bloomington: Indiana University Press, 1994), chapter 5. For major Canadian studies, see Bruce S. Elliott, *Irish Migrants in the Canadas: A New Approach*, 2nd ed. (Montreal and Kingston: McGill-Queen's University Press, 2004); Bouchard, *Quelques arpents d'Amérique*; Randy W. Widdis, *With Scarcely a Ripple: Anglo-Canadian Migration into the United States and Western Canada, 1880–1920* (Montreal and Kingston: McGill-Queen's University Press, 1998).

25 See Mark Granovetter, "The Strength of Weak Ties: A Network Theory Revisited," *Sociological Theory* 1 (1983): 201–33. Specifically, Granovetter argues that "weak ties have a special role in a person's opportunity for mobility" – that there is a "structural tendency for those to whom one is only weakly tied to have better access to job information one does not already have. Acquaintances, as compared

to close friends, are more prone to move in different circles than oneself" (205). Also see, Mark Granovetter, "The Strength of Weak Ties," *American Journal of Sociology* 78, no. 6 (1973): 1369–73.

26 Peter Baskerville, "Familiar Strangers: Urban Families with Boarders, Canada, 1901," *Social Science History* 25, no. 3 (2001): 321–46.

27 The levels of statistical significance reported in table 7.2 consider that the samples of dwellings are cluster samples of individuals, as discussed in the introduction to this volume. We expect little within-dwelling homogeneity in age or gender, but the native-born and immigrants tend to cluster in separate dwellings, although by no means exclusively. As expected, the confidence intervals for the nativity coefficient are somewhat wider than those resulting from models assuming simple random sampling of individuals. Those for age and gender barely differ. See Michael Davern, Steven Ruggles, and Tami Swenson, "Drawing Statistical Inferences from Historical Census Data, 1850–1950," *Demography* 46, no. 3 (2009): 589–60. A number of binary logistic models were examined with the dependent variables one of the three main household situation categories. The results very largely conform to the interpretations presented here.

28 On historical residence patterns of the aged, see Lisa Dillon, chapter 8 in this book, and her *The Shady Side of Fifty: Age and Old Age in Late Victorian Canada and the United States* (Montreal and Kingston: McGill-Queen's University Press, 2008), chapter 4. Also see Steven Ruggles, "Multigenerational Families in Nineteenth-Century America," *Continuity and Change* 18, no. 6 (2003): 139–65.

29 On historical ethnic endogamy, see Madeline A. Richard. *Ethnic Groups and Marital Choices* (Vancouver: UBC Press, 1991); and Madeline A. Kalbach, "Ethnicity and the Altar," in Madeline A. Kalbach and Warren E. Kalbach (eds.), *Perspectives on Ethnicity in Canada: A Reader* (Toronto: Harcourt, 2000), 111–20.

30 The models in table 7.2 also generate statistics (likelihood ratio chi-square) that allow one to evaluate the overall "fit" of a given model to the array of data, and so evaluate the relative importance of any variable to that fit. In both census years, 1901 and 1911, age was by far the most important contributor to the fit of the models, due to the high probability that children resided with parents and the aged in extended and lone-headed households. Next most important was nativity, followed by gender differences. Among immigrants in 1901, age differences again had the predominant influence on household experiences, but the effects of gender and the timing of immigration were barely distinguishable. In 1911, after age, gender assumed a much greater influence among immigrants in conditioning household situations, followed by period of immigration.

31 I thank Byron Moldofsky both for advice on these maps and for their production.

32 For purposes of this analysis, the Prairies are defined in 1911 as the populations of Manitoba and the new provinces of Alberta and Saskatchewan (which joined Confederation in 1905). The two new provinces were made up of four districts of the North West Territories (NWT), Athabasca, Assiniboia, Alberta, and Saskatchewan. As an approximation in 1901, the corresponding region is defined as the enumerated populations given for Manitoba, Athabasca, and the NWT. The 1901 Prairies sample probably represents a slightly larger area and population

than a more refined definition would, but the additional territory was sparsely populated. The Maritimes is defined in each year as Prince Edward Island, New Brunswick, and Nova Scotia. The excluded portions of the samples are those of the Yukon and part of the NWT, which represented less than one-half a per cent of the total in each year.

33 Regional variation in urban residence was high in both years, with a low fifth or so of the 1901 Prairies population in villages, towns, and cities, and just less than a third in 1911, and a high of 48% (in BC) in 1901 and 52% in 1911. Ontario and Quebec were more similar, with 39% and 36% urban residents, respectively; just over a quarter of the population of the Maritimes was urban in 1901, although by 1911 the proportions in Ontario and Quebec had risen to 50% and 44%, and in the Prairies and the Maritimes, 28% and 30%, respectively. See also Kalback and McVey, *The Demographic Basis*, 98–105.

34 See John Herd Thompson, *Forging the Prairie West* (Don Mills, ON: Oxford University Press, 1998), chapter 5.

35 Burke first identified the regional gradients for 1901, in "Transitions in Household and Family Structure."

36 For the strong tendency to concentrate on urban boarding and lodging, see Peter Baskerville, "Familiar Strangers" and references therein. For single parenthood, see Bettina Bradbury "Canadian Children Who Lived with One Parent," chapter 8, in Eric Sager and Peter Baskerville (eds.), *Household Counts*, 247–301. The rise of the primary individual is a later twentieth-century phenomenon. See Ruggles, "The Demography of the Unrelated Individual."

37 Leroy O. Stone showed that the Maritime provinces had negative interprovincial migration ratios (losses exceeded gains) for the first 30 years of the twentieth century, while Ontario and the West gained especially Saskatchewan and Alberta (in 1901 and 1911, respectively). Stone, *Migration in Canada: Regional Aspects* (Ottawa: Government Printing Office, 1961), 138.

38 The uneven regional immigrant presence is also evident in regional sex ratios. In both census years, men outnumbered women about six to four in BC, while the ratio rose in the Prairies from 54% male in 1901 to match BC in 1911. The other three regions had nearly balanced sex ratios, reflecting the predominance of the native-born in each.

39 See Thompson, *Forging the Prairie West*, chapter 5. Also, more generally, see Gérard Bouchard, "Family Reproduction in New Rural Areas: Outline of a North American Model," *Canadian Historical Review* 75, no. 4 (1994): 475–510. Some of these census-enumerated, lone-headed householders may have been members of the same families, fathers and brothers, who reported to the census enumerator that they were independent households on different, adjacent prairie properties in order to establish landed claims, although they may have mostly resided together. I thank Doug Thompson for this suggestion.

40 In several publications, Eric Sager and Peter Baskerville have examined the intention of the census designers and administrators to include the variable and undertaken its analyses for 1901. See Eric Sager and Peter Baskerville, "Unemployment, Living Standards, and the Working-Class Family in Urban Canada in 1901,"

History of the Family 2, no. 3 (1997): 229–54; and Peter Baskerville, "Displaying the Working Class: The 1901 Census of Canada," *Historical Methods* 33, no. 4 (2000): 229–34. A succinct statement of the class implications of the variable is in Eric Sager and Christopher Morier, "Immigrants, Ethnicity and Earnings in 1901: Revisiting the Vertical Mosaic," *Canadian Historical Review* 83, no. 2 (2002): 196–229.

41 The User Guides of each census sample provide detailed and flexible numerical codes, although they differ in key ways. The coding adopted here is based on a 1911 code scheme provided on the data file, labelled Chief Occupation Code 1, which was the first part of a three-part code used by the Census to classify occupations by sector into twelve categories – agriculture; building trades; domestic and personal service; civil and municipal service; fisheries; hunting and trapping; forestry and lumbering; manufacturing: mechanical and textiles; manufacturing: food and clothing; mining; professional, trade, and merchandising; and finally, transportation. The detailed occupation codes provided in the 1901 User Guide were then recoded to match the 1911 sector labels as closely as possible. There was some inevitable loss of comparability, mainly due to ambiguous 1901 categories, such as "General and Unspecified Labour," which were left unclassified, rather than arbitrarily assigned. They represented about 8% of those age 15 and older with an enumerated occupation. This differential loss means that, in 1911, the sample of the labour force includes 55% of those aged 15 and older, compared with 47% in 1901. In 1911, this labour force was 87% male, and in 1901, 84% of the labour force was male.

42 Sylvester, "Rural to Urban Migration"; Larry McCann, "Seasons of Labor: Family, Work, and Land in a Nineteenth-Century Nova Scotia Shipbuilding Community," *History of the Family* 4, no. 4 (2000): 485–527; Bouchard, *Quelques arpents d'Amérique,* chapters II and X–XIII.

43 For example, 60% of those age 15 or over in agriculture in 1901 and 70% in 1911 worked on their own account, while nearly 90% of domestic and civil workers were employees in both years. These were the sectors in which one employment status group was most concentrated; with the exception of the service workers, who were mainly employees, every sector had a clear presence of each class in each year.

44 This is so with one minor difference: the foreign-born labour force in 1911 appears to have been slightly, but significantly more likely to reside in lone-headed households than the native-born, but this was not so among the larger population.

45 We chose the professional, trade, and transportation category as the reference category due to its omnibus character; it represented about a fifth of the labour force in both years. It is primarily a trade and transportation category. Trade and merchandising represented over half of the individuals in each year with those in transportation over a quarter in 1901 and over a third in 1911. Professionals were 22% and 12% in 1901 and 1911, respectively.

46 Considering these labour force and regional patterns leads one to wonder about the yet more complex question of their interaction in influencing household situations. We might expect that the household situations associated with working

in a given occupational sector or class situation in one region might differ from those in another. We examined multinomial models that incorporated explicit interactions between the regions and occupational sectors. They are complex models, but it turns out that the statistically significant results are few and almost identical for each census year. Only three combinations of region and location in the labour force significantly affected the relative likelihood of individuals living in lone-headed households: in BC and in Ontario, those working in the non-agricultural primary sector had the greatest likelihood to be living in lone-headed households, while those in Quebec working in agriculture were much less likely be in lone-headed households. As for the relative likelihood of extended household residence, making a living in agriculture in three regions (Ontario, Quebec, and the Prairies) lowered the relative chances, with those farming on the Prairies being least likely to be living in extended households. As in earlier analysis, extended household residence was unusually common in the Maritimes. Cross-sectional data (not reported) indicate that extended households were most common among Maritime farmers. In general, the models confirm that regional locations exerted a marked influence on individual household experiences both independently and in association with particular labour force circumstances.

47 If we include the small category of those enumerated as living on their own means, that is, on independent incomes, then class differences between them and each of the others are very distinct and of interest, but this does not change the implications for the three main class categories considered here. See Darroch, "Canadian Households in Transition."

48 Frédéric Le Play, *L'organisation de la famille selon le vrai modèle signalé par l'histoire de toutes les races et de tous les temps* (Tours: A. Mame et fils, 1884). For recent studies based on new databases, see Ruggles, "Reconsidering the Northwest European Family System" – wherein Ruggles provides a tidy overview of relevant classical writing; and Siegfried Gruber and Mikolaj Szoltysek, "Stem Families, Joint Families, and the European Pattern: How Much of a Reconsideration Do We Need?" *MPIDR Working Paper WP 2011-001*, Jan. (2001): 1–34.

49 Richard Harris, "The Impact of Self-Building on the Social Geography of Toronto, 1901–1913: A Challenge for Urban Theory," *Transactions, Institute of British Geographers* 15, no. 4 (1990): 387–402; and *Creeping Conformity: How Canada Became Suburban, 1900–1960* (Toronto: University of Toronto Press, 2004). For BC, see Deryck W. Holdsworth, "House and Home in Vancouver: Images of West Coast Urbanism," in Gilbert A. Stelter and Alan F.J. Artibise (eds.), *The Canadian City: Essays in Urban History* (Toronto: McClelland and Stewart, 1966; reprinted by Macmillan, 1979). I thank Eric Sager for bringing the BC circumstances to my attention.

50 A substantial literature traces the ethnic variations in household size and composition, but the clearest demonstration of the historically consequential relationship are the studies by Thornton and Olson of the implications of ethnicity for family life and especially for infant and child mortality in Montreal. Among a number of studies, see Sherry Olson and Patricia Thornton: "Mobilité et structure démographique dans la région montréalaise, 1840 à 1900," in Christian Des-

sureault, John Dickenson, and Joseph Goy (eds.), *Famille et marché XVIe–XXe siècles* (Montreal: Septentrion, 2003), 341–54; "A Deadly Discrimination among Montreal Infants, 1860–1900," *Continuity and Change* 16, no. 1 (2001): 95–135; and *Peopling the North American City: Montreal, 1840–1900* (Montreal and Kingston: McGill-Queen's University Press, 2011).

51 For an exception, see Wetherell et al., "Social Networks, Kinship, and Community in Eastern Europe."

52 Bouchard, *Quelques arpents d'Amérique*, 266–76.

53 Ibid., Table XXI-4. Married daughters tended to reside within the circles of their spouses' families. Bouchard further argues that the high rates of individual and family migration, which characterized not only Quebec but much of nineteenth- and early twentieth-century North America, were integral features of this system, rather than destabilizing.

54 Peter Gossage, *Families in Transition: Industry and Population in Nineteenth-Century Saint-Hyacinthe* (Montreal and Kingston: McGill-Queen's University Press, 1999), 122–34; quotation is from 131.

55 Sherry Olson, "Pour se créer un avenir: Stratégies de couple Montréalais au XIX siècle," *Revue d'histoire de l'Amérique française* 51, no. 3 (1998): 357–89; and Jason Gilliland, "Modeling Residential Mobility in Montreal, 1860–1900," *Historical Methods* 31, no. 1 (1998): 27–42.

56 Nancy Grey Osterud documents a similar system in which powerful norms of mutual aid and tight kinship relations, largely sustained by women, engendered mostly nuclear household residences in a nineteenth-century farming community of New York State. Osterud, *Bonds of Community: The Lives of Farm Women in Nineteenth-Century New York* (Ithaca, NY: Cornell University Press, 1991).

57 On occupational pluralism, see McCann, "Seasons of Labor." The earlier work is Peter McGahan, Dianne O'Keefe, and F.K. Donnelly, *Family and Household in Mid-nineteenth Century New Brunswick* (St John, NB: University of New Brunswick, 1986). Although we discuss the Maritimes as a single region, like the others, it was in fact a diverse area. Nevertheless, each of the three provinces, Nova Scotia, New Brunswick, and Prince Edward Island, had the highest rates of extended household residence in Canada in 1901 and in 1911.

— · 8 · —

Aging and Social Reproduction in Canada, 1901–11

LISA DILLON

Elderly parents played important roles in social reproduction prior to the twentieth century in Canada. During the eighteenth and nineteenth centuries, most elderly parents continued to meet parental responsibilities as they aged, mediating children's transitions to adulthood by supporting them as unmarried adults and aiding their establishment through the disposition of family property. Although various scholars have demonstrated the continuing importance of intergenerational exchange by the end of the Victorian period, new research on the 1901 Canadian census suggests that by the turn of the twentieth century, family interdependence was becoming less predicated on co-residence. To what extent did these trends prevail during the busy first decade of the twentieth century? Did the significant shifts between 1901 and 1911 – heightened immigration, westward expansion, market development, and increased industrialization – diminish or augment co-residential family interdependence? This chapter addresses such questions concerning social reproduction in the context of the family as Canadians entered the twentieth century. The following analysis compares the socio-economic status and living arrangements of the elderly in 1901 and 1911, drawing upon the Census of Canada for those two years. Our research examines factors associated with the household status of aged women and men and co-residence with children, highlighting change as well as continuity since 1901, in addition to gender, ethnoreligious, and regional disparities.

Literature Review

The important role of elderly family members in social reproduction in North America has been addressed at length, yet for Canada, most of our knowledge is confined to the nineteenth century. The Canadian scholarly literature on historical old age itself has been steadily growing since the 1980s, with a continued focus on the institutionalization of the elderly or the development of pension policies. Most of these researchers have reserved some words for the situation of elderly women and men outside institutions at the dawn of the twentieth century. Social histories of particular Canadian communities written in recent decades also serve as important sources of information on the position of the elderly within Canadian families. Canadian social historians have generally depicted the elderly as important decision makers, stressing the primacy of parental control as well as cooperation between generations.[1] Historians of the elderly in Canada state that most men at the turn of the twentieth century continued to work into old age, that elderly persons maintained their own households in large numbers, and that families remained the first source of support for elderly persons in need.[2] This literature tends to emphasize gender differences, with elderly women more easily finding a continued place in the family.[3] The lives of the elderly were marked by considerable diversity in other ways, on the basis of class, race, ethnicity, religion, family history, past fertility, and property ownership.[4]

For their part, US scholars have produced a wealth of research on the household and economic status of the elderly over a long time period, and these studies generally agree on an association between elevated economic status and multigenerational co-residence, as well as the influence of demographic opportunity on living arrangements.[5] Other scholars have argued that rising wages resulting from the industrial revolution improved the elderly's ability to finance their own retirement.[6] The changing destinies of the elderly during the most recent century continue to inspire debate among US researchers. In articles published between 2007 and 2010, Steven Ruggles and also Brian Gratton and Myron Gutmann identified a sharp decline in the elderly's co-residence with children throughout the twentieth century, with the steepest decline happening after 1940.[7] Ruggles argued that such changes resulted from increased opportunities for children to establish themselves in independent livelihoods and a concomitant, dramatic decline in patriarchal power: the ability of elderly parents, namely, elderly fathers, to insist upon prolonged co-residence with dependent children diminished as children found alternative means to transition to adulthood and work life. Since both articles highlight the importance of economic change in explaining this decline, the interpretative differences among these scholars are those of emphasis. Gratton and Gutmann focus equally on decisions made by elderly persons as well as their children, while Ruggles decisively foregrounds children's changing priorities. Ruggles disputes assertions that most intergenerational co-residence of the elderly and adult children happened as a result of "nuclear reincorporation" (the elderly moving back in with children), reasoning that since the majority of households that contained elderly members were headed by that elderly person, these households could not have been formed through nuclear reincorporation. Evidence from Gratton and Gutmann and Ruggles shows more agreement than disagreement, particularly their findings that intergenerational co-residence before 1940 was associated with the elevated economic status of either generation.[8] Research produced by Ruggles and Gratton and Gutmann alike encourages greater attention to *temporal shifts* in the co-residential patterns of the Canadian elderly and their children into the twentieth century.

As the nineteenth century drew to a close and the new century dawned, as Canada expanded geographically to the west, as new immigrants arrived, urban centres grew, and increasing numbers of Canadians turned to industrial and commercial work, some evidence suggests that the nature of intergenerational cooperation was shifting. First, the diversity of living arrangements reported by elderly women appears to have increased by the turn of the century: "from 1871 to 1901, the percentage of Canadian women living as boarders, siblings, other relatives or employees of the household head increased from 5% to 16%. Changes in elderly women's living arrangements from the late nineteenth century ... represented a residential separation of generations and an impulse to nuclearization and independent living."[9] Second, recent research suggests that some men adopted a practice of life-cycle saving to finance an independent old age, a practice that may have served as a growing alternative to co-residence with children.[10] Third, and finally, research indicates the important role of regional economies in differentiating the living arrangements and family reproductive strategies pursued by elderly men and women. Gordon Darroch and Michael Ornstein demonstrated important regional variations in household complexity in 1871, arguing that household complexity was minimized in contexts where markets offered alternatives to dependence on the family farm.[11] In general, it seems that French Canadian family practices were more oriented towards the establishment of children early in the family life cycle: in addition to the French Canadian Catholic tradition of early marriage, French Canadian parents used the *donation* and other inheritance practices to transmit the farm or other property on to the next generation during their own lifetime.[12] French Canadian patterns describe the dominant patterns in Quebec. In Ontario, in contrast, the elderly seemed to retain control of their household to a later point in their life course. For example, the proportion of elderly widows who headed their own homes in 1901 Ontario (41%) outstripped the proportion doing so in Quebec (27%).[13] Smaller proportions of elderly male household heads in rural Quebec lived with dependent adult children than did elderly men in Ontario, perhaps the result of the relatively early age at marriage among French Canadian children. Instead, in Ontario researchers have discerned "a vanguard of men who accumulated the resources necessary to finance their own retirement."[14] Darroch and Ornstein noted high proportions of stemlike households in Nova Scotia, as well as Quebec and New Brunswick in 1871, arguing that such households were probably formed by "recently widowed parents moving in with the son's family"; research by Katie Pickles and Timothy Lewis also suggests high rates of intergenerational co-residence in rural Nova Scotia and New Brunswick.[15] Other research on the Maritimes towards the close of the nineteenth century suggests that young persons who migrated on a seasonal or temporary basis would resume co-residence with their aging parents at one point.[16] In the Prairie provinces, homesteading regulations and traditions may have hindered independent residence by aging females and enforced their co-residence with adult children; federal government land distribution rules permitted women to homestead only if they had dependent minor children.[17] On the other hand, research findings from Montcalm, Manitoba, suggest that a growing proportion of elderly persons were living apart from their adult children in village situations.[18] Research on the living conditions of the elderly in British Columbia indicates still other patterns: in this context, many elderly persons were aging bachelors who lived especially precarious lives, with fewer family and community attachments to sustain them.[19] Davies writes, "The dominance of resource-based industries meant that British Columbia had a significant population of elderly single labouring men ... aged and impoverished castoffs of resource capitalism."[20] Thus, ample evidence suggests that strong regional disparities may have characterized the living arrangements of elderly women and men across Canada at the beginning of the twentieth century.

Hypotheses

The Canadian and US literature on aging and social reproduction suggests that we will discover a continued trend towards co-residential separation of the generations between 1901 and 1911, with the incidence of intergenerational co-residence remaining high. Nevertheless, westward expansion, increased industrialization, and market development offered alternatives to intergenerational interdependence for either generation and may have increased the diversity of living arrangements observed among the elderly and decreased the incidence of intergenerational co-residence. We also expect to encounter important regional differences, with increased proportions of elderly women as well as elderly men heading their own households in Ontario and decreased proportions doing so in the Maritimes. The development of the western Canadian provinces by 1911 will afford better opportunities to explore whether truly western patterns of intergenerational co-residence existed, namely, a high proportion of elderly men living alone in the west and, particularly, in British Columbia. The question remains: can these regional differences be explained by underlying ethnoreligious or occupational class differences?

Data and Methodology

The data employed in this study are drawn from the 1871, 1901, and 1911 censuses of Canada. The 1871 Canadian census sample provides some statistical comparisons with the nineteenth-century period (as seen in tables 8.1 and 8.2). The 1871 national sample was created by Gordon Darroch and Michael Ornstein at the Institute of Social Research, York University, in 1979; the base sample includes over 45,000 observations.[21] The bulk of the analysis in this chapter focuses on the first decade of the twentieth century, and draws upon the 1901 and 1911 censuses. The 1901 Canadian census national file is a 5 per cent sample of the 1901 Canadian census created by the Canadian Families Project (University of Victoria) and released in 2001.[22] This 5 per cent sample is a nationally representative, geographically stratified sample, clustered by dwelling in order to provide the possibility of studying the characteristics of co-residents, and featuring extensive geocoding at the district and subdistrict level. The 1911 Canadian census national file, described in the introduction to this volume, is based on a similar sample design also accompanied by geocoding. Overall, the 1901 Canadian census sample includes 265,288 cases, while the 1911 census sample includes 371,373 cases. The elderly persons studied in this chapter are defined as persons aged 65 years or more, a group numbering 13,036 in 1901 and 16,118 in 1911. Both census samples comprise all variables included in the personal census schedule, while the 1901 census also includes variables drawn from the property schedule. Comparability of the two census samples is good: both censuses include a wide range of common variables, including the usual demographic and sociocultural variables (age, sex, marital status, ethnicity, religion, birthplace) as well as economic variables (occupation, industry, relation to the means of production). The analyses in this chapter are conducted at the household level; in the vast majority of cases (e.g., 95% in 1911), individuals residing in private homes lived in a dwelling that included only one household. On account of differences in the way collective dwellings were sampled for the 1901 and 1911 databases, this chapter focuses on elderly persons living in private households and excludes the 2 per cent to 4 per cent of elderly persons who were living in institutions and other large dwellings in 1901 and 1911.

Research Results

Portrait of the Elderly in Canada, 1901 and 1911

Demographic comparisons of elderly persons in 1901 and 1911 in Canada are perhaps most striking for their continuity rather than change: in both census years, about a third of men and women were "old old," or over 75; few changes occurred with respect to marital status other than the emergence of a tiny proportion of divorced elderly persons by 1911; the percentage of elderly women in charge of their own household as spouses of the household head or household heads in their own right remained the same (about half), while three-quarters of elderly men headed their own homes in both census years. These continuities are contrasted by changes in nativity status, ethnoreligious identity, and language, as well as their geographical distribution. Although the first decade of the twentieth century was marked by significantly higher immigration rates than preceding decades, the proportion of foreign-born elderly persons was falling: in 1901, 34 per cent of older women and 38 per cent of older men had been born outside Canada; by 1911, just over a quarter of women and men over 65 were foreign-born. Immigration to Canada after the turn of the century was a young person's game: over half of immigrants who arrived in Canada between 1901 and 1911 were aged 20 to 39 years. The elderly population in 1911 had, instead, witnessed the gradual dying off of their peers of old immigrant stock, leaving an increasingly large native-born population of old folks. With the passage of time, a greater proportion of elderly persons reported being able to both read and write. The widening diversity of immigrants coming to Canada did modestly enhance the cultural diversity of the elderly population by 1911, by which time almost a tenth of elderly women and men spoke neither English nor French, favouring a different language such as German, Gaelic, a host of Aboriginal languages including Cree and Ojibway, or Scandinavian languages, notably Icelandic, Norwegian, or Swedish. Unfortunately, our ability to analyse indigenous and Afro-Canadian elderly persons is limited, as the 1911 sample includes just 232 elderly Aboriginal persons and just thirty-nine black elderly women and men.

Alongside increased immigration to Canada between 1901 and 1911 came the development of the western provinces and the aging of populations in the Maritimes. The western provinces of Canada, in 1911, were disproportionately comprised of persons in their 20s and 30s, whereas the opposite was true in the Maritimes. Three times as many Prince Edward Islanders were 65 to 69 years old compared with British Columbians (3% vs. 1%). Elderly women and men as a whole in 1911, as in 1901, were concentrated in Quebec and Ontario. The addition of population totals for villages, towns, and cities to the 1901 and 1911 samples has permitted the creation of a compatible rural/urban status variable for both census years. Compared with the gradual population shifts discussed above, the proportion of elderly women living in cities of 3,000 persons or more rose significantly in just ten years, from almost a quarter in 1901 to almost a third in 1911. In both years, somewhat fewer elderly men resided in cities, but the percentage of those who did reside in cities also rose notably, from about a fifth in 1901 to a quarter in 1911.

Gender cleavages in residential and demographic patterns were sustained from 1901 to 1911: greater proportions of elderly men headed their own households in both census years, while across the decade, consistently twice as many women were widowed and more than twice as many lived as parents of the household head. Furthermore, in both census years, about twice as many elderly men as women reported the ability to speak both French and English. Only in terms of literacy did an admittedly small gender gap in 1901 narrow by 1911, by which time four-fifths of elderly men and women alike declared literacy. The greatest gender cleavage between elderly women and men concerns the proportion reporting paid labour. In both census years, just 7 per cent to 8 per cent of women aged 65 years or more listed an occupation on the census return, while three-quarters of their male counterparts in 1901 (56% if we set aside those simultaneously reporting retirement) and 68 per cent of aged men in 1911 did so. The 1911 census did instruct enumerators to record women's occupations, specifying remunerative work in addition to housework in her own home; the 1911 census also specified that "a person in charge of a farm should be returned as farmer, whether he owns it or operates it as a tenant, renter or cropper." For this reason, one of the largest groups of women who did report occupations in 1901 and 1911 reported the occupation "farmer," although the proportion doing so fell from 46 per cent to 37 per cent during this interval.[23] Instead, in 1911, slightly greater percentages of women stated that they worked as employees or worked on their own account. Differences in the recording of retirement in the 1901 and 1911 censuses will necessitate a more detailed analysis of the occupation strings in the 1911 sample to identify all retired men and, thus, allow a true comparison of older men's labour force participation in 1901 and 1911.

Living Arrangements and Social Reproduction

The preceding analysis has demonstrated both demographic continuities and changes in terms of nativity and geographical distribution. Changes intro-

Table 8.1 · Marital and household status of women aged 65+ years (%), Canada, 1871, 1901, 1911

	1871	*1901*	*1911*
SPOUSE PRESENT			
Spouse of household head, children present	25	19	17
Spouse of household head, no children present	14	14	15
Parent or parent-in-law of household head	4	5	
SPOUSE ABSENT			
Head of household, no children present	9	8	8
Head of household, children present	10	11	10
Parent or parent-in-law of household head	37	29	27
Boarder, lodger, tenant, no children		4	3
Sibling/sib-in-law of household head, no children		4	5
Other relative, no children present	1	3	4
Employees, no children present		2	1
OTHER HOUSEHOLD STATUSES	4	2	5
N	1,061	6,282	7,835

Sources: Gordon Darroch and Michael Ornstein, Canadian Historical Mobility Project. National Sample of the 1871 Census of Canada, York Institute for Social Research and Department of Sociology, York University, 1979, http://datalib.chass.utoronto.ca/major/canpumf.htm; Canadian Families Project database (CFP), 1901; and CCRI 1911 microdata database.

Note: Includes all individuals residing in dwellings housing 30 or fewer people.

duced by the decade of heightened immigration and urbanization influenced younger cohorts more significantly: the lives of the elderly were changing moderately, but the lives of their children were changing much more rapidly. How did these shifts influence social reproductive strategies at the dawn of the twentieth century? The key way to address this question is through the study of living arrangements.

Tables 8.1 and 8.2 compare the distribution of elderly women and men across a series of predominant marital and household statuses. The majority of elderly women and men lived as household heads or spouses of the household head, with or without children present, or as the parent of the household head. Within these categories, substantial variation occurred between elderly women and elderly men; as noted earlier, in both 1901 and 1911, about 40 per cent of men 65 years or more continued to live as they had in middle age, with both a spouse and children, while less than a fifth of elderly women did so. In contrast, larger percentages of elderly women lived as the parent or parent-in-law of the household head, as well as in a variety of other household statuses such as sibling

Table 8.2 · Marital and household status of men aged 65+ years (%), Canada, 1871, 1901, 1911

	1871	*1901*	*1911*
SPOUSE PRESENT			
Head of household, children present	53	40	38
Head of household, no children present	13	20	23
Parent or parent-in-law of household head	3	5	6
SPOUSE ABSENT			
Head of household, no children present	6	7	6
Head of household, children present	9	10	8
Parent or parent-in-law of household head	12	10	9
Boarder, lodger, tenant, no children		3	3
Sibling or sibling-in-law of household head, no children		1	2
OTHER HOUSEHOLD STATUSES	4	4	5
N	1,239	6,664	8,283

Sources: Gordon Darroch and Michael Ornstein, Canadian Historical Mobility Project. National Sample of the 1871 Census of Canada, York Institute for Social Research and Department of Sociology, York University, 1979, http://datalib.chass.utoronto.ca/major/canpumf.htm; Canadian Families Project database (CFP), 1901; and CCRI 1911 microdata database.

Note: Includes all individuals residing in dwellings housing 30 or fewer people.

or other relative. Widowhood ushered in change for both elderly women and men, as less than a fifth of elderly women and men headed households in the absence of their spouse. The proportion of elderly women living as a widowed parent or parent-in-law of the household head diminished from 29 per cent in 1901 to 27 per cent by 1911; this decline is more notable when understood as part of a downward trend since 1871, when 37 per cent of widowed elderly mothers lived in their children's households. Instead, by 1911, slightly more elderly women were distributed in less typical household statuses, including sibling and other relative, and more married elderly women were living with their husband as married parents or parents-in-law of the household head. By 1911, slightly fewer elderly women and men alike lived in their own homes as a married couple with children present and just 1 per cent more elderly women but 3 per cent more elderly men lived in empty-nest households than was the case in 1901. The proportion of elderly men living in empty-nest households, in fact, had been growing steadily since the late nineteenth century: between 1871 and 1911, the proportion of older men found in this living arrangement almost doubled, from 13 per cent to 23 per cent; this forty-year increase was paralleled by a forty-year decline in the proportion of elderly men heading households with co-resident dependent children, which fell from over half in 1871 (53%) to 38 per cent in 1911.

Thus, small but systematic changes can be observed between 1901 and 1911: the falling proportion of elderly women living as parents of the household head and the rising proportion of aged men living in empty-nest households. These modest but consistent changes between 1901 and 1911 garner greater interest when we introduce region to the analysis. At the turn of the century, the proportion of elderly women heading their own households, with or without children present, varied notably across the Canadian provinces (see table 8.3). Up to 19 per cent of women headed their own households in the Maritime provinces, Quebec, and Manitoba, while this proportion attained a quarter in Ontario and 29 per cent in British Columbia (albeit, with only 70 cases to analyse). Conversely, only 30 per cent of aged women over 65 in Ontario in 1901 lived as the parent of the household head, but up to 41 per cent lived in a son's or daughter's home in New Brunswick, Nova Scotia, Quebec, or Manitoba. Ten years later, Ontario's elderly women were still the high water mark in terms of household headship in Canada. In 1911, almost a quarter of aged women in Ontario headed their own households, compared with just 10 per cent to 17 per cent in the Maritimes and Quebec, and 15 per cent in Manitoba. The larger population of elderly women now living west of Manitoba permits greater analysis and comparison of the western provinces. In British Columbia, the proportion of elderly women heading households had declined to resemble levels observed in Quebec and Prince Edward Island. In contrast, a notable proportion (41%) of elderly women in British Columbia were aging in place with their husbands, with or without children present; only a third of elderly women did so in the Maritimes, Quebec, Ontario, Saskatchewan, and Alberta, while almost as many did so in Manitoba. With the exception of Ontario, the prairie and eastern provinces were more prominent with respect to the proportion of elderly women living as parent of the household head: about a third did so across Nova Scotia, New Brunswick, Prince Edward Island, Quebec, and Manitoba, while even greater proportions lived in the home of a child in Saskatchewan (44%) and Alberta (41%). In this regard, elderly women in Ontario (29%) and British Columbia (31%) seem of a piece, with a slightly reduced proportion living as parent of the household head.

The prominence of Ontario's aged women as heads of their own households in both census years is also evident when we examine maps showing subdistrict variations below the level of province. Figures 8.1 and 8.2 show the proportion of elderly women in 1901 and 1911 heading their own household by census district across Canada, in central Canada and the Maritimes, as well

Table 8.3 · Household status of women aged 65+ years (%), by province or territory, Canada, 1901 and 1911

	1901								
	NB	*NS*	*PEI*	*QC*	*ON*	*MB*	*Org' Terr*	*BC*	*Unorg' Terr*
Spouse of head, children	20	19	24	19	20	18	14	11	25
Spouse of head, no children	10	11	7	15	14	18	22	13	
Household head, +/- children	14	18	19	15	24	13	12	29	50
Parent/parent-in-law of head	41	34	31	35	30	39	31	34	
Other household status	15	18	20	16	12	11	22	13	25
N	420	818	144	1,851	2,773	143	59	70	4

	1911									
	NB	*NS*	*PEI*	*QC*	*ON*	*MB*	*SK*	*AB*	*BC*	*Yukon & NWT*
Spouse of head, children	20	17	20	16	17	18	16	16	22	10
Spouse of head, no children	14	14	11	15	16	20	18	17	19	30
Household head, +/- children	15	17	10	14	23	15	9	13	11	20
Parent/parent-in-law of head	34	33	34	34	29	34	44	41	31	10
Other household status	18	20	25	21	15	13	13	12	17	30
N	496	919	197	2,163	3,368	213	159	134	176	10

Sources: CFP 1901 and CCRI 1911 microdata databases.

as in the Toronto and Montreal areas. These maps indicate a concentration of higher headship proportions in Ontario and generally lower proportions in other provinces such as Quebec. In both census years, there are also interesting variations within the provinces, with select districts across the Maritimes and the Prairie provinces manifesting higher proportions of elderly women heading households. For example, in 1911, we also see areas of higher headship proportions within Nova Scotia, New Brunswick, Manitoba, and Alberta. The district of Hants and Halifax in Nova Scotia, the districts of St John and Charlotte in New Brunswick, the St Anne and St Antoine districts of Montreal, the Montcalm district of Quebec, the Macdonald and Portage-la-Prairie districts of Manitoba, Strathcona and Macleod districts of Alberta, and the Nanaimo district of British Columbia all show elevated proportions of elderly women heading households. In many instances, these proportions are asso-

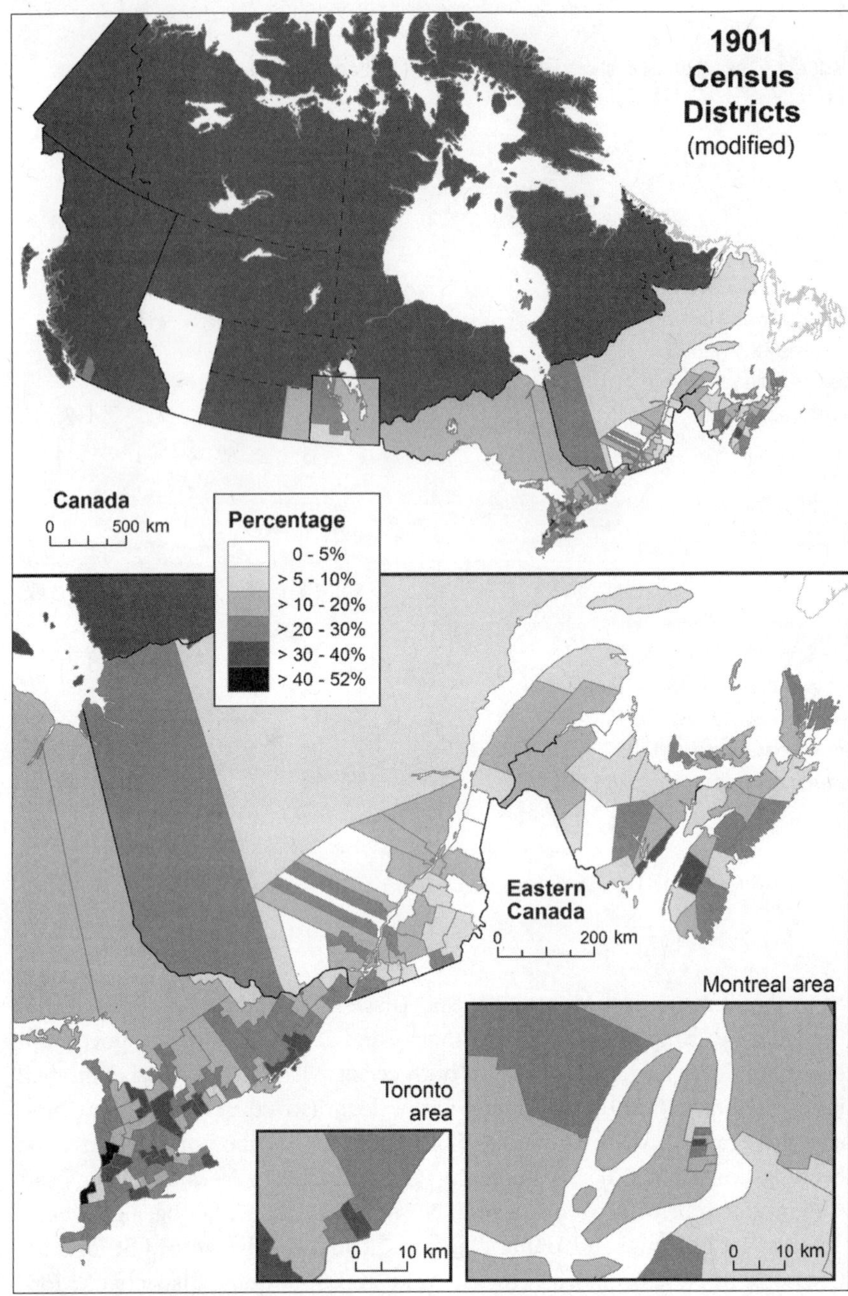

Figure 8.1 · Women heads of household aged 65+, by modified census districts: Canada, Eastern Canada, Montreal area, and Toronto area, 1901.

Sources: Canadian Families Project database, CFP 1901 (http://web.uvic.ca/hrd/CFP/data/index.html), and GIS files from the Historical Atlas of Canada Data Dissemination Project, Department of Geography and Program in Planning, University of Toronto (www.historicalatlas.ca).

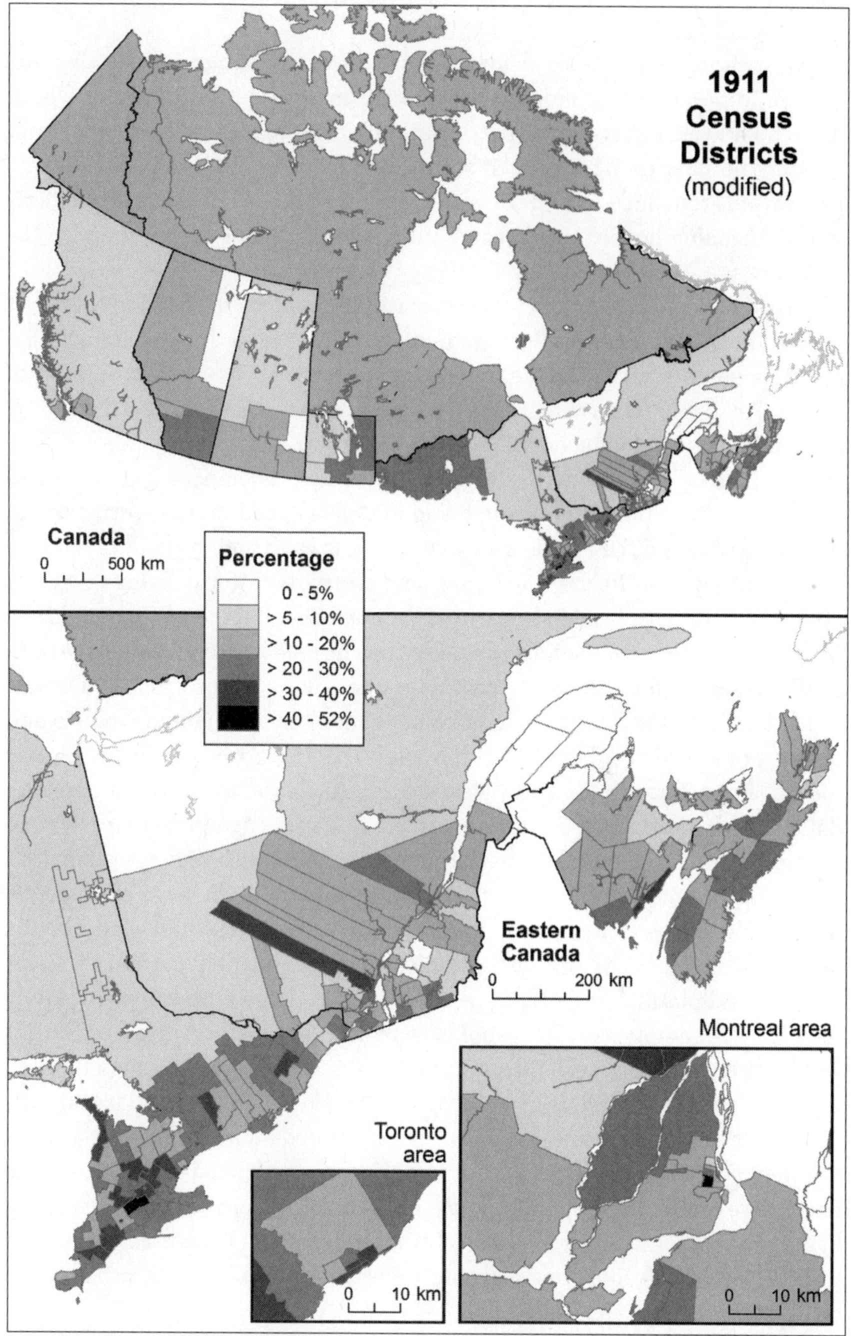

Figure 8.2 · Women heads of household aged 65+, by modified census districts: Canada, Eastern Canada, Montreal area, and Toronto area, 1911.

Source: CCRI geographical database.

ciated with urban residence, as in the case of Montreal and St John. A more general impression that emerges from these maps, however, is rising female household headship across districts, both in Ontario and Quebec, with an increasing number of "dark grey" districts. A certain heterogeneity of headship proportions remained in Ontario and Quebec, while the proportion of elderly women heading households became more homogeneous across space in the Maritimes.

A regional comparison of elderly men's household statuses in 1901 and 1911 yields quite a different set of geographical contrasts from those characterizing elderly women. Canadian elderly women seem to fall into two groups, with "dependence" characterizing those in the Maritimes, Quebec, and the Prairie provinces, and "independence" characterizing those in Ontario. With elderly men, on the other hand, we find strong residential differences between those living in the Maritimes and those living in Quebec, and more similarities between Ontario and the Prairie provinces (table 8.4). In both 1901 and 1911, over half of elderly men in the Maritimes, and nearly two-thirds living in Prince Edward Island both headed households and resided with dependent children. In Quebec, on the other hand, fewer aged men headed households at all, in both census years. At the turn of the century, 71 per cent of elderly men in Quebec headed households compared with 79 per cent of elderly men in Ontario and 81 per cent in Prince Edward Island. By 1911, the proportion of Quebec elderly men heading households had fallen slightly to 68 per cent; the proportion doing so in Ontario and the Maritimes also fell very slightly, but elderly men in these provinces continued to head households in much higher proportions than men in Quebec. For their part, Quebec elderly men were consistently more likely to reside as parent or parent-in-law of the household head: about a fifth did so in both 1901 and 1911. Another notable residential pattern concerns empty-nest households. At the turn of the century, large proportions of elderly men living in empty-nest households were found in the organized territories and British Columbia: from 32 per cent to 45 per cent of elderly men in these regions headed households in the absence of children. Between 1901 and 1911, elderly men in Ontario and Manitoba demonstrated a similar residential shift: like their counterparts in the west in 1901, by 1911, aged men in these provinces were increasingly heading empty-nest households. Finally, elderly men living in the western regions were more likely than elderly men in central and eastern Canada to live in "other" living arrangements, such as living with other kin or boarding.

The maps in figures 8.3 and 8.4 display the proportion of elderly men heading households with co-resident children across Canadian districts in 1901 and 1911 respectively. These spatial representations show the lower proportions of

Table 8.4 · Household status of men aged 65+ years (%), by province or territory, Canada, 1901 and 1911

	1901								
	NB	*NS*	*PEI*	*QC*	*ON*	*MB*	*Org' Terr*	*BC*	*Unorg' Terr*
Household head	74	79	81	71	79	75	80	78	78
With children	54	54	62	45	51	47	48	33	56
Without children	20	25	19	26	27	29	32	45	22
Parent/parent-in-law of head	16	12	14	20	13	15	9	7	0
Other household status	10	9	5	9	9	10	11	15	22
N	481	725	154	1,873	3,052	161	88	121	9

	1911									
	NB	*NS*	*PEI*	*QC*	*ON*	*MB*	*SK*	*AB*	*BC*	*Yukon & NWT*
Spouse of head, children	20	17	20	16	17	18	16	16	22	10
Household head	75	77	79	68	77	77	71	78	69	80
With children	51	52	57	42	46	46	38	39	39	33
Without children	24	25	22	26	31	31	33	39	30	47
Parent/parent-in-law of head	16	13	14	19	14	13	21	10	10	0
Other household status	9	10	7	13	9	9	8	13	21	20
N	563	871	199	2,229	3,475	283	224	169	255	15

Sources: CFP 1901 and CCRI 1911 microdata databases.

western Canadian elderly men heading households in the presence of children in both census years. Nevertheless, elderly men living in certain 1901 and 1911 Manitoba districts such as Selkirk did remain in charge of their own homes with co-resident children in greater proportions than their neighbours further to the west. Within central Canada, the ten-year decrease in the proportion of elderly men heading households with co-resident children is made clear by the smaller number of "dark grey" districts in the 1911 map. The 1901 map of Ontario and Quebec elderly men's living arrangements is a patchwork, with some districts showing 40 per cent to 45 per cent of older men heading households with co-resident children adjacent to other districts exhibiting 60 per cent to 70 per cent of elderly men doing so. In the 1911 map, the differences across districts are more muted; we see more homogeneity of light grey tones from district to district within Ontario, albeit with some higher percentages

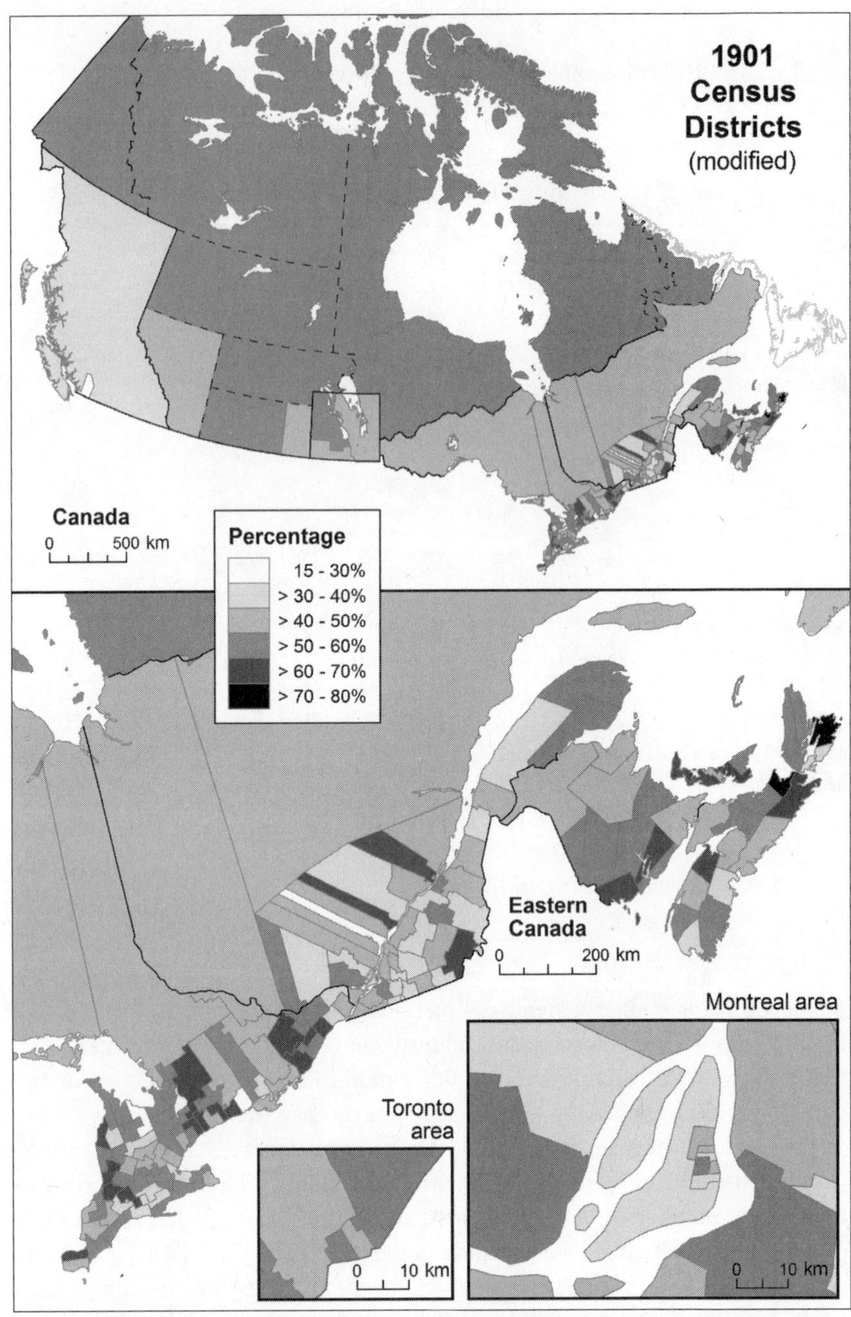

Figure 8.3 · Men aged 65+ who were both heads of household and living with children, by modified census districts, Canada, 1901.

Sources: Canadian Families Project database, CFP 1901, and GIS files from the Historical Atlas of Canada Data Dissemination Project, Department of Geography and Program in Planning, University of Toronto.

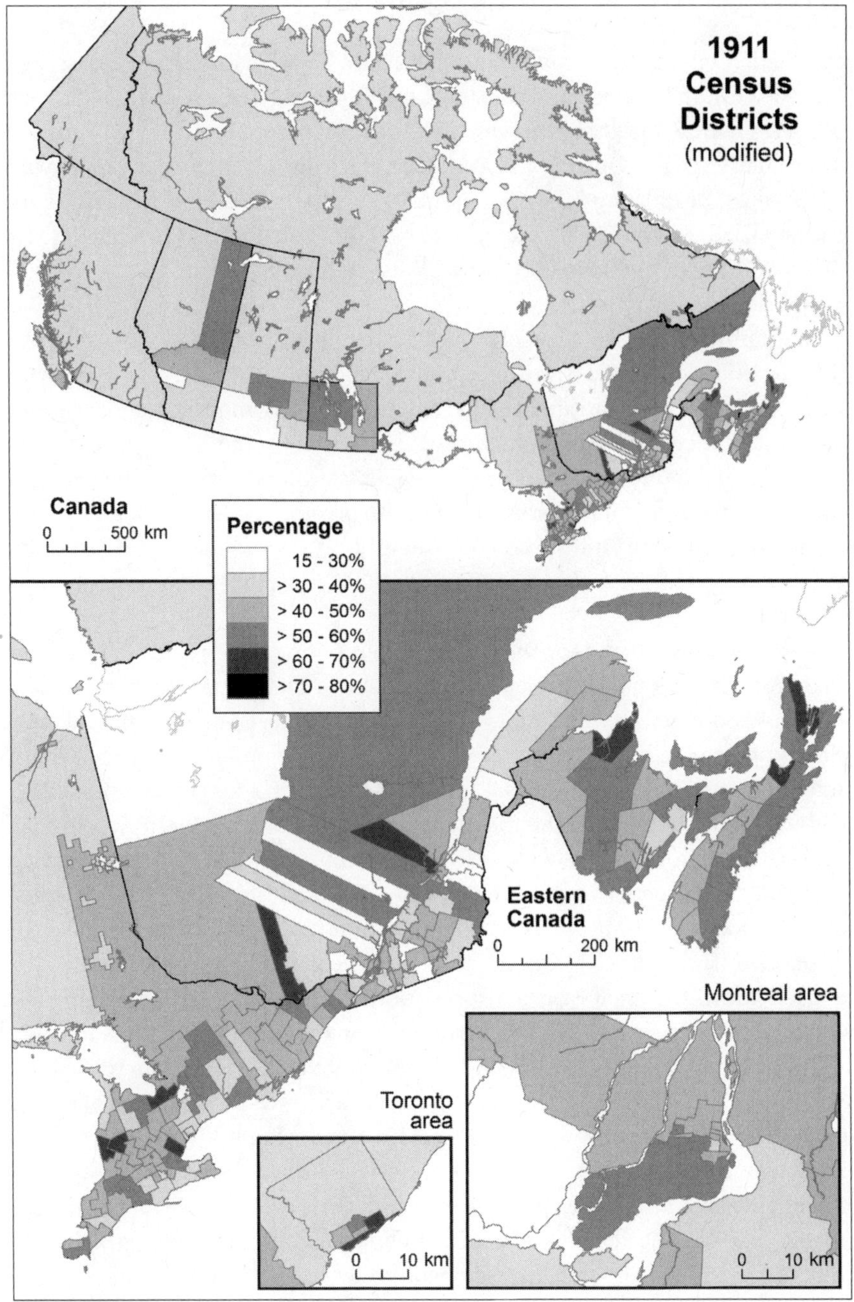

Figure 8.4 · Men aged 65+ who were both heads of household and living with children, by modified census districts, Canada, 1911.

Source: CCRI geographical database.

in middle Ontario, in Toronto South, Toronto East, Halton, Huron East, and Huron West. In both census years, men over 65 living in the Maritime districts headed their own households with co-resident children in greater proportion than elderly men in Quebec and even than those in the Ontario districts, with the greatest proportions showing up in and around Cape Breton, in Antigonish, and Cape Breton North/Victoria, also south in Shelburne/Queen's, in parts of New Brunwick (Gloucester, York, Westmoreland) and in Prince Edward Island (Prince and Queen's).

In summary, we see a general picture of intergenerational co-residential interdependence in the Maritimes and Quebec for elderly men, albeit with headship more concentrated in the hands of elderly men in the Maritimes and more concentrated in the hands of children in Quebec. Intergenerational co-residential interdependence is also evident in the Maritimes, Quebec, and the Prairie provinces for elderly women, with greater residential independence for elderly women in Ontario and more empty-nest households for elderly men in Ontario and in the west.

Predicting Household Headship: Descriptive Analysis

Many of the regional contrasts discussed above focus our attention on two social phenomena: the residential independence of never-married or widowed elderly women, a minority pattern subject to variation, is contrasted with a similarly varying pattern among elderly men, their chances of co-residing with dependent children. The following analysis focuses on these two groups. Among never-married or widowed elderly women, the proportion heading households fluctuated in accordance with many factors other than province of residence, and in many cases the proportion doing so exceeded provincial disparities (see table 8.5). The single or widowed elderly women who headed households in the greatest proportions were those who listed an occupation on the census, lived in rural non-farm areas or were non-white (40% to 63%). Almost 40% of elderly women who had immigrated to Canada from the United States, England, Ireland, or Scotland headed their own homes. Finally, over a third of widowed or never-married elderly women who lived in Ontario or in cities; who spoke English only; or who were English-, Scottish-, or Irish-Protestant or Irish-Catholic headed households. Elderly men's household headship, in this case specifically with co-resident children, presents a demographically and geographically different yet socioculturally similar profile to that of aged women. Between 45% and 67% of elderly men who were aged 60 to 69 years; were married; were born in the Maritimes, the western provinces, Ireland, or Scotland; were Protestant or Irish-Catholic; lived in the Maritime provinces; or were employers or farmers headed households with co-resident children.[24]

Table 8.5 · Headship status of widowed and never-married women and all men aged 65+ years (%), by select characteristics, Canada, 1901 and 1911

	Widows/Never married women: Head		*Men: Head of household with children*	
	1901	*1911*	*1901*	*1911*
All	18	18	50	45
AGE (years)				
65–69	38	38	60	55
70–74	33	32	50	46
75–80	31	26	42	36
80+	18	20	30	30
MARITAL STATUS				
Widowed, divorced, separated	33	33	35	33
Never married	19	17	3	3
VISIBLE MINORITY STATUS				
White	31	30	50	46
Non-white	42	40	39	45
MIGRANT STATUS				
Immigrated from outside Canada	37	36	50	44
Migrated from province of birth	33	30	52	42
Living in province of birth	28	28	49	47
BIRTHPLACE				
Prince Edward Island	26	22	52	55
Nova Scotia	26	27	55	52
New Brunswick	21	23	54	49
Quebec	34	23	45	41
Ontario	38	35	51	48
West (MB, SK, AB, BC, NWT)	41	21	43	48
Other Canada, incl. Nfld	30	27	29	54
United States	41	37	36	36
England	39	38	48	43
Ireland	38	39	55	46
Scotland	36	37	55	49
Other Europe	26	21	40	41
RELIGION AND ETHNICITY				
English Protestant	35	35	49	45
Scottish Protestant	35	35	58	49
Irish Protestant	36	32	55	48
Irish Catholic	36	36	58	57

/continued

Table 8.5 · continued

	Widows/Never married women: Head		*Men: Head of household with children*	
	1901	*1911*	*1901*	*1911*
German	33	29	41	43
French Catholic	20	20	45	41
Other	31	30	47	45
LITERACY				
Literate (reads and writes)	34	33	52	47
Illiterate or can read but not write	23	21	41	39
LANGUAGE SPOKEN				
Speaks English only	36	35	53	47
Speaks French only	20	19	41	38
Speaks English and French	29	27	49	53
Other language	20	26	34	44
RURAL/URBAN STATUS				
Living in city 3,000+ persons	39	36	50	48
Rural	28	27	50	45
Rural non-farm	45	47	42	38
Rural farm	15	9	53	49
PROVINCE OF RESIDENCE				
Prince Edward Island	28	17	62	57
Nova Scotia	27	27	54	52
New Brunswick	22	26	54	51
Quebec	24	23	45	41
Ontario	39	38	51	46
Manitoba	25	29	47	46
Territories	24		49	
Saskatchewan		17		38
Alberta		24		39
Yukon and Northwest territories		40		33
British Columbia	41	23	33	39
OCCUPATION LISTED				
No occupation listed on census	27	28	22	26
Occupation listed on census	63	53	58	55
OCCUPATION/CLASS STATUS				
Employer only			63	67
Employee only			49	47
Farmer			63	59

/continued

Table 8.5 · continued

	Widows/Never married women: Head		*Men: Head of household with children*	
	1901	*1911*	*1901*	*1911*
Other own account			57	51
Other occupation/status			42	42
No occupation listed on census			22	26
HOUSEHOLD CONTAINS BOARDERS				
No boarder present	33	31	52	47
Boarder(s) present	23	25	30	30
HOUSEHOLD CONTAINS SERVANTS				
No servant present	33	31	51	46
Servant(s) present	22	22	43	37
N	3,675	4,605	6,664	8,283

Sources: CFP 1901 and CCRI 1911 microdata databases.

Notable proportions of such men were also literate, lived in Ontario, lived in cities or on rural farms, and spoke English or English and French.

This descriptive analysis suggests several complexities associated with household headship and co-residence with children among the elderly. With respect to race and paid labour, elderly female household headship was seemingly associated with economically vulnerable populations or the need to support oneself. On the other hand, elderly female household headship was also definitively associated with an anglophone cultural identity and residence in Ontario. Elderly male household heads with resident dependent children were more concentrated in the Maritime provinces. This pattern for men was also connected to an earlier phase in the life course, as much older and widowed men were less often found heading households with dependent children. Although region was responsible for much differentiation in the household statuses of elderly men and women, ethnoreligious identity, age, marital status, occupational status, and urban/rural status also played important roles. Did these cultural and socio-economic factors, in fact, erase much of the observed regional differentiation?

Predicting Household Headship: Multivariate Analysis

Table 8.6 presents a multivariate analysis on the probability that never-married or widowed women aged 65 years or more would head a household in 1901

Table 8.6 · Logistic regression on the probability of heading a household, by select characteristics, never-married or widowed women aged 65+ years, Canada, 1901 and 1911

	Model 1		*Model 2*	
	Exp (B)	*Sig*	*Exp (B)*	*Sig*
PROVINCE OF RESIDENCE				
Prince Edward Island	0.442	0.	0.759	0.403
Nova Scotia	0.589	0.	0.948	0.783
New Brunswick	0.512	0.	0.94	0.764
Quebec	0.504	0.	0.7	0.004
Ontario	1		1	
Manitoba	0.601	0.003	0.617	0.017
Territories in 1901	0.515	0.104	0.307	0.025
Saskatchewan in 1911	0.318	0.	0.414	0.01
Alberta in 1911	0.509	0.013	0.548	0.057
British Columbia	0.657	0.028	0.452	0.
Yukon and Northwest territories in 1911	1.074	0.938	0.378	0.444
AGE (years)				
65–69			1	
70–74			0.789	0.001
75–80			0.68	0.
80+			0.42	0.
MARITAL STATUS				
Never married			0.311	0.
Widowed, divorced, separated			1	
BIRTHPLACE				
Prince Edward Island			1.025	0.942
Nova Scotia			0.739	0.152
New Brunswick			0.661	0.079
Quebec			1.573	0.003
West (MB, SK, AB, BC, NWT)			1.309	0.405
Other Canada, incl. Nfld			0.574	0.164
United States			1.12	0.566
England			1.043	0.725
Ireland			1.257	0.064
Scotland			1.151	0.3
Other Europe			0.655	0.044
Other			2.245	0.212
Ontario			1	

/continued

Table 8.6 · continued

	Model 1		Model 2	
	Exp (B)	Sig	Exp (B)	Sig
RELIGION AND ETHNICITY				
English Protestant			1.554	0.026
Scottish Protestant			1.782	0.005
Irish Protestant			1.331	0.17
Irish Catholic			1.507	0.056
German			1.513	0.075
Other			1.611	0.014
French Catholic			1	
LITERACY				
Illiterate or can read but not write			0.744	0.
Literate (reads and writes)			1	
LANGUAGE SPOKEN				
Speaks French only			0.545	0.003
Speaks English and French			0.657	0.017
Other language			1.009	0.963
Speaks English only			1	
RURAL-URBAN STATUS				
Living in city 3,000+ persons			7.109	0.
Rural non-farm			10.981	0.
Rural farm			1	
OCCUPATION LISTED				
Occupation listed on census			9.253	0.
No occupation listed on census			1	
HOUSEHOLD CONTAINS BOARDERS				
Boarder(s) present			0.474	0.
No boarder present			1	
HOUSEHOLD CONTAINS SERVANTS				
Servant(s) present			0.439	0.
No servant present			1	
N	8,280		8,092	
-2 Log Likelihood	10,011		7,789	
Model Chi-square	190		2,206	

Sources: CFP 1901 and CCRI 1911 microdata databases.

Note: Exp (B) = Odds Ratios; Sig = Observed Significance Level. A low significance level allows us to reject the null hypothesis of no effect.

and 1911. In this analysis of aged women, census year proved insignificant and was dropped from both model 1 and model 2. Province of residence exhibited strong, significant associations with household headship when entered alone in the regression. Elderly women living in Saskatchewan (in 1911), Prince Edward Island, Alberta (in 1911), Quebec, Manitoba, New Brunswick and Nova Scotia were half as likely to head households as their counterparts in Ontario (table 8.6, model 1). By presenting province of residence alone in model 1, we are able to see what happens to the odds ratios for province of residence once we include a host of demographic, cultural, and economic variables in the next model. In model 2, many of the provincial odds ratios have drawn closer to the reference category of Ontario, and many of the effects have been rendered insignificant, mainly in the case of the Maritime provinces. Visible minority status and immigrant/migrant status proved insignificant and were dropped from model 2.

Several of the positive associations with aged female household headship observed in the descriptive analysis have been maintained in this multivariate analysis, including being aged 65 to 69, widowed, Anglo-Protestant, literate, living in urban or rural non-farm areas, and listing an occupation on the census return (table 8.6, model 2). Holding all factors constant, aged female household headship was still negatively associated with increasing age, being born in Quebec, being single or married, French Catholic, speaking French only, and living with boarders or servants. The strongest effect concerns living in rural non-farm areas: women who lived in rural contexts but not on a farm were more than ten times more likely to head their own households as their counterparts who lived on farms. The next most important factor was occupation: aged women who listed an occupation on the census return were over nine times more likely to head their own households compared with women who did not list an occupation. Elderly women who lived in cities had seven times the odds of heading their own households as women in rural farm areas. Widowhood was the next more important variable, with never married women 0.311 times as likely to head households as their widowed counterparts. By entering different combinations of variables into the regression analysis, we see that it was place of birth, ethnoreligious identity, and urban-rural-farm status that mitigated many of the provincial effects. Yet, although Protestant identity was positively associated with household headship among elderly women, cultural identity was not as important overall as demography/life-course factors, the dynamics of family life in relation to rural contexts, and the economic need to work.

At first glance, the passage of time from 1901 to 1911 affected elderly men's living arrangements to a greater extent than seen with elderly women: table

8.7, model 3 shows that aged men in 1901 had 1.167 times the odds of heading households with dependent children compared with their counterparts in 1911, when only province of residence is also included in the model. In this model, many results for province of residence are significant: as seen in the descriptive analysis, elderly men living in the Maritime provinces had 1.151 to 1.548 times the odds of heading households with co-resident children as their counterparts in Ontario, while elderly men living in the Prairie provinces and in British Columbia had 0.636 to 0.711 times the odds of Ontarians heading such households. Once again, as seen with elderly women, differences between the Maritime provinces, Quebec, and Ontario are eliminated once we introduce a variety of demographic, cultural, and socio-economic variables to the regression model, while differences between the western provinces and Ontario remain. The impact of census year becomes insignificant and is dropped from the model (table 8.7, model 4). Migrant status and language spoken prove insignificant and were also dropped from the model.

Many of the effects observed independently in the cross-tabulation remain in this multivariate analysis. Setting aside groups that were small, such as never-married men or men born in the west, the strongest associations are observed with, in order of importance, occupational class status, urban residence, and Irish ethnicity, followed by age and marital status. Among different occupational groups, elderly farmers had the greatest chances of heading households with co-resident children, followed by elderly men who reported employer only status (0.669 the odds of heading households with children compared with farmers) and, excluding farmers, other elderly men who worked on their own account (0.551 odds) (table 8.7, model 4). With farmer status controlled, the other group of elderly men who had large and significant odds of co-residing with children were urban dwellers: elderly men who lived in cities that numbered 3,000 persons or more had 1.707 times the odds of heading households with co-resident children as their rural counterparts. Irish Catholic men and, to a lesser extent, Irish Protestant men had respectively 1.609 and 1.208 times the odds of heading households with dependent children as French Catholic men, while Canadian men of German origin had smaller odds of doing so (0.715). Irish Catholic men's pronounced tendency to head households with co-resident children was maintained over this ten-year period, whereas declines in this behaviour are evident among other ethnoreligious groups. As a result, when controlling for ethnoreligious identity, the odds ratios for time itself change. The effect of time, thus, represents the changing chances of different ethnicities of heading households with lingering children. Subsequent to these socio-economic and cultural effects, elderly men's household headship with co-resident children remained, in part, a function of the life course,

Table 8.7 · Logistic regression on the probability of heading a household, by select characteristics, men aged 65+ years, Canada, 1901 and 1911

	Model 3		*Model 4*	
	Exp (B)	*Sig*	*Exp (B)*	*Sig*
CENSUS YEAR				
1901	1.167	0.		
1911	1			
PROVINCE OF RESIDENCE				
British Columbia	0.636	0.	0.749	0.03
Manitoba	0.925	0.427	0.877	0.251
New Brunswick	1.151	0.035	1.041	0.769
Nova Scotia	1.197	0.001	1.039	0.785
Prince Edward Island	1.548	0.	1.217	0.357
Quebec	0.803	0.	0.921	0.322
Territories in 1901	0.919	0.68	1.008	0.974
Saskatchewan in 1911	0.711	0.015	0.598	0.001
Alberta in 1911	0.713	0.035	0.665	0.029
Yukon and Northwest territories in 1911	0.57	0.306	0.646	0.555
Ontario	1		1	
AGE (years)				
65–69			1	
70–74			0.702	0.
75–80			0.52	0.
80+			0.435	0.
MARITAL STATUS				
Never married			0.025	0.
Widowed, divorced, separated			0.549	0.
Married, spouse present			1	
BIRTHPLACE				
Prince Edward Island			1.201	0.411
Nova Scotia			1.243	0.143
New Brunswick			1.203	0.235
Quebec			1.083	0.439
West (MB, SK, AB, BC, NWT)			1.971	0.002
Other Canada, incl. Nfld			1.108	0.704
United States			0.737	0.039
England			1.106	0.21
Ireland			1.134	0.154
Scotland			1.342	0.003

/continued

Table 8.7 · continued

	Model 3		Model 4	
	Exp (B)	*Sig*	*Exp (B)*	*Sig*
Other Europe			0.966	0.758
Other			0.502	0.099
Ontario			1	
RELIGION AND ETHNICITY				
English Protestant			0.95	0.555
Scottish Protestant			1.181	0.081
Irish Protestant			1.208	0.049
Irish Catholic			1.609	0.
German			0.715	0.003
Other			1.104	0.263
French Catholic			1	
LITERACY				
Illiterate or can read but not write			0.836	0.001
Literate (reads and writes)			1	
RURAL/URBAN STATUS				
Living in city 3,000+ persons			1.707	0.
Rural			1	
OCCUPATION/CLASS STATUS				
Employer only			0.669	0.049
Employee only			0.46	0.
Other own account			0.551	0.
Other occupation/status			0.419	0.
No occupation listed on census			0.225	0.
Farmer			1	
HOUSEHOLD CONTAINS BOARDERS				
Boarder(s) present			0.542	0.
No boarder present			1	
HOUSEHOLD CONTAINS SERVANTS				
Servant(s) present			0.796	0.001
No servant present			1	
N	14,947		14,841	
-2 Log Likelihood	20,565		17,078	
Model Chi-Square	114		3,459	

Sources: CFP 1901 and CCRI 1911 microdata databases.

Note: Exp (B) = Odds Ratios; Sig = Observed Significance Level. A low significance level allows us to reject the null hypothesis of no effect.

decreasing steadily with age and reduced by half in the case of widowers compared with married men. Elderly men who lived in households that contained boarders or servants were less likely to head households with co-resident children. Other characteristics that were negatively associated with household headship with co-resident children include residence in Saskatchewan or Alberta and illiteracy.

The residential patterns of elderly women and men alike were strongly influenced by whether or not they reported paid labour, and for elderly men, the type of paid labour. The urban/rural context was also significantly associated with aged men's and women's household patterns, albeit in different ways, with rural non-farm residence favouring elderly women's household headship and urban residence favouring men's household headship with children (with farmer status controlled). Although ethnic identity was also an important determinant for both women and men, marital status and age were the next most important factors influencing elderly women's household headship, while these same variables were less important for men's chances of co-residing with dependent children than was their ethnic identity.

Discussion and Conclusion

Although recent US studies of transformations in the lives of the elderly spanning the twentieth century have focused on large trends, by focusing on the relatively short period 1901 to 1911 in Canada, this analysis has encouraged attention to more subtle changes. At first glance, the continuities between 1901 and 1911 command our attention. In both census years, the majority of elderly persons across the country continued to reside with family, the majority of elderly men continued to head their own households, and less than one-fifth of elderly women and men headed households in the absence of their spouse. Gender disparities evident in 1901 prevailed in 1911: more elderly women than men resided as dependants in the households of their children, a sizeable proportion of elderly men continued to live as they had in middle age, with both a wife and dependent children, vastly more elderly men than women reported an occupation to the census taker – despite the option to indicate retirement – and twice as many elderly men as women spoke both English and French. As observed in earlier decades, elderly men's reduced likelihood of widowhood and marriage to wives younger than themselves combined to prolong midlife circumstances into older age, whereas elderly women experienced greater periods of family dependency.[25] It would appear that some elderly francophone men had learned some English in the course of paid labour, whereas francophone females functioned in a more unilingual environment.

Some of the more nuanced shifts we observed between 1901 and 1911 reflect the fact that the elderly were an increasingly native-born group relative to the general population, more were aging in their province of birth, somewhat more were reporting the ability to both read and write, and modestly more spoke a language other than English or French. Definitional differences in the recording of occupations in 1901 and 1911 hinder our comparisons of elderly men's labour force participation in these two years, although statistics seem to indicate a modest drop in the proportion of elderly men describing themselves as farmers in 1911 compared with 1901. One of the most striking changes between 1901 and 1911 concerns the increasing percentage of elderly persons, particularly women, living in cities. The consistently greater proportion of elderly women than men living in cities may suggest that upon widowhood, some elderly women moved to towns or cities rather than remain in a rural context. Although James Struthers wrote of urban contexts as more risky settings for the elderly, enhancing the possibilities of poverty, unemployment, and high rents, older women may have found greater means of survival in the urban environment.[26] In terms of living arrangements, one of the most interesting changes between 1901 and 1911 concerns the 5 per cent decline in the proportion of elderly women living as dependants in a child's household. Although this change is modest, it is consistent with an earlier decline witnessed across the latter third of the nineteenth century. With elderly men, we also see a steadily growing trend towards empty nest households, a shift also rooted in the late nineteenth century.

Our descriptive portrait of the elderly at the beginning of the twentieth century depicts strong differences in the living arrangements of the elderly across regions. Aging as a national experience was tilted towards the central and Maritime provinces, the provinces with the largest share of elderly persons across the country due to high rates of outmigration by young persons combined with moderate fertility rates. Differences across space are at first evident when mapping the elderly's household statuses across provinces and districts. The proportion of aged women heading their own households varied a great deal across Canada's regions in 1901 and 1911, with almost a quarter of Ontario's elderly women heading their own households. Some of Ontario's elderly mothers may have better exploited farm ownership to retain control of their own homes: of the 7 per cent who reported occupations, over half of those declared themselves to be farmers (the remainder were scattered in a variety of occupations including dressmaker, housekeeper, boarding house keeper, and proprietor). However, the vast majority of Ontario's aged female household heads lived in either rural non-farm settings (50%) or urban settings (42%), so continued farm residence and farm operation with the assistance of children does not really explain this unique Ontario pattern. Furthermore, elderly female heads in Ontario were not especially more likely to co-reside with children than their counterparts in other provinces: 58 per cent did so compared with 54 per cent in Quebec, 56 per cent in British Columbia, and 61 per cent in Nova Scotia. Instead, the answer seems to lie in social patterns revealed by place of birth. The power of province to predict household headship is partly mitigated when including place of birth in the regression model. Cross-tabulating place of birth with province reveals distinctions between Ontario and the Maritime provinces. Most elderly women living in Nova Scotia, New Brunswick, and Prince Edward Island (over four in five) were born in that same province of residence. About a third of Ontario's elderly women, on the other hand, hailed from England, Ireland, or Scotland. Women born in Ireland or Scotland were significantly more likely to head households than women born in Ontario; elderly women who were born in England were also more likely to head households than elderly women born in Ontario, but at levels less significant. Thus, much of Ontario's elderly female household headship emerges from the tendency of Ontario-resident but British- and Irish-born older women to do so. The gradual rise in women's financial activities following passage of married women's property laws in various Canadian provinces during the second half of the nineteenth century may have encouraged residential independence. Ontario's married women's property legislation of 1872, 1873, and 1884 resembled the married women's property laws passed in Britain; perhaps British-born elderly women living in Ontario held greater expectations about their control over property and household headship.[27] Peter Baskerville's analysis of women's probated wealth and will making in Hamilton, Ontario, and Victoria, British Columbia, shows a rise in women's percentage of all probated wealth as well as will making in both cities following passage of the married women's property laws. The percentage of probated decedents who were women was higher in Hamilton in 1911 than in Victoria between 1910 and 1913; this result may help explain Ontario elderly women's particularly advantaged position with respect to household headship.[28]

If we look to the other side of the country, less than half as many elderly women in British Columbia headed households as their Ontario counterparts, despite the fact that even more of BC's elderly women were born in England, Ireland, or Scotland. Those who did managed their own households for different reasons than we see in Ontario. The 11 per cent of elderly women who headed households in British Columbia did not tend to report occupations, but were more likely to live with boarders: 41 per cent of elderly female household heads in British Columbia lived with boarders compared with only a tenth of their counterparts in Ontario. This surplus is understandable in light of the large proportion of boarders and lodgers in British Columbia: a quarter of all BC residents in 1911 were boarders or lodgers compared with just 7 per cent of Ontario's residents. British Columbia's elderly women took advantage of BC's relatively large population of unattached individuals in need of housing to maintain a home based on revenue from a boarder or lodger. Nevertheless, elderly female household heads in British Columbia remained a minority. The household experiences of elderly women in Canada's westernmost province were more notable for the proportion aging in place with their husbands, with or without children: four in ten elderly women in British Columbia did so compared with about a third of their counterparts back east. This distinction is related to differences in the marital status profile of elderly women in British Columbia. A more favourable age gap between husbands and wives in British Columbia – BC's elderly wives were 1.5 years older than their husbands, on average, while Ontario's elderly wives were 1.88 years younger than their husbands, on average – meant that somewhat fewer elderly women in British Columbia lived in a state of widowhood (49% vs. 40% in Ontario). Accordingly, older women in this province spent a longer time co-parenting alongside their husbands in a home of their own, and spent less time living as dependants of their children. In contrast to the experiences of aging women in Ontario and British Columbia, larger proportions of elderly women lived as parents of the household head in the Maritimes, Quebec, Manitoba, Saskatchewan, and Alberta; these findings resonate with evidence in the secondary literature showing patterns of elderly female dependence in the east and west. District variations in 1911 largely mirror the provincial disparities, with some exceptions; urban districts in provinces such as Quebec and New Brunswick showed some counter-provincial trends of elevated headship percentages for elderly women living in those areas.

Elderly men's regional residential patterns were distinct from those of elderly women. The greatest proportion of elderly men heading households with dependent children could be found in the Maritimes, perhaps signalling children's later age at marriage and greater dependency on their parents in these regions. This finding resonates with Timothy Lewis's general emphasis on the stability and importance of farm families in Burton County, New Brunswick.[29] Elderly men living in the west were far more likely to live by themselves. This particular residential pattern signalled independence but not necessarily wealth. For example, Megan Davies has carefully documented the unique character of elderly men in British Columbia at the end of the nineteenth century and beginning of the twentieth. Many of them were lifelong bachelors who originally moved to British Columbia in search of labour in resource industries and who continued living in old age as they had in youth: in outlying areas, occupying a shack, and managing to sustain themselves through hunting and fishing.[30] Davies's qualitative explorations are well borne out by the quantitative evidence presented here.

Aged men residing in Quebec and Ontario were also notably distinct in ways that confirm our hypotheses: elderly men in Ontario were far more likely to live in empty-nest households, whereas elderly men in Quebec were much more likely than elderly men in Ontario to live as parents of the household head. Evidence and insights from secondary sources help to explain the Quebec-Ontario distinctions. According to Gérard Bouchard, the occurrence of multigenerational households in late nineteenth-century and early twentieth-century Saguenay was "le cas classique des cultivateurs agés ayant transmis l'exploitation principale à un fils successeur qui a habité avec ses parents jusqu'à leur décès. C'est ensuite le cas de fils ou des filles mariées qui ont vécu avec leur famille avant de pouvoir s'établir."[31] Bouchard did not provide statistics on household co-residence of parents and adult children, but he did show that the proportion of married sons residing in the same parish as their parents remained steady between the end of the nineteenth century and 1911 at 88 per cent and 94 per cent respectively.[32] James Snell noted that the 1866 Quebec Civil Code mandated support for parents long before Ontario and other provinces developed filial responsibility laws.[33] In the early twentieth century, writes Snell, "the family culture of Quebec was perceived to be particularly authoritative, and traditional values to be fully functioning." Snell goes on to quote a federal civil servant writing in 1932 about the adoption of old age pensions in Quebec: "'The situation in Quebec does not lend itself to comparison with other provinces, due to filial reasons. The young people of Quebec, particularly among the French-speaking, consider it not only a duty but a privilege to care for the aged. This characteristic is perhaps more pronounced in the Province of Quebec than in any other province.'"[34] Snell saw this presumption as a cultural stereotype, but the preceding regional statistics suggest some truth to this assumption. Snell evoked an alternate mechanism linked to high fertility that might also explain the distinct patterns observed in Quebec: he noted that in other provinces, a diminishing fertility rate and compression of spaces between births "could result in a lack of 'fit' in timing between the parents' willingness to turn over primary control of the property and the son's readiness to take over, particularly when adult sons were aware of the opportunities for social and economic independence in rapidly growing urban communities."[35]

Although slowly declining, Quebec fertility rates were nonetheless higher than those in other provinces in both 1901 and 1911; as a result, demographic conditions unique to Quebec families may have facilitated their adherence to traditional inheritance and co-residential mechanisms longer than their counterparts in other provinces. Even though Quebec rural communities were experiencing high rates of outmigration, both to New England and to Montreal, the system of transferring family property to one son while accommodating other children in other ways may have prevailed longer in Quebec than in the rest of Canada. With respect to the Saguenay region, in particular, Bouchard, in fact, argues that the cultural habit of proximate residence and intergenerational aide continued even when it was no longer economically optimal, when, during the early twentieth century, the best arable land was already settled and attempts to create farms on less arable land were leading to poverty.[36] Thus, evidence from Quebec resonates with Steven Ruggles's suggestion that a lag occurred between the advent of alternative economic opportunities for children and the change in cultural values esteeming intergenerational co-residence.

Turning from Quebec to Ontario, we also find results that resonate with Ontario community studies. Edgar-André Montigny wrote an optimistic assessment of the economic status of the elderly in late nineteenth-century Brockville, Ontario, stating, "At least a portion of Brockville's aged population possessed substantial amounts of wealth" as evidenced by their wills.[37] As children came of age in Ontario, they may have found more alternatives to the family farm economy than they did in other parts of Canada. As early as 1871, Gordon Darroch and Michael Ornstein argue, "Among the provinces, Ontario ... presented the widest array of nonfarm options for full-time wage-work."[38] The reasons for the high proportion of empty nests in Ontario is also consonant with research by Livio Di Matteo and Peter George on older men's economic behaviour: Di Matteo and George determined that, as early as the period 1872–1902, men in Wentworth County had begun to develop "the pattern of accumulating assets during youth and middle age for use in old age." They go on to note that the existence of this pattern in Wentworth County is understandable in light of "the increasing urbanization of the county and the rise of non-farm employment opportunities, the decline of agricultural employment ... and the rise in holdings of financial assets."[39]

Although regional disparities are clear from our bivariate analyses, only multivariate analyses can demonstrate whether these geographical differences were really rooted in other characteristics that differed across space. Our multivariate analyses focused on two sensitive household indicators: the chances that elderly women would head their own households and that aged men would head households with co-resident dependent children. Our results demonstrated, in fact, the primacy of several demographic, economic, and social factors over region. For elderly women, living in rural non-farm areas, reporting paid labour, living in cities, and being widowed were all factors strongly associated with the odds of heading a household. These odds were all more important than region, although Quebec or western residence remained significantly and negatively associated with household headship compared with living in Ontario. Our logistic regressions for aged men focused on their odds of heading households with co-resident dependent children. With elderly men, as with elderly women, introducing a host of demographic, economic, and social variables into the multivariate analysis eliminated the regional differences between men living in Ontario and men living in the Maritimes, although distinctions between Ontario and the western provinces remained. Among men, farmers, employers, non-farming men who worked on their own account, urban dwellers, and Irish Catholic and Irish Protestant men had the greatest odds of heading households with dependent children present. Men with resources and property, either in farming or urban contexts, were more likely to live with dependent children who had an inheritance to anticipate.

These multivariate analyses, thus, present a complementary perspective on the elderly's household statuses compared with the view provided by a bivariate geographical analysis. The reduced tendency of elderly women to head their own households in the Canadian west relative to elderly women in Ontario is maintained even when taking a variety of other factors into account: perhaps the strong orientation of the Prairie provinces to the farm economy and restrictive federal land distribution rules hindered the opportunities of elderly women to sustain independent households west of Ontario. The prairie farm economy may also explain the tendency of elderly men not to co-reside with dependent children in 1911 Saskatchewan and Alberta, even when controlling for other variables. Did single adult children in these new provinces move away from their fathers' household more quickly, responding to land acquisition opportunities? Maritime-Quebec-Ontario differences, on the other hand, are alternatively represented by place of birth and ethnoreligious identity; in the case of elderly women and men, place of birth and ethnoreligious identity as well as urban-rural-farm status mirrored and sometimes mitigated the effects of region. The development of the western Canadian provinces created new environments for aging but not necessarily more advantageous or innovative ones; west of Ontario, elderly women did not find heightened chances to maintain their own households, with the exception of a small number of boarding house keepers in British Columbia. Meanwhile, the traditional contours of aging prevailed, with widowhood, increased old age, and paid labour exacting costs or presenting opportunities.

The shifts explored in this national and provincial analysis encourage further speculation about how the lives of Canada's elderly were changing at the dawn of the twentieth century. As the elderly became an increasingly native-born group, did they feel disconnected from the incoming generation of young immigrants, who were not the children of anyone they knew? On the other hand, larger proportions of elderly men and women were aging in the same province in which they were born. Were these persons benefiting from increased residential stability, or were they confining their lifetime movements to within their own province? What were the residential pathways typically experienced by elderly persons and how did these change over time? What happened to family generations after they residentially separated, did they remain geographically proximate or were parents and children separated by many miles? To answer such questions of family reproduction more directly, future research must turn to linked census data, data that promise to shed light on the origins and destinies of family generations as they confronted the new world of the twentieth century.

Notes

1 Gérard Bouchard, "Mobile Populations, Stable Communities: Social and Demographic Processes in the Rural Parishes of the Saguenay, 1840–1911," *Continuity and Change* 6, no. 1 (1991): 59–86; Gérard Bouchard, *Quelques arpents d'Amérique: Population, économie, famille au Saguenay, 1838–1971* (Montreal: Boréal, 1996), 200–5, 262, 266; J.I. Little, *Crofters and Habitants: Settler Society, Economy and Culture in a Quebec Township, 1848–1881* (Montreal and Kingston: McGill-Queen's University Press, 1991), 121–3. See also David Gagan, *Hopeful Travellers: Families, Land, and Social Change in Mid-Victorian Peel County, Canada West* (Toronto: University of Toronto Press, 1981), 62; A. Gordon Darroch and Michael Ornstein, "Family and Household in Nineteenth-Century Canada: Regional Patterns and Regional Economies," *Journal of Family History* 9, no. 2 (1984): 158–77, esp. 164. Gordon Darroch and Lee Soltow, *Property and Inequality in Victorian Ontario: Structural Patterns and Cultural Communities in the 1871 Census* (Toronto: University of Toronto Press, 1994), 11; Bruce S. Elliott, *Irish Migrants in the Canadas: A New Approach* (Montreal and Kingston: McGill-Queen's University Press, 1988), 195–8, 237.

2 James G. Snell, *The Citizen's Wage: The State and the Elderly in Canada, 1900–1951* (Toronto: University of Toronto Press, 1996), 20–3, 28–9; Edgar-André Montigny, *Foisted upon the Government? State Responsibilities, Family Obligations and the Care of the Dependent Aged in Late Nineteenth-Century Ontario* (Montreal and Kingston: McGill-Queen's University Press, 1997), 42–5, 53, 63, 72–4.

3 Megan Davies, *Into the House of Old: A History of Residential Care in British Columbia* (Montreal and Kingston: McGill-Queen's University Press, 2003), 39; Snell, *The Citizen's Wage*, 23–4.

4 Lisa Dillon, *The Shady Side of Fifty: Age and Old Age in Late Victorian Canada and the United States* (Montreal and Kingston: McGill-Queen's University Press, 2008), 146–59, 167–78, 187–92, 205–12.

5 Daniel Scott Smith, "Life Course, Norms and the Family System of Older Americans in 1900," *Journal of Family History* 4, no. 3 (1979): 285–98; Steven Ruggles, *Prolonged Connections: The Rise of the Extended Family in Nineteenth-Century England and America* (Madison: University of Wisconsin Press, 1987), 11; Steven Ruggles, "The Transformation of American Family Structure," *American Historical Review* 99, no. 1 (1994), 103–28; Steven Ruggles, "Multigenerational Families in Nineteenth-Century America," *Continuity and Change* 18, no. 1 (2003): 139–65.

6 Brian Gratton and Frances M. Rotondo, "Industrialization, the Family Economy and the Economic Status of the American Elderly," *Social Science History* 15, no. 3 (1991): 337–62; Brian Gratton, "The Poverty of Impoverishment Theory: The Economic Well-being of the Elderly, 1890–1950," *Journal of Economic History* 26, no. 1 (1996): 39–61; Cheryl Elman, "Turn-of-the-Century Dependence and Interdependence: Roles of Teens in Family Economies of the Aged," *Journal of Family History* 18, no. 1 (1993): 65–85; Carole Haber and Brian Gratton, *Old Age and the Search for Security: An American Social History* (Bloomington: Indiana University Press, 1994): 81.

7 Steven Ruggles, "The Decline of Intergenerational Coresidence in the United States, 1850 to 2000," *American Sociological Review* 72, no. 6 (2007): 964–89; Brian Gratton and Myron P. Gutmann, "Emptying the Nest: Older Men in the United States, 1880–2000," *Population and Development Review* 36, no. 2 (2010): 331–56. See also Steven Ruggles, "Reconsidering the Northwest European Family System: Living Arrangements of the Aged in Comparative Historical Perspective," *Population and Development Review* 35, no. 2 (2009): 249–73.

8 Ruggles, "The Decline of Intergenerational Coresidence," 973–5; Gratton and Gutmann, "Emptying the Nest," 346–9.

9 Dillon, *The Shady Side of Fifty*, 143.

10 Lisa Dillon, Brian Gratton, and Jon Moen, "Retirement at the Turn of the Twentieth Century: A Canadian Perspective," *Canadian Historical Review* 91, no. 1 (2010): 59.

11 Darroch and Ornstein, "Family and Household in Nineteenth-Century Canada," 167.

12 Bouchard, *Quelques arpents d'Amérique*, 200–10; Dillon et al., "Retirement at the Turn of the Twentieth Century," 58.

13 Dillon, *The Shady Side of Fifty*, 169.

14 Dillon et al., "Retirement at the Turn of the Twentieth Century," 58.

15 Darroch and Ornstein, "Family and Household in Nineteenth-Century Canada," 163–6. Also see Timothy D. Lewis, "Rooted in the Soil: Farm Family Persistence in Burton Parish, Sunbury County, New Brunswick, 1851–1901," *Acadiensis* 31, no. 1 (2001): 35–54, esp. 37, 49; Katie Pickles, "Locating Widows in Mid-Nineteenth-Century Pictou County, Nova Scotia," *Journal of Historical Geography* 30 (2004): 70–86, esp. 79.

16 Alan A. Brookes, "Out-Migration from the Maritimes Provinces, 1860–1900: Some Preliminary Considerations," *Acadiensis* (Spring 1976): 26–55, esp. 37.
17 Sarah Carter, *The Importance of Being Monogamous: Marriage and Nation Building in Western Canada to 1915* (Edmonton: University of Alberta Press, 2008), 74–8.
18 Kenneth Michael Sylvester, *The Limits of Rural Capitalism: Family, Culture and Markets in Montcalm, Manitoba, 1870–1940* (Toronto: University of Toronto Press, 2001), 147.
19 Davies, *Into the House of Old*, 16–27; Snell, *The Citizen's Wage*, 23–4.
20 Davies, *Into the House of Old*, 16.
21 This base sample is obtained in SPSS by setting WEIGHT=SAMPWGT.
22 Eric W. Sager, Douglas K. Thompson, and Marc Trottier, *The National Sample of the 1901 Census of Canada: User's Guide* (Victoria: University of Victoria, 2002).
23 Canada, Department of Agriculture and Statistics, *Fifth Census of Canada, 1911: Instructions to Officers, Commissioners and Enumerators* (Ottawa: Government Printing Bureau, 1911), 31.
24 The category "own account" used in tables 8.7 and 8.9 denotes all men reporting "own account" status *other than* farmers, who are placed in their own category.
25 Dillon, *The Shady Side of Fifty*, 135–6, 144–5, 188, 198.
26 James Struthers, *The Limits of Affluence: Welfare in Ontario, 1920–1970* (Toronto: University of Toronto Press, 1994), 52.
27 Peter Baskerville, *A Silent Revolution? Gender and Wealth in English Canada, 1860–1930* (Montreal and Kingston: McGill-Queen's University Press, 2008), 5.
28 Baskerville, *A Silent Revolution?* 23, 25, 263: Table 1.1.
29 Lewis, "Rooted in the Soil," 37.
30 Davies, *Into the House of Old*, 19–26; see also Snell, *The Citizen's Wage*, 61–3.
31 Bouchard, *Quelques arpents d'Amérique*, 262.
32 Ibid., 266–71.
33 Snell, *The Citizen's Wage*, 77.
34 Ibid., 82.
35 Ibid., 103.
36 Bouchard, *Quelques arpents d'Amérique*, 271.
37 Montigny, *Foisted upon the Government?* 56–7.
38 Darroch and Ornstein, "Family and Household in Nineteenth-Century Canada," 167.
39 Livio Di Matteo and Peter George, "Patterns and Determinants of Wealth among Probated Decedents in Wentworth County, Ontario, 1872–1902," *Histoire sociale/Social History* 31, no. 61 (1998): 30–1.

— · 9 · —

Geography of Encounter: Immigration, Ethnic Diversity, and Interethnic Relations within Quebec, 1881–1911[1]

DANIELLE GAUVREAU AND
PATRICIA THORNTON

Growing ethnic diversity and multiculturalism in recent years has aroused heated public debate in Quebec, as in many other Western countries, on whether to severely limit immigration and on how to "accommodate" cultural diversity and integrate immigrants from diverse origins. These have become hot policy and research issues, but frequently, they are based on an inadequate appreciation of how past waves of immigrants have been integrated in Quebec. Notwithstanding much work by historians and social scientists on specific immigrant ethnic groups in the past, and acknowledgment of Montreal's ethnic diversity long before the 1960s,[2] there has been no provincewide demographic or genetic historical overview of diversity and integration.[3] There remains an impression that, before 1960, compared with most of Canada, Quebec was rather homogeneously French, and the diversity insofar as it exists there has been perceived in terms of a simple duality: French versus English, or Protestant versus Catholic. A long view of cultural diversity and immigrant integration provides a needed perspective on the current situation.

This chapter addresses the broad question of encounter between people of different ethnoreligious communities in the past, in terms of the extent to which different groups shared (or did not share) a common space. How geographically segregated were the different cultural communities across Quebec? What does a fine-grained picture of their distribution reveal about opportunities for interaction? Through the lens of major ethnoreligious groups, we examine residential patterns from large regions to small census subdistricts (CSDs), and in different milieus (i.e., rural farm, rural non-farm, and urban) as well as the degree of co-residence within the family and household. In this way, we explore the opportunity that individuals from different groups had to meet and mix, and the ways in which they were integrated into households and into small residential communities.

We start by explaining how we define and measure cultural/ethnic diversity and integration and how we operationalize these definitions and measures using data from the 1911 and 1881 Canadian censuses. The 1911 census allows us to see the impacts of the first major wave of immigrants to Quebec from non-traditional sources by taking advantage of the new Canadian Century Research Infrastructure (CCRI) geographical information systems (GIS) to map cultural diversity at the CSD level and the 5 per cent sample of census microdata to model probabilities of encounter. The 1881 census serves as a reference for comparison since it is available in digital form in its entirety, and occurs before the new dawn of immigration but after the major wave of British and American immigration, at a time when more people were actually leaving Quebec than arriving there.[4] After sketching how cultural interaction has been framed in the literature, we provide a brief overview of the history of immigration and cultural diversity in Quebec, before embarking on our main purpose – to examine the probabilities of cross-cultural encounter across Quebec within the household, within the neighbourhood, and within a city or a region.

First, we examine the geography of encounter at the level of 64 census districts (CDs) and more than 1,000 census subdistricts (there were 1,169 CSDs in 1911). Using descriptive statistical measures and maps, we see how segregated or how intermingled the major ethnoreligious groups were across Quebec in 1911 and how they had changed since 1881. In the next section, we employ a micro-approach in examining cultural "mixity" within private households – an intimate level of cultural interaction where groups share domestic space, eating at the same table, sharing experiences, as well as the most intimate spaces of all between married couples, their bed. We examine whether mixity within households stems from intermarriage or the presence of kin or non-kin, and which ethnoreligious groups are more likely to mix. The main focus is a multilevel model of the odds of living in a "mixed" household that combines the effects of household characteristics with the effects of contextual variables measured at the level of more than 120 geographical areas defined also by milieu called census areas.

This represents a first attempt to articulate the probabilities of encounter between ethnoreligious groups at different scales – within the family, within the neighbourhood or region, and within rural farm, rural non-farm, and urban milieus – and it demonstrates the need for a variety of measures to bring these encounters to light. Simple descriptive measures of residential segregation and cultural diversity combined with multilevel modelling at the level of the household and larger milieu offer new power to grasp the scale phenomenon and connect the macro with the micro. This allows us to inquire into the behavioural choices of late nineteenth- and early twentieth-century Quebec households, to distinguish the social dimensions of ethnic differences, and to challenge some of our assumptions about the meaning of "diversity" and "integration" in Quebec today and in the past. To what extent was Quebec culturally, linguistically, and religiously homogeneous compared with the rest of Canada? Does the notion of cultural duality – whether it is of "two founding peoples" as reflected in the 1960s report of the Royal Commission on Biculturalism and Bilingualism or the "two solitudes" immortalized in Hugh McLennan's 1945 novel – adequately reflect the true nature of cultural identities and divisions in Quebec in the late nineteenth and early twentieth centuries?[5]

Defining and Measuring Cultural Diversity and Mixity

Canadian censuses are unique in the richness of information they contain on cultural diversity. For each individual, religion and place of birth have been recorded since 1852; ethnic or national origin since 1871; year of immigration, language spoken, and ability to speak English and/or French since 1901. Despite long-standing scepticism over the validity of the concept of "ethnic group" or "ethnic identity," driven by concerns of essentialism and naturalism, denying its existence does not make the phenomenon disappear.[6] In both the past and the present, the concept of "ethnicity" actually serves to make sense of many practices, policies, and social relations. Ethnicity – the subjective sense of community based on a shared origin, history, and culture – is and has been in Quebec an important dimension of group identity regardless of whether a common ancestry objectively exists. Although it would be desirable to use subjective criteria, nineteenth- and early twentieth-century censuses force us to use artificially constructed categories such as "national origin" that oblige populations to cast themselves into prescribed categories, often reinforcing official state-making "social imaginaries" of ethnic composition.[7] Despite the "warp," by defining things in ways that made sense at the time, religion, "origins," and language were given a significance in Canada that was totally unlike the cultural politics of statistics that emerged in France, the United States, the United Kingdom, or Australia.[8]

The published census requires that we use these variables as separate identifiers; however, census microdata allow us to examine how language, religion, and national origin combine in a more dynamic and nuanced analysis of diversity that more accurately reflects the fault lines of social relations and institutional organization. Language and religion are among the most often explored referents in present-day and historical studies of ethnicity. In Montreal, and across Quebec, they resonated in newspapers throughout the nineteenth century; formal institutions such as schools, hospitals, military units, and cemeteries were all organized along language and religious lines. Nevertheless, neither religion (Catholic vs. Protestant) nor language (English vs. French) on its own is sufficient to reflect the political and social fabric, even before cultural variations became more complex in the twentieth century. Rather, we need a cross-cutting of these dimensions, which combine religion and national origin. The latter can be used as a surrogate for language since data on language per se are not available before 1901. The major ethnoreligious groups in this period can be conceived in terms of the following: French Catholic, British Catholic, British Protestant, Jewish, and Other, with Other broken down, where numbers permit, into Native Indians, non-Jewish other Europeans (mostly Catholic), and a residual, amorphous group. We argue that these groupings reflect the major political, cultural, and institutional cleavages in Quebec before the 1960s. This representation, however, most certainly, understates the cultural diversity and, hence, the extent of cross-cultural mixing within households in Quebec.

Geographically, cultural diversity and cultural interaction across Quebec are examined at the level of CSDs and larger spatial units that are aggregations of CSDs. We use three different measures: the first two measure the relative difference in the way ethnoreligious groups are distributed across space, yielding values for each spatial unit; the third measures how each ethnoreligious group is distributed relative to each other ethnic group yielding a single measure for each paired group across all spatial units. The concentration index (CI) shows the degree to which an ethnoreligious group is concentrated in each area relative to its representation in the population as a whole. The diversity index (DI) measures the proportional combinations of ethnicities within each area relative to the entire population. Residential segregation (RS) measures the degree of overlap of one group relative to another group across space. These rather simple statistical devices enable us to examine diversity and segregation at a variety of geographical scales, milieus, and social dimensions.

Within households, "cultural diversity" or "mixity" is defined as having at least one resident individual with a different ethnoreligious background than the household head.[9] Our main interest is in "private" households, defined as those with a conjugal unit at their core. Institutions and large boarding houses offer spaces where new immigrants congregate and different groups may co-reside; however, they do not represent the same type of intimate relations, nor the intimate relations experienced by most people, and so, they do not reflect the most profound forms of integration. We know from Peter Baskerville that many lodgers and boarders living in private households, just like servants and other non-kin, are what he calls "familiar strangers," people living "as part of families," who more frequently share cultural properties of the heads of the families within which they are living than do the people living in large boarding houses and hotels.[10] It is these family situations that we wanted to study, and so we excluded large households composed of more than thirty individuals (mostly institutions or hotels) and we excluded households with more than three boarders, which we believed constituted more commercial settings than family ones and which expanded considerably in number and size between 1881 and 1911.[11] We then used the definition of a "census family" to select households with a family unit at their core: couples with or without children or a single parent with child(ren). Other family members (kin) or unrelated members (non-kin) in such households are considered additional members of these households. In this context, mixity or diversity can result from intermarriage or it can be the outcome of the presence of live-in domestics or boarders. Clearly, diversity has quite a different meaning between husband and wife, between master or mistress and servant, and between a widow and her boarders: signifying different forms of interethnic relations and reflecting different personal circumstances and stages of life. These measures of diversity and mixity can reveal nothing of the quality and nature of different forms of interethnic relations. We should keep in mind that the high turnover among servants and boarders suggests that a larger share of the population than is revealed at the time of a census may have experienced intercultural encounter at some point.

Cultural interaction and intermarriage are often explained in terms of three general notions: (1) individual cultural preferences to mix within or outside the group, (2) structural opportunities to meet members of one's own group, and (3) the influence of third parties on socializing and marriage behaviour.[12] For example, members of different ethnoreligious groups may have different norms and values that form a barrier to cultural interaction (individual preferences), they may live in homogeneous neighbourhoods (structural opportunities), and the community to which members of the group belong may oppose out-marriage and even socialization outside the group (third-party influence). These can be most usefully combined into a two-fold distinction between (1) *cultural* arguments that relate to norms, values, and preferences that people have regarding interaction and marriage with "other" groups, and (2) *structural* arguments that address opportunities that people have to interact with and/or marry inside or outside the group. Individual preferences and third-party influences are both considered cultural determinants, and although the distinction between cultural and structural determinants is conceptually meaningful, in practice, indicators for one may reflect both. For example, the size of the group in a neighbourhood is a structural factor, but where people live is also a choice that people make and, in this sense, preferences come into play. This is the way we incorporate them in the multilevel modelling.

Some Background and Context

When New France became a British colony in 1759, the population numbered about 70,000. There were a few thousand Aboriginals. The remainder were almost all French Canadians: descended from about 8,500 permanent French settlers who came in the seventeenth century.[13] These French settlers were strung out along the St Lawrence River Valley, with subsequent generations gradually carving out farms further inland. Less is known about the subsequent period of American and British immigration because of the relative paucity of Protestant records and the difficulties of tracking these mobile populations.[14] In the first fifty years following the Conquest, only a relatively small number arrived, and most of these people settled in Quebec City and Montreal and their immediate surroundings. With the arrival of the Loyalists fleeing the United States after the War of Independence, but especially with the flood of immigrants from England, Ireland, and Scotland after 1815, border regions such as the Eastern Townships (Estrie), the Ottawa Valley (Outaouais), the Gaspé Peninsula (Gaspésie), and the Montreal Plain close to the US border were all settled for the first time by Europeans. By 1851, French Canadians constituted barely three-quarters of Quebec's population, and they were concentrated in the St Lawrence Valley, "hemmed in, surrounded by a British cordon," as the geographer Raoul Blanchard described the situation.[15]

There is the common perception that those of "British" origin were mostly Scots and English Protestants, when in fact, the Irish dominated numerically. Present from the outset, but with massive entries in 1831, 1847, and 1849, the Irish constituted in 1851 two-thirds of all British immigrants; the majority of them were Catholic. The cross-cutting nature of religious and linguistic divides in Quebec placed Irish Catholics in a pivotal position, sharing their religion with the majority French population and their language with the economically powerful Protestants. In a situation where religious differences were firmly institutionalized (not just for worship but the provision of a whole array of social services from schools to hospitals to housing and caring for the marginalized), Irish Catholics in Quebec rapidly produced their own set of institutions becoming a distinctive third community, making it important in Quebec to distinguish British Catholics from British Protestants. And they provided a model for the integration of later immigrant groups.[16]

Despite this broad pattern of separation, there was much internal movement of people that contributed to mixing among groups. Long before 1850, periods of disruptions around the time of the Conquest (1759–65), and the upheavals (especially around 1840), saw massive movement of militia, migrant labourers, and colonizers – and a consequent mixing of peoples. The major change came after 1851, however, when the seigneurial lands along the St Lawrence Valley could no longer absorb the growing French Canadian population, now six or seven generations deep. As roads and railway lines developed, French Canadians exploded in every direction: some leaving for factories in New England, others moving into recently surveyed township lands where they mingled with British and American settlers, still others moved towards cities, especially to Canada's premier industrial metropolis, Montreal, and its rich commercial agricultural hinterland. In the early twentieth century, forest regions were opened up further north deliberately for French Canadian colonization such as in Saguenay-Lac Saint Jean and Temiscamingue.[17] This suggests a complex geography of settlement and encounter. Adding to this mix was a new wave of immigrants arriving at the very end of the nineteenth century, many from non-traditional sources, immigrants whose mother tongue was neither French nor English. Some of these, like the Italians, Ukrainians, and Poles were Catholic, but many were Yiddish-speaking Jews from Eastern Europe. Most came to Montreal, attracted by the opportunities of a large cosmopolitan industrial metropolis.

The censuses show that compared with Upper Canada in 1851, and the rest of Canada in 1881 and 1911, Lower Canada/Quebec was not more homogeneous before the turn of the twentieth century. Overall, immigrants represented a much smaller proportion of the total population in Quebec than elsewhere, but this was entirely due to the much earlier immigration: only 10 per cent of Quebec's population in 1851 were people who were not born in Quebec, dropping to 6 per cent in 1881, and rising a little to just over 7 per cent in 1911, while roughly one-quarter of the population in the more recently settled Upper Canada (1851 census) or rest of Canada (1881 and 1911 censuses) were born elsewhere. It was not until 1911 that Quebec stands out as being ethnically more homogeneous, and even then, it is no less homogeneous than most of Atlantic Canada. In 1881, the dominant ethnic group (French in Quebec, British elsewhere) consti-

Figure 9.1 (opposite) · Immigrants and population of non-French ethnic origin: Regional and municipal trends, Quebec, 1851–1911.

Sources: Census of Canada, 1852, 1861, 1871, 1881, 1891, 1901, 1911, published tables.

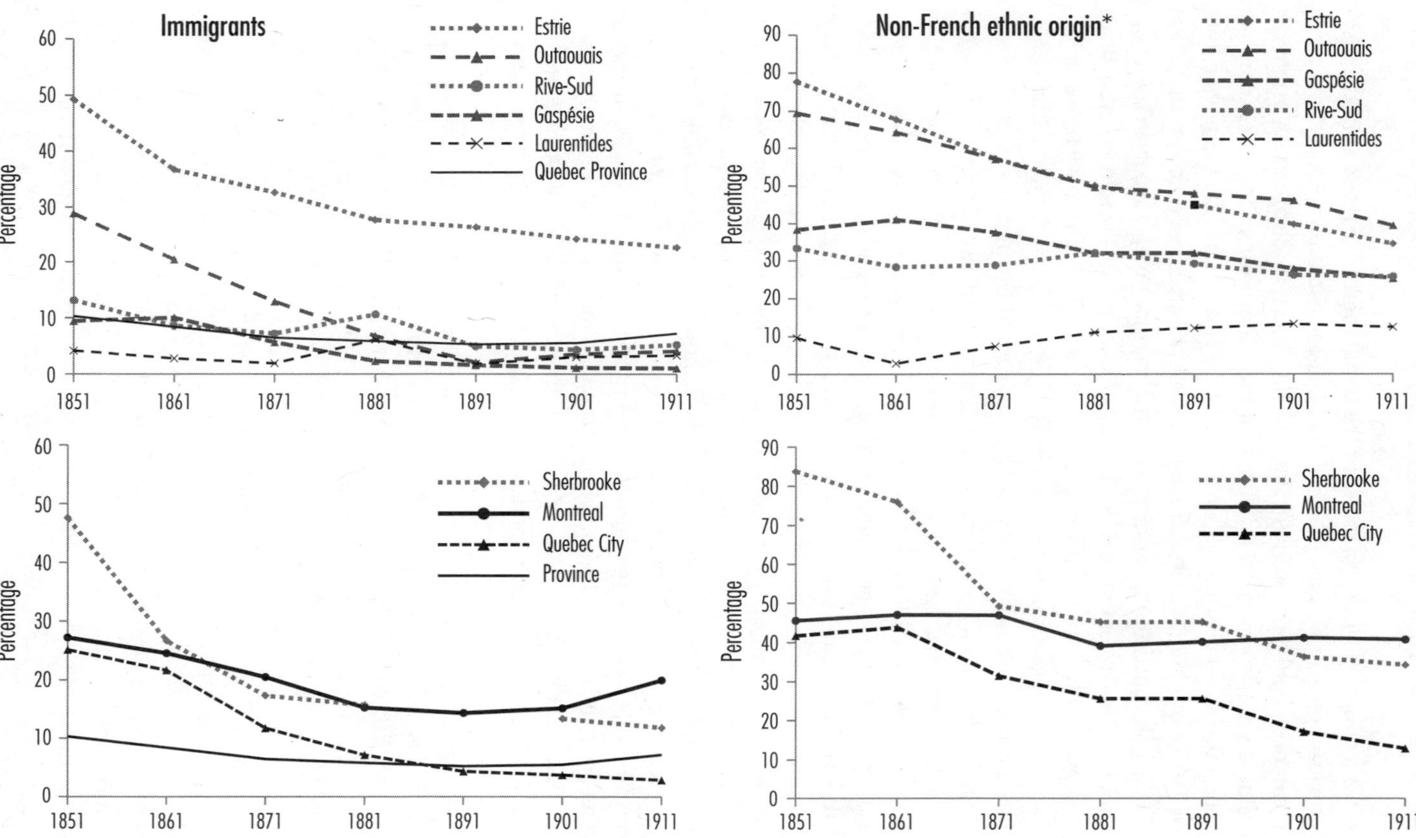
Immigrants
Estrie
Outaouais
Rive-Sud
Gaspésie
Laurentides
Quebec Province
Percentage
Sherbrooke
Montreal
Quebec City
Province
Non-French ethnic origin*
Estrie
Outaouais
Gaspésie
Rive-Sud
Laurentides
Sherbrooke
Montreal
Quebec City

tuted a similar proportion (78%) of the population of Quebec as in the rest of Canada; however, by 1911, the French in Quebec had grown to be 80 per cent of the entire population, while in the rest of Canada, those of British origin constituted only 69 per cent. It is more in the composition of the non-dominant group that Quebec differs from much of the rest of Canada. In Quebec, those of British origin dominated the far more populous non-French group. In 1851, the British constituted one-quarter of the population of Quebec; in 1881, 19 per cent; and 16 per cent in 1911. In the rest of Canada, as a whole, the non-British group was always more diverse, and outside of New Brunswick and Eastern Ontario, not predominantly French. The "Other" group (of neither British nor French origin) comprised less than 2 per cent of the population of Quebec in 1881, doubling to 3.6 per cent in 1911; whereas in the rest of Canada, as a whole, "Other" comprised 13 per cent of the entire population in 1881, and 19 per cent by 1911. Figure 9.1, based on the published aggregate census data from 1851 to 1911, tracks the geographical patterns and trends focusing on the three largest cities and five non-city regions where diversity was greatest. Figure 9.2 shows the locations of the major cities and the regions developed by the BALSAC project based on aggregations of adjacent CSDs whose boundaries can be standardized over the entire period (1851–1951) so that comparisons can be made over time. The Projet BALSAC and the Laboratoire de géographie historique du Centre interuniversitaire d'études québecoises (CIEQ) identify twenty-four regions that can be consistently constituted from the census. Montreal and Quebec City are each regions of their own. We have separated out Sherbrooke from its surrounding region of Estrie. One region, Îles de la Madeleine, is excluded here, as its population is very small and it lies too far off the east coast of Gaspésie to be shown on the map.

Figure 9.1 shows a different and more complex story of cultural diversity that is neither homogeneously French nor a simple duality. As late as 1881, non-French people by origin formed the majority of the population in the Eastern Townships (Estrie) and the Ottawa Valley (Outaouais); and more than a third of the population of the Gaspésie and the plain south of Montreal (Rive-Sud). The remaining sixteen regions (figure 9.2) were more than 90 per cent French.[18] Montreal, Quebec City, and Sherbrooke, the three largest cities, all were more than 40 per cent non-French. As the port of disembarkation of all immigrants, Quebec City was much more diverse than often perceived, especially before 1871, when its lumber trade and shipping were thriving. In most places, the proportion of immigrants and persons of non-French "racial or tribal" origin fell consistently after the 1860s, when all arable township lands had been taken up, and French Canadians were added to the mix. This is most dramatic in the Eastern Townships, and its main city of Sherbrooke, as well as in the Ottawa

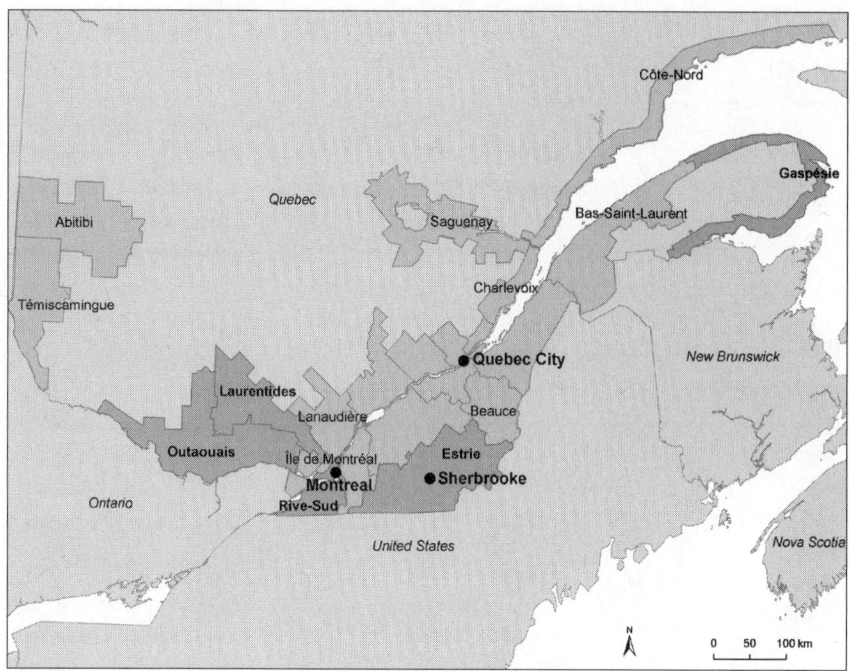

Figure 9.2 · Quebec: Regions and major cities. These regions have been developed as part of the BALSAC database of generationally linked marriages for the entire Catholic population of Quebec from the beginning of European settlement to the present. The map is based on an original base map created by the Laboratoire de géographie historique du Centre interuniversitaire d'études québécoises (CIEQ) at l'Université Laval.

Valley. Only the regions of Montreal and adjacent Rive-Sud and the Laurentians (Laurentides) maintained or expanded their non-French and immigrant proportions.

Table 9.1, based on the digital censuses of 1881 and 1911, focuses on changes in the pattern and composition of immigrants to Quebec.[19] The 1881 census reflects the effects of the post-Conquest wave of newcomers from Britain and the United States, while the 1911 census shows the recent turn-of-the-century immigration from more diverse sources. In 1881, four-fifths of those who were not born in Canada were of British origin; by 1911, this proportion was only half. Of British-born immigrants, in 1881, half were born in Ireland, but by 1911, the Irish-born were fewer than 8 per cent of the British-born immigrants, and two-thirds were born in England. Most of the remaining immigrants were a mixture of Jews (increasing from 1% to 16%) and non-Jews (mostly Cath-

Table 9.1 · Immigrants in Quebec, by ethnic origin and milieu (rural farm, rural non-farm, and urban), 1881 and 1911

	1881		*1911*		*1881*	*1911*	*1911*
	Total population	*Immigrants*	*Total population*	*Immigrants*	*Portion of group who are immigrants (%)*		*Arrived in last 10 years (%)*
All *n*	1,358,222	78,351	103,109	7,808			
All %	100.0	100.0	100.0	100.0	5.8	7.6	72.8
BY ETHNIC ORIGIN							
French	78.5	14.5	80.3	15.0	1.0	1.4	68.7
English	6.1	24.7	7.7	32.9	7.2	32.3	74.6
Irish	9.1	39.9	5.0	9.5	11.7	14.5	38.2
Scottish	4.0	15.5	2.8	9.5	4.5	25.8	72.1
Jewish	0.1	0.7	1.8	16.0	52.0	67.7	78.6
NW Europe	0.8	2.9	0.8	5.3	23.5	50.7	80.2
S Europe	0.1	0.4	0.5	5.0	30.7	73.1	84.0
E Europe	—	0.0	0.3	2.9	55.2	80.7	95.5
Other	1.3	1.4	0.8	3.8	29.1	7.6	76.8
BRITISH ORIGIN BY RELIGION							
British Catholic	6.8	28.5	4.8	10.8	23.5	17.2	51.6
British Protestant	12.4	51.6	9.7	36.6	23.3	28.6	71.9

	1881		*1911*		*1911*		
	Canadian-born (%)	*Immigrants (%)*	*Canadian-born (%)*	*Immigrants (%)*	*Year of Immigration*		
					Before 1860 (%)	1860–79 (%)	1880 and after (%)
BY MILIEU							
Rural farm	52.6	35.7	39.1	9.6	33.3	15.6	6.8
Rural non-farm	27.8	20.3	23.2	12.3	19.5	9.4	10.2
Urban	19.6	44.0	37.7	78.1	47.2	75.0	83.0

Sources: Census of Canada microdata, 1881 (entire); CCRI 1911 microdata database.

Note: Urban places in both censuses are standardized as villages, towns, or cities with more than 3,000 people. The 1881 Census of Canada microdata for all of Canada was collected in its entirety by the Church of Christ and the Latter-Day Saints (LDS). It was cleaned and coded for researchers by the *North Atlantic Population Project* (NAPP), 2008. Version 2.0 can be accessed by researchers at the Université de Montréal Département de démographie, http://www.prdh.umontreal.ca/census/en/member/download.aspx.

olics) from Southern and Eastern Europe. Overall, the non-French, non-British group grew from 5 per cent of all those who were not born in Canada in the 1881 census to one-third of the foreign-born by 1911.

The wave of mostly British settlers arriving between 1815 and 1860 settled predominantly in rural areas. For three decades thereafter, opportunities in Quebec were meagre compared with those in the United States, where the rural frontier was still expanding and industrialization was proceeding more rapidly, so most immigrants to Quebec and many who were born there left.[20] By the 1880s, growing industrialization meant that new opportunities were mostly in urban centres. By 1881, 44 per cent of all those who were living in Quebec but were not born there lived in urban places; however, by the turn of the twentieth century, rapidly growing opportunities in manufacturing, primarily in Montreal, attracted a new wave of immigrants. According to the 1911 census, close to three-quarters of those who were not born in Quebec had arrived within the previous ten years, and 78 per cent of all immigrants in Quebec were living in urban places. A striking difference between 1881 and 1911 is the proportion of each ethnic group who were themselves immigrants. Not surprisingly, only 1 per cent of people who were French by origin in either census year were immigrants. Yet, while only 7 per cent of the British population in Quebec in 1881 were not born there, by 1911, one-quarter of the Scots and one-third of those of English origin in Quebec were immigrants. Those claiming Jewish, Eastern European, or southern European origin were predominantly foreign-born in both censuses (half in 1881, 70%–80% in 1911), and of those from northwestern Europe, less than half were foreign-born.

The Geography of Encounter

To appreciate the geography of encounter across Quebec, we need a much finer grained geography than that of regions. In 1911, when we have the GIS at the level of the CSD, we can map immigrants and ethnic groups at the level of the 1,167 census subdistricts. At this scale, we chose to use the entire published census, because a 5% sample, even a geographically stratified one, is prone to unacceptable sample error given the small size of many CSDs. The published census does not allow us to distinguish between British Catholics and British Protestants; we, therefore, aggregated the data into three gross categories by origin: French, British, and Other. Figure 9.3 shows the relative concentration of each of these groups by CSD across Quebec, while figure 9.4 shows the overlap and mixing of cultural groups. In both cases, the boundaries of each CSD are suppressed so that patterns can emerge more clearly.

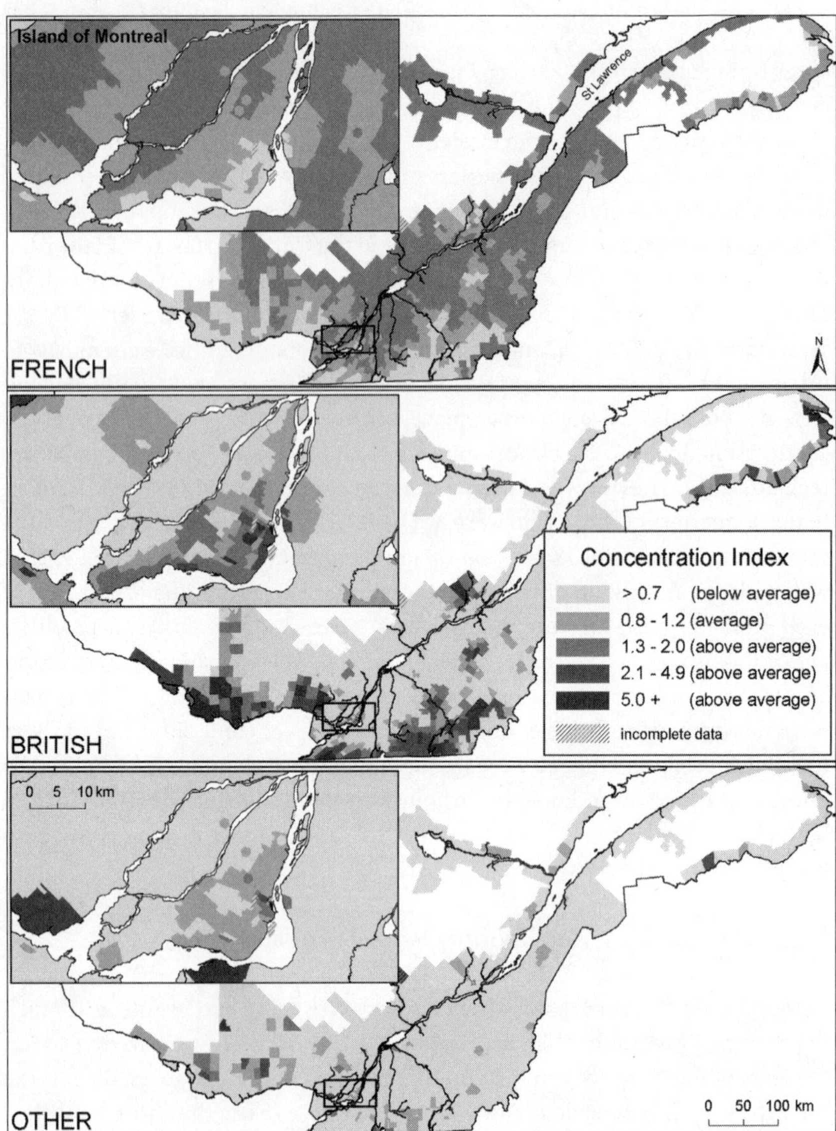

Figure 9.3 · Quebec and Island of Montreal: Concentration of French, British, and other ethnic groups, by census subdistrict, 1911. The concentration index (CI) is the ratio of the percentage in each ethnic group in the CSD to average percentage in the province as a whole: a value of 1 means the CSD had exactly the same proportion as the provincial average; < 1 means less than expected, and > 1 more than expected. A CI value of 5 would mean there was five times the average concentration, CI of 0.2 would mean one-fifth the average concentration. The areas shaded the lightest have less than average concentrations; those shaded darker have higher than average concentrations. CSD boundaries have been suppressed to avoid confusion. There were 1,167 populated CSDs in Quebec in 1911.

Source: Based on calculations from Census of Canada, 1911, vol. II, Table 7, 256–315; also available on the CCRI website.

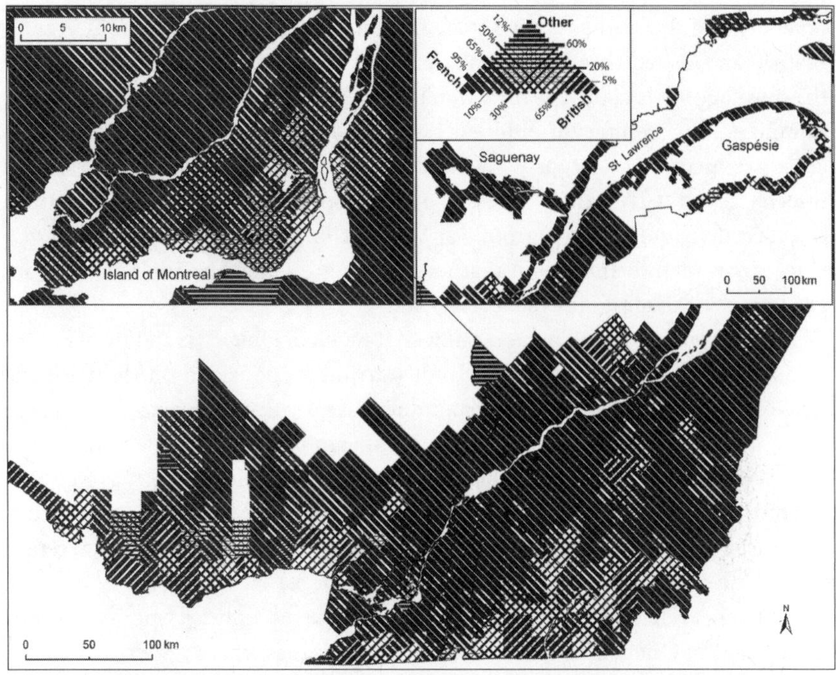

Figure 9.4 · Distribution and mixing of three major ethnic groups (French, British, other) in Quebec, Island of Montreal, Saguenay, and Gaspésie, by census subdistrict, 1911. The direction of the lines denotes which ethnic group dominates (French, British, or other), while the intensity of the lines denotes the relative proportion. CSD boundaries have been suppressed to avoid confusion. There were 1,167 populated CSDs in Quebec in 1911.

Source: Census of Canada, 1911, vol. II, Table 7, 256–315; also available on the CCRI website.

Before discussing the maps, we need to consider how the complementary ideas of concentration and diversity are measured in the two maps and the problem of representing statistically and visually CSDs of very different population size and area. The concentration index (CI; see figure 9.3), more often known as a location quotient, is calculated as the ratio of the proportion of an ethnoreligious group in a CSD to its proportion in the entire province. This produces relative values, where 1 means a CSD has exactly the same proportion of the ethnoreligious group as the entire province does; values less than 1 mean that the group is underrepresented, greater than 1 mean that the group is overrepresented. The maps must be interpreted with caution, since the darkness of shading of one group relative to another is inversely related to the size or dominance of the group overall.[21] The difference in shading within each group, however, is a reflection of its relative concentration. Figure 9.4 looks at diversity and shows the relative contribution of each ethnic group (i.e., French, British, and Other) through a combination of line shading and intensity. Where the line shading is all in one direction this means one group is overwhelmingly dominant. Where lines of different directions combine this means that these areas are mixed. The intensity of the shading reflects the relative contribution of each group. Given their different overall representation in the population, the class divisions for each group vary. A much more detailed and clearer version of this map (using colours rather than line shading and more continuous gradations of shading) is available on-line.

The maps in figures 9.3 and 9.4 show that much of Quebec is solidly of French origin. Almost all the seigneurial lands outside of the Island of Montreal and Quebec City and immediate surroundings are French. However, the French are also strongly represented in the township lands away from the St Lawrence Valley, where there are significant concentrations of British settlers, as well as in the most recently settled frontier zones of the Saguenay and the north shore of the Gaspé Peninsula. Just over 80 per cent of the Quebec population is French; half of the 1,167 CSDs are almost entirely (> 97.5%) French, while 12 per cent are entirely French. People of British origin make up only 14.7 per cent of the population of Quebec; however, there are many areas where the British are the dominant group: in 10 CSDs, the British make up more than 90 per cent of the population; in 33 CSDs, they make up more than 75 per cent, and in 108 CSDs, they are more than half. Even today, the British are concentrated, as Blanchard implied, around peripheral zones: in the areas adjacent to the border with the United States, especially in the Eastern Townships (Estrie region) and Huntingdon County (Rive-Sud region); up the Ottawa Valley (Outaouais region) in Pontiac and Wright counties, and in the southern parts of the Gaspésie region, especially in Bonaventure County. Those of British origin are also concentrated in Montreal. Moreover, there are other distinct pockets such as around Quebec City, showing a finely grained pattern of concentration and mixing that is disguised at larger scales.

The Other group, despite their very small numbers overall (3.3%), are even more highly concentrated in certain areas. The most visible and numerous are the Indian reserves as well as more remote regions where European settlement has barely penetrated: especially the upper reaches of the Ottawa Valley and Temiscamingue. All but two of the fourteen CSDs where more than half the population is of "Other" origin, are Indian communities. However, there are pockets of Other groups, such as the concentration of Jewish people in Ste Sophie (Terrebonne County), Jews and Poles in the remotest part of Montcalm, Austro-Hungarians in Rimouski, and Italians in Ashford and L'Islet. In the Montreal wards of St Louis, St Laurent, and most especially, St Joseph, Jews and Italians bring the proportion of Others to between 40 per cent and 70 per cent of the entire population of the most populated CSDs. There are also rural communities of Dutch and Germans, larger than the British or French groups, in Mississquoi along the US border and in Mulgrave and Bowman in Labelle County in the Ottawa Valley. Each group must carry a particular story of chain migration and settlement; each its own story of interethnic relations.

Zones of mixing (figure 9.4) are the mirror image of the more familiar map of concentration (figure 9.3). Not surprisingly, mixing is greatest in the boundary zones between areas where ethnoreligious groups are most highly concentrated. However, mixing or overlap or intermingling occurs exclusively in areas bordering core areas of British or Other settlement, reflecting a one-way process of expansion of the six- or seven-generation deep French Canadian population out of their St Lawrence lowland heartland due to population pressure. Mixing is also greatest in the cities, which have always attracted immigrants both old (British) and new (Jews, Southern and Eastern European "Others"). Scale is important here. Gaspésie and Montreal are both very mixed, but in reality, the cultural communities are highly segregated within these regions, with adjacent villages or small city blocks and neighbourhoods almost exclusively of one group or another. At what scale does diversity or segregation affect the likelihood that different cultural communities might come into contact or the likelihood of households being mixed?

In interpreting the maps, we must consider that some small areas have huge populations and some large areas, relatively few. The median population of the more than 1,100 CSDs is just over 1,000 people; however, CSDs vary in size from fewer than 100 (only 7 CSDs) to more than 10,000 (26 CSDs). The largest CSDs are all cities or wards of cities, a few in Montreal have more than 40,000 people by 1911.[22] Since the French and Native Indians are more often concentrated in rural places, which are much larger in area than the small villages, towns, and cities, the map gives undue emphasis to the presence of these groups, and the measures to their concentration. By comparison, the British are most concentrated in rural areas with small populations and also overrepresented in cities like Montreal. Recent immigrant groups (especially Jews and Italians) are more often found in Montreal. To give greater visual prominence to these small but highly populated areas we have created a separate inset for Montreal.

To compare the situation in 1911 with that in 1881, and to measure more precisely the varying degree of ethnoreligious diversity along a more varied set of dimensions across Quebec, we constructed a diversity index (DI).[23] To distinguish between Catholics and Protestants of British origin, as well as between Jews and non-Jews from other European as well as British origins, we used the census microdata. Since for 1911 this is only a 5 per cent sample, we had to aggregate the data into larger spatial units less prone to sampling error than CSDs. Widely employed in species ecology, the diversity or heterogeneity index is calculated for each area as 1 minus the sum of the squared proportions in each group: in this case, French, British Catholic, British Protestant, and Other. The diversity index (DI) for each census district varies little whether the Other group is considered as a whole or broken down into Jews, Native Indians, and Others. The DI can be interpreted as a measure of the probability of people belonging to different groups coming into contact within an area. To reduce the distorting effect on the DI of areas of different population size, to approximate the context in which decisions about where to live might have been made, and to compare places over time, we used census districts broken down between their rural farm, rural non-farm (mostly villages and small towns of < 3,000 people), and urban settings (> 3,000). Within Montreal, we used wards (CSDs) that were closer in population size to these rural CDs. There were 121 such areas in 1911, and 132 in 1881.

The diversity index produces a value between 0 and 1. Zero means the area is homogeneous (only one group); the higher the number the more heterogeneous the area is.[24] In Quebec, in 1911, DI values ranged between 0 and .72, with the average for all 121 areas being .22. Surprisingly, the level of diversity had not changed overall from 1881, when the maximum DI value (.74) and the average DI value for all 132 CAs (.23) were almost identical to the values thirty years later.[25] Nevertheless, some shifts had occurred, and by 1911 eight areas were completely homogeneous, (with DI values of 0) compared with only one area in 1881. The DI values are mapped for 1911 census districts in figure 9.5. We believe that CDs broken down by milieu-specific census areas as spatial units reflect the geographical context within which potential contact between ethnoreligious groups might have taken place and we, therefore, use these milieu units in the multilevel analysis and the DI for each unit as a structural macro-level variable to predict the likelihood of mixity within domestic families and households in the multilevel analysis reported in the next section.

To measure the extent of residential segregation (RS) of each ethnoreligious group with respect to each other ethnoreligious group, we calculated the proportion of the population that would have to be redistributed from one census area to another for the distribution of two groups to be the same. This measure is known as the segregation index (SI) when the categories are spatial; otherwise it is known as the index of dissimilarity.[26] The higher the SI value, the greater the degree of residential segregation and the less the groups overlap. The SI measure is highly sensitive to the number of spatial units (or categories) across which the population is distributed: SI values generated from finer grained districting were much greater than for coarser districting, as can be

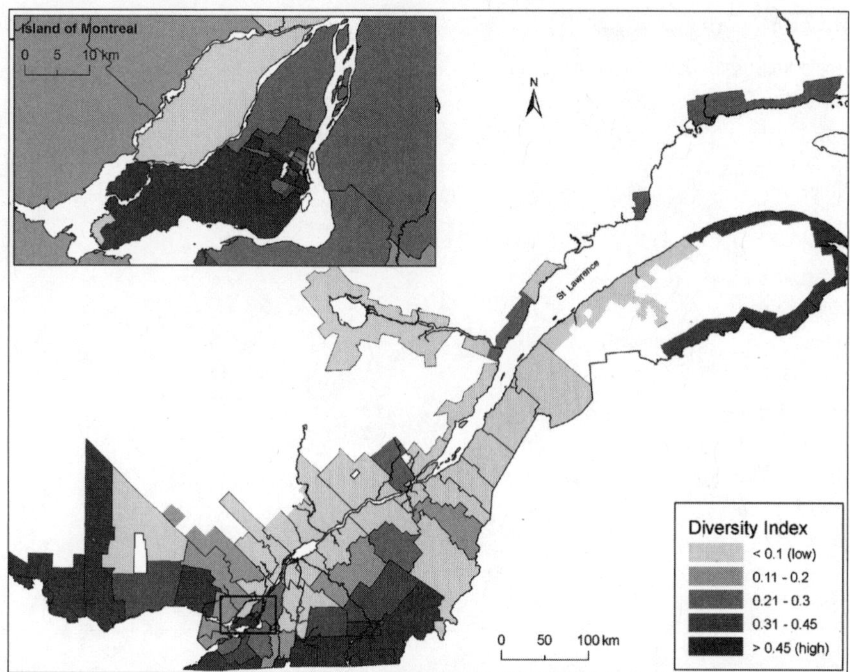

Figure 9.5 · Ethnoreligious diversity: Quebec and Island of Montreal, by census districts, 1911. The diversity index (DI) is explained in the text, but low values reflect low levels of ethnic diversity and, hence, little potential for ethnic mixing; high values reflect higher levels of ethnic diversity and, hence, greater opportunities for ethnic mixing.

Sources: CCRI 1911 microdata database, and GIS of census districts, CCRI geographical database. A beta version of the GIS for Quebec was made available by Marc St Hilaire and Laurent Richard at CIEQ (Centre interuniversitaire d'études québécoises at Université Laval).

seen for 1881 in table 9.2.[27] SI values are much higher (and, hence, there is greater apparent segregation and less overlap) in the top panel when 814 CSDs were used compared with when the 132 CAs were used (in the lower panel). The difference between the values at the two scales reflects the fine-grained nature of residential segregation, evident in figures 9.3 and 9.4, and shows how this is disguised when we aggregate to larger spatial areas, as in figure 9.5. However, to compare the degree of segregation between the six ethnoreligious groups in 1881 with 1911, we need to use the same geographical scale, and since the sample size is too small for CSDs in 1911 (when we are dependent on the 5% sample), we use the coarser district level. The segregation index is less sensitive to sampling than to scale. The results at the two periods are displayed in the lower panel of table 9.2.

Table 9.2 · Residential segregation of ethnoreligious communities (% that would have to move to have the same distribution), Quebec, 1881 and 1911

By census subdistrict				
1881	*French*	*British Catholic*	*British Protestant*	*Jewish*
French	x			
British Catholic	63	x		
British Protestant	74	46	x	
Other	70	61	58	
Jewish	91	76	75	x
Native Indian	94	95	97	100
Other European	64	54	49	77
Number of CSDs (814)				

By census area[a]				
1881	*French*	*British Catholic*	*British Protestant*	*Jewish*
French	x			
British Catholic	48	x		
British Protestant	59	34	x	
Other	56	42	38	
Jewish	83	63	69	x
Native Indian	83	81	82	97
Other European	52	33	30	68
Number of areas (132)				
1911				
French	x			
British Catholic	48	x		
British Protestant	57	33	x	
Other	54	40	42	
Jewish	77	67	71	x
Native Indian	87	85	86	98
Other European	52	30	30	62
Number of areas (121)				

Sources: Census of Canada microdata, 1881 (entire); CCRI 1911 microdata database.

Note: The higher the value, the greater the degree of residential segregation between two groups, the lower the degree of geographical overlap, and the lower the potential for the two groups to meet and mix.

a Census areas are defined in the chapter.

We are struck by the stability in residential segregation, overall, in Quebec between 1881 and 1911, which suggests that the problems of small numbers for small ethnic groups in the CCRI 5 per cent sample are not a major problem. The pattern of segregation is similar to what we might expect from the geography of settlement, the size of each ethnoreligious group, and the perceived cultural distance between specific groups. The Native Indian population is the most segregated from every other group (no overlap for 82%) but especially segregated from the Jewish group (97%), which is consistent with their geographical separation and their cultural distance. The segregation between British Catholics and French Catholics (48%) is less than between British Protestants and French Catholics (59%) but greater than between British Catholics and British Protestants (34%). This is consistent with findings from much more finely grained analysis within Montreal.[28] The residual group (with a SI of 30%) within the "Other" group is much less segregated than the Native Indian (63%) and Jewish (83%) populations with respect to the British (Catholics or Protestants). This reflects their close geographical proximity and the similarity in their ethnic origin and/or religion since many are Americans of British origin, or Europeans of either Protestant or Catholic faith.

Moving to the household level, if we look at which groups are more likely to mix with each other group within the household, we can see in table 9.3 from the choice of marriage partners (based on microdata) the impact of the same structural and cultural factors on the propensity to marry within the group (endogamy) and the preferences for particular groups for those who married out (exogamy). Among all groups, there is a high degree of endogamy, ranging from 60 per cent to 99 per cent of couples in 1881 and 1911, and greater intermarriage between some groups than others. One might interpret these as cultural preferences, yet they are also affected to various degrees by structural variables that determine opportunity such as the sizes of the groups and sex ratios. The differential in levels of endogamy for husbands compared with wives of the same ethnoreligious group is consistent with the nature of their skewed sex ratios: we find higher exogamy among British Catholic wives, especially in the 1881 census, where the sex ratio is 94.9 men for every hundred women; however, exogamy is lower among wives where the sex ratios strongly favour men, as for British Protestants and Others.

As with residential segregation, the pattern of endogamy/exogamy is very similar in 1881 and 1911, but the differences are consistent with what we know about changes in the composition of ethnic and immigrant groups at these two points in time. The recently arrived Jewish population, many of whom were married on arrival, and the more culturally distinct "Other" populations mostly of Southern and Eastern European origins show higher levels of endog-

Table 9.3 · Ethnoreligious intermarriage: Ethnoreligious identity of marriage partners (%), Quebec, 1881 and 1911

Ethnoreligious identity of marriage partners, 1881

Origin of spouse	*French Catholic*		*British Catholic*		*British Protestant*		*Jewish*		*Other*		*Sex ratio*
	Hus.	*Wife*	*Hus.*	*Wife*	*Hus.*	*Wife*	*Hus.*	*Wife*	*Hus.*	*Wife*	*H/100W*
French Catholic	98.1	97.9	16.3	16.4	2.8	2.4	2.9	.0	20.4	12.0	99.8
British Catholic	1.3	1.2	80.6	76.5	3.0	1.1	.0	.8	4.5	3.1	94.9
British Protestant	.4	.5	2.3	5.9	91.7	94.4	.8	.0	15.4	20.4	103.0
Jewish	.0	.0	.0	.0	.0	.0	96.3	99.2	.0	.0	103.0
Other	.2	.4	.8	1.2	2.5	2.1	.0	.0	59.7	64.5	108.2
Total	*100*	*100*	*100*	*100*	*100*	*100*	*100*	*100*	*100*	*100*	*100.0*

Ethnoreligious identity of marriage partners, 1911

Origin of spouse	*French Catholic*		*British Catholic*		*British Protestant*		*Jewish*		*Other*		*Sex ratio*
	Hus.	*Wife*	*Hus.*	*Wife*	*Hus.*	*Wife*	*Hus.*	*Wife*	*Hus.*	*Wife*	*H/100W*
French Catholic	98.6	98.2	19.4	16.9	2.9	2.2	.0	.0	11.8	6.2	99.6
British Catholic	.9	1.0	75.7	74.3	2.5	.9	.0	.0	3.2	3.6	98.2
British Protestant	.3	.4	2.4	6.5	91.9	94.4	.0	.4	8.4	9.5	102.6
Jewish	.0	.0	.0	.0	.1	.0	99.6	99.6	.0	.2	100.0
Other	.2	.4	2.5	2.3	2.6	2.5	.4	.0	76.6	80.5	105.0
Total	*100*	*100*	*100*	*100*	*100*	*100*	*100*	*100*	*100*	*100*	*100.0*

Sources: Census of Canada microdata, 1881 (entire); CCRI 1911 microdata database.

Includes only households with three or fewer boarders.

amy in 1911 compared with 1881. British Catholics (mostly Irish) have somewhat lower levels of endogamy in 1911, reflecting their diminished "Otherness" in light of the trainloads of Italians, Chinese, and Eastern European Jews arriving in Quebec and flooding into Montreal, as well as their diminishing size. Not only do more Irish women marry out because they outnumber men, especially in 1881, but men and women who marry out choose different partners. Irish Catholic women are more likely than Irish men to choose a Protestant mate, perhaps with an eye to upward social mobility, or because they may have spent time as servants in Protestant homes and neighbourhoods. Alternatively, prospects are gendered, for example, an Irish Catholic woman may be more attractive and attracted as a wife to a Protestant man than an Irish Catholic man as a husband to a Protestant woman.

Multilevel Modelling of Household Mixity

In this section, we examine how the overall picture of cultural diversity may have come into play in the daily life of ordinary families and dwellings in Quebec. We are interested in the most intimate kinds of interactions, those that occur when people share domestic space, perhaps eat at the same table, share conversations, histories, and hopes, and in the case of couples, share the same bed. How are these affected by structural processes operating at a larger scale or by the characteristics of the households themselves? We ask questions such as the following: To what extent did the composition of households reflect the presence of different cultural communities within various settings? Were the most common forms of diversity within households associated with intermarriage, or with the presence of non-kin members who may have worked as domestics or have been included as boarders? What household factors were more (or less) conducive to incorporating members from other cultural communities?

To identify the households included in our study for the 1911 sample, we first removed institutions and large households, as defined in the CCRI sample, and then we removed the 273 remaining households with more than three boarders. We also excluded 768 households with only one individual, and problematic ones with no head (453) or more than one head (219), which could not easily be fixed. There remained 16,233 households with a family unit at their core, which represents 83 per cent of all households included in the CCRI sample for the province of Quebec. Of these households, 89 per cent are composed of a couple with or without child(ren) and the remaining 11 per cent of "census families" are single-parent families.

With no direct information regarding the relationship between household members, the 1881 census is more difficult to use in this way. We relied on a variable built into the file by Lisa Dillon, that is, a unique family identifier (FAMID) given to all members of a household who have the same surname. Within FAMIDs, we identified married couples on the basis of marital status and age, along with their children, and single parents (usually widowed), along with their children.[29] These families are embedded into households with as many FAMIDs as there are different surnames listed. As in 1911, we retained in our analyses only households where the first FAMID was a census family, which resulted in our including 85 per cent of the households (217,011). Of these, 87 per cent are composed of couples with or without children and 13 per cent are single parents with children, almost the same proportion as in 1911. The slightly larger proportion of single-parent families in 1881 is most likely due to a drop in adult mortality between 1881 and 1911, but it may also result from the indirect way in which we identified census families in 1881. Institutions and large households were removed using the same criteria as in 1911; households with more than three boarders were excluded, as were households with individuals displaying different FAMIDs and who were recorded with an occupation other than servants, if there were more than three such people.

Table 9.4 describes the distribution of the independent variables used in the multilevel modelling of mixity as well as the proportions of households that are mixed according to each of these characteristics taken separately. The first group of variables pertains to the individual households, while the contextual variables aim at capturing the characteristics of the geographical areas in which these households are situated. Table 9.5 provides additional information on the distribution of households in the various milieus. We briefly describe these tables before turning to the multivariate analysis of household mixity.

One of the most important changes between 1881 and 1911 is the declining proportion of heads of household who are farmers and the significant increase of the urban type of milieu (table 9.4). They both attest to the significant urbanization taking place within Quebec during this period. The new immigration wave – dominated by males,[30] more often directed towards cities and more diversified than before – combines with rural-to-urban migration to bring about changes to the population characteristics. The ethnoreligious composition and the DI are two population characteristics that changed, especially when examined by milieu: they indicate, for 1911, an increased concentration of all ethnoreligious groups in the urban milieu, including the French, and the overrepresentation of urban milieus among areas with high cultural diversity (table 9.5). Measured at the contextual level, the sex ratio is designed to reflect the regional consequences of migration patterns, both international and internal. Fewer than 92 men for every 100 women identifies areas with surpluses of women, more often in urban and rural non-farm settings, which attract young local women to work as domestics or where widow-headed households may be able to remain viable economic units. The declining proportion of female-dominant urban contexts between 1881 and 1911 is linked to the increasing masculinity ratio of the immigrant population from new sources of immigration (tables 9.4 and 9.5). Finally, it is worth mentioning that single-parent families tended to concentrate in urban and rural non-farm areas when headed by a woman and in rural areas when headed by a man, which points to differentiated gender roles and greater opportunities for women to survive without

Table 9.4 · Determinants of ethnoreligious mixity within households, Quebec, 1881 and 1911

		1881		*1911*	
		All households (%)	*Portion of hhds mixed (%)*	*All households (%)*	*Portion of hhds mixed (%)*
Number of households		215,455	5.9	15,776	5.9
HOUSEHOLD VARIABLES					
Domestic unit	Couple headed	87.4	6.0	91.9	5.8
	Male head	7.0	4.3	3.5	4.0
	Female head	5.6	5.7	4.6	8.6
Ethnoreligious background of head	French	78.9	2.3	80.1	2.5
	British Catholic	6.5	21.8	4.4	30.3
	British Protestant	12.8	14.9	10.8	14.2
	Jewish	0.1	34.0	1.6	6.6
	Other	1.7	40.7	3.1	28.8
Age of head (years)	< 35	33.1	5.6	24.6	5.1
	35–49	33.5	6.3	32.7	5.9
	≥ 50	33.4	5.7	42.7	6.3
Head farmer		46.3	3.9	35.2	3.9
Presence of other kin or non-kin	Yes	23.9	11.2	26.5	11.8
CONTEXTUAL VARIABLES					
Milieu	Urban	22.9	10.1	39.3	8.0
	Rural non-farm	29.6	5.6	24.6	5.2
	Rural farm	47.5	4.0	36.1	3.9
Sex ratio (M per 100F)	Female dominant < 92	36.2	8.0	21.8	5.6
	Balanced 92–108	33.1	5.0	39.5	6.9
	Male dominant > 108	30.7	4.3	38.7	5.0
Diversity index	Very low < .1	32.7	2.0	33.8	1.7
	Moderate .1–.399	29.4	4.4	29.5	5.2
	High ≥ .4	37.9	10.3	36.7	10.2

Sources: Census of Canada microdata, 1881 (entire); CCRI 1911 database.

Includes only households with three or fewer boarders.

Table 9.5 · Characteristics of population by different milieus (urban, rural non-farm, and rural farm), Quebec, 1881 and 1911

		1881			1911		
		Urban	*Rural non-farm*	*Rural farm*	*Urban*	*Rural non-farm*	*Rural farm*
Number of households		49,365	63,685	102,405	6,202	3,883	5,691
Row percentage		22.9	29.6	47.5	39.3	24.6	36.1
HOUSEHOLD VARIABLES (row percentages)							
Domestic unit	Couple headed	22.4	28.8	48.9	39.3	24.3	36.4
	Male head	17.7	31.2	51.1	26.5	26.8	46.7
	Female head	38.1	39.4	22.5	49.7	28.6	21.7
Ethnoreligious background of head	French	20.1	31.4	48.5	34.6	26.5	38.9
	British Catholic	45.4	18.2	36.4	61.4	11.3	27.3
	British Protestant	29.2	22.2	48.6	52.9	19.1	28.0
	Jewish	92.3	6.4	1.3	95.8	1.9	2.3
	Other	20.0	46.0	34.0	53.1	26.5	20.4
Age of head (years)	< 35	25.0	32.9	42.1	43.3	27.6	29.1
	35–49	23.6	28.0	48.4	43.0	24.3	32.7
	≥ 50	20.2	27.8	52.0	34.3	23.1	42.6
Head farmer		0.0	0.0	100.0	0.8	0.0	99.2
Presence of other kin or non-kin	Yes	26.3	23.3	50.4	43.5	20.7	35.8
CONTEXTUAL VARIABLES (row percentages)							
Sex ratio (M per100F)	Female dominant < 92	53.9	46.0	0.1	39.7	55.4	4.9
	Balanced 92–108	10.3	39.0	50.7	64.6	16.3	19.1
	Male dominant > 108	0.0	0.0	100.0	13.2	15.8	71.0
Diversity index	Very low < .1	1.9	33.0	65.1	17.9	29.8	52.3
	Moderate .1 to .399	18.9	38.8	42.3	32.6	28.9	38.5
	High ≥ .4	44.2	19.4	36.4	64.4	16.4	19.2

Sources: Census of Canada microdata, 1881 (entire); CCRI 1911 microdata database.

Includes only households with three or fewer boarders.

a spouse in a city or village where they can more easily make a living (table 9.5). The significant increase in the proportion of households with additional kin or non-kin that are urban in 1911 is yet another consequence of the recent migration patterns (table 9.5).

We now turn to the mixity figures provided in table 9.4 for each characteristic taken separately. The overall proportion of mixed households, those with at least one person of a different ethnoreligious group than the head of household, is 5.9 per cent at the two census years.[31] Despite some differences in the way households are defined between the two censuses, cultural diversity within the household appears to be as common in 1911 as it was in 1881. This in itself is an interesting result since the immigration patterns in the two periods immediately preceding the census are quite different. In considering whether this 5.9 per cent is a large proportion or not, we must remember that because we excluded large households and large boarding houses, which include somewhat more immigrants than domestic households do, this must represent a minimum estimate of the level of cultural diversity within households. Moreover, the high turnover of servants and boarders may mean that a much larger proportion of people actually spent time in a mixed household.

The proportion of mixed households varies enormously according to the ethnoreligious identity of the head of household, which is consistent with structural factors and cultural preferences previously found and discussed in residential segregation at the neighbourhood level and intermarriage at the micro-level. Most striking is the low level of mixity within households headed by French Canadians, but this group is so large and far more residentially segregated than the British group that structurally there is very little need and less opportunity, in many cases, for its members to seek a spouse outside the group, compared, say, with the smaller Irish Catholic group (even smaller by 1911). The diversity index computed at the contextual level is explicitly designed to measure the relative opportunity for interaction among groups. The similarity between the map of the diversity by CD (figure 9.5) and the map of proportions of households that are mixed by the same CDs (figure 9.6) is striking. It suggests that when opportunities for interaction increase, so do the proportions of mixed households. It also suggests that diversity varies widely across Quebec as well as by milieu, and together these factors would be expected to play a major role in determining the opportunities that households might have to incorporate individuals from other ethnoreligious groups.

Not surprisingly, urban settings display higher levels of household mixity, which may result from a greater level of diversity, a propensity for immigrants to settle in urban places, and the presence of more unattached individuals from various cultural backgrounds (table 9.4). Slightly more households headed by

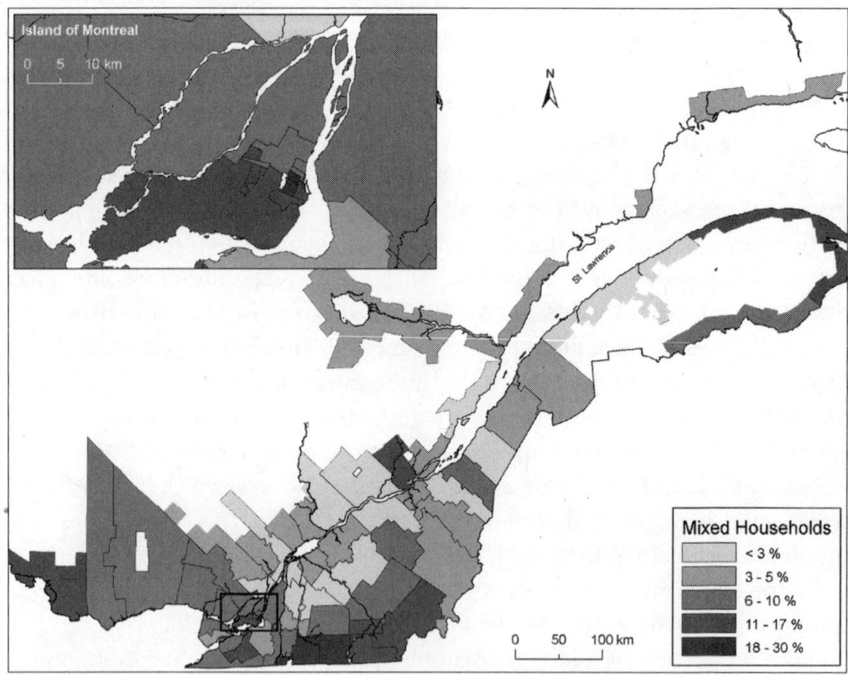

Figure 9.6 · Mixed households (with at least one person of another ethnoreligious group) as a percentage of all households: Quebec and Island of Montreal, by census districts, 1911. Based on 16,233 domestic households with three or fewer boarders.

Sources: CCRI 1911 microdata database, and GIS of census districts, CCRI geographical database.

couples are mixed, partly because intermarriage is fully visible in this situation as opposed to single-parent families where the surviving parent of a mixed marriage may share the ethnic or religious identity of the children. Mixity is more common in households headed by women than by men, most likely because the child's ethnic origin in the census is traced through the paternal line. Nevertheless, Bettina Bradbury has demonstrated that single-parent families have specific needs that may lead to taking in individuals such as domestics (in the case of widowers) or boarders (in the case of widows).[32] The addition of such people is likely to increase the chance of one member being of a different cultural background from the head of household. The proportions of mixed households seen in table 9.4 seem to reflect these various processes: there are higher proportions of mixed households in female-led households compared with in male-headed households and highest of all in households where kin or non-kin are present. In 1911, when we can use the "relation to head" variable to distinguish between kin and non-kin in the household, the proportion of households that are mixed is much higher when non-kin are present than when kin alone are present.

If we try to further characterize the source of mixity in various types of households (figures not shown here), we find that between two-thirds and three-quarters of mixed situations for couple-based households originated from the couple itself rather than from the presence of kin or non-kin in the household or the children only. Cultural mixity within single-parent families, especially in urban areas where they abound, is indeed, more often due to the presence of kin or non-kin. Couple-based households in urban areas are also more likely to be mixed due to the presence of kin or non-kin members, which points to the greater diversity of the urban milieu and, thus, increased chances of close cultural interaction in this milieu.

Multilevel modelling seems particularly appropriate to account for variations in household mixity associated with both cultural and structural attributes of individual households and the largely structural attributes of the milieu in which the households are located. Five attributes have been taken into account at the household level, as categorized in table 9.4. The context is defined as a geographical area: one of 64 census districts (which remained almost the same over the period) subdivided by the characteristics of its constituent census subdistricts into those parts that are predominantly rural farm, rural non-farm, or urban. Rural non-farm census areas closely correspond to distinct CSDs for villages and small towns of fewer than 3,000 inhabitants, but enclaves do exist within some CSDs. Urban includes CSDs that make up towns of more than 3,000 people or are part of large cities like Montreal that are composed of numerous CSDs, or wards. Where there are insufficient households in a particular milieu of a given CD (only a problem in 1911), contiguous areas or milieus are combined and this is why there are ten fewer census areas in 1911 (121) than in 1881 (131). After verifying that multicollinearity is not a problem, the following three variables have been retained to characterize the context: the type of milieu, the overall sex ratio of the CA, and the diversity of the CA (as shown in table 9.4).[33]

The reason for defining census areas not just in terms of census districts but also milieu was based on the notion that opportunity structures differed markedly between farm census areas (CAs), rural non-farm CAs, and urban CAs, and this would be reflected in the composition of their populations. This is supported by the strong differences that all the variables displayed by milieu (as seen in table 9.5 and already discussed). The number of census areas is relatively similar in 1881 and 1911, but the numbers of households are much greater in 1881 when the data pertain to the entire set of households (215,455).

Although the number of households (15,776) in 1911 is sufficient to perform the analyses, one has to keep in mind that the much larger size in 1881 makes it easier for the parameters to be statistically significant, especially when it comes to the effects of the interaction among variables.

The null model in the multilevel analyses (see table 9.6) shows that 18.0 per cent of the variation in cultural diversity within households is accounted for by the contextual level in 1881 and 20.6 per cent is in 1911. These numbers indicate that intrinsic characteristics such as the geographical location of a context, for example, being close or not to a boarder or in a colonization area, or an area with a particular industrial base or history of settlement and contact, or the fact that the population is predominantly urban or rural, do indeed, play a significant role in explaining household mixity in 1881 as well as in 1911. When computed within the structure of the multilevel analysis, the proportions of mixed households are, again, very similar with 5.0 per cent in 1881 and 5.3 per cent in 1911. Most of the factors used in the model have a similar impact in 1881 and 1911, although a few yield different results at the two dates.[34] The impact of the household characteristics on mixity remains almost identical when contextual variables are added, which suggests that their effect is distinct and additive to the impact at the household level. There are more significant interaction effects in 1881 than in 1911, but this may well be due to the much larger number of cases available for 1881.

As expected, given the importance of intermarriage as a source of mixity, households with a couple at their head are about twice as likely as households with single-parent families at their core to be culturally mixed. This is true in the case of both male and female single-parent heads of household in 1881 but only for male-headed single-parent households in 1911; in both cases, however, female-headed households are more likely to be mixed than are male-headed households. Widow-led households are more likely to take in boarders and, given the rise in immigrants and urbanization by the time of the 1911 census, family-based boarding may have increased. As expected, the presence of additional members to the core census family is associated with much more mixity, and the pattern is the same for both 1881 and 1911. Results for 1911 (not shown here) indicate that this result holds for each category of kin and non-kin taken separately, but the odds ratio is much higher in the case of non-kin than in the case of kin. Many of these non-related individuals are domestics or boarders who are more likely to be recent immigrants and to belong to a different cultural group.[35]

Structural effects are the most obvious in that every ethnoreligious group is more likely than the French to be the head of a mixed household. The only exception to that pattern is for the Jewish community in 1911, when the odds

Table 9.6 · Household and contextual determinants of the likelihood of living in a culturally mixed household (mixity), Quebec, 1881 and 1911

	1881			*Census*		
	Null Model	*Model 1*	*Model 2*	*Null Model*	*Model 1*	*Model 2*
HOUSEHOLD VARIABLES		*n* = 215,455			*n* = 15,776	
Domestic unit (couple-head)						
Male head		0.49 ***	0.49 ***		0.56 **	0.56 **
Female head		0.55 ***	0.56 ***		1.06	1.05
Ethnoreligious origin of head (French)						
British Catholic		9.93 ***	9.89 ***		17.32 ***	15.32 ***
British Protestant		6.00 ***	5.92 ***		5.01 ***	4.35 ***
Jewish		11.91 ***	11.83 ***		1.56	1.39
Other		28.30 ***	28.36 ***		13.16 ***	11.54 ***
Age of head (< 35 years)						
35–49		1.03	1.03		0.89	0.89
≥ 50		0.96	0.96		0.79 **	0.80 **
Head farmer (non-farmer)						
Farmer		0.61 ***	0.68 ***		0.71 **	0.98
Presence of kin or non-kin (none)						
Extended kin or non-kin present		2.97 ***	2.98 ***		3.58 ***	3.56 ***
CONTEXTUAL VARIABLES		*n* = 131			*n* = 121	
Milieu (rural non-farm)						
Rural farm			0.73 *			0.97
Urban			1.35 *			0.96
Sex ratio M per 100F (balanced)						
Female dominant			0.90			1.04
Male dominant			1.12			1.02
Diversity index (homogeneous)						
Moderate diversity			1.27 **			2.07 ***
Most diversified			1.58 ***			2.38 ***
Variance at group level	18.0%	6.1%	5.2%	20.6%	6.4%	4.3%

Sources: Census of Canada microdata, 1881 (entire); CCRI 1911 microdata database.

Note: Reference category for which the odds are 1.00 and to which the other odds ratios are relative are in parentheses.

* $p < .05$; ** $p < .01$; *** $p < .001$.

ratio is slightly higher for Jews than for French, but not significant. Although much larger in size in 1911 than 1881, the Jewish community is still relatively small in Quebec but highly concentrated, and the recent immigrants are much more traditional in character, religiously and economically, and many were already married at the time of immigration. Results for the diversity index at the contextual level also show very clearly that cultural diversity within households is more common (1.5 to two times) when there are more opportunities for such interaction in the immediate neighbourhood.

The two sociodemographic factors, the age group of the head at the household level and the sex ratio at the contextual level, yield few significant results. Unbalanced sex ratios stemming from internal and international migration (whether producing surpluses of women or men) are not significantly or consistently associated with different probabilities of mixity, perhaps because so many French Canadians are involved in internal migration and the favoured residential arrangement for young immigrants remains to live with relatives or other acquaintances from the same cultural group. This situation seems consistent with the importance of family and community networks in the modalities of migration, which has been shown both at the international and internal levels.[36] Even though the results for the age of the head of the household must be interpreted with caution due to possible flaws in defining the head of the household in the two different censuses, table 9.6 suggests that, for 1911 only, households with older heads are significantly less likely to be mixed compared with households with young heads. This most likely reflects the fact that immigrants (all recent in 1911) are younger.

As we might suspect, mixed households are less common when the head of household is a farmer, but in 1911, the effect disappears once milieu is included. Milieu is significant only in 1881, and even then, its effect disappears when interaction terms are added to the model. This suggests that cultural diversity within the household is not restricted to urban areas. By 1911, non-French cultural communities within rural settings are sufficiently long-standing for integration to have occurred.

Table 9.7 displays the results for significant interactions between household and contextual variables in 1881 and in 1911.[37] There are more of these significant interactions in 1881 than in 1911 (probably because of the larger sample size), and most of them involve variables pertaining to the structure of households. The one effect that is present in both 1881 and 1911 involves the interaction between household type and milieu. The reference category is a couple-based household in a rural non-farm milieu. Couple-based households do not differ in their propensity to be mixed according to the milieu where they live (neither in 1881 nor in 1911), but single-parent families do. Female-headed

Table 9.7 · Household and contextual determinants of the likelihood of living in a culturally mixed household (mixity), including significant interaction effects, Quebec, 1881 and 1911

	1881			1911		
	Main effects	*Interaction with milieu*		*Main effects*	*Interaction with milieu*	
		Rural farm	*Urban*		*Rural farm*	*Urban*
HOUSEHOLD VARIABLES						
Domestic unit (couple-head)						
Male head	0.43 ***	1.33 **	1.46 **	0.75	0.62	3.32 **
Female head	0.64 **	1.37 **	1.59 ***	0.13 **	2.85 **	2.49 **
Ethnoreligious origin of head (French)						
British Catholic	20.99 ***	0.57 ***	0.29 ***	15.78 ***		
British Protestant	4.76 ***	0.85 **	1.73 ***	4.38 ***		
Jewish	5.39 **	12.34	2.33	1.42		
Other	13.92 ***	2.25 ***	5.33 ***	11.89 ***		
Age of head (< 35 years)						
35–49	1.03			0.88		
≥ 50	0.97			0.80 **		
Head farmer (non-farmer)						
Farmer	0.66 ***			1.01		
Presence of other kin or non-kin (none)						
Extended kin or non-kin present	2.79 ***	.78 ***	1.46 ***	3.53 ***	0.86	1.11
CONTEXTUAL VARIABLES		*n* = 131			*n* = 121	
Milieu (rural non-farm)						
Rural farm	0.85					
Urban	1.06					
Sex ratio M per 100F (balanced)						
Female dominant	0.90					
Male dominant	1.14					

/continued

households are consistently more likely to be mixed in urban (1.59 in 1881; 2.49 in 1911) and rural farm areas (1.37 in 1881; 2.85 in 1911); the opposite prevails in rural non-farm areas (0.64 and 0.13, respectively, in 1881 and 1911). These results point to the greater opportunities for women heads of household to make a living in the city as boarding house keepers and the need for the few women heads of household in rural areas to hire complementary workers; in

Table 9.7 · continued

	Main effects	Interaction with domestic unit (couple head)		Main effects	Interaction with domestic unit (couple head)	
		Male head	Female head		Male head	Female head
Diversity index Low < .1						
Moderate .1 to .399	1.34 **	0.95	0.63 **	2.01 ***	0.58	4.62
High ≥ .4	1.80 ***	0.90	0.62 ***	2.37 ***	0.38	2.01
Variance at group level		4.7%			4.3%	

Sources: Census of Canada microdata, 1881 (entire); CCRI 1911 microdata database.

Note: Reference category for which the odds are 1.00 and to which the other odds ratios are relative are in parentheses.

* $p < .05$; ** $p < .01$; *** $p < .001$.

rural villages and non-farm areas, widows – and widowers at 0.43 in 1881 and 0.75 in 1911 – can probably cope more easily with their situation, and boarding is less common as people living in closer proximity provide adequate support for the widowed to live on their own. Differentiated gender roles are most likely linked also to greater probabilities of mixity among male-headed households in the cities (1.46 and 3.32 in 1881 and 1911, respectively) and in the rural farm areas (at 1.33 in 1881 only).

Interaction between the household type and the diversity index at the contextual level shows that the positive impact of diversity on mixity is only true for couple-based households in 1881, probably because higher levels of diversity significantly increase the probability of intermarriage. No matter in what milieu they were living, families headed by single parents were always less likely than couples living in the least diverse milieu to experience household mixity, which points to the significance of intermarriage as a source of mixity regardless of how diverse the region. Although the results are not significant in 1911, they seem to suggest that female-headed census families (4.62) are no longer in that situation, being at least as likely to display cultural mixity as couple-based households (2.01).

Not surprisingly, French Canadians are unlikely to head mixed families in every type of milieu. All other ethnoreligious heads display higher mixity levels when their households are located in rural non-farm milieus compared with rural farm and urban, but in 1881 only, and not for the Jewish community which was then very small. Most likely, in 1911, the greater diversity of the urban milieu is counterbalanced by the larger size of the groups, which allows minorities to live among their own kind in those urban surroundings.

The presence of kin or non-kin is linked to greater cultural diversity within households in both the urban (1.46) and rural non-farm (2.79) milieus; the significantly lower odds in the rural farm milieu (0.78) suggests that this category is probably mostly composed of kin rather than non-kin, which we cannot properly distinguish in 1881. Consistent with previous results showing almost no difference between milieus, there is no difference in the level of mixity for households without kin or non-kin regardless of milieu.

To summarize, multilevel analyses confirm the importance of contextual variables in accounting for variations in household mixity, both on their own and in addition to household characteristics. The models are relatively stable between 1881 and 1911. They point to the importance of structural factors, especially the size of the ethnoreligious groups and the diversity of the ethnic composition of the area at the contextual level, as well as the type of households (whether couple-based or single-parent families) and the presence of non-family members within the household. Although couple-based households are more likely to be mixed, given the importance of intermarriage as a source of mixity, female-headed households are no longer associated with lower levels of mixity in 1911, which may reflect increased opportunities for taking in boarders, especially in the urban areas due to greater mobility. In itself, at the contextual level, the milieu where households are located does not yield significant differences in mixity, but when combined with household-level characteristics, it is present in almost all significant interaction terms. Despite the similar levels and the presence of the same significant factors in 1881 and 1911, we cannot assume that the nature of mixity in rural and urban areas in 1881 and 1911 has not changed, since we are unable to distinguish in 1881 between the effect of kin and non-kin.

Conclusion

Cultural diversity varied a lot across Quebec at the turn of the twentieth century but, despite significant changes between the two census dates, the degree of diversity remained surprisingly similar in 1881 and 1911. This conclusion remains whether we are looking at the degree of diversity at the scale of the census subdistrict, BALSAC regions, or even the province as a whole, or in the percentages of domestic households that are mixed, or in the degree of segregation between the major ethnoreligious groups. The changes reflect the diversification of immigration and the increasingly urban destination of immigrants, particularly Montreal, which initiates a pattern that is still in place today. Other changes lie in the differences between genders and their propensity to marry out or to live in a mixed household.

Overall, the findings support the theory that structural factors, largely explained by the history of settlement, have a major bearing on the propensity for cultures and ethnoreligious groups to mix. These are visible both at the household level and the broader level of *milieu de vie*. It appears that proximity of groups living in villages may reduce the need for individuals from groups different from the head of the household's group to live in family settings in that milieu. With the death of a spouse, families faced a structural challenge that, among other things, led widows in the cities to take in boarders and widowers to hire domestics or welcome other family members or non-kin to help with domestic chores, and this increased the probability of incorporating someone with a different ethnoreligious identity into the household. These undertakings were largely absent from villages and small towns. By 1911, even more opportunities had opened up for women heads of household to use such a strategy, which contributes further to a gender difference in the propensity to mix.

With respect to the prevailing image that the French Canadian population was homogeneous, this chapter suggests that geography (residential segregation) and size rather than cultural preference go a long way in explaining their low degree of cultural mixing compared with smaller groups that are relatively widely dispersed. Still, for the Jewish population in Quebec, cultural preference combined with a high degree of spatial concentration are likely responsible for the extremely low levels of mixity within Jewish households in 1911, as well as their high degree of spatial segregation compared with their situation in 1881. The picture of cultural diversity in Quebec is more complex than the notion of two solitudes, with several groups remaining relatively separate from each other and mixing in different ways with other groups. Irish Catholics and Jews are particularly interesting in this respect, able to maintain separate identities over much of the nineteenth century and to marry predominantly within the group despite their size. Apart from Native Indians and Jews, the "Other" group in 1881 was clearly not homogeneous or separate. By 1911, even though Others is composed of several different groups, especially newly arrived immigrants from non-traditional sources, which are more distinct and residentially segregated. Future analyses using the 1921 through 1941 newly available samples of the census will serve to test some of the trends depicted for 1911, especially the consequences of the growing concentration of immigrants in Montreal and the long-term effects of previous cultural diversity in rural areas and villages within Quebec.

This research suggests that milieu and residential segregation are important in determining the propensity to mix within the most intimate spaces and, hence, the opportunity that individuals from different ethnoreligious groups had to meet and mix matters. It is much less clear whether mixity within households is a good indicator of cultural integration or whether living together but separately, the famous Canadian mosaic, produces not one Quebec nation but multiple and overlapping Quebec identities.

Notes

1 This research is part of a larger project entitled "Diversity, Cross-Cultural Relations, and Integration: A Socio-demographic and Demo-genetic Study of Quebec, 1760–1940," conducted with Hélène Vézina (Université du Québec à Chicoutimi), in collaboration with Sherry Olson (McGill University). We wish to thank the Social Sciences and Humanities Research Council of Canada for their financial support of the project. Special thanks go to Anne Bourgeois, Ph.D. student in demography, who performed the multilevel analyses as well as for her tremendous work in manipulating the 1881 census to identify census family units, and to Sherry Olson for her valuable comments on an earlier draft. Thanks also to Marc St-Hilaire and Laurent Richard for providing the detailed maps for 1911; and to two research assistants, Marc-Antoine Côté-Marcil and cartographer Brian Armstrong.

2 On the history of Montreal, see Paul-André Linteau, *Histoire de Montréal depuis la Confédération*, 2nd ed. (Montreal: Boréal, 2000). For examples of work on the Irish, see Robert Grace, "Irish Immigration and Settlement in a Catholic City: Quebec, 1842–61," *Canadian Historical Review* 84, no. 2 (2003): 217–52; Cecil J. Houston and William Smyth, *Irish Emigration and Canadian Settlement* (Toronto: University of Toronto Press, 1990); and Sherry Olson and Patricia Thornton, "The Challenge of the Irish Catholic Community in Nineteenth-Century Montreal," *Histoire sociale/Social History* 35, no. 70 (2002): 333–64. For the Jews, see Michael Brown, *Jew or Juif? Jews, French Canadians, and Anglo-Canadians, 1759–1914* (Philadelphia, PA: Jewish Publication Society, 1987); Ira Robinson, "Historical Introduction to the Jewish Community of Quebec/Introduction à l'histoire de la communauté juive du Québec," http://www.federationcja.org/en/jewish_montreal/history. For the Italians, see Nicole Malpas, "Destination: Montréal – L'étude de l'émigration en provenance de Casacalenda (Molise)," *Cahiers québécois de démographie* 26, no. 2 (1997): 155–89; Bruno Ramirez, *The Italians of Montreal: From Sojourning to Settlement, 1900–1921* (Montreal: Editions du Courant, 1980). A few examples of work acknowledging ethnic diversity and interaction at this time are Sherry Simon, *Translating Montreal: Episodes in the Life of a Divided City* (Montreal: McGill-Queen's University Press, 2006) which looks at literature; Pierre Anctil, "Finding a Balance in a Dual Society: The Jews of Quebec," in Ezra Mendelsohn (ed.), *Jews and the State: Dangerous Alliances and the Perils of Privilege* (Oxford: Oxford University Press, 2003), 70–87; Roderick McLeod and Mary Anne

Poutanen, *A Meeting of the People: School Boards and Protestant Communities in Quebec, 1801–1998* (Montreal: McGill-Queen's University Press, 2004) refer to complexity in the Townships of religious and language diversity and to the intense issues in the 1900s about schooling of Jewish pupils.

3 One of the only overviews is based on published census data. See Victor Piché, "Immigration et rapports ethniques au Canada et au Québec: Pour sortir de l'ornière triangulaire," in Guy Brunet, Michel Oris, and Alain Bideau (eds.), *Les minorités: Une démographie culturelle et politique, XVIIIe–XXe siècles/Minorities: A Cultural and Political Demography, 18th–20th Centuries* (New York: Peter Lang, 2004), 399–428.

4 The 1881 census microdata for all of Canada were collected by the Mormons. They were cleaned and made available by the North Atlantic Population Project and Minnesota Population Center. *National Sample of the 1881 Census of Canada, Version 2.0.* Montreal: Département de Démographie, Université de Montréal [distributor], 2008.

5 Canada, Royal Commission on Bilingualism and Biculturalism, *Report of the Royal Commission on Bilingualism and Biculturalism* (Ottawa: Queen's Printer, 1967–69); Hugh MacLennan, *Two Solitudes* (Toronto: Collins, 1945).

6 Guenther Roth and Claus Wittich (eds.), *Max Weber: Economy and Society* (New York: Bedminister Press, 1968); Danielle Juteau, "Theorising Ethnicity and Ethnic Communalisations at the Margins: From Québec to the World System," *Nations and Nationalism* 2 (1996): 45–66.

7 Bruce Curtis, *The Politics of Population: State Formation, Statistics, and the Census of Canada, 1840–1875* (Toronto: University of Toronto Press, 2000). Throughout this period, the question in the census on ethnic origin was posed in terms of the "racial or tribal" origin on the father's side.

8 These variables provide a national self-description that is rich in details on ethnic diversity. See, e.g., Edward N. Herberg, *Ethnic Groups in Canada: Adaptations and Transitions* (Toronto: Nelson, 1989); Burton W. Hurd, *Origin, Birthplace, Nationality and Language of the Canadian People: A Census Study Based on the Census of 1921 and Supplementary Data* (Ottawa: Dominion Bureau of Statistics, 1929); John Kralt, "Ethnic Origins in the Canadian Census, 1871–1986," in Shiva S. Halli, Frank Trovato, and Leo Driedger (eds.), *Ethnic Demography: Canadian Immigrant, Racial and Cultural Variations* (Ottawa: Carleton University Press, 1990), 13–29.

9 Households with missing information for one or more members were excluded from the regression models but, fortunately, this situation was not very frequent (0.6% of the population). A very small number of French Protestants were included within the main French category and a small number of Americans, larger in 1881 than 1911, were excluded due to the uncertainty about their origin relative to other members of the household.

10 Peter Baskerville, "Familiar Strangers: Urban Families with Boarders in Canada, 1901," *Social Science History* 25 (2001): 321–46. Others who point to the similarity in ethnic background of boarders and boarding house keepers are Robert F. Harney, "Boarding and Belonging," *Urban History Review* 78, no. 2 (1978): 8–37;

Valérie Laflamme, *Vivre en ville et prendre pension à Québec* (Paris: L'Harmattan, 2007); and Richard Harris, "The End Justified the Means: Boarding and Rooming in a City of Homes, 1891–1951," *Journal of Social History* 26 (2009): 56–86.

11 The decision to concentrate on family-based households leads to excluding more immigrants than the native-born as immigrants are more likely to live in hotels and boarding houses. Nevertheless, our analyses include over 80% of the immigrant population.

12 Matthijs Kalmijn, "Intermarriage and Homogamy: Causes, Patterns, Trends," *Annual Review of Sociology* 24 (1998): 395–421; Matthijs Kalmijn and Frank Van Tubergen, "Ethnic Intermarriage in the Netherlands: Confirmations and Refutation of Accepted Insights," *European Journal of Population* 22 (2006): 371–97.

13 Even they were not as genetically homogeneous as formally believed. The *Registre de la population du Québec ancien* and the BALSAC database of marriages have confirmed the contribution of Native Indian and Acadian groups to the diversity of the Quebec population as well as the diversity of the original French stock. See Hubert Charbonneau, Bertrand Desjardins, André Guillemette, Yves Landry, Jacques Légaré, and François Nault, *Naissance d'une population: Les Français établis au Canada au XVIIe siècle* (Montreal and Paris: Presses de l'Université de Montréal and Presses Universitaires de France, Institut National d'Études Démographiques, Travaux et Documents, Cahier no. 118, 1987); Gérard Bouchard, "Représentations de la population et de la société québécoises: L'apprentissage de la diversité," *Cahiers québécois de démographie* 19 (1990): 7–28; Claudia Moreau, Hélène Vézina, Vania Yotova, Robert Hamon, Peter de Knijff, Daniel Sinnett, and Damian Labuda, "Genetic Heterogeneity in Regional Populations of Quebec: Parental Lineages in the Gaspé Peninsula," *American Journal of Physical Anthropology* 139 (2009): 512–22.

14 Ronald Rudin, *The Forgotten Quebecers: A History of English-Speaking Quebec, 1750–1980* (Quebec: Institut québécois de recherche sur la culture, 1985).

15 Raoul Blanchard, *Le Canada français* (Montreal: Librairie Arthème Fayard, 1960).

16 Sherry Olson and Patricia Thornton show how Irish Catholics in Montreal rapidly developed their own institutions and maintained distinctive demographic, residential, and employment characteristics. See their "The Challenge of the Irish Catholic Community in Nineteenth-Century Montreal," and *Peopling the North American City: Montreal 1840–1900* (Montreal: McGill-Queen's University Press, 2011).

17 Serge Courville (ed.), *Atlas historique du Québec: Population et territoire* (Quebec: Les Presses de l'Université Laval, 1996); Clermont Dugas, "Composition et évolution ethniques des régions périphériques du Québec," *Cahiers québécois de démographie* 19 (1990): 113–21; Yves Roby, *Les Franco-Américains de la Nouvelle-Angleterre, 1760–1930* (Quebec: Septentrion, 1990).

18 The percentage of non-French origin before 1871 is calculated as the residual of the percentage born in Canada of French Origin, the only information provided in census publications.

19 Compared with the published census, the CCRI 5% sample underrepresents some ethnic groups (e.g., French, British, Jewish), while other smaller groups

are overrepresented (e.g., the group "Other"). Some of the difference between the published census and the manuscript sample result from the inability to cross-reference categories: Jewish, e.g., is classified by us if their religion is Jewish regardless of how their ethnic origin is recorded.

20 Patricia Thornton, "The Exodus: Leaving Home in the Age of Industry," in Rod MacLeod (ed.), *Canada: Confederation to Present* (Calgary: Chinook Multimedia, 2001), CD-ROM.

21 The highest possible concentration index (CI) for French Canadians, given their numerical dominance, is 1.25, while even a small increase in the "Other" group (less than 4% of the population) would produce a much larger increase in their concentration index (or CI).

22 Eight CSDs with very small populations have been amalgamated with adjacent ones.

23 The diversity index (DI), also known as the Shannon Index after the mathematician who first developed it, is calculated $DI = 1 - \Sigma p_i^2$, where p is the proportion of each ethnic group in area i and Σp_i^2 is the sum of the squared proportions of each ethnic group in area i. It makes no difference if the other group is divided among Jewish, American, Native Indian, and Other. See Claude E. Shannon, "A Mathematical Theory of Communication," *Bell System Technical Journal* 27 (1948): 623–56; Robert H. MacArthur, *Geographical Ecology: Patterns in the Distribution of Species* (Princeton: Princeton University Press, 1972). For its application in the case of interethnic relations and intermarriage, see John Lievens, "Interethnic Marriage: Bringing in the Context through Multilevel Modelling," *European Journal of Population* 14 (1998): 117–55.

24 The maximum value varies according to the number of categories, in this case the maximum value is 0.83 not 1.

25 Gilliland et al. found that modifying the boundaries made no difference to the values. So, the fact that the boundaries are not identical in the two periods should have no effect on comparisons between the two periods. See Jason Gilliland, Sherry Olson, and Danielle Gauvreau, "Did Segregation Increase as the City Expanded? The Case of Montreal, 1880–1901," *Social Science History* 35 (2011): 505–41. Moreover, it seems that the values themselves are robust to differences in population size between areas as long as population size is large enough to avoid sampling errors.

26 The segregation index (SI) measures the proportion of a population that needs to be redistributed for two distributions to be the same. SI is calculated,

$$SI = 0.5 \sum_{i=0}^{n} \left(\frac{bc_i}{BC_T} - \frac{f_i}{F_T} \right)$$

where n is the number of districts; bc_i is, e.g., the British Catholic population of district I; f_i is the French Catholic population of district I; Bc_T is the total British Catholic population; and F_T is the total French Catholic population. For a discussion of this measure and how it is applied to urban residential segregation, see Jason Gilliland and Sherry Olson, "Residential Segregation in the Industrializing City: Montreal, 1880," *Urban Geography* 31, no. 1 (2010): 28–58; and Gilliland et al., "Did Segregation Increase as the City Expanded?"

27 This is a widely recognized problem. See Otis D. Duncan and Beverly Duncan, "A Methodological Analysis of Segregation Indexes," *American Sociological Review* 20 (1955): 210–21; and Alan Walks and Larry S. Bourne, "Ghettos in Canada's Cities? Racial Segregation, Ethnic Enclaves and Poverty Concentration in Canadian Urban Areas," *Canadian Geographer* 50 (2006): 273–97. Gilliland et al., in "Did Segregation Increase as the City Expanded?" have shown that while scale mattered, boundary modification did not, and so we were careful to ensure roughly similar numbers of units in both census years.

28 Olson and Thornton, *Peopling the North American City*; and Gilliland et al., "Did Segregation Increase as the City Expanded?" The persistence over time (1881–1901) was also something Gilliland et al. and Olson and Thornton found for Montreal.

29 Single parents are widowed or married individuals with children listed with them who display the proper age difference.

30 The sex ratio of immigrants in Quebec in 1911 was 125 men for every 100 women compared with only 105 men per 100 women in 1881.

31 Since we categorized individuals into one of only five major ethnoreligious groups (i.e., French Catholic, British Catholic, British Protestant, Jewish, and Other), excluding all households where any member was recorded of American rather than Old World origin, we clearly understate "mixity," especially within the heterogeneous "Other" group. However, we feel this is minimized since the other European and Native Indian populations are geographically distinct and the American group is excluded altogether since we are unable to ascertain their true identity, which could be any of the following groups: French Catholic, British Catholic, British Protestant, or other European.

32 Bettina Bradbury, *Working Families: Age, Gender, and Daily Survival in Industrializing Montreal* (Toronto: University of Toronto Press, 2007).

33 It is almost impossible for the diversity index to reach the value 1; in our case, 0.1 and 0.4 were reasonable cut-off points given the distribution of values.

34 Associations are reported in table 9.6 as odds ratios (exponents of the coefficients): values significantly greater than 1 mean that the cases in this category are more likely than the reference category to belong to mixed households, while values significantly less than 1 mean that they are less likely than the reference category to belong to mixed households.

35 Danielle Gauvreau, Patricia Thornton, and Sherry Olson, "The Harsh Welcome of an Industrial City: Immigrant Women in Montreal, 1880–1900," *Histoire sociale/Social History* 40 (2007): 345–80.

36 France Gagnon, "Les migrations internes vers Montréal au XIXe siècle: Un bilan," *Cahiers québécois de démographie* 21 (1992): 31–49; Ramirez, *The Italians of Montreal*; Malpas, "Destination: Montréal."

37 We conducted many tests to verify various terms of interaction and only show the results that proved to be significant.

PART IV

Locales in Transition

— · 10 · —

Trois-Rivières and Its People: A Portrait of a Smaller City in Transition at the Beginning of the Twentieth Century

CLAUDE BELLAVANCE AND FRANCE NORMAND

Relatively few specialized studies examine the populations of Canada's smaller urban centres. Yet, if major cities have attracted the bulk of the attention, smaller cities are not without interest. They, too, experienced – albeit often after a certain delay and with varying degrees of intensity – most of the major transformations that accompanied the massive process of industrialization that marked the final decades of the nineteenth century and the first third of the twentieth. These include fundamental changes in the structure of work, as well as changes related to reproductive behaviour, access to education, population migrations, the physical environment, and sociospatial differentiation. If their history does not always have the same impact as that of major metropolises, smaller cities, nevertheless, offer particularly good opportunities to apply systematic approaches such as the recomposition of a population and its built environment. In this spirit, we have treated Trois-Rivières as a sort of retrospective social laboratory, where we can attempt to take full advantage of the potential offered by such a context of enquiry. To date, we have collected nominative information on all residents of the city and the surrounding area from 1851 to 1911. Our principal source is the Canadian census, carried out every ten years and providing information on a little over 12,000 households, comprising some 67,000 individuals. This chapter represents a provisional overview of our first set of explorations and the focus is on the first decade of the twentieth century.[1]

One of the first French colonial towns in North America, Trois-Rivières long remained a small trading post and administrative centre.[2] In the middle of the

1800s, the city experienced its first major industrial development, as large-scale exploitation of the forestry resources in its hinterland began. The lumber trade was unequivocally the economic motor for the region at the moment when the economic crisis of 1870 hit, with its harsh and lasting impact on international commerce. Up until the end of the century, industrial activity remained fragile. Trois-Rivières was passing through a difficult period and turned to its traditional urban functions. In the 1890s, however, the context once again became progressively more favourable to industrial development and urban growth. Ambitious projects were dreamed up, in collaboration with Canadian and American businessmen, mainly seeking to control and promote the natural riches of the Canadian Shield, hydroelectricity, and forest resources, in particular, as well as to profit from abundant labour resources. Several sawmills were founded at the mouth of the St Maurice River, walking distance from the heart of the city, providing work for hundreds of men. A modern company was founded on the northern boundary of the city, breathing new life into its historic steel industry. By 1907, the industrial vocation of Trois-Rivières had been confirmed, with the creation of a new generation of factories, notably, in the textile and paper sectors.

Taking advantage of abundant job opportunities, the population of Trois-Rivières increased dramatically during the first decades of the twentieth century. People came from far and wide to work in Trois-Rivières, from the surrounding countryside and other regions of Quebec and Canada, and even from foreign countries. Such strong growth did not occur without exerting significant pressure on the old urban infrastructure. The great fire of 1908 almost completely destroyed the downtown. About one-third of the city's buildings were damaged or destroyed, and reconstruction represented a significant challenge from the perspectives of both resources and coordination.[3]

This demographic analysis examines the first decade of the twentieth century in Trois-Rivières, a period of transition that is not yet well understood, situated as it is between the first phase of industrialization and the industrial boom that would follow. Over the course of these ten years, the population of Trois-Rivières increased by more than a third. Until now, the historiography of the region has primarily concentrated on the industrial development of the region's dominant urban centre as well as on the evolution of the built environment and the urban landscape.[4] Our approach focuses, instead, on the composition and characteristics of the population, marrying both macro- and micro-social approaches. We proceed in three stages. First we provide an overview of the population of Trois-Rivières in 1901. Were the residents born in the city? Was it a relatively young population? How did the people earn their living? Next, we examine in detail the education of girls and the participation of women in the workforce, notably, in the fields of teaching and domestic ser-

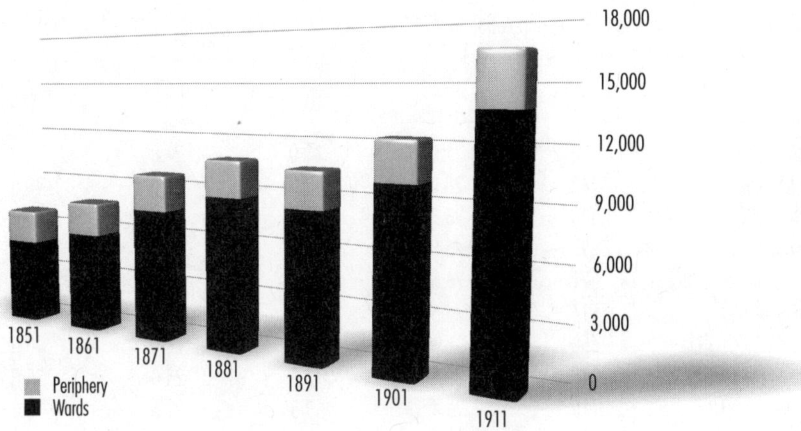

Figure 10.1 · Trois-Rivières: Changes in the population (city wards and periphery), 1851–1911. The surrounding area is composed of subsectors of the Parish of Trois-Rivières (Banlieue and des Forges sectors) as well as Sainte-Marthe-du-Cap-de-la-Madeleine.

Sources: published Canadian census tables.

vice. Third, and finally, we look at minority groups within the community of Trois-Rivières.

In parallel, we also sought to use these detailed explorations of Trois-Rivières during the first decade of the twentieth century to test the heuristic potential of the 1911 sample (5%) of the Canadian Century Research Infrastructure (CCRI). Briefly put, we gathered data for the entire population (see above) completely independently of the research undertaken for the constitution of CCRI sample; all of the manuscript census tracts were processed again. Furthermore, we chose not to use the data from the CCRI sample, but only to note those individuals and households in our complete data set that also appear in the sample. This has the advantage of neutralizing the differences between the two sets of data (differences appearing during the collection or the correction and coding of the data).

Families, Ages, and Occupations: An Overview

There were about 12,000 individuals living in Trois-Rivières and its surrounding area in 1901, a number that would increase by 4,500 over the next decade. The main urban centre of the Mauricie region was truly taking off, although the regional population had been stagnant since the 1870s (see figure 10.1). Some families lived on farms. However, farm households were largely concentrated

Table 10.1 · Age (in years) of the population in 1911 in 10 Canadian cities of similar size to Trois-Rivières

	n	*Mean*	*Quartile 25*	*Median*	*Quartile 75*
Brandon (MB)	738	21.0	3.0	21.0	33.0
Guelph (ON)	762	28.0	12.0	26.0	40.0
Lachine (QC)	548	23.9	8.0	21.5	35.0
Moncton (NB)	595	26.8	11.0	22.0	40.0
New Westminster (BC)	821	26.8	13.0	26.0	38.0
Sherbrooke (QC)	914	24.5	8.0	22.0	37.0
St Catharines (ON)	650	28.6	14.0	26.0	40.0
Sydney (NS)	943	26.1	13.0	24.0	35.0
Trois-Rivières (QC)	718	25.4	9.8	21.0	38.0
Windsor (ON)	908	29.3	14.0	26.0	43.0
All	*7,597*	*26.1*	*10.0*	*24.0*	*38.0*

Source: CCRI 1911 database.

on the city's periphery, notably, in Sainte-Marthe-du-Cap-de-la-Madeleine, in the neighbourhood of the Chemin des Forges, and along the St Lawrence River and the Chemin Ste-Marguerite. Farm families represented 0.9 per cent of Trois-Rivières households in 1901 and 0.4 per cent ten years later. The following analysis and calculations, therefore, deal only with the urban neighbourhoods of Trois-Rivières: the wards of Trois-Rivières, in 1901, and the sub-districts corresponding to the limits of the *cité*, in 1911.

The distribution of the Trois-Rivières population according to age and gender is structurally rather similar regardless of whether the 5 per cent sample or the full census is used; there are, nevertheless, some differences, notably, among individuals in their 30s and their 60s (see our comments below on the distribution of the active workforce according to age and gender and figure 10.4). The population of Trois-Rivières at the beginning of the twentieth century was very young (see table 10.1 and figure 10.2). Half had yet to reach the age of majority (21 years), while only a quarter was older than 38 years. In 1911, a quarter of the city's residents were children less than 10 years old. A comparison with other Canadian cities ranks Trois-Rivières among the youngest. It is difficult to imagine, in the midst of today's aging population, such omnipresent youth, whether at work, in public, or at home.

A significant number of the residents of Trois-Rivières were relative newcomers in 1901. In fact, more than four of every ten adults declared that they had been born in the countryside: 37 per cent when including children, com-

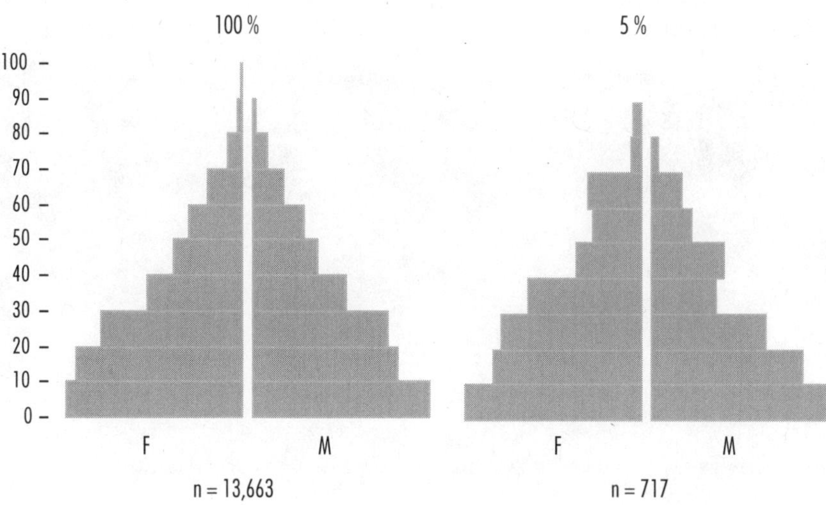

Figure 10.2 · Trois-Rivières: Age-gender pyramids, comparing manuscript census data and CCRI 1911 5% sample.

Source: Complete data collection by the authors of the Canadian manuscript census rolls for 1911 and the CCRI 1911 microdata database.

pared with 43 per cent for individuals aged 21 and older. (This information was only collected in 1901. To avoid distorting the results, the members of households whose head was a farmer have been excluded from these calculations.) People had moved into the city, attracted by the urban lifestyle and the availability of work. For several decades already, rural areas had no longer been able to absorb the available workforce, resulting in thousands of their population moving to the Canadian west or the United States. The urbanization of Quebec, of which Trois-Rivières was an active part at the beginning of the twentieth century, did much to slow these migratory trends.

How did residents of Trois-Rivières earn a living during the Belle Époque? To begin with, the sawmills at the mouth of the St Maurice River employed at least a thousand workers. Since the 1880s, the municipality had sought to attract manufacturers by offering tax exemptions and lands. If this policy had a negative impact on public finances, it encouraged the establishment of factories in a variety of sectors, such as the manufacturing of water pipes, axes, shovels, and shoes. The arrival of Wabasso, in 1907, breathed new life into the city's economy. At the official opening of its factory the following year, it was estimated that some 750 people would be employed there.[5] Three years

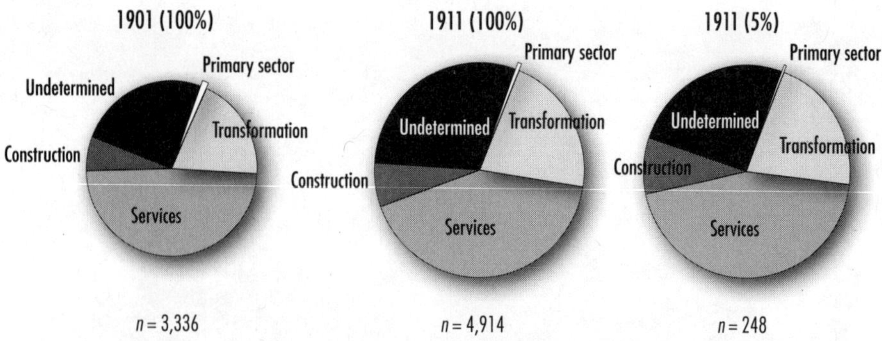

Figure 10.3 · Trois-Rivières: Population in workforce, by employment sector, 1901, 1911, and 1911 5% sample.

Sources: Complete data collection by the authors of the Canadian manuscript census rolls for 1901 and 1911 and CCRI 1911 microdata database.

later, textile manufacturer Diamond Whitewear, a subsidiary specialized in the sewing of undergarments for women, began providing work for about 250 people, including 225 women.

If the city's industrial vocation became increasingly clear in these years, commerce, services, and construction remained important sources of employment. In 1901, 210 individuals in Trois-Rivières declared employment related to construction and that number rose to 323 by 1911; however, these figures likely underestimate the number of men working in construction since an important portion of day labourers (originally entered in the "Undetermined" sector) were probably employed on the city's construction sites. The reconstruction of the downtown following the 1908 fire brought about intense activity. In 1910, a group of American industrialists (the Grès Falls Co. Ltd.) opened a pulp and paper mill at Cap-de-la-Madeleine. In 1911, construction began on a large chemical paste and kraft paper factory on Île de la Potherie. These projects and the boost they gave to the housing sector provided employment to several hundred construction workers. The rise in the population stimulated commercial activity and the demand for services, with these sectors providing about one out of every two jobs in 1901 (see figure 10.3). However, the strong growth experienced by Trois-Rivières during the first decades of the twentieth century also had negative effects; notably, it caused a structural crisis in housing.

The distribution of workers by occupational sector underwent a significant transformation during the first decade of the twentieth century. The service sector, with a little more than four workers out of every ten in 1911, lost sig-

Table 10.2 · Active population in Trois-Rivières by employment category (*n* and %), Canada 1901 and 1911

	1901 (100%)	*1911 (100%)*	*1911 (5%)*	*1901 (100%)*	*1911 (100%)*	*1911 (5%)*
Farmers	23	29	1	0.7%	0.6%	0.4%
Domestic servants	254	195	7	7.6%	4.0%	2.8%
Businessmen	42	48	1	1.3%	1.0%	0.4%
Unskilled manual trades	857	1,330	54	25.7%	27.0%	21.8%
Semi-skilled or skilled manual trades	1,022	1,562	79	30.6%	31.8%	31.9%
Non-manual trades	579	874	54	17.4%	17.8%	21.8%
Foremen, managers, etc.	31	127	7	0.9%	2.6%	2.8%
Religious occupations	70	118	7	2.1%	2.4%	2.8%
Technical and scientific workers	90	144	10	2.7%	2.9%	4.0%
Small landholders	310	406	25	9.3%	8.3%	10.1%
Professionals	44	58	3	1.3%	1.2%	1.2%
Others	13	27	0	0.4%	0.5%	0.0%
Total	*3,335*	*4,918*	*248*	*100%*	*100%*	*100%*

Sources: Complete data collection by the authors of the Canadian manuscript census rolls for 1901 and 1911 and CCRI 1911 microdata database.

nificant ground to the manufacturing and "undetermined" sectors (the latter referring to workers for whom the sources do not allow a specific sector to be identified). However, it is almost certain that the vast majority of these men and women (including 1,200 day labourers) worked in factories and on construction sites. Only 180 individuals were associated with the textile subsector; meanwhile, in 1911, Wabasso employed at least 500 people, and perhaps even over a thousand.[6] Thus, the transformation of the economic structure of Trois-Rivières appears to have been well under way. The process would continue into the 1920s with the growth in industrial production. Wayagamack Pulp and Paper Ltd. would soon begin production but had not yet done so when the 1911 census was taken. Other larger establishments would come to Trois-Rivières over the years, so many that in 1930 the city declared itself the "world capital of the pulp and paper industry." The population of Trois-Rivières and surrounding areas reached 46,000 in 1931, compared with a little more than 16,500 in 1911.

Applying the law of large numbers, the gaps found between the distributions of types of work in the case of trades experiencing labour shortages should not be surprising. By contrast, the underrepresentation of unskilled manual trades (day labourers) in the sample is more difficult to explain. Nevertheless, whether we consider commerce or services, construction or manufacturing, small salaried trades predominated in Trois-Rivières (see table 10.2). The annual salary of these workers was relatively low in 1901: about $72 for domestic servants, $290 for unspecialized manual trades, and $300 for more highly skilled and non-manual trades. Next, comprising about 310 merchants and artisans, came a group of small property owners, as well as technical and scientific workers (90 individuals), which included engineers, accountants, and cullers. Their annual salary, like that of some 30 foremen, managers, and inspectors employed by the largest businesses and some public services, was around $600 in 1901. Finally, the city's 44 professionals and its 42 industrialists (businessmen) and owners of large businesses enjoyed annual incomes of between $1,500 and $1,800, that is, five or six times more than in the small trades and between 20 and 25 times that of domestic servants. Salaries increased significantly during the first decade of the twentieth century (by 33%, if the median salary for all categories is compared), for example, that of day labourers rose from $290 to $400.

Stimulated by economic activity, the size of the workforce grew significantly faster than the general population. Employed residents of Trois-Rivières were proportionally 8 per cent more numerous in 1911 than ten years earlier. This change is mainly explained by an increased mobilization of youth old enough to work, as well as of young adults (figure 10.4); however, the possibility that residents of Trois-Rivières, in 1911, had a greater propensity to answer questions relating to employment cannot be dismissed. The distribution according to gender and age was significantly different in the case of those aged 21 to 38, which also constituted the largest group of those employed. In large part, the explanation lies in the oversampling of institutional residences, notably religious communities. It is likely that this also explains certain differences in the distribution of the population itself according to age and gender (see figure 10.2).

In the 10–16 and 16–21 age cohorts, the proportions of employed males (891 and 835, respectively, in 1911, compared with 903 for the population as a whole) were lower than the proportions of employed females. Girls aged 10 to 16 years comprised the cohort which, proportionally, was most sought after by employers. In 1911, they had actually almost achieved parity with male youth. Overall, between 1901 and 1911, in Trois-Rivières, women increased their participation in the workforce in an even more significant manner than men (increase of 56% vs. 44.5%). There were 1,200 female workers and employees in 1911, compared with 770 in 1901. In almost all cases, however, marriage interrupted women's participation in the workforce. Indeed, among adults (21 years and older), only three married women out of every 100 declared employment in 1901 (4 did in 1911), while at least one-half of single women had a job.

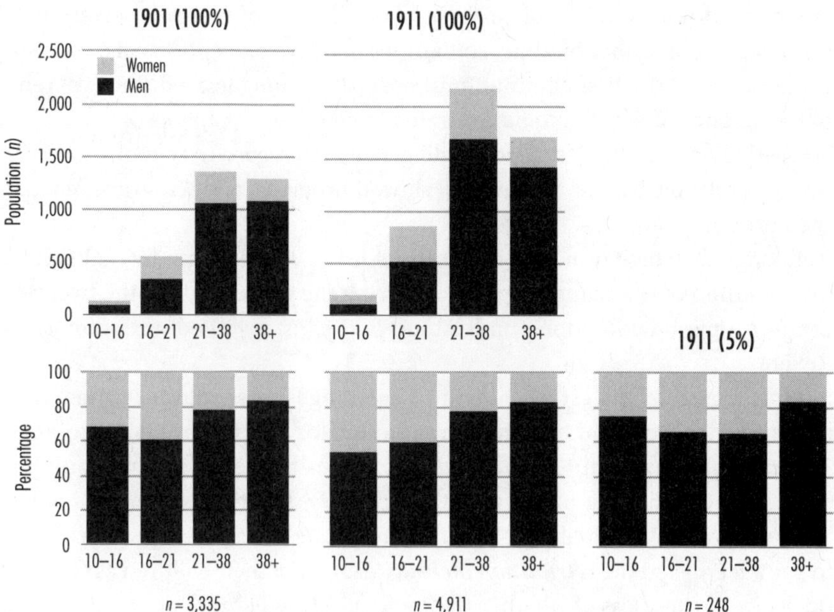

Figure 10.4 · Trois-Rivières: Population in workforce, by sex and age group, 1901, 1911, and 1911 5% sample.

Sources: Complete data collection by the authors of the Canadian manuscript census rolls for 1901 and 1911 and CCRI 1911 microdata database.

Universal Education?

As with the participation of women in the workforce, the education of girls was an important question at the beginning of the twentieth century. The two issues were linked to changes in reproductive behaviour.[7] The most recent works on the history of education in the Mauricie region indicate that, at the beginning of the twentieth century, the network of elementary schools was already well established, even if not all families attributed the same importance to education.[8] In general, the level of school attendance appears to have been greater in urban areas than in the countryside. Aside from its public schools, Trois-Rivières had well-regarded private institutions, the seminary for boys and the Ursuline convent for girls, and in 1908, the Ursulines also opened a normal school dedicated to the training of female teachers. Meanwhile, although the children in Trois-Rivières appear to have been better educated than their rural counterparts, it should be remembered that, in 1901, the majority still did not complete the prescribed four years of elementary education and a large number did not even complete three.[9] For all sorts of reasons – overcrowding, insufficient school funding, sometimes negative perceptions of continuing studies beyond the first communion, especially among less-educated parents, the reluctance of families to be separated from children capable of performing household chores, etc. – the lack of diligence with regard to school attendance was a significant barrier to learning, slowed progress, and with time, encouraged dropping out.

Taking advantage of nominative census lists, we will begin by highlighting the evolution of the school population during the first decade of the twentieth century, a period still poorly understood in the history of education in Trois-Rivières.

With regard to the establishment of age ranges, it should be remembered that the school year and information gathering for the census did not coincide. The population was surveyed for the 1901 census between June 1900 and June 1901. At the beginning of the twentieth century, strictly speaking, school attendance was not mandatory. Rather, data exist because parents were required to pay a fee, called the *rétribution mensuelle* for all of their children aged 7 to 13 (inclusive), regardless of whether they actually attended school.

Taking the entire period 1901–11 into account, a large concentration of students in the age range of 7 to 13 years becomes evident. As shown in figure 10.5, the vast majority of the children in this cohort (approximately 80%) were attending school. In 1901, the ratio "number of children in school in relation to the total of children of the same age" was rising by age group: only 35 per cent of the youngest children (6-year-olds) were attending school, compared with 68 per cent of 7-year-olds and 85 per cent of 8-year-olds. The school attendance curve plateaus for children between the ages of 9 and 12 years, when nearly all of them were attending school (almost 90%), only to dip precipitously afterwards. If the results obtained from the CCRI 5 per cent sample are less precise, they nevertheless, show the same trends.

Adolescence most often marked the end of schooling. Thus, more than three-quarters of Trois-Rivières 13-year-olds attended school in 1901, but this proportion drops suddenly to less than two-thirds by the age of 14, as soon as parents were no longer under an obligation to contribute to school expenses. An interesting discovery is the following: contrary to what other researchers have previously observed with regard to students in the public school system, it seems that boys stayed in school longer than girls once the private system is taken into account.

At the age of 17, when the gap between the sexes appears to have been the largest with regard to school attendance, the proportion of boys attending school was a full two times higher than that of girls! The most highly educated

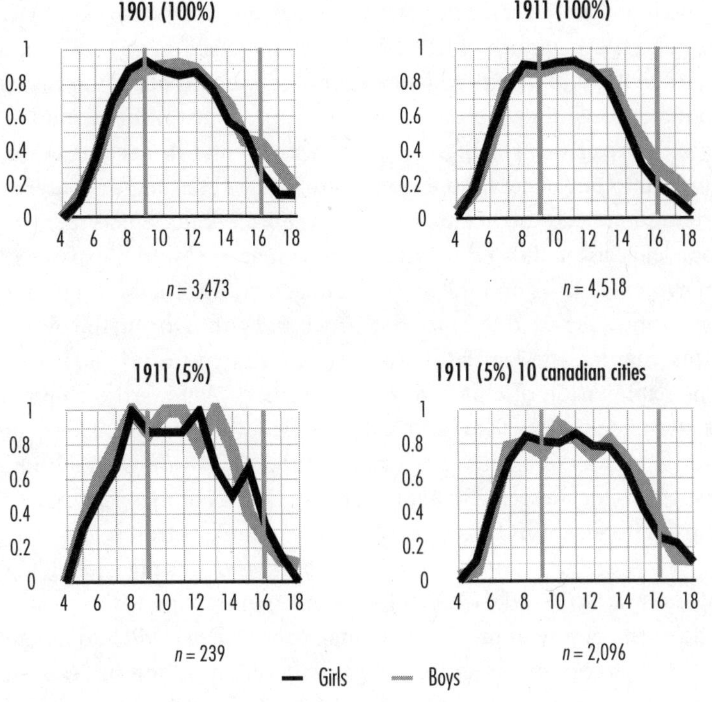

Figure 10.5 · Trois-Rivières and 10 Canadian cities (1911 only): School attendance rates, by age and gender, 1901 and 1911.

Sources: Complete data collection by the authors of the Canadian manuscript census rolls for 1901 and 1911 and CCRI 1911 microdata database.

young men, as might be expected, mostly belonged to the higher social strata, and they were by all appearances called on to conserve their privileged position once their education was completed.

What about the many school-aged children who ultimately did not have a chance to pursue an education? Take, for example, the approximately 360 youth aged 7 to 14 years who did not attend school in 1901 (19.2% of their age group). Their non-attendance can be explained, above all, by the lack of available classrooms, a direct result of the significant demographic growth associated with industrialization. Who were these children who were left on the educational sidelines? And what were they doing with their time? Our sources do not provide all of the answers to these questions. It must be said that "non-productive" activities were of little interest to the state, and they are not well reflected in inventories, leading to a tendency to underestimate their significance. However, helping with household tasks appears to have been particularly common. Given the size and the structure of the households in question, all signs point to the likelihood that children who remained at home were expected to provide domestic labour or look after a member of the family (most often a younger sibling or an older relative). Having to choose which child to keep at home, parents, according to our observations, most often turned to their daughters.

The information collected by census takers is more telling. Since 1885, industrial labour legislation allowed for the employment of children capable of reading from age 12 for boys and the age of 14 for girls. In 1910, the minimum age for factory work was raised to 14 for both boys and girls. During the period covered by this chapter, the legislation, in effect, included no provisions for preventing the exploitation of children in other sectors. Among the children who did not attend school in 1901, about one in five was already part of the urban proletariat by way of a skilled or unskilled job. Boys worked mainly as day labourers, clerks, or messengers, while girls worked as domestic servants, chamber maids in hotels, or in factories (especially in the fabrication of gloves for Balcer Glove). A certain number were in the process of getting a job; a few were learning their father's trade, while others were apprenticing with a master artisan outside of the family home. In all, demand for low-priced child labour existed in various sectors of the city's economy (without taking undeclared work into account). About 10 per cent of the Trois-Rivières children who did not attend school in 1901 – and practically all of those less than 10 years of age – had never received basic instruction and did not know how to read or write.

This initial analysis highlights the strides that remained to be taken before universal education would be achieved. Nevertheless, the attitude of parents to educational opportunities for their children does not appear to have been at all resistant. To the contrary, given the tiny number of families who kept more than one school-aged child at home (only two working-class households with low incomes), it appears that the people of Trois-Rivières made significant efforts to educate their children, albeit with limited success. The problem to be overcome was, therefore, not one of mentalities; rather, it was economic in nature.

Education levels did not progress much between 1901 and 1911, as can be seen in figure 10.5. Among the school-aged population (7 to 14 years old at the beginning of the census year), the rate of school attendance increased by a mere 1.6 per cent over the ten years, a significant slowdown when the statistics available for the end of the 1890s are also taken into account. For the public schools only, Jocelyne Murray calculates that the proportion fell from 75 per cent in 1896 to 82 per cent in 1900–01.[10] Children were starting school, on average, a little earlier than before (47% of children aged 6 were registered in 1911, compared with 35% in 1901), but collectively, they abandoned their studies at a much younger age than they had before. The portrait degrades further if the reduction of full-time enrolment numbers are taken into account (10-month basis): according to the data in the census, 85 per cent of students aged 7 to 14 had completed the school year in 1901, compared with only 77 per cent in 1911.

The proportion of school-aged children who stayed at home compared with those who were employed remained largely stable from the start to the finish of the decade 1901–11. Children's work, always a marginal phenomenon, retained the same palliative role for the family economy. It was especially prevalent in those households most touched by poverty. As they had earlier, young girls mostly worked as domestic servants or as seamstresses in factories. The production of gloves remained a particularly important employment opportunity in Trois-Rivières, but the recent arrival of Diamond Whitewear, thanks to its policy of paid training and its short probationary period, seems to have begun attracting more new recruits to the fabrication of undergarments. Diamond Whitewear opened its doors in Trois-Rivières in 1910. From the start, the firm used the local press to publicize the working conditions in its factory and to recruit female workers: learning the trade at $2.25 per week, a probationary period lasting between one and two months, a salary of between $6 and $9 per week for permanent staff. However, in practice, employees did "piece work," and the salaries paid were significantly lower than those advertised. According to information gathered from the 1911 census, none of the workers declared a weekly salary greater than $5 for a sixty-hour week.[11]

More broadly, as shown above, employers took increasing advantage of the presence of a pool of female labour: between 1901 and 1911, the proportion of girls aged 11 to 14 who worked in factories almost doubled. Thus, the opening of new factories exerted a significant pressure on school attendance, particularly for girls.

Factory work was not, however, the only source of employment for girls and women. By changing the level of observation, we will examine in detail two occupations where women were in the majority, beginning with those who were responsible for educating young boys and girls.

Teaching and Domestic Service: Two Female Professions

A Young, Single, Female Teacher, Just Passing through the Profession?

In contrast to the surrounding countryside where laypeople, working in rural schools, predominated at the beginning of the twentieth century, education in Trois-Rivières was already well under the responsibility of religious orders. In 1901, 85 per cent of the teaching staff in Trois-Rivières was made up of members of religious orders (Ursuline nuns and Christian Brothers), and they further consolidated their near-monopoly over the years to come (92% in 1911). In additional to their private boarding school, however, the Ursulines were responsible for the administration of all the public schools for girls in Trois-Rivières after 1891. On occasion, the order would employ laypeople.[12]

In the period 1901–11, the total number of teachers increased more rapidly than the population as a whole. There were 152 teachers for a resident population of 9,980 in Trois-Rivières at the time of the 1901 census, compared with 284 for a population of 13,663 in 1911. These teachers declared their profession as follows (in order of importance): *instituteur(trices), professeur(es) d'école, professeur(es) de musique,* high school teacher, *maître(sse) privé(e)* and *instructeur.* Throughout the decade, women were resolutely at the forefront of the teaching profession. At the turn of the twentieth century, seven teachers out of ten in Trois-Rivières were women, and the proportion would increase to more than eight out of ten a decade later. The place of women within the field of education should not be at all surprising, since according to the conceptions of the period, women's intrinsic qualities naturally predisposed them to such professions. Thus, female professions (teacher, nurse, midwife) should ideally be capable of being placed within the "extension of maternal duties" (seeing to the education of children, providing care, giving birth).[13] The idea that teaching merely represented a temporary source of employment for women – a provisional occupation to be pursued while waiting for marriage – remained widespread in the world of education. According to the studies undertaken by Marta Danylewycz, on Montreal, the argument that teaching was only a temporary occupation may even have been evoked by educational authorities in order to justify keeping teachers' salaries as low as possible.[14] Beyond the discourse, to what extent did the image of a young, single, female teacher practising her profession for only a short time correspond to the reality in Trois-Rivières? Looking at the facts, the female teachers in our study looked nothing like this image put forward by the school commissioners.

The contributions made by teaching orders will be put aside for the moment. It goes without saying that these nuns and brothers who had chosen to dedicate their life to the service of education largely remained faithful to their mission. Instability is, therefore, not to be found in their professional itineraries. But what of the twenty female lay teachers working in Trois-Rivières at the start of the century? (In the CCRI 1911 5 per cent sample, there are only three female lay teachers in Trois-Rivières.) To begin with, our research has revealed that these lay teachers were far from being distinguished by their youth. Indeed, half of them were more than 30 years old, and not one was under 21. It is impossible to determine the exact moment when these women entered the teaching profession, but we do know that in many cases their commitment was a long-term one. About one in two of these teachers remained in her position for more than ten years, and some remained until retirement. Take Miss Georgina A., a well-known example in the world of teaching in Trois-Rivières in her day. In 1896, Miss Georgina A., school mistress, placed an advertisement in *Le Trifluvien*, a local newspaper, for her elementary school located at 41 Rue St-Olivier.[15] Since the young woman remained there for several years (the school was located just to the north of the zone that would later be destroyed by fire), it is relatively easy to follow her across subsequent censuses. Georgina A. was born into a family of modest means (her father, a simple gardener, could neither read nor write). In 1901, she had not moved; she lived with her parents and ten other members of her family in the building that also served as a schoolhouse. Ten years later, at the age of 34, Georgina A. was still at her post. Having stayed single, her life had, nevertheless, changed significantly with the death of her parents, which left her with sole responsibility for two nieces and one nephew whom she had to care for with her single income. At the time of her death, in 1934, Georgina A. had dedicated more than forty years of her adult life to teaching.[16] Her case was in no way exceptional: many other female teachers would likewise pursue their careers rather than marry, while fulfilling the obligation of providing for their loved ones.

It was not uncommon to find more than one teacher within the same family. Moreover, it can be assumed that before the opening of the first normal school for the training of teachers in the region, following in the footsteps of a sister who was already working in education must have represented one of the best paths to the profession. In 1901, 28-year-old Victoria V. and her younger sister Clara, both teachers, lived with their father (an uneducated carter) in an attached house on rue De Niverville. In the 1891 census, Victoria V. is described as a "primary school teacher." At the time, Clara was only 12 years old, attending school, but her other sister, 24-year-old Anna, also taught at the primary level. We find that the experiences of the three G. sisters show certain similarities, and they all had an interest in teaching. In 1891, Hermine and Alphonsine G. were teachers, and their sister Elmire was a dressmaker. They were all single, their father was deceased, and they lived in the same house as their mother. By the time of the next census, in 1901, Hermine, the oldest, had replaced her mother (likely deceased) as head of household. Hermine and Alphonsine were still teachers, while Emire had abandoned her dressmaking career to follow in the footsteps of her sisters. One decade later, they were still living together on Rue Gervais. After at least twenty years of service, Hermine and Alphonsine G., then aged 55 and 45, respectively, in 1911, had never abandoned teaching, but Elmire G., the least experienced of the three, was out of work. The same spirit of collaboration continued to reign within the family, which had been recently enlarged by the arrival of the youngest sister, Élizabeth, an unemployed widow, and her son Albert. By chance, their nephew was able to contribute to the family finances thanks to his full-time job in a cotton mill.

There are numerous other examples Trois-Rivières of careers dedicated to education. Even if almost all of the female teachers that we have been able to follow remained single, many would eventually find themselves supporting a family. Meanwhile, with a typical salary of $150 a year – the median salary paid to female teachers in Trois-Rivières in 1901, including French- and English-language schools in both the private and public systems – lay teachers could depend only on a low rate of remuneration, one that was just slightly above that of domestic servants. To make ends meet, ensure stability, or simply out of filial duty, these female teachers had to share resources and lodgings with family members.[17]

Occupation: Domestic Servant

Domestic service, in Canada as in most Western countries, constituted a long-standing employment sector for women. Women represented more than 80 per cent of domestic servants employed in Trois-Rivières in 1901. They represented a rather homogeneous group in Trois-Rivières: most were young and almost all were single, living in their employer's house, and as a result, they earned very modest wages for their work. By cross-referencing the variables "family name" and "relationship to the head of household," we have been able to determine that less than 20 per cent of the female domestic servants working in Trois-Rivières at this time lived with their fathers. As salaried workers, they could, of course, theoretically move freely within the labour market. In practice, however, their precarious situation – accentuated by a lower-than-average literacy rate – presented a real barrier to such mobility.

Generally seen as unattractive and marginal work, domestic service was used by the city's elite not only as a means of avoiding irksome tasks but also to distinguish itself socially. The work of domestic servants covered a vast range of activities, from housework (e.g., cooking, cleaning, gardening, and a multitude of maintenance and repair duties) to the care of children and adults. Numbering 254 individuals in Trois-Rivières in 1901, household servants would, nevertheless, view their relative numbers significantly reduced in the following years. We include in the category "domestic servants" all individuals who declared their occupation as *domestique, bonne, serviteur, servante, cuisinière,* or *valet/garçon d'écurie,* and who (1) specified the existence of an employment relationship and (2) indicated their status as a domestic servant in response to the question regarding "relationship to the head of household." The few mentions of *femmes de ménage, homme de palier,* or other equivalent workers who worked independently or for lodging establishments were placed under "unskilled manual trades." Over ten years, domestic servants as a proportion of the total population dropped by 44 per cent, to 195 in 1911; there were 7 in the 5 per cent sample. A closer examination of the situation of domestic service and how it evolved over the years provides some clues as to why.

What set domestic service apart was the fact that the work took place in a residence, in a private – and highly intimate – sphere of family life. It is not easy to imagine the relationships that these young girls developed within their new living spaces, but it can be assumed that this integration into the new context often involved significant challenges. Indeed, at least a third of the domestic servants working in the city in 1901 did not come from Trois-Rivières. They were drawn mainly from the surrounding countryside and, to a lesser extent, from the rest of Canada or other countries. The flow of the rural residents to the city in search of work is a well-known phenomenon for the period, but in the absence of specific studies on domestic servants at the turn of the century, it is impossible to say whether the workers in question migrated by themselves or as part of a family. How did they experience this change in environment? The statistics do not say, but our research suggests, at the very least, that the conditions of recruitment may have had a determining effect on the candidates' adaptation. Thus, some experiences appear to have been better oriented to a rapid adaptation: being hired into a household with other servants (37% of observed cases), for example, must have encouraged the establishment of social relations and facilitated integration from the outset. Likewise, belonging to a family network, which can be observed in situations such as those where servants worked for uncles or brothers, or even the presence of several related servants within the same household, doubtlessly helped allow for the preservation of a personal attachment and family unity.

If, as we have seen, the model of service to individuals predominated, a non-negligible part of domestic labour, nevertheless, took place in religious communities – at the seminary, the convent, the orphanage, or other institutions – as much by laypeople as by nuns who described themselves as "servants" (even if they did not earn any revenue for their labour). The strong presence of women in domestic service does not, of course, mean that there were no men. In 1901, in Trois-Rivières, about fifty men worked as domestic servants. In contrast to women, these men were recruited primarily from older age groups (about a third of them were older than 38 years) and earned an average salary at least twice as high as women domestics.

Domestic service was rapidly transformed during the first decade of the century. The high concentration of the mass of workers, as described above, is not the only indication of the profession's decline that we have been able to identify. While the number of households in Trois-Rivières increased by more than a third between 1901 and 1911, the number of households employing servants reached a plateau. How should we interpret this change? Was it a sign of the influx of working-class families that accompanied the recent economic boom? Or was it a manifestation of a slide in the standard of living among the higher social classes? What is certain is that households henceforth had to make due with fewer hands on deck and that, overall, employers tended to occupy a lower level in the social hierarchy (fall in the number of businessmen in favour of small landholders).

In parallel, the evolution of the group of domestic servants suggests a certain reorientation towards a less qualified workforce. In this regard, two divergent tendencies emerged: the collapse of male domestic service, which dropped by more than 95 per cent between 1901 and 1911, and a drop in the age of female servants – the number of employees younger than age 16 increased by about 40 per cent.

Minorities

Unsurprisingly, at the beginning of the twentieth century, francophones constituted the great majority of the population of Trois-Rivières and greatly influenced its destiny. Francophones dominated the major institutions, and francophone elites had a massive presence in local and regional politics.[18] Representing 97 per cent of the city's faithful, the Catholic Church also exerted a great influence, as much on material life as in the symbolic and spiritual spheres. That being said, the city was also home to an anglophone community as well as immigrant families of rather diverse origins. We have identified members of the anglophone community using declarations of origin and nationality.

Compared with Montreal or Quebec City, there were relatively few anglophones in Trois-Rivières, just under 500 individuals in 1901, or about one out of every twenty residents. Nevertheless, anglophones were able to create their own community, with all of the basic institutions (notably, schools and places of worship), as well as ensure their cultural reproduction over the generations (they could easily find a spouse within the community or by looking to the anglophone populations of Quebec City or elsewhere). The anglophones of Trois-Rivières generally enjoyed a social status and resources that were clearly above average. Their massive presence in certain types of employment suggests that they were much more educated than the majority of francophones. Anglophones were particularly numerous in technical and scientific professions (e.g., engineers and cullers), as well as in supervisory positions (foremen, managers, etc.). They often engaged in non-manual labour (e.g., clerks, bookkeepers). By contrast, they were greatly underrepresented in the world of manual labour (among day labourers, in particular). Largely absent from small businesses and artisanal production, anglophones, nevertheless, exerted a significant influence among businessmen. On average, in 1901, their annual revenue was about double that of the city's other residents – $687 compared with $321, while the median annual salary in Trois-Rivières was $400 for anglophones and $240 for everyone else. In 1911, the average annual salary for anglophones in Trois-Rivières was $709 compared with $380 for everyone else, while the median annual salary for anglophones was $550 compared with $314 for everyone else. Proportionally, anglophones were three and a half times more likely to be among the highest-paid citizens. The best-paying jobs were defined here as those in the highest decile (the highest 10%) for annual salary: $624 and more in 1901 and $778 and more in 1911.

Although there was not, strictly speaking, an "English neighbourhood" in Trois-Rivières at the beginning of the twentieth century, the members of the anglophone community generally tended to favour certain neighbourhoods or streets.

The situation was radically different for other non-francophone ethnic groups. Their smaller numbers (see table 10.3) and the diversity of their cultures greatly lowered their chances of reproducing as a community in a city the size of Trois-Rivières. Their participation in economic and social life depended on the daily use of French and English. The transmission from one generation to the next of their culture of origin (notably, their mother tongue) rested entirely on the family, school being in this case a significant force for assimilation and integration.

To identify ethnic origin, we used, as with the anglophone community, declarations regarding origin and nationality. About three out of four individuals in Trois-Rivières who were of neither French nor British origin were born outside of Canada. The others were most often the children of these immigrants. Only nine of the 65 heads of household of this group were born in Quebec (six of them declared German ancestry, two Jewish, and the last Huron). Immigrants from France integrated after the first generation. In 1911, forty-eight of them were members of a teaching religious order who had arrived in Trois-Rivières a few years before. Their arrival explains the great increase in French immigrants and, in large part, that of the whole of the non-anglophone minority population. Had it not been for the forty-eight francophone nuns, the increase in the number of residents of Trois-Rivières who were non-anglophone immigrants between 1901 and 1911 would have been about 50 per cent, while the population as a whole increased by 37 per cent during the same period.

Painting the portrait of such a disparate group of ethnic minorities is no easy matter. In general, these men and women held low-paying jobs. Their salaries

Table 10.3 · Ethnic origins of non-anglophone minority groups in Trois-Rivières, Canada, 1901 and 1911

	1901	*1911*
Germans	20	12
West Indians, etc.	0	5
Austrians	8	0
Belgians	0	7
Chinese	9	17
French	26	66
Greeks	0	7
Dutch	1	2
Hurons	5	0
Italians	1	0
Jews	11	18
Luxembourgers	1	1
Norwegians	0	14
Poles	3	5
Syrians	5	29
Total	*90*	*183*

Sources: Complete data collection by the authors of the Canadian manuscript census rolls for 1901 and 1911and authors' calculations.

were most often about half of that of a day labourer. Some were, nevertheless, able to get a leg up, by opening a small business, for example. Many of them were also likely to try their hand at something new, each pursuing his or her own speciality.

Below, we examine a few groups more closely. This will allow for a certain number of common traits to be identified, despite the great diversity.

Jews, Syrians, and Chinese

Established in Trois-Rivières since the second half of the eighteenth century, the "Hart dynasty" was a symbol of the Jewish population of Trois-Rivières. Well known for their dynamism and their business spirit, the Harts belonged to the social elite. From father to son, they played a central role in the regional economy up until the 1880s. With time, however, the descendants were not able to preserve their identity. Some chose to emigrate, but those who decided to stay were progressively assimilated. At the beginning of the twentieth century, almost all of the Hart families still living in Trois-Rivières had converted to Catholicism, had begun to use both English and French, and had adopted

Canadian nationality. The previous generation of Harts had principally declared themselves Anglo-Protestant. In the 1901 census, representatives of the Hart family declared English as their mother tongue, but then also indicated that they spoke French fluently, and only one man and two women still declared themselves to be of Jewish origin. If the Harts captured the imagination of their contemporaries, they were, nevertheless, not at all representative of the typical trajectory of immigrant groups that settled in Trois-Rivières.

Three other Jewish households were recorded in the 1901 census in Trois-Rivières. As with many other immigrants, their integration did not mean that they had been completely acculturated. The first, the G. family, was composed of first-generation Russian immigrants who had arrived in Canada with their only son Moses some twenty years earlier. Over the years, the G. family established itself in its host society and began adopting local customs, but without turning its back on its culture of origin. Seven children were born to the marriage and would grow up in the city. When the time came, each of the children was sent to school and learned French and English (it should not be forgotten that at the time, the English language was a very powerful force in the business world of Trois-Rivières). Nevertheless, all family members spoke fluent Hebrew and conserved their religion of origin. The father had become a small businessman, an occupation that encouraged integration. The attitude of the two other Jewish households – one were Romanians and the other, German-speaking Poles – was very similar. The only significant difference was that the settlement of the head of the family came at least a year before the arrival of other family members and household servants.

Most of the Jewish immigrants who followed also undertook commercial activities to the point that, by 1911, practically all Jews in Trois-Rivières of working age declared their occupation as shopkeeper, retailer, sales clerk, or pedlar. One of them set himself apart because of the size of his revenues: Moses G. had become the owner of a clothing store in the city's downtown, in the heart of the newly rebuilt commercial district. Married to a young Canadian-born woman of Jewish origin, he founded his own family. Like his father before him, Moses transmitted his cultural heritage to his children (native tongue and religious affiliation), while allowing his children to learn French and English at a young age. Was this a sign of his desire to fit into the larger society? Henceforth, he gallicized his first name to Moïse.

Compared with Jews, Syrians immigrated to Trois-Rivières in much greater numbers during the first decade of the twentieth century. In 1901, there was only one Syrian household, composed of five individuals; while in 1911, there were twenty-nine individuals, in five or six households. The behaviour of the Syrians was not, however, fundamentally different from that of other minority groups in Trois-Rivières. Syrians were highly cohesive and responded to the same need for mutual assistance. Almost all of the Syrian families practised chain migration. Although on a broader scale, the pattern was the same as that observed among the Romanian and Polish Jews: first, a man or a young couple (never a single woman) established themselves in a home and opened a clothing store. Next, following the birth of the first children, and once the business was prosperous enough to support stable employment and a home, relatives were called on to join them in Canada. Gradually, these relatives would arrive to increase the ranks of the early arrivals and take their turn ensuring the survival of the family network.

The majority of Syrians recorded in Trois-Rivières in 1911 were Orthodox Christians, but a small number declared themselves Catholics.[19] The group maintained a certain distance with regard to the host society. During the years covered by this analysis, the Syrians married only among themselves. As for the sole older individual who remained single, it seems that he also sought out the presence of his compatriots, since he chose to become a lodger with a young (apparently unrelated) Syrian family, who arrived in Canada shortly after him. The significant concentration of Syrian households established in the same area or within short walking distance of each other also suggests the existence of a strong ethnic solidarity.

How were these newcomers perceived by the rest of the city's population? Few traces remain of either acceptance or rejection. The testimony of a contemporary who "believed that Syrian and Jewish pedlars should be taxed, but hesitated to see these marginal citizens penalized,"[20] nevertheless, suggests that like elsewhere, these foreigners were the object of different forms of exclusion. However, well integrated into economic activity, and too small in number to present a threat, these newcomers were not victims of ostracism or antisemitic demonstrations as could be the case in other, larger urban centres.[21]

The Chinese also figured among those "visible" minorities whose numbers increased substantially during the first decade of the twentieth century. Omnipresent in the laundry sector, the Chinese in Trois-Rivières almost all worked in positions related to cleaning or ironing.[22] Given that women were banned from entering the country, the Chinese population of Trois-Rivières was entirely male, adult, and with at most one exception, single. It was spread across all of the city's neighbourhoods, following the demand for laundry services in the city. Although spread out, the Chinese do not appear themselves to have been disposed to breaking contact with their community and to living in isolation. They formed a homogeneous group, functioned in an autonomous fashion, and resolutely employed each other. In 1911, out of seventeen residents of Chinese origin, sixteen lived behind their businesses with their countrymen;

for all of the households, the place of residence was the same as the place of work.

Conclusion

As we postulated at the beginning of this chapter, Trois-Rivières, indeed, appears to have been a city in transition in the early years of the twentieth century. First, even if traditional urban functions remained significant, signs of decisive structural change were clearly being manifested, beginning with the increasing importance of industrial work and the growth in population that followed. Furthermore, the rural roots of a large portion of residents were themselves the expression of another form of transition, that of the changing relationship to shared time and living space that accompanied urbanization and the adoption of the factory, the store, or the office as a place of work.

The comparison with the systematically gathered 1911 census sample of 5 per cent prepared by the CCRI shows that, while the sample provides a less precise image of reality, the portrait it does provide is, nevertheless, largely a faithful one. Most of the questions explored above could not have been studied using only the data from published censuses. The ability to put variables into relation on the basis of individual persons and households, therefore, reveals itself to be a considerable advantage compared with the published aggregate tables. That being said, it should be kept in mind that the sampling of microdata was not conceived for use in micro-historical approaches. Census microdata do not allow for following cohorts of individuals over time, as we have done above for female teachers, for example. At the scale of a small city of 15,000 residents, the occurrences in a distribution were sometimes too small in number for the results to be conclusive. Finally, certain anomalies like those we discovered for the age of the labour force cannot be explained simply by the law of large numbers. We believe that the overrepresentation of institutions (which increased the weight of members of female religious orders) is the most likely cause and that the methodological notes prepared by those responsible for the sampling strategy used by the CCRI team must be taken very seriously.

There are several avenues for further research, which have been hardly touched in this chapter and which definitely deserve further attention, including the questions of housing, the configuration of social networks, neighbourhood relations, and more broadly, sociospatial differentiation in the city. Cartography and the pairing of data from the census, insurance maps, municipal taxation rolls, and commercial directories for the city are currently under way. No doubt, this will open quite stimulating perspectives for our analyses of the case of Trois-Rivières.

As with earlier censuses, the ones undertaken in Canada at the turn of the twentieth century mobilized thousands of individuals over an immense territory tasked with collecting and then compiling a vast range of statistics. The objectives of those who initiated this gigantic operation, namely, government officials, were to have a complete inventory of the Canadian population and to better know its characteristics. After the publication of the results, contemporaries used the aggregate tables to discuss and interpret the major trends of the time, inspiring often vigorous debates which the newspapers of the time recorded.[23] About ninety years later, the manuscript lists of a census were released to the public. As a result, the census was given a second life, one that went far beyond the initial objectives. Direct access to the original declarations has since allowed historians to establish individual relationships, where the whole of the information gathered until then had been isolated from its context. Making use of this rich documentation, we have been able to identify the major structural changes under way while highlighting the sociodemographic characteristics and the living conditions of many residents of Trois-Rivières who – because of their occupations or their minority status – would otherwise have left but the smallest of traces in the collective memory. It is our hope that their descendants will have the same opportunity.[24]

Notes

1 This chapter was translated by Steven Watt. This text is a revised and augmented version of Claude Bellavance and France Normand, "La population de Trois-Rivières il y a cent ans," in Jean Roy and Lucia Ferretti (eds.), *Nouvelles pages trifluviennes* (Quebec City: Septentrion, 2009), 23–52. The following organizations have provided financial support to our research: the Fondation de l'Université du Québec à Trois-Rivières, the city of Trois-Rivières, and the Centre interuniversitaire d'études québécoises (which manages funds provided by the Comité de suivi de la CSM de l'UQTR). We would like to thank all those who participated in the collection of microdata from the census, notably, Marie-Line Audet, Benoît Bourbeau, Chantale Dureau, and Catherine Lampron-Desaulniers.

2 See René Hardy and Normand Séguin, *Histoire de la Mauricie* (Quebec City: Institut québécois de recherche sur la culture, 2004), 41–90.

3 On the devastation caused by the fire, see Daniel Robert and Jean Roy, "22 juin 1908: Le grand incendie de Trois-Rivières," *Patrimoine trifluvien*, no. 15 (June 2005): 4–24.

4 On the industrialization of the city, see among others, Jacques Belleau, *L'industrialisation de Trois-Rivières, 1905–1925*, M.A. thesis, Quebec Studies (UQTR, 1979); SCAP, "Le patrimoine industriel et manufacturier de Trois-Rivières, XVIIe–XXe siècles," *Patrimoine trifluvien*, no. 12 (June 2002), 24 pp. There are

also detailed studies on other themes such as municipal management, working-class housing, cultural life, and associations. See, e.g., Mireille Lehoux, Élus municipaux et promotion industrielle à Trois-Rivières, 1870–1920, M.A. thesis, Quebec Studies (UQTR, 1994); Hélène Desnoyers, *Le logement ouvrier à Trois-Rivières, 1845–1945: L'exemple du secteur Hertel,* M.A. thesis, Quebec Studies (UQTR, 1988); Alain Gamelin, René Hardy, Jean Roy, Normand Séguin, and Guy Toupin, *Trois-Rivières illustrée* (Trois-Rivières: La Corporation des fêtes du 350e anniversaire, 1984).

5 Hardy and Séguin, *Histoire de la Mauricie,* 575.

6 Pierre Lanthier and Alain Gamelin, *L'industrialisation de la Mauricie: Dossier statistique et chronologique, 1870–1975* (Trois-Rivières: UQTR, Groupe de recherche sur la Mauricie, 1981), 452.

7 The literature on the evolution of fertility in the context of industrialization is abundant. For the case of Quebec, see esp. Danielle Gauvreau and Peter Gossage, "Avoir moins d'enfants au tournant du XXe siècle: Une réalité même au Québec," *Revue d'histoire de l'Amérique française* 54, no. 1 (2000): 39–65; as well as Peter Gossage, Danielle Gauvreau, and Diane Gervais, *D'une exception à l'autre: La fécondité des Québécoises, 1870–1970* (Montreal: Boréal, 2007).

8 For an overview of education in the Mauricie region in the second half of the nineteenth century, see Jocelyne Murray, *Apprendre à lire et à compter: École et société en Mauricie, 1850–1900* (Sillery: Septentrion, 1999). See also Hardy and Séguin, *Histoire de la Mauricie,* 466–71 and 776ff.

9 Hardy and Séguin, *Histoire de la Mauricie,* Table 7.5, "Inscription des élèves au cours élémentaire par degrés d'enseignement pour 1900–1901," 203.

10 Murray, *Apprendre à lire et à compter,* 584.

11 *Le Bien Public* (28 Oct. 1910): 6.

12 Murray, *Apprendre à lire et à compter,* 106.

13 For a more in-depth analysis of recognizing women's work, the potential for an activity to be designated as a trade or profession, and the social construction of "qualifications," see Delphine Gardey, "Perspectives historiques," in Margaret Maruani (ed.), *Les nouvelles frontières de l'inégalité: Hommes et femmes sur le marché du travail* (Paris: La découverte/MAGE, 1999), 23–37.

14 Marta Danylewycz, "Sexes et classes sociales dans l'enseignement: Le cas de Montréal à la fin du 19e siècle," in Nadia Fahmy-Eid and Micheline Dumont (eds.), *Maîtresses de maison, maîtresses d'école : Femmes, famille et éducation dans l'histoire du Québec* (Montreal: Boréal, 1983), 93–118.

15 *Le Trifluvien* (28 Aug. 1894), 3, cited in René-Hardy, "Mauricie: Bases de données en histoire régionale en ligne." http://mauricie.cieq.ca/index.php?p=hardy_collection.

16 SCAP, "Les petites écoles à Trois-Rivières, XVIIe–XXe siècles," *Patrimoine trifluvien,* no. 5 (April 1995): 19.

17 The various forms of domestic arrangements which allowed single women to develop networks of mutual aid and to adapt to the precarious living conditions brought about by industrialization have been studied in the province's two major cities, Montreal and Quebec City. In particular, see Bettina Bradbury, *Familles*

ouvrières à Montréal: Âge, genre et survie quotidienne des ménages pendant la phase d'industrialisation (Montreal: Boréal, 1995), and Valerie Laflamme, "Vivre en famille ou en pension: Stratégies résidentielles et réseaux d'accueil," *Cahiers québécois de démographie* 37, no. 1 (2008): 61–96.

18 François Guérard, "Les notables trifluviens au dernier tiers du 19e siècle: Stratégies matrimoniales et pratiques distinctives dans un contexte d'urbanisation," *RHAF* 42, no. 1 (1988): 27–46.

19 The process of "Syrian-Lebanese" migration at the end of the nineteenth century and the beginning of the twentieth is better understood thanks to the work of Brian Aboud. Beginning in 1882, immigrants from Bilad al-Sham (present-day Syria) arrived at Montreal. In the space of only a few years, families of Syrian origin settled in several cities in Quebec, including Trois-Rivières, Sherbrooke, and Rouyn. "Historical" Syria broadly corresponded to "the present-day territories of Syria, Lebanon, Jordan and Israel, as well as the occupied Palestinian territories of the West Bank and Gaza. According to Canadian immigration statistics, about 6,000 individuals from Bilad al-Sham entered Canada before 1915. They were recorded as Arabs, Surians or Turks … Contrary to popular belief, the majority of the first Syrian-Lebanese immigrants were Christians and not Muslims. They belonged to one of the numerous Eastern Rite churches: Melkite Greek Catholic, Maronite Catholic, Anticohian Orthodox (also called "Syrian" and "Greek"), Syriac Orthodox and Catholic." Brian Aboud, "Min Zamaan – Depuis longtemps: La communauté syrienne-libanaise à Montréal de 1882 à 1940," Centre d'histoire de Montréal, http://ville.montreal.qc.ca/portal/page?_pageid=2497,3090574&_dad=portal&_schema=PORTAL.

20 See *Le Bien Public* (8 April 1910): 6, cited in René-Hardy, "Mauricie."

21 A much-discussed incident was the looting of the businesses of Jewish storekeepers in Quebec City in 1910, following a public speech by a notorious antisemite, Jacques-Édouard Plamondon. This notary notably incited his listeners to boycott Jewish businesses. His speech inspired lively debates in the local press. Plamondon was ultimately charged with defamatory libel, leading to a trial that attracted extensive press coverage. At the time Quebec City was home to about 75 Jewish families, who were mainly involved in business. See Sylvio Normand, "Plamondon, Jacques-Édouard," *Dictionary of Canadian Biography* (1921–1930), vol. XV (Quebec: Université Laval; and Toronto: University of Toronto Press, 2000).

22 At the beginning of the century, Chinese-managed laundries could be found throughout the country, no doubt because of the low start-up costs associated with this type of business.

23 C. Bellavance and F. Normand, "Documenter et 'informer' les recensements canadiens: Le dossier des données contextuelles de 1911 dans l'IRCS," *Cahiers québécois de démographie* 34, no. 2 (2005): 329–47.

24 As we know, the Canadian government recently made the long-form census voluntary, attracting criticism from both the scientific community and public administrators.

— · 11 · —

A New Look at Confederation: Shifting Population Dynamics and Newfoundland's Relationship with Canada, 1869–1949

TERRY QUINLAN AND SEAN T. CADIGAN

Men, hurrah for our own native Isle, Newfoundland,
Not a stranger shall hold one inch of her strand;
Her face turns to Britain, her Back to the Gulf,
Come near at your peril, Canadian Wolf![1]

This stanza from an anti-Confederate song of the 1860s, still a local favourite, suggests that geography and history divided Newfoundland and Labrador from its neighbour Canada. In 1869, then Premier (later Sir) Frederick B.T. Carter fought a general election on Confederation, which met defeat (21 seats to 9).[2] This resounding loss suggests that the song's perspective might have had some validity at the time. Eighty years later, the Confederates won the day through two referendums, but by a slender margin. The literature has assumed that a significant regional and sectarian divide in 1949 helped mostly rural Protestants to raise the banner of Confederation over the supposedly Irish Roman Catholic hearth of the Avalon Peninsula.

Analysis of census data allows us to revisit this assumption about sectarianism. It is more likely that the anti-Confederates of 1948–49 had misunderstood how the years since 1869 had witnessed a fundamental shift in the nature of Newfoundland economy and society. Demographically, Newfoundland had shifted westward, partially as a result of the drive to diversify landward its economy from dependence on the fishery. Perhaps the most important part of this shift was that, by 1949, Newfoundland no longer had its back to Canada. A population of Canadian origin lived on the west coast, Canadian capital was important to Newfoundland development, and Canadian Maritime centres such as Halifax were becoming important metropoles in western and southern Newfoundland trade. Mining and forestry even led to labour mobility between Cape Breton and Newfoundland. By 1949, the Gulf of St Lawrence was a highway rather than a barrier between Newfoundland and Canada.

Taking a Second Look

Historians usually understand the outcomes of Newfoundland's battles over Confederation in the 1860s and 1940s as a matter of political leadership. Charles F. Bennett gets the credit for the anti-Confederate campaign of 1869; although 76 years old, he mounted a vigorous fight against Confederation.[3] Similarly, Joseph Roberts "Joey" Smallwood became the charismatic prophet of the 1948 campaign for Confederation. At the level of political rhetoric, sectarian divisions and mercantile influence appear to have been critical factors in the struggles over union with Canada.[4] Few studies concede that the voters were important agents in the struggle over Confederation, but rather, that they were passive audiences for prominent political figures. The Canadian Century Research Infrastructure (CCRI) data permit investigation of cross-sections of this audience because the manuscript census contains important contextual information about the life of each and every person.

Unique data provided by the CCRI allow an assessment of how the changing nature of the voters themselves might help to explain the difference in outcomes between the 1860s and 1940s. As part of the CCRI project, the Atlantic Centre at Memorial University of Newfoundland, in joint partnership with the Government of Newfoundland and Labrador's Statistics Agency, developed not only the standard 3 per cent to 5 per cent sample for other Atlantic provinces, but also all available records for the pre-Confederation Newfoundland censuses for 1911, 1921, 1935, and 1945. Such a complete record of twentieth-century nominative data is very rare, if not entirely unique.

Prior to joining Confederation in 1949, Newfoundland and Labrador conducted its own census, usually every ten years, typically at the same intervals as the Canadian censuses were taken. However, not all the schedules survived, particularly not those for 1911 (see table 11.1). Overall, only 11 per cent of records are available for the 1911 census, compared with 79 per cent for 1921, 100 per cent for 1935, and 99 per cent for 1945.

Although missing records limit what may be done with the Newfoundland portion of the CCRI, it nevertheless permits unparalleled studies at the individual, household, and community levels. Such a detailed analysis is simply not possible with existing data sources such as the published census recapitula-

Table 11.1 · Surviving census records (%), by district and year, Newfoundland, 1911–45

District (1911)	*1911*	*1921*	*1935*	*1945*
St John's East	58	90	100	97
St George's	49	93	100	100
St George's Bay	99	87	100	100
Humber	—	100	100	100
Codroy Valley	—	99	100	100
Fogo	18	15	100	100
Port de Grave	14	87	100	100
Trinity	11	93	100	100
Bonavista	10	4	100	100
St Barbe	—	100	99	100
Harbour Main	—	100	100	100
Carbonear	—	100	100	100
Ferryland	—	100	100	100
Burgeo and LaPoile	—	100	100	100
Placentia and St Mary's	—	100	100	100
Twillingate	—	99	100	100
St John's West	—	97	100	100
Burin	—	96	100	100
Harbour Grace	—	95	100	100
Fortune Bay	—	90	100	100
Bay de Verde	—	—	100	100
Labrador	—	—	94	100
Total	*11*	*79*	*100*	*99*

Sources: Census of Newfoundland, 1911 to 1945; CCRI 1911 microdata database.

tion, where identifiable individual or household information is unavailable, and community summaries are too general to allow for meaningful analysis. A case in point: one question of interest, place of birth, is only published using broad categories such as "British colonies." Within the Newfoundland portion of the CCRI, the specific community is captured whenever so reported.

The infrastructure permits detailed examination of how individual decisions multiplied over even relatively small groups may have an impact beyond the scope one would expect from their population. In 1948, the choice to join with Canada was put to the people of Newfoundland and Labrador. The first referendum, on 3 June 1948, actually resulted in a lead, but not a majority, for a return to Responsible Government (44.6% vs. 41.1% for Confederation with

Table 11.2 · Referendum results (n and %), Newfoundland, June and July 1948

Date	*Option*	*Votes*	
		n	%
3 JUNE 1948	Responsible Government	69,400	44.6
	Confederation with Canada	64,066	41.1
	Commission of Government	22,311	14.3
	Total	*155,777*	*100.0*
22 JULY 1948	Confederation with Canada	78,323	52.3
	Responsible Government	71,334	47.7
	Total	*149,657*	*100.0*

Source: Encyclopedia of Newfoundland, vol. I (St John's: Newfoundland Book Publishers, 1981), 722–3.

Canada, and 14.3% for a continuation of the existing Commission of Government; see table 11.2).

It was only after a second referendum, a month and a half later, on 22 July, with the removal of the Commission of Government from the ballot that Confederation surpassed Responsible Government by a slim majority (52.3% vs. 47.7%). In the end, fewer than 7,000 votes separated the two choices (78,323 for Confederation vs. 71,334 for Responsible Government out of 149,657 votes counted). Newfoundland officially joined Canada the following year, on 31 March 1949.[5]

Major Factors

To better understand the various factors that may have affected the vote in 1948, we turn to the 1945 census. This was the last census before the referendum, and it better represents the population at the time of the vote than any other source. The census categories allow correlations to help identify some of the major influences on the various voter groups across regions. Table 11.3 shows the correlation between each factor and the percentage voting in favour of Confederation in the 25 electoral districts (results are weighted to more accurately reflect population differences across districts). A positive correlation is identified with voting for Confederation, whereas a negative correlation is identified with voting against. Statistical significance levels are provided to

Table 11.3 · Correlation of selected demographic characteristics, according to the 1945 census, and the results of Newfoundland's second 1948 referendum

1945 Census	*Correlation*	*Significance*
GEOGRAPHY		
Avalon Peninsula	-.836 **	.000
Average distance from St John's (ordinal)	.789 **	.000
Average longitude (ordinal)	.769 **	.000
RELIGION		
Roman Catholic	-.729 **	.000
Church of England	.421 *	.036
United Church	.433 *	.031
LITERACY		
Can read and write	-.720 **	.000
> 8 years of schooling age 10+ years	-.652 **	.000
Attending school age 5–14 years	-.344	.093
OCCUPATION		
Service	-.634 **	.001
Logging	.600 **	.002
Fishing, hunting, and trapping	.537 **	.006
Professional	-.443 *	.026
Construction	-.440 *	.028
Manufacturing and mechanical	-.415 *	.039
Transportation and communication	-.339	.098
Labourers	-.328	.109
UNEMPLOYMENT AND SELF-EMPLOYMENT		
Occupation groups with higher than average weeks unemployed[a]	.601 **	.001
Own accounts	.504 *	.010
DWELLING AND HOUSEHOLD		
Average rooms per dwelling	-.509 **	.009
Average monthly rent of tenant-occupied dwellings	-.409 *	.042
Average value of owner-occupied dwellings	-.482 *	.015
Average persons per household	.018	.930
PLACE OF BIRTH		
Born in district	.393	.052
INCOME		
Per capita income	-.354	.083

Source: Census of Newfoundland, 1945; *Encyclopedia of Newfoundland*, vol. I (St John's: Newfoundland Book Publishers, 1981), 723.

a Occupation groups with higher than average weeks unemployed include fishing, hunting and trapping, logging, mining and quarrying, construction, and labourers; * Correlation is significant at the .05 level (2-tailed); ** Correlation is significant at the .01 level (2-tailed).

Table 11.4 · Confederation vs. Responsible Government: Results of second Newfoundland 1948 referendum, by district, all Avalon Peninsula and Roman Catholics (%)

Electoral district	*Confed*	*Avalon Peninsula*	*Roman Catholic*
GROUP 1: CONFEDERATION WITH CANADA			
St George's–Port au Port	57		77
Placentia West	55		56
Humber	69		30
Burin	85		30
Fortune Bay and Hermitage	81		26
Grand Falls	56		25
Carbonear–Bay de Verde	53	Y	24
White Bay	76		20
Bonavista South	52		15
St Barbe	79		14
Fogo	62		11
Labrador	78		11
Bonavista North	74		10
Trinity South	60	Y	8
Green Bay	71		6
Trinity North	65		5
Twillingate	75		2
Burgeo and LaPoile	89		1
GROUP 2: RESPONSIBLE GOVERNMENT			
Ferryland	15	Y	98
Placentia and St Mary's	18	Y	92
Harbour Main–Bell Island	17	Y	57
St John's East	31	Y	51
St John's West	33	Y	46
Harbour Grace	38	Y	22
Port de Grave	49	Y	20

Source: Census of Newfoundland, 1945; *Encyclopedia of Newfoundland*, vol. I (St John's: Newfoundland Book Publishers, 1981), 723.

help assess degree of association, with those significant at 1 per cent and 5 per cent specifically identified.

The highest correlation to voting preference is whether or not the district was located on the Avalon Peninsula (-.836, .000; see table 11.3). Other computed variables related to geographical distance from St John's are also significant. Average distance from St John's (ordinal) and average longitude showed similar results (.789 and .769, both highly significant at .000); ordinal scales are used to measure relative distance of districts from St John's, with values ranging from 1 to 25, where 25 is the total number of districts. Literacy is also correlated to voting patterns with "can read and write" highly significant (-.720, .000). However, this is related to geography, with the urban centre of St John's and other areas nearby on the Avalon having higher rates of literacy than more outlying areas. Also, the percentage of individuals stating their religion as Roman Catholic is also correlated strongly to voting preference (-.729, .000). While historians tend to assume that this is evidence of sectarianism in the fight over Confederation, the Roman Catholic vote reflects a fundamental divide in the economic and social geography of Newfoundland voters.

Table 11.4, showing the referendum result by district, helps demonstrate these findings. For example, with only two exceptions, districts on the Avalon Peninsula voted against Confederation and districts off the peninsula voted in favour. Similarly, the three districts that had, by a wide margin, the least votes for Confederation (Ferryland, Placentia and St Mary's, and Harbour Main–Bell Island at 15 per cent, 18 per cent, and 17 per cent, respectively) were also largely Roman Catholic (98%, 92%, and 57%, respectively). St George's–Port au Port, to be discussed later, is one of only two Roman Catholic districts (77%) to vote for Confederation, as did Placentia West (56% Roman Catholic). Therefore, two main factors can be identified with voting preference, each highly significant at .000: geography, with whether or not the district was on the Avalon Peninsula (-.836), distance from St John's (.789), and longitude (.769); and religion, with Roman Catholic (-.729).

The 1869 Vote as Background

We must be cautious in accepting early nineteenth-century British views that the struggle for colonial self-government in Newfoundland was by a priest-ridden unruly Irish rabble. Irish Roman Catholics had dominated the settlement of the Avalon Peninsula – St John's, Placentia, the coastal communities in between, and parts of Carbonear and Harbour Grace – as they followed Irish merchants or sought waged employment in the bank fisheries or the seal hunt. English West Country Protestants tended to settle around West Country merchants' premises on the northeast coast. Although immigration dried up in the depression following the Napoleonic Wars, a few Irish continued to trickle into St John's. While early Roman Catholic bishops tried to contain fishing servants' discontent about merchant credit practices and harsh employment, newer clerics, from the 1820s, channelled their discontent into support for colonial self-government. By 1855, Philip Francis Little, a Roman Catholic from Prince Edward Island, with his bishop, Thomas Mullock, had won the battle for Responsible Government through an economic development platform and alliance with Wesleyan Methodists for state support of their schools. Sectarianism cropped up in the early 1860s, but often as bickering within denominations. By 1865, the main debate was about how Newfoundland's economic diversification should be secured. A Conservative–Liberal alliance under Frederick Carter and Ambrose Shea argued that Canadian help was necessary. Shea was a Roman Catholic Liberal, but lost the support of Bishop Mullock, who sided with Bennett in the election of 1869.[6]

Bennett led the anti-Confederation forces, but the success of his fight had little to do with sectarianism. The anti-Confederate appeal may be appreciated by considering the rest of their era's anthem:

> Cheap tea and molasses they say they will give,
> All taxes taken off that the poor man may live –
> Cheap nails and cheap lumber, our coffins to make,
> And homespun to mend our old clothes when they break.
>
> If they take off all taxes, how then will they meet
> The heavy expenses on Army and fleet?
> Just give them the chance to get into the scrap,
> They'll show you the trick with pen, ink and red tape.
>
> Would you barter the right that your fathers have won?
> No! let them descend from father to son.
> For a few thousand dollars Canadian gold
> Don't let it be said that our birthright was sold.

Bennett argued that if Newfoundland had tremendous interior resources awaiting development then it made no sense to place them in Canadian hands. Bennett, a St John's merchant and industrialist, had been a vocal proponent of interior development. His success in defeating Confederation in 1869 lay in his portrayal of Carter and Shea as "political iscariots" willing to betray Newfoundland's resources into the hands of Canadians.[7]

A commitment to a colonial national policy of economic development grew out of the defeat of the vote on Confederation in 1869, and it had important consequences for the subsequent rematch in 1948. The policy promoted the economic and social bifurcation of Newfoundland along regional lines. Newfoundland's national policy resembled Canada's: build a railway to open up interior and westward resources funded partially by tariffs that would also protect local manufacturing. Such resources would prompt industrial development and the growth of a consumer market, eventually removing the need to protect domestic manufacturing. Throughout the later nineteenth century, the development of the railway helped to foster some landward industrial diversification in forestry and mining, with concomitant settlement. However, such development was never strong enough to support a domestic market large enough to sustain local manufacturing without protection. The Avalon Peninsula remained the home of people of Irish–Roman Catholic descent, but by the 1940s, their economic interests were tied increasingly to an urban rather than sectarian basis in protected manufacturing and the railway. Tariffs sheltered St John's manufacturing at the expense of rural fishing people and the loggers who worked in the newer forestry sector.[8]

The divide between town and country rather than sectarianism defined Newfoundland politics. Particularly on the northeast coast, fishers supported the populist Fishermen's Protective Union (FPU), which opposed development policies that primarily benefited St John's. Conservative political parties courted working-class support through the patronage of railway contracts and defence of protected manufacturing. The Liberals limped along with FPU support, becoming primarily the courtiers of outside capital in railway development and forestry, the latest being the British firm of Armstrong, Whitworth, and Company in the development of a second pulp and paper complex on the west coast's Humber River.[9]

Newfoundland's "national" policy aimed to develop westward resources for the benefit of the St John's region, but it actually contributed to the development of a population that had other interests. The national policy included asserting more control over portions of the northern and western coasts of Newfoundland largely controlled by France for fishing purposed under the Treaty of Utrecht (1713) and the Treaty of Versailles (1783). Neither France nor Newfoundland could settle this "French Shore," although Newfoundland gained limited rights to do so within one half-mile of the high tide water mark in 1869 (see figure 11.1). The French Shore kept Newfoundland's "Back to the Gulf," but the colonial government steadily pressured Britain to negotiate for its control over the shore's resources. It was not until 1904 that international strategic considerations led France to agree to give up its treaty rights to the French Shore in return for access to fisheries, bait, and ports in Newfoundland during the summer, but subject to Newfoundland law, and without the right to use the shore in their fisheries.[10]

Although Newfoundland gained control over the French Shore, a population of largely Canadian and French origin had already developed there. From

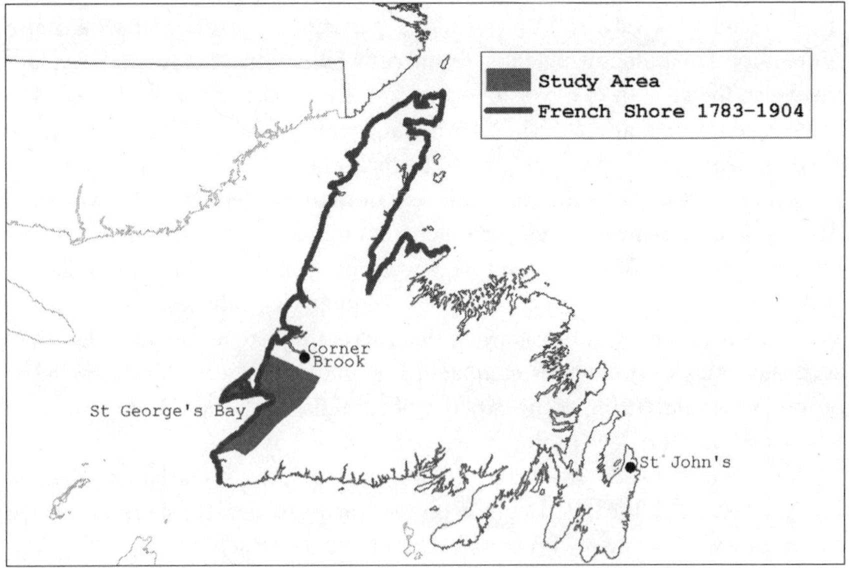

Figure 11.1 · Newfoundland study area, showing French Shore (1783–1904), as well as St George's Bay, Corner Brook, and St John's.

Source: Newfoundland and Labrador Statistics Agency.

1820, Roman Catholic Acadian migrants from the west coast of Cape Breton had been settling the area from St George's Bay to Bonne Bay. Mi'kmaq had been migrating to the west coast from Cape Breton from as early as 1763, but more Mi'kmaq began to arrive, settling across from Sandy Point, having fled Cape Breton where they suffered from the effects of overhunting. The Roman Catholic community of the west coast became more complex after 1840 as kin groups of Highland Scottish settlers from Prince Edward Island and Inverness County, Cape Breton, came in search of better land. Newfoundlanders also moved to the west coast to escape the troubled fisheries of their homes after 1870, searching for new opportunities in the herring fisheries and timber industries of Bonne Bay and Humber Sound. These settlers dealt increasingly with Halifax mercantile firms, often to the jealousy of St John's merchants. Other settlers from the south coast of Newfoundland and from the Maritimes came to exploit the previously untouched forests of the coast. Especially important was the establishment of a large sawmill by Halifax investors at Corner Brook, worth more than $40,000 in 1865. The attraction of the growing sawmilling industry, as well as the better agricultural resources of places such as the Codroy

Valley, meant that west coast settlement also spread into the interior shores of the coast's great bays, St George's, Bonne Bay, and the Bay of Islands.[11]

Canadian People: St George's Bay

The CCRI database allows consideration of the broader significance of these demographic developments on the west coast. Table 11.1 indicates that the St George's district was one of two districts with the highest proportions of available 1911 records (49% compared with St John's East, with 58%). Most importantly, for a specific subregion of the St George's district, the St George's Bay area, virtually all records survived and, thus, form part of the CCRI database (99%). This area includes Port au Port, a peninsula at the north end of St George's Bay. The bay area, including the peninsula, permits a community study of the newer population of the west coast.

Figure 11.2 demonstrates the difference between St George's and other districts.[12] On average, those born in "British colonies" and "other foreign" account for only 0.5 per cent and 0.3 per cent, respectively, of the overall population. However, in St George's they comprise much larger proportions, 2.5 per cent and 0.9 per cent, respectively.

The manuscript census records allow for a better understanding of the population than the corresponding published numbers, as the published tables often do not provide the level of detail necessary for meaningful analysis. For example, the place of birth reported in the publication is summarized using only the following categories: Newfoundland, England, Scotland, Ireland, British colonies, and foreign states. Not surprisingly, virtually all of those listed under British colonies are actually from Canada.

Published results may also be misleading, undercounting the number of foreign-born. In the census records for the community study area, 284 individuals were identified as being born outside of Newfoundland compared with only 175 counted as such in the corresponding published tabulations. A review of discrepancies at the community level reveals that this occurs most often when the year of immigration is not provided. It seems that the year of immigration was used at the time the census publications were originally compiled to help identify foreign-born people, so when this information was not provided, the place of birth was often overlooked. Although we do not have complete manuscripts for all other areas, the records we do have indicate that similar undercounting occurs elsewhere.

Unlike census results, the CCRI database allows different types of analysis such as precise identification of the latitude and longitude of origin-destination pairs for geospatial analysis. This identification permits assessment of flows of

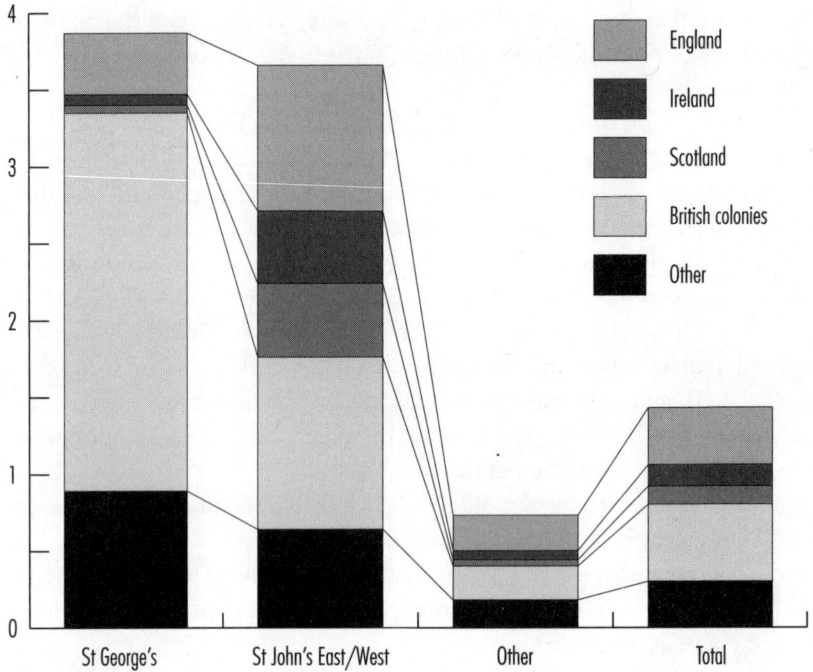

Figure 11.2 · Population of Newfoundland: Place of birth by district (% of population), 1911.
Source: 1911 Census of Newfoundland.

family groups and populations across space and time in tremendous detail, and in relationship to all other variables at the level of the individual person. The complex interplay of town, country, nationality, religion, and other variables – even family name – provides rich historical context that is simply not possible in any published format.

The application of the underlying census records to the findings of figure 11.2, then, helps clarify the data for St George's Bay. For example, a comparison by time period shows that much of the in-migration to the area from outside Newfoundland occurred for those born prior to 1850 (see table 11.5). The foreign-born comprise 42 per cent of the population of that age group, compared with only 3 per cent of those born since 1850.

Two aspects of the nature and scope of migration are clear. First, since young married couples and unattached individuals are generally more apt to migrate, this dates the period of largest in-migration to the area from outside the colony to the 1870s at the latest. Second, one would expect that many of the people

Table 11.5 · Population of St George's Bay, Newfoundland: All and foreign-born of (*n* and %), 1911

Year of birth	*Population*	*Foreign-born*	*Per cent*
Prior to 1830	22	12	55
1830 to 1839	90	45	50
1840 to 1849	178	66	37
Subtotal: prior to 1850	290	123	42
1850 to 1859	293	28	10
1860 to 1869	444	30	7
1870 to 1879	560	32	6
1880 to 1889	772	24	3
1890 to 1899	1,350	23	2
1900 to 1911	2,123	21	1
Subtotal: 1850 to 1911	5,542	158	3
Not available	5	3	60
Total	*5,837*	*284*	5

Source: CCRI 1911 microdata database.

born locally thereafter are children or grandchildren of those earlier settlers. Further examination of the source areas for those early settlers can explain much more about the overall population than their numbers imply.

Using the manuscript census allows us to assess town of birth, as opposed to just country. In over 90 per cent of cases, this additional information is complete in some form. In cases where it is not, or the information provided is a region as opposed to a community, the required detail may often be obtained from the corresponding record for the same individual in a later census year. This is made possible because the Newfoundland pre-Confederation records have been linked across the four census years of 1911, 1921, 1935, and 1945. The community of birth question on the Newfoundland census, then, is particularly useful for tracing many of the early settlers of St George's Bay.

Birth Location

Birth locations are summarized in table 11.6. For the period prior to 1850, the vast majority of these who were "foreign-born" were from Cape Breton, Nova Scotia, with over a third from the communities of the Margaree River, located

Table 11.6 · Population of St George's Bay, Newfoundland: Place and period of birth

Place of birth	*Period of birth*					
	< 1850		*1850–1911*		*N/A*	*Total*
	n	%	n	%		
Newfoundland and Labrador	167	100	5,381	100	2	5,550
Within district	136	81	5,057	94	1	5,194
Elsewhere	31	19	324	6	1	356
Foreign	123	100	158	100	3	284
Nova Scotia	92	75	53	34		145
Cape Breton	88	72	38	24		126
Margaree	45	37	9	6		54
Elsewhere	32	26	25	16		57
Not specified	11	9	4	3		15
Elsewhere	2	2	13	8		15
Not specified	2	2	2	1		4
Elsewhere in Canada	7	6	12	8		19
Prince Edward Island			9	6		9
New Brunswick	2	2	1	1		3
Quebec	5	4	2	1		7
France	11	9	49	31	2	62
St Pierre	1	1	11	7	2	14
Elsewhere	3	2	3	2		6
Not specified	7	6	35	22		42
British Isles	11	9	27	17	1	39
England	7	6	21	13	1	29
Ireland	3	2	3	2		6
Channel Islands	1	1	3	2		4
United States			11	7		11
Other foreign	2	2	6	4		8
Not specified			3	2		3
Total	*290*		*5,542*		5	*5,837*

Source: CCRI 1911 microdata database.

Note: Percentages do not always total 100 because of rounding.

on the west coast of Cape Breton Island (45 out of 123). For the period from 1850 to 1911, France surpassed Cape Breton as the single largest source area. However, for a high percentage of these, the community is not specified, so it is unclear if these are from the French island of St Pierre (including Miquelon), or France itself.

Family Name

Family names also tell us much about origins. Table 11.7 shows the most common surnames in St George's Bay in the 1911 census. For many of these individuals, the earliest place of birth from the 1911 census records is often Inverness County, on the western shore of Cape Breton Island, and specifically the community of Margaree or nearby Broad Cove. Sydney, near the ferry terminal to Newfoundland, is also represented, as are Quebec's Magdalen Islands.

The family names of those born locally are also useful. However, as they are descendants of earlier settlers that pre-date the scope of the 1911 census, their origins cannot be known directly from the manuscript itself. Nevertheless, from investigating other sources, we learn that many of the names here are Acadian (French) or anglicizations.[13] Family history researchers have been able to trace some of these names to Jersey, in the Channel Islands.[14] As well, each of the top seven names is common among Mi'kmaq First Nation bands in this area of the province.[15] Scottish kin groups from Cape Breton are also represented.[16]

The 1948 Vote

The St George's Bay area was unique in that it had a large population of Canadian origin. However, the whole thrust of the national policy had been to reorient the Newfoundland economy towards the North American continent, and Canada in particular, in ways that would have a broader cultural impact. The development of mining, especially of iron ore at Bell Island, for example, more closely tied Newfoundland to the steel industry of Cape Breton. Many Newfoundlanders worked in the Maritimes, especially in Cape Breton, many settling permanently but others often returning to Newfoundland. The construction of the pulp and paper complex at Corner Brook on the west coast, and related logging activities, created a regional labour market around the rim of the Gulf of St Lawrence, and the opportunities of the forestry sector continued to attract Canadian capitalists such as the Nova Scotian Harry Crowe, who became prominent in Newfoundland political life. Although Canadian industrialists such as the Reids and political adventurers such as A.B. Morine might

Table 11.7 · Population of St George's Bay, Newfoundland: Incidence of last names (*n*) by year of first occurrence, with place of birth and indicating whether name was of French origin

Last name	*Frequency*	*First*	*Place of birth*	*Prov*	*Orig*[a]
Benoit, Bennett	403	1831	Bay St George[b]		F
LeJeune, Young	333	1829	Sydney	NS	F
LeBlanc, White	290	1824	Margaree	NS	F
Hynes	136	1845	Sandy Point		
Marche, March	125	1835	Port au Port		F
Gaudet, Gaudon	124	1850	Stephenville		F
Alexander	107	1842	St George's		F
Jesso	104	1818	Sydney	NS	F
Huelin	98	1840	Crabbes		F
Shears	97	1829	Robinsons Head		
Guillaume, Gillam	98	1838	River Brook		F
Gillis	90	1837	Broad Cove	NS	
Legge	86	1831	Crabbes		
Cormier	76	1830	Margaree	NS	F
Morris	76	1841	Crabbes/St George's		
McIsaac	70	1839	Margaree	NS	
LeRoi, King	69	1846	Margaree	NS	F
McDonald	68	1833	Inverness	NS	
Hall	66	1838	Grand River		
Renouf	66	1841	Robinsons Head		F
Gale	62	1858	Robinsons Head		
LeRoux	61	1862	St George's		F
Butt	60	1818	St George's		
Messervey	59	1834	Sandy Point		F
Blanchard	55	1836	Margaree	NS	F
AuCoin, O'Quinn	54	1827	Margaree	NS	F
Bourgeois	53	1833	Magdalen Islands	PQ	F
Harvey	53	1845	Isle aux Morts		
Chaffey	52	1849	Crabbes		
Parsons	52	1854	Sandy Point		
Madore	50	1855	St George's		F
Subtotal	3,193				
Other	2,644				
Total	*5,837*				

Source: CCRI 1911 microdata database.

a F denotes French (Acadian) or anglicization of French; b Also Margaree, NS, 1834.

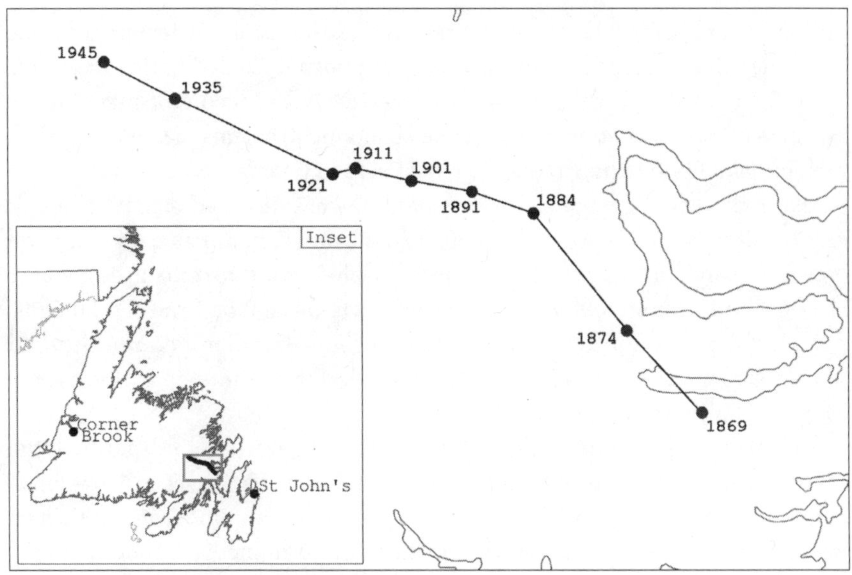

Figure 11.3 · Newfoundland: Population centroid, 1869–1945.

Source: Newfoundland and Labrador Statistics Agency, using 1869 to 1945 Census of Newfoundland.

acquire poor reputations, Crowe's paternalistic and progressive labour practices earned him much admiration among the loggers of White Bay. Canada and Canadians did not always appear as wolves among the sheep.[17]

In the years between 1869 and 1945, Newfoundland's population grew sizably from 146,536 to 321,819.[18] Not only had the population grown, but it was leaving St John's behind as people moved westward. Internal migration became considerable and significant over time. The demographic centre of the colony was changing, as demonstrated in figure 11.3, moving to the west and north, much of it associated with forestry, away from the historic population centres of St John's and the Avalon Peninsula.

By 1945, the second largest centre was now Corner Brook, the pulp and paper town on the west coast. The historic communities that comprise the present-day extent of the City of Corner Brook had increased from just "a handful" of people in 1860 to 12,757 by 1945.[19]

In short, by 1945, as compared with 1869, Newfoundland could no longer be said to have "Her face turn[ed] to Britain, her back to the Gulf." One could argue that by the end of the Second World War in 1945, Newfoundland was figuratively, at least from a population location perspective, now turned partly around. This change affected the second battle for Confederation. Most voters on the Avalon Peninsula favoured a return to Responsible Government, while the remainder of the island and Labrador supported Confederation (see table 11.4). Exposed daily to the anxieties expressed in the media of many in the business community about the possible economic problems of Confederation, including higher taxation and loss of local industry, people on the Avalon Peninsula, regardless of religious denomination, were disposed against Confederation. Smallwood, however, had portrayed Confederation as a way for rural Newfoundlanders to get out from under a plutocratic merchant-dominated political and economic system. In the districts of Humber and Grand Falls, pulp and paper companies were opposed to Confederation because they did not want to come under a more exacting federal taxation regime; this opposition probably encouraged loggers to support Smallwood.[20]

There is much wisdom in the arguments that the wartime prosperity of the 1940s and the related presence of American and Canadian bases in Newfoundland and Labrador meant that many people had no appetite for a return to Responsible Government.[21] However, these more immediate factors simply reinforced a deeper shift in the nature of Newfoundland society. Such change is evident in the changes in religion. The Roman Catholic population had dropped considerably, down from 42 per cent to 33 per cent of the total population (61,040 out of 146,536 in the 1869 census vs. 106,006 out of 321,819 in 1945). This was largely due to out-migration of the Irish, as demonstrated in the decline of the Avalon Peninsula population as a percentage of the total. Many of the Irish from this area migrated to major US cities such as Boston and other centres.[22]

The southern Avalon districts of Ferryland and Placentia and St Mary's, districts with populations almost exclusively of Irish and Roman Catholic origin, voted almost completely against Confederation. Highly unusual political circumstances must be considered in these cases. Ferryland was the home district of Major Peter Cashin, the firebrand opponent of Confederation. Cashin was a local favourite, originally from Cape Broyle, and he was the son of Sir Michael Cashin, a prominent opponent of the old Liberal party of Sir Richard Squires. Placentia and St Mary's was the home district of the Roman Catholic Archbishop Edward P. Roche, who was perhaps the most publicly bitter opponent of Confederation and did everything he could to fight it in 1948.[23]

The easternmost extremity of old Newfoundland remained anti-Confederation. However, new factors dominated the political climate of 1948, most notably the changing, more Canadian-oriented nature of the population overall. If the population distribution (and voting rights) had remained the same in 1948 as they were in 1869, the results could have been considerably different, resulting in the defeat of the Confederation option. This is demonstrated in table

Table 11.8 · Results of second Newfoundland 1948 referendum, by district: Actual vs. estimates using 1869 population distribution

Electoral district	*1945 Census population*	*Actual 1948 vote*		
		Confederation	*Total*	*Per cent*
Bonavista North	12,978	3,466	4,653	74.5
Bonavista South	11,584	2,730	5,260	51.9
Burgeo and LaPoile	9,357	3,296	3,707	88.9
Burin	10,940	4,079	4,801	85.0
Carbonear–Bay de Verde	12,825	2,705	5,132	52.7
Ferryland	6,346	612	3,965	15.4
Fogo	10,077	2,438	3,937	61.9
Fortune Bay and Hermitage	11,445	3,675	4,515	81.4
Grand Falls	19,458	6,228	11,030	56.5
Green Bay	8,606	2,392	3,352	71.4
Harbour Grace	7,249	1,206	3,201	37.7
Harbour Main–Bell Island	17,549	1,431	8,215	17.4
Placentia and St Mary's	9,448	920	5,001	18.4
Placentia West	9,653	2,067	3,771	54.8
Port de Grave	8,278	1,565	3,191	49.0
St John's East	28,821	4,895	15,679	31.2
St John's West	36,435	6,193	18,706	33.1
Trinity North	12,808	3,153	4,844	65.1
Trinity South	10,983	2,593	4,302	60.3
Twillingate	9,566	2,524	3,354	75.3
Humber	20,560	7,133	10,378	68.7
Labrador	5,525	2,681	3,447	77.8
St Barbe	13,074	2,353	2,986	78.8
St George's–Port au Port	7,509	3,817	6,728	56.7
White Bay	10,745	4,171	5,502	75.8
Total	*321,819*	*78,323*	*149,657*	*52.3*

Electoral district	*1869 census population*	*Estimate using 1869 distribution*		
		Confederation	*Total*	*Per cent*
Bonavista North	4,655	1,243	1,669	74.5
Bonavista South	6,905	1,627	3,135	51.9
Burgeo and LaPoile	5,119	1,803	2,028	88.9

/*continued*

Table 11.8 · continued

Electoral district	*1869 census population*	*Estimate using 1869 distribution*		
		Confederation	*Total*	*Per cent*
Burin	5,560	2,073	2,440	85.0
Carbonear–Bay de Verde	14,215	2,998	5,688	52.7
Ferryland	6,672	643	4,169	15.4
Fogo	4,426	1,071	1,729	61.9
Fortune Bay and Hermitage	5,024	1,613	1,982	81.4
Grand Falls	62	20	35	56.5
Green Bay	3,325	924	1,295	71.4
Harbour Grace	9,617	1,600	4,247	37.7
Harbour Main–Bell Island	7,046	574	3,298	17.4
Placentia and St Mary's	4,572	445	2,420	18.4
Placentia West	4,921	1,054	1,922	54.8
Port de Grave	10,636	2,011	4,100	49.0
St John's East	15,708	2,668	8,545	31.2
St John's West	13,720	2,332	7,044	33.1
Trinity North	7,368	1,814	2,787	65.1
Trinity South	4,924	1,163	1,929	60.3
Twillingate	5,254	1,387	1,842	75.3
Humber	947	X	X	X
Labrador	1,420	X	X	X
St Barbe	920	X	X	X
St George's–Port au Port	2,131	X	X	X
White Bay	1,389	X	X	X
Total	*146,536*	*29,063*	*62,304*	*46.6*

Source: Census of Newfoundland, 1869 and 1945; *Encyclopedia of Newfoundland*, vol. I (St John's: Newfoundland Book Publishers, 1981), 723.

Note: Estimates using 1869 distribution do not always match percentages because of rounding.

11.8. By applying the 1869 population to the 1948 referendum results by district, and excluding those districts with no right to vote in 1869, we find that the proportion of the population for Confederation would have dropped to only 46.6 per cent. Furthermore, this calculation does not adjust for the decline in the proportion of Roman Catholics within districts. Therefore, one would expect that the differences would have been even greater and the option of a return to Responsible Government would have won by an even more substantial margin.

It is important to remember that economic considerations were more prominent than sectarian ones in the campaigns for and against Confederation in 1869 and in 1948. For much of the Avalon Peninsula, the question was to what extent St John's privileged status under the old national policy could be preserved in a union with Canada. The anti-Confederates argued, rightly as it turned out, that manufacturing would be hard pressed to survive, a disconcerting prospect for the working-class population of the northern Avalon Peninsula. Although analytically less significant, there is still correlation between occupational status and voting in the second 1948 referendum. What is most noticeable is the association of logging (almost exclusively an occupation of those who lived outside the Avalon Peninsula) and fishing with the vote for Confederation, while people who worked in government and other services, almost completely concentrated on the Avalon Peninsula, were even more likely to have voted against it (see table 11.3).

Conclusion

Overall, statistical analysis based on the CCRI database derived from the 1945 Newfoundland and Labrador census correlating with voter preferences at the district level suggests that the major issues that distinguished between voters for and against Confederation were geography and religion. Voters near St John's, the capital, and elsewhere on the Avalon Peninsula voted, for the most part, against Confederation. All districts off the peninsula voted in favour. Similarly, voters of Roman Catholic faith tended to vote against, whereas Protestants tended to vote for joining Canada. The view that sectarianism in the campaign helped to create a split between the Avalon Peninsula and the rest of Newfoundland and Labrador's voting districts is a long-standing shibboleth in the literature on its experience with Confederation.

A demographic analysis of the 1911 manuscript census for the St George's area suggests caution in too easily accepting this view. This west coast district voted in favour of Confederation, despite being largely Roman Catholic. Analysis of the complete CCRI census records for a specific region of this district, St George's Bay, including the bay itself as well as the Port au Port Peninsula, better reveals the true nature of these differences. Many of the inhabitants of this area were born in either Nova Scotia or France.

The people of St George's had strong family ties to Canada. The increased settlement of this west coast district reflected an overall reorientation of Newfoundland away from the Atlantic and towards the continent. In the short term, this fostered a colonial desire for autonomy and a rejection of Confederation in 1869. However, the dynamic of continental reorientation continued as the interior and westward parts of Newfoundland developed and became more populated. While on the west coast, economic links to Canadian centres strengthened, much of the Avalon Peninsula's economy increasingly depended on the expansion of manufacturing at the expense of rural areas. It was largely a coincidence of historical geography that this more urban economy dovetailed with the most significant concentration of the descendants of Irish Roman Catholics. Although there were vocal advocates of sectarian opposition to Confederation in 1869 and in 1948, it is significant that most feared the "Canadian wolf" for economic reasons; by 1948, there were more people in rural areas who also feared the wolves of St John's. Canada, by contrast, was the home of neighbours and distant cousins.

Notes

1 "The Anti-Confederate Song," http://www.heritage.nf.ca/law/song.html.

2 James K. Hiller, "Confederation Defeated: The Newfoundland Election of 1869," in James K. Hiller and Peter Neary (eds.), *Newfoundland in the Nineteenth and Twentieth Centuries: Essays in Interpretation* (Toronto: University of Toronto Press, 1980), 87–8.

3 James Hiller, "Bennett, Charles James Fox," in *Dictionary of Canadian Biography Online*, http://www.biographi.ca/EN/ShowBio.asp?BioId=39490.

4 Hiller, "Confederation Defeated," 69; Richard Gwyn, *Smallwood: The Unlikely Revolutionary* (Toronto: McClelland and Stewart, 1968), 91, 96.

5 Diane P. Janes, "Confederation," in *Encyclopedia of Newfoundland and Labrador*, vol. 1 (St John's: Newfoundland Book Publishers, 1981), 497–502.

6 Gertrude E. Gunn, *The Political History of Newfoundland, 1832–1864* (Toronto: University of Toronto Press, 1966), 120–7, 143–75; John Mannion, "Irish Migration and Settlement in Newfoundland: The Formative Phase, 1697–1732," *Newfoundland Studies* 17, no. 2 (2001): 257–93; John Mannion, "Waterford and the South of England: Spatial Patterns in Shipping Commerce, 1766–1777," *International Journal of Maritime History* 6, no. 2 (1994): 115–31; John Mannion, "Irish Merchants Abroad: The Newfoundland Experience, 1750–1850," *Newfoundland Studies* 2, no. 2 (1986): 127–90; and W. Gordon Handcock. *Soe longe as there comes noe women: Origins of English Settlement in Newfoundland* (St John's: Breakwater, 1989); John Mannion, "St John's," in R. Cole Harris (ed.), *Historical Atlas of Canada*, vol. 1, *From the Beginning to 1800* (Toronto: University of Toronto Press, 1987), plate 27; John Mannion, "'... Notoriously Disaffected to the Government ...': British Allegations of Irish Disloyalty in Eighteenth-Century Newfoundland," *Newfoundland Studies* 16, no. 1 (2000), 1–29; Philip McCann, "Bishop Fleming and the Politicization of the Irish Roman Catholics in Newfoundland, 1830–1850," in Terrence Murphy and Cyril J. Byrne (eds.), *Religion*

and Identity: The Experience of Irish and Scottish Catholics in Atlantic Canada (St John's: Jesperson, 1987), 81–98; E.C. Moulton, "Constitutional Crisis and Civil Strife in Newfoundland, February to November 1861," *Canadian Historical Review* 48, no. 3 (1967): 251–72; Hiller, "Confederation Defeated," 71; Sean Cadigan, "A Shift in Economic Culture: The Impact of Enclave Industrialization on Newfoundland, 1855–1880," paper presented to the Atlantic Canada Studies Conference, Moncton, May 1996.

7 Hiller, "Bennett, Charles James Fox."

8 James K. Hiller, "The Railway and Local Politics in Newfoundland, 1870–1901," in Hiller and Neary, *Newfoundland*, 130; John Joy, "The Growth and Development of Trades and Manufacturing in St John's, 1870–1914," unpublished M.A. thesis, Memorial University of Newfoundland, 1977; David Alexander, "Newfoundland's Traditional Economy and Development to 1934," in Hiller and Neary, *Newfoundland*, 17–39.

9 David Alexander, "Development and Dependence in Newfoundland, 1880–1970," in David Alexander, compiled by Eric W. Sager, Lewis R. Fischer, and Stuart O. Pierson, *Atlantic Canada and Confederation: Essays in Canadian Political Economy* (Toronto: University of Toronto Press, 1983), 3–32; Ian D.H. McDonald, "*To Each His Own*": *William Coaker and the Fishermen's Protective Union in Newfoundland Politics, 1908–1925*, ed. by J.K. Hiller (St John's: Institute of Social and Economic Research, 1987); J.K. Hiller, "The Politics of Newsprint: The Newfoundland Pulp and Paper Industry, 1915–1939," *Acadiensis* 19, no. 2 (1990): 3–19.

10 J.K. Hiller, "The Newfoundland Fisheries Issue in Anglo-French Treaties, 1713–1904," *Journal of Imperial and Commonwealth History* 24, no. 1 (1996): 1–23; W. Gordon Handcock, "English Migration to Newfoundland," in John Mannion (ed.), *The Peopling of Newfoundland: Essays in Historical Geography* (St John's: Institute of Social and Economic Research, 1977), 15–48; J.K. Hiller, "Bond, Bait, and Bounties: The Newfoundland Government and the Negotiation of the Entente Cordiale," in J.K. Hiller and Christopher English, *Newfoundland and the Entente Cordiale, 1904–2004: Proceedings of a Symposium Held in St John's and Corner Brook, Newfoundland and Labrador, 16–20 September 2004* (St John's: Faculty of Arts Publications, Memorial University of Newfoundland, 2007), 77–94.

11 Rosemary E. Ommer, "Highlands Scots Migration to Southwestern Newfoundland: A Study of Kinship," in Mannion, *The Peopling of Newfoundland*, 212–33; and John J. Mannion, "Settlers and Traders in Western Newfoundland," in Mannion, ibid., 234–75; Gary R. Butler, "L'Acadie et la France se rencontrent: Le peuplement franco-acadien de la baie St-Georges, Terre-Neuve," *Newfoundland Studies* 10, no. 2 (1994): 180–207; Dennis A. Bartels and Olaf U. Janzen, "Micmac Migration to Western Newfoundland," *Canadian Journal of Native Studies* 10, no. 1 (1990): 71–96.

12 British colonies include any British possession outside the British Isles (e.g., Canada, Australia, New Zealand). The Isles themselves (England, Ireland, Scotland and Wales, which are not listed separately in the publications) are not included here. Foreign countries comprise any other non-British possession such

as, in this case, France (such as the French islands of St Pierre and Miquelon off Newfoundland's south coast), the United States, Norway, Germany, Italy, Spain, and Switzerland.

13 E.R. Seary, assisted by Sheila M.P. Lynch, *Family Names of the Island of Newfoundland* (St John's: J.R. Smallwood Centre for Newfoundland Studies, 1977; reprint, Montreal and Kingston: McGill-Queen's University Press, 1988), 35, 200, 262, 275, 344, 544, 561. Alexander is an anglicization of Alexandre; see Kirk R. Butt, *Early Settlers of Bay St George*, vol. I, *The Inner Bay* (Whitby, ON: Boonen Books, 2009), 257.

14 Family names associated with Jersey, Channel Islands, include Guillame/Gillam, Harvey, Huelin, Messervey, and Renouf. See Seary, *Family Names*, 205, 235, 262, 355, 440; and Butt, *Early Settlers*, vol. I, 147–8, 167–70, 182–6, and vol. II, *The Outer Bay* (Whitby, ON: Boonen Books, 2009), 155–6, 180.

15 "FNI Member Bands," Federation of Newfoundland Indians, http://www.fni.nf.ca/bands.asp (accessed 21 Sept. 2010).

16 Scottish family names include Gillis, McIsaac, and McDonald. See Seary, *Family Names*, 206, 327–8, 332; and Butt, *Early Settlers*, vol. II, 252–3, 261; for an examination of Scottish migration to Newfoundland via Cape Breton, see Ommer, "Highlands Scots," 212–33.

17 Ron Crawley, "Off to Sydney: Newfoundlanders Emigrate to Industrial Cape Breton, 1890–1914," *Acadiensis* 17, no. 2 (1988): 27–51; Sean Cadigan, "A Nova Scotian in White Bay: Forestry Restructuring in a Newfoundland Case Study," paper accepted for presentation at the Atlantic Canada Studies Conference XV, Fredericton, May 2005, but not presented due to weather-related travel difficulties. Presented instead to History department seminar series, Memorial University, Oct. 2005.

18 Government of Newfoundland, *The Eleventh Census of Newfoundland and Labrador, 1945*, vol. I, *Population* (Ottawa: Dominion Bureau of Statistics, 1949), 1.

19 "Corner Brook," in *Encyclopedia of Newfoundland and Labrador*, vol. I (St John's: Newfoundland Book Publishers, 1981), 536–42; calculated by the authors based on applying present-day municipal boundaries to 1945 census results.

20 J.K. Hiller, *Confederation: Deciding Newfoundland's Future, 1934 to 1949* (St John's: Newfoundland Historical Society, 1998), 50.

21 The most important statement about the impact of the war on Newfoundland is Peter Neary, *Newfoundland in the North Atlantic World, 1929–1949* (Montreal and Kingston: McGill-Queen's University Press, 1988). Malcolm MacLeod has also examined the manner in which war drew Newfoundland and Canada together in *Peace of the Continent* (St John's: Harry Cuff Publications, 1986). MacLeod comes close to stating that there was inevitability in the relationship, which is a different view from that argued here. See also Malcolm MacLeod, *Nearer than Neighbours: Newfoundland and Canada before Confederation* (St John's: Harry Cuff Publications, 1982); and W.J. Chafe, *I've Been Working on the Railroad: Memories of a Railwayman, 1911–1962* (St John's: Harry Cuff Publications, 1987), 94.

22 Harvey Mitchell, "Canada's Negotiations with Newfoundland, 1887–1895," *Canadian Historical Review* 40 (1959): 291.

23 John Edward Fitzgerald, "Archbishop E.P. Roche, J.R. Smallwood, and Denominational Rights in Newfoundland Education, 1948," *CCHA Historical Studies* 65 (1999): 33; Fitzgerald, "'The True Father of Confederation,' Archbishop E.P. Roche, Term 17, and Newfoundland's Union with Canada," *Newfoundland Studies* 14, no. 2 (1998), 188–219; "Cashin, Maj. Peter J.," *Encyclopedia of Newfoundland and Labrador*, vol. 1, 380–1.

— · 12 · —

Individual and Familial Life Courses in Quebec City, 1871–1911: Some Considerations on Two Biographical Data Sets

MARC ST-HILAIRE, LAURENT RICHARD, AND RICHARD MARCOUX

According to the 1871 Canadian census, Sophie Saint-Pierre, who was then only 5 years old but the eldest child of the family, was living with her parents Jean (a blacksmith) and Sophie, along with one brother and two sisters, in their house on Sainte-Monique Street in Quebec City's modest ward of St Sauveur.[1] At the same census, Albert Patry, aged 10, the youngest of his family, was also living with his parents François (a butcher) and Caroline, along with a brother and a sister, in their home on Sainte-Élizabeth Street, some 200 metres from the Saint-Pierres. In 1881, Sophie and Albert were still living with their parents. Sophie was working as a manufacturing employee and her brother as a blacksmith, probably with their father, who was by then a widower. Albert, the sole child living at home with his parents at this time, was working as a carter. Sophie and Albert were married in the parish church of St Sauveur on 12 August 1884, Albert declaring himself to be a carter and Sophie, unsurprisingly, declaring no occupation. They had at least fourteen children prior to the 1911 census, by which time Albert was 51 and Sophie was 45, and they were living together with their ten remaining children (newborn to 24 years old), only six blocks farther south in the same ward in which they were living in 1871. Albert was at that point a labourer, a modest occupation for supporting a twelve-person household, but the four eldest children were also participating in the paid labour force – as milliner, labourer, or shoemaker – and almost certainly were contributing additional income to the household economy.

If such a life course does not appear on the face of it to be exceptional, in fact, it was quite unusual. The Patrys were part of the few, among the roughly eight hundred 10-year-old boys and seven hundred 5-year-old girls found in the 1871 census for Quebec City, who were still living in Quebec City in 1911, and only one of the three couples formed from those 1,500 individuals who spent a majority of their lives in the Old Capital. Was the Patrys' destiny written in the warm and bright blue May sky of the emerging French Canadian capital or in the cold, grey, snow-clouded December sky of a slowly industrializing late Victorian mid-sized city? Or, was it the result of a chain of decisions, made by their parents prior to their adulthood and by themselves thereafter, based on some rationale for assessing individual and familial resources and needs, and the expected – and positively perceived – results? If definitive answers to such questions are not readily found, some essential clues may be drawn from the analysis of socio-economic and cultural information found in Canadian censuses. Using a longitudinal data set drawn from the 1871–1911 census microdata, we attempt to establish to what extent socio-economic factors as given by censuses mark out individual and family life courses. In view of the limits herein, not every dimension of social and economic life that can be drawn from the censuses is considered in this chapter. Our focus is on one aspect of residential itineraries, that is, staying within the city limits or not, an issue of particular interest in the context of Quebec City's deeply altered urban fabric during this period.

Residential mobility is only one aspect of individuals' and families' strategies aimed at maintaining or improving their material conditions or social status; however, it is a fundamental one and has received much scholarly attention for a number of decades.[2] At one level, for instance, within a city, mobility may be driven simply by the need for a more suitable dwelling (its size and number of rooms or dwelling facilities; proximity to employment, to services, or to other resources; or proximity to a culturally familiar group) or by the desire to improve social status (to live in a ward better fitting one's self-image). Of course, these rationales vary with household resources. Although the same considerations may be in play for those moving beyond a municipal boundary as for those who move within it, economic circumstances usually loom large in moves beyond a commuting belt, except for when the move is made mainly for educational purposes (including apprenticeship) or following exogamous marriages (where one of the parties to the union is from outside the area under consideration). Moving house requires individual and familial resources, both material and social, and such moves are determined by existing information about and perceptions of the intended destinations.[3] Decisions to leave a given community should relate to the conditions one faced prior to moving, conditions that longitudinal census microdata allow us to partially and broadly assess.

The Context

From the mid-nineteenth century to the beginning of the twentieth, Quebec City experienced a deep economic restructuring along with a major turnover of population.[4] In 1850, the city's flourishing economy was based on administration, transportation, commerce, and shipbuilding, and each one of these sectors faced strongly decline in the 1850s and 1860s. The colonial capital was transferred to Ottawa, in 1865, along with the civil servants attached to public administration, and just six years before the imperial garrison sailed back to Great Britain, removing a substantial source of income to local merchants and other service providers. The transportation sector suffered a major blow, with the harbour facing hard competition from Montreal, following the digging of the St Lawrence channel, which allowed transatlantic ships to bypass Quebec City and sail directly to the colonial metropolis. With the decrease of seafaring transportation, commerce (especially wholesale commerce) faced difficulties maintaining its level of activity. Finally, the sea shanties almost collapsed between 1850 and 1880, as they missed the change from wooden sailing ships to steam-powered, iron ones. In addition to these problems, and partly because it was not connected to the continental railway system until the end of the 1870s, Quebec City only slowly shifted to industrial production (especially in leather and clothing, two sectors employing an important female labour force). Facing the decline of its previously main economic sectors and the slow emergence of a labour-intensive industrial one, the population of Quebec City almost stagnated between 1860 and 1900, growing from 57,400 to only 68,800 inhabitants in those forty years (implying a mean annual increase of 4 per thousand, the lowest among major Canadian cities for that period). Moreover, because of highly differentiated net migration rates among ethnoreligious groups (null for French Catholics, quite negative for both Irish Catholics and Anglo-Protestants), the cultural composition of Quebec City changed dramatically during the forty years being examined here, leading to a quasi–French Canadian homogeneity early in the beginning the twentieth century (86% in 1911, compared with 60% in 1861). The higher French Catholic migration rates were not due, as it might be thought, to relatively lower outmigration, but to much higher in-migration, thanks to rural-to-urban movement from regions surrounding the capital city (in 1901, half of the city's French Canadians over 30 years of age declared that they were born in a rural setting, which is more than twice the proportion of other cultural groups, mostly the Irish who arrived after the Great Famine). Other cultural groups could not count on such rural-to-urban movement. Along with the French Canadianization of the city, the demographic fabric of Quebec City was modified by an increasing feminization which can be related to the industrialization of its economy (the overall sex ratio changed from 932‰ to 859‰ or 93.2% to 85.9% between 1861 and 1911).

The major economic and demographic changes experienced by City of Quebec in this era had undoubted impact on the life courses of individuals and families. For instance, according to what is known about migration parameters, we have every reason to expect that the occupational composition of those who left the city was quite different from that of the stayers, especially in the context of the decline of specific economic sectors; for example, we know that there were 112 caulkers, a typical wooden ship building trade monopolized by French Canadians (96%), in the city in 1871, and by 1881 this number was down to twenty-five. In the context of a family economy, it is likely that labour market conditions led families that had more resident boys than girls to leave in greater proportions or encouraged larger numbers of young males than females to leave the city as individual migrants. Concerning cultural belonging (ethnoreligious group), we can also wonder to what extent members of the Irish Catholic and Anglo-Protestant communities left as family units or as individuals. And what about those who remained? To what extent and how did they differ from those who left? Regarding gender, for example, a smaller proportion of women married than of men, but what distinguished women who married from those who did not? Were the latter simply all single females financially helping their parents? Indeed, looking at who stayed and who left leads one to take into consideration many aspects of their lives. When aggregated, these collective biographies help us to better understand the formation of the city's industrializing labour force as well as its evolving cultural (ethnoreligious) composition. Regarding the latter, examining population history can also help in understanding the urbanization of Quebec City's French Canadians, a prerequisite for a more complete historical account of the subsequent French Canadianization of Quebec society as a whole.

The Data

To explore those processes, we use biographies of a cohort of female and male children based on age and sex at the 1871 census (5-year-old girls and 10-year-old boys), built from the information found in the four subsequent censuses. These data come from the 100 per cent sample of Quebec City's census microdata, 1852 to 1911 (total population from 45,900 to 78,700), entered for the aims of the Population et histoire sociale de la ville de Québec project. As a complement, we also use the marriage records for the City of Quebec, 1850–1910 (all denominations; 33,700 marriage certificates, provided by the BALSAC project), to allow linkage of single young adults in their original families to couples at the head of new families ten years later (necessary for the girls because they lose their maiden names at marriage).

The 1871 census microdata contain 824 boys aged 10 years and 733 girls aged 5 years with legible names (12 were not), enumerated into 1,454 households (12% of the city's households). The sex ratio of the cohort is exceptionally high. It is due to visible rounding of ages for the boys: they represent 40 per cent of the 9- to 11-year-old population while the 5-year-old girls are much closer to expected numbers, being 30 per cent of the girls aged 4–6. This imbalance contributes to the overall sex ratio of 1,054 males to 1,000 females among the children present in all the 1871 families covered by this study.

In 1871, most of these children were living in a household led by at least one of their parents; twenty-one were in a household led by another adult, and fourteen were in one of three institutions (orphanage or asylum). Of the main body, six boys and twenty-two girls were children of one or another member of the citadel garrison, which departed a few weeks after the census was taken, and were thus excluded from the study group, leaving 818 boys and 711 girls as the starting point for the linkage to subsequent censuses. The linkage was done following a four-step procedure entailing a name-based search of each child into the following census and into the marriage records. The information pertaining to the whole household (names, ages, birthplace, marital status, apparent or given relationship to head) was used to overcome intercensus spelling variations or names substitutions that may have affected the individual searched for.[5] Linkage with marriage records was based on nominative information, marital status, age (minor/major), and parents' survival. Table 12.1 shows the results of this operation.

Roughly half of the individuals in the study are lost at each ten-year interval prior to their reaching the age of 25–30, with the diminution quickly becoming smaller thereafter. Linkage rates by matrimonial status indicate that the linked sample for boys is quite representative of the total population by age. For girls, there are wider variations, with single women being slightly overrepresented and widows relatively underrepresented (especially in 1911) in the linked sample. What is striking here is the very high proportion of single women in the population, which reflects the lowering sex ratio for Quebec City in this period. It must be emphasized here that married women could only be linked thanks to the use of marriage certificates. For the girls, 161 first marriage records were found and 184 first marriage records were found for the boys, that is, the same proportion for both sexes (23%). Forty other linked men, declared married in the census, evidently were married somewhere else since no marriage certificate for them was found in Quebec City. The linkage rate would have been higher if we could have used marriage records for counties surrounding Quebec City: if marriages generally took place within the bride's

Table 12.1 · Quebec City sample cohort: Marital status, 1871–1911

		5-year-old girls				*10-year-old boys*			
		n	%	*% in city*	*% of group*	n	%	*% in city*	*% of group*
1871	Single	711	100.0		100.0	818	100.0		100.0
1881	Single	349	100.0	99.8	52.2	372	95.1	94.6	67.5
	Married	0	0.0	0.2	0.0	19	4.9	5.2	86.4
	Widowed	0	0.0	0.0	—	0	0.0	0.2	0.0
	Total/% of 1871	349	49.1	100.0	52.2	391	47.8	100.0	67.8
	Theoretical *N*/%	678	51.5			780	50.1		
1891	Single	104	58.4	55.9	24.8	69	34.0	30.0	35.9
	Married	71	39.9	42.7	23.2	130	64.0	67.6	35.5
	Widowed	3	1.7	1.4	37.5	4	2.0	2.4	21.1
	Total/% of 1871	178	25.0	100.0	24.3	203	24.8	100.0	35.1
	Theoretical *N*/%	625	28.5			720	28.2		
1901	Single	44	37.3	34.3	23.4	21	14.2	14.9	26.6
	Married	72	60.2	62.1	22.5	122	81.8	81.1	35.2
	Widowed	3	2.5	3.6	16.7	6	4.0	4.0	26.1
	Total/% of 1871	119	16.7	100.0	22.6	149	18.2	100.0	33.2
	Theoretical *N*/%	571	20.8			657	22.7		
1911	Single	26	31.0	24.7	16.1	4	4.7	10.6	8.0
	Married	56	66.7	69.2	16.7	75	87.2	84.1	22.7
	Widowed	2	2.4	6.1	6.1	7	8.1	5.3	25.9
	Total/% of 1871	84	11.8	100.0	15.7	86	10.5	100.0	21.0
	Theoretical *N*/%	505	16.6			579	14.9		

Sources: Population et histoire sociale de la ville de Québec project (PHSVQ).

Theoretical *N* = number of surviving individuals at the end of the period according to life tables available for the decade. See Robert Bourbeau and Jacques Légaré, *Évolution de la mortalité au Canada et au Québec, 1831–1931: Essai de mesure par génération* (Montreal: Presses de l'Université de Montréal, 1982).

% in city = % of population of expected age ± one year (based on 1,275 to 2,090 women and 919 to 1,792 men).

% of group = % of individuals expected to be in that age group in subsequent censuses, e.g., the 149 linked men in 1901, no matter their declared age, represent 1/3 of the 449 men in the city declaring an age of 40 – which, here again, shows the overrepresentation in the sample of boys aged 10 compared with girls aged 5.

parish, a small proportion were celebrated elsewhere. Regarding widows, the low linkage rate reflects the variability of ways in which they were recorded (maiden name, both first and last names of the spouse, spouse's last name only), thus lowering the chances of finding them in a subsequent census.

The linked sample represents a good proportion of age/marital status groups within Quebec City: more than half of girls aged 15 in 1881, nearly a sixth of 45-year-old women in 1911, two-thirds of 20-year-old men in 1881, and more than a fifth of men aged 50 in 1911. Although they give a very rough idea of in-migration levels by ages in the city, those proportions can hardly be seen as comprehensive measures because of the approximate way in which ages were declared to the enumerator; inquiries that are a lot more systematic are needed to get a good measure of the whole population turnover for this period.

According to ethnoreligious groups, the sample is quite representative of Quebec City's cultural composition in 1871. Nevertheless, Irish Catholics are very slightly underrepresented (at 16% instead of 18%) in favour of French Canadians (at 68% instead of 66%), while at the end of the period under study, this representativeness is slightly modified: in 1911, the sample underrepresents French Canadians (82% instead of 86%) in favour of Anglo-Protestants (10% instead of 5%). Ethnicity is processed here like has been done for Montreal by Sherry Olson, Patricia Thornton, and Danielle Gauvreau.[6] In addition to Anglo-Protestants (non-Catholics with British origins), Irish Catholics and French Canadians (Catholic), there are very few people belonging to other ethnoreligious groups (3%), mostly English and Scottish Catholics (Anglo-Catholics), Germans (any religion), and non-Catholic French Canadians.

Finally, we can ask what biases do we face using the linkage results? Since we focus on mobility, and since death records have not yet been scrutinized to control for individual absences in a following census, the available life tables have been applied to the local population to estimate the denominators of potential links (these are the theoretical numbers in table 12.1). Such an exercise gives a maximum total outmigration of 83 per cent to 85 per cent over forty years for the 1871 sampled population, a level similar to that previously reported for the Quebec City.[7] The progression of the proportions of the persistent population (those who stayed) is also consistent with what is known, whereby the 1870s and 1880s were the worst decades for outmigration from Quebec City as a whole. If the general figures seem reliable, the linkage is, nevertheless, affected by two biases. The first has to do with family size: since the linkage procedures used information about the composition of the entire household, the chances of finding a matching record is greater for families with more members than for smaller families. In addition, individuals who were living in a household not led by their parents or in an institution are also ill represented. Thanks to the high volume of information we could count on to make a decision when possible matches were found, for over 2,918 searches into one or another census, only thirty-five links were not made because of ambiguities or because they were considered too risky (for cases with common names). But six of these ambiguities affect the thirty-five children who were not found in their family in 1871, contributing to a limited linkage rate for this group of just 17 per cent (6/35) for the 1871–81 interval.

The following analyses are based on 170 to 740 more or less complete biographies over the 1871 to 1911 period. However, in order to work on more homogeneous groups, for consistency of statistical analysis over the cohort, we decided to put aside children living in households led by someone other than their parents, leaving, for our multivariate analyses, 797 boys and 697 girls.

Living (or Not) in the Transforming City

Working with longitudinal data is without doubt the optimal way to gain an understanding of the transformations in a city's sociodemographic structure as revealed by census-based transversal snapshots. Longitudinal data allow analysis at a very fine scale, following individual biographies according to the life course. Very few urban history studies are based on this kind of data, major exceptions in a Canadian perspective being the works of Sherry Olson, Patricia Thornton, and Danielle Gauvreau, who produced individual longitudinal data sets from census microdata and marriage records for a sample of Montrealers between 1861 and 1901.[8] Nevertheless, if the biographies constructed from census microdata provide a great deal of information, they do not reveal everything. Their main deficiency when attempting to analyse population dynamics is that they are silent on kin relations that bind a household and its members to others.[9] As a consequence, this chapter limits its exploration of individual destinies to considering only first-degree kin relationships within households and, exceptionally, between cohort households and their immediate neighbours. Being based on censuses, the life courses are examined here by decades. After some description of the sample, the analyses focus on factors such as ethnoreligious belonging, occupation, and composition of the family to try to determine the circumstances that were associated with the continuing presence of individuals in the City of Quebec, while taking into account the transformations of the local context.

Depending on Parents' Fate: The 1871–81 Decade

During the first decade that we are examining here, the members of our cohort pass from no autonomy at all to a relatively independent adulthood for men, even though they remain minors in the eyes of the law until they reach the age

Table 12.2 · Quebec City sample cohort: Marital status and autonomy of those who were present (in the census) and those who were absent, 1871–1911

				1871	*1881*	*1891*	*1901*	*1911*
BOYS	Present	Single	Within his original family	797	349	64	15	1
			Out of family	21	23	5	6	3
		Married/	In an autonomous household		15	129	124	81
		widowed	Co-resident within parents' household		4	5	4	1
		Total		*818*	*391*	*203*	*149*	*86*
	Absent	Single	Individual only		64	76	10	4
			Individual and family		345	66	12	8
		Married/	Couple only		2	25	28	39
		widowed	Couple and family		1	15	1	2
			Deceased		0	2	3	7
		Ambiguity/too risky link			15	4	0	3
		Total			*427*	*188*	*54*	*63*
GIRLS	Present	Single	Within her original family	697	339	102	41	12
			Out of family	14	10	2	3	14
		Married/	In an autonomous household		0	68	73	57
		widowed	Co-resident within parents' household		0	6	2	1
		Total		*711*	*349*	*178*	*119*	*84*
	Absent	Single	Individual only		56	38	8	0
			Individual and family		299	96	14	9
		Married/	Couple only			18	27	19
		widowed	Couple and family			16	6	1
			Deceased			0	2	4
		Ambiguity/too risky link			6	3	2	2
		Total			*361*	*171*	*59*	*35*

Source: PHSVQ, census micro-data, 1871–1911.

Note: This table has been compiled by ethnoreligious group; data not shown but used in the text.

of 21 years. Consequently, a large number of them share their parents' fate, as shown in table 12.2, which disaggregates the situation of the cohort members according to their appearance in the following census, their marital status, and their "autonomy" from their parents. For instance, of the 818 boys present in 1871, there were 349 males living as singles with at least one of their parents in

1881, while twenty-three were living in a household not headed by at least one of their parents, fifteen were married and heads of their own household, and four were married and living in their parents' household. When the individual is absent, the situation is more uncertain. If single (i.e., no record of marriage has been found), the individual may have left the city alone, or with his or her parents, or may be deceased. If married, we may know the person's status because he or she was recorded as married on a previous census or because a record of marriage prior to the next census was found; however, the individual may have left the city with a spouse only or along with his or her parents, or may be deceased, with the surviving spouse being declared widow or widower in the following census. For the 1871 boys, for instance, sixty-four are absent in 1881, although their original families are present; 345 other single males and their original families are absent in 1881; two others got married after 1871 (marriage certificates were found), but they and their wives were absent in 1881, although their original families were still in Quebec City. A marriage certificate was found for one other man, but he, his wife, and his original family were all absent in 1881. An "absent person" may also result from a linkage ambiguity, a respondent's or an enumerator's error in the original records, or a mistake made in our data entry. There is no way to control for these eventualities.

Table 12.2 indicates that seven children out of eight in 1881, whether male or female, were with their original family, whether living with them within the city or having left with them. The 15-year-old girls still present almost all lived with their parents; 42 per cent were going to school, 15 per cent were participating in the paid-labour force, with the remaining ones declared neither as attending school nor as working. These proportions are quite different from those for the rest of the city, where 33 per cent of the same-aged girls were going to school and 23 per cent were paid workers. As was the case in Montreal,[10] many more 15-year-girls were in school among Quebec City's Anglo-Protestants (68%) and Irish Catholics (60%) than among French Canadians (35%). As a consequence, only 5 per cent to 9 per cent of Anglo-Protestant and Irish Catholic girls declared a paid job compared with 35 per cent of French Canadian ones, a tribute to a well-documented labour-based, family economy.[11]

Regarding autonomy, the situation was not so different for the persistent young men who were now 20 years old (except for the 15 who married and headed new households): 90 per cent were living with their parents. Because of their age, far fewer were still at school (7%), and 85 per cent were reportedly in paid work. Those who were at school, roughly proportionally distributed among the cultural (ethnoreligious) groups, were mostly the sons of professionals, merchants, or high-level public administrators (only 4 out of the 23 who were in school were the sons of manual workers); schooling for them appears to have been a sure key to social reproduction. The young men who were part of the paid labour force were mostly manual workers (69%; with 36% in skilled trades and many apprentices among them); a quarter were unskilled, non-manual workers (including many clerks). We find, however, that those proportions were quite different by ethnoreligious group: among the unskilled non-manual workers in this group of men, 63 per cent were Anglo-Protestant (we find clerks here, too, but fewer store clerks and many more bookkeepers), 25 per cent were French Canadians, and 11 per cent were Irish Catholics. The proportions of unskilled manual workers were the reverse of these, respectively, 7 per cent, 28 per cent, and 60 per cent. Olson, Thornton, and Gauvreau's work on Montreal shows a similar differentiation in occupational structure for the three main ethnoreligious communities.[12] The proportions in the labour force and the socio-occupational distributions were quite close to Quebec City's overall, 20-year-old male population, with two exceptions: there were fewer unskilled non-manual workers in the city as a whole (20%) and the proportion of students was a bit lower (5%). Finally, nineteen of the young men in the sample got married between 1871 and 1881, and they were all French Canadians.[13] Half were skilled manual workers, a quarter were unskilled, and a quarter were in non-manual jobs or were small entrepreneurs. This occupational distribution seems to indicate a more secure economic situation, allowing these men to start up new families. Nevertheless, their independence was not complete: four of them still lived within their parents' households, four others next door to them, and another four immediately adjacent to their spouse's parents. For two others, the brother-in-law was either living within or next door to the new couple's household. In short, as pointed out by Olson and Bradbury for Montreal and Hareven for French Canadians in New England, intergenerational and familial interdependence remained vividly present beyond the marriage boundary.[14] A bit more than a half of the 1871 cohort were not found in census data for 1881.

Fully comparable data on linkage or persistence rates in North American cities are very rare since methodology differs from one author to another. The closest to that for Quebec City is probably Jason Gilliland's work on Montreal.[15] For the period 1861–1901, Gilliland found the mean decennial persistence rate for households in Montreal to be 59 per cent, almost in reverse proportions by ethnoreligious group compared with Quebec City (69% Anglo-Protestant, 57% French Canadian, and 52% Irish Catholic). Lower persistence rates in Quebec City are likely due to its far worse economic situation; Montreal offered many more opportunities than the Old Capital.

As shown in table 12.3, the variations in linkage by cultural groups differ reasonably, especially for the Anglo-Protestants of whom a much larger por-

Table 12.3 · Quebec City sample cohort: Marital status and ethnoreligious group of those who stayed (present in the census), 1871–1911

			1871	*1881*	*1891*	*1901*	*1911*
Anglo-Protestants	Boys	Single	100	38	9	2	1
		Married			8	12	9
		Total	*100*	*38*	*17*	*14*	*10*
	Girls	Single	81	34	12	6	3
		Married			4	4	4
		Total	*81*	*34*	*16*	*10*	*7*
French Canadians (Catholic)	Boys	Single	539	244	38	14	2
		Married		19	108	101	66
		Total	*539*	*263*	*146*	*115*	*68*
	Girls	Single	497	259	81	34	21
		Married			66	69	51
		Total	*497*	*259*	*147*	*103*	*72*
Irish Catholics	Boys	Single	148	75	19	5	1
		Married			15	12	5
		Total	*148*	*75*	*34*	*17*	*6*
	Girls	Single	111	47	9	2	1
		Married			3	2	2
		Total	*111*	*47*	*12*	*4*	*3*
Others	Boys	Single	31	15	3		
		Married			3	3	2
		Total	*31*	*15*	*6*	*3*	*2*
	Girls	Single	21	9	2	2	2
		Married			1		
		Total	*21*	*9*	*3*	*2*	*2*

Source: PHSVQ, census microdata, 1871–1911.

Note: Ethnoreligious group unknown for one 1871 girl; individual and family absent in 1881.

tion of the community was absent from Quebec City (60%) than of Irish Catholics (53%) or French Canadians (50%). Most of the absentees (85%) clearly left the city accompanying their parents, and only 2 per cent of losses were due to linkage difficulties. The remaining 13 per cent are individuals not found even though their parents were still present in the city. Some of these were deceased (an estimated 4.6%, or 21 boys and 18 girls). Altogether, this leaves some twenty-eight girls and thirty boys neither located in their family nor in the city (4% of the whole cohort). Although we have no way of knowing their familial situation in 1871, it is worth noting that the estimated numbers of absent youngsters are quite similar to the numbers of 15-year-old girls and single, 20-year-old boys not living with their family in the city in 1881 (respectively, 3.6% and 5.0%). It is likely that they appear elsewhere as boarders, living outside their natal families in order to work or as apprentices, or working as household servants, or living as co-residents in a household headed by a sibling or another relative. Along with the absent singles, we find three recently married men, who apparently left the city with their wives, while the original families of two of them remained in Quebec City. One returned soon, residing again in the city where we find him remarrying in 1884.

The preceding account relates to the situation of our cohort of individual males and females in 1881. Since most of them shared their parents' circumstances, looking at their family characteristics in 1871 may help to better understand their life courses. Tables 12.4 and 12.5 indicate two fundamental attributes of these by ethnoreligious group, one economic (occupation of male head of household) and the other sociodemographic (gendered composition of the family).[16] Regarding the latter, we also examine the activity of children. Overall (see table 12.4), we first note that, even though the members of the garrison are not considered in the analysis, a much smaller proportion of the Anglo-Protestant families than other cultural groups were persistent. It is likely that the city's loss of military and administrative functions also affected some people gravitating around these British groups. Regarding occupations, the distribution indicates the extent to which the socioprofessional structure within the Quebec City varied according to cultural belonging in almost the same way as has been found for Montreal: Anglo-Protestants occupied the top categories in greater proportions, French Canadians dominated in the skilled manual occupations, in manufacturing and in the trades (shipbuilding and general construction), and Irish Catholics were concentrated in unskilled positions, among others, those needed by maritime transportation. The geography of the Quebec City is characterized by a sharp cultural differentiation superimposed on the socioeconomic one: French Canadians live mostly in the industrial wards along the St Charles River, the Irish live along the St Lawrence waterfront (where they monopolize the labouring occupations of stevedores and timber towers), and Anglo-Protestants live in the nice parts of the walled city and the Montcalm ward.[17]

Second, distributions by cultural group and presence in the city reveal some discrepancies between the persistent and absent families, although not a consistent pattern. Considering the literature on urban transiency literature, it is

Table 12.4 · Quebec City sample, male heads of household: Occupations, in 1871, of those who stayed and those who left, according to ethnoreligious group and presence in the 1881 census (%)[a]

Occupational category	*Anglo-Protestants*		*French Canadians*		*Irish Catholics*		*Total*[b]	
	Present	*Absent*	*Present*	*Absent*	*Present*	*Absent*	*Present*	*Absent*
Skilled non-manuals	14.1	15.4	6.6	3.1	9.9	4.2	8.2	5.2
Unskilled non- manuals	14.1	12.1	4.9	3.8	5.8	5.3	6.3	5.2
Small entrepreneurs	16.5	16.5	13.4	10.7	9.9	5.3	13.3	10.8
Skilled manuals	32.9	29.7	49.3	46.8	14.0	16.8	41.5	39.6
Semi- and unskilled manuals	22.4	26.4	25.8	35.5	60.3	68.4	30.7	39.2
Valid *N*	85	91	531	391	121	95	765	594

Source: PHSVQ, census micro-data, 1871–1911.

a Found in the 1881 census, the parents of individually absent children are included in the "Present" category; b Includes all ethnoreligious groups.

no surprise that both French Canadians and the Irish in higher occupational status categories tended to stay in the city in larger proportions than others, but the pattern is less obvious among Anglo-Protestants. The difference is reversed, however, for skilled manual workers, with the Irish somewhat more likely to be absent, contrary to conventional expectations. Only at the bottom of the occupational status distribution is the expected pattern consistently respected, those in unskilled manual being less numerous among the persistent families for all cultural groups, but especially for the French Canadians. Crude occupation distributions, thus, give strong, but not definitive clues regarding persistence rates.

In a context of a gendered labour market and of family economies, the number, sex, and age of children count heavily among the household resources. The labour-intensive industrial urban economy of the city, in large part based on the female workforce, could be expected to encourage families with more female teenagers or young adults to stay in the city,[18] especially the French Canadians who were more concentrated in industrial jobs. By contrast, families with boys should have been favoured within the Irish Catholic community, since the specific segment of the labour market in which they were concentrated, transportation, was strongly male dominated. Our results are consistent with these hypotheses when we consider children over 9 years old as a whole. Among French Canadians, we find a higher sex ratio for the absent families and among Irish Catholics, a lower one, although for the former the

Table 12.5 · Quebec City sample cohort: Sex ratio by age group, in 1871, according to ethnoreligious group and child's presence in 1881 census, together with proportions at school and at work

Age (years)	*Anglo-Protestants*				*French Canadians*				*Irish Catholics*			
	Present		*Absent*		*Present*		*Absent*		*Present*		*Absent*	
	n	‰	n	‰	n	‰	n	‰	n	‰	n	‰
0–4	82	1,278	91	750	601	983	360	925	153	1068	87	1,071
5–9	129	573	118	532	918	553	600	563	216	701	169	408
0–9	*211*	*788*	*209*	*620*	*1,519*	*699*	*960*	*681*	*369*	*836*	*256*	*580*
10–14	148	1,792	117	2,250	873	2,052	550	2,526	224	2,613	153	2,825
15–19	72	1,000	48	1,000	451	996	225	940	81	1,132	39	857
20–29	37	947	15	1,500	165	1,171	81	929	27	1,455	32	882
10–29	*257*	*1,380*	*180*	*1,727*	*1,489*	*1,532*	*856*	*1,726*	*332*	*1,991*	*224*	*1,872*
Total	468	1,071	389	995	3,008	1,030	1,816	1,052	701	1,247	480	1,000
% 15–29 at school (women)	16.4 (16.4)		19.0 (26.7)		12.1 (8.8)		8.2 (8.2)		17.6 (22.4)		15.5 (13.1)	
% 15–29 at work (women)	39.1 (12.7)		36.5 (0.0)		33.9 (14.1)		41.8 (24.1)		45.4 (24.5)		50.7 (34.2)	

Source: PHSVQ, census micro-data, 1871–1911.

patterns were not entirely consistent by age subgroups. Perhaps what is more significant than the number of children and their sex was what contribution they made to the household economy, or whether, instead, the family had invested in their education.

Table 12.5 shows that the activity of 15- to 29-year-old children differs depending on their persistence in Quebec City, especially for French Canadians and the Irish. Both groups had higher rates of school attendance along with lower rates of children at work in 1871 if they were still in Quebec City in 1881. The overall rates for children at work were 65 per cent for sons and 23 per cent for daughters of absent families, and 57 per cent for sons and 15 per cent for daughters of persistent families; these rates resemble those reported for Montreal.[19] The propensity to be at school appears to be consistent with the occupational status of the still present and absent families, that is, longer schooling for children is associated with higher occupational status of the parents. Similarly, we find that fewer children in school entailed more working members of the

Table 12.6 · Quebec City sample cohort: Likelihood of having left the city by 1881 (absent from census) relative to selected 1871 characteristics

Variable	*Value*	*Exp (B)*	*Sig.*
Ethnoreligious group	Irish Catholic	0.724	.07
	Anglo-Protestant	1.537	.02
	Other	1.102	.75
	French Canadian	R	
Family size (*n*)	2–4	1.818	.00
	5–7	R	
	8–9	0.541	.00
	10+	0.522	.00
Occupation	Skilled non-manual	0.329	.00
	Unskilled non-manual	0.403	.01
	Small entrepreneur	0.392	.00
	Skilled manual	0.501	.01
	Unskilled manual	0.599	.06
	Not given/do not work	R	
Age of head (years)	20–29	0.731	.23
	30–39	1.193	.20
	40–49	R	
	50–59	0.796	.16
	60+	1.307	.40
Children sex ratio	Girls only	0.600	.05
	1–49	1.013	.95
	50–99	0.779	.19
	100	R	
	101–200	0.804	.25
	201–899	0.650	.05
	Boys only	1.335	.25

Source: PHSVQ, census microdata, 1871–1911.

R = reference category.

household, and the absent families seemed more dependent on the income of their children prior to leaving the city.

Several features of the census records of 1871 couples deserve further examination. In this analysis, we undertake logistic regression comparing 1871 household characteristics of cohort members still present in 1881 with those of the absent young people (see table 12.6). Based on a number of prior examinations of the data, the independent variables included in the analysis are the number of persons within the biological family, the head of household's marital status, the sex ratio of the children within the family, the head of household's occupational status, and ethnoreligious affiliation (see table 12.6). No matter the order in which they are entered into the regression models, we find that the variables with statistically significant effects are always the same. The ethnoreligious group comes first, with Anglo-Protestants being a lot more likely to be absent by 1881 than individuals in the other groups, and confirming the bivariate distributions already discussed. Second, the relative importance of the head of household's occupational status category is confirmed, especially for the highest occupational categories. Sex ratio among the children also has an effect, but in an inconsistent way, paralleling the bivariate distributions. However, if the regression includes only French Canadians (data not shown), the effect of sex ratios among children is very clear: the probability of being absent in 1881 decreased as the number of male to female children decreased.

Finally, family size seems to play a strong role: the larger the family, the higher was the probability of an individual being present in the 1881 census data for Quebec City. This might be associated with the head of household's age (heads of households persisting to 1881 were 4.4 years older on average in 1871 than heads who were absent, which is consistent with the literature); however, we find that head of household's age did not play a consistent or statistically significant role.[20] Thus, we have to conclude that a combined effect of family size and the linkage bias favouring larger families probably is involved in these results, as mentioned earlier. The effect of family size on moving might be determined by a fact as trivial as that moving a larger household demands more resources than moving a smaller one, and is as much of a determinant as the insurance in facing domestic needs that the availability of more earners in the family provides. The variables entered into the model correctly predict 65% of the cases in the logistic regression.

Settling Down: The 1881–91 Decade

During the second decade being examined here, the cohort members are expected to have gained much independence, once they reached the age of 25 or 30, passing from adolescence or young adulthood to complete adulthood. This was a period of key choices, which played a major role in setting the paths for the rest of their lives: to marry or not, to become parent, to try to find a "serious," if not entirely secure and lasting means of making a living, to settle somewhere. Of course, as argued earlier, such choices are not made with complete independence, and the cohort members are still associated intimately – some would write intricately – to their immediate family and kin networks. Table 12.2 gives a first indication of the extent to which the members of this cohort are living on their own: 18 per cent of these young men who were single in 1881 (64/349) and 30 per cent of young women who were single in 1881 (102/339) were still living with their parents in 1891, while at least half of the men and a third of the women made what was perhaps the biggest decision of their lives by getting married in the interval. And they did it at quite young ages, on average the young women married at 21 years and the men at 23 to 24 years, although apparently the non-French members of our cohort married somewhat later (the averages for non-French Canadians are based on very limited numbers). Otherwise age at marriage for the cohort members is consistent with what has been found in Montreal for the same period.[21] Among the married couples in this cohort present in Quebec City in 1891, 145 had already started their families (with 2.1 to 2.7 children, on average).

The proportion of those absent in 1891 is quite similar to the preceding decade (at 49%), reflecting an economic situation that had not improved. Indeed, calculated from aggregate census data and general mortality by ethnoreligious group, net outmigration rates for Quebec City were even higher by a few points in the 1880s than in the 1870s. The proportions absent still varied considerably by cultural group. The Irish Catholics were the most affected (with an absence rate of 62%), followed by the Anglo-Protestants (54%), and still further behind, the French Canadians (at 44%). Being concentrated in the Champlain ward, facing a harbour still in decline, the Irish community suffered a true haemorrhage that contributed to its depopulation (its crude number decreased by 36% between 1871 and 1901); in this connection, we observe that from 1885 to 1891 alone, the exports of square timber from Quebec City fell by a third of what they were between 1867 and 1872, while the exports of planks fell by half.[22]

In addition to the few unlinked or deceased persons, the absentees left as unmarried members of their original families (45%), as members of married couples (21%), or as a family's only absent member (32%), with differences among ethnoreligious groups largely due to the younger ages at marriage among French Canadians. These culturally differentiated rates of outmigration led to an increasingly French Canadian sample, comprising 77 per cent of the cohort in 1891, with only 12 per cent of the cohort Irish and 9 per cent Anglo-Protestant in that census year. The high proportion of the cohort members leaving as individuals, about fifty-two men and eighteen women, once we control for expected mortality, is as indicative of the increasing prevalence of independence among the male cohort, as it is of the economic difficulties into which the City of Quebec was sinking.

Marriage records give some clues about the destinations of these outmigrants, marriage fields reflecting migration fields quite well. We know that in the Saguenay region, for example, nearly 80 per cent of exogamous marriage fields correspond to migration fields, short distances being overrepresented compared with longer ones. Seen from place in particular (as Quebec City here), residences located in stagnating or declining zones may be roughly associated with an in-migration field, residences located in growing zones with an outmigration field; thus, recently departed families often appear in the marriage records of the place where they were living previously, the groom returning to marry the bride he knew before leaving.[23] According to the records for 9,400 marriages celebrated in the Quebec City between 1871 and 1891 (implying a bride residing in the city), of which 1,500 were exogamous unions, grooms declared residences from an array of 410 places all over the continent. As expected, most were located within Quebec (81%), with Montreal representing a sixth of all locations (22% for the Anglo-Protestants, 16% for others). Grouped by sub-continental regions, the overall figures are sharply differentiated by cultural groups. Outside Quebec City, a good share of the Irish remained within the area, especially in the neighbouring town of Sillery into which Quebec City's harbour extends. When leaving Quebec as a whole, Anglo-Protestants rather preferred to share in the expansion of Canada, while French Canadians who left tended to contribute to US industrial production in New England or to the resources economy of the Midwest. The distribution of the places of residence of US French Canadian grooms is consistent with the distribution of French Canadians in the United States as estimated by Jean Lamarre and with the literature regarding this ethnic emigration.[24] What is rather new here, however, is the substantial level of the urban, as opposed to rural, outmigration to the United States. For the Irish, too, our results suggest a US-urban oriented movement more than a Canadian one. Marriage records for the sample cohort provide a similar picture.

Finally, marriage records also help us understand the gender-differentiated persistence rate according to marital status: of eighteen women in the cohort who were married during the decade and whose grooms were not residing in Quebec City, seventeen were no longer in Quebec City in 1891.

Tables 12.7 and 12.8 give cohort members' occupations (for males) and family composition (for males and females), comparing those who were absent from Quebec City in 1891 with those who were still there. Regarding occupations, only crude numbers are indicated for the non–French Canadians given their rather small numbers. The general distribution in 1891 differs only slightly from the city's overall occupational structure (men, aged 29–31; data not shown), except for the small entrepreneurs, who were less numerous in the city, and for

Table 12.7 · Quebec City sample, males: Occupational profile of those who stayed and those who had left by 1881 and 1891, according to ethnoreligious group and presence status in 1891[a]

		Anglo-Protestants			*French Canadians*			*Irish Catholics*			*Total*[b]		
	Presence status in 1891	*Present*		*Absent*	*Present*		*Absent*	*Present*		*Absent*	*Present*		*Absent*
	Situation in …	*1891*	*1881*	*1881*	*1891* n (%)	*1881* n (%)	*1881* n (%)	*1891*	*1881*	*1881*	*1891* n (%)	*1881* n (%)	*1881* n (%)
Occupation (all marital status)	Skilled non-manuals	2	1		11 (7.7)	1 (0.7)	2 (1.9)				13 (6.7)	2 (1.1)	2 (1.3)
	Unskilled non-manuals	6	9	11	16 (11.2)	23 (16.8)	26 (24.3)	5	4	3	29 (14.9)	40 (21.4)	40 (25.5)
	Small entrepreneurs	2		1	18 (12.6)	5 (3.6)		1		1	22 (11.3)	5 (2.7)	2 (1.3)
	Skilled manuals	2	4	3	59 (41.3)	58 (42.3)	47 (43.9)	8	7	7	70 (35.9)	70 (37.4)	57 (36.3)
	Unskilled manuals	1	1	3	38 (26.6)	40 (29.2)	24 (22.4)	19	16	20	59 (30.3)	58 (31.0)	47 (29.9)
	At school	1	1		1 (0.7)	10 (7.3)	8 (7.5)		1	1	2 (1.0)	12 (6.4)	9 (5.7)
	Valid *N* (100.0%)	14	16	18	143	137	107	33	28	32	195	187	157
Occupational mobility (1881–91)[c]	Upward	2			32 (25.4)			1			35 (21.0)		
	Downward	0			9 (7.1)			2			11 (6.6)		

Source: PHSVQ, census microdata, 1871–1911.

a Occupations of women not shown because only 15% of female cohort declared an occupation in 1881, 11% 1891, and 3% in both years. Occupational structure of female cohort members' husbands in 1891 is similar to male cohort members' for that year; it is not displayed because their occupation in 1881, and thus their occupational mobility, is unknown (i.e., their biographies have not been reconstructed); b Includes all ethnoreligious belongings; c 100% = *N* of individuals whose occupation is known in both years (total = 167).

those in skilled manual work, who are marginally more. By cultural group, the distribution is again consistent with that of a decade earlier, with the French Canadians mid-way between the generally higher-status Anglo-Protestants and lower-status Irish Catholics. More surprising is that the differences in the 1881 distributions between those who were absent and those persistent in 1891 were tiny (except for some unskilled non-manual workers, who tended to be less numerous among those who stayed). This is as if one's occupation at age 20 was of little direct influence on later life events. This trend is accentuated for the French Canadians, whose unskilled manual workers were relatively more numerous among those who stayed than among those who left. It appears, rather, as if the occupational history of the cohort members played the key role. That is, between the ages of 20 and 30 years, the chances of staying were greater among those young men who seem to have succeeded in anchoring if not improving their position within the local economy, as shown by the upward occupational mobility. Persistence in staying in a place and upward social mobility in North American urban history have been associated in virtually all of the numerous studies on those topics.[25] Of 167 men whose occupations for both 1881 and 1891 are known (and excluding students), forty-six (28%) declared jobs belonging to a different status category from the original one, in most cases, a higher status one. Cases of upward mobility imply a shift from unskilled to skilled manual work (13 men), from skilled manual work to small entrepreneurs (12 men), or from unskilled non-manual work to either small entrepreneurs or to skilled non-manual jobs (9 men, mostly a result of clerks transferring to other occupations). As a sign of their relative occupational success, we see that 78 per cent of these young men were married in 1891, compared with 67 per cent married for the rest of the cohort. Downward mobility is mostly a result of moves from skilled to unskilled manual work (8 out of 11 men; 7 of them were married in 1891). Although this whole picture provides an image of stability or even improvement, the Irish Catholics still experienced more difficulties maintaining themselves, again reflecting the problems that the maritime transportation sector was facing.

About half of the cohort members still present in Quebec City in 1881 shared their parents' fate before or up to 1891: nearly a quarter of those still present in 1891 were living with their parents, while more than another quarter had likely left with their original family. Moreover, if we assume that newly formed couples and their original families somehow contribute to their reciprocal well-being, then parents' resources have to be considered, too, in assessing the factors influencing cohort members' persistence in staying in Quebec City. In this regard, we find rather puzzling the occupational structure of the fathers of never-married cohort members who were living with their parents in 1881 (data not shown) according to their presence or absence status in 1891. Indeed, it appears to be in the opposite direction to our expectation. Unlike the fathers' occupational distribution in 1871, skilled workers were more numerous among fathers who were no longer in Quebec City than among those still there (45% to 38%), as were skilled non-manual workers (12% to 9%), while those fathers who occupied unskilled manual jobs were notably more numerous among the persistent (35%) than among the absent families (27%). Only small entrepreneurs, and not statistically significantly, were more frequent among parents present in 1891 than among those absent. We return later to these unexpected patterns.

Demographic attributes of the original family in 1881 (see table 12.8) are partly consistent with the results for the 1871–81 decade regarding children's sex ratios and their participation in the paid workforce. Children attending school in 1881 were as much to be found in the families who had left by 1891 as in the ones still present in the city (with higher proportions of young women than men, especially for the non-francophones), and were working to a similar degree (much greater proportion of men working than women). As in 1871, many more Anglo-Protestant children were attending school than the children in other cultural groups, a larger portion of French Canadian single female youngsters were paid workers, and the child sex ratio for Irish Catholics was higher in the families that stayed than in the ones who left. However, some other results for 1881 show no consistent trends compared with the previous decade, especially regarding family sex ratio of the French Canadian children, which was quite a bit higher for persistent families than for absent ones. The patterns for families with single cohort members in 1891 are, nevertheless, quite consistent with what we might expect, regarding children's sex ratios and for the level of participation in the paid workforce. The family economies of Anglo-Protestants relied a good deal less on their children's earnings, while the proportions of paid workers among French Canadian and Irish Catholic children were much higher, with the daughters' contributions to a family economy being larger for the French.

Family ties are also evident in residential organization where married cohort members resided with their parents (data not tabulated): 8 per cent of cohort married women and 7 per cent of men lived as couples with their biological parents, another 7 per cent of married women had at least one surviving parent within their families and similarly for men, and another 26 per cent of couples resided next door to the parents of one or the other spouse (13% for both). Due to methodological differences in the processing of household structure, those figures are hardly comparable with the distributions obtained by Gordon Darroch and Michael Ornstein at the Canadian scale in 1871; let's just point out that their findings for stemlike family household were far fewer in their 1871

Table 12.8 · Quebec City sample cohort: Demographic profile of those who stayed and those who left, in 1881 and 1891, according to ethnoreligious group and presence status in 1891

		Anglo-Protestants		*French Canadians*		*Irish Catholics*		*Total*[a]	
	Presence status in 1891	*Present*	*Absent*	*Present*	*Absent*	*Present*	*Absent*	*Present*	*Absent*
Single children aged 15–29 years in original family (1881)	*n*	85	91	671	546	110	159	889	851
	Sex ratio	889	1,116	1,151	943	1,750	1,524	1,195	1,091
	% at school	16.5	19.8	11.6	11.9	7.3	11.9	11.5	12.3
	(women)	(20.0)	(32.6)	(14.7)	(12.8)	(12.5)	(20.6)	(15.1)	(16.0)
	% at work	42.4	45.1	59.0	55.9	51.8	50.9	56.5	54.1
	(women)	(13.3)	(4.7)	(28.2)	(30.6)	(10.0)	(15.9)	(24.2)	(24.8)
Single children aged 15–29 years in original family (1891)	*n*	43		263		65		382	
	Sex ratio	792		623		1,097		690	
	% at work	37.2		52.9		52.3		50.3	
	(women)	(8.3)		(31.5)		(22.6)		(27.0)	
Children in founded family (1891)	Families	6		127		12		148	
	Average *n* of children	2.5		2.7		2.1		2.6	

Source: PHSVQ, census micro-data, 1871–1911.

a Includes all ethnoreligious groups.

sample (3% for urban households), but they refer to all households while our findings refer to a specific moment in the life cycle of young couples.[26]

Taking these variables together in logistic regression, two main factors emerge as explanatory variables of the likelihood of a person being present in the 1891 census for Quebec City: ethnicity and occupation (data not shown). The first one is obviously related to the Irish exodus. Combined with occupation and other parameters, being Irish in 1881 increased two-fold the probability of leaving Quebec City by 1891. There is no surprise here given what has been said regarding both the ethnic segmentation of the labour market in the city and the serious problems that harbour activities faced in the 1870s and 1880s. Occupation is less obvious. Being engaged in an unskilled job in 1881 diminished the probability of being absent in 1891 by a third. To some extent, such a situation may be understood in the context of a second possible explanation regarding children's work in 1871, that is, that families able to count on some secure resources were more able than those without sufficient means to plan a move to some other place offering better opportunities. In this interpretation, assuming that occupational skills represent key family resources, families headed by unskilled workers can be expected to be more limited in their choices and may have had no alternative but to stay in City of Quebec since they simply did not have the means to leave. And, seemingly, just to survive, they really needed to be able to count on their children's earnings, however modest, and on their web of local social relationships (or social capital).

The Aggregate Generations: The 1891–1901 Decade

During the third decade of the study, our cohort members matured into established adults, likely in the middle of their lives, whether heading a still growing family, or as a prominent single member of their original family, or living on their own, alone, or with some unrelated co-resident(s). They were often fully integrated into the productive system, occupying jobs in which they had gained valuable experience, or managing a home that both sustained them and reproduced the city's labour force. In the intergenerational transmission process, they also began to be increasingly involved in the care of their aging parents. To meet all those familial and societal obligations, married members of the cohort might also have begun to count on their offspring's assistance. Thus, because of the resources required and because of the consequences for related individuals, leaving Quebec City became less and less an easy option to consider as a way of maintaining the family's well-being.

Modifying conditions are reflected in the persistence rates of cohort members. Three-quarters of the 1891 men and two-thirds of the women were found in the 1901 census. This difference is likely due, in large part, to marriages not celebrated within the city limits (changed names of married woman between two censuses) and to exogamous marriages (where the groom resided outside the city, with his bride following him after the marriage). Persistence rates also vary largely by ethnoreligious group. As in the 1880s, Irish Catholics experienced the highest absence rate (at 54%), which was double that of both French Canadians (26%) and Anglo-Protestants (27%), and again, contributing to the increasing French Canadian proportion of the sample (81% in 1901). The Irish rate is consistent with the continuing limited level of employment in harbour activities, despite some modest improvement in the local economy. In effect, probably thanks to the end of the crisis of the Atlantic economy and to the national policy instituted by the Canadian federal government, the 1891–1901 decade witnessed a higher population growth rate than previous decades (8%), with net migration even becoming slightly positive. Between 1881 and 1901, the number of industrial workers in the city grew from 7,500 to nearly 10,000, thanks especially to the leather sector (mostly shoes).[27] Apart from the two unlinked persons due to ambiguities and five deceased, the missing individuals left Quebec City as lone single individuals (16%), as single members within their original family (26%), or as members of a married couple (58%). According to life tables, the now absent lone individuals would have included five men and six women deceased during the decade, implying that five men and two women left on their own, a dramatic reduction compared with the previous decade. Among the 173 single cohort members in 1891 (104 women, 69 men), thirty-six women and twenty-seven men married prior to the next census. That would be the last significant decennial marriage movement within the cohort we are examining here.

Tables 12.9 and 12.10 show the data for both the decades 1891–1901 and 1901–11; the numbers for ethnoreligious groups other than French Canadian were very small and are not given here. The occupational structure of our male cohort in 1901 was quite representative of that of the males of Quebec City aged 39–41 years (data not shown here). Both groups were distributed quite evenly between the three higher-status categories with the modal one being that of skilled manual work. The difference is that for each of those four categories, the proportions were slightly smaller within the city than in the sample, leaving the last one (unskilled manual) rather underrepresented in the sample (21% against 29% in the city), likely reflecting the association between persistence in staying in Quebec City and upward occupational mobility. Unlike the decade 1881–91, the 1891 occupational structure of cohort members remaining in the city in 1901 differs in relative terms from the absentees' occupational distribution, in a way that could be expected (unskilled labourers leave in higher proportions). However, the numbers for those who left are so small that any conclusive assertion would be hazardous. Still, the progression in occupational

Table 12.9 · Quebec City sample, males: Occupational profile (*n* and %) in 1891, 1901, and 1911 of those who stayed and those who left, according to ethnoreligious group and presence status in 1901 and 1911[a]

		1891–1901 decade, n (%)						1901–1911 decade, n (%)					
		French Canadians Presence status in 1901			Total Presence status in 1901			French Canadians Presence status in 1911			Total Presence status in 1911		
		Present		Absent	Present		Absent	Present		Absent	Present		Absent
	Situation in ...	*1901*	*1891*	*1891*	*1901*	*1891*	*1891*	*1911*	*1901*	*1901*	*1911*	*1901*	*1901*
Occupation	Skilled non-manuals	15	7	4	21	9	4	13	11	4	17	16	5
(all marital status)		(13.6)	(6.1)	(13.8)	(14.6)	(6.2)	(8.2)	(21.0)	(16.4)	(9.3)	(22.7)	(18.8)	(8.6)
	Unskilled non-manuals	12	12	4	17	20	9	4	7	5	5	10	7
		(10.9)	(10.5)	(13.8)	(11.8)	(13.7)	(18.4)	(6.5)	(10.4)	(11.6)	(6.7)	(11.8)	(12.1)
	Small entrepreneurs	14	17	1	18	20	2	6	10	4	8	12	7
		(12.7)	(14.9)	(3.4)	(12.5)	(13.7)	(4.1)	(9.7)	(14.9)	(9.3)	(10.7)	(14.1)	(12.1)
	Skilled manuals	49	49	10	57	54	16	21	28	21	24	30	25
		(44.5)	(43.0)	(34.5)	(39.6)	(37.0)	(32.7)	(33.9)	(41.8)	(48.8)	(32.0)	(35.3)	(43.1)
	Unskilled manuals	20	28	10	31	41	18	18	11	9	21	17	14
		(18.2)	(24.6)	(34.5)	(21.5)	(28.1)	(36.7)	(29.0)	(16.4)	(20.9)	(28.0)	(20.0)	(24.1)
	At school		1 (0.9)			2 (!.14)							
	Valid *N* (100.0%)	110	114	29	144	146	49	62	67	43	75	85	58
Occupational	Upward	20 (18.3)			26 (18.6)			9 (14.8)			10 (13.5)		
mobility[b]	Downward	7 (6.4)			8 (5.7)			12 (19.7)			14 (18.9)		

Source: PHSVQ, census micro-data, 1871–1911.

a Occupations of women cohort not shown because only 22% declared an occupation in 1891, 14% in 1901, and 9% in both years; b 100% = *N* of individuals whose occupation is known in both years.

Table 12.10 · Quebec City sample cohort: Demographic profile of those who stayed and those who left, in 1891, 1901, and 1911, according to ethnoreligious group and presence status in 1901 and 1911

		1891–1901 decade						*1901–1911 decade*					
		French Canadians Presence status in 1901			*Total[a] Presence status in 1901*			*French Canadians Presence status in 1911*			*Total[a] Presence status in 1911*		
		Present		*Absent*	*Present*		*Absent*	*Present*		*Absent*	*Present*		*Absent*
	Situation in . . .	*1901*	*1891*	*1891*	*1901*	*1891*	*1891*	*1911*	*1901*	*1901*	*1911*	*1901*	*1901*
Single children aged ≥ 15 years in original families	*n*	98	188	75	125	243	139	29	72	37	33	91	54
	Sex ratio	463	621	630	471	688	695	318	385	850	320	400	800
	% at work	55.1	53.7	50.7	52.0	50.6	49.6	41.4	50.0	56.3	37.5	48.3	52.1
	(women)	(35.8)	(32.8)	(28.3)	(30.6)	(27.8)	(25.6)	(31.8)	(34.7)	(26.3)	(28.0)	(30.6)	(20.7)
Children in founded families	Families	149	102	25	177	116	32	100	122	36	117	130	47
	Average *n* of children	4.5	2.7	2.5	4.4	2.6	2.6	4.9	4.7	4.0	4.8	4.5	4.1
	Aged ≥ 10 years	254	b	b	285	b	b	227	192	60	265	207	76
	Sex ratio	1,065			1,065			1,340	1,157	875	1,304	1,134	949
	% at school	59.5			60.1			15.5	59.7	61.0	16.0	60.2	61.3
	(girls)	(58.5)			(58.7)			(8.3)	(60.7)	(56.3)	(10.5)	(58.8)	(61.5)
	% at work	23.8			22.6			55.8	24.1	20.3	55.0	22.3	21.3
	(girls)	(17.9)			(15.9)			(40.6)	(19.1)	(9.4)	(38.6)	(17.5)	(7.7)

Source: PHSVQ, census microdata, 1871–1911.

a Includes all ethnoreligious groups; b < 20.

history gives some indication of influence, the shift in ten years witnessing a notable displacement towards higher occupational categories. For the 140 male cohort members for whom occupations are known in both 1891 and 1901 (109 for the French Canadians), we find their mobility moves very neatly upwards.

Regarding children's participation in the labour market (see table 12.10), the results are consistent with the preceding ones, despite the diminishing number of children in the original families, which makes definitive conclusions difficult (especially for the non-French). There was very little overall variation between the families of single cohort members in 1891 whether they are still in Quebec City in 1901 or not. The clearer difference was between cultural groups, French Canadians and Irish Catholics still counting more on their children's paid labour than Anglo-Protestants, a difference mostly due to the work of daughters. For the French Canadians especially, the sex ratio among children at this point was rather lower for the families that stayed than for the families that left, reflecting as much the aging of the cohort members, as the high level of singlehood among the women members. Those patterns were accentuated in 1901. The image of single "unemployed" women responsible for household domestic tasks and the care of their aging parents (and maybe remaining siblings), thus, appears more and more clearly once they have passed their 30th birthday. This more focused and lasting interdependence between generations within nuclear families is also revealed for the married cohort members. There were fewer couples living within their parents' household in 1901 (3%) than in 1891, reflecting the increasing economic independence of couples and the increasing mortality of their parents. Nevertheless, a quarter of the married cohort members had at least one surviving parent residing with them, as many men's parents as women's, a proportion that is a good deal higher than it was in 1891.

Entering all the basic variables into the logistic regression at once results in only one significant factor – being an Irish Catholic – that appears to have modified the odds of a person being absent over the decade, which increased four-fold the probability of an individual not persisting in Quebec City to 1901. These restricted effects reveal the limits of crude census data as predictors of persistence when the group under study becomes more heterogeneous (increasing variation in marital statuses, in household composition, and so on). If we had been able to add to the model a range of specific, derived variables, we surely would have improved the fit and predictive capacity of the results.

Thinking of Children: The 1901–11 Decade

During the 1901–11 decade, our cohort of women and men reached or were in their 40s. Men were at their peak occupational skills; however, they would have begun to feel the effects of age and years of heavy work. Women would soon stop bearing children (or likely were, at least, hoping to do so) and waited for the moment when child care would be less overwhelming. If parents still counted on their children to help with the demands of everyday family life, they surely also worried about launching them into independent lives. In fact, these cohort members were at a similar stage in their life course as their own parents were when we selected them for this study, but now in an improved economic context. Moving away from Quebec City was still an option, but was considered as much for the prospects of their offspring as for their own benefit. Regarding the context, the city's economy offered wider opportunities at the beginning of the twentieth century: clothing industries (among them corsets) and services, in particular, had expanded the labour market, and population growth reached 13 per thousand in the new century's first decade, a rate not witnessed since the 1850s.

Even though the overall local conditions were improved, persistence rates for our cohort stayed quite stable. Between 1901 and 1911, seven out of ten of the women and six out of ten of the men remained in Quebec City; these proportions rose to four-fifths and two-thirds, respectively, if we take estimated mortality into account. Again, persistence rates varied strongly according to ethnoreligious affiliation, from 80 per cent for the Anglo-Protestants to 73 per cent for the French Canadian and 47 per cent for the Irish, the latter group still showing an absentee rate at least two times higher than for the other groups. The Irish haemorrhage thus continued, principally due to the continuing decline of harbour activities related to the wood products sector; for example, wood exports continued to fall at the beginning of the twentieth century, from 160 million board feet in 1900 to less than 60 million board feet by 1910.[28] In addition to the five individuals not found due to ambiguous links and the eleven deceased, a quarter of the absentees left while they were still single, mostly along with their remaining families, and three-quarters of them left married, mostly men. This last result may be compared with what happened in the previous decades. In fact, if the married cohort members were in 1901 at similar stages in their life course as their parents were in 1871, we may expect to find similar outmigration rates for this subgroup. Actually, however, 86 per cent of 1881 absentees left with their original families, a good deal higher rate than the proportion in 1901–11. However, since this rate was only 58 per cent in the 1891–1901 decade, it shows that even better economic conditions do not completely change life-course related migration dynamics. With regard to outmigration, it is worth noting further that according to marriage records for the period 1891–1910, the marriage fields (and thus likely the migration fields) did not change from the 1871–90 period, with Anglo-Protestants still favouring

Canadian destinations outside Quebec, and the Irish and French Canadians favouring the Unites States, with New England the destination of 70 per cent of the latter.

The 1911 occupational structure for male cohort members (see table 12.9) differs in some ways from all of Quebec City's males aged 49–51 (not shown). Although the numbers are quite small, we find that if proportions within upper-status categories were similar (2% to 3% discrepancies), the gaps were more sizable for the two lower-status groups: 38 per cent in the sample compared with 30 per cent of the entire city's skilled manual workers and 21 per cent versus 30 per cent for unskilled manual labourers. Such differences were likely due to the duration of residence within Quebec City, which was shorter for the general population than for the cohort members, who in addition had experienced upward occupational mobility in previous decades. Again, for this decade, the 1901 occupational structure of those in the cohort who were present in 1911 does not differ significantly from those who were absent. Moreover, this time, occupational mobility seems to have played no role, since there is no obvious trend for the seventy-four persons for whom occupations are known for both 1901 and 1911 (61 were French Canadians). The few cases of mobility were even downward, something rather unexpected, but hardly conclusive given the small numbers. For female cohort members, occupations were seldom registered, even for singles, and are known for only eleven of them, almost all of whom were skilled manual workers (milliners and seamstresses), but included one unskilled manual labourer (manufacturing employee) and one woman running a boarding house. Seven of these women were single, one was widowed, and three were married (but two were listed without enumerated husbands). The nineteen other single women declared no occupation. Altogether, thirteen single women were living with one or both parents while eleven others were living with one or more siblings; as in 1901, this residential pattern was a good deal more common for women than for the men. For married cohort members, intergenerational co-residence was still frequent, a quarter having one or another parent living with them (more frequently the mother). If the co-residence proportion was still high if not actually increasing, kin-related neighbours were less and less common, and none was found in 1911, as if it were the case that for established couples familial solidarities no longer required close residential propinquity.

An examination of demographic characteristics (table 12.10) generally supports the preceding interpretation. For cohort members still within their original families, even among the few remaining in Quebec City in 1901, the sex ratio among the children was consistent with what was expected, that is, generally low and still lower for the persistent families over the decade. We find a different pattern for the families founded by the cohort members. The sex ratio among their children aged 10 years and over in 1901 was higher in the families that were still in Quebec City in 1911 than for the ones that had left (considering only French Canadians, since numbers for other groups are too small), a result that is contrary to what may have been expected considering the economic structure favouring female work. But, like in previous decades, children within persistent families attended school in higher proportions and took part in the paid labour force in smaller proportions than children within the families that were no longer in Quebec City. In 1911, persistent families reveal an even higher sex ratio for teenagers and adult children. This is, of course, partly due to older ages at marriage for men, but that is not a sufficient explanation. Perhaps it is simply that the better economic conditions generated more job opportunities for members of urban families, no matter what the gender of their children. It is worth noting, too, that the gap in the proportion of working children was narrowed between the Anglo-Protestant group and the two others, despite the fact that the proportion of working girls was also reduced.

As in the case the previous decades, logistic regression employing just the enumerated 1901 variables only identifies ethnicity as a predictive factor for being present in the city in 1911. No other direct variable provides a significant odds ratio. But as we noted earlier, the results of such a multivariate model might be quite different if we included historically and theoretically specified derived variables.

Conclusion

Despite the challenges, following 1,500 individuals over a forty-year time span through these rich data for Quebec City yields valuable insights into the social and spatial dynamics affecting individuals and families within a wider urban economic and cultural context and on a very fine scale. Were their migratory destinies written in the sky? Or did they have some control of them? One could answer "yes" – or "no" – to both questions. From an individual point of view, their childhood (the 1871–81 decade) experiences were linked to their parents' conditions and strategies and, thus, in this sense, they had no control at all on their own destiny. Certainly, they were elements of their families' life situations and taken into account in the formulating of family strategies, but as children, they had little say in the actual decisions. Getting older, they gained some relative autonomy in terms of their "value" as a family resource, put into service on behalf of the family's material and social well-being; in other terms, they became a form of "capital," as valuable as their talent and training (in the house, in school, in a factory, or somewhere else). That is likely why so many young men (and some girls) left the city alone in their 20s, earning their own wages outside of Quebec City, but remitting some of them to help with their family's needs. Often being "strangers" in some other city, these transients indeed unwillingly fuelled the perception that their contemporaries had of a floating proletariat jeopardizing the stability of the urban industrializing world. From a family economy perspective, however, the mobility of these young adult children was a consequence of the necessary flexibility of the family to ensure its maintenance. This family-centred, ultimate aim leads to what Gordon Darroch calls the "family and community auspices of migration" or Gérard Bouchard, the "dynamique communautaire."[29] If they remained in the city and married, the members of our cohort were quickly faced with an array of circumstances that their parents also faced when they were children. However, they also had lower outmigration rates because they had acquired more experience in the local, urban context than their parents' generation earlier and, probably, were able to take advantage of wider social and economic networks. The fact that the local economy improved compared with the 1870s and 1880s surely also promoted the diminution of outmigration.

The unexpected character of the comparisons between the occupational distributions of those who left and those who were still in Quebec City over the decades is probably the most surprising aspect of this study. We expected that those who left would be in families affected by more fragile and insecure conditions. The occupational distribution in 1871 was consistent with that notion, but for subsequent decades not as clearly, especially the 1881–91 decade, when French Canadian unskilled manual workers were more numerous among the cohort members still present than among the absent ones, a distribution that is similar for the fathers of the cohort members. Other sources have been entered through the PHVSQ project, such as the 1871 and 1901 city directories and the 1901 tax roll; however, as for the more complete occupational information given by the censuses for 1901 onwards (place of work, self-employment, wages), we made the choice of using only consistent variables through the whole period. Since we rely on the simple census occupation titles to assess economic positions, we may not fully recognize changed economic circumstances in these data; it is possible that if we enlisted complementary sources, we would discover a more nuanced picture.

The repetition of the unexpected distributions through time must be considered seriously. The main reason we can imagine such historical consistency in this respect follows from a recognition of the resources needed to migrate. Moving demands some means: some cash to pay for transportation, a place to reside at the destination, some cash to pay for a new beginning in a new location. Thus, the poorest are least likely to be able to afford to move. The fact that those who moved were counting on their children's earning capacity in greater proportions than the families who stayed supports this idea. It is also consistent with previous research that we conducted on rural-to-urban movement to Quebec City. Using the 1901 census question on the type of place of birth (rural or urban) as an indicator of movement to the city, our previous research showed that a good share of the in-migration was not undertaken by the poorest rural dwellers, but by those who were already enjoying decent living standards, those, in other words, who could count on enough resources to consider a decision to migrate.[30] That result is consistent with what has been reported for Quebec City outmigrants: those who have more to offer on the labour market (skilled workers) were more likely to integrate into any growing urban economy than other workers and they were more likely to have the financial resources to move. Finally, regarding the local, urban context, a parallel could be drawn with our knowledge of the process of rural exodus. The classical works on rural depopulation show that labour surpluses in the countryside do not leave all at once, skilled and unskilled, manual and non-manual workers. Rather, the more fragile portion leaves first, that is, the farm labourers, departing when they can still have enough resources to do so or are simply forced to. In Quebec City, the local economy began to suffer seriously during the 1860s. Thus, the most insecure part of the workforce was likely to be among the first to leave, in the late 1860s and the 1870s, a tendency that may be reflected in the 1871–81 absentees' occupational structure.

The results also shed some light on the evolution of Quebec City's demographic composition. On the cultural side, the growing French Canadianization of the city did not occur following similar non-French outmigration processes. The Irish Catholics and the Anglo-Protestants experienced sharply different itineraries out of the city. After the sudden decrease in numbers in the 1870s, accompanying the loss of the city's administrative functions, the Anglo-Protestants had high persistence rates thanks to their better socio-economic status within the urban fabric. For their part, the Irish Catholic community experienced a much harder transition. Constrained to the lower levels of the occupational structure, most of them had to take advantage of their migratory experience to leave for urban settings offering better economic opportunities, especially for the harbour workers, as revealed by the works of P. Bischoff.[31] For most of them, Quebec City had simply been the North American gateway to their transatlantic voyage. Finally, the French Canadians, if they experienced higher persistence rates, were nevertheless, affected by an important turnover, urban families being attracted by US industrial towns in numbers similar to their rural co-nationals. Only at the end of the period were they rather less likely to leave, but at about the same rates as the Anglo-Protestants.

If the cohort that we have followed for over forty years for this chapter is considered a starting point, much remains to be done to provide a full picture of Quebec City's population during its industrializing period, hopefully with more complete biographical material drawn both from censuses and from vital records in order to control for the familial dimension of households' strategies. From a geographical point of view, for instance, it would be possible to study family clustering and spatial relationships (or the family as a territorial agency), something rather unexplored in North American historiography. Or, from a demographic point of view, it would be possible, too, to get a better idea of the transitions in reproductive behaviour according to cultural community affiliations. In each instance, what has been accomplished for Montreal (especially by Olson and Thornton) will provide highly valuable points of reference, as will the studies of other regions and industrial towns (e.g., Saint-Hyacinthe, Sherbrooke, Trois-Rivières), deepening our comprehension of the history of how Quebec society was made.

Notes

1 The authors are grateful to Catherine Chabot, Marie-Ève Harton, and Jeannette Larouche for their assistance with the preparation of this chapter. The research was funded by the Fonds québécois de recherche sur la société et la culture (FQRSC) through its grant to the Population et histoire sociale de la ville de Québec project (www.phsvq.cieq.ulaval.ca).

2 It is impossible to give a short list of references regarding social and spatial mobility, especially in the context of industrialization and growing urbanization. Some large "new" social history research projects were initiated in the 1960s and 1970s for a number of US metropolis, using census microdata, city directories, and assessment rolls to examine the topic. For a review of those pioneering works in their day, see Lawrence E. Hazelrigg, "Occupational Mobility in Nineteenth-Century U.S. Cities: A Review of Some Evidence," *Social Forces* 53, no. 1 (1974): 21–32; for another good review of the subject, see Howard P. Chudacoff, "A Reconsideration of Geographical Mobility in American Urban History," *Virginia Magazine of History and Biography* 102, no. 4 (1994): 501–18. For a European example, see Sune Akerman, "Swedish Migration and Social Mobility: The Tale of Three Cities," *Social Science History* 1, no. 2 (1977): 178–209.

3 Migration, household organization, and family history during industrialization are topics that have led to a huge scholarly production and naming some authors is surely unfair to a lot of others; however, one cannot ignore the works of Tamara Hareven, especially her *Families, History, and Social Change: Life-Course and Cross-Cultural Perspectives* (Boulder, CO: Westview Press, 2000). In Quebec and Canada, some authors who must be cited for cities include the following: on Hamilton, Ontario, Michael Katz, *The People of Hamilton, Canada West: Family*

and Class in a Mid-Nineteenth-Century City (Cambridge, MA: Harvard University Press, 1975); on Montreal, Bettina Bradbury, *Familles ouvrières à Montréal: Âge, genre et survie quotidienne pendant la phase d'industrialisation* (Montreal: Boréal, 1995), as well as the inspiring and major very recent contribution on Montreal by Sherry Olson and Patricia Thornton, *Peopling the North American City: Montreal, 1840–1900* (Montreal and Kingston: McGill-Queen's University Press, 2011); and on Saint-Hyacinthe, Peter Gossage, *Families in Transition: Industry and Population in Nineteenth-Century Saint-Hyacinthe* (Montreal and Kingston: McGill-Queen's University Press, 1999). For rural or semi-urban settings, see Gérard Bouchard on the Saguenay region, at least, *Quelques arpents d'Amérique: Population, économie, famille au Saguenay (1838–1971)* (Montreal: Boréal, 1996).

4 On the economic restructuring of the city, see chapters 8 and 13 of Marc Vallières, Yvon Desloges, Fernand Harvey, Andrée Héroux, Réginald Auger, and Sophie-Laurence Lamontagne, *Histoire de Québec et sa région*, vol. II, *1792–1939* (Quebec: Presses de l'Université Laval, 2008). On the transformation of its stagnating population, see Marc St-Hilaire and Richard Marcoux, "Le ralentissement démographique," in S. Courville and R. Garon (eds.), *Québec: Ville et capitale* (Quebec: Presses de l'Université Laval, 2010), 172–9.

5 On names variations within birth, marriage, and death records, see, e.g., Gérard Bouchard and Raymond Roy, "Les variations nominatives dans les registres paroissiaux du Saguenay," *Annales de démographie historique* 89 (1982): 354–68.

6 See Olson and Thornton, *Peopling the North American City*; Danielle Gauvreau and Sherry Olson, "Mobilité sociale dans une ville industrielle nord-américaine: Montréal, 1880–1900," *Annales de démographie historique* 115 (2008): 89–114.

7 St-Hilaire and Marcoux, "Le ralentissement démographique," 174.

8 See Olson and Thornton, *Peopling the North American City*; Gauvreau and Olson, "Mobilité sociale." Jason Gilliland used a subset of these data to study residential mobility in Montreal between 1861 and 1901; see his "Modeling Residential Mobility in Montreal, 1860–1900," *Historical Methods* 31, no. 1 (1998): 27–42. The biographies that Gilliland used are richer, especially for economic dimensions of family biographies, than the ones we use here.

9 For an example on the benefit of using individual biographies enhanced by kin relations and other social and economic information, see Sherry Olson, "'Pour se créer un avenir': Stratégies de couples montréalais au XIXe siècle," *Revue d'histoire de l'Amérique française* 51, no. 3 (1998): 357–89. For Quebec City, a pilot project is under way to develop the methodology to link the seven censuses (1852–1911) to the BALSAC population register. See Marc St-Hilaire and Hélène Vézina, "Between Household and Family: The Use of Marriage Records to Link Census Data (Quebec City, 1852–1911)," unpublished paper presented at the RECORDLINK Workshop, University of Guelph, May 2010. The data work for this chapter was conducted for that work.

10 Gauvreau and Olson, "Mobilité sociale," 108. In Quebec City, differences follow the same pattern in 1901. For details regarding schooling and work among Quebec City's children in 1901, see Richard Marcoux, "Entre l'école et la fabrique:

Une analyse exploratoire de la fréquentation scolaire et du travail des enfants dans la ville de Québec en 1901," in Maria Cosio, Richard Marcoux, Marc Pilon, and André Quesnel (eds.), *Éducation, famille et dynamiques démographiques* (Paris: CIRED, 2003), 125–51.

11 The overall percentages of paid working girls in Quebec City are of the same order as in Montreal at the same census. See Bradbury, *Familles ouvrières*, 171–4.

12 For 1881, see Gauvreau and Olson, "Mobilité sociale," 95–6; for 1901, see Olson and Thornton, *Peopling the North American City.*

13 Younger ages at marriage for French Canadians have already been noted in Montreal by Bradbury, *Familles ouvrières*, 67–71; and by Sherry Olson and Patricia Thornton, "Familles montréalaises du XIXe siècle: Trois cultures, trois trajectoires," *Cahiers québécois de démographie* 21, no. 2 (1992): 67.

14 Olson, "'Pour se créer un avenir,'" 12–13; Bradbury, *Familles ouvrières*, 85–8; Hareven, *Families, History, and Social Change.*

15 Gilliland, "Modeling Residential Mobility."

16 Based on Erickson, Goldthorpe, and Portocarrero, seven class categories, as reported in Charles Fleury, *Les classes d'Erickson, Goldthorpe et Portocarrero (EGP)* (Quebec: Programme PHSVQ, 2000).

17 For a more detailed presentation of the urban occupational structure between 1871 and 1901 and its spatial distribution, see Nicolas Lanouette, "Québec comme laboratoire urbain: Transformations socioprofessionnelles et industrialisation dans la ville de Québec, 1871–1901," *Cahiers de géographie du Québec* 52, no. 145 (2008): 43–61.

18 Mobility within the Saguenay region (1901–21) was strongly influenced by the composition of the family, with the sex ratio for children over 9 years old (boys to girls) among mobile couples being 21% higher among those going to the pioneer fringe than among those going to the city. See Marc St-Hilaire, *Peuplement et dynamique migratoire au Saguenay, 1840–1960* (Quebec: Presses de l'Université Laval, 1996), 196–8. It is suggested, too, by Sylvester's finding, using the 1901 place of birth census question: the odds that rural-born women would have lived in an urban setting were 21% higher than for men in 1901. See Kenneth Sylvester, "Rural to Urban Migration: Finding Household Complexity in a New World Environment," in Eric E. Sager and Peter Baskerville (eds.), *Household Counts: Canadian Households and Families in 1901* (Toronto: University of Toronto Press, 2007), 147–79, esp. 160–3.

19 See Bradbury for Montreal, in *Familles ouvrières*, 153–66.

20 Higher urban migration rates for younger people are well documented, especially for single males. For families, it was also the case in the Saguenay, where 40% of newly married couples moved within their first ten years of common life. See St-Hilaire, *Peuplement et dynamique migratoire*, 164–5.

21 See Bradbury, *Familles ouvrières*, 67–9.

22 See Vallières et al., *Histoire de Québec*, vol. II, 1097–9.

23 See Marc St-Hilaire, "Espace économique et espace social dans le Québec du XIXe siècle: De la vie de relation aux réseaux de sociabilité," in Yves Frenette,

Martin Pâquet, and Jean Lamarre (eds.), *Les parcours de l'histoire: Hommage à Yves Roby* (Quebec: Presses de l'Université Laval, 2002), 176–7.

24 See Jean Lamarre, "La présence des Canadiens français dans le Midwest américain, 1860–1930: Une évaluation," in T. Wien, C. Vidal, and Y. Frenette (eds.), *De Québec à l'Amérique française: Histoire et mémoire* (Quebec: Presses de l'Université Laval, 2006), 530–45, 540; and Bruno Ramirez, with the collaboration of Yves Otis, *La Ruée vers le Sud: Migrations du Canada vers les États-Unis, 1840–1930* (Montreal: Boréal, 2003).

25 See the classical studies by Stephan Thernstrom (on Boston: *The Other Bostonians; Poverty and Progress in the American Metropolis, 1880–1970* (Cambridge, MA: Harvard University Press, 1973), Howard Chudacoff (on Omaha: *Mobile Americans: Residential and Social Mobility in Omaha, 1880–1920* (New York: Oxford University Press, 1972), and Michael Katz (*The People of Hamilton*). For an early instance, see Alwyn Barr, "Occupational and Geographic Mobility in San Antonio, 1870–1900," *Social Science Quarterly* 51, no. 2 (1970): 396–403.

26 See G. Darroch and M. Ornstein, "Family Co-residence in Canada in 1871: Family Life Cycles, Occupations, and Networks of Mutual Aid," *Historical Papers/Communications historiques* 18, no. 1 (1983): 30–55.

27 See Vallières et al., *Histoire de Québec*, vol. II, 1146–8.

28 Ibid., 1002–4.

29 A. Gordon Darroch, "Migrants in the Nineteenth Century: Fugitives or Families in Motion?" *Journal of Family History* 6, no. 3 (1981): 257–77. Gérard Bouchard, "La dynamique communautaire et l'évolution des sociétés rurales québécoises aux 19e et 20e siècles: Construction d'un modèle," *Revue d'histoire de l'Amérique française* 40, no. 1 (1986): 51–71; the model has been developed based on data relating to rural settings; nevertheless, the model is applicable to urban society. Both articles examine mobility in both rural and urban contexts to show how migrations are dictated by the goals of the family and not primarily by those of the individual.

30 Those results have not been published yet. Marc St-Hilaire and Richard Marcoux, "Spatial and Social Integration of Rural Dwellers to the City: Quebec City, 1901," paper presented at the Social Science History Association Conference, St Louis, Missouri, 2002.

31 Peter C. Bischoff, *Les débardeurs au port de Québec: Tableau des luttes syndicales, 1831–1902* (Montreal: Hurtubise, 2009).

PART V

Markets and Mobility: Class, Ethnicity, Gender

— · 13 · —

Labour Market Dynamics in Canada, 1891–1911: A First Look from New Census Samples

KRIS INWOOD, MARY MacKINNON, AND CHRIS MINNS[1]

The decades spanning the transition from the nineteenth to twentieth centuries saw dynamic changes in the size and structure of North American labour markets.[2] In both Canada and the United States, international and internal migration altered demographic profiles and the spatial distribution of the population. Rapid expansion took place in the cities and in previously thinly settled regions, particularly western Canada. The Canadian population rose by more than 50 per cent between 1891 and 1911, while the population of urban areas more than doubled.[3] Newcomers fuelled much of the growth, as North America experienced a substantial surge in immigration from 1891 to 1911, with Canada receiving historically unprecedented numbers of immigrants from 1903 onwards.[4] Immigration possibilities are usually thought of as being attractive mainly to unskilled young workers, but improving school attendance in both Britain and the rest of Europe expanded the numbers of potential emigrants with some education. In Canada, too, educational attainment rose with the expansion of school provision and the establishment of an increasing number of secondary schools.

These supply changes were accompanied by changes on the demand side. In the United States, Claudia Goldin and Lawrence Katz argue, skill-biased technological change in the early twentieth century created a particularly rapid growth in the numbers of workers in sectors using new technology and methods, with a supply response following in fairly short order.[5] We might expect a similar, if somewhat lagged, pattern in Canada. Skill shortages would have been most acute in newly settled and rapidly growing western Canada. Moreover, increases in the size of firms in many sectors suggest that Canada experienced an expansion and articulation of managerial activities and changes in the organization of firms with additional implications for the structure of pay.[6]

Scholars already have generated evidence on the patterns of wages, earnings, and skill premia in Canada for this period.[7] For the most part, however, the available data have not allowed the identification of earnings and employment outcomes associated with personal characteristics that are of interest. Indeed, for the earlier years, wage data are largely limited to blue-collar workers in the manufacturing or construction sectors. The age of workers, for example, is particularly relevant to understanding the structure of occupations and pay and the effect of changes in labour supply and demand. Young workers with recent education and fewer job-specific skills, for example, may have benefited disproportionately from technological change that increased the demand for new skills.[8] It is known that around the turn of the century schools increased both the technical training they offered and secondary school academic subjects but the consequences for young workers are so far unknown.[9] The impact of immigration is likely to have varied with skill and age. Differences in cohort size have implications for earnings patterns. Changes in demand, and the extent of human capital investment both before and after entering employment, affect how employment and especially earnings capacity evolves with age, as well as differences between cohorts at any point in time.

Hitherto, we have not been able to document the long-run effects of these and other changing labour market conditions because life-cycle evidence has been lacking. Very recently, however, large random samples from successive Canadian censuses have been constructed. The new data open a window that allows, for the first time, a more comprehensive examination of occupational and earnings dynamics in Canada before the First World War.

In this chapter, we trace the evolution of employment and earnings in Canada over two decades using random samples of the censuses of 1891, 1901, and 1911. The availability of successive cross-sections of the Census of Canada supports an exploration of career dynamics for synthetic cohorts of both Canadians and foreign-born men. We document the evolution of occupations and earnings for the largest groups of Canadian workers, and examine how the spatial distribution of workers changed during this time of rapid population growth. The 1901 and 1911 censuses are particularly valuable because they asked respondents to report earnings. We use this information to describe changes to the structure of wages for male workers. We identify the wage implications of individual characteristics; document how pay was related to ethnicity, religion, and national origin; and analyse how these relationships evolved between 1901 and 1911. We also use evidence on the occupational and spatial composition of cohorts to compute a preliminary estimate of the sources of earnings growth over the life cycle. Our goals are to identify the broad patterns that will frame the direction of future research and to provide preliminary evidence on issues that invite more intensive investigation.

Representative samples have been drawn from the 1891, 1901, and 1911 censuses of Canada. The Canadian Families Project (CFP), headquartered at the University of Victoria, created a 5 per cent sample from the 1901 census.[10] The Canadian Century Research Infrastructure (CCRI) project, led by a team at the University of Ottawa, constructed a 5 per cent sample of the 1911 census.[11] The University of Guelph built the 1891 sample with a general density of 5 per cent (10% for the western provinces and eastern cities of Toronto, Montreal, and Halifax).[12] The 1901 sample has been available since 2003; the 1911 data became available in 2010; and the 1891 sample was completed in 2011. Given the rapid population increase of the first decade of the twentieth century, especially in western Canada, the number of working-age adults is much larger in the 1911 sample than for the earlier samples.

In all cases, individual dwellings provide the sample points. Enumeration was broadly similar although some differences in the census questions influence our handling of the data. Earnings and hours of work are reported in 1901 and 1911 but not 1891. As we will see below, about 80 per cent of production workers reported earnings in both 1901 and 1911. Hours of work are provided by the majority of employees in 1911, but not in 1901; intertemporal earnings comparisons are, therefore, made on the basis of annual earnings rather than the hourly wage.

Occupations are reported in all three censuses but the nature of the enumerations and procedures used to code occupations varies. The instructions to enumerators for acceptable occupational responses became much more elaborate in 1891, and remained more directing than in earlier censuses. The contemporary processing of data into reportable categories of occupation is visible through the codes introduced post-enumeration onto the manuscript pages in 1891 and 1911. The teams constructing data during the past ten years have brought the occupations into various modern classification systems based on the original alpha strings recorded by enumerators.

The 1901 team cast their data into a standard format based on a 1989 Statistics Canada Classification and Dictionary of Occupations (itself an adaptation of ISCO categories), organized around twenty-seven two-digit categories. The 1891 and 1911 samples implement versions of a classification system introduced by the 1950 United States census (and available for all historical census samples in that country).[13] The 1950 system recognizes nine major occupational groups. Its implementation on 1891 data involves a larger number of subcategories reflecting the variety of occupational strings returned by enumerators. As we are mainly interested in broad changes in the Canadian labour market, for the present chapter, we have collapsed the occupational structure into seven broad categories: professional occupations and proprietors, clerical jobs, craft workers, operatives, service workers, farm workers, and labourers. For 1911, we are unable to separate farm labourers from farm managers or owner-operators.

Changes in Regional Labour Supply, 1891–1911

We begin our analysis by considering changes in the relative supply of labour across Canada. The arrival of internal and international migrants in locations offering high earnings would, all else being equal, lead to reduced wage premia in locations where labour demand was initially high. Interregional migration offered an avenue for individuals to move to high-wage regions and to realize significant earnings growth over time. Changing location may have coincided with a movement from one occupational sector to another – leaving farm work to become a city store or bank clerk, for example.[14] For much of the later nineteenth century, these kinds of moves were often associated with emigration from Canada to the United States. Between 1870 and 1900, the number of Canadian-born individuals living in the United States increased by 240 per cent – and then not at all from 1900 to 1910.[15] The change in migrant pattern reflects, in part, the opening of the Canadian west which expanded the range of in-country choices for the footloose, and even allowed some expatriate Canadians to return to Canada.[16] Migration towards the Canadian west, of course, was associated with an expansion of prairie agriculture. Although the pecuniary returns to homesteading in the west are difficult to measure, it is clear that from the mid-1890s western farming was increasingly attractive to eastern Canadians.

We document the regional distribution of the adult male labour force in table 13.1. We focus on three large groups: Ontario-born anglophones, Quebec-born francophones, and the foreign-born (most of whom came from the United Kingdom). Ontario anglophones are the largest group of native English-speakers in Canada. The range of service and industrial employment within Ontario increased considerably in this period, and a good number of the locally born also migrated to western Canada and to the United States. Most Canadian francophones came from Quebec. Evidence of an earnings disadvantage for Montreal francophones stretches back to the early nineteenth century.[17] The foreign-born in Canada were primarily of British origin. This is particularly true of those arriving before 1901, a group that we will focus on in order to trace post-arrival economic mobility. Cross-sectional analysis of economic

Table 13.1 · Male labour force: Ontario-born, Quebec-born, anglophones and francophones, and foreign-born, by age group and by province or region, Canada, 1891–1911

	British Columbia	*Northwest*	*Manitoba*	*Ontario*	*Quebec*	*Maritimes*
1891						
All	3	2	4	46	28	18
O-born, A	1	1	4	92	1	0.1
Q-born, Fr	0.2	0.1	1	5	93	0.3
F-born	10	4	8	61	12	7
1901						
All	5	4	5	42	28	16
O-born, A	2	2	6	88	1	0.1
O-born, A, 21–25 yrs	2	3	7	87	1	0.2
O-born, A, 26–30 yrs	3	3	7	86	1	0.1
O-born, A, 31–35 yrs	3	3	8	84	1	0.3
Q-born, Fr	0.2	0.5	1	5	93	0.5
F-born	17	12	11	44	12	5
F-born, arrived 1891–1901, 21–30 yrs	31	21	16	18	11	3
1911						
All	9	14	7	34	24	11
O-born, A	4	11	5	79	1	0.1
O-born, A, 31–35 yrs	5	15	7	72	1	0.1
O-born, A, 36–40 yrs	5	12	7	75	1	0.2
O-born, A, 41–45 yrs	5	10	6	78	1	0.1
Q-born, Fr	0.1	1	0.4	3	95	0.3
F-born	20	28	12	29	8	2
F-born, arrived 1891–1901, 31–40 yrs	31	24	12	21	11	2

Sources: 1891 Census Project, http://www.census1891.ca/; Canadian Families Project database, CFP 1901; and CCRI 1911 microdata database.

Note: Results for 1891 are calculated using sample weights. Percentages may not always total 100 because of rounding.

O-born = Ontario-born; Q-born = Quebec-born; F-born = foreign-born; A = Anglophones; Fr = francophones; Yrs = years.

outcomes for this group in 1901 has suggested relatively slow labour market assimilation in spite of having broadly favourable characteristics.[18]

A comparison of the 1891 and 1901 data in table 13.1 indicates that only a small proportion of Ontario anglophones and Quebec francophones relocated to the west during the 1890s. The western region did gain a noticeably larger proportion of the foreign-born by 1901 and more so after 1901 as western settlement advanced more rapidly. About 10 per cent of Ontario anglophones moved west over this decade; the newly established Northwest (i.e., the provinces of Saskatchewan and Alberta) were the primary destinations. In contrast, as is well known, Quebec francophones did not participate in the western movement to any significant degree. Alan Green, Mary MacKinnon, and Chris Minns find that limited language skills and low levels of education (as approximated by literacy rates) were an impediment to western migration.[19] These characteristics may also have slowed occupational mobility within Quebec.

As one would expect, the location of the foreign-born was highly responsive to changing opportunities. British Columbia was attractive to immigrants as early as 1891. By 1911, about 60 per cent of the foreign-born in Canada were to be found west of Ontario. The farm sector attracted much of this western movement, but high wages in a range of occupations also contributed to the appeal of rapidly growing labour markets in western Canada.

Census data allow us to explore the regional distribution of workers by age cohort. In table 13.1 we trace the shares of young Ontario-born anglophones between 1901 and 1911. The westward shift over the decade is particularly sharp among those aged 21 to 30 in 1901. This effect is more muted among older cohorts. It would appear that westward movement may have been an especially important influence on labour market outcomes for Ontario men entering employment at the very beginning of the twentieth century. We also examine the mobility of the foreign-born within Canada. By 1911, only a slight shift in the location of this cohort is apparent, with a small increase in the prairie Northwest and Ontario, and a small decrease in the share in Manitoba. The distinct locational patterns of the immigrant population in 1901 and 1911 appear to be driven by differences between reasonably long-lasting choices made by young adults in each cohort, rather than movement over time.

Occupation over the Life Course

The 1901 and 1911 census samples allow us to examine changes in occupation and earnings at the micro-level. It is possible to trace successive cohorts of Canadian men's careers as they evolved with age. We begin by summarizing the occupational distribution for Ontario-born anglophone and Quebec-born francophone males aged 16 to 65 in the three censuses. Table 13.2 shows broadly similar occupational breakdowns for all groups.

About one-third of men were engaged in farming. Ontario anglophones were more often in skilled occupations (professional and proprietor, clerical, craft); the difference is roughly 5 percentage points in all three years. This was mirrored by a higher share of Quebec francophones in semi-skilled and unskilled occupations (operatives and labourers). The distribution of occupations

Table 13.2 · Occupations of Ontario-born anglophones and Quebec-born francophones, Canada, 1891, 1901, 1911

	Ontario-born anglophone			*Quebec-born francophone*		
	1891	*1901*	*1911*	*1891*	*1901*	*1911*
Proprietor/professional	8	8	10	7	7	8
Clerical	6	7	9	3	4	5
Craft	12	11	13	12	11	14
Operative	6	8	7	7	9	7
Service	1	2	2	2	2	2
Farm	41	37	37	40	36	34
Labour	9	16	11	13	19	18
No occupation category	18	10	12	15	12	13
n	49,073	27,984	33,811	22,536	18,072	21,506

Sources: 1891 Census Project; CFP 1901; and CCRI 1911 microdata database.

Note: Results for 1891 are calculated using sample weights. Percentages may not always total 100 because of rounding.

across categories changed little over the twenty years. The "unclassified" or "no occupation" category is a partial exception. Included here are occupational responses not easily placed within the seven occupational categories used in table 13.2 (e.g., "gentlemen") as well as non-occupational responses such as "student." As there may be some interest in seeing how the unoccupied share varies over the life cycle (perhaps following unusual patterns of investment in human capital while young and then retirement when old), or between anglophones and francophones, we do not exclude these responses from our analysis.[20] The finding of broad similarities between the occupational distribution of Ontario anglophones and Quebec francophones, at least at this level of aggregation, is intriguing. Indeed, they were more alike than those of immigrants and locally born in the northern United States in the same period.[21]

We provide a detailed breakdown of occupational patterns over time for "synthetic cohorts" – samples of men from the same birth year interval in successive census returns – in Appendix table 13.A1. For these calculations, operatives, service workers, and labourers have been aggregated into a semi-skilled/unskilled category. Figure 13.1 presents this information by age cohorts for Ontario anglophone men.

Younger cohorts experienced a significant rise in the share of those who were farming over time; later cohorts were, however, less likely to be engaged in the farming sector at any given age. The data also show a sharp rise with age in the

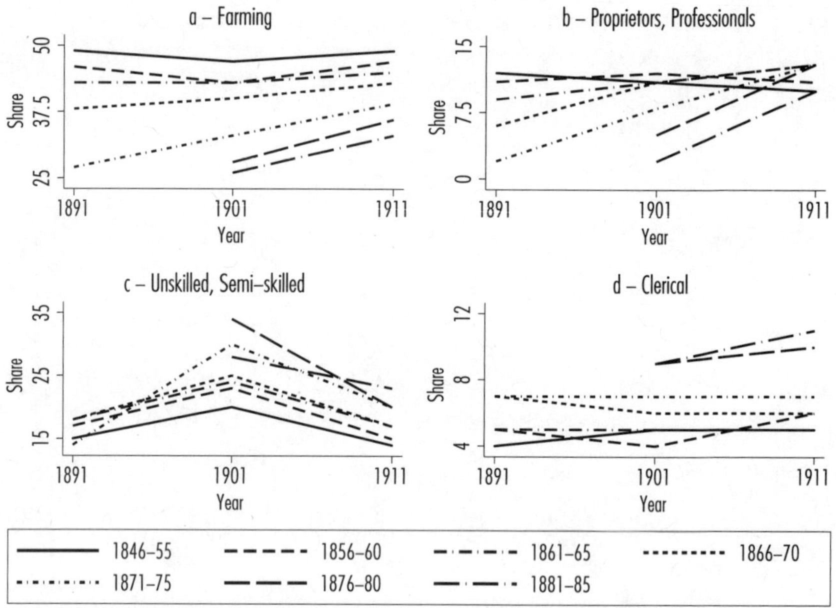

Figure 13.1 · Ontario anglophones in the active workforce, by occupation sector, 1891–1911, and by birth cohort.

Source: Table 13.A1.

share in proprietor and professional occupations for men born after 1870, and young men in 1911 were more likely to be in this sector than in 1891 or 1901. The proportion in semi-skilled and unskilled workers fell from 1901 to 1911, while patterns for clerical work show a modest rate of entry over time, with the youngest cohorts more likely to be found in this range of jobs. If the 1890s were a time of labour market stress, the first decade of the twentieth century allowed many to move up the ladder a bit. Taken as a whole, occupations where access to resources and financial capital were important – farming, the professions, proprietorship – saw considerable cohort entry over time. For other sectors, there appears to have been relatively little entry or departure, although the younger cohorts were more likely to have the skills for clerical work and were less likely to be "stuck" as labourers or operatives.

For Quebec-born francophones (see figure 13.2), the rise in the farming share is less sharp, and the cohort differences are smaller. Entry into professional and proprietor occupations looks broadly similar as found for Ontario anglophones. Employment in semi-skilled and unskilled occupations declines

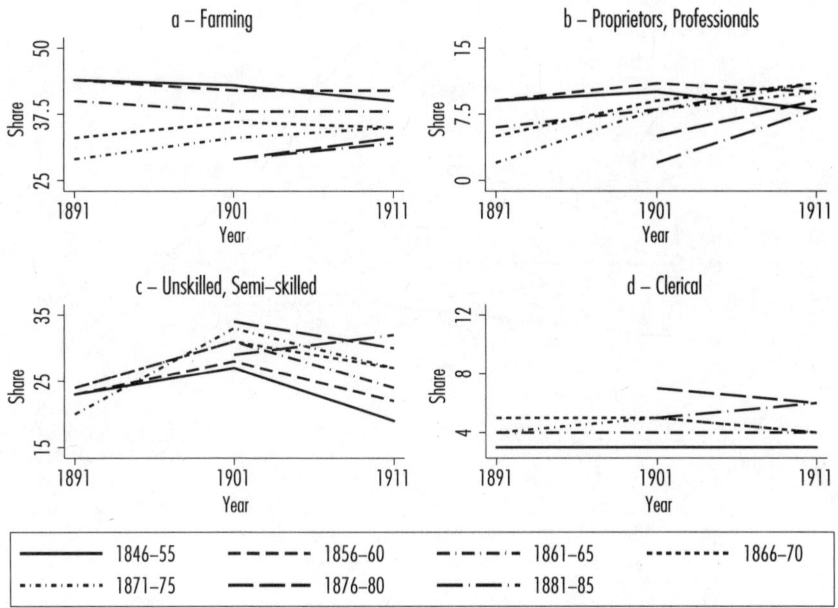

Figure 13.2 · Quebec francophones in the active workforce, by occupation sector, 1891–1911, and by by birth cohort.

Source: Calculated from Table 13.A1.

less between 1901 and 1911 than for the Ontario-born group, with the youngest cohorts holding high shares in these occupations in 1911. Among francophones, there is some evidence of higher rates of clerical employment among the youngest cohorts, but rates are much lower than for Ontario anglophones in those years. Human capital and skills were surely important in allowing access to the clerical sector and escape from unskilled work.

It seems possible that lower educational attainment delayed the advancement of Quebec francophones. Indeed, the increased importance of human capital and, therefore, the burden of its deficiency, may have contributed to the growing gap between anglophones and francophones in Quebec after 1901.[22]

Comparisons of school attendance across provinces are inevitably imprecise; however, it does appear that Ontario had the highest proportion of children reporting school attendance. At age 13, 74 per cent of Quebecers reported school attendance, which is 10 points below the Ontario rate (the rate for francophones in Quebec was even lower). In Ontario, during the first decade of the twentieth century, total enrolment in publicly controlled schools

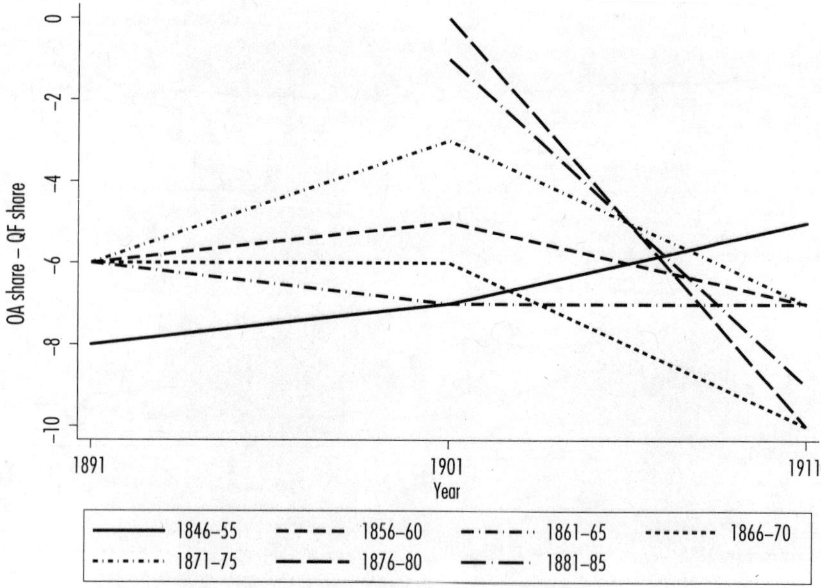

Figure 13.3 · Share of unskilled and semi-skilled workers: Ontario anglophones vs. Quebec francophones, 1891–1911, and by birth cohort.

Source: Calculated from Table 13.A1.

kept pace with the growth of the juvenile (aged 5–19 years) population (both rose by about 5%), while enrolments in the urban high schools and collegiate institutes increased more than 40 per cent.[23] Quebec's 24 per cent increase in pupils at publicly controlled schools and 21 per cent increase at classical colleges did *not* keep pace with the 34 per cent increase in its juvenile population. It is, therefore, likely that the gap in educational attainment between Quebec francophones and Ontario anglophones was rising, at least in the later part of the period.[24]

Figure 13.3 traces differences in the unskilled/semi-skilled share of occupations between Ontario anglophones and Quebec francophones. Ontario anglophones were almost uniformly less likely to be found at the bottom of the occupational distribution. The widening gap between 1901 and 1911 for the two youngest cohorts is particularly notable. This pattern suggests that young anglophone Ontarians managed to respond more effectively to changes in the demand for skill, realizing a greater share of the potential benefits. The early twentieth century is typically painted as a good time to have been a young

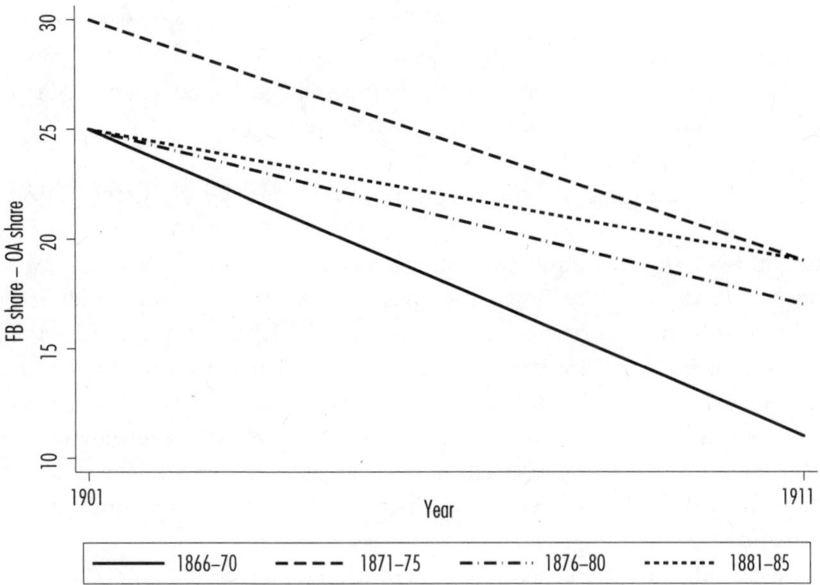

Figure 13.4 · Share of unskilled and semi-skilled workers: Foreign-born vs. Ontario anglophones, 1901 and 1911, and by birth cohort.

Source: Calculated from Tables 13.A1 and 13.A2.

Canadian, with much discussion of a growing sense of self-confidence and enthusiasm for various nation-building projects.[25] The detailed evidence of labour market change suggests that this optimism was firmly rooted in the work and career experiences of many young men, particularly in the anglophone population.

Evidence for the foreign-born in Appendix table 13.A2 shows occupational shifts from 1901 to 1911 broadly similar to those of Canadian-born men. The proportion of men in farming and professional/proprietor occupations increased, and the share in unskilled and semi-skilled work declined. The patterns of change varied less by age cohort among the foreign-born than among the Canadian-born. For example, the share of professionals and proprietors rose less rapidly between 1901 and 1911. It would seem that occupational assimilation, at least in terms of rate of change, was fairly similar for immigrants of the same arrival vintage regardless of their ages. This suggests to us that overall economic conditions in Canada probably had more of an impact on immigrants than how recently they had completed school or their job training.

Comparing the unskilled and semi-skilled share of immigrants with Ontario anglophones (see figure 13.4) shows that all the foreign-born cohorts enjoyed reductions in their relative share in the bottom categories, but continued to be overrepresented in labouring and operative work in 1911.

The Structure of Canadian Earnings, 1901 and 1911: Occupations

Recent research provides important evidence on changes in wages and earnings in Canada in the early twentieth century. Alan Green and David Green report results based on unpublished census material for 1911 onwards, while Herbert Emery and Clint Levitt construct nominal and real wage series from data published in the *Labour Gazette*.[26] We begin our analysis of earnings by documenting the basic patterns in the census samples before turning to consider the evolution of pay with age and, for targeted age cohorts, the evolution of pay over time. Table 13.3 summarizes earnings information from both the 1901 and 1911 censuses.

The sample for this purpose consists of adult men aged 16 to 65 with a recognized occupation. More than 80 per cent of men in the clerical, craft, operative, and labouring categories indicate earnings in both 1901 and 1911. In these sectors, we are fairly confident that the data give a reasonable portrayal of the range of pay on offer; it is likely that the same types of workers report pay in both years. Workers in services also report pay with high frequency, although admittedly, they are more likely to receive additional non-monetary compensation (such as food, lodging, and clothing) than clerical and production workers. The professional/proprietor and farming groups include many who received compensation mainly in the form of retained earnings rather than salary or wages; it is no surprise that their shares reporting earnings are lower. Indeed, only wage earners were required to report compensation.[27]

Table 13.3 shows that the rankings of occupational groups are the same in 1901 and 1911 for average and median earnings, and that these follow the expected pattern, as reported previously for 1901 by Green, MacKinnon, and Minns.[28] Table 13.4 uses the earnings information in table 13.3 to calculate the change in nominal wages from 1901 to 1911 in each of four categories. These calculations suggest that the skill premium in Canada narrowed between 1901 and 1911. The fastest rate of nominal earnings growth was in the labourer category, and the slowest was among clerical workers, who are relatively well paid. Evidence of wage compression between skilled and unskilled workers is consistent with evidence reported by Green and Green, who draw evidence on earnings from unpublished census materials.[29] Table 13.4 also reports the coefficient of variation on earnings within each occupational group in 1901 and 1911. For manual

Table 13.3 · Nominal earnings of males, by occupation group, Canada, 1901 and 1911

	1901			*1911*		
	Mean (sd)	*Median*	n *(% with earnings)*	*Mean (sd)*	*Median*	n *(% with earnings)*
Proprietor/ professional	864 (872)	600	3,121 (50)	1,185 (1,020)	960	4,731 (54)
Clerical	542 (378)	480	3,953 (85)	785 (610)	660	6,251 (81)
Craft	483 (318)	450	7,452 (83)	723 (405)	685	11,393 (80)
Operative	423 (325)	375	6,047 (80)	627 (430)	600	6,556 (82)
Service	366 (279)	300	1,584 (75)	577 (364)	520	2,451 (80)
Farm	216 (277)	150	3,225 (12)	378 (389)	300	6,614 (19)
Labour	276 (183)	250	12,619 (83)	469 (258)	450	15,497 (80)
All	*414 (408)*	*320*	*38,610*	*640 (541)*	*533*	*55,717*

Sources: CFP 1901 and CCRI 1911 microdata database.

Note: Standard errors in parentheses.

Table 13.4 · Selected occupation categories: Changes in earnings between 1901 and 1911

	Mean ratio, 1911/1901	*Median ratio, 1911/1901*	*CV, 1901*	*CV, 1911*
Clerical	1.45	1.38	0.79	0.92
Craft	1.50	1.52	0.71	0.59
Operative	1.48	1.60	0.87	0.72
Labour	1.70	1.80	0.73	0.57

Sources: CFP 1901 and CCRI 1911 microdata database.

CV = coefficient of variation.

workers (craft, operative, labourer), the data suggest a narrowing of earnings dispersion, while the opposite is true for the clerical sector.

The patterns in table 13.4 imply that the net effect of supply and demand changes was a rise in wages for male workers in manual occupations, especially those with lower skills. This is consistent with rapid investment in urban and western Canadian infrastructure and in the export of goods which could have created a strong (if possibly temporary) need for less-skilled workers in a variety of occupations and industries. While the average clerical worker was slipping relative to less-skilled workers, there is also evidence of a rising range of pay within the clerical sector. At the first pass, this is consistent with a story of occupational change and increasing returns to intermediate activities that are typically thought to have gained in importance as firm size and complexity grew. The number of relatively simple jobs at the bottom of the clerical ladder expanded, but so did more responsible positions (such as bank clerks) towards the top of it. This is also a trend one might expect to see with the advent of internal labour markets for white-collar employment within firms. Junior jobs for young men hoping to move up in the white-collar world could be very low-paid while, to maintain honesty and work incentives for the more experienced, at least some men had to be paid above their marginal product later in their career. Formal pensions were still rare except at very large firms like the Canadian Pacific Railway, so pension rights would not have contributed greatly to any shift of earnings across the age profile.[30]

The Structure of Canadian Earnings, 1901 and 1911: Regions

The census data provide evidence on nominal wages adjusted for cost of living with two readily available indices. The MacKinnon-Minns estimate, used to compute Real (1), relies mainly on contract prices paid by federal penitentiaries. Real (2) uses the Emery-Levitt cost-of-living estimates, which derive from prices reported in the *Labour Gazette*.[31] Real earnings are benchmarked to indicate implied purchasing power in Ontario in 1901. We limit our attention here to wages in urban areas for which the cost-of-living evidence is most directly relevant. For this purpose farm workers, for whom the earnings evidence is least complete, are excluded.

Table 13.5 summarizes earnings in 1901 by Canadian region. The same data expressed in table 13.6 as regional ratios relative to Ontario replicate the east-west gradient in nominal wages found by Emery and Levitt.[32] After controlling for regional differences in the cost of living, Maritime earnings are about 10 to 15 per cent lower than earnings in Ontario or Quebec. Real earnings in Manitoba are 10 to 25 per cent above those in Central Canada, while the premium further west is less consistent. Reported earnings are low in Alberta and Saskatchewan (the Northwest) in 1901 although this is based on a small number of observations. Another complication arises for 1911. Nominal wages in the Northwest are similar to those of Manitoba, but different sources provide conflicting evidence for the cost of living. For British Columbia, there is a significant decline in relative nominal wages from 1901 to 1911, and both sources of living costs agree that these fell considerably less. The combined effect is to bring real wages in British Columbia a bit below comparable estimates for Cen-

Table 13.5 · Urban male non-farm workers: Earnings, Canada and by province or region, 1901 and 1911

	1901				*1911*			
	Nominal	*Real (1)*	*Real (2)*	n	*Nominal*	*Real (1)*	*Real (2)*	n
British Columbia	679 (602)	485 (430)	561 (498)	1,276	797 (548)	429 (295)	420 (289)	3,109
Northwest	549 (676)	392 (483)	422 (520)	253	841 (633)	584 (440)	470 (354)	3,309
Manitoba	694 (733)	574 (606)	547 (577)	699	921 (835)	606 (550)	580 (526)	2,645
Ontario	469 (365)	469 (365)	469 (365)	8,916	680 (578)	482 (410)	511 (434)	15,244
Quebec	519 (553)	480 (512)	489 (522)	6,465	671 (560)	460 (383)	516 (431)	10,069
Maritimes	434 (382)	391 (344)	443 (389)	2,393	561 (390)	395 (274)	442 (307)	3,242
Canada	503 (477)	467 (433)	480 (444)	20,002	708 (591)	482 (403)	500 (416)	37,618

Sources: CFP 1901 and CCRI 1911 microdata database.

Note: Real (1) is deflated using methodology from Chris Minns and Mary MacKinnon, "The Costs of Doing Hard Time: A Penitentiary-Based Regional Price Index for Canada, 1883–1923," *Canadian Journal of Economics* 40 (2007): 528–60. Real (2) is deflated using methodology from J.C. Herbert Emery and Clint Levitt, "Cost of Living, Real Wages, and Real Incomes in Thirteen Canadian Cities, 1900–1950," *Canadian Journal of Economics* 35 (2002): 115–37. Standard errors in parentheses.

Table 13.6 · Urban male non-farm workers: Relative regional earnings (Ontario = 100), Canada, 1901 and 1911

	1901			*1911*		
	Nominal	*Real (1)*	*Real (2)*	*Nominal*	*Real (1)*	*Real (2)*
British Columbia	145	103	120	117	89	82
Northwest	117	84	90	124	121	92
Manitoba	148	122	117	135	126	114
Ontario	100	100	100	100	100	100
Quebec	111	102	104	99	95	101
Maritimes	93	83	94	83	82	86

Sources: CFP 1901 and CCRI 1911 microdata databases.

Note: Real (1) is deflated using methodology from Chris Minns and Mary MacKinnon, "The Costs of Doing Hard Time: A Penitentiary-Based Regional Price Index for Canada, 1883–1923," *Canadian Journal of Economics* 40 (2007): 528–60. Real (2) is deflated using methodology from J.C. Herbert Emery and Clint Levitt, "Cost of Living, Real Wages, and Real Incomes in Thirteen Canadian Cities, 1900–1950," *Canadian Journal of Economics* 35 (2002): 115–37.

Table 13.7 · Regional skill premia: Nominal earnings, clerical workers vs. operatives (labourers), by province or region, 1901 and 1911

	1901			1911		
	Nominal earnings, clerical	*Nominal earnings, operative*	*Ratio clerical/ operative*	*Nominal earnings, clerical*	*Nominal earnings, operative*	*Ratio clerical/ operative*
British Columbia	807	570	1.42	1,000	769	1.30
Northwest	511	333	1.53	959	734	1.31
Manitoba	738	599	1.23	960	752	1.28
Ontario	532	410	1.30	744	601	1.24
Quebec	569	446	1.28	738	623	1.18
Maritimes	485	386	1.26	611	520	1.18

Sources: CFP 1901 and CCRI 1911 microdata databases.

tral Canada. Rapid migration to British Columbia, therefore, appears to have been effective in reducing the sharp disequilibrium observed in 1901.

Differences in supply and demand for skilled and unskilled workers across Canada might lead to distinctive regional patterns of skill premia. We investigate this possibility in table 13.7 in which we report the ratio of nominal earnings between clerical workers and operatives (labourers). These are calculated for each region in 1901 and 1911. Here we find further evidence of an east-west gradient, with the relative earnings of clerical workers higher further west. The gradient appears to be somewhat flatter in 1911 than in 1901. Part of the decline in the national skill premia documented in table 13.4 originates with falling wages for white-collar work in western provinces.

Earnings over the Life Course, 1901–11

Labour economists have drawn attention to a range of issues in understanding how earnings evolve over the employment career. One set of concerns is primarily empirical: how "humped" are earnings profiles over the life cycle, and what functional form is most appropriate for making comparisons between groups and over time?[33] The shape of life-cycle earnings profiles speaks to fundamental questions regarding the importance of various forms of human capital, the structure of compensation, and other employment attributes. These point to a set of questions that are particularly interesting in the context of the early twentieth-century Canadian labour market. The extent to which workers entered employment with human capital acquired from schooling or other forms of training can affect initial earnings and the rate at which earnings rise with experience. Increased schooling among young workers entering employment after 1901 could have shifted the pattern of wage profiles across age cohorts. Another form of human capital is on-the-job experience. Part of the rise in earnings associated with time in employment reflects a return to experience. Whether this is concentrated in the first few years of employment or extended for most of the working life reflects opportunities for on-the-job acquisition of skills and their portability to different work environments. For example, in large enterprises, managers need a wider range of skills as they move up, and this is likely a source of sustained earnings growth. A final point of consideration is whether or not earnings profiles have an inverted U-shape at the beginning and end of the career. This pattern might be most evident at both ends of the age range in jobs where physical strength or manual dexterity is important.

Relatively little is known about the shape of earnings over the life cycle in the early twentieth century. Evidence for employees of the Canadian Pacific Railway in this period suggests that earnings rose sharply until the mid- to early 20s and then were fairly flat at higher ages.[34] Given that workers moved across sectors in response to opportunities, studies limited to a single (large) firm or industry are likely to understate the extent of cumulative earnings growth. Other studies of labour market outcomes in this period are based mainly on single cross-sections from census or other labour force data.[35] Age-earnings profiles estimated using these sources assume that longitudinal wage or earnings growth can be approximated through variation by age in a snapshot at one point in time. The new census samples provide evidence on a broad range of occupations and activities; the presence of earnings information in two cross-sections allows us to trace cohort outcomes over time. To our knowledge, no other studies of early twentieth-century labour markets have been able to generate lifetime earnings evidence of this type.

Figures 13.5 and 13.6 summarize earnings growth for Ontario-born anglophones and Quebec-born francophones from 1901 to 1911 (the raw data are given in Appendix table 13.A3). The lines trace the growth in real earnings between these two dates for five cohorts. Figure 13.5 shows that earnings growth was especially strong among men aged 16 to 25 in 1901 (i.e., born 1881–85) and that clerical workers aged 21 to 25 in 1901 enjoyed more sustained earnings growth than operatives. Real earnings growth was slower for those born before 1876 (i.e., aged at least 25 in 1901), with little return to experience for those remaining in operative work. The pattern for Quebec francophones is less settled. Very young clerical workers (i.e., aged 16 to 20 in 1901) saw large increases

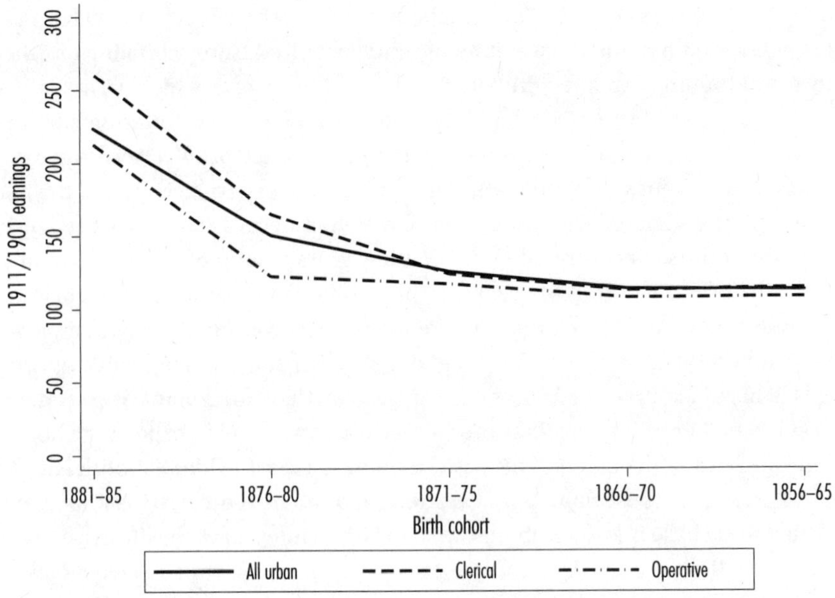

Figure 13.5 · Ontario anglophones, earnings growth: All urban, clerical, and operative, 1901–1911, and by birth cohort.

Source: Calculated from Table 13.A3.

Figure 13.6 (opposite, above) · Quebec francophones, earnings growth: All urban, clerical, and operative, 1901–11, and by birth cohort.

Source: Calculated from Table 13.A3.

Figure 13.7 (opposite, below) · Relative cohort growth, Ontario anglophones vs. Quebec francophones: All urban, clerical, and operative, 1901–11, and by birth cohort.

Source: Calculated from Table 13.A3.

in earnings, although their income was still lower than that of operatives in the next two age cohorts. Taken together, these figures show that men aged 16 to 25 in 1901 enjoyed faster intertemporal earnings growth than older cohorts. If the twentieth century was thought to belong to Canada, contemporaries had particularly good reason to think it would belong to the rising generation of more skilled young workers. To highlight comparisons between the Ontario and Quebec groups, figure 13.7 traces relative growth rates for age cohorts.

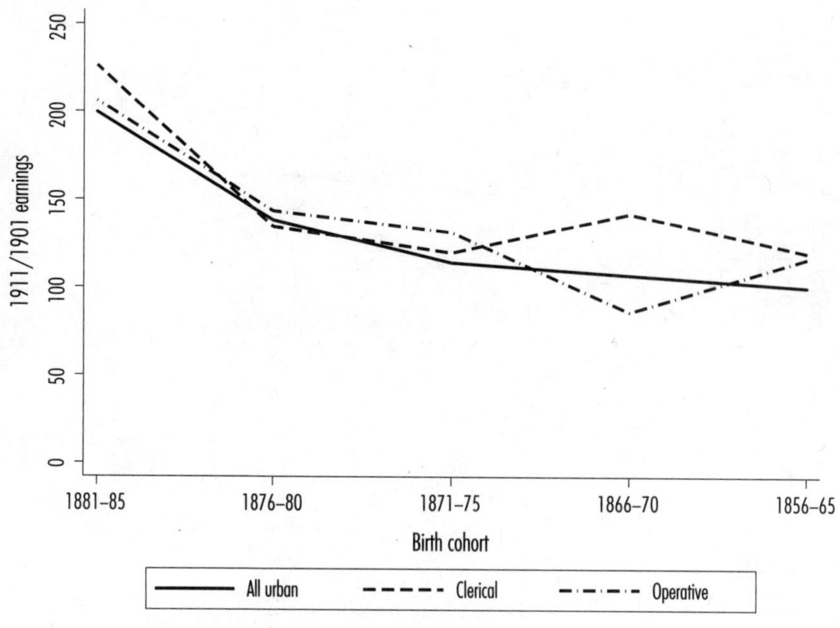
1911/1901 earnings
250
200
150
100
50
0
1881–85
1876–80
1871–75
1866–70
1856–65
Birth cohort
All urban
Clerical
Operative

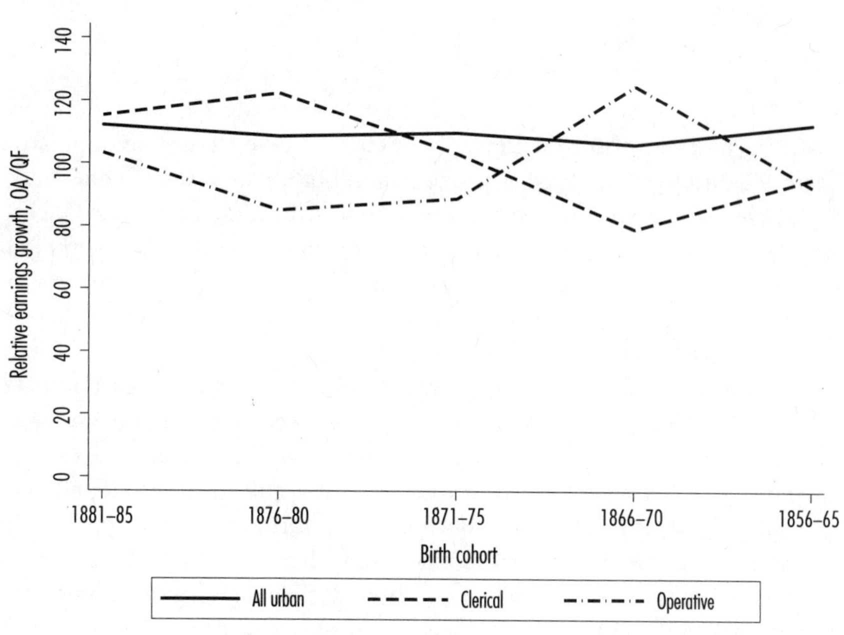
Relative earnings growth, OA/QF
140
120
100
80
60
40
20
0
1881–85
1876–80
1871–75
1866–70
1856–65
Birth cohort
All urban
Clerical
Operative

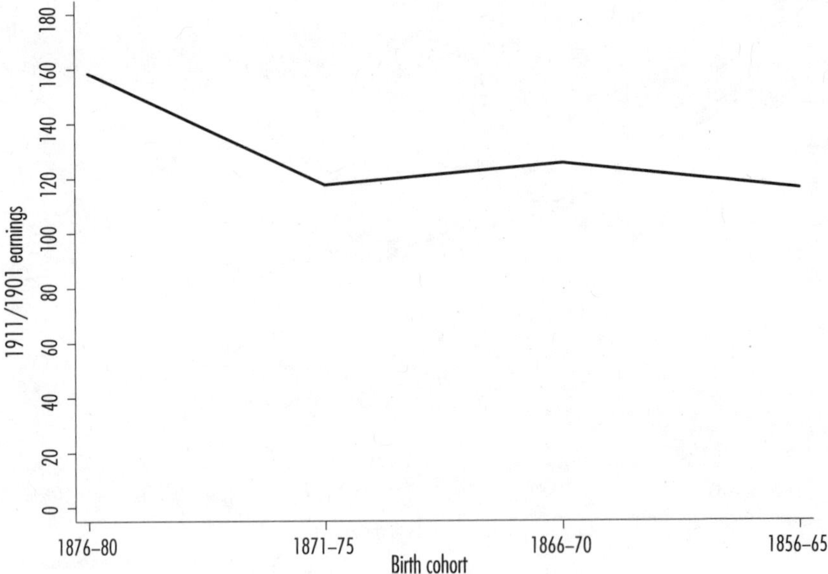

Figure 13.8 · Foreign-born arrivals 1901–1911: Earnings growth, by birth cohort.
Source: Calculated from Table 13.A3.

This comparison shows that Ontario anglophones in all cohorts enjoyed faster earnings growth over time. The picture for the clerical and operative sectors is more complicated – young cohorts of Ontario anglophone workers in clerical employment gained much more with time than their Quebec counterparts (a pattern that does not appear to hold for semi-skilled workers in the operative sector). In 1901, Quebec francophones had lower earnings than Ontario anglophones of the same age; the subsequent decade saw further divergence between the two groups.

We have also generated earnings growth profiles for the foreign-born. We focus on immigrants who arrived in Canada between 1891 and 1901, and were at least 21 years of age in 1901. We start at a higher age band in order to exclude migrants who arrived in Canada as young children. Due to the smaller number of migrants in each age cell, we do not report sector-specific patterns as in the previous figures. Figure 13.8 shows that much as with the two native-born groups, earnings growth for the foreign-born declines after age 25. Comparing immigrants to the Ontario-born (figure 13.9) suggests little evidence of earnings assimilation over time, with the 1871–75 cohort experiencing slower earnings growth than native-born Ontario anglophones.

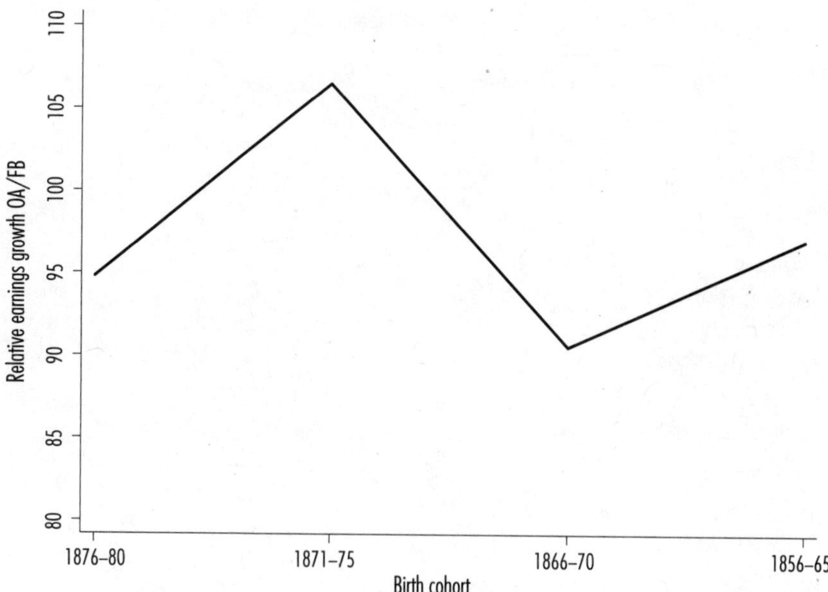

Figure 13.9 · Ontario anglophones vs. Ontario foreign-born: Relative earnings growth, by birth cohort.
Source: Calculated from Table 13.A3.

These results are consistent with the occupational evidence presented above, and further support the view that the mainly British immigrant population in Canada experienced sluggish labour market assimilation.

Sources of Earnings Growth

In this section, we compute a statistical decomposition of earnings in 1901 and 1911 for specific birth cohorts. This takes the form of an Oaxaca decomposition, a technique used frequently in the economics literature to identify sources of differences between groups.[36] Equation (1) and the text that follows outline this technique. We write the difference in (log) earnings as follows:

$$Y_1 - Y_0 = (a_1 - a_0) + (b_1 - b_0)x_0 + (x_1 - x_0)\,b_1 \qquad (1)$$

In Equation (1), Y_1 and Y_0 are average log earnings of an age cohort in 1911 and 1910, respectively. We estimate regressions of the log of earnings against a set of dummy variables for region and occupational sector in both census years. These regressions yield the constant terms (a_1 and a_0), and vectors of

Table 13.8 · Analysis of changes in earnings growth: Ontario-born anglophones, by age cohort, 1901–11

	Born 1881–85	*Born 1876–80*	*Born 1871–75*
Log earnings 1901	5.38	5.91	6.11
Log earnings 1911	6.18	6.26	6.28
Difference	*.80*	*.35*	*.17*
Contribution of			
Change in region	.05	.03	.02
Change in sector	.03	.05	.04
Total change in characteristics	*.09*	*.08*	*.06*
Change in regional return	-.001	-.001	.01
Change in sector return	.31	.12	.04
Total change in returns	*.31*	*.12*	*.05*
Change in constant (secular change in real wage for age group)	*.41*	*.15*	*.06*

Sources: CFP 1901 and CCRI 1911 microdata databases.

Note: Calculated from estimation of the model in Equation (1).

coefficients (b_1 and b_0) used in the decomposition in Equation (1). Finally, mean characteristics for age cohorts at both dates (x_1 and x_0) are combined with coefficient estimates to compute the decomposition. The results of this exercise yield crude estimates of the contribution of different sources to intertemporal earnings growth. The difference in the constant term shows the secular increase in earnings over time with age for the reference group (for Ontario-born anglophones, this is labourers resident in Ontario). The second term is the effect of changes in the return to occupation sector and location. For example, if the earnings premium associated with clerical work rises over time, or earnings in the Northwest rise relative to earnings in Ontario, these effects will be captured by positive differences in the b terms. The third term gives the contribution of occupational and geographical mobility. If cohorts migrate towards high-earnings regions, or increase their share in high-earnings occupations, these will lead to positive values for $(x_1 - x_0)\, b_1$.

We focus our analysis on the three age cohorts that we observe in both 1901 and 1911 that have significant intertemporal earnings growth: urban-resident men born 1881–85, 1876–80, and 1871–75. We undertake the analysis for both Ontario-born anglophones and Quebec-born francophones. Table 13.8 summarizes the main results of the regression results for the Ontario cohorts.[37]

Table 13.9 · Analysis of changes in earnings growth: Quebec-born francophones, by age cohort, 1901–11

	Born 1881–85	*Born 1876–80*	*Born 1871–75*
Log earnings 1901	5.21	5.72	5.99
Log earnings 1911	5.99	6.04	6.04
Difference	*.78*	*.32*	*.05*
Contribution of			
Change in region	-.004	.002	.01
Change in sector	.01	.0002	-.03
Total change in characteristics	*.004*	*.002*	*-.02*
Change in regional return	-.004	-.001	-.02
Change in sector return	.33	.16	.08
Total change in returns	*.32*	*.16*	*.06*
Change in constant (secular change in real wage for age group)	*.45*	*.16*	*.02*

Sources: CFP 1901 and CCRI 1911 microdata databases.

Note: Calculated from estimation of the model in Equation (1).

For the youngest group (born 1881–85), the steep age-earnings profile is evident even for unskilled workers. Those not in labouring occupations get a considerable extra kick from more rapid earnings growth in other sectors. Sectoral and regional movement together brought about a 9 log point increase in earnings. As we move to the next age cohort (born 1876–80), earnings growth over the ten years is slower. The breakdown between characteristics, returns, and the secular trend is similar to those from the youngest group, although all of these effects are slightly smaller in absolute terms. For those born between 1871 and 1875 (aged 26 to 30 in 1901), the constant term plays a much smaller role. There was much less earnings growth (on average) above age 26, but what there was more likely came from being in a sector (clerical) with sustained earnings growth, or intersectoral mobility. Taken together, these effects account for about two-thirds of earnings growth (.06 + .05 / .17) in this cohort.

Francophones (see table 13.9) appear to get similar secular changes in earnings (from a lower base) as Ontario anglophones, and they also benefit from changes in the returns to the sector they are in. Strikingly absent in this set of decompositions is evidence of a substantial benefit from migration and occupational mobility. These effects account for a fair share of earnings growth in the youngest of the Ontario cohorts but otherwise appear to have been of modest

Table 13.10 · Analysis of changes in earnings growth: Foreign-born, by age cohort, 1901–11

	Born 1876–80	*Born 1871–75*	*Born 1866–70*
Log earnings 1901	5.64	5.77	5.83
Log earnings 1911	6.12	6.03	6.05
Difference	*.48*	*.26*	*.22*
Contribution of			
Change in region	.05	-.01	.03
Change in sector	.05	.01	.01
Total change in characteristics	*.10*	*-.003*	*.04*
Change in regional return	.06	.05	.08
Change in sector return	.10	.12	.14
Total change in returns	*.16*	*.17*	*.22*
Change in constant (secular change in real wage for age group)	*.23*	*.09*	*-.04*

Sources: CFP 1901 and CCRI 1911 microdata databases.

Note: Calculated from estimation of the model in Equation (1).

importance for Ontario men. One can also see that had Quebec francophones enjoyed the same degree of occupational and geographical mobility as anglophones, they would have had faster intertemporal earnings growth than the Ontario-born group, and some earnings convergence between the two would have occurred.

Finally, we report the results of a similar decomposition for the foreign-born (see table 13.10). For the youngest immigrant cohort (aged 21–25 in 1901), earnings growth was about 13 log points above that of native-born cohorts of the same age, with roughly similar proportions allocated to characteristics and returns. For both the 1871–75 and 1866–70 immigrant cohorts, we find that changes in regional and sector returns account for the bulk of earnings growth, with less importance attached to changes in characteristics than for Ontario anglophones. There are several possible interpretations of this result. One is reduced discrimination against foreigners (mainly of British origin) outside of Central Canada and in more skilled occupations.[38] Another is that immigrants invested greater amounts in sector-specific skills (perhaps compensating for limited pre-migration human capital formation), rather than investing in secondary migration or further occupational mobility once in Canada. If part of immigrant earnings convergence is due to the accumulation of country-specific skills, immigrants may have structured their careers so that more of these returns were specific to an occupational sector. It is difficult to draw any conclusions regarding the self-selection of immigrants to Canada from this evidence. They appear to have enjoyed somewhat faster earnings growth than the native-born, but the two older cohorts remained about 20 log points below the native-born after at least ten years of residence in Canada. While US evidence suggests that immigrant convergence with the native-born drew heavily on intersectoral mobility, Canadian immigrants appear to have benefited from particularly strong intrasector earnings growth.[39]

Conclusion

The recent availability of large random samples from successive censuses allows us, for the first time, to examine the labour market in Canada during the years 1891 to 1911 from a life-cyle perspective using synthetic cohort analysis. The ability to follow the experience of particular cohorts through time depends, critically, on the availability of samples from successive censuses. We can now begin to understand labour market outcomes (employment, occupation, income) in relation to personal characteristics (age, education, language, and so on) and to do so in a way that disentangles life-cycle effects from broader changes in the historical context. The new data, therefore, make possible a signficant advance in analytical potential. We have been able to identify several previously unrecognized features of the Canadian labour market before the First World War.

Following lifetime outcomes for individual age and ethnic groups in the 1891, 1901, and 1911 census enumerations reveals how geographical mobility relates to economic mobility. We document how internal and international migration responded to changing opportuntities across Canada during the period of rapid western settlement. Neither Ontario-born anglophones nor Quebec-born francophones moved to western Canada in significant numbers during the 1890s. By the end of that decade, the share of the foreign-born in the west had begun to increase, and it increased significantly after 1901. The same was true for Ontario-born anglophones, especially among the younger cohorts. The considerable western movement of Ontario anglophones reinforces Patrick Coe and Herbert Emery's finding that Canada's national labour market emerged early in the twentieth century.[40] Quebec-born francophones, however, appear not to have benefited equally from this development as they did not move to western Canada in significant numbers even during the 1901–11 boom.

Migration, the spread of secondary schooling, and changes in technology and firm organization are expected to have altered the relative supply and demand for skilled workers early in the twentieth century. One manifestation of these changes was a marked shift in occupational mix over the twenty years. Ontario-born anglophones increasingly entered professional, proprietor, and even farming occupations although, admittedly, later cohorts were less likely to be farming than earlier ones at the same age. Younger cohorts were much more likely to be employed in the clerical sector, even though the movement into clerical work of older cohorts through a process of career mobility was limited. Quebec-born francophones enjoyed broadly similar occupational transitions – an increasing share in farming and proprietorship, and a decreasing share in unskilled or semi-skilled occupations – but they were more likely than comparable Ontario-born cohorts to remain at the bottom of the occupational ladder. Foreign-born men were predominantly occupied in unskilled and semi-skilled work in 1901. All immigrant cohorts show considerable movement out of this sector by 1911, but they remain much more likely to be in low-end work even after ten or twenty years of residence in Canada.

Changes in the supply and demand for skills may also be expected to precipitate changes in the structure of wages and earnings. We see this, albeit imperfectly, through the 1901 and 1911 record of individual earnings for most employees (including the growing numbers in white-collar work who do not feature in many surveys of the industrial workforce). Clerical earnings increased rapidly. Earnings in unskilled and semi-skilled work grew even more quickly. This is consistent with an economy undergoing *both* a structural transformation that expanded the number and variety of clerical roles *and* a strong demand for lower-skilled workers because of the construction and export boom. The national skill premium, or differential between unskilled/semi-skilled and clerical earnings, diminished, in part, because of a noticeable decline in the large western wage premium – perhaps reflecting the combined supply effects of increasing levels of education and westward migration.[41]

Finally, synthetic cohort evidence on earnings sheds new light on the nature of the earnings life cycle in the early twentieth century, and how different groups were affected by the broader economic changes of the period. Younger men in 1901 appear to have benefited most; their rates of earnings growth between 1901 and 1911 were much larger than for for older cohorts. Ontario-born men older than 25 years in 1901 experienced more modest earnings growth, and much of that flowed from their geographical and occupational mobility. Quebec-born francophones had slower earnings growth than their Ontario-born anglophone counterparts. Lower levels of occupational and especially regional mobility would appear to account for much of the gap. The earnings growth of foreign-born workers drew heavily upon improved returns to skill and location.

The broad patterns of labour market change visible from the new Canadian census samples for 1891, 1901, and 1911 suggest a number of possible extensions for future research. The data will sustain, for example, more fine-grained and complex multivariate analysis on many of the points identified above. A particular issue of importance that invites further attention is immigrant labour market assimilation.[42] A second question, which we have not explored here, is whether or not the larger changes in the Canadian economy may also have made the labour market more or less segmented by personal characteristics. Increased scale of activity and higher proportions of foreign and internal migrants decreased the likelihood that potential employers would have known potential employees. This may have made observable characteristics (such as ethnic origin, religion, or age) more important in hiring decisions. However, as employers became more used to a wider range of people seeking work in a tighter labour market towards 1911, there may have been greater willingness to hire across traditional ethnic or denominational lines.

Two additonal topics that we have only begun to address in this chapter are of particular importance and likely to receive attention in coming years. The availability of multiple census cross-sections now makes possible a complete analysis of earnings and employment differences between anglophones and francophones in the early twentieth century. Understanding the disadvantaged labour market position of francophones throughout the twentieth century continues to be one of the most important challenges for Canadian social scientists and historians. Our preliminary review of the new census samples points to the importance of a relatively slow francophone improvement in educational achievements and relatively weak mobility within Canada. A more comprehensive analysis is needed to confirm or reject these observations arising from our preliminary analysis.

Finally, we are now able to see clearly that the dominant narrative of the Canadian economy in this period requires some nuancing if not outright revision. It is true that western Canada expanded enormously and that the national economy accelerated robustly.[43] The importance of this macro-dynamic, of course, should not distract from equally dramatic changes occurring within individual industries and regions, even in eastern Canada.[44] We are now in a position to extend this debate to the labour market. Preliminary analysis in this chapter suggests that the extensive growth of the labour market after 1900 was accompanied by a number of complex changes associated with intensification, human capital development, and skill-biased technological change. Further research using individual-level evidence is needed to develop a new meta-narrative in which we recognize more clearly both extensive and intensive changes in the labour market and the importance of their interaction for the life outcomes of those Canadians who experienced the transformational decades 1891 to 1911.

Table 13.A1 · Occupations of native-born Ontario anglophones and Quebec francophones, by age cohort, 1891–1911

		Ontario anglophones			*Quebec francophones*		
				1891			
1901	*1911*	*1891*	*1901*	*1911*			
Born 1846–55	Prop/prof	12	11	10	9	10	8
[*n* 1891 = 7,904]	Clerical	4	5	5	3	3	3
[*n* 1901 = 3,326]	Craft	14	13	11	15	12	12
[*n* 1911 = 2,914]	Farm	49	47	49	44	43	40
	Unskilled/semi-skilled	15	20	14	23	27	19
	No category	5	4	11	6	5	17
Born 1856–60	Prop/prof	11	12	11	9	11	10
[*n* 1891 = 6,131]	Clerical	5	4	6	3	3	3
[*n* 1901 = 2,478]	Craft	15	14	13	14	13	14
[*n* 1911 = 2,455]	Farm	46	43	47	44	42	42
	Unskilled/semi-skilled	17	23	15	23	28	22
	No category	7	3	8	6	3	10
Born 1861–65	Prop/prof	9	11	13	6	8	11
[*n* 1891 = 8,531]	Clerical	5	5	5	4	4	4
[*n* 1901 = 3,196]	Craft	14	13	13	14	15	15
[*n* 1911 = 2,864]	Farm	43	43	45	40	38	38
	Unskilled/semi-skilled	18	23	17	24	31	24
	No category	11	4	6	10	5	8
Born 1866–1870	Prop/prof	6	11	13	5	9	11
[*n* 1891 = 10,039]	Clerical	7	6	6	5	5	4
[*n* 1901 = 3,327]	Craft	12	13	15	12	14	16
[*n* 1911 = 3,103]	Farm	38	40	43	33	36	35
	Unskilled/semi-skilled	18	25	17	24	31	27
	No category	20	4	6	20	7	7

/continued

Table 13.A1 · continued

		Ontario anglophones			*Quebec francophones*		
		1891	*1901*	*1911*	*1891*	*1901*	*1911*
Born 1871–75	Prop/prof	2	8	13	2	8	10
[*n* 1891 = 10,884]	Clerical	7	7	7	4	5	4
[*n* 1901 = 4,036]	Craft	8	13	15	6	13	18
[*n* 1911 = 3,568]	Farm	27	33	39	29	33	35
	Unskilled/semi-skilled	14	30	20	20	33	27
	No category	41	8	7	39	8	6
Born 1876–80	Prop/prof		5	13		5	9
[*n* 1901 = 4,725]	Clerical		9	10		7	6
[*n* 1911 = 4,160]	Craft		10	14		10	18
	Farm		28	36		29	33
	Unskilled/semi-skilled		34	20		34	30
	No category		13	7		15	6
Born 1881–85	Prop/prof		2	10		2	8
[*n* 1901 = 5,081]	Clerical		9	11		5	6
[*n* 1911 = 4,679]	Craft		6	15		5	15
	Farm		26	33		29	32
	Unskilled/semi-skilled		28	23		29	32
	No category		28	8		31	7
Born 1886–90	Prop/prof			6			6
[*n* 1911 = 5,198]	Clerical			12			6
	Craft			12			13
	Farm			32			29
	Unskilled/semi-skilled			25			32
	No category			12			13
Born 1891–95	Prop/prof			2			3
[*n* 1911 = 4,870]	Clerical			12			6
	Craft			7			7
	Farm			28			30
	Unskilled/semi-skilled			19			26
	No category			32			29

Sources: 1891 Census Project; CFP 1901 database; CCRI 1911 microdata database.

Note: Results for 1891 are calculated using sample weights.

Table 13.A2 · Occupations of foreign-born who arrived in Canada between 1891 and 1901, by age cohort, 1901 and 1911

		1901	*1911*
Born 1861–65	Prop/prof	10	11
[*n* 1901 = 547]	Clerical	5	6
[*n* 1911 = 442]	Craft	11	12
	Farm	22	38
	Unskilled/semi-skilled	49	28
	No category	4	5
Born 1866–70	Prop/prof	10	14
[*n* 1901 = 694]	Clerical	5	7
[*n* 1911 = 603]	Craft	11	11
	Farm	16	28
	Unskilled/semi-skilled	55	36
	No category	4	5
Born 1871–75	Prop/prof	10	11
[*n* 1901 = 969]	Clerical	5	7
[*n* 1911 = 785]	Craft	9	12
	Farm	17	26
	Unskilled/semi-skilled	55	37
	No category	4	6
Born 1876–80	Prop/prof	5	10
[*n* 1901 = 797]	Clerical	6	9
[*n* 1911 = 856]	Craft	8	13
	Farm	14	24
	Unskilled/semi-skilled	59	39
	No category	9	5

Sources: CFP 1901 and CCRI 1911 microdata databases.

Table 13.A3 · Ontario-born anglophones, Quebec-born francophones, and foreign-born who arrived in Canada between 1891 and 1901: Earnings by age cohort and occupation (all, clerical, and operative), 1901 and 1911

		Ontario-born anglophones		*Quebec-born francophones*		*Foreign-born, arriving 1891–1901*	
		1901	*1911*	*1901*	*1911*	*1901*	*1911*
Born 1856–65	All wage obs.	597 (440) [1,238]	673 (702) [1,327]	519 (407) [958]	520 (509) [856]	482 (440) [261]	560 (683) [227]
	Clerical	751 (346) [176]	859 (908) [182]	657 (393) [84]	787 (911) [56]		
	Operative	549 (419) [187]	593 (869) [128]	473 (351) [152]	551 (713) [86]		
Born 1866–70	All wage obs.	581 (463) [779]	660 (634) [900]	516 (418) [568]	551 (690) [521]	464 (385) [196]	582 (729) [225]
	Clerical	678 (303) [134]	763 (591) [138]	652 (302) [70]	926 (1,619) [31]		
	Operative	477 (165) [149]	513 (467) [86]	511 (289) [107]	440 (240) [64]		
Born 1871–75	All wage obs.	507 (286) [1,128]	635 (497) [1,085]	456 (289) [677]	520 (480) [730]	426 (339) [308]	501 (366) [297]
	Clerical	599 (244) [216]	740 (607) [165]	553 (252) [94]	662 (647) [62]		
	Operative	464 (194) [225]	542 (367) [145]	417 (159) [142]	548 (716) [101]		
Born 1876–80	All wage obs.	407 (196) [1,320]	611 (427) [1,416]	356 (177) [818]	492 (338) [824]	358 (237) [263]	567 (659) [348]
	Clerical	448 (180) [322]	738 (498) [302]	423 (197) [137]	569 (277) [100]		
	Operative	398 (220) [313]	486 (198) [212]	343 (135) [181]	492 (254) [105]		
Born 1881–85	All wage obs.	248 (129) [1,184]	557 (359) [1759]	221 (134) [738]	441 (213) [1,065]		
	Clerical	251 (119) [334]	655 (464) [405]	228 (122) [124]	516 (319) [139]		
	Operative	232 (121) [322]	494 (226) [274]	209 (131) [211]	431 (167) [169]		

/continued

Table 13.A3 · continued

		Ontario-born anglophones		Quebec-born francophones		Foreign-born, arriving 1891–1901	
		1901	1911	1901	1911	1901	1911
Born 1886–90	All wage obs.		453 (301) [1,909]		382 (199) [1,170]		
	Clerical		464 (237) [486]		446 (342) [116]		
	Operative		416 (162) [361]		387 (157) [178]		
Born 1891–95	All wage obs.		282 (151) [1,358]		252 (174) [995]		
	Clerical		282 (143) [485]		233 (117) [180]		
	Operative		255 (130) [259]		230 (134) [188]		

Sources: CFP 1901 and CCRI 1911 microdata databases.

Note: Standard error in parentheses; number of observations in brackets.

Notes

1 Mary MacKinnon died while working on this study. Readers will recognize the ways in which this chapter builds on her earlier work and the importance of her many contributions to the understanding of historical labour markets. We miss her greatly.

2 We thank Gordon Darroch, Rowena Gray, and participants at the Canadian Economics Association Annual Conference, 28–30 May 2010, Quebec City, Quebec, for comments on a previous draft of this chapter.

3 Social Science Federation of Canada and Statistics Canada, *Historical Statistics of Canada*, 2nd ed. (Ottawa: Statistics Canada, 1983), A1 and A68.

4 Ibid., A350.

5 Claudia Goldin and Lawrence F. Katz, "Technology, Skill, and the Wage Structure: Insights from the Past," *American Economic Review* 86 (1996): 252–7.

6 Ian Drummond, *Progress without Planning: The Economic History of Ontario from Confederation to the Second World War* (Toronto: University of Toronto Press, 1987); Graham Lowe, "'The Enormous File': The Evolution of the Modern Office in Early Twentieth-Century Canada," *Archivaria* 19 (Winter 1985): 137–51,

and *Women in the Administrative Revolution: The Feminization of Clerical Work* (Toronto: University of Toronto Press, 1987); Peter Baskerville and Graham Taylor, *A Concise History of Canadian Business* (Toronto: Oxford University Press, 1994).

7 Robert C. Allen, "Real Incomes in the English-Speaking World, 1879–1913," in George Grantham and Mary MacKinnon (eds.), *Labour Market Evolution: The Economic History of Market Integration, Wage Flexibility and the Employment Relation* (London: Routledge, 1994), 107–38; J.C. Herbert Emery and Clint Levitt, "Cost of Living, Real Wages, and Real Incomes in Thirteen Canadian Cities, 1900–1950," *Canadian Journal of Economics* 35 (2002): 115–37; J.C. Herbert Emery, K. Inwood, and H. Thille, "Hecksher-Ohlin in Canada: New Estimates of Regional Wages and Land Prices," *Australian Economic History Review* 47 (2007): 22–48.

8 Canada, Royal Commission on Industrial Training and Technical Education, *Report of the Commissioners* (Ottawa: King's Printer, 1913).

9 Robert M. Stamp, *The Schools of Ontario, 1876–1976* (Toronto: University of Toronto Press, 1976).

10 Canadian Families Project, http://web.uvic.ca/hrd/cfp/.

11 Canada Century Research Infrastructure Project, http://ccri.library.ualberta.ca/.

12 The 1891 Census Project, http://www.census1891.ca/.

13 Coding based on the NAPP-HISCO classification system is also available; however, for this chapter we use the 1950 US classification system.

14 Duncan McDowell, *Quick to the Frontier: Canada's Royal Bank* (Toronto: McClelland and Stewart, 1993).

15 Leon E. Truesdell, *The Canadian Born in the United States: An Analysis of the Statistics of the Canadian Element in the Population of the United States 1850 to 1930* (New Haven: Yale University Press, 1943), Table 2.

16 Randy W. Widdis, *With Scarcely a Ripple: Anglo-Canadian Migration into the United States and Western Canada, 1880–1920* (Montreal and Kingston: McGill-Queen's University Press, 1998): 290–336.

17 Michael Baker and Gillian Hamilton, "Écarts salariaux entre francophones et anglophones à Montréal au 19e siècle," *L'Actualité économique* 76 (2000): 75–111.

18 Alan G. Green and Mary MacKinnon, "The Slow Assimilation of British Immigrants in Canada: Evidence from Montreal and Toronto, 1901," *Explorations in Economic History* 38 (2000): 315–38. Choosing to live in Canada rather than the United States was a plausible choice for British emigrants; see Alan G. Green, Mary MacKinnon, and Chris Minns, "Dominion or Republic? Migrants to North America from the United Kingdom, 1870–1910," *Economic History Review* 55 (2002): 666–96.

19 Alan G. Green, Mary MacKinnon, and Chris Minns, "Conspicuous by Their Absence: French Canadians and the Settlement of the Canadian West," *Journal of Economic History* 65 (2005): 822–49.

20 Peter A. Baskerville and Eric Sager, *Unwilling Idlers: The Urban Unemployed and Their Families in Late Victorian Canada* (Toronto: University of Toronto Press, 1998).

21 Chris Minns, "Income, Cohort Effects, and Occupational Mobility: A New Look at Immigration to the United States at the Turn of the 20th Century," *Explorations in Economic History* 37 (2000): 326–50.

22 Mary MacKinnon, "Unilingues ou bilingues? Les Montréalais sur le marché du travail en 1901," *L'Actualité économique* 76 (2000): 137–58.

23 Canada, Dominion Bureau of Statistics, Education Statistics Branch, *Historical Statistical Survey of Education in Canada* (Ottawa: King's Printer, 1921), Tables 4, 5, 27, and 99.

24 Ibid., Tables 4, 5, 44, and 99.

25 O.D. Skelton, "General Economic History," in A. Shortt and A. Doughty (eds.), *Canada and Its Provinces*, vol. 9, part 1 (Toronto: Glasgow, Brook, 1914), 95–276.

26 Alan G. Green and David Green, "Canada's Wage Structure in the First Half of the Twentieth Century (with Comparisons to the United States and Great Britain)," paper presented to the Canadian Economics Association Annual Conference, 2–5 June 2011, Ottawa; Emery and Levitt, "Cost of Living."

27 The instructions to 1901 census officers state: "Entries under the heading of Wage Earners [which includes the columns where earnings were recorded] will be made ... for each person named in column 3 who is employed in any industrial or other occupation and is paid salary, wages, or other money allowance for his or her service, and whether employed by piece-work or by time (hour, day, week, etc.), at home, in a factory, or elsewhere." See Canada, Census Office, *Fourth Census of Canada, 1901: Instructions to Officers, Commissioners and Enumerators* (Ottawa: Department of Agriculture, 1901), para. 62.

28 Green, MacKinnon, and Minns, "Dominion or Republic?"

29 Green and Green, "Canada's Wage Structure."

30 Kenneth Bryden, *Old Age Pensions and Policy-Making in Canada* (Kingston and Montreal: McGill-Queen's University Press, 1977); Mary MacKinnon, "Providing for Faithful Servants: Pensions at the Canadian Pacific Railway," *Social Science History* 21 (1997): 59–83. Queen's University, Industrial Relations Section, "Industrial Retirement Plans in Canada," *Bulletin* no. 1 (Kingston: Queen's University, 1938).

31 Emery and Levitt, "Cost of Living"; Chris Minns and Mary MacKinnon, "The Costs of Doing Hard Time: A Penitentiary-Based Regional Price Index for Canada, 1883–1923," *Canadian Journal of Economics* 40 (2007): 528–60.

32 Emery and Levitt, "Cost of Living."

33 Kevin M. Murphy and Finis Welch, "Empirical Age-Earnings Profiles," *Journal of Labor Economics* 8 (1990): 202–29.

34 Mary MacKinnon, "New Evidence on Canadian Wage Rates, 1900–1930," *Canadian Journal of Economics* 29 (1996): 114–31.

35 Green and MacKinnon; "The Slow Assimilation of British Immigrants"; Timothy J. Hatton, "The Immigrant Assimilation Puzzle in Late Nineteenth-Century America," *Journal of Economic History* 57 (1997): 34–62.

36 Ronald Oaxaca, "Male-Female Wage Differentials in Urban Labor Markets," *International Economic Review* 14 (1973): 693–709.

37 The regression results underlying the visual representation that follows are available in an extended working paper version of this chapter: see Kris Inwood, Mary MacKinnon, and Chris Minns, "Labour Market Dynamics in Canada: A First Look from New Census Samples," *LSE Economic History Department Working Paper 148* (2010).

38 Jason Dean, *Three Essays on the Economic Integration of Canadian Immigrants*, doctoral dissertation, McGill University, 2010.

39 Minns, "Income, Cohort Effects, and Occupational Mobility."

40 Patrick J. Coe and J.C. Herbert Emery, "The Dis-Integrating Canadian Labour Market? The Extent of the Market Then and Now," *Canadian Journal of Economics* 37, no. 4 (2004): 879–97.

41 High school enrolment nearly doubled in each of the western provinces between 1905 and 1911. The ratio of classrooms to population aged 5–19 years in Alberta and Saskatchewan remained similar to that of eastern Canada in spite of the challenge of a very rapidly growing population. See Canada, *Historical Statistical Survey of Education in Canada*, Tables 10, and 28–32.

42 Jason Dean reports an initial investigation based on 1901 and 1911 census samples. Dean, *Three Essays*.

43 Kris Inwood and Thanasis Stengos, "Discontinuities in Canadian Economic Growth, 1870–1985," *Explorations in Economic History* 28 (1991): 274–86; Skelton, "General Economic History"; M.C. Urquhart, "New Estimates of Gross National Product, Canada, 1870–1926: Some Implications for Canadian Development," in Stanley Engerman and Robert Gallman (eds.) *Long-Term Factors in American Economic Growth* (Chicago: University of Chicago Press, 1986), 9–88.

44 Drummond, *Progress without Planning*.

— · 14 · —

The Vertical Mosaic Anticipated: Ancestral Origin, Occupational Status, and Earnings in Canada before 1914

CHARLES JONES AND STELLA PARK

Much sociological scholarship on immigration is focused on the period since the 1990s. This leads to research on Canada's biggest cities and suburbs where there are high proportions of recent immigrants and where graduate students as well as journalists are naturally drawn to a field of study that combines human interest with equity issues and policy relevance. Yet, large-scale immigration is neither a new nor a recent phenomenon and the surge into Canada that took place over the first decade of the twentieth century, towards the end of the "classical period" of immigration to the Americas, has lessons for the present. Then, as now, immigration seemed to be hitting unprecedented levels. Then, as now, there were concerns about immigrants from countries from which there had been little previous recruitment. Then, as now, it was feared that immigrant ghettoes might achieve a critical mass and become self-sustaining cultural communities whose inhabitants might never assimilate to Canadian values. Then, as now, there were concerns about the "quality" of recent immigrants as well as about human trafficking. There are, of course, many differences between the two periods but one advantage of studying processes that occurred a century ago is that we know how things turned out.

Total immigration to Canada exceeded 100,000 in 1903 – for the first time since the previous record achieved in the early 1880s. It peaked at just over 402,000 in 1913 (over 5% of the 1911 population), giving national leaders grounds for considerable optimism. It seemed that the opening up of the prairies and the "wheat boom" together with industrialization in eastern Canada could be the basis for something much better than the long depression and continued loss of population to the United States that had occupied the last quarter of the preceding century.

Bringing farm workers in and getting the wheat out required rail transport. The Canadian Pacific Railway had been open for through traffic since 1886, and work was progressing on the Canadian Northern, Grand Trunk, and National Transcontinental lines, the northern route now known as the Canadian National Railway.[1]

Although not part of any government plan, Canada's industrialization was proceeding rapidly along with that of the United States. Increased productivity associated with the replacement of iron by steel, the large-scale use of electricity and of industrial chemistry has been termed the "second phase of the Industrial Revolution."[2] The age of steam was at its peak and, while much transportation was still horse-based, motorcars and trucks as well as electric tramways were beginning to make their appearance on North American streets. Montreal and Toronto, but also smaller Canadian cities such as Hamilton, Brantford, and Valleyfield, were already important centres of manufacturing, and the first generating stations were in place at Lachine and Niagara Falls.[3] Such industrialization required skilled tradesmen as well as factory and office workers.

All that said, the most important elements of the national project were agricultural, mostly linked with opening up the prairies to the expanded production of hardy strains of wheat. Official pronouncements at the time repeatedly stated that more people were needed to work the land, and Canada actively recruited farmers from continental Europe as well as from the United States. Few immigrants came from France, which itself was an immigrant-receiving country at that time.

Advertisements in a range of languages offered 160 acres of free land to settlers together with subsidized transport to the west. At the same time, however, immigration policy officially discouraged what was then called "Oriental" immigration. Such workers had been welcome, although only as what we might now call "guest workers," for the mining industry and construction of the Canadian Pacific railroad twenty or thirty years previously. By 1908, there was considerable resistance to "Asiatic" immigration as well as general unease about overall numbers of immigrants from non-traditional countries of origin.[4] Census snapshots show that the share of foreign-born people in Canada grew from 13 per cent in 1901 to 22 per cent in 1911. By this time, immigration policy had become more restrictive as illustrated by this official statement published in 1913 by the Department of the Interior: "Canada seeks immigration from the British Isles, the United States and certain continental countries such as France, Belgium, Holland, Denmark (including Iceland), Norway, Sweden,

Switzerland and Germany. At various times during the past two decades efforts have also been made in Finland, Russia and Austro-Hungary. At present the advertising propaganda does not include the last three countries mentioned ... Canada does not seek the immigration of Southern Europeans or Asiatics of any race, and those who come to Canada from such countries are attracted by the industrial conditions here or are induced to come by employers of labour, such as railway contractors."[5]

Population Growth in the West

The total population of the prairies almost doubled in the five years after 1901 and more than doubled in the five years after 1906.[6] Over the first decade of the twentieth century, Saskatchewan and Alberta (newly created as provinces in 1905) each quintupled their populations.[7] Manitoba's population started from a higher base and increased less dramatically, not quite doubling between 1901 and 1911.[8] British Columbia differed from other provinces in many ways but it, too, more than doubled its population between 1901 and 1911, largely due to immigration.[9]

The picture is less dramatic in eastern Canada, where the two biggest provinces grew only modestly, and New Brunswick and Nova Scotia held their own. The exception is Prince Edward Island, where the population count declined by around 10 per cent. Populations also declined significantly in the North West Territories.[10]

In 1891, only one-third of Canadians were living in towns or cities, but twenty years later almost half the population was urban.[11] This rapid urbanization reflected population movements as well as the economic transformations associated with industrialization. It also created opportunities for skilled and unskilled labour in the building trades as well as in the construction of urban infrastructure. The expansion of towns and cities together with declines in some rural populations was very striking to contemporary observers, particularly to the agricultural interests personified by John MacDougall, who wrote:

> Canada during the last decennial census period increased in population by 1,833,523, yet her rural growth was only 574,878, while her urban expansion was 1,258,645. She added 34.13 per cent to her total population during the decade, but only 17.16 to her people in the country, though 62.25 to those in town and city. We are apt to think of the prairies as purely agricultural regions, yet Saskatchewan, adding 389 per cent to her rural population, added 648 per cent to her urban population; and Alberta, increasing by 344 per cent in rural growth, increased by 588 per cent in urban growth.[12]

As well as opening up the west and the northern prairies, railroads were built to service extractive or manufacturing industries and their settlements. In many cases, the new townships that sprung up along railway lines were populated by some of the people who had been involved in railroad construction and who then shifted into other lines of work.

Canadian transcontinental rail capacity was considerably overbuilt and boom was followed by bust.[13] Yet, the construction and operation of new railways generated significant demand for lumber, coal, steel, and foreign investment.[14] Over 21 million railway sleepers and over 600,000 poles were purchased by railroad and electric companies in 1912: clearly, a stimulus for the forest products industry. By 1917, Canada had over 38,000 miles of steam railway track and 1,700 miles of electric railways.[15] Hydroelectric plants were built at Niagara Falls and at Lachine near Montreal. Newly built steel works in Cape Breton Island, Hamilton, and Sault Ste Marie employed salaried workers in establishments organized with modern forms of industrial production. Many of the jobs related to this wave of industrialization were specialized and the demand for labour fluctuated over the pre-1914 years. In general, however, Quebec, Ontario, and the west experienced strong demand for all kinds of labour, particularly in construction.

The expansion, westernization, and urbanization of Canada's population involved relatively small but symbolically significant changes in the ancestral background of the population: this was the case particularly in the west but also in the major urban centres of eastern Canada. The United States experienced a similar great wave of immigration, generally considered as the "classic" era from 1890 to the beginning of the Great War. Many of these immigrants were from unfamiliar parts of the world: southern and Eastern Europe, even from China and Japan. Nativist popular reactions are illustrated by book titles such as *The Russian Jew in the United States*, *The Italian in America*, *The Slav Invasion*, *Chinese Immigration*, and *The Problem of the Immigrant*. *Chautauquan* magazine in 1903–04 included a series of articles on the "Racial Composition of the American People," by John R. Commons.[16] Such changes were of considerable public interest to Canadians, as demonstrated by articles in the *Toronto Star* and other periodicals. James S. Woodsworth published a concerned although broadly sympathetic book, *Strangers within Our Gates; or, Coming Canadians*, in 1908, and census and immigration figures were reported on by government officials in successive numbers of the *Canada Year Book*.[17] The choice of tabulations to be carried out and the commentaries upon them clearly indicate that the writers were attempting to understand the large social changes of the time. By 1913, not surprisingly, given the British Columbia Legislature's history of anti-Oriental legislation and the 1907 riots in Vancouver, there was particular interest in using the 1911 census and other data to monitor the consequences of recent immigration policies regarding Chinese, East Indians, and Japanese, as well as in the number and geographical distribution of the Chinese population.

Terminologies for ancestral origin have varied over the years. One modern usage applies "race" or "visible minority" as a term for distinctions based on physical appearance, while the term "ethnicity" is used for distinctions based on culture or identity.[18] The 1901 census had a question about skin colour, and the instructions to enumerators leave little doubt that officials of the time thought in terms of biologically determined races.[19] This question was never asked again, although the 1911 census retained the "racial or tribal origin" column that had been used in 1871, 1881, and 1901. Data from this question were reported simply as "origin" in the *Canada Year Book* of 1913, but by 1918, soon after the founding of the Dominion Bureau of Statistics, the published report of the interdecade *Census of Prairie Provinces* included tables that classified people according to their "racial origins,"[20] while a special report from the 1911 census, published in 1915, shows the "racial origins" of Canadian residents born in the United States.[21]

Returning to the situation at 1911, the phrase printed on the enumeration form was, "Racial or tribal origin" ("Origine selon la race ou la tribu"). Instructions to enumerators regarding this question suggest some of the groups that were of special interest to census officials at the time:

> The racial or tribal origin column 14 is usually traced through the father as in English, Scotch, Irish, Welsh, French, German, Italian, Danish, Swedish, Norwegian, Bohemian, Ruthenian,[22] Bukovinian, Galician, Bulgarian, Chinese, Japanese, Polish, Jewish, etc. A person whose father is English but whose mother is Scotch, Irish, Welsh or other race will be ranked as English, and so will any of the others. In the case of Indians the origin is traced through the mother and the names of the tribes should be given as "Chipewa," "Cree," etc. The children begotten of white and black or yellow races will be classed as Negro or Mongolian (Chinese or Japanese) as the case may be.[23]

The 1913 *Canada Year Book* compares 1901 with 1911 by grouping the detailed responses to the racial or tribal origin question in a table called "Origins of the People" where some of the more populated categories were French, English, Irish, Scotch (sic), German, Austro-Hungarian, Scandinavian, Indian (Aboriginal), Jewish, Dutch, Italian, Russian, Dutch, Chinese and "Negro" (sic).[24] Bukowinians (sometimes spelled Bukovinians) had been reported under "Austrian" for 1901, while Ruthenians had been counted with Galicians. However, these groups were listed separately for 1911 – clearly, a response to the explosive

Table 14.1 · Origins of the people living in Canada in 1901 and 1911, with increases over 10 years and as percentage of population

Origins			*Increase in 10 Years*			
	1901	*1911*	*Absolute increase*	*Percent increase*	*Percent share at 1901*	*Percent share at 1911*
English	1,260,899	1,823,150	562,251	44.6	23.5	25.3
Irish	988,721	1,050,384	61,663	6.2	18.4	14.6
Scotch	800,154	997,880	197,726	24.7	14.9	13.9
Welsh	13,135	24,848	11,713	89.2	0.2	0.3
Other British	286	723	437	152.8	0.0	0.0
All British	3,063,195	3,896,985	833,790	27.2	57.0	54.1
French	1,649,371	2,054,890	405,519	24.6	30.7	28.5
German	310,501	393,320	82,819	26.7	5.8	5.5
Austrian	10,947	42,535	31,588	288.6	0.2	0.6
Bukowinian[a]	(1)	9,960	9,960	(1)	—	0.1
Galician	5,682	35,158	29,476	518.8	0.1	0.5
Hungarian	1,549	11,605	10,056	649.2	0.0	0.2
Ruthenian[b]	(2)	29,845	29,845	(2)	—	0.4
Austro-Hungarian	18,178	129,103	110,925	610.2	0.3	1.8
Belgian	2,994	9,593	6,599	220.4	0.1	0.1
Bulgarian and Romanian	354	5,875	5,521	1559.6	0.0	0.1
Chinese	17,312	27,774	10,462	60.4	0.3	0.4
Dutch	33,845	54,986	21,141	62.5	0.6	0.8
Finnish	2,502	15,497	12,995	519.4	0.1	0.2
Grecian (sic)	291	3,594	3,303	1135.1	0.0	0.1
Hindu	—	2,342	2,342	—	—	0.0

/continued

increase in immigration from this part of Eastern Europe.[25] As we have seen, the instructions to enumerators for 1911 make specific reference to Galicians, Ruthenians, etc., which indicates official interest in them, likely arising from print media discussions of Slav immigration as well as the prairie censuses of 1906. As with earlier and later Canadian censuses, the categories used in official reports mix criteria of skin colour ("Negro"), religion (Jewish, Hindu), and birthplace or nationality (Austrian, Belgian, British Dominions, Russian).[26]

Table 14.1, reproduced from the 1913 *Canada Year Book*, shows how the balance of immigration, emigration, and natural increase affected the absolute and

Table 14.1 · continued

Origins	*Increase in 10 Years*					
	1901	*1911*	*Absolute increase*	*Percent increase*	*Percent share at 1901*	*Percent share at 1911*
Indian (sic)[c]	127,941	105,492	-22,449	-17.6	2.4	1.5
Italian	10,834	45,411	34,577	319.2	0.2	0.6
Japanese	4,738	9,021	4,283	90.4	0.1	0.1
Jewish	16,131	75,681	59,550	369.2	0.3	1.1
Negro (sic)	17,437	16,877	-560	-3.2	0.3	0.2
Polish	6,285	33,365	27,080	430.9	0.1	0.5
Russian	19,825	43,142	23,317	117.6	0.4	0.6
Scandinavian	31,042	107,535	76,493	246.4	0.6	1.5
Swiss	3,865	6,625	2,760	71.4	0.1	0.1
Turkish	1,681	3,880	2,199	130.8	0.0	0.1
Various	1,454	18,310	16,844	1158.5	0.0	0.3
Unspecified	31,539	147,345	115,806	367.2	0.6	2.0
Total population	*5,371,315*	*7,206,643*	*1,835,328*		*100.0*	*100.0*

Source: *Canada Year Book*, 1913, 69; reproduction of Table 15, "Origins of the People." http://www66.statcan.gc.ca/eng/acyb_c1913-eng.aspx.

a Included in the general term Austrian in 1901; b Included in the general term Galician in 1901; c Included half-breeds (sic) in 1901 but not in 1911.

relative sizes of ancestral-origin groups. A "Canadian" category is conspicuous by its absence since the census authorities were interested in the balance of ancestral-origin groups making up the country's population. The French-origin category increased by 25 per cent from the previous census, but since this was less than the 34 per cent growth in Canada's population overall, the relative share of those of French origin had slightly declined. The British-origin group taken together increased by 27 per cent and remained numerically dominant, at 54 per cent of the 1911 population, albeit with a slightly reduced share. Those identified as English-origin increased by almost 50 per cent,[27] while the Irish- and Scots-origin populations increased by 6 per cent and 25 per cent, respectively: their proportional shares declining.

North American Indians showed an 18 per cent decline partly because of changes in the method of counting mixed ancestry.[28] African Canadians ("Negro" category in the *Canada Year Book*'s vocabulary and mainly located in eastern Canada) slightly decreased in numbers, continuing the decline from the 1871 and 1881 counts. While slavery had been practised in eastern Canada into the early 1800s, most people of African ancestry in Canada were in the Maritime provinces or Ontario, in many cases because their forebears had taken the side of the British in the American Revolution or the War of 1812, or had escaped from slavery along the Underground Railroad. Black Nova Scotians were mostly in and around Halifax, including the "Africville" settlement in the Bedford Basin, with smaller numbers living in other parts of the province.[29] A few African Canadians also lived in Ontario towns such as Hamilton, London, and Oakville. Compared with African Americans in the United States, they had higher levels of literacy but they still tended to work in lower-level jobs and/or farm marginal agricultural land and occupy very low-quality housing.[30]

Some smaller ancestral-origin groups made significant gains in numbers between 1901 and 1911. The well-established German-origin group increased by 25 per cent compared with a six-fold increase (from a much smaller base) among the broad group of Austro-Hungarians. The Italian population tripled in size, the Polish one quadrupled, and the Finnish quintupled, while the Scandinavians more than doubled and the Jewish-origin population increased by 369 per cent. If we group Galicians and Ruthenians together since they likely include many of those later identifying as Ukrainians, their population increased ninefold between 1901 and 1911. Writing about similar immigrant groups in the United States at this time, Brian Gratton describes how very different many of these people would have seemed to the native-born: "Rural, rough folk, unlettered, the great majority of the new arrivals had no understanding of English ... Most were young single males, footloose and fancy free, and most intending to return to their home countries after making a pile of money."[31]

Chinese and Japanese ancestral-origin groups increased by 60 per cent and 90 per cent, respectively, albeit from relatively small bases, reaching population sizes, in Canada as a whole, of 27,774 and 9,021, respectively. Since this population of East Asian origin was mostly located in British Columbia, about half of it in segregated neighbourhoods of Vancouver and Victoria, and largely composed of Chinese men of working age who were perceived to undercut wage rates, it was exceptionally noticeable. Certainly, the visibility of East Asians had become the occasion of a tightening up of immigration regulations, as discussed in some detail in the *Canada Year Book* of 1913.[32]

With hindsight, we know that a decade later, after the economic slowdown that started just before the Great War, after the Russian Revolution and territorial reorganizations according to the peace treaty at Versailles, after the wheat boom ended and the bankruptcy and nationalization of the Canadian Northern and Grand Trunk railways, and after the Winnipeg General Strike of 1919, among other economic and political events, the Chinese Immigration Act of 1923 would severely restrict the legal entry of all Chinese except for merchants, diplomats, and students.[33] The optimism of the first decade of the twentieth century was to be followed by many years of retrenchment.

Results from the 1911 Census Sample Data

We have seen that published materials of the time tell of large-scale immigration and impressive population growth. This had been encouraged by official narratives of the wheat boom and the "last best west" as well as by continuing railroad construction. Those who migrated to homestead in the west were attracted by the prospect of free or low-priced agricultural land.[34] But migration was also fuelled by urbanization and the shift towards modern manufacturing practices in the east, particularly in the Montreal and Toronto regions. This created employment opportunities for skilled and professional as well as unskilled workers: the former having higher levels of human capital (e.g., ability to speak English or French where relevant, literacy, work experience, apprenticeship experience, advanced training) than the latter. Those with lesser amounts of human capital or those who faced barriers because of their geographical origin, ethnolinguistic background, gender, or religious affiliation were at risk of ending up working long hours as factory workers and/or doing dirty and dangerous jobs in construction camps, lumbering, or mining.

The foreign-born of British or American ancestral origin would have been at an advantage compared with other recent immigrants. They spoke the dominant official language; most were literate and many had served apprenticeships and/or were used to the patterns of work discipline in an industrial society. Longer established groups, including charter groups and others such as Germans would also have been advantaged in these ways. Contrast this with the foreign-born from ancestral origin groups such as Chinese, Eastern European, Italian, or Scandinavian who came from less-industrialized regions and many of whom spoke only their own languages and/or were illiterate.[35]

Then, as now, people did better or worse according to their talents, or what economists call "human capital," which includes language skills, literacy, nativity, and years since immigration if foreign-born. However, job levels and income attained were also affected by ancestral origins, community ties, and gender, over and above the effects of human capital endowments. In the remainder of this chapter, we show the extent to which such ascribed characteristics were linked to the occupational achievements of Canadians before 1914.

Aside from Aboriginal peoples and the British and French charter groups, we focus on selected single-origin groups of which German was by far the most numerous. Smaller single-origin groups included (in order of 1911 population size) Scandinavians, Jews, Dutch, Italians, Russians, Austrians, Galicians, Poles, and Ruthenians.[36] The Chinese-origin population was only slightly smaller than the Ruthenian but, as we shall see, Chinese in Canada at that time were almost entirely men of working age. The African Canadian ("Negro") population was about the same size as the Finnish-origin group and, as already mentioned, was almost unique in that there were fewer of them in 1911 than in 1901.[37] After grouping English, Irish, Scottish, and Welsh under British, all other single-origin groups discerned by the 1911 census authorities had population sizes under 12,000. Because of this we shall give them only minimal attention.[38]

Sociologists have looked at social mobility partly in terms of the processes by which societies change and partly in terms of the degree to which adult social and economic status depends on factors such as family background, family size, ethnicity, education, and gender.[39] The two perspectives are interlinked, and both relate to immigration and other forms of geographical mobility. Later in this chapter, we shall show how some ethnic groups were overrepresented in less desirable jobs.[40] Before demonstrating such associations between status outcomes and ethnic group membership, it is important first to examine the composition of Canada's ancestral-origin groups in 1911, including their very different histories of immigration, their varying sex ratios, age structures, geographical distribution, literacy rates, and living arrangements. In so doing, we focus on the major ancestral-origin groups: those with significant population size in 1911. We arrange them somewhat differently from the manner of table 14.1, placing the British and French groups first, then the three groups distinguishable by physical appearance (Aboriginals, Blacks, Chinese and Japanese), and finally the remainder of the larger single-origin groups in alphabetical order, with one exception – Galicians and Ruthenians are placed directly beneath Austrians because of the overlapping regional and ethnic identities of these groups that are likely to have included high proportions of people from what is now Ukraine.[41]

Behind Aboriginals and the French, with over 97 per cent born in Canada, three-quarters of the British-origin group were Canadian-born, which is similar to the Dutch and the Germans. Within the British group, those of English origin were more likely to be recent immigrants than the Irish or the Scots. Other groups had well under 20 per cent born in Canada, with some almost entirely foreign-born, for example, Chinese, Italians, and Jews, as well as most of the groups from the Austro-Hungarian and Russian empires of the time. Among those non-charter groups that were relatively new to Canada at 1911, half of Ruthenians had immigrated before 1902 and half of Chinese before 1903. Considered in the aggregate, groups such as these had at least a decade

Table 14.2 · Major ancestral-origin groups: Immigrants according to number of years in Canada and Canadian-born, Canada, 1911

1911 Census sample	*Years in Canada / Nativity*				
	0–4 yrs (%)	*5–9 yrs* (%)	*10–14 yrs* (%)	*15+ yrs* (%)	*Cdn-born* (%)
ORIGIN					
British	10.1	6.2	1.6	7.7	74.4
French	0.9	0.6	0.3	0.6	97.6
Aboriginal	0.6	0.2	0.0	0.3	99.0
Black	12.3	3.1	1.7	5.1	77.8
Chinese	31.2	23.5	22.6	21.4	1.3
Japanese	32.9	30.4	20.8	15.4	0.6
Dutch	9.2	3.8	0.9	1.7	84.5
German	11.6	10.2	3.5	8.8	65.9
Austrian	52.8	24.6	14.8	3.6	4.3
Galician	36.4	35.9	20.6	2.6	4.5
Ruthenian	19.8	34.3	36.3	3.9	5.6
Finnish	53.2	26.9	10.2	4.7	5.0
Italian	50.5	24.1	9.2	7.8	8.4
Jewish	29.7	34.5	10.7	12.7	12.3
Polish	43.7	26.9	10.8	6.3	12.3
Russian	35.8	15.4	29.2	7.0	12.6
Norwegian	50.8	36.0	4.7	3.5	5.0
Swedish	44.3	29.8	8.5	10.0	7.3
Other	19.1	12.6	5.2	5.6	57.5
Total	*9.8*	*6.4*	*2.3*	*5.7*	*75.9*

Source: CCRI 1911 microdata database, weighted data.

Note: Both sexes, aged 10+ years. Percentages may not always total 100 because of rounding.

to form communities adapted to life in Canada. Austrians, Finns, Italians, and Norwegians, however, had a median arrival year of 1907, meaning that half of their members had arrived in the four years before the 1911 enumeration. Given that it can take several years to recover from the costs of immigration, we would expect members of these groups to be worse off and likely in low-status jobs.

Canadians of French origin were concentrated in eastern Canada, in Quebec, of course, but also in parts of the Maritime provinces and Ontario. The English and other British-origin groups were well represented in all provinces. More

Table 14.3 · Major ancestral-origin groups according to where they lived: Urban (major, minor, small) and rural, Canada, 1911

1911 Census sample	*Urban-rural classification*			
	Major urban (%)	*Minor urban (%)*	*Small urban (%)*	*Rural (%)*
ORIGIN				
British	25.4	21.1	4.0	49.5
French	21.5	17.8	3.6	57.1
Aboriginal	0.7	1.8	1.2	96.3
Black	19.8	33.2	0.5	46.5
Chinese	39.9	18.8	4.1	37.1
Japanese	30.4	4.7	0.5	64.4
Dutch	9.5	17.2	2.7	70.6
German	12.0	18.9	4.1	65.1
Austrian	17.5	17.2	4.7	60.6
Galician	9.2	9.1	4.1	77.7
Ruthenian	14.1	5.9	0.3	79.8
Finnish	5.4	34.7	0.2	59.8
Italian	36.0	31.2	2.2	30.6
Jewish	84.9	9.0	1.2	4.9
Polish	36.8	17.4	3.9	41.9
Russian	14.2	5.8	5.0	75.0
Norwegian	6.9	9.3	6.0	77.9
Swedish	10.6	15.0	4.8	69.6
Other	28.4	17.0	5.2	49.5
Total	*23.7*	*19.3*	*3.8*	*53.2*

Source: CCRI 1911 microdata database, weighted data.

Note: Both sexes, aged 10+ years.

recently arrived groups such as Eastern Europeans were mostly in Manitoba and the west, although some settled in eastern urban centres including the home of the new steel plant, Sydney, Nova Scotia.[42]

Census officials devoted several tables to descriptions of the Chinese-origin population in 1901 and 1911.[43] Seventy per cent of those of Chinese origin in 1911 were enumerated in British Columbia, 10 per cent in Ontario, and 6 per cent in Alberta. Even Quebec was home to over 1,000 Chinese in 1901, and this number had grown to 1,578 by 1911. The Chinese-origin group stands out very sharply because of its skewed sex ratio: over all age groups, in 1911, there were sixty men for every woman, a ratio directly related to the immigration policies of the time.

A quarter of a century previously, Chinese workers had been well represented in the work camps associated with construction of the Canadian Pacific railroad and, before that, in the goldfields. We know that 38 per cent of Chinese working in Canada in 1881 were miners and 36 per cent were labourers.[44] By 1911, however, only 15 per cent of all Chinese were enumerated in the kind of large single units that are likely to have been work camps. And of more than 100,000 men counted in such large enumeration units, the Chinese constituted only 4 per cent, a slightly smaller share than that of Italians (at 6%). In fact, over half the men enumerated in such "group quarters" in 1911 were of British or French origin.

We have seen that urbanization was a major trend over the first decade of the twentieth century. Canada still thought of itself as a strongly rural society, and in many ways it was, but by 1911, a quarter of the population lived in major urban centres and a further 19 per cent lived in minor urban centres, leaving just over half in rural areas. Given the numerical dominance of the British and French groups, these overall figures describe their distribution reasonably well, with roughly a quarter of the British in major urban centres compared with one fifth of the French. As one might expect, the French-origin population was somewhat more rural-based (57% rural compared with 50% rural for the British).

Other ancestral-origin groups differed considerably in their propensity to live in urban or rural areas. Overall, the Chinese-origin group was roughly equally split between major urban (40%) and rural (37%) areas. However, if we focus only on British Columbia, we find that half of the Chinese-origin group was in major or minor urban areas, mostly in Vancouver and Victoria, with the other half rural. In Ontario, by contrast, 98 per cent of the small but significant Chinese population was enumerated in urban areas.

Other ethnic-origin groups had their own patterns of urban-rural location. Galicians and Ruthenians were about 80 per cent rural, reflecting the fact that most of them had been encouraged to come to Canada in search of land to homestead. In similar fashion, Germans and Austrians were, respectively, 65 per cent and 60 per cent rural. Only 30.6 per cent of Italians and 5 per cent of Jews lived in rural areas. In other words, these two groups were least likely to be living in rural areas compared with other ethnic origin groups.

What Kind of People Moved to the Western/Prairie Provinces?

The "last best west," a term used in Canada's publicity for recruiting immigrants, achieved massive population growth in the first decade of the twenti-

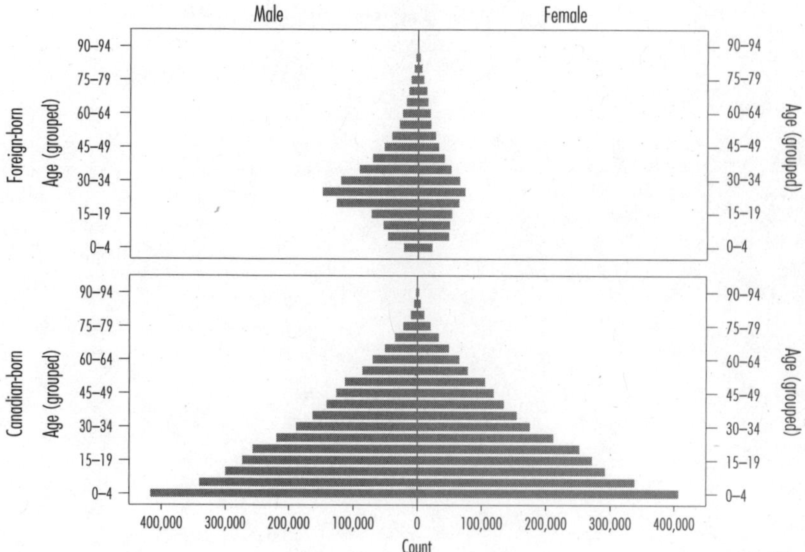

Figure 14.1 · Age-gender pyramids for Canadian-born and foreign-born population 10 years of age and older, Canada, 1911.

Source: CCRI 1911 microdata database.

eth century and did so to a large extent through recruiting British and other foreign-born immigrants. In fact, over half (55%) of the foreign-born aged 10 and over in 1911 were located west of Ontario, compared with one-third in Ontario and most of the remainder (9%) in Quebec, while hardly any were in the Maritimes.

The west was also settled by people born in Canada, and most of these interprovincial migrants, in 1911, were Ontario-born.[45] One in five of those enumerated in the west were Ontario-born but only 6 per cent had been born in Quebec or the Maritimes. Only 12 per cent of those aged 10 and over living west of Ontario in 1911 were born there. A quarter were born in the British Isles, and a further 36 per cent were non-British immigrants. British Columbia, as part of the west, had broadly the same pattern of in-migration, with the added features that many of its foreign-born were Asians and many of its Canadian-born were Aboriginals.

Sex Ratios

It was remarked at the time that the sex ratio among the foreign-born in 1911 was 158 men to every 100 women. The 1913 *Canada Year Book* devotes several

Table 14.4 · Major ancestral-origin groups: Number of males and females and sex ratios, Canada, 1911

1911 Census sample	*Sex of person enumerated*		
	Male	*Female*	*Sex ratio*
ORIGIN			
British	1,623,770	1,417,058	1.2
French	734,360	700,568	1.1
Aboriginal	35,820	35,266	1.0
Black	7,024	6,964	1.0
Chinese	27,056	450	60.1
Japanese	7,388	914	8.1
Dutch	21,096	17,838	1.2
German	155,900	136,262	1.1
Austrian	20,096	7,212	2.8
Galician	16,050	8,390	1.9
Ruthenian	12,132	8,978	1.4
Finnish	9,620	3,104	3.1
Italian	31,124	6,854	4.5
Jewish	29,194	25,186	1.2
Polish	16,698	8,294	2.0
Russian	18,770	10,518	1.8
Norwegian	21,162	10,666	2.0
Swedish	25,080	10,874	2.3
Other	137,734	100,226	1.4

Source: CCRI 1911 microdata database, weighted data.

Note: Both sexes, aged 10+ years.

tables and paragraphs of discussion to this issue, noting that Saskatchewan, Alberta, and British Columbia, along with the Yukon, were very different from the eastern provinces in terms of sex ratios and the proportion of foreign-born, with Manitoba being mid-way between Ontario and the west in this regard. Figure 14.1 shows population pyramids for the Canadian-born and foreign-born aged 10 and over in 1911. The lower panel provides the classic symmetrical picture of a high fertility population but, as the upper section shows, the foreign-born population at that time included large numbers of men in their 20s and 30s with markedly fewer women. While some might have left wives and children behind, many of the foreign-born were clearly unpartnered young men seeking economic opportunity. As one might expect of such a population, the rate per 1,000 of convictions for public drunkenness doubled over the first decade of the twentieth century.[46] It is likely that they contributed to the demand for sex trade workers.[47]

Table 14.4 shows sex ratios by ancestral origin among the foreign-born in Canada who were aged 10 and over in 1911. The sex ratio among Chinese is extreme, at sixty men for every woman, compared with most other ethnic origin groups, such as the large group of British immigrants, which had a more modest but still unbalanced ratio of 1.15 men for every woman. Given the small number of Chinese merchants and professionals whose families were exempt from the head tax, many Chinese lived as bachelors in rooming houses. Other ancestral-origin groups with sex ratios of at least 2:1 include Austrians, Finns, Italians, and Swedes, over half of whose members had arrived within the five years before the 1911 enumeration.

High levels of literacy are important for a modern industrial society but not essential for most jobs in basic labouring or farming. The 1911 census asked two simple questions about reading and writing ability, in any language, for persons aged 5 and older.[48] These data are quite crude since some informants might report that members of their household are literate when they can only read or write a few words. Alternatively, some census enumerators might rely too much on their impressions or their racial stereotypes. These arguments were evaluated in the 1920s, and it was concluded that the literacy data were, on the whole, accurate.[49]

Literacy rates among the major ancestral groups we have been discussing are given in table 14.5. For each ancestral-origin group, the table shows the percentages enumerated as being able to read and write in any language, as well as the percentages whose first language was neither English nor French.

Northern European groups as well as the British were highest in literacy, with rates of 95 per cent and over. The French group was somewhat lower, and African Canadians were about level with the French, having near 85 per cent of men able to read and write. Markedly lower rates were recorded for Eastern and southern European groups such as Galicians, Italians, Ruthenians, and Russians, as well as for Chinese, Japanese, and Aboriginals. The Chinese had around the same incidence of literacy as Italians and Poles, around 70 per cent, while Jews were somewhat behind the northern Europeans. There were high rates of illiteracy in any language (rates of one-third or more) among several groups whose numbers in Canada had doubled or tripled over the previous decade. This was a matter of lively debate about the "quality" of immigrants in the United States as well as in Canada, with nativists arguing that the national stock would be weakened by admitting large numbers of illiterates.[50]

Table 14.5 · Major ancestral-origin groups, males and females: Literacy (in any language) and use of non-official languages, Canada, 1911

1911 Census sample	*Gender*			
	Male		*Female*	
	Literacy & first language spoken		*Literacy & first language spoken*	
	Can read & write (%)	*Non-official language(s) (%)*	*Can read & write (%)*	*Non-official language(s) (%)*
ORIGIN				
British	97.9	2.3	98.0	2.4
French	85.3	1.4	89.9	1.4
Aboriginal	44.9	78.7	40.9	81.6
Black	87.8	4.3	84.2	4.2
Chinese	67.8	72.2	72.1	82.2
Japanese	56.6	86.1	79.4	84.2
Dutch	95.0	6.8	95.6	8.1
German	95.7	41.4	95.6	41.0
Austrian	68.1	80.7	65.1	79.4
Galician	61.4	84.9	42.3	87.2
Ruthenian	53.9	92.1	36.6	93.9
Finnish	90.1	65.7	92.1	63.1
Italian	72.4	69.0	74.0	57.9
Jewish	90.7	38.2	82.5	43.7
Polish	66.9	78.8	62.6	73.4
Russian	61.7	82.6	51.6	84.0
Norwegian	96.6	21.8	95.9	25.0
Swedish	95.1	33.4	97.0	32.6
Other	91.0	23.1	94.2	14.2
Total	92.0	10.9	93.6	8.2

Source: CCRI 1911 microdata database, weighted data.

Note: Both sexes, aged 10+ years.

There is a rough relationship between the pattern of literacy across ancestral-origin groups and that of non-official languages. Table 14.5 shows the percentage of each ancestral-origin group that was commonly speaking a language other than English or French. There is high prevalence of non–official language speakers, well over 50 per cent, among Eastern and southern Europeans some of whom, as we have seen, included large proportions of very recent immigrants.[51] Putting this pattern together with that concerning literacy, the census enumerations represent several ancestral-origin groups as having relatively low levels of human capital so far as work in mainstream Canadian society was concerned. We would, therefore, expect that members of these groups would find work either in ethnic communities where their command of a non-official language could be an asset rather than a handicap or in agriculture and/or unskilled labour, neither of which required much beyond physical endurance. Of course, immigrants at that time were not selected for their literacy or language skills; nevertheless, illiteracy and inability to speak an official language, where they occurred, helped to define these "new Canadians" as being of different "stock."

Occupational Status

As usual among sociologists, we define social position mostly in terms of a person's means of earning a living, where lower social position is inferred from unskilled labouring work and higher status from proprietorship as well as skilled, managerial, or professional paid activities where the individual has some degree of authority and/or autonomy. We are greatly helped by the fact that the census authorities coded the 1911 data into occupational level as well as into industry.

Occupational information was coded into "the particular industry or place where the worker is employed." The census used twelve broad industrial categories of which agriculture was dominant followed at some distance by building/construction and transportation. Just under 40 per cent of men of British or French origin were employed in the farming sector, as were about half of the Galicians and Germans and well over half of the Dutch, Ruthenians, and Norwegians. Recent immigrant groups with hardly any representation in the farming sector included the Japanese, Italians, and Jews. The most common industries for Japanese men were hunting/fishing and forestry, while Jewish men tended to work in trade and merchandizing or in the manufacturing of food or clothing including fancy goods, umbrellas, harnesses, musical instruments, and furs. Around one-third of the Austrians, Galicians, and Italians worked in transportation, likely the railways. Interestingly, most of the Chinese were no longer working in railway construction, 40 per cent of them being employed in the domestic or personal service category, with around 10 per cent each in agriculture, hunting/fishing, and forestry.[52]

Women enumerated as working at an occupation most commonly provided domestic or personal services in or outside a household. One-third of the women of British or French origin but three-quarters of Black women were in jobs of this kind. Like their male counterparts, Jewish women who worked tended to be in trade and manufacturing of food and clothing or in trade and merchandizing.

More important for the study of status, information about occupation was also coded into "class or rank of the worker" within each industry. We interpret this as the overall level of the enumerated person's job. The coding instructions of the time make it clear that a global judgment was required: "In classifying the entries in columns 17 and 22 the clerk should take into consideration the evidence in the other columns of the schedule, such as relationship to head of family, age, sex and whether employer, employee or working on own account. The amount of salary or wages received should also be considered."[53]

Occupation is a good indicator of social status for men as well as for most never-married adult women. It is not such a good indicator for farm proprietors or homesteaders since we have little information about the relative size of farm establishments. That said, agricultural proprietors were generally considered much superior to agricultural labourers so, within the agricultural sector at least, being a farm proprietor, however small, is better than being a farm labourer. The census forms provided less information for proprietors and own account workers since they were not asked to provide information on wages or hours and weeks worked.

The most common three categories of "class or rank of worker" account for over 85 per cent of non-farm male workers. These are (1) owners, proprietors, manufacturers, contractors, and anyone working on own account (37%); (2) workers, makers, operators, operatives, journeymen, millwrights, skilled workers of all kinds (25%); and (3) labourers, unskilled, messengers, cleaners, haulers (25%). Of the remaining rank categories, the most frequent were various kinds of supervisory or clerical positions: (4) superintendents, assistant superintendents, purchasing agents, head housekeepers, chief clerks, and (5) bookkeepers, stenographers, office clerks, cashiers, timekeepers.

We have grouped the ten categories of "class or rank of worker" into four broad job levels consisting of self-employed owners and proprietors, managerial and supervisory employees/clerical workers, skilled employees, and unskilled labourers.

Self-employed owners and proprietors were mostly homesteaders or farm owners, but the category also includes many kinds of artisans working on their own account as well as professionals. Most proprietors did not report earnings since that question was directed at those who were paid wages or salaries. To be one's own master was a valued status in Victorian and Edwardian times but, given wide variations in farm or business size, the category would have been quite heterogeneous as regards the economic status it conferred.[54] The high

Table 14.6 · Major ancestral-origin groups: Broad job levels, Canada, 1911

1911 Census sample	*Broad job levels*				
	Self-employed owners (%)	*Clerical & supervisory (%)*	*Skilled employees (%)*	*Unskilled labourers (%)*	*Ratio of skilled to unskilled employees*
ORIGIN					
British	41.8	11.8	26.6	19.9	1.3
French	46.5	6.6	24.0	22.9	1.0
Aboriginal	59.3	1.8	7.7	31.2	0.2
Black	29.0	5.6	17.0	48.4	0.4
Chinese	16.2	3.0	31.1	49.7	0.6
Japanese	8.5	3.2	38.0	50.3	0.8
Dutch	58.3	5.6	14.4	21.6	0.7
German	57.1	6.5	18.5	17.8	1.0
Austrian	19.6	1.4	15.8	63.1	0.3
Galician	44.8	1.3	4.0	49.9	0.1
Ruthenian	65.4	1.5	3.6	29.5	0.1
Finnish	11.6	3.2	25.9	59.3	0.4
Italian	10.1	3.4	15.1	71.4	0.2
Jewish	40.0	7.3	43.0	9.6	4.5
Polish	19.9	3.8	15.2	61.1	0.2
Russian	42.5	1.7	9.2	46.6	0.2
Norwegian	59.5	2.5	13.3	24.7	0.5
Swedish	37.1	5.1	18.3	39.5	0.5
Other	41.6	9.1	20.9	28.4	0.7
Total	*42.8*	*9.3*	*24.4*	*23.5*	*1.0*

Source: CCRI 1911 microdata database, weighted data.

Note: Men aged 20–64 years.

percentages of proprietors among Aboriginals, Dutch, Germans, Norwegians, and Ruthenians likely reflect the extent to which these groups tended to be farmers. The three remaining broad job levels are easier to understand in terms of relative status; all refer to employed persons receiving wages or a salary, although they differ in terms of authority, skills, and wage levels. Interpreting the broad job categories through this lens, men of British origin had the highest percentage in supervisory and managerial work, with Aboriginals, Blacks, Chinese, Japanese, and some of the recent European immigrant groups having the lowest. Around 40 per cent of Jews were skilled employees, and only about one in ten worked as an unskilled labourer. Italians emerge as the origin group with the highest percentage in unskilled work and, therefore, with the lowest average occupational status. Looking at each ancestral-origin group's ratio of skilled to unskilled workers among men, the Jewish group is clearly highest, with recent immigrant groups from southern and Eastern Europe being the lowest. Galicians and Ruthenians, for example, had roughly one skilled worker for every ten unskilled workers compared with the British-origin group that had thirteen skilled workers for every ten unskilled.

Whether in urban or rural settings, unskilled labour was generally considered low status. We, therefore, learn something about group inequality by predicting the odds of a man's being in unskilled labour, rather than being a proprietor, manager, supervisor, clerk, or skilled worker, from his ancestral origin as well as from indicators of his age, immigration status, literacy, and religion (Protestant or otherwise[55]). Since the ancestral-origin groups were far from evenly distributed over Canada's regions, we carried out logistic regression results separately by province.[56] Among other things, this demonstrates that certain groups were completely unrepresented in particular provinces; for example, Quebec had few or no Galician or Ruthenian men aged 20 to 64, while British Columbia had few African Canadians or Austrians.

Recent immigrants had higher odds of working in unskilled labour, as did men aged between 20 and 35, while Protestants had lower odds of being in such low-status work. These variables controlled, ancestral origin still had strong links with the odds of being in unskilled work. All these comparisons are made with reference to those of British ancestral origin. African Canadians had markedly higher odds of working as labourers, as did Aboriginals, Austrians, Italians, Poles, and Russians. Confirming the descriptive results shown in table 14.6, Jews had markedly lower odds of being unskilled labourers, while those of French-origin were significantly more likely to be unskilled labourers – but only in Ontario.[57]

Weeks Worked and Weekly Earnings in 1910

The 1911 census questions on earnings, weeks of work, and hours of work were directed at wage earners (*employés*) rather than at proprietors or own-account workers.[58] More than half of male wage earners and over a third of women wage earners reported working a sixty-hour week. Two-thirds of these women and a slightly smaller percentage of the men worked fifty or more weeks in 1910; the most common response indicated working the full fifty-two weeks of the year. A major exception here were those of Aboriginal origin, who typically worked a much smaller number of weeks in their chief occupation or trade, presumably because their waged work was seasonal.

Table 14.7 · Median 1910 weekly employee earnings according to broad job levels, by province, Canada, 1911

1911 Census sample	*Broad job levels*			
	Unskilled labourers	*Skilled employees*	*Clerical and supervisory*	*Total*
	1910 Weekly earnings	*1910 Weekly earnings*	*1910 Weekly earnings*	*1910 Weekly earnings*
	Median ($)	*Median ($)*	*Median ($)*	*Median ($)*
PROVINCE				
Nova Scotia	8.33	11.54	13.85	10.00
Prince Edward Island	6.56	8.65	11.60	8.00
New Brunswick	8.08	11.11	13.92	9.60
Quebec	9.00	12.00	15.38	11.54
Ontario	9.62	12.69	16.83	11.92
Manitoba	10.21	16.15	19.23	13.85
Saskatchewan	9.62	16.67	19.23	13.46
Alberta	12.46	17.50	20.00	15.00
British Columbia	12.50	18.46	21.25	16.00
Total	*9.62*	*13.46*	*17.31*	*12.00*

Source: CCRI 1911 microdata database, weighted data.

Note: Men aged 20–64 years.

Given the seasonality of much work before 1914, the weekly wage would have been a meaningful concept to people at the time. It, therefore, makes more sense to talk about weekly than annual earnings and to use the median for group averages. Table 14.7 shows that earnings differed markedly by province, with the strong east-west gradient that has been discussed by economic historians.[59] This must be borne in mind since we analyse nominal wages without any adjustments for east-west or urban-rural differentials in cost of living. Weekly earnings differed by job level, with skilled employees obtaining a "skill premium" of 40 per cent over the unskilled, and clerical and supervisory employees earning an "authority premium" of 80 per cent over the same group.

Prince Edward Island paid the lowest wages, at an average of $8.00 per week (only $6.56 for unskilled labourers), while Manitoba and Saskatchewan were both paying over $13.00 a week ($10.21 and $9.62 for unskilled labourers, respectively). The low level of earnings in PEI is consistent with its loss of population between 1901 and 1911. At around $12.50 a week, unskilled labourers in

Table 14.8 · Major ancestral-origin groups in Maritime provinces, Quebec, and Ontario: Median 1910 weekly earnings according to broad job levels

1911 Census sample Maritime provinces, Quebec, and Ontario	*Broad job levels*			
	Unskilled labourers	*Skilled employees*	*Clerical and supervisory*	*Total*
	1910 Earnings Median ($)	*1910 Earnings Median ($)*	*1910 Earnings Median ($)*	*1910 Earnings Median ($)*
ORIGIN				
British	9.00	12.31	16.35	11.54
French	9.00	12.00	13.85	10.58
Aboriginal	9.38	12.00	—	9.60
Black	8.65	10.00	8.40	9.00
Chinese	6.00	6.73	—	6.00
Japanese	—	—	—	—
Dutch	8.00	12.00	19.23	10.00
German	8.40	12.00	16.00	11.00
Austrian	10.77	13.08	—	11.54
Galician	10.00	—	—	10.00
Ruthenian	12.00	—	—	12.00
Finnish	11.94	15.00	—	12.00
Italian	10.00	13.46	14.42	10.00
Jewish	10.00	12.00	18.46	12.00
Polish	10.00	12.00	—	10.00
Russian	10.00	11.06	—	10.00
Norwegian	12.50	13.46	—	12.96
Swedish	10.58	16.39	17.31	14.00
Other	9.23	12.00	17.31	10.96
Total	*9.00*	*12.00*	*15.63*	*11.54*

Source: CCRI 1911 microdata database, weighted data.

Note: Men aged 20–64 years. Averages calculated from 10 or fewer unweighted cases are not shown.

Alberta and British Columbia earned slightly more than skilled workers in the Maritime provinces – a differential that makes the low rate of western settlement from the Maritimes rather puzzling, although we must also remember that eastern Canadians have had a long history of temporary or permanent migration to the "Boston states" of New England and many would have had family ties there.[60]

Table 14.9 · Major ancestral-origin groups in Prairie provinces and British Columbia: Median 1910 weekly earnings according to broad job levels

1911 Census sample Prairie provinces and British Columbia	*Broad job levels*			
	Unskilled labourers	*Skilled employees*	*Clerical and supervisory*	*Total*
	1910 Earnings Median ($)	*1910 Earnings Median ($)*	*1910 Earnings Median ($)*	*1910 Earnings Median ($)*
ORIGIN				
British	11.88	18.00	20.77	16.35
French	11.54	18.27	23.08	15.00
Aboriginal	8.65	13.17	—	10.00
Black	12.22	—	—	13.85
Chinese	9.23	9.23	8.37	9.23
Japanese	9.62	17.50	—	11.25
Dutch	12.00	18.85	22.62	14.40
German	12.00	18.46	20.08	15.00
Austrian	11.84	15.00	13.75	12.50
Galician	11.25	11.79	—	11.54
Ruthenian	12.00	15.00	—	12.50
Finnish	15.00	23.08	—	18.00
Italian	14.29	17.31	18.46	15.00
Jewish	12.50	15.00	—	15.00
Polish	11.54	13.85	13.64	11.67
Russian	12.69	15.00	—	13.46
Norwegian	12.19	19.14	—	15.00
Swedish	13.71	18.00	19.23	15.00
Other	11.07	18.46	22.12	15.00
Total	*11.54*	*17.31*	*20.00*	*15.00*

Source: CCRI 1911 microdata database, weighted data.

Note: Men aged 20–64 years. Averages calculated from 10 or fewer unweighted cases are not shown.

We have already shown that ancestral origin was linked to the ranking of jobs as well as to geographical distributions. Groups whose males had greater odds of being in unskilled manual work included Aboriginals, African Canadians, Austrians, Italians, Poles, and Russians, while there were hardly any African Canadians in the west, few Chinese and hardly any Japanese in eastern Canada, and very few Jews in rural areas. Given these lumpy distributions, it makes sense to look at eastern and western Canada separately when examining ancestral-origin differences in wages. Thus, table 14.8 shows average weekly wages for men by ancestral origin and job level for eastern Canada (Maritime provinces, Quebec, and Ontario), while table 14.9 provides the corresponding information for the west. Over all groups of employees, the average weekly earnings were $11.54 in eastern Canada but $15.00 in the west, with "premiums" for skilled over unskilled work of 30 per cent in the east compared with 50 per cent in the west, a difference that reflects the greater demand for skilled workers in the booming economy of western Canada before 1914.

As before, we used median rather than mean incomes. This avoids having our results biased by "outlier" income values that might be due to special circumstances or transcription errors. We have blanked out those figures where average earnings were based on ten or fewer employees in the 1911 census sample. This protects us from drawing conclusions based on only a few cases. The pattern of blanked-out cells reminds us, yet again, about the uneven geographical distribution of ancestral-origin groups. Several groups have little or no representation at the higher job levels in eastern or western Canada. Thus, most Eastern European groups are conspicuous by their absence from clerical and supervisory positions. This reflects their recent immigration as well as their concentration in farming and, in some cases, their lower levels of relevant human capital factors such as literacy and proficiency in English or French. The same is true for Aboriginals, a group that was strongly racialized at the time.

Wage inequality based on ancestral origin is most clearly demonstrated by working out the ratio of each group's average weekly earnings to that of the British-origin group. We control for the general east-to-west gradient in earnings and cost of living by doing this separately for the eastern and western halves of the country. Thus, African Canadian labourers earned more in western Canada than in they did in the east, but in both parts of the country they earned about the same as those of British origin. Among unskilled workers, at least, there seems to have been comparatively little variation in weekly earnings by ancestral origin, the major exception being that Chinese labourers earned markedly less than almost all other groups – a fact that made them attractive to employers as a source of low-wage labour but also contributed to the strong resentment expressed towards the Chinese by other workers. In eastern Canada, the relatively small number of Chinese labourers earned only 67 per cent of the weekly wage for those of British origin, while in the west they earned 78 cents on the dollar. Aboriginal-origin labourers also did badly in the west, reporting slightly lower weekly earnings than the Chinese; in the east, however, they earned about the same as those of British origin.

Patterns of earnings inequality are different at the higher job levels of skilled and clerical or supervisory work. In eastern Canada, French-origin employees, mostly in Quebec, had the same average weekly earnings ($9.00) as those of British origin. Even among skilled workers, they earned 97 per cent of the comparable British wage. Clerical and supervisory work, however, paid men of French origin only 66 per cent of what it paid those of British descent, a difference that could be due to many factors, most obviously the dominance of English in the highest-paying occupations.[61] This is the British-French income gap that was to be remarked on fifty years later by scholars writing in the 1960s and 1970s. It is interesting that those of Dutch or German origin earned premiums for skill and authority in much the same way as the British.

While African Canadian labourers earned about the same as the British-origin comparison group, those who were in skilled work, at least in eastern Canada, earned only 80 per cent of British-origin men's weekly earnings, and those in clerical or supervisory occupations earned only 50 cents on the dollar. The Chinese in both parts of the country also failed to obtain any significant wage premium for being in skilled or clerical/supervisory occupations. In both eastern and western Canada, Chinese weekly earnings were roughly half those for comparable British-origin men.

Overall, then, income differences linked to ancestral origin in 1910 are complicated by the fact that most owners and proprietors or those working on their own account obeyed the census instructions and did not report their earnings. Further difficulties are caused by the highly uneven geographical distribution of certain ancestral-origin groups across industries, job levels, and provinces. Nevertheless, the census data clearly show the economic marginalization of the Chinese as well as the fact that in several other ancestral-origin groups, particularly the French, the earnings differential versus those of British origin was greatest among clerical-supervisory employees, less marked among skilled workers, and relatively small among unskilled labourers.

Conclusion

This chapter has focused on the fortunes of Canada's various ancestral-origin groups towards the end of the "wheat boom" and "second Industrial Revolution" decade that opened the twentieth century. Although British and French heritages still overwhelmingly defined the nation, new groups from Eastern, northern, and southern Europe established viable ethnic communities in Montreal, southern Ontario, and western Canada over this period, while the Chinese and Japanese, in spite of discriminatory legislation, continued to increase their numbers, the Chinese even establishing communities in eastern Canada. Aboriginals and African Canadians, almost entirely Canadian-born, were the only populations to decline in absolute numbers. It is hardly surprising that Asian or continental European immigrants should continue to speak their native languages or even that the foreign-born were disproportionately men of working age. It is less well recollected, although extensively discussed at the time, that several of these new ancestral-origin groups were over 30 per cent illiterate in any language, a fact that helped to justify race-theory linked concerns of the time on both sides of the Canada-US border. Large proportions of new Canadian groups lived in rural areas in 1911, although there were major exceptions such as Jews, who settled almost entirely in urban areas, and Chinese, half of whom lived in the greater Vancouver and Victoria areas, as well as Italians. Rural settlement was natural for those who had come to homestead, but some members of groups that had been recruited as potential farmers ended up as labourers. Except for the Jewish group, the foreign-born had greater odds of being in unskilled manual work particularly if they were very recent immigrants, illiterate, or speakers of non-official languages. In the broader context of a generally increasing wage gradient from eastern to western provinces such unskilled labourers earned markedly less than skilled employees who, in turn, earned much less than clerical, supervisory, and managerial staff. But, even within provinces and within these broad job levels, there are clear effects of ancestral origin upon earnings. In a pattern reminiscent of the "glass ceiling" ancestral-origin linked earnings differences,[62] for example, the British-French earnings gap, was essentially zero among unskilled labourers, and small among skilled employees but very significant among clerical, supervisory, and managerial staff. The pattern was much stronger among racialized groups such as African Canadians in eastern Canada and Aboriginals in the west. It was stronger still among Chinese immigrants both in eastern Canada and in the west, suggesting that members of these groups either did not get into occupations with the highest levels of skill and authority within a given job level or that their earnings did not reflect it when they did. Taken together, these results show that many of the "ethnic" differences in social and economic status that have preoccupied Canadian sociologists in the post-1960s period were already present well before 1914.

Notes

1 See T.D. Regehr, *The Canadian Northern Railway: Pioneer Road of the Northern Prairies, 1895–1918* (Toronto: Macmillan, 1976).

2 Marvin McInnis, "Engineering Expertise and the Canadian Exploitation of the Technology of the Second Industrial Revolution," in Jonas Ljungberg and Jan-Pieter Smits (eds.), *Technology and Human Capital in Historical Perspective* (Basingstoke: Palgrave Macmillan, 2004), 49–78.

3 See Ronald H. Walder and Daniel Hiebert, "The Developing Industrial Heartland: 1871–1891," in Louise Gentilcore (ed.), *The Historical Atlas of Canada*, vol. II, *The Land Transformed, 1800-1891* (Toronto: University of Toronto Press, 1993), Plate 48.

4 Australia, Canada, and the United States all experienced local exclusionary movements directed against Asians. See Roderick D. McKenzie, *Oriental Exclusion: The Effect of American Immigration Laws, Regulations, and Judicial Decisions upon the Chinese and Japanese on the American Pacific Coast* (New York: American Group, Institute of Pacific Relations, 1927). See also James Morton, *In the Sea of Sterile Mountains* (Vancouver: J.J. Douglas, 1974).

5 Canada, Department of the Interior, *Immigration Facts and Figures* (Ottawa: King's Printer, 1913), 7. The pamphlet goes on to state, "Canada advertises only for farmers, farm labourers and female domestic servants, and these are the only classes who are guaranteed employment on arrival." This and other publications followed from the Immigration Act (An Act Respecting Immigration, assented to 4th May, 1910) as well as from An Act to Amend the Act Respecting Immigration, assented to 4th April 1911. See Canada, Department of the Interior, *The Law and Regulations of Canada Respecting Immigration and Immigrants: Issued by the Superintendent of Immigration, Ottawa* (Ottawa: King's Printer, 1911).

6 See Ernest H. Godfrey, "Fifty Years of Canadian Progress as Illustrated by Official Statistics, 1867 to 1917," *Journal of the Royal Statistical Society* 83, no. 1 (1920): 20. The same material had been published as Part III of Canada, Census and Statistics Office, *Canada Year Book 1918* (Ottawa: Census and Statistics Office), 33–72.

7 From 91,279 to 492,432 for Saskatchewan, and from 73,002 to 374,663 for Alberta. See Canada. Census and Statistics Office. *Canada Year Book, 1913* (Ottawa: Census and Statistics Office), 56 and 52, respectively.

8 From 255,211 to 455,614 (ibid., 52).

9 From 178,657 to 392,480 (ibid.).

10 Tables from the 1913 *Canada Year Book* show that in the province of Quebec the population rose from 1,648,898 to 2,003,232 (ibid., 54), while in Ontario it went from 2,182,947 to 2,523,274 (ibid., 53). Nova Scotia went from 459,574 to 492,338 and New Brunswick from 331,120 to 351,889. The population in PEI declined from 103,259 to 93,728. The Yukon population declined from 27,219 to 8,512 and that of the North West Territories dropped from 20,129 to 18,481. *Canada Year Book, 1913*, 52–6.

11 The proportion urban in 1911 was 46%. Godfrey, "Fifty Years," 11. This is lamented throughout John MacDougall, *Rural Life in Canada: Its Trend and Tasks* (Toronto: Westminster Co., 1913).

12 MacDougall, *Rural Life in Canada*, 22.

13 The Canadian Northern had been bailed out by the Government of Canada in 1913 and was later nationalized in a forced merger with the Grand Trunk that had

gone bankrupt in 1919. The Canadian National Railway remained under government ownership until 1995.

14 See Michael B. Katz and Mark J. Stern, *One Nation Divisible: What America Was and What It Is Becoming* (New York: Russell Sage Foundation, 2006), 35, for the United States at the end of the nineteenth century.

15 Godfrey, "Fifty Years."

16 These titles are taken from James S. Woodsworth, *Strangers within Our Gates; or, Coming Canadians* (Toronto: Missionary Society of the Methodist Church of Canada, 1908), 7.

17 At that time, government statisticians worked under the authority of legislation such as the Census and Statistics Act of 1905. The Dominion Bureau of Statistics was created in 1918.

18 Pierre van del Berghe, *Race and Racism: A Comparative Perspective* (New York: Wiley, 1967).

19 The 1901 census included a question about "Colour" (column 5). Canada, Census Office, *Fourth Census of Canada, 1901: Instructions to Officers, Commissioners and Enumerators* (Ottawa: Department of Agriculture, 1901), para. 47.

20 See Canada, *Census of Prairie Provinces: Population and Agriculture, Manitoba, Saskatchewan, Alberta, 1916* (Ottawa: King's Printer, 1918), 224ff, Table XXVII: "Languages spoken by the population ten years of age and over, born within the Empire and resident in the Prairie Provinces, June 1916, classified according to racial origins and sex, by provinces."

21 Canada, Department of Trade and Commerce, Census and Statistics Office, *Special Report on the Foreign-Born Population, Abstracted from the Records of the Fifth Census of Canada, June 1911* (Ottawa: Government Printing Bureau, 1915). See this for the table of racial origin of the immigrants born in the US (30–1). There is also a table of foreign-born Jews in Canada at 1911 classified according to nativity and citizenship (32).

22 The term "Ruthenians" can mean "Little Russians." See Peter Roberts, *Immigrant Races in North America* (New York: Young Men's Christian Association Press, 1910), 49.

23 Canada, Department of Agriculture and Statistics, *Fifth Census of Canada, 1911: Instructions to Officers, Commissioners and Enumerators* (Ottawa: Government Printing Bureau, 1911).

24 *Canada Year Book, 1913*, 69: Table 15.

25 Groups enumerated as Austrians, Galicians, Bukowinians, or Ruthenians likely included many Ukrainians. The 1911 sample data show 87% of Galicians and 70% of Ruthenians enumerated as Catholics rather than as Orthodox Christians. See Vladimir J. Kaye, *Early Ukrainian Settlements in Canada, 1895–1900* (Toronto: University of Toronto Press, 1964). See also Lubomyr Luciuk and Stella Hryniuk (eds.), *Canada's Ukrainians: Negotiating an Identity* (Toronto: University of Toronto Press, 1991).

26 The entries are grouped on a geographical-racial basis. See Norman B. Ryder, "The Interpretation of Origin Statistics," *Canadian Journal of Economics and Political Science* 21, no. 4 (1955): 466–79.

27 The increase in the population of English origin was discussed in Canada, Census and Statistics Office, *Canada Year Book, 1922–23* (Ottawa: Census and Statistics Office). It is confirmed by the similar increase in the population that described their religion as Anglican.

28 Aboriginals of mixed parentage were counted as Indians in 1901.

29 See Donald H. Clairmont and Dennis W. Magill, *Africville: The Life and Death of a Canadian Black Community* (Toronto: McClelland and Stewart, 1974).

30 See Anne Milan and Kelly Tran, "Blacks in Canada: A Long History," *Canadian Social Trends*, no. 72. (Ottawa: Statistics Canada, 2004), cat. no. 11-008. Robin W. Winks, *The Blacks in Canada: A History*, 2nd ed. (Kingston and Montreal: McGill-Queen's University Press, 1997).

31 Brian Gratton, "Race, the Children of Immigrants, and Social Science Theory," *Journal of American Ethnic History* 21, no. 4 (2002): 75.

32 See Canada, *Royal Commission on Chinese and Japanese Immigration* (Ottawa: King's Printer, 1902).

33 The anti-Chinese consequences of Canada's 1923 Immigration Act were similar to those of the US Immigration Act of 1924. See McKenzie, *Oriental Exclusion.*

34 The Government of Canada published advertisements in many European languages, including those with Cyrillic script, to the effect that agricultural land was freely available in the Prairie provinces. Difficult social conditions in Eastern Europe together with a reduced supply of free agricultural land in the United States contributed to the success of these advertising efforts.

35 See Woodsworth, *Strangers within Our Gates*, 245–6.

36 The terms "Austrian" and "Hungarian" as well as "Romanian" or "Russian" could include several more specific ethnic identities. The term "Ruthenian" has both linguistic and religious as well as territorial connotations. Some scholars might wish to group Galicians with Ruthenians and Bukowinians as a broader Ukrainian group, although Ukraine did not exist as a political unit at that time and "Ukrainian" seems to have been first used as an official "racial origin" category in the published report of the 1916 *Census of Prairie Provinces.* We have followed the example of the 1911 census and treated these groups separately.

37 There would likely have been two-way movement across the border but there appears to have been long-term net emigration of African Canadians, either to the United States or to other destinations. Weighted estimates from the 1911 census sample indicate that 3,912 "Blacks" in Canada were foreign-born: over 1,000 being enumerated in Ontario and another 1,000 in the prairies.

38 These smaller groups include Bukowinians, Belgians, Japanese, Swiss, Bulgarians/Rumanians (considered together), Turks, Greeks, and "Hindus" (sic). The census reports had grouped Bukowinians under the general term "Austrians" in the 1901 population counts.

39 This approach stems from Peter M. Blau and Otis Dudley Duncan, *The American Occupational Structure* (New York: Wiley, 1967). See also Monica Boyd, John Goyder, Frank E. Jones, Hugh A. McRoberts, Peter C. Pineo, and John Porter, *Ascription and Achievement* (Ottawa: Carleton University Press, 1985).

40 For those analyses that bear upon employment and wages, we restrict the sample to those aged between 20 and 64 years, and often to men within that subpopulation.

41 Bukowinians who were to be grouped with Galicians, Ruthenians, and Ukrainians in tables from the 1921 census are not included here because of their relatively low population count in 1911.

42 The Sydney steel plant on Cape Breton Island provided semi-detached company houses on Victoria Road.

43 *Canada Year Book, 1913*, 112.

44 The total number of Chinese in Canada in 1881 was 4,383. These figures are from the 100 per cent sample from the 1881 Census of Canada at http://www.chass.utoronto.ca/datalib.

45 Leroy Stone writes, "Canada's ethnic composition was also affected by migration between the Provinces. Each of the three Maritime Provinces had negative inter-provincial migration ratios for the first thirty years of the twentieth century while Ontario and the Western Provinces all saw gains, the most spectacular being in Saskatchewan and Alberta between 1901 and 1911." Leroy O. Stone, *Migration in Canada: Regional Aspects* (Ottawa: Government Printing Office, 1969), 138.

46 Godfrey, "Fifty Years."

47 The census underenumerates the numbers of sex workers. See Patrick Dunae, "Geographies of Sexual Commerce and the Production of Prostitutional Space: Victoria, British Columbia, 1860–1914," *Journal of the Canadian Historical Association* 19, no. 1 (2008): 115–42.

48 The US Census of the time asked the same questions.

49 See Canada, Dominion Bureau of Statistics, *Illiteracy and School Attendance in Canada: A Study of the Census of 1921 with Supplementary Data* (Ottawa: King's Printer, 1926).

50 In 1911, the US Immigration Commission, formed in 1907, published, *The Children of Immigrants in Schools*, and also issued its recommendations in a paper, referred to as the "the Dillingham Report." The subsequent Burnett-Dillingham Bill, passed in February 1917, over a Presidential veto, incorporated a literacy test into US immigration procedures. See selected articles on *Restriction of Immigration, Compiled by Edith M. Phelps* (New York: H.W. Wilson, 1920). For an account of Canadian attitudes to immigrants, see Donald H. Avery, *Reluctant Host: Canada's Response to Immigrant Workers, 1896–1994* (Toronto: McClelland and Stewart, 1995).

51 This was commented upon at the time, as well as after the 1916 and 1921 censuses.

52 Domestic or personal service occupations included houseworkers, barbers, hotelmen, hospital workers, laundry employees, cemetery employees, undertakers, stable men, etc.

53 Canada, "Fifth Census of Canada 1911: Instructions to Occupation Editors – Index to Occupations," by E.S. MacPhail. Unpublished internal document.

54 See, e.g., Andrea Tyree, J Walter Freiberg, Kenneth Ong, Dagmar Raczynski, Norma Shosid, and Donna Ver Steeg, "The Dickensian Occupational Structure," *Sociological Inquiry* 41, no. 1 (1971): 95–106.

55 Including religion as a predictor raises difficulties since the Jewish ancestral-origin group had been defined in terms of the enumerated religion. The impact on estimates of the effect of being Jewish is negligible.

56 These logistic regression analyses are not shown here.

57 Since very few Canadians of French origin were Protestants, any barriers associated with being of French origin will overlap with those linked to religion.

58 Column 23: Weeks employed in 1910 in chief occupation or trade. Column 25: Hours of working time per week at chief occupation. Column 27: Total earnings in 1910 from chief occupation or trade. There were similar questions about hours of working per week and 1910 weeks of working per year and 1910 earnings in relation to other paid work, if any. Some 20% of self-employed or own-account workers provided information in response to these questions but we have not used their data here.

59 Marvin McInnis, "Regional Income Differentials in Canada, 1911–1961," *Journal of Economic History* 26, no. 4 (1966): 586–8.

60 Katz and Stern make a similar comment in regard to the relatively small number of internal migrants from the Southern United States to the North at that time.

61 The pattern is different in the west, where the French-origin population was much smaller.

62 A "glass ceiling" pattern of equality is one where there is a widening gap with increasing seniority between gender or ethnic groups in earnings or authority. Group differences may be quite small at lower levels of seniority but they become much greater later in the career. The picture in Canada at 1911 is considerably muddied by the fact that many minority groups were composed almost entirely of very recent immigrants.

— · 15 · —

Canada's Immigrants in 1911: A Class Analysis

ERIC W. SAGER

Introduction: The Analytical Challenge

In the first decade of the twentieth century, Canadians saw more newcomers entering their country than ever before. Between 1901 and 1911, the total population grew by 34 per cent; immigration exceeded emigration, and by 1911, more than one in every five people living in Canada had been born outside of the country. Anglo-Canadian reaction to these immigrants was a stew of ambiguity and contradiction. The newcomers erased the disappointments of previous decades, answered the perceived need for a larger labour force, and filled much of the prairies with farmers. Clifford Sifton's "stalwart peasant in a sheep-skin coat, born on the soil" had arrived, and politicians rejoiced.[1] From many perspectives, however, immigrants were a problem: instead of farming, many of them took to the cities and often to the slums; those who came from Europe or Asia brought customs and traditions that appeared threatening; and the army of the unemployed drew heavily on immigrant recruits.

The Anglo-Canadian lens, filtered by ethnic and racial consciousness, often washed out the class position of immigrants. J.S. Woodsworth offers one example of the resulting confusion. His examination of the "strangers within our gates" begins with a tentative class analysis. In the immigrant ship crossing the Atlantic, he wrote, "all classes and types are represented." Those interested in "social problems" must study the first-, second-, and third-class decks. In the first-class deck was "that weedy-looking young fellow with a cigarette, who has never done anything all his life." In the second- and third-class decks were the real workers, whose courage and endurance were a gift to their new country.[2] The rest of Woodsworth's famous book organizes immigrants by national or ethnic origin, where ethnicity trumps class, and the initial optimism about workers largely evaporates: "The general law seems to be that cheap labor tends to drive out higher-priced labor and lower the standards of living."[3] Moreover, "immigration means a very heavy burden upon all our charitable institutions."[4] Even British immigrants were suspect: "the trouble has been largely with the *class* of immigrants who have come ... England has sent us largely the failures of the cities."[5]

The contradictions and racisms of a century ago are tempting and easy targets. If analysis were to end with such "unpacking," the historian of the early twenty-first century might well be vulnerable to accusations of complacency and condescension. Echoes of Woodsworth's general law may easily be found today, for racial discrimination has not ended, and an official obsession with the quality or "class" of immigrants has evolved into systematic exclusion of the economically undesirable and the admission of "temporary migrant workers" to meet "short-term skill and labour needs."[6] No less pertinent, as an antidote to complacency, is the extent of what we have yet to learn about those same immigrants that Woodsworth studied a century ago. We have a corpus of excellent studies of immigrants and immigration, of course. I suggest, however, that we know more about ethnicity and racialization than we do about the class position or the fate of immigrants in labour markets. Even where class is significant to the analysis, the analytical gaze is framed by the cultural matrices of family, gender, religion, and ethnic associations.[7]

How much do we really know about the occupations, incomes, standards of living or class composition of the immigrants of Canada's "wheat boom" decade? We do know that while many immigrants tried farming, the majority of them ended up as proletarians, expanding the labour force in manufacturing, the resource sector, or general labouring. But that is not to say very much: that statement applies equally to the Canadian-born. The undergraduate student who reads our survey histories must be forgiven for concluding that immigrants were an unskilled, low-wage proletariat, especially if they came from Europe or Asia. The "dangerous foreigners" described by Donald Avery were crowded into low-wage, unpleasant, and dangerous jobs.[8] Women immigrants were streamed into domestic service or low-wage factory jobs. Continental Europeans, especially, ended up on "the wrong side of the tracks" in cities, or in resource-industry bunkhouses.[9] Textbooks tend to mix the discussion of where immigrants were in the labour force with cultural stereotyping, which can easily blur the distinction between observer's gaze and immigrants' condition. "Business people," for example, were enthusiastic about immigrants, "seeing them as ideal candidates for the hard, low-wage labour needed in factories, resource industries, and homes."[10] This is true enough, with respect to both the employer's gaze and the actual employment of many immigrants, but we must remember that employers also hired immigrants into high-wage jobs and that many of those employers were also immigrants themselves.

Labour historians offer a corrective to the equation of immigrants with low wages and lack of skills. In railways, steel, and other industries, employers recruited skilled workers, foremen, and managers from Britain and offered them above-average wages.[11] T.W. Acheson offered another corrective many years ago: immigrants were at the top of the social hierarchy! In 1885, 49 per cent of Canada's industrial elite had been born outside Canada; by 1910, that proportion had fallen, but it was still at 26 per cent.[12] Immigrants contributed as much or more to the formation of the nation's bourgeoisie as they did to the formation of a working class. At this point, ethnicity re-enters the frame: the elite were not *any* immigrants – they were disproportionately English, Scots, or Irish rather than continental Europeans or Asians, and they were Protestants rather than Catholics. Proletarians, it follows, were disproportionately from non-British groups and religions other than Protestant Christianity. Out of such observation of disproportionality came the "vertical mosaic" metaphor, which neatly captured the Canadian conception of an ethnic-based social stratification. There were "distinct ethnic classes": "That a mosaic, not a melting pot, was the best description of the new Canada could not disguise the vertical character of ethnic relations."[13] This is not far from Woodsworth's mixing of class and race a century ago, when he wrote, "The competition of races *is* the competition of standards of living."[14]

It is unlikely that any single metaphor can capture the complexities of class or ethnicity, still less the way in which they interacted with each other. One merit of the work of economic historians who study immigrants is that they eschew the grand metaphor in favour of precisely specified definitions of "assimilation," labour-market participation, and even "quality." Among other things, economic history decomposes the category "immigrant" and even "British immigrant." In Canada's biggest cities, in 1901, British immigrants were underrepresented in white-collar jobs, and they moved slowly towards wage parity with native-born English-speaking Canadians; yet British immigrants had no difficulty obtaining craft jobs. The fate of British immigrants in labour markets varied significantly among English, Irish, and Scots, and by religious background, when other characteristics are held constant. Ethnicity mattered, but in ways that varied by location and group.[15] Since no single pattern emerges, there is no opportunity for recomposition into a summarizing metaphor. If there is a risk in such close and technically sophisticated empirical scrutiny, it is that both class and ethnicity get blurred, as merely two of many "variables" in the labour-market experience of immigrants. Statistical significance is not always the same as historical significance. Immigrants to Canada were enmeshed in a mutually reinforcing interaction of class with ethnicity that preceded their arrival in Canada and shaped their entire life experience.

Such reflections are prompted, in part, by the sudden explosion of new information on Canada's population in the first half of the twentieth century. The national samples of census microdata created by the Canadian Century Research Infrastructure (CCRI) project allow us to move beyond specific ethnic groups, specific locations, or time-specific snapshots. Such empirical riches present us with challenges and opportunities, and not least is the challenge of historical significance: can we use these "data" while avoiding what C. Wright Mills referred to as abstracted empiricism? Shall we be content with more refined unpacking of the racisms and discriminatory actions of our forebears, as these were manifested in labour markets? Or, is there another *problematique*, a historical and theoretical strategy that puts "data" and "variables" in the frame of changing relations of class, power, and inequality?

If there is such a strategy, it involves granting a renewed priority to macro-social evidence, the national benchmarks of immigrant experience, as well as the local patterns of work, wages, housing, and other material conditions among immigrant families and households. These come first and should inform the undergraduate textbooks and immigrant histories of the future. Almost none of these benchmarks or patterns can be found in the tables in the published census volumes for 1911.[16] Whether the analysis is bivariate or multivariate, the national microdata sample for 1911 is indispensable to the research on immigrants. Of key importance is the analysis of immigrants by class, occupation, and earnings, none of which could be attempted without the 1911 national microdata.

Class, Ethnicity, and Immigrants

Users of the CCRI national sample of the 1911 census must be aware of the CCRI sampling strategy. Dwellings were sampled in three strata. Dwellings of less than thirty persons were selected with equal probability. For dwellings with thirty-one or more residents, in which a majority of persons were deemed to be unrelated, one in every ten respondents was selected. In large multi-unit dwellings, where a majority resided in identifiable household units, one in four units was selected at random and all residents of the selected unit were sampled. Since many immigrants were likely to be found in large dwellings, the analysis in this chapter includes large dwellings, but the appropriate weights are applied; dwellings of thirty or less = 20; large single-unit dwellings = 10; large multi-unit dwellings = 4.

The 1911 census gives us two key facts about immigrants prior to their arrival in Canada: the date of their birth and the country of their birth. Almost half of those born outside Canada were born in Britain; 26 per cent were born in Europe and 19 per cent in the United States. Taken as a whole, immigrants differed in key respects from the Canadian-born. They were less likely to be children, and more than two-thirds of them were aged between 20 and 59 years. Recent immigrants brought children more often than they brought elders, and cohorts above age 50 were underrepresented among recent immigrants. Had you looked at the immigrants disembarking in Halifax or Montreal, you would have seen a largely male population. Over 62 per cent of all immigrants were men, and among the newest arrivals – those whose year of immigration was 1911 – 70 per cent were men. Two of every three of the newly arrived adult men were single.

The immigrant population included relatively few children and elders. In 1911, only 15.5 per cent of immigrants were under the age of 15; by contrast, 37.9 per cent of those born in Canada were under 15. Only 5 per cent of immigrants who had arrived in Canada in 1908 or after were aged 50 or over; among the Canadian-born, 21 per cent were 50 or over. Among all immigrants aged 20 and over, regardless of their date of arrival in Canada, 32.3 per cent were single; among the Canadian-born of similar age, 30.9 per cent were single. This is the broad demographic context for all reactions to the immigrants of the early twentieth century. Into a society, at a specific moment in its history of class, gender, race, and family, came a newcomer population that comprised large numbers of single men.

Despite contemporary concerns that immigrants were swelling the ranks of the unemployed, immigrants did find jobs in Canada. Their labour-force participation rate in 1911 was higher than for the Canadian-born, as it had been in 1901: two-thirds of all immigrants (aged 15 and over) had a reported occupation, compared with 53 per cent for the Canadian-born. The higher labour-force participation rate for immigrants is explained, in part, by the higher proportion of men in the immigrant population; however, among both men and women, the labour-force participation of immigrants was higher than for the Canadian-born. Among immigrant men, 92.0 per cent had a reported occupation compared with 86.6 per cent of Canadian-born men. Among women, 19.0 per cent of immigrants had a reported occupation compared with 17.9 per cent of women born in Canada.

Immigrants found employment, but what can we say about their class position? Like the 1901 census, the 1911 census offers more than one way of an-

Table 15.1 · Immigrants and Canadian-born by class (weighted %): Employer, employee, and working on own account, Canada, 1911

Class	*Immigrants*	*Canadian-born*
Employer	5.1	6.4
Employee	67.6	54.2
Working on own account	25.0	35.6
Other	2.3	3.7
Weighted total *N*	848,754	1,836,354

Source: CCRI 1911 microdata database.

Note: Percentages may not always total 100 because of rounding. Weighted *N*'s are inflated by the weighting replication procedure.

swering the question. All persons in the labour force were recorded as being employers, employees, or "working on own account." Employers were individuals who "employ helpers other than domestic servants in their own business." An employee was "a person who works for salary or wages," and this class included general managers and domestic servants, but not those such as lawyers or physicians who worked for fees. Those "working on own account" were "independent workers who neither receive pay, salaries nor regular wages" and who employ no helpers, such as farmers, lawyers, small shopkeepers. Some enumerators were not able to treat these categories as mutually exclusive; in the following analysis those who were said to be both employers and self-employed (working on own account) are grouped with employers.

The first conclusion is that immigrants appeared in all of these categories of class (see table 15.1). Most of the Canadian-born were employees, and so were most of the foreign-born. Some immigrants were employers, and their contribution to the employer class should not be underestimated: one of every four employers in Canada in 1911 was an immigrant. Immigrants were represented in all social classes and in the labour force as a whole; but, when they entered the labour force, they were entering a social structure that they shared with the Canadian-born.

The second conclusion is perhaps more surprising. There appears to have been a change in the position of immigrants since 1901. There was little difference between immigrants and Canadian-born in 1901, when immigrants were neither overrepresented among employees, nor underrepresented among employers.[17] In 1911, however, immigrants were less likely than the Canadian-born to be employers, less likely to be self-employed, and more likely to be employees.[18] The category "living on own means" does not exist in 1911, as it did in

Table 15.2 · Immigrants, recent immigrants, and Canadian-born (weighted %) by census-defined occupation "classes" (0–9), Canada, 1911

Occupation "class"	*Immigrants*	*Recent immigrants*	*Canadian-born*
0. Owner of business/self-employed	30.4	18.8	43.5
1. Managers, assistant managers	0.8	0.5	0.8
2. Superintendents, assistant superintendents, supervisors	1.6	1.0	3.0
3. Foremen, bosses, paymasters, treasurers	1.5	1.0	1.4
4. Agents, brokers, commission men	1.0	0.6	1.3
5. Inspectors, weighers, graders	2.1	1.6	1.7
6. Employees, workers, operators, skilled workers	26.6	27.4	24.3
7. Clerks, companions, timekeepers	1.9	1.9	2.7
8. Apprentices, helpers, learners, assistants	0.6	0.5	0.7
9. Labourers, unskilled, messengers, teamsters	33.5	46.6	20.6
Weighted total *N*	841,466	270,504	1,814,832

Source: CCRI 1911 microdata database.

1901. The 1911 enumerators were told to enter "income" in column 17, the occupation column, for persons who were not employed but lived on an "independent income" such as investment or pension income; the definition in 1911 was less likely than that in 1901 to allow enumerators to include impoverished people who had no jobs but were surviving on small savings. Immigrants were underrepresented among those with independent incomes. While immigrants were 18.8 per cent of those who had "income" (in column 17), they were 23 per cent of the population overall and 33 per cent of the labour force.

The 1911 census offers another window into class, unique to this census. The census office applied its own coding system to all recorded occupations. The set of codes is subtle and flexible. It is composed of three codes, each entered onto the census form and included as three fields in the CCRI national sample. The first code assigns each occupation to a "general main division," or economic sector, of which there are eleven. The second code "refers to the class of worker," assigning to each person with an occupation a code from 0 through 9 in an implied hierarchy. The third code, of two digits, is applied to each "trade" or occupation. Table 15.2 uses the second of these codes and shows that immigrants were represented at all points in this occupation-class scale. Immigrants were less likely to be business owners (the first category in table 15.2) than the Canadian-born. In this category, most of the immigrants (73%) were farmers, but the underrepresentation of immigrants in the business/self-employed cat-

Table 15.3 · Immigrants, recent immigrants, and Canadian-born (weighted %) by occupation sector, Canada, 1911

Sector	*Immigrants*	*Recent immigrants (1908 and after)*	*Canadian-born*
Agriculture	30.0	25.4	37.2
Building trades	9.6	10.9	8.4
Domestic and personal service	9.2	11.0	6.9
Civil and municipal service	4.4	4.8	4.0
Fisheries, hunting	0.9	0.4	1.9
Forestry, lumbering	3.9	4.0	4.5
Manufactures: mechanical, textiles	7.0	7.8	6.0
Manufactures: food, clothing	5.6	5.1	6.9
Mining	3.9	4.4	1.8
Professional pursuits	2.8	2.2	3.1
Trade and merchandising	10.1	7.7	12.1
Transportation	12.5	16.2	7.3
Weighted total *N*	841,342	270,322	1,813,680

Source: CCRI 1911 microdata database.

egory is the result of their underrepresentation in farming. Immigrants were less likely than the Canadian-born to hold white-collar jobs (superintendents, agents, clerks), and more likely to be labourers. This is particularly true of recent immigrants (defined here as those who arrived in 1908 or after).

Immigrants did not create a working class but, more than their Canadian-born neighbours, they were in that class. They were much less likely than the Canadian-born to be farmers, and entry into farming was clearly slow, as the low proportion of farmers among the most recent immigrants suggests (see table 15.3). Building trades, domestic service, and transportation were important sectors for immigrants. These patterns are similar to those for immigrants in 1901, with one exception. In 1911, immigrants were not overrepresented in manufacturing, as they were in 1901. Immigrants were predominantly urban-dwellers, and they were over-represented in labouring occupations: here is the basis for the exaggerated perception at the time and since that immigrants were unskilled labourers. If you lived in a Canadian town or city in 1911, and you observed the recent immigrants in your city, the odds were quite strong that you were observing a man who was a labourer.

If you observed those immigrant labourers from a distance, before you heard them speak and before you could identify their language, you would not have been able to predict their ethnicity. They came from a wide range of birthplaces and backgrounds. The population of immigrants differed from the Canadian-born in one very obvious way: they included very few French Catholics. If we remove French-origin and French Canadian Catholics from the analysis, one striking difference between the Canadian-born and immigrants is the much higher proportion of English Anglicans among the immigrants (22.0% of non-French immigrants compared with only 9.5% among the Canadian-born). There were fewer Irish, either Catholic or Protestant, among the foreign-born than among the Canadian-born, and there were more Europeans, both Catholics and Protestants, in the immigrant population than among the Canadian-born. Continental Europeans were arriving in a society in which language and ethnicity were key markers of identity. However, they were outnumbered by English, Scots, and Irish immigrants: there were almost twice as many immigrants from the British Isles as there were continental Europeans.

Did the ethnicity of immigrants determine their class position? How strong was the association between ethnicity and class? The answer is that there was a relationship, but not a strong one. Most ethnoreligious groups appeared in all three main social classes, in proportions similar to their share in the total employed population (the "All" column in table 15.4). In only a few figures of table 15.4 is there a marked "overrepresentation" of an ethnoreligious group. European Catholics were more likely to be employees and less likely to be employers or self-employed than if their ethnicity made no difference. Immigrants of Asian origin were more likely to be employers – presumably small-business employers who hired other Asian immigrants. A more refined analysis, based on the census-defined occupation "class" categories used in table 15.2, confirms the point that ethnoreligious groups were represented in all categories. Among the labourers, for instance, there were English Anglicans, English Methodists, Scots Presbyterians, and Irish Protestants, as well as European Catholics. The odds that a European Catholic immigrant would end up as a labourer were somewhat higher than for an English immigrant. Occupation "classes" were not, however, ethnic enclaves. English, Irish, and Scots of various religious affiliations were half of all immigrant labourers, and in that class they far outnumbered the Europeans.

There was no ethnically determined class hierarchy among immigrants to Canada.[19] Most immigrants were wage-earning employees who entered a large and diverse working class, where the material conditions of life varied enormously. Within every broad occupation category, moreover, there were enormous variations, none of which was ethnically determined. The labourer category, for instance, included the low-wage "mucker" hired by municipalities for street improvements; many of these men were English immigrants. It

Table 15.4 · Immigrants in the labour force (weighted %) by ethnoreligious group and class, Canada, 1911

Ethnoreligion	*Employer*	*Employee*	*Own account*	*All immigrants*
English C of E	19.0	24.9	15.9	22.3
English Methodist	8.5	6.2	7.2	6.6
English other	10.6	9.9	8.3	9.5
French Catholic	2.8	2.2	2.7	2.4
Scots Presbyterian	11.8	10.6	8.4	10.1
Scots other	3.9	3.7	3.2	3.6
Irish Catholic	2.7	3.1	2.7	3.0
Irish Protestant	7.1	4.7	5.6	5.0
German Lutheran	2.9	1.6	4.5	2.4
German other	5.4	2.5	8.2	4.0
European Catholic	4.7	13.0	10.7	11.9
European Protestant	6.1	7.6	14.8	9.4
Asian	5.2	4.9	1.5	4.0
Other	9.3	5.2	6.2	5.8
Weighted *N*	41,744	556,128	203,358	819,664

Source: CCRI 1911 microdata database.

also included Paul Floris, a Hungarian immigrant living in Hamilton, a factory "labourer" who reported his annual earnings to be $1,250 – more than double the mean earnings for all Hamilton men in 1911.[20]

Class and Urban Space: Hamilton, Ontario

Immigrants, whatever their birthplace and ethnicity, were not separated from other Canadians. Images of immigrants crowding into urban ghettoes, boarding houses, and hinterland bunkhouses should not obscure the extent of immigrant dispersal across urban space and across the spatial map of class. As census databases grow, and especially as we acquire more complete-coverage data sets for specific locations or entire nation states, the subject of spatial distribution and segregation is being reopened. For 1911, at the end of the "wheat boom" immigration, the City of Hamilton offers an opportunity for a tentative foray into the subject. Here I make use of the complete-coverage database from the 1911 enumeration for Hamilton and the adjacent Ancaster and Barton townships (85,068 persons). Although we possess complete-coverage data sets for other Canadian cities, I have selected Hamilton because it was a major

Table 15.5 · Hamilton, Ontario, by wards in 1911: Canadian-born, immigrants, recent immigrants, and total (% and *N*)

Ward	*Canadian-born*	*Immigrants*	*Recent immigrants (1908 and after)*	*Total population*	N
Ward 1	11.8	8.1	8.3	10.4	8,889
Ward 2	7.5	6.4	6.7	7.1	6,043
Ward 3	12.4	9.5	9.7	11.4	9,677
Ward 4	13.8	12.8	11.6	13.4	11,434
Ward 5	5.8	6.9	7.0	6.2	5,271
Ward 6	12.3	12.9	13.5	12.6	10,679
Ward 7	14.9	16.5	17.3	15.5	13,202
Ward 8	6.5	13.2	13.2	8.9	7,549
Hamilton city	3.6	3.5	3.1	3.6	3,046
Hamilton west	4.7	3.5	3.6	4.3	3,636
Ancaster	1.1	1.0	1.0	1.1	899
Barton	5.6	5.6	5.0	5.6	4,743

Source: Hamilton complete count data, 1991.

Note: There is no weighting by household size in the Hamilton database.

manufacturing city and a magnet for immigrants, and because my experiment with segregation measures may be of wider interest, since this city has already attracted the attention of historians.

The 1911 census suggests that 36 per cent of Hamilton residents were first-generation immigrants. To what extent were these immigrants clustered into specific neighbourhoods? Table 15.5 shows the distribution of immigrants by ward for 1911 (the database includes two subsets of the population where the ward was not stated, as well as Ancaster and Barton). Immigrants, including recent immigrants, lived in all wards in Hamilton, and were significantly over-represented only in Ward 8. It is striking how closely the distribution of immigrants mirrors the distribution of non-immigrants. A standard measure of unevenness of groups across spatial units is the index of dissimilarity: the index for immigrants in table 15.5 is only .10. To achieve perfect evenness – a proportionately even distribution of immigrants and non-immigrants in all wards – would have required that one in every ten immigrants move to another ward.

The ward, with its average population of over 7,000, is a rather blunt category. The real segregation of immigrants might well have occurred in smaller neighbourhoods within wards. To test for this possibility, I have looked at the smallest census tracts – the census subdistricts – within each ward. The result

Table 15.6 · Hamilton, Ontario, all wards in 1911: Dissimilarity index (DI) for ethnic groups relative to English group

Ethnic group	*DI*	N
English		40,267
Scots	.07	15,931
Irish Catholic	.24	6,598
Irish Protestant	.07	8,751
French	.19	1,155
German	.06	4,994
Italian	.41	1,444
Russian	.39	791
Jew	.35	805

Source: Hamilton complete count data, 1911.

is forty-eight spatial units, with an average of 1,772 people in each. The pattern shown in table 15.5 remains intact: immigrants appear in all of these small neighbourhoods, and the dissimilarity index is only .17.

While immigrants were dispersed across the city, ethnic groups, and especially continental Europeans, tended to be concentrated in space. Table 15.6 presents the dissimilarity indices for eight groups (including both immigrants and Canadian-born): their spatial segregation is compared with that of people of English origin. How many persons of Italian origin, for instance, would need to move in order to have the same relative distribution across wards as people of English origin? The Scots, Irish Protestants, and Germans appeared in all city wards in roughly the same proportions as did the English. However, Italians, Russians, and Jews were distributed unevenly across the city. Almost two-thirds of the Italians were concentrated in two wards, Ward 8 and Ward 4. Similarly high concentrations of Europeans appear at the subdistrict level; for example, 57 per cent of Italians lived in two of the forty-eight subdistricts. The dissimilarity index for Italians compared with English across the forty-eight subdistricts is .70. Spatial clustering is a complex subject, and we should not ignore the extent of dispersal, even where there was a high degree of concentration. There were people of Italian origin living in all of Hamilton's wards, and in twenty-seven of forty-eight subdistricts.

Are these indices unusually large or not? An informed answer must await other studies of residential dispersion for Canadian cities in the early twentieth century. No doubt the concentration of groups of people of Asian origin living in Vancouver and Victoria in 1911 was greater. Eighty years later, Italians in Toronto were even more concentrated than Italians in Hamilton in 1911; across census tracts for 1991, the dissimilarity index for Italians in inner-city Toronto, relative to the English, was .68.[21] One benchmark for very high segregation is the black-white segregation in US cities, which in 1940 ranged from .60 to .95.[22]

The pattern, then, is immigrant dispersal, with degrees of clustering for specific ethnic groups. What did this pattern of dispersal and separation mean for the lived experience of immigrants? In the analysis of spatial segregation, it is advisable to use more than the dissimilarity index, since spatial segregation is too complex to be measured by a single summary statistic.[23] In this context, we can deploy the interaction index (*P*), which measures the extent of exposure of one group to others. Residential exposure refers to the degree of potential contact, or the possibility of interaction, between minority and majority group members within geographical areas of the city.[24] The *P* value always falls between 0 and 1: it is the probability that a randomly selected person from the same neighbourhood will be a member of group Y. Because 36 per cent of the population of Hamilton were immigrants in 1911 does not mean that the Canadian-born and immigrants regularly encountered each other on the streets where they lived; it could be that the immigrants were separated in ways that minimized contact. The interaction index for Hamilton wards suggests that the exposure was high: the *P* for the exposure of immigrants to Canadian-born in Hamilton wards was .63, which means that a randomly selected person in a ward where an immigrant lived had a 63 per cent chance of being Canadian-born. From the perspective of the Canadian-born, the probability of encountering an immigrant in the same ward was .35.

Immigrants and Canadian-born encountered each other regularly, in workplaces and in their neighbourhoods. Whatever their origins, however, they were distanced from members of other classes. The interaction index is often deployed in the analysis of ethnic or racial distancing in urban space, but the measure can have some utility in class analysis. The *P* value for the exposure of immigrant labourers to immigrant employers in Hamilton wards was a mere .029, reflecting the concentration of employers in wards 1, 2, and 3, and the concentration of labourers in wards 4, 6, and 7, and in Barton. The residential distancing of immigrant blue-collar workers (employees in manufacturing or transportation) and immigrant employers was equally extreme: they lived in different parts of the city. The interaction index for blue-collar immigrants relative to employer immigrants was .027. If we add together employees, those living on income, and the self-employed, the distance between these groups and the "blue collar" working class remains: the interaction index for blue-collar workers relative to these three groups was .10. Immigrant workers in manufacturing and transportation were also separated residentially from immigrant employees in white-collar jobs (clerical, sales, service): the *P* value for the exposure of the former to the latter was .16. Similar results were obtained at the level of the forty-eight census subdistricts; the *P* value for the sum of blue-collar workers plus labourers relative to employers across the forty-eight subdistricts is .0256.

Hamilton was not a city of immigrant or ethnic ghettoes. Working-class neighbourhoods were heterogeneous mixes of both immigrants and Canadian-born, and of ethnic groups living in close proximity. This mixing is visible at the micro-level scale of a single census subdistrict. As an example, I take the subdistrict with the largest proportion of immigrants. Of the 3,657 people living in East Hamilton in Ward 8 (district 77, enumeration area 20), two-thirds were immigrants. They lived within walking distance of the east-end industrial zone between Barton Street and the lakeshore, in one of the densely populated areas where developers had built working-class housing in recent decades. In this small area, enumerator W.J. Roberts found Armenians, Austrians, Bulgarians, Germans, Galicians, Hungarians, Italians, Lithuanians, Poles, and even a few Chinese. He also found many English, Scots, and Irish. Although one would have heard many languages in the streets and shops, the majority language of the neighbourhood was English. There were, of course, small concentrations of chain migrants. At 198 Sherman Avenue, Roberts the enumerator found seventeen Armenian men, all of them moulders or labourers in foundries, and he listed one of them as the head of the household. Next door, at 197 Sherman, lived Benito Martini, an Italian labourer, and his wife Rosina and their four children. The Martini household also included three young Italian men, listed as boarders. Nearby, at 195 and 201 Sherman, the occupants were all Italian. Here was a small Italian and Armenian neighbourhood, but it was not exclusively so, for at 193 Sherman lived an English Newfoundlander, John Holmes, with his wife, three daughters, a grand-daughter, and his father-in-law. Also next door to the Italians, at 205 Sherman, lived Herbert Corser, an English watchmaker, with his wife and daughter. Perhaps these people met and mingled further down Sherman Avenue, where Michael Foley and his wife Julia, Irish Catholics, operated a grocery store. It was a short walk to the multi-ethnic shops and churches on Barton Street East, which bisected the census subdistrict.

This neighbourhood, if it was such (for we cannot assume that a sense of community existed where there was such diversity), was not unusually poor. Fifteen census subdistricts had lower mean earnings. The one common characteristic of the population in this urban space was the homogeneity of class: 91 per cent of those with jobs were workers in manufacturing or transportation. There were 107 white-collar workers, a small number of shopkeepers, and hardly any employers (most of those listed as such were shopkeepers).

Four kilometres from Benito Martini and his family, residing at 29 Hunter Street West in West Hamilton, was another Italian immigrant, Edward Cantania, who lived with his wife and daughter and four lodgers. Cantania was a foreman in an electrical works. He had been in Canada for eleven years and had done well: he reported his annual earnings to be $2,000. Cantania was probably as close as a recent European employee could come to the bourgeoisie of Hamilton. Only three-quarters of a kilometre away from Cantania was Herkimer Street and the home of the Scots Presbyterian William Vallance, a leading iron merchant who had been in business in Hamilton since 1853. In Vallance's household were his wife, three sons, his daughter, his son-in-law, and three domestic servants. Vallance's immediate neighbours on Herkimer were all English, Scots, or Irish, and the immigrants among them had been in Canada for many decades. This was the area of Ward 2 that in the early 1900s "retained streets with exclusive airs which had been implanted in the 1850s."[25] The small area bounded by Aberdeen on the south, Hunter on the north, Bay on the west, and John on the east was not ethnically homogeneous, however. Among the immigrants – 29 per cent of the area's population – were a few Germans, Italians, and Russians, and a Polish Jew. In coming years, more of Hamilton's wealthy citizens would gradually move west, into the new Westdale development with its covenants forbidding sales to blacks, Asians, and most continental Europeans. In 1911, William Vallance lived in a neighbourhood where class and wealth sufficed to exclude more than a handful of non-British immigrants. The ability to choose one's neighbours was a privilege of class. Immigrants could enjoy that privilege, but in order to do so, they had to move out of the working class.

Moving out of the working class was possible for a minority of immigrants, but it took time. Benito Martini had been in Canada only five years; Edward Cantania had been in Canada for eleven years. Did the passage of time affect the probability of movement between classes? The question cannot be answered at all definitively when using the static portrait of individuals captured in a single census, and in the future, nominal linkage systems will allow us to track the same individuals across censuses. For the moment, however, we can offer a few observations. If the passage of time made a difference, we would expect to see a different distribution of immigrants by class and by time since arrival: wage-earning workers would be clustered among the recent arrivals in Canada; immigrants who were employers would appear more frequently in later years. Figure 15.1 suggests that time did matter: new arrivals were almost all employees, in blue-collar jobs (manufacturing, transportation, resources),

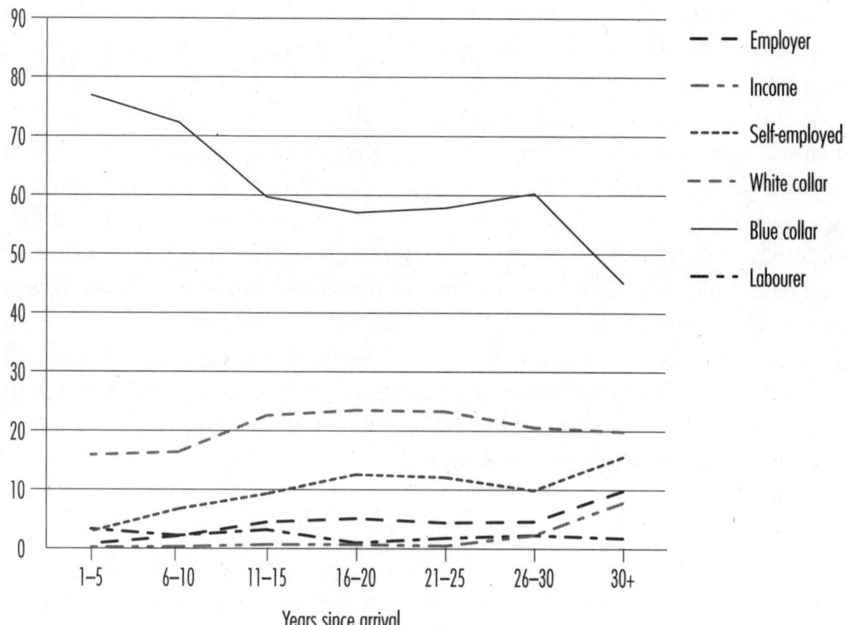

Figure 15.1 · Hamilton, Ontario, 1911: Class distribution of immigrants in the workforce, by years since arrival in Canada.

Source: Hamilton complete count data, 1911, CCRI Project, University of Victoria.

white-collar jobs, or labouring. Most immigrant employers (62%) had been in Canada for twenty-one years or more. Recently arrived adults had almost no chance of being employers and were much less likely to be self-employed than those who had been in Canada for several years. Similar results appear when controlling for the age of immigrants. For immigrants in their 30s, for instance, the chances of being an employer or self-employed were much better for those who had been in Canada since childhood than for recent arrivals.

The measures used in the preceding paragraphs apply only to Hamilton's immigrants. If we look at the entire population of the city, we find similar levels of dissimilarity and interaction. Across Hamilton wards, the dissimilarity index for labourers relative to employers, including both immigrants and Canadian-born, was .34; the dissimilarity index for blue-collar workers relative to employers was .37, and the interaction index for blue-collar workers and labourers taken together relative to employers was .04.

Time influenced the chances of movement between classes and across the urban landscape of class, but among immigrants the employers and self-employed remained a minority, however long they had lived in Canada. By 1911, housing and residential location reinforced, more intensely than ever before, class position and the lived experience of class. For both immigrants and the Canadian-born, class divisions were imprinted more deeply on urban space as the old commercial town evolved into an industrial city. In Hamilton, between 1840 and 1872, Robert Kristofferson observed "the maintenance of residential patterns in which masters and men lived and worked as members of the same organic community."[26] Michael Katz, observing the Hamilton of 1851, saw "people of all degrees of wealth" dwelling in close proximity to each other, "the poor and the affluent intermingling on the same streets."[27] No such conclusions can be drawn for the Hamilton of 1911. In sixty years, the social ecology of the city had been transformed.

Class and Earnings

Outside the population of farmers and other self-employed persons, the most obvious correlate of class is earned income. Canadian censuses began reporting the annual earnings of employees (and frequently also for employers and self-employed) as early as 1901.[28] Since the majority of immigrants became employees rather than farmers, wage earnings rather than land were the first small step in the pursuit of prosperity. Immigrants were well aware that wage earnings existed in temporal and spatial dimensions. With the passage of time and the acquisition of experience, they expected that their wage earnings would improve. In labour markets known to vary by region, moving to the right location could be essential to earning adequate wages.

Where did immigrants fit in the highly unequal distribution of annual earnings in 1911? At the level of national benchmarks, we would expect that the mean earnings of immigrants would be higher than the earnings of the Canadian-born, for two obvious reasons: men earned more than women, and immigrants were disproportionately male; and immigrants tended to move to high-wage regions of the country. This pattern is confirmed (see table 15.7), but there is a sharp contrast with 1901. By 1911, the gap between the means had diminished: an 18 per cent advantage for immigrant men and an 8 per cent advantage for immigrant women in 1901 had fallen to a 3 per cent difference for both groups in 1911.[29] A complete explanation for the narrowing of the earnings gap between immigrants and Canadian-born would require extensive analysis, but the change is related, at least in part, to the higher proportion of very recent immigrants in 1911, and to the fact that the immigrants of 1911 were

Table 15.7 · Immigrant and Canadian-born employees, men and women: Mean annual earnings, Canada, 1901 and 1911

	1901 mean ($)	*Std dev*	N	*1911 mean ($)*	*Std dev*	*Unweighted* N
Immigrant men	437.41	342.9	7,245	609.24	479.5	22,666
Canadian-born men	370.58	275.8	25,146	578.64	791.0	36,460
Immigrant women	194.78	153.8	1,139	310.50	305.4	2,942
Canadian-born women	180.23	131.1	6,816	302.86	302.7	9,744

Source: CFP 1901 and CCRI 1911 microdata databases. Means and standard deviations for 1911 are weighted.

younger than those of 1901. While the mean age of male immigrants in 1901 was 40, in 1911 it was 32; in 1911, 44 per cent of immigrants had arrived in the previous five years, while in 1901 this proportion was only 19 per cent.

As in 1901, these national benchmarks are not the sum of similar patterns across all provinces. In the Prairie provinces and British Columbia, mean immigrant earnings were far below the mean earnings for the Canadian-born. In British Columbia, for example, the earnings of Canadian-born males were 31 per cent higher than for male immigrants, and Canadian-born women had an 8 per cent earnings advantage. Meanwhile, in the three Prairie provinces, taken together, the mean earnings of Canadian-born men were 28 per cent above the mean for immigrant men, and the mean for Canadian-born women was 27 per cent above the mean for immigrant women.[30] In Ontario, in contrast to 1901, the earnings of those who were born in Canada were slightly higher than the earnings of immigrants. Only in Quebec and the Maritime provinces were the mean earnings of immigrants above those of the Canadian-born.

Mean annual earnings are a national benchmark, but the mean is a highly abstract number in the context of such large standard deviations. The deviations in 1911 are much larger than they were in 1901, and they are driven in part by the influences of region, age, and occupational structures that varied across provinces. The deviations reflect a remarkably wide dispersion of annual earnings, even within the working class, defined for the moment simply as all waged or salaried employees. The national sample of the 1901 census yields a gini coefficient of .35 for all male employees; the gini coefficient for all male employees had not changed in ten years – it was .35 in 1911. If women employees are included, the gini coefficient rises to .37. Given that high incomes are not included in this analysis – all employers are excluded – the earnings inequality in Canada in 1911 was extreme, and higher than a century later.

Table 15.8 · All male employees and all immigrant male employees: Gini coefficients by province or region in Canada and for Hamilton, Ontario, 1911

Region	*All male employees*	*All immigrant male employees*
Maritime provinces	.35	.33
Quebec	.34	.32
Ontario	.34	.32
Prairie provinces	.35	.33
British Columbia	.32	.32
Hamilton	.26	.26

Source: CCRI 1911 microdata database and Hamilton complete count data, 1911.

Table 15.9 · Variables associated with earnings, Canada, 1911: Summary of regression analysis

Main effects (no. of categories)/ Categories	*F (main effects) and unstandardized B*	*Std. error*	*Sig.*	*Eta²*
CLASS (4)	16505.67		.000	.035
Employer	347.44	4.851	.000	
Employee/not labourer	-184.74	2.912	.000	
Employee-labourer	-383.61	2.930	.000	
Own account	—		—	
SEX (2)	37250.85		.000	.026
Male	360.16	1.866	.000	
Female	—		—	
ECONOMIC SECTOR (9)	2575.33		.000	.015
Professions	416.01	4.303	.000	
Trades/retail	326.93	2.687	.000	
Manufacturing	225.52	2.559	.000	
Building/construction	177.34	2.676	.000	
Resources	146.03	2.714	.000	
Transportation	242.26	2.627	.000	
Domestic service	224.88	2.996	.000	
Civil/municipal	312.78	3.216	.000	
Agriculture	—		—	
REGION (5)	3583.88		.000	.010
Maritimes	-272.98	2.908	.000	
Quebec	-113.82	2.907	.000	

/continued

Table 15.9 · continued

Main effects (no. of categories)/ Categories	*F (main effects) and unstandardized B*	*Std. error*	*Sig.*	*Eta²*
Ontario	-151.78	2.442	.000	
Prairies	1.21	2.720	.656	
BC	—			
ETHNORELIGION (8)	637.89		.000	.003
English C of E	99.58	2.972	.000	
English other	111.04	2.878	.000	
French Catholic	16.39	3.116	.000	
Scots	139.54	2.924	.000	
Irish Catholic	115.59	3.553	.000	
Irish Protestant	107.31	3.268	.000	
European	52.29	3.058	.000	
Other	—		—	
AGE SQUARED	6.38		.012	.000
IMMIGRANT OR NOT (2)	308.92		.000	.000
Born in Canada	28.34	1.612	.000	
Immigrant	—		—	
Adjusted R^2 = .097				

Source: CCRI 1911 microdata database.

The gini coefficients are influenced by the extreme variations in wage levels across provinces. The simplest way to control for regional variation is to observe the gini coefficients within regions, and even within specific locations where there are sufficient cases. The coefficients indicate a very high degree of earnings inequality in all regions, and a smaller dispersion in Hamilton (see table 15.8). In most regions, earnings inequality was slightly less extreme among immigrants than among the Canadian-born. The wave of immigrants was not contributing to a rise in income inequality. Inequality was a stable condition of the capitalist economy which absorbed the labour of both immigrants and Canadian-born.

Economic inequality interacted with and reinforced cultural assumptions about the identities, status, and innate talents of ethnic groups in the immigrant wave. But, economic inequality cut across all ethnic groups: it was a condition of gender and class. There is more than one statistical method that allows assessment of the relative importance of multiple conditions of earnings inequality. The simplest approach is regression (using the GLM procedure in SPSS). Table 15.9 summarizes the regression of six categorical variables and one covariate (age) on annual earnings. There are eight ethnoreligious categories. Class is entered as four categories: employers (1,645 cases), employees who were not general labourers (40,817), employees who were labourers (27,368), and self-employed (3,686). Normally, one would not use the earnings data for employers and self-employed, since census enumerators reported earnings consistently only for employees. Nevertheless, earnings are reported for 26 per cent of all employers and 13 per cent of those "working on own account" (the proportions are higher if we look at employers and self-employed outside agriculture). Employers who reported earnings were not representative of all employers: large capitalist employers rarely reported annual earnings. The use of these categories of class may be justified here, so long as it is understood that the category "employer" refers only to small employers. The categories do not embrace all social classes, and the importance of class will be underestimated in the results.

The results indicate that all seven variables are significantly associated with the dependent variable, earnings. The earnings advantages of employers over employees and self-employed, and of men over women, are strongly confirmed. The signs are positive for all economic sectors, indicating an earnings advantage for all groups outside agriculture (the reference category). The signs are negative for Ontario, Quebec, and the Maritimes, confirming the expected earnings advantage for people living in British Columbia. All major ethnoreligious groups had an advantage over the reference category, a mix of minority religions and visible minority groups. The reference category for ethnoreligious identity includes 5,177 cases: Aboriginal Canadians, Asians, Jews, and unspecified "Canadians."

As in 1901, the earnings of people who were born in Canada were higher than the earnings of immigrants; where bivariate analysis suggested an apparent earnings advantage on the part of immigrants, the apparent advantage disappears in the presence of other factors. Did the passage of time affect immigrant earnings, allowing them to move closer to the earnings of their Canadian-born neighbours? A tentative answer to this question requires a separate regression, comprising only immigrants. The answer is negative, as it was for 1901: in a regression of six variables (sex, birthplace, region, occupation sector, age, and years since migration) on annual earnings for immigrants, all variables are significant except for two: years since migration and age. As in 1901, Asian-origin workers were particularly disadvantaged. With Asians and other non-Europeans as the control variable (n = 1,351), all other birthplace groups had higher earnings and all were statistically significant.

Partial eta squared is the effect-size measure, and it offers an indication of the relative importance of each variable in explaining the total variance. The weakest contributors are ethnoreligious identity and the immigrant/not immigrant dichotomy. The substantial contributors are gender and class.

Class and gender were fundamental to the material condition of both immigrants and people born in Canada, in a way that ethnicity was not. Class and gender were the bases of material inequality, social divisions, and even segregations in time and space. Class and gender defined the parameters of entry to occupations and all other material conditions of life. Ethnicity interacted with class and gender, shaping and reinforcing their definition and boundaries, but ethnicity was not a hierarchy independent of the class formation in which it existed. Immigrants themselves continued to seek protection in ethnic associations, and "to think in terms of ethnic exclusion and difference," but in the decade after 1911, many more of them crossed the boundaries of ethnic belonging.[31] By 1919, if not before, the loyalty of class was bold and explicit: "this body of workers recognize no alien but the capitalist."[32] This new consciousness of class was planted in the material conditions both of immigrants and those born in Canada as recorded so comprehensively in the census of 1911.

Notes

1 Clifford Sifton, "The Immigrants Canada Wants," *Maclean's Magazine*, 1 April 1922; reprinted in Howard Palmer (ed.), *Immigration and the Rise of Multiculturalism* (Toronto: Copp Clark, 1975), 35.

2 J.S. Woodsworth, *Strangers within Our Gates, or Coming Canadians* (Toronto: University of Toronto Press, 1972; first published 1909), 32–3.

3 Ibid., 184.

4 Ibid., 187.

5 Ibid., 46. The emphasis is Woodsworth's.

6 Human Resources and Skill Development Canada, "Hiring Foreign Workers in Canada," http://www.hrsdc.gc.ca/eng/workplaceskills/foreign_workers/pamphlet/tfwp_pamphlet.shtml.

7 Royden Loewen and Gerald Friesen, *Immigrants in Prairie Cities: Ethnic Diversity in Twentieth-Century Canada* (Toronto: University of Toronto Press, 2009), 13–33. The category "class" has recurring priority for Loewen and Friesen: "Within a few years, income, housing and ethnicity were linked in a single category – class – in people's consciousness" (51). Immigrants, according to Harney and Troper, "did not fit [into the] North American class structure, only its stereotypes." Robert Harney and Harold Troper, *Immigrants: A Portrait of Urban Experience, 1890–1930* (Toronto: Van Nostrand Reinhold, 1975), 53.

8 Donald Avery, *"Dangerous Foreigners": European Immigrant Workers and Labour Radicalism in Canada, 1896–1932* (Toronto: McClelland and Stewart,

1979); Donald Avery, *Reluctant Host: Canada's Response to Immigrant Workers, 1896–1994* (Toronto: McClelland and Stewart, 1995).

9 Daniel Hiebert, "Class, Ethnicity and Residential Structure: The Social Geography of Winnipeg, 1901–1921," *Journal of Historical Geography* 17 (1991): 56–86; Edmund Bradwin, *The Bunkhouse Man: A Study of Work and Pay in the Camps of Canada, 1903–1914* (New York: Columbia University Press, 1928).

10 Margaret Conrad and Alvin Finkel, *Canada: A National History* (Toronto: Pearson Longman, 2007), 243. See also Raymond Blake, Jeffrey Keshen, Norman Knowles, and Barbara Messamore, *Narrating a Nation: Canadian History Post-Confederation* (Toronto: McGraw-Hill Ryerson, 2011), 111.

11 Paul Craven and Tom Traves, "Dimensions of Paternalism: Discipline and Culture in Canadian Railway Operations in the 1850s," in Craig Heron and Robert Storey (eds.), *On the Job: Confronting the Labour Process in Canada* (Kingston and Montreal: McGill-Queen's University Press, 1986), 60; Craig Heron, *Working in Steel: The Early Years in Canada, 1883–1935* (Toronto: McClelland and Stewart, 1988), 74ff; Craig Heron, "Factory Workers," in Paul Craven (ed.), *Labouring Lives: Work and Workers in Nineteenth-Century Ontario* (Toronto: University of Toronto Press, 1995), 512; Joy Parr, *The Gender of Breadwinners: Women, Men, and Change in Two Industrial Towns* (Toronto: University of Toronto Press, 1990), 18–19; Robert Kristofferson, *Craft Capitalism: Craftworkers and Early Industrialization in Hamilton, Ontario, 1840–1872* (Toronto: University of Toronto Press, 2007), 62.

12 T.W. Acheson, "Changing Social Origins of the Canadian Industrial Elite, 1880–1910," *Business History Review* 47, no. 2 (1973), 193.

13 Ramsay Cook, "The Triumph and Trials of Materialism," in Craig Brown (ed.), *The Illustrated History of Canada* (Toronto: Lester and Orpen Dennys, 1987), 391.

14 Woodsworth, *Strangers*, 186.

15 Alan G. Green, Mary McKinnon, and Chris Minns, "Dominion or Republic? Migrants to North America from the United Kingdom, 1870–1910," *Economic History Review* 55, no. 4 (2002): 666–96; Alan Green and Mary McKinnon, "The Slow Assimilation of British Immigrants in Canada: Evidence from Montreal and Toronto, 1901," *Explorations in Economic History* 38 (2001): 315–38.

16 See Canada, Census and Statistics Office, *Fifth Census of Canada, 1911*, vol. II, *Religions, Origins, Birthplace, Citizenship, Literacy and Infirmities by Provinces, Districts and Sub-districts* (Ottawa: C.H. Parmelee, 1912). The most finely grained detail is given in the section on "Birthplace and Citizenship," where Tables XV, XVI, and XVII show birthplace by district, by cities and towns over 7,000, and by province.

17 Eric W. Sager and Christopher Morier, "Immigrants, Ethnicity, and Earnings in 1901: Revisiting Canada's Vertical Mosaic," *Canadian Historical Review* 83, no. 2 (2002): 202–3.

18 The chi square is significant and the contingency coefficient is .138 (which is a contrast with the similar table for 1901).

19 The literature on ethnicity and class is abundant. For some references, see Sager and Morier, "Immigrants, Ethnicity, and Earnings," 196n4. See also Rick Helmes-Hayes and James Curtis (eds.), *The Vertical Mosaic Revisited* (Toronto: University

of Toronto Press, 1998). Moving far beyond the metaphorical mosaic are labour historians and historians of women, for whom the intersection of ethnicity and class remains a major theme. See, e.g., Katrina Srigley, *Breadwinning Daughters: Young Working Women in a Depression-Era City, 1929–1939* (Toronto: University of Toronto Press, 2010); Joan Sangster, *Transforming Labour: Women and Work in Postwar Canada* (Toronto: University of Toronto Press, 2010); Lara Campbell, *Respectable Citizens: Gender, Family, and Unemployment in Ontario's Great Depression* (Toronto: University of Toronto Press, 2009). Sociologists' interest in class and ethnicity is displayed in *Canadian Ethnic Studies* and other journals; see also Vic Satzewich and Nikolais Liodakis, *"Race" and Ethnicity in Canada* (Don Mills, ON: Oxford University Press, 2010).

20 This Hungarian labourer is in District 77, subdistrict 11, page 20, line 16. The Automated Genealogy transcriber has transcribed the surname as Horis, but there is no such Hungarian surname in the voluminous Radixindex of Hungarian genealogy.

21 Brian K. Ray, "Plural Geographies in Canadian Cities: Interpreting Immigrant Residential Spaces in Toronto and Montreal," *Canadian Journal of Regional Science* 22, nos 1 & 2 (1999): 77. A very useful tool for comparative analysis, including an introduction to the key measures, is Jordan Stanger-Ross, *City Stats*, http://citystats.uvic.ca/.

22 This is the range for nineteen cities, as reported in Douglas S. Massey, "Origins of Economic Disparities: The Historical Role of Housing Segregation," in James H. Carr and Nandinee K. Kutty (eds.), *Segregation: The Rising Costs for America* (New York: Routledge, 2008), 42. The seminal work is Karl E. Taeuber and Alma F. Taeuber, *Negroes in Cities: Residential Segregation and Neighborhood Change* (Chicago: Aldine, 1965).

23 Vaughan Robinson, "Lieberson's Isolation Index: A Case Study Evaluation," *Area* 12, no. 4 (1980): 307–12.

24 Ray, "Plural Geographies," 72.

25 John C. Weaver, *Hamilton: An illustrated History* (Toronto: Lorimer, 1982), 103.

26 Kristofferson, *Craft Capitalism*, 14.

27 Michael B. Katz, *The People of Hamilton, Canada West: Family and Class in a Mid-Nineteenth-Century City* (Cambridge, MA: Harvard University Press, 1975), 23.

28 We cannot, however, examine incomes exactly, for we know nothing about non-wage sources of income.

29 Table 15.7 reports earnings for those said to be employees in column 20, as well as those who have positive responses in both columns 20 and 21 (working on own account); employers and those "working on own account" only are omitted.

30 In order to exclude a small number of highly improbable extreme numbers (likely due to data entry error) in the earnings field in the 1911 database, I selected only earnings greater than 10 and less than 50,000 dollars.

31 Loewen and Friesen, *Immigrants in Prairie Cities*, 54.

32 Resolution at the founding convention of the One Big Union, Calgary, March 1919, cited in Avery, *Dangerous Foreigners*, 80.

— · 16 · —

The Worth of Children and Women: Life Insurance in Early Twentieth-Century Canada

PETER BASKERVILLE

In the late nineteenth century, life insurance came of age in Canada. In 1869, twenty-three mostly foreign-based companies sold life insurance in the young nation. By 1911, forty-three predominately Canadian-based companies were active in the business, and total insurance in force had increased from $36 million in 1869 to just under a billion dollars in 1911. In the first decade of the twentieth century, the increase in policies outpaced population growth by a factor of 2.5, and per capita expenditure on life insurance increased by 75 per cent. Indeed, one contemporary believed that he lived in an era that exhibited a "mania for life insurance." While historians know something about growth trends and the major companies involved in that business – although not nearly as much as we might wish – we know next to nothing about the people who bought life insurance.[1]

By 1911, companies marketed two major types of life insurance: ordinary life and industrial. Ordinary life appealed to middle-class heads of household who, on average, purchased policies in excess of $1,500 and paid for their policies on a yearly basis. From the insurance company's viewpoint, these policies were cheap to administer. A second type of life insurance, pioneered in England by Prudential and in the United States by Prudential and the Metropolitan, offered cheaper insurance to working-class families, and it was payable weekly or monthly to company agents who collected at their clients' doorsteps. Administrative costs were much higher in this business, and for that reason many companies stayed clear of that market. But, for those that entered and survived the time it took to build a viable client base, the profits were substantial.[2] Indeed, as

Table 16.1 · Growth of industrial and ordinary life insurance in Canada, 1900–20

Year	*Number of policies*		*Decadal growth rate*	
	Industrial	*Ordinary*	*Industrial*	*Ordinary*
1900	144,601	251,639	—	—
1910	686,000	619,197	4.7x	2.5x
1920	2,319,860	1,253,764	3.4x	2.0x

Source: Neufeld, *Financial System*, 276; Canada, House of Commons, *Sessional Papers*, 1911, vol. 45, no. 8, XLIII, Life Insurance in Canada for 1910.

table 16.1 demonstrates, by 1911, Canadians held more industrial than ordinary life policies.

Most overviews of the insurance business focus on the sale and management of ordinary policies. The industrial life policies, however, filled needs not met by ordinary life policies. As a vice president of Metropolitan Life, a large industrial insurer based in the United States, stated, "Women and children of the wage earning population, by reason of their needs for lesser amounts of insurance, make up the larger numbers of Industrial policy holders."[3] "Child insurance in this country is always called industrial insurance," a Canadian senator informed his colleagues in 1895.[4] This chapter takes a close look at the women and especially the children who held such insurance. Almost nothing has been written on insured women and only a little more on insured children. Viviana Zelizer has argued that the purchase of insurance for children is best understood as "a measure of the emerging 'sacralization' of children's lives." She examined a number of debates about the morality of insuring children that took place in the late nineteenth and early twentieth centuries and concluded that the desire for children's insurance among working-class families reflected a growing sense, first evident in middle-class families, that children were more than economic assets. Adopting the language of Lawrence Stone, she pointed to the rise of "affective individualism" among working-class families. In this context, the purchase of insurance for children is best seen as a symbolic marker of profound cultural change: by the late nineteenth century, working-class, like middle-class families before them, had redefined a child's value. Zelizer based this interpretation on a rich body of qualitative commentaries drawn from newspapers, congressional and state inquiries, court records, and insurance company correspondence, drawn, in other words, from middle- and upper-class commentators.[5]

This chapter does not take issue with the broad context within which Zelizer places children's insurance. It may well be that a child's value was being redefined in this era. One might wonder, however, about the causal direction explicit in Zelizer's focus. For her, working-class families simply followed the lead of their more progressive middle-class counterparts. This form of trickle-down social change has been critiqued from many directions.[6] As well, for Zelizer, working-class families are faceless and homogeneous. The possibility that such families might exhibit a whole spectrum of behaviours is not entertained. Who among the working class insured their children? Who were the working-class women who took out insurance? This chapter argues that cultural and economic differences within the working class underlay decisions to purchase industrial insurance in early twentieth-century Canada and that these purchases contributed to and were markers of changing gendered behaviour in the public sphere.

We begin with a discussion of the major source used, a 5 per cent sample of the nominal returns from the 1911 Canadian census, compiled by the Canadian Century Research Infrastructure (CCRI) project.[7] Then follows a descriptive overview of insurance holders in Canada in 1911, with special focus on women and children. Finally, the chapter provides preliminary explanations for the user profiles highlighted in the previous section and suggestions for further research.

The Source: The CCRI 1911 Sample

The 1911 Canadian census is unique among national censuses in Canada, the United States, and Great Britain in asking three questions relating to insurance. This was the only year that these questions were asked of all people in Canada. We do not have any direct information as to why questions relating to insurance were posed in 1911. However, very likely it was a fallout from the royal commission set up by the Canadian government to look into investment and management practices of life insurance companies operating in Canada. This commission, headed by Duncan Byron MacTavish was struck in 1906 following a similar investigation in New York State. The MacTavish Commission reported in 1907. One of the recurring themes of the investigation was the need for increased publicity concerning the operations of insurance companies.[8] The three 1911 census questions relating to insurance reflect that focus: amount of insurance on life; amount of insurance against accident or sickness; and cost of insurance in census year. Several newspapers at the time mentioned this new set of queries, but the questions in general did not elicit much public debate, and the census authorities decided to leave insurance questions out of the 1921 census.[9]

Table 16.2 · Number and value of insurance policies: 1911 5% (weighted) census sample and government reports compared

Policy characteristics	*1911 5% Census sample*	*1910/11 Sessional Papers*
Insurance holders/policies (*n*)	780,010	1,305,197
Total amount of insurance in force	$1,177,312,880	$1,022,934,253
Average value insurance per individual/policy	$1,509	$784

Source: CCRI 1911 microdata database. Neufeld, *Financial System*, 276; Canada, House of Commons, 1911, *Sessional Papers*, vol. 45, no. 8, LXVII–LXVIII.

Note: For information on the weighting procedures used, see CCRI, On-line Contextual Database, http://ccri.library.ualberta.ca/, esp. Database-sampling. Weighting is necessary because the sample includes two types of large dwellings (31+ individuals, composed of single units and multifamily units), which were sampled differently from dwellings comprised of 30 and fewer individuals. Unless otherwise noted, all tabulations are weighted samples using the following formula: for dwellings of less than 31 residents, weight = 20; large single-unit dwellings (> 30 residents), weight = 10; large multi-unit dwellings (> 30 residents), weight = 4.

There were several reasons for this decision. In about 1918, census authorities did a review of census-taking practices preparatory to finalizing questions for the 1921 census. They wished to devise a cost-effective happy medium between too few questions to make the enumeration process worthwhile and too many that might render the enterprise too costly. As the report's authors put it, "Care, therefore, should be exercised ... to keep the schedules down. Particularly," they continued, "does this hold of questions on which information can be obtained through other sources. The census schedules, in short, should be delimited in correlation to the whole field of statistics, and on the further principle that there is a point in the number of questions below which it is wasteful to fall and beyond which it is dangerous to rise."

Among the most "notable omissions" were the insurance questions. In the opinion of the report's authors, the replies to these questions were "very inadequate" – although precise reasons for this view were relegated to a separate memo which has yet to be uncovered. Moreover, and importantly, the report continued, "It would be better to obtain the data from the 65 insurance companies involved than from the several millions of policy holders ... in view of the failure of the 1911 experiment." They concluded that in the future it would be better to obtain the information from insurance companies. This, of course, suited the companies who would, once again, have control of the data that they considered suitable for public consumption.[10]

A comparison of the replies to the insurance questions in the 1911 census with information that companies provided the state at the end of 1910 suggests that there were, indeed, some inconsistencies between the companies' statistics and the census data. Our 5 per cent weighted sample suggests that 780,010 Canadians possessed life insurance in 1910. The average value of a life insurance policy was $1,463. As table 16.2 indicates, the total value of insurance in force is acceptably close, but the policy numbers and average values are seemingly quite divergent. There are probably three main factors that account for most of the differences. The first is that the units measured are different in each source. The census provides a figure for policy holders; the company statistics provide figures for policies. It is difficult to estimate the extent to which individuals held more than one policy, although it seems clear that many did. Estimates vary from 7 to 50 per cent, depending on the type of policy and the nature of the provider – main-line insurance company or fraternal society – and none of these estimates are very convincing on a national level.[11] Second, part of the divergences can be accounted for by what appears to be an underestimation of the amount of industrial insurance in force. Industrial policies were worth, on average, $119 in Canada at the end of 1910, and there were some 686,000 such policies in force. If, from the 1911 census sample, we select all individuals with policies worth $500 or less, the number represents about a third of all policyholders.[12] Yet, we know that industrial policies exceeded ordinary policies in 1910. The third factor is suggested by comments in the press at the time of the enumeration. The Prescott *Journal*, in Ontario, advised its readers to have the insurance information "on hand" for the census enumerator. Yet, as the Kingston *Daily Standard* observed, not everyone was so prepared: "enumerators are unable to get the necessary information [on insurance] ... very few wives know anything concerning their husband's insurance." Since the enumerators generally called when husbands were at work, the paper urged husbands to leave the correct information with their wives.[13]

I conclude, first, that the figures are closer than they appear to be especially because of the different units measured. Second, I think that the issue concerning the ignorance of wives was probably overstated and reflected more the gendered ideology of the era rather than a significant problem in reporting.[14] Finally, on the basis of the relative undercounting of industrial insurance participation (even acknowledging the units of measurement problem), I conclude that the census underestimates working-class (industrial) life insurance policies. This is a bias that is probably consistent with a wider underestimation of the poorer working class in censuses in that period. The large number of cases extant will, nevertheless, yield meaningful results.[15]

Profile of the Insured

Advertisements from Toronto's *Globe* in the mid-1890s suggest that insurance companies were quite happy to insure women (see figure 16.1). Such ads

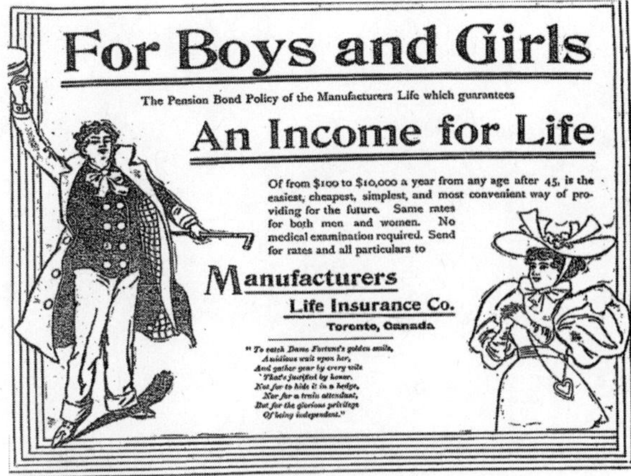

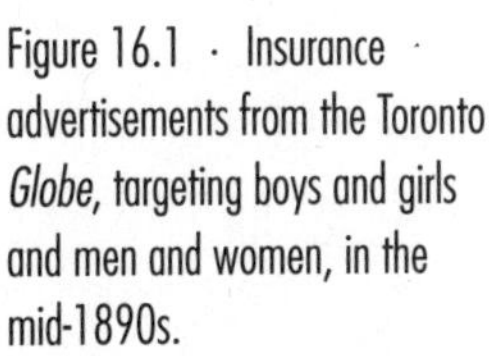
Figure 16.1 · Insurance advertisements from the Toronto *Globe*, targeting boys and girls and men and women, in the mid-1890s.

Source: Toronto *Globe*, 9 March 1895, 16; 16 Nov. 1895, 10; 4 April 1896, 4.

targeted "young persons of both sexes." As the illustrations reproduced here suggest, ads stressed insurance as an investment opportunity rather than as a means for providing for dependants after death. Women and men were encouraged to save "not for to hide it in a hedge, nor for a train attendant but for the glorious privilege of being independent."[16] Were women attracted to these ads?

Figure 16.2 indicates what few of us would find surprising: men's lives were much more apt to be insured than were the lives of women. One of every twenty women (5%) had life insurance in Canada in 1911 compared with one of every six men (17%).

It is instructive, as well, to look at the broad geographical distribution of the insured population. As figure 16.3 illustrates, life insurance was not popular in rural areas. Land substituted as an asset that could provide a livelihood on the death of the male head and obviously it was extremely rare for rural women,

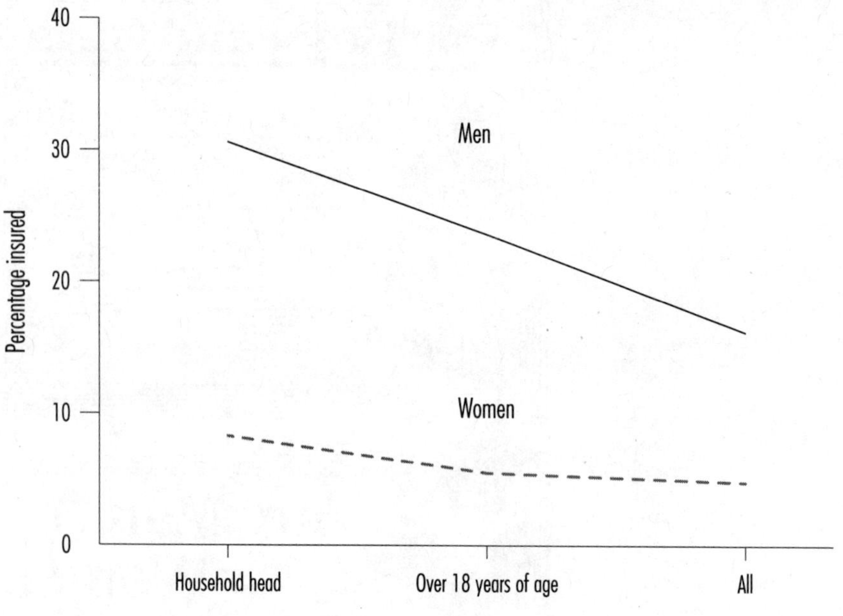
Men
Women
Percentage insured
40
30
20
10
0
Household head
Over 18 years of age
All

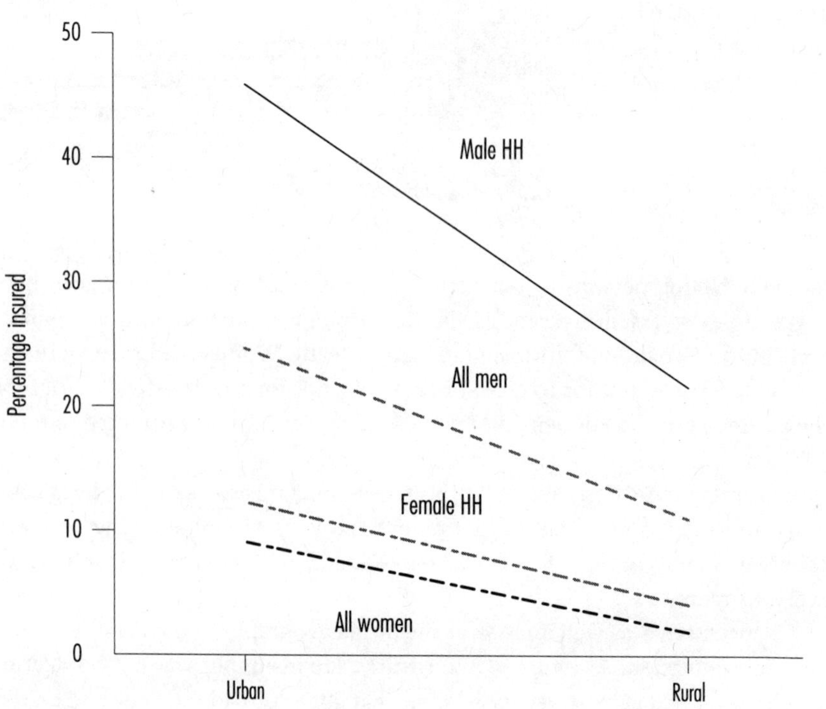
Male HH
All men
Female HH
All women
Percentage insured
50
40
30
20
10
0
Urban
Rural

whether heads of household or not, to be insured. If, in the first years of the twentieth century, life insurance was a barometer for a rising middle class, it was an attribute of that class missing from rural Canada. The rest of this chapter, therefore, will focus on urban Canada – which is where most people who had life insurance lived.

The data displayed in table 16.3 point to the very different social/demographic characteristics of insured men and women. Most insured women were single; most insured men were married. Most insured men were household heads; most insured women were daughters or wives. Most insured men had a paid occupation; most insured women did not. Interestingly, for those with occupations, insured men and women both bulk in the manufacturing sector. And, finally, insured men were, on average, older than insured women.

This simple table opens up several avenues for investigation. Who were the single women with life insurance? Were they all dependant daughters living in a nuclear family? Or were many "business girls" who through their work contributed to the family's economic well-being? A November 1911 article in the *Globe* argued that three-quarters of the 40,000 "working girls [in Toronto] have home responsibilities ... girls are left to make their own living and support others as well." "Supposing," the writer continued, "through death the family are left without any means of support, would it not have been wise that the business girl and supporter of the family should have carried life insurance?"[17] Many of the women working in business took the *Globe*'s article to heart. Women who worked were about two times more likely to have life insurance than those who did not have an identifiable occupation, and 78 per cent of working women with life insurance were single. Fully two-thirds (or 66%) of single women with occupations and life insurance were daughters living at home (80% of those who lived at home had fathers who were employees). Some 30 per cent lived outside of a nuclear family. The correlation of insured single working women living at home in a working-class family suggests that such insurance very likely did provide a safeguard against a loss of wages attendant on death.

Figure 16.2 (opposite, above) · Gender and life insurance policyholders: Household heads, those over 18 years of age, and all, Canada, 1911.

Sources: CCRI 1911 microdata database.

Figure 16.3 (opposite, below) · Insured population of Canada: All men, all women, whether head of household (HH), and according to urban or rural place of residence, 1911.

Sources: CCRI 1911 microdata database.

Table 16.3 · Demographic characteristics of the insured in urban Canada, 1911[a]

Characteristics	*Men (weighted* N = *359,682)*	*Women (weighted* N = *124,672)*
CIVIL STATUS (%)		
Married	66	40
Single	32	53
Widowed	2	7
RELATION TO HEAD OF HOUSE (%)		
Head	64	6
Wife	—	37
Son/daughter	22	45
Boarder	9	4
OCCUPATION GROUP (%)		
Have occupation	84	21
Manufacturing	40	44
Manager/professional	20	12
Sales	11	9
Service	5	18
AVERAGE AGE (years)	34	27

Source: CCRI 1911 microdata database.

a The table reports all ages for those who lived in communities of 2,000+ people.

Jane Synge's interviews with women who worked in the early twentieth century in Hamilton, Ontario, provide another very suggestive source that nicely supplements the census in the following way. The census is pretty much restricted to identifying familial relationships at the household level. We do not know, from the 1911 census, whether "business girls" sent money "home" to another household. Synge's interviews, however, suggest that such practice was extremely common in this era.[18] It might be inferred, then, that working women with life insurance were providers for more than simply themselves, even if they did not live in a nuclear setting, and that the life insurance they held provided the possibility of support for others in the event of their death.

As table 16.3 shows, female heads of household represented only a small proportion of the women with insurance. But, as a group, female heads with children were more likely than most other women to insure themselves, presumably to leave some legacy to their dependants; of urban female heads of household with children, 16% purchased insurance for themselves compared with just over 10% for all urban women.

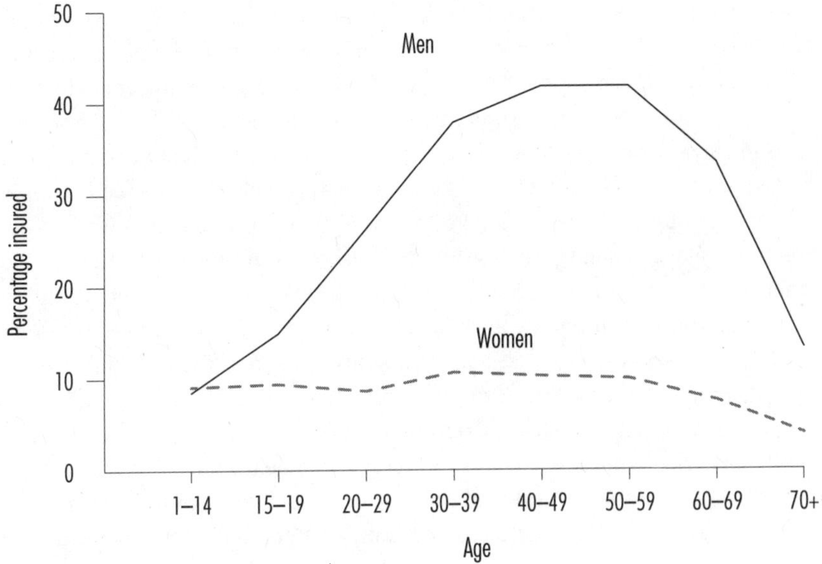

Figure 16.4 · Life insurance policyholders in Canada: Gender and age, 1911.

Sources: CCRI 1911 microdata database.

It is interesting, too, that the average age of an insured woman was quite a bit younger than that of an insured man. As figure 16.4 indicates, the age distribution for men follows a well-documented hump shape with the odds of having life insurance changing over the course of the life cycle.[19] There is a hint of such a process for women, as well. Perhaps the most interesting observation, however, relates to the chances of having life insurance before the age of 15. Just about one in ten urban children in Canada had life insurance in 1911. Perhaps even more interesting is the fact that the chances of having life insurance at the ages 1 to 14 are slightly greater for female than for male children. Parents were virtually gender blind when they insured their children. Why, before the age of puberty, would a female have been worth at least as much as a male?

To answer this question one must address a slightly broader query and that is why would children's lives be insured in the first place? Some thought that it was in order to murder them for the money. In the opinion of the *Globe*, "any life insurance other than on the supporter of a family has a questionable appearance." "In England," the *Globe*'s editorialist pointed out in March 1895, "within the past ten years, where child insurance was allowed to have full sway, many murders of innocent children have been brought to light, and these crimes were shown to have been committed simply for the gain of four or five pounds … In Ontario the law at present sanctions child insurance and it is a question if it would not be wise to put a stop to the business before it acquires a firm hold and before any serious case arises calling for active measures."[20] By the time of the 1906 Royal Commission on Life Insurance, legislation had been passed in Ontario – which was copied in other provincial jurisdictions – that set limits to the worth of policies on children up to the age of 10 years and only allowed parents to take out such policies on children who were more than a year old. Nonetheless, the commissioners were eager to learn all they could about industrial insurance and especially children's insurance. The commission discovered that London Life devoted half its resources to that line of insurance and found it to be very profitable. One commissioner wondered if "child insurance is an incentive to neglect of children by parents who are viciously inclined?"[21] Another worried whether "it tends to increase the death rate with the children insured?" One company representative thought such an idea to be "simply ridiculous."[22] Another, John Richter, from London Life, replied that since the law restricted the amount of the insurance that one could purchase, "dangerous results" were prevented. If, however, there were no limits then Richter was not as confident: "any good thing was capable of abuse" and the companies had no way of constructing reliable death tables for that class of insurance since the children were inspected rather than medically examined.[23]

Current literature argues that children's insurance appealed more to the working class than the middle class primarily because the insurance could ensure a decent burial.[24] "It is principally and was primarily a burial insurance," one insurance representative informed the MacTavish Commission in 1906.[25] The supposition was, Senator Tilley affirmed, "that the industrial insurance is placed on children who for the most part reside in the poorer parts of the city" and whose domestic condition "is not on a very high plane."[26] However, this hypothesis has yet to be tested with disaggregated data. So, the first question to answer is: who was most likely to insure their children?

Figure 16.5 (opposite, above) · Workforce status of families with insured children under 15 years of age: Employer, employee, or self-employed, Canada, 1911.

Sources: CCRI 1911 microdata database.

Figure 16.6 (opposite, below) · Employee-headed families with insured children under 15 years of age in relation to level of income (deciles), Canada, 1911.

Sources: CCRI 1911 microdata database.

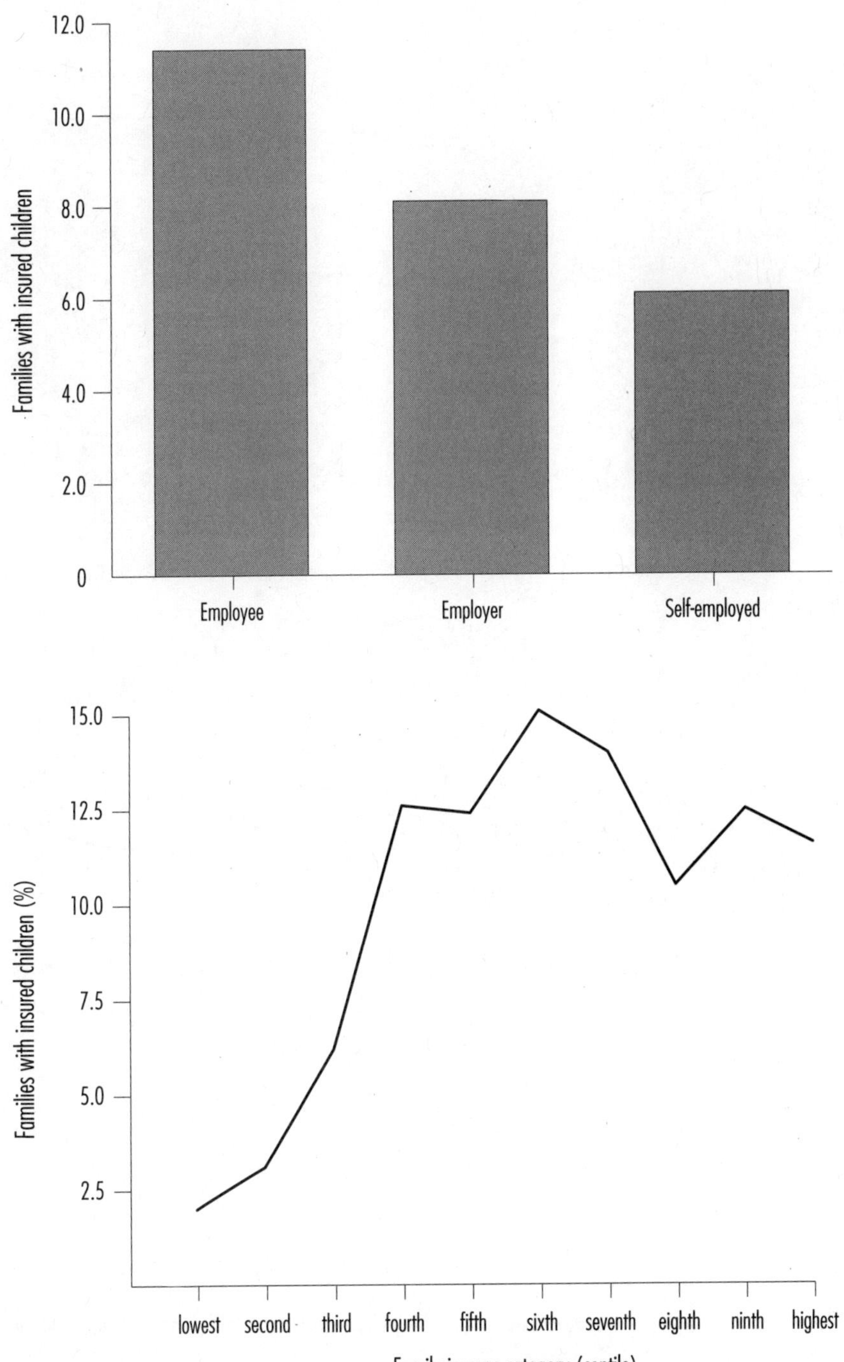
12.0
10.0
8.0
6.0
4.0
2.0
0
Families with insured children
Employee
Employer
Self-employed
15.0
12.5
10.0
7.5
5.0
2.5
Families with insured children (%)
lowest
second
third
fourth
fifth
sixth
seventh
eighth
ninth
highest
Family income category (centile)

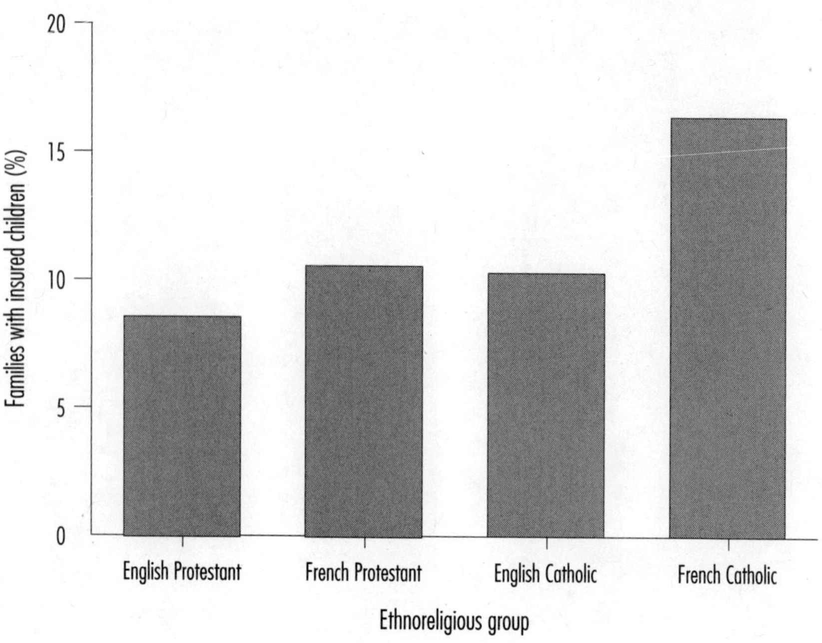

Families with insured children (%)
20
15
10
5
0
English Protestant
French Protestant
English Catholic
French Catholic
Ethnoreligious group

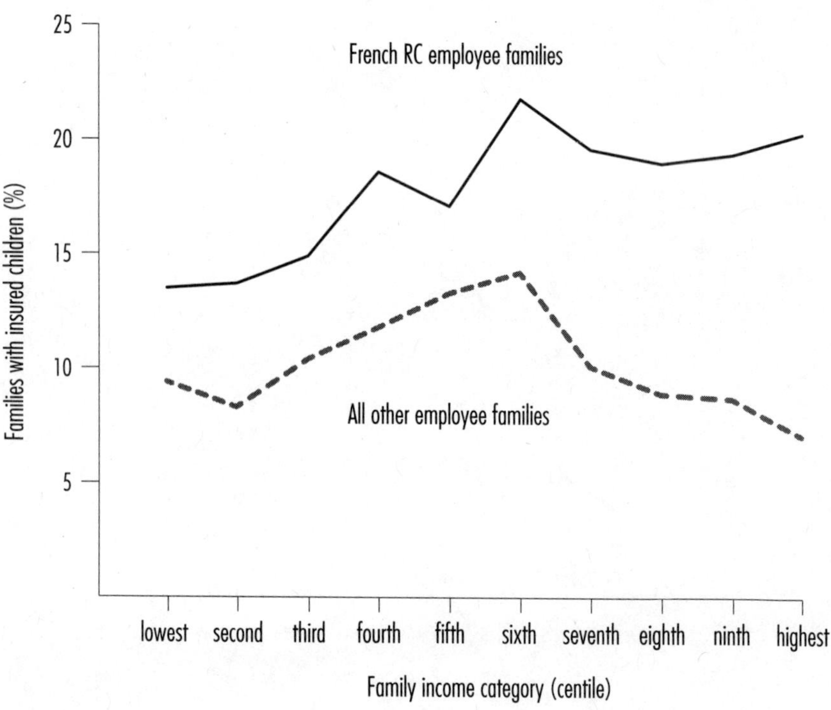

Families with insured children (%)
25
20
15
10
5
French RC employee families
All other employee families
lowest
second
third
fourth
fifth
sixth
seventh
eighth
ninth
highest
Family income category (centile)

The 1911 census asked whether one was an employer, employee, or self-employed. As figure 16.5 demonstrates, clearly, employees were most likely to insure their children and to that extent current literature is confirmed. But, income levels varied greatly among employees. Some working-class families were quite well off. So, then, were poor employees the ones who mainly insured their children – presumably to ensure a proper burial? The 1911 census provides information on the incomes of (primarily) employees. Using that information, figure 16.6 shows the relationship between family income of employee-headed families and insuring children; family income refers to the total of all income earned by members of the nuclear family living in the household.[27] Here we find evidence that somewhat refines current views: employees with middling family incomes were the most likely to insure their children, while those closer to the bottom were the least likely to do so. Clearly, infant insurance appealed primarily to those in income categories that one would assume were themselves sufficient to ensure a decent church burial. Income levels are useful for predicting who might be most likely to insure their children but not in the way formulated in the current literature.

Class and income characteristics go some way to determining who insured their children. As the data in figure 16.7 suggest, however, a possibly more powerful determinant was of a cultural nature. The odds of insuring one's children varied significantly according to ethnoreligious affiliation. The results are really quite intriguing. French Roman Catholic families were about two times more likely to insure their children than were English Protestant families.

When, as in figure 16.8, we compare income status and tendency to insure for French Catholics and others, we find quite different profiles especially on the tail where the higher-income families resided. No matter the income group, French Catholic families were more apt than other families to insure their younger offspring. As well, figure 16.8 suggests that income levels did not seem to matter as much for the tendency of French Catholics to insure children as they did for non–French Catholic families.

Figure 16.7 (opposite, above) · All urban families with insured children under 15 years of age in relation to ethnoreligious group (English Protestant, French Protestant, English Catholic, French Catholic), Canada, 1911. This figure is based on all families, not just employee-headed families.

Sources: CCRI 1911 microdata database.

Figure 16.8 (opposite, below) · Employee-headed families with insured children under 15 years of age in relation to level of income (deciles): French Catholic and all others, Canada, 1911.

Sources: CCRI 1911 microdata database.

Table 16.4 · Demographic characteristics of insured/not insured children (under 15 years of age) and household heads (HH) of families with children insuring/not insuring their children, Canada, 1911: Logistic regression of odds

Variables	*Children under 15 years*	*Families with children under 15/ household head*
	Log odds of being insured	*Log odds of insuring young child*
CITY POPULATION	*	*
2000–10,000	0.7 *	0.7
10,001–50,000	1.1 *	1.2 *
50,001–100,000	1.1 *	1.1 *
Ref. cat.: 100,000+		
SEX	*	*
Female	1.1 *	2.0 *
Ref. cat.: Men		
ETHNORELIGIOUS GROUP	*	*
Irish Catholics	1.1 *	1.1 *
Other English Catholics	1.2 *	1.4 *
French Protestants	0.2 *	1.6 *
French Catholics	2.1 *	2.0 *
Ref. cat.: English Protestants		
OCCUPATION CATEGORY: Household head	*	*
White-collar employee	2.3 *	1.7 *
White-collar employer	2.3 *	1.9 *
White-collar own-account	1.7 *	2.0 *
Blue-collar employee	2.4 *	2.1 *
Blue-collar employer	3.0 *	2.6 *
Ref. cat.: Blue-collar own account		

/continued

We could go on with a series of simple comparisons, but what we really want to know here is how powerful was ethnoreligion as a predictor of insuring children in the presence of all other socio-economic variables? To explore that we need to engage with multivariate analysis and especially with logistic regressions, which help to control for unbalanced numbers on the dependent variable, in this case, a small number of families with insured children versus a much larger number of families without insured children.

Table 16.4 shows the results of logistic regressions with all children under 15 years of age and all families with children under 15 years of age as the de-

Table 16.4 · continued

Variables	*Children under 15 years*	*Families with children under 15/ household head*
	Log odds of being insured	*Log odds of insuring young child*
FAMILY EARNINGS CATEGORY (centile)	*	*
Lowest tenth	2.3 *	1.3 *
Second	2.3 *	1.3 *
Third	0.9 *	1.3 *
Fourth	1.9 *	1.8 *
Fifth	1.4 *	1.7 *
Sixth	1.8 *	2.1 *
Seventh	1.4 *	1.6 *
Eighth	1.3 *	1.4 *
Ninth	1.1 *	1.3 *
Ref. cat.: Highest tenth		
RATIO OF DEPENDANTS TO EARNERS IN FAMILY	1.1 *	1.3 *
SCHOOL/EMPLOYMENT STATUS	*	—
Unemployed not in school	1.0	
Employed not in school	1.7 *	
Ref. cat.: in school		

Source: CCRI 1911 microdata database.

Note: The occupational categories have been constructed using the relationship to means questions on the 1911 census: whether one was an employer, employee, or on "own account" (self-employed). Blue-collar employees were generally trades and factory workers; white-collar employees were generally office and professional workers. Dependants in a family refer to members of the nuclear family who, according to the 1911 census returns, were not working outside the household. Earners were members of the nuclear family who were recorded as working outside the household. Standard errors of the B coefficient are used to evaluate the statistical significance of the independent variables, and changes in the likelihood estimates were used to determine whether the inclusion of a given variable improves the fit of the model.

Not significant means $p > .05$; * $p < .02$; ** p between .02 and .05.

pendent variables. The size of the urban area mattered most in the smallest of communities, where people were the least likely to insure their children. These communities of from 2,000 to 10,000 inhabitants were the closest to farming areas and, indeed, the number of farmers living in them, not surprisingly, was higher than for the other sized communities in the regression. As we have seen, rural families were the least likely of all to insure their children, and the city variable confirms that observation. The logistic run for children under 15 confirmed the small tendency to insure female children more often than male

Table 16.5 · Demographic characteristics of insured/not insured household heads (HH) of non-French Roman Catholic (RC) families with children (under 15 years of age) and of household heads of French Roman Catholic families with children insuring/not insuring their young children, Canada, 1911: Logistic regression of odds with children insured/not insured as the dependent variable

Variables	*Non-French Roman Catholic families with children under 15/household head*	*French Roman Catholic families with children under 15/household head*
	Log odds of being insured	*Log odds of insuring young child*
CITY POPULATION	*	*
2000–10,000	0.5 *	1.0
10,001–50,000	0.9	1.8 *
50,001–100,000	1.1 *	1.0
Ref. cat.: 100,000+		
SEX	*	*
Female	2.0 *	2.8 *
Ref. cat.: Men		
ETHNORELIGIOUS GROUP	*	*
Irish Catholics	1.1 *	
Other English Catholics	1.4 *	
French Protestants	1.6 *	
Ref. cat.: English Protestants		
OCCUPATION CATEGORY: Household head	*	*
White-collar employee	1.3 *	3.0 *
White-collar employer	1.2 *	3.1 *
White-collar own account	1.4 *	3.2 *
Blue-collar employee	1.8 *	2.6 *
Blue-collar employer	1.8 *	4.1 *
Ref. cat.: Blue-collar own account		

/continued

children. This finding confirms what the simple cross-tabulation in figure 16.3 suggests: knowing the child's sex is of little help in predicting whether that child had life insurance. The ethnoreligious category is fairly flat in both runs except that French Catholics were about twice as likely as English Protestants to insure their children. In the presence of a number of other characteristics, the exceptional tendency of French Catholics to insure their children continues to stand out. Might this mean that the Catholic religion prized children more than other religions did? I am not aware of literature on this issue, but work

Table 16.5 · continued

Variables	*Non-French Roman Catholic families with children under 15/household head*	*French Roman Catholic families with children under 15/household head*
	Log odds of being insured	*Log odds of insuring young child*
FAMILY EARNINGS CATEGORY (centile)	*	*
Lowest tenth	1.6*	0.8
Second	1.5*	0.9
Third	1.6*	0.9
Fourth	2.1*	1.3*
Fifth	2.3*	1.1
Sixth	2.4*	1.6*
Seventh	1.8*	1.3*
Eighth	1.5*	1.3*
Ninth	1.4*	1.3*
Ref. cat.: Highest tenth		
RATIO OF DEPENDANTS TO EARNERS IN FAMILY	1.4*	1.2*

Source: CCRI 1911 microdata database.

Note: The table is based on all families, not just employee-headed families.

Not significant (ns) means $p > .05$; ns removed from the equation using the backward stepwise likelihood ratio procedure; * $p < .02$; ** p between .02 and .05.

has been done on Methodists and their changing view of children towards a more affective emotional bonding, and indeed, Methodists were the second most likely to insure their children in urban Canada in 1911.[28] The findings with regard to income confirm that middle- to upper middle-income earners most often insured their children. Interestingly, however, it did make a difference if a family had a relatively high number of dependants to earners: in those families, children were more often insured perhaps to safeguard income. Relatedly, it mattered whether or not a child was employed or in school; the logistic regression was run for ages 7–14 and 1–14, and the results were the same for school/employment status. Those who were out of school and employed were 1.7 times more likely to be insured than those who were in school.

It is instructive to compare the odds of non–French Catholic families insuring their children compared with French Catholic families (see table 16.5). Would the same set of factors explain the tendency to insure in both groups?

The answer is "No." Those French Catholic families who insured their children bulked in small to lower medium-sized cities, whereas other families were spread widely over all city sizes except for those under 10,000. There is a different profile for occupational categories: the tendency for French Catholic families to insure children is strong across occupational categories; for non–French Catholic families, this relationship is relatively weak. It is at present not clear why French Canadian Catholic blue-collar self-employed workers did not insure their children to an extent comparable with other French Catholics. Very interestingly, the two variables that measure aspects of wealth are, in the case of French Catholic families, relatively undramatic.

Two related logistic regressions were run with insured/not insured children as the dependent variable (as per table 16.4) selecting for just French Catholic children, and in a second regression, all other children.[29] Although proportionately more of the French Catholic children than other children were in the workforce (2.9% vs. 2.0%), the regression on French Catholic children discarded both the school/employment variable and the dependant-to-earner ratio as not significant. French Catholic families did not insure children for primarily economic reasons. The run with all other (non–French Catholic) children included both the school/employment and the dependant-to-earner ratio variables as relatively quite significant: children who were employed and not in school were two times more likely to be insured than children in school (sig .00); the dependant-to-earner ratio was 1.2 and significant at the .05 level. For these families, the insurable worth of children was closely related to economic measures. Put simply, wealth was not a significant a predictor of the odds of a French Catholic family insuring their children, and the reverse was very much the case for non–French Canadian families.

Discussion

Children

Our descriptive analysis has uncovered a fair amount concerning who was most apt to insure their children in early twentieth-century urban Canada. French Catholic children represented 43 per cent of all insured children but only 27 per cent of all children under the age of 15. The question is: why were French Catholic families so much more likely to insure their children than families of all other ethnoreligious groups in urban Canada? Economic and class issues seem not to be a sufficient explanation. One strong possibility is that they insured them because their children were relatively the most likely to die and that the insurance would provide a proper burial for those children. There are compelling reasons to run with this explanation. Much work has been done on infant death in Canada (and elsewhere), and the findings are clear that French Catholic children weré, indeed, more likely to die than children of other families. In Montreal, at the beginning of the twentieth century, one-quarter of all babies died before their first birthday, and the death rate for French Catholic babies was 42 per cent higher than for Irish Catholics or Anglo-Protestants.[30] Investigations of death rates have found that economic contexts account for little variation. That would be consistent with the flat spread across family income levels of insured French Catholic children. Research has well established that cultural explanations for differential infant deaths, reinforced by degree of cultural segregation, provide the most compelling explanations. It is hard to test cultural segregation using the 5% CCRI sample, but in Montreal's six census districts where French Catholics were a simple majority, the tendency for people to insure their children was generally higher than in those districts where another ethnoreligious group was the larger. Length of breastfeeding was perhaps the most important cultural behaviour affecting infant death rates. French Catholic mothers gave up breastfeeding more quickly than Protestant mothers and more quickly even than Irish Catholic mothers. Milk was not pasteurized at this time, and the earlier a baby was weaned the greater the risk of death from unsafe milk. All of these general factors sit well with the propensity of French Catholics to insure their children.[31]

There are, however, reasons for not resting content at this point. In the first place, we are comparing aggregate numbers (death rates and rates of insurance), and as such, the analysis is susceptible to the dangers of ecological fallacy. At a more concrete level, insurance companies were quite content to ignore children under the age of one year for the very good reason that those were the children most apt to die. If a child survived to age one, than his or her odds of living longer increased, although it was not until about the age of 5 that the threat of childhood death eased significantly.

What is interesting in our data is that the frequency of insurance by year for those under 15 increased somewhat over time. Indeed, a logistic regression run with ages for those under 15 divided into five categories showed that the older the child was the greater the odds of being insured. Interestingly, this finding undercuts much "informed" opinion in the early twentieth century. Various insurance experts and concerned social workers argued that the "volume of business" came in the younger years. As C.G. Harvey of the Union Life Insurance Company told the Royal Commission on Insurance, "probably there is more insurance at the first age of the table than at any other age."[32] Social workers, naturally, would emphasize that presumed truth simply because insuring at such a young and vulnerable age fed the fears of child murders by "vicious parents." Here we are confronted with a possible problem with the census as a source.

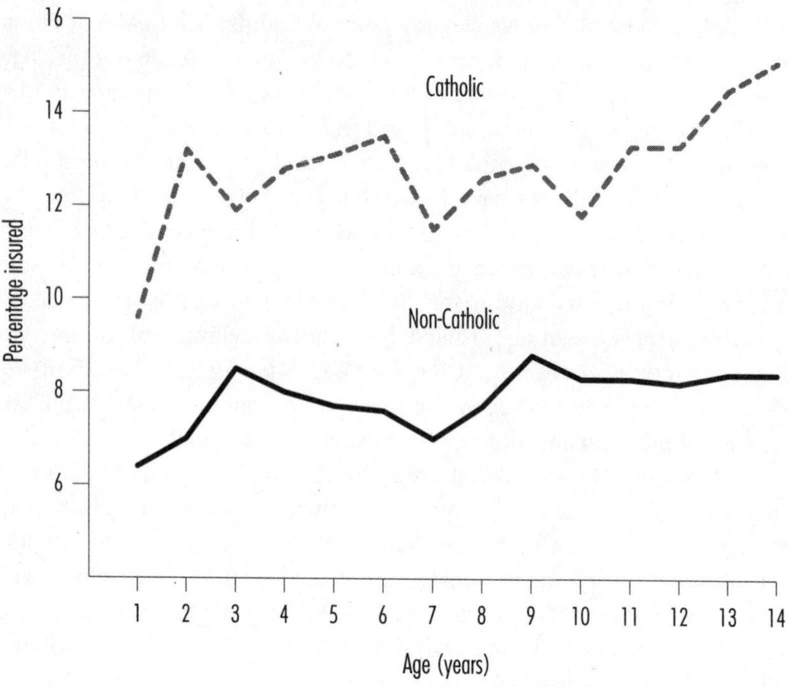

Figure 16.9 · Insured children of urban families, by age: French Catholic and all other families, Canada, 1911. *Sources*: CCRI 1911 microdata database.

Testimony at the MacTavish Commission from insurance representatives was fairly consistent on stating that the younger ages were more often insured. The census does not support those comments. In the face of negative social commentary on insuring the very young, some mothers may have been reluctant to admit to insuring their youngest children, and as a result, the census might undercount the extent of insurance at younger ages. Access to insurance company files would seem to be the only way to resolve this issue.

As figure 16.9 reveals, the trend towards insuring older children was most marked for French Catholics. This trend suggests that there might be several reasons for insuring what we are calling children here (under 15 years of age). Those at younger ages were insured more to cover the costs of burials and those at older ages were insured more to provide a backup for earnings and work lost on death. A logistic regression run on children aged one to 9 threw out the ratio of dependants to earners and maintained the flat income findings, continuing to suggest that economic issues did not push the desire for insuring children at that age. A logistic regression run with only French Catholic children 10 to 14 years of age, while maintaining a flat income trend, did show a somewhat stronger probability for insuring as the number of dependants increased relative to the number of earners (Exp(B) = 1.2 SIG .05). This lends some support for the view that reasons changed over time for insuring children. An asset protection program might have underlay insuring children aged 10 and over. In fact, the tendency for upper age single teenagers (between the ages of 15 and 19) to be insured for both French Catholic and other families increased, as well, further supporting the economic argument.

There are other possibilities that might help explain why French Catholics were more likely to insure their children. Pope Leo XIII's social encyclical Rerum Novarum (On the Condition of the Working Classes, 1891) stressed to Catholics the benefits to be gained from the formation of voluntary and benefit associations. Following the encyclical, there was a sharp rise in Catholic voluntary and fraternal benefit societies.[33] Catholic benefit associations, no matter their size, were linked heavily to parishes and actively supported by the clergy.[34] Societies like the Catholic Mutual Benefit Society and other like-minded associations were woven into the fabric of parish culture.

This may well prove to be a fruitful line of research; however, benefit societies were not alone. Some insurance companies also courted Catholics, suggesting that they were aware of the propensity of Catholics to buy industrial insurance. One main-line insurance company even quoted "His Holiness Leo XIII on Life Insurance" in its advertisements. The same company, the Metropolitan, also established a system of free nursing advice for young mothers in Quebec and elsewhere.[35] Moreover, one would want to control for these Catholic benefit associations by investigating the degree to which they were more or less prolific than Protestant societies at this time. As well, the literature assessing the impact of the Rerum Novarum on social and labour activities in Quebec is at best contested. Some argue that it had little impact; others suggest that in some areas it had a more positive influence.[36] Finally, while the fact of clergy participation may prove to be a differentiating factor, we need to investigate operations at the parish level to be sure.

Certainly, parish priests abounded in Quebec: in 1890, there was one priest for every 510 Catholics in the province.[37] Moreover, from the perspective of parish activity, it is intriguing that almost one-quarter of French Catholic families with young children who lived in small to medium-sized communities – those large enough not to be dominated by farmers but small enough to maintain aspects of small town neighbourhood life – insured their children. As figure 16.10 demonstrates (and the logistic regression suggested in table 16.5) this incidence is far higher than for any other sized urban community.

If we just select Quebec, then 27.2 per cent of French Catholic families in communities with a population between 10,000 and 50,000 insured their

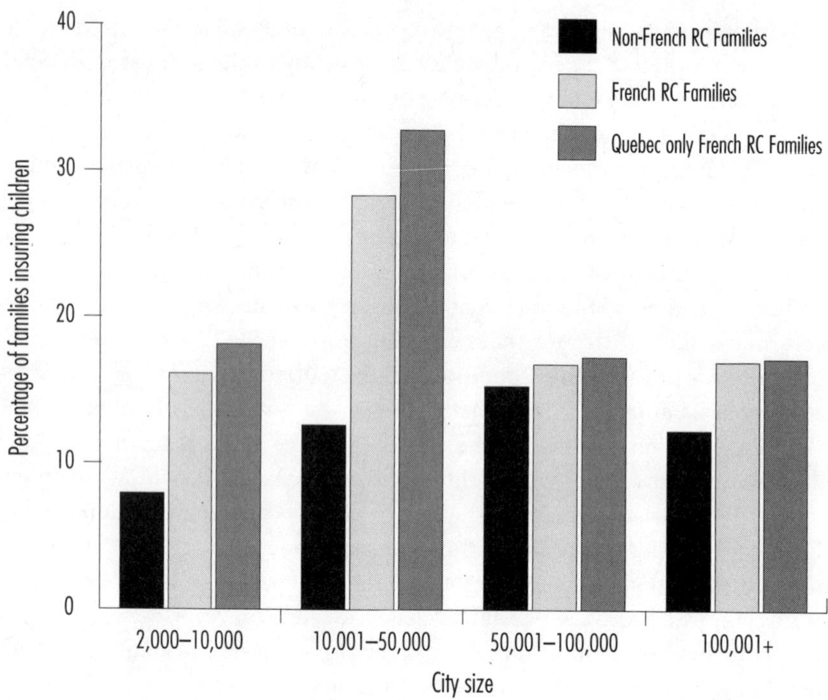

Figure 16.10 · Employee-headed families with insured children under 15 years of age in relation to size of city: Non-French Catholics (RC), French Catholics, and French Catholics in Quebec, 1911. RC = Roman Catholic.
Sources: CCRI 1911 microdata database

children, and if we just consider employee-headed French Catholic families in Quebec, the proportion insuring their children rises to over 30 per cent. In these moderately sized communities, the parish might have been a strong focal point for social activities and the clergy might have exercised a relatively greater degree of influence, both inside and outside of Quebec, than in larger, more dispersed urban environments.[38] One of the highest rates of such insurance was in Trois-Rivières (where 36% of French Catholic families insured their children), a diocese undergoing expansion under the energetic leadership of Monseigneur François-Xavier Cloutier, a person described by the diocese's historian as "le second fondateur du diocèse."[39] The Rerum Novarum encouraged the Church "to create new ways of promoting the interests of the poor" and perhaps infant insurance is one example of that encouragement.

Economic motives might also have prompted parish pressure to purchase burial insurance. Such pressure was of two sorts: top down and bottom up. In the nineteenth century, Catholic families were faced with increasing costs for burial-related expenses. Some insurance executives testified before the MacTavish Commission that even insurance payoffs were not sufficient to cover rising burial costs. Indeed, Catholic cemeteries seemed organized, in part, along the lines of ability to pay. In 1891, in Montreal, it cost about a year's salary for a skilled working man to purchase/lease the rights to a family plot for ninety-nine years in the Notre-Dame des Neiges cemetery. Catholic cemeteries did have areas for the burial of those who could not afford to pay, but such burials were for only five years and were denied the rites of commemoration.[40] The lighting of candles and conducting prayers also cost money. As early as the mid-nineteenth century, parishioners in Notre Dame in Montreal protested high burial costs and the denial of consecration for families who could not afford those expenses. One response from church officials was the introduction of burial societies, one of the most popular of which was L'Union de prières et de la bonne mort, established in the 1850s. By the late nineteenth century, for a fee of about 25 cents a year, a member in good standing could be buried at no cost, but the grave was granted for the short period of five years. Most people buried there were married women or widows, and there was another temporary section for children.[41] Burial societies and main-line company industrial insurance provided Catholic families the promise of at least a modest burial and parish officials the promise of some remuneration.

The dominant explanation for insuring children is one or a combination of the following: to have money to replace an income provider and/or to indicate a new appreciation for a child's life – the spread of a middle-class affective perspective with regard to raising children. This chapter suggests that both might have some explanatory power but, at the same time, other forces of an ethnocultural sort were operative, arguably independently of the other two causes and account for much of the tendency for insuring children. Ethnocultural beliefs and behaviours operated both directly and indirectly on the tendency to insure children. Infant deaths were relatively high in French Roman Catholic families because of a strong tendency to stop breastfeeding at an early age, thereby exposing babies to unpasteurized milk. The high incidence of death prompted a high rate of children's insurance, facilitating a decent burial and demonstrating the affection felt by parents towards their children. At the same time, parish priests may have encouraged the insuring of children and, in relatively small communities where a very high incidence of child insurance was in force, they may have been quite successful in their efforts.

Women

There may well be a link between the sale of insurance for children and the expansion of sales to women. Insurance companies advertised for women's business. As we have pointed out, "business girls" were purchasers of such insurance. Tellingly, an official in one large industrial company stated, "Many are first insured, as children, in the Industrial Department; then as they grow up and join the ranks of workers or housewives ... they ... graduate into the Ordinary Department."[42] Clearly, it made sense to insurance companies to insure youngsters, not simply in anticipation of immediate profits, but also in anticipation of insurance becoming a normal part of both a man's and a woman's life as they aged. Of all females aged over 15 (as with those under 15), none were more likely to have life insurance than single female French Catholics whether formally employed or not: one in ten of such urban women were insured compared with one in fourteen for the rest. They continued to be insured disproportionately to their numbers in the total population even after the age of 15. All other major religions were either underrepresented in the insured column compared with their proportion of the population or the variance was miniscule.

Insurance companies were not the only financial enterprises seeking women's business. Financial institutions courted women, assuring them that they would deal with them independently from their husbands. The Birbeck Loan and Savings Company of London, Ontario, set up local boards for women in Toronto and Ottawa in this period. Aemilius Jarvis and Company, a member of the Toronto Stock Exchange, openly advertised for the business of "the Woman Investor." "We are always glad to have women investors consult with us either personally or by letter," the company promised, "no matter how small the sum may be that they have to invest." By 1911, Ontario women were as apt to invest in bank stock and, yes, insurance stock, as their male counterparts. A "Business girl" wrote in an article in *Saturday Night,* in June 1912, "now-a-days ... stocks and bonds and property have become part and parcel of [the business girls'] life ... You will hear [mining stocks] discussed with such a familiarity as would make our grandmothers rise up in holy horror and wonder to what a pass the gentler sex has reached when they mingle with business men with a freedom unthought of in their day."[43]

Insurance companies were clearly aware of these trends. Far from stressing how insurance would protect dependants in the event of death, they stressed, instead, the advantages of insurance as an investment for women: offering "an income for life" and promising the security "of being independent." In what may have been an appeal to parents to purchase on their child's behalf, one company argued that "no greater service can be done to young persons of either sex than to teach them the value of a dollar and how they may ... best invest it for future needs." Rates were the same for men and women. A woman could independently from her husband set up a "pension" that could pay from $100 to $10,000 per year after age 45.[44] Having life insurance was marketed as a right and necessity for the modern independent woman.

It is important to underline that girls as well as boys under 10 years of age were insured to the virtually same extent and at the same cash value. There was no gender bias operative here. A cynic might comment that the cost of burial was the same and financial reasons, not an explicit recognition of gender equality, was what was really at work. Yet, that view is too quick by half. According girls the right to as dignified a burial as that for boys is symbolic of more than a generalized appreciation for what Zelizer and others term the "priceless" child. The fact that, in this context, girls were not second-class citizens is potentially quite significant. As we have briefly suggested here, the late nineteenth and early twentieth centuries in Canada and elsewhere in the British North American world was a time of great change for women in economic and financial matters, as well as a time of great ferment for increased civil and political rights.[45] The marketing of insurance to women and children must be seen in that context. Not all girls who were insured died young. Most became adults and many of them, as we have seen, continued to insure themselves, thus, indicating in a tangible way a strong sense of self-worth and a desire to be financially independent. The purchase of insurance for children and by women is best seen as a symbolic marker of changing gendered behaviour in the public sphere.[46]

Notes

1 E.P. Neufield, *The Financial System of Canada: Its Growth and Development* (Toronto: MacMillan, 1972), 244–5; Canada, House of Commons, *Sessional Papers*, 1911, vol. 45, no. 4, Sessional Paper no. 8, Life Insurance Companies, v; *Canada Board of Inquiry into Cost of Living* (Ottawa: Government of Canada, 1915), 1015; quote from Toronto *Globe*, 13 March 1895, 4.

2 Louis Dublin, *A Family of Thirty Million: The Story of the Metropolitan Life Insurance Company* (New York: Metropolitan Life Insurance Co., 1943); Canada, Report of the Royal Commission on Insurance, *Minutes of Evidence* (hereafter RCI) (Ottawa: Government of Canada, 1907), C.G. Harvey, Union Life, 1: 673; John Richter, London Life, 2: 1515–16. Toronto *Globe*, 21 Nov. 1901, 9, Crown Life Insurance Co.

3 Dublin, *A Family*, 466.

4 *Debates of the Senate of the Dominion of Canada* (Ottawa: Government of Canada); McClelan, 11 June 1895, 257.

5 Viviana Zelizer, "The Price and Value of Children: The Case of Children's Insurance," *American Journal of Sociology* 86, no. 5 (1981): 1036–56; Viviana Zelizer, *Pricing the Priceless Child: The Changing Social Value of Children* (New York: Basic Books, 1985).

6 Julie-Marie Strange, "'She Cried a Very Little': Death, Grief and Mourning in Working-Class Culture, 1880–1914," *Social History* 27, no. 2 (2002): 143–61.

7 This project was funded by the Canada Foundation for Innovation and the provinces of British Columbia, Ontario, Quebec, and Newfoundland and Labrador. For an overview of the Canadian Century Research Infrastructure project, see the special issue of *Historical Methods: A Journal of Quantitative and Interdisciplinary History* 40, no. 2 (2007): 54–103, and the two introductory chapters to this volume.

8 *Report of the Royal Commission on Life Insurance*, passim. *Globe*, 27 Feb. 1907, 4.

9 The instructions to the enumerator emphasized that if a person "'male or female' carries insurance upon his or her life, whether in an 'old line company' an assessment company or fraternal organization the total value of the policies in force at June 1 1911 will be entered." Canada, Department of Agriculture and Statistics, *Fifth Census of Canada, 1911: Instructions to Officers, Commissioners and Enumerators* (Ottawa: Government Printing Bureau, 1911), 37.

10 Memo on the Taking of the 1921 Census, not dated (circa 1918), Canadian Century Research Infrastructure Project, Archives, University of Alberta.

11 For the high-end estimate, see Jason Kaufman, "The Political Economy of Interdenominational Competition in Late Nineteenth-Century American Cities," *Journal of Urban History* 28, no. 4 (2002): 463n18. A somewhat lower estimate is Don Doyle, "The Social Functions of Voluntary Associations in a Nineteenth-Century American Town," *Social Science History* 1, no. 3 (1977): 339, 352. David Beito, *From Mutual Aid to Welfare State: Fraternal Societies and Social Services* (Durham: University of North Carolina Press, 2000), 22, cautions that not every fraternal member had life insurance. Shawn Everett Kantor and Price V. Fishback, "Precautionary Saving, Insurance and the Origins of Workers' Compensation," *Journal of Political Economy* 104, no. 2 (1996): 425, give statistics relating to multiple policies within households. Dublin (*A Family*, 471) claims that a significant proportion of Metropolitan's policyholders owned insurance in other companies and fraternal societies. My thanks to George and Herb Emery for their comments on this issue.

12 Industrial policies rarely exceeded $500.

13 Canadian Century Research Infrastructure, On-line Contextual Database, http://ccri.library.ualberta.ca/. Prescott *Journal*, 18 May 1911, 1; Kingston *Daily Standard*, 7 June 1911, 2.

14 For an extended discussion of women's ability to manage money in this period, see Peter Baskerville, *A Silent Revolution? Gender and Wealth in English Canada, 1860–1930* (Montreal and Kingston: McGill-Queen's University Press, 2008).

15 According to Livio Di Matteo and Herb Emery ("Wealth and Demand for Life Insurance: Evidence from Ontario, 1892," *Explorations in Economic History* 39 [2002]: 455), 18% of men were insured in 1901. Of all men in the CCRI 1911 census sample, 16% were insured. This suggests a possible undercount in the census sample, especially since overall rates of insurance participation were increasing in this period.

16 *Globe*, 9 March 1895, 16; 16 Nov. 1895, 10; 4 April 1896, 4.

17 *Globe*, 25 Nov. 1911, 11.

18 Jane Synge, "The Transition from School to Work: Growing Up Working Class in Early 20th Century Hamilton, Ontario," in K. Ishwaran (ed.), *Childhood and Adolescence in Canada* (Toronto: McGraw-Hill, 1979).

19 Matteo and Emery, "Wealth and Demand."

20 *Globe*, 13 March 1895, 4; 2 July 1895, 4.

21 RCI, 2: 1515–16.

22 RCI, C.G. Harvey, 1: 654.

23 RCI, Richter, 2: 1516–17.

24 Zelizer, "The Price."

25 RCI, Harvey, 1: 649.

26 RCI, Tilley, 2: 1517.

27 Family income refers to the total of all income earned by members of the nuclear family living in the household.

28 Neil Semple, "'The Nurture and Admonition of the Lord': Nineteenth-Century Canadian Methodism's Response to Childhood," *Histoire sociale/Social History* 14 (1981): 157–75.

29 The regressions are available from the author.

30 Patricia Thornton and Sherry Olsen "A Deadly Discrimination among Montreal Infants, 1860–1900," *Continuity and Change* 16, no. 1 (2001): 127.

31 For Canadian literature on this issue, see Patricia Thornton and Sherry Olsen: "Family Contexts of Fertility and Infant Survival in Nineteenth-Century Montreal," *Journal of Family History* 16, no. 4 (1991): 401–17, and "A Deadly Discrimination," 95–135; Michael E. Mercier and Christopher G. Boone, "Infant Mortality in Ottawa, Canada, 1901: Assessing Cultural, Economic and Environmental Factors," *Journal of Historical Geography* 28, no. 4 (2002): 486–507; Denyse Baillargeon, *Babies for the Nation: The Medicalization of Motherhood in Quebec, 1910–1970* (Waterloo: Wilfrid Laurier Press, 2009), esp. 30–9. For an international literature, see Evelien C. Walhout, "Is Breast Best? Evaluating Breastfeeding Patterns and Causes of Infant Death in a Dutch Province in the Period 1875–1900," *History of the Family* 15 (2010): 76–90; Gunnar Thorvaldsen, "Was There a European Breastfeeding Pattern?" *History of the Family* 13 (2008): 283–95; Kwang-Sun Lee, "Infant Mortality Decline in the Late Nineteenth and Early Twentieth Centuries: The Role of Market Milk," *Perspectives in Biology and Medicine* 50, no. 4 (2007): 585–602; Frans Van Poppel, Iona Schellekens, and Aart C. Liefbroer, "Religious Differentials in Infant and Child Morality in Holland, 1855–1912," *Population Studies* 56 (2002): 277–89; Renzo Derosas, "Watch Out for the Children! Differential Infant Mortality of Jews and Catholics in Nineteenth-Century Venice," *Historical Methods* 36, no. 3 (2003): 130; Beatrice Morning, "Motherhood, Milk and Money: Infant Mortality in Pre-Industrial Finland," *Social History of Medicine* 11, no. 2 (1998): 177–96.

32 RCI 1: 649.

33 My thanks to Mark McGowan for pointing me in this direction.

34 For an example of a Catholic parish's involvement in burial societies, see John Belcham, "Priests, Publicans and the Irish Poor: Ethnic Enterprise and Migrant

Networks in Mid-Nineteenth Century Liverpool," *Immigrants and Minorities* 23, nos 2–3 (2005): 207–31.

35 Manufacturer's Life, *Globe*, 6 April 1895, 16. In fact, the connection was a bit of a stretch: the actual quote used in the advertisement referred to inheritance not life insurance per se. On nursing services, see Denyse Baillargeon, "Les rapports médecins-infirmières et l'implication de la Métropolitaine dans la lutte contre la mortalité infantile, 1909–1953," *Canadian Historical Review* 77, no. 1 (1999): 33–61, and Dublin, *A Family*, 430–1.

36 For a general and fairly positive overview, see John C. Super, "Rerum Novarum in Mexico and Quebec," *Revista de Historia de América* 126 (2000): 63–84. For more critical accounts, see Pierre Savard, "Rerum Novarum au Canada français: Des fruits tardifs et divers," in Richard Jean and Louis O'Nell (eds.), *La question sociale hier et aujourd'hui: Colloque du centenaire de Rerum novarum* (Sainte-Foy: Presses de L'Université Laval, 1993), passim.

37 Paul-André Linteau, René Durocher, and Jean-Claude Robert, *Histoire du Québec Contemporaine*, vol. 1 (Montreal: Boreal, 1989), 43.

38 One historian claimed that the city in Quebec was "the tomb of Quebec Catholicism," quoted in Savard, "Rerum Novarum," 81.

39 Jean Panneton, *Le diocèse de Trois-Rivières, 1852–2002* (Sillery: Septentrion, 2002), cited in Fernand Harvey, "Note Critique: L'historiographie diocèsaine recent au Québec," *Etudes d'histoire religieuse* 72 (2006): 99.

40 For literature on pauper burials in Great Britain, see Julie-Marie Strange, "'Only a Pauper Whom Nobody Owns': Reassessing the Pauper Grave, 1880–1914," *Past and Present* 178, no. 1 (2003): 148–75, and Elizabeth Hurren and Steve King, "'Begging for a Burial': Form, Function and Conflict in Nineteenth-Century Pauper Burial," *Social History* 30, no. 3 (2005): 321–41.

41 Meredith Watkins, "The Cemetery and Cultural Memory: Montreal, 1860–1900," *Urban History Review* 31, no. 1 (2002): 52–63. Petit manuel des Associés de l'union de prières et de la bonne mort, Montreal, 1873, http://cihm_04796/cihm_04796.pdf. Sherry Olsen provided many references and thoughtful direction.

42 Dublin, *A Family*, 464.

43 *Monetary Times*, 4 May 1894, 1386; *Saturday Night*, 17 May 1913, 18, and 8 June 1912, 29–30.

44 *Globe*, 9 March 1895, 16; 26 Oct. 1895, 19; 16 Nov. 1895, 10; 4 April 1896, 4.

45 Studies of bequeathment strategies on the part of urban fathers have determined that daughters as well as sons began to receive similarly sized bequests in this era. See Baskerville, *A Silent Revolution?* for a fuller discussion of women's financial and economic behaviour in this period.

46 Another, related symbolic marker is the fact that by the end of the nineteenth century women "were being referenced as individuals" on tombstones instead of being identified as the wife of Mr ... Meredith Watkins, "The Cemetery and Cultural Memory: Montreal Region," M.A. thesis, McGill University, 1999, 84–5.

CONTRIBUTORS

PETER BASKERVILLE holds a Research Chair in Modern Western Canadian History at the University of Alberta and is professor emeritus at the University of Victoria. He has written on 19th and 20th century Canadian gender, business, labour, and social history. He published *A Silent Revolution?: Gender and Wealth in English Canada, 1860–1930* with McGill-Queen's University Press, in 2008. He is currently writing a book on social relations in 19th and 20th century Perth County, Ontario.

CLAUDE BELLAVANCE has taught economic history at l'Université du Québec à Trois-Rivières since 1991. He is a member of the Centre interuniversitaire d'études québécoises, of which he was the director for many years. He participated in the construction of the IRCS-CCRI and is currently working on the development of the integrated infrastructure of historical microdata of the population of Quebec (1621–1965). His areas of specialization range from the history of electricity to urban history and to regional history. His latest book is titled *Histoire du Centre-du-Québec* (with Yvan Rousseau and Jean Roy; Presses de l'Université Laval, 2013).

SEAN T. CADIGAN is a professor in the Department of History, Memorial University, St. John's, Newfoundland and Labrador. His book *Newfoundland and Labrador: A History* (University of Toronto Press, 2009) won the J.W. Dafoe Book Prize in 2010. Cadigan's research focuses on the social, economic, and environmental history of fishing, forestry, and offshore oil and gas development in Newfoundland and Labrador. His latest book is *Death on Two Fronts: National Tragedies and the Fate of Democracy in Newfoundland, 1914–34* (Allen Lane Canada).

GORDON DARROCH is professor emeritus of sociology, York University. He is credited as being one of the pioneers in the development of national historical census micro-databases. He has authored historical studies on ethnic communities, social mobility and inequalities, families and households, and children's lives. A recent publication appeared in *Popolazione e Storia* (Italian Society of Historical Demography, 2010). He is currently writing a book on migration and mobility in 19th century Ontario.

LISA DILLON is an associate professor in the Département de démographie, Université de Montréal, and co-director of the Programme de recherche en démographie historique. Her research encompasses the populations of Quebec and Canada, from the 17th to the 20th centuries, and addresses fertility, marriage, kinship, living arrangements, and life course transitions. She is the author of *The Shady Side of Fifty: Age and Old Age in Late Victorian Canada and the United States* (MQUP, 2008); her current research addresses sibling influences on marriage and fertility, the living arrangements of single urban Canadians, social mobility, and longitudinal database development.

CHAD GAFFIELD is a professor of history at the University of Ottawa where he has been on leave since his appointment in 2006 as president of the Social Sciences and Humanities Research Council of Canada. His research focuses on the ways demographic, economic, and cultural changes have influenced, and been influenced by, institutional and political history. In addition to his role as principal investigator for the Canadian Century Research Infrastructure project (2002–08), Gaffield has led a variety of major research initiatives since the 1980s involving universities and partner organizations across Canada and internationally.

DANIELLE GAUVREAU is a professor in the Department of Sociology and Anthropology at Concordia University and is currently the director of the Quebec Interuniversity Centre for Social Statistics. Her interests in population studies and social history merge to address issues like the fertility transition and the baby boom in Quebec, adaptation of youth in industrializing Montreal, and the making of cultural diversity within Quebec. She is the author of *La fécondité des Québécoises, 1870–1970: D'une exception à l'autre* (coauthors Diane Gervais and Peter Gossage; Montréal, Boréal, 2007).

GUSTAVE GOLDMANN is an adjunct professor in the Faculty of Graduate Studies at the University of Ottawa. He is also an adjunct professor in the School of Public Policy and Administration at Carleton University. His fields of study include Aboriginal demography, the settlement and absorption of immigrants, and subjects related to ethnic groups and ethnic identity. He recently published chapters in *Challenges of Migration in Canada* (2013, Ertler and Imbert, editors), *The International Handbook on Rural Demography* (2012, Laszlo and Curtis, editors) and *The Changing Canadian Population* (2011, Fong and Edmonston, editors) on these topics.

ADAM JAY GREEN is the acting director of research at the Canadian Security Intelligence Review Committee, and is an adjunct professor of history at the University of Ottawa. His academic interests include Canadian identity, Canadian-American relations, the Social Gospel, and Canada in the 1960s. He has published in various academic journals on each of these topics.

KRIS INWOOD is professor of economics and of history at the University of Guelph. His interests extend to the economic history of labour markets, productivity, physical well-being, and the reconstruction of population from individual records. He recently published (with M. Hamilton) "The Aboriginal Population and the 1891 Census of Canada," in P. Axelsson and P. Skold, eds., *Indigenous Peoples and Demography: The Complex Relation Between Identity and Statistics* (Berghahn, 2011).

CHARLES JONES is a professor of sociology at the University of Toronto. He has a long-standing interest in families, social mobility, and the sociology of occupations. Most recently he has been analyzing data from Canada's National Longitudinal Survey of Children and Youth. He is currently working on the use of sample data from past censuses (1871 to 2006) from Canada and other countries to test hypotheses related to family, gender, and migration, as well as work and occupations. His interests are illustrated in books such as *The Images of Occupational Prestige*, *Lives of Their Own*, and *The Futures of the Family.*

MARY MacKINNON (d. 2010) was professor of economics at McGill University, Montreal. She was an economic historian who wrote primarily about labour markets and economic policy in Canada and the United Kingdom between 1860 and 1939. She published the influential collection *Labour Market Evolution* (Routledge, 1994, with George Grantham) and was the author of numerous articles including "English Poor Law and the Crusade Against Outrelief" (*Journal of Economic History*, 1987) and "New Evidence on Canadian Wage Rates, 1900–1930" (*Canadian Journal of Economics*, 1996).

RICHARD MARCOUX, a professor of demography at the University Laval (Sociology Dept.), concentrates his research work on African social demography while co-directing the Population et histoire sociale de la ville de Québec project with Marc St-Hilaire. Relating to this field of research, he has authored many articles on child labour and demographic transformations in Quebec City. He recently edited *Mémoires et démographie: Regards croisés au Sud et au Nord* (Presses de l'Université Laval, 2009) and co-edited *Villes du Sud: Dynamiques, diversités et enjeux démographiques et sociaux* (Éditions des archives contemporaines, 2009).

CHRIS MINNS is senior lecturer in economic history at the London School of Economics and Political Science. His main research interests are in the operation of labour markets in history, with particular emphasis on migration, education, and training in the past. He has recently published "The Price of Human Capital in a Pre-industrial Economy: Premiums and Apprenticeship Contracts in 18th Century England" (*Explorations in Economic History*, 2013, with Patrick Wallis).

BYRON MOLDOFSKY is the manager of the GIS and Cartography Office in the Department of Geography, University of Toronto. He was the production coordinator for the Historical Atlas of Canada from 1983 to 1993, and was the University of Toronto project coordinator for the geography team of the CCRI. He has worked widely on GIS and atlas projects in Canada, both historical and contemporary, and recently published another chapter about the CCRI in *Historical GIS Research in Canada, Calgary* (University of Calgary Press, 2013).

FRANCE NORMAND is a professor of social and economic history at l'Université du Québec à Trois-Rivières and a researcher at the Centre interuniversitaire d'études québécoises (CIEQ). Her research interests cover maritime history, population history, and the history of the family. She is currently involved in the development of the integrated infrastructure of historical microdata of the population of Quebec (1621–1965). She recently published "Une vocation maritime pour les populations littorales de l'estuaire et du golfe du Saint-Laurent à la fin du XIXe siècle?" in N. Landry, J. Péret and T. Sauzeau, *Développement comparé des littoraux du golfe du St-Laurent et du Centre-Ouest français* (Institut d'études acadiennes, 2012), 85–97.

STELLA PARK is a project manager/research associate at the Mowat Centre, School of Public Policy and Governance at the University of Toronto. Her fields of research include immigration, labour market, non-profit sector, and health.

She has published in the *Canadian Review of Social Policy, Canadian Journal on Aging, Toronto Star, Canadian Diversity*, and *Toronto Immigrant Employment Data Initiative (TIEDI)* analytical reports. She completed her MA and PhD coursework in sociology at the University of Toronto.

TERRY QUINLAN is senior statistician with the Government of Newfoundland and Labrador Statistics Agency and CCRI Coordinator for Atlantic Canada. He led the technical team that developed the System of Community Accounts, a web-based data-sharing infrastructure within a well-being model framework. This garnered both the Government of Newfoundland and Labrador Public Service Award of Excellence (2002) and the National IPAC Award for Innovative Management (2003). He created a provincewide automated genealogy system for genetic research at Memorial University, for which he won a second Public Service Award (2009).

LAURENT RICHARD has been a research professional at l'Université Laval since 2000. He is one of the former CCRI project coordinators, and also worked at Statistics Canada as an analyst. GIS, data analysis, and IT-related projects are his main fields of research. He is currently associated with the works of the Observatoire démographique et statistique de l'espace francophone (ODSEF), directed by Richard Marcoux, and of the Population et histoire sociale de la ville de Québec project (PHSVQ).

KATHARINE ROLLWAGEN is an L.R. Wilson Assistant Professor in Canadian History at McMaster University. Her research examines the social and cultural influence of corporate entities, from her current work on the impacts of consumer culture and employment on youth to earlier research on notions of gender, class, and community in Canadian company towns. She is currently revising her thesis, "The Market That Just Grew Up: How Eaton's Fashioned the Teenaged Consumer in Mid-Twentieth-Century Canada," for publication.

EVELYN S. RUPPERT is a senior lecturer and director of research in the Department of Sociology, Goldsmiths, University of London, and from 2008 to 2013 was a senior research fellow at the Centre for Research on Socio-cultural Change (CRESC), a collaboration between the Open University and the University of Manchester. She is a data sociologist and her research focuses on how different methods and digital data are constituted and mobilized to know and manage populations. Ruppert is also a founding editor of the Sage journal, *Big Data & Society: Critical Interdisciplinary Inquiries.*

ERIC W. SAGER is a professor of history at the University of Victoria. He has written two books about the history of the shipping industry in Atlantic Canada. He was director of the Canadian Families Project (1996–2002), which created a national sample of the 1901 population census of Canada. His work with Canadian census microdata has yielded two coauthored books and articles on domestic servants, women teachers, and immigrants.

MARC ST-HILAIRE is a professor of geography at l'Université Laval. His work deals with Northeastern American historical geography and more specifically relates to population geography (19th and 20th centuries). He recently co-edited *Les traces de la Nouvelle-France au Québec et en Poitou-Charentes* (Presses de l'Université Laval, 2008) and *La francophonie nord-américaine* (Atlas historique du Québec, Presses de l'Université Laval, 2012), and is currently co-editing with Claude Bellavance another volume of the Atlas historique du Québec dedicated to Quebec's urbanization.

PATRICIA THORNTON is professor emerita in the Department of Geography, Planning and Environment at Concordia University. Her research has focused on the extent and impact of outmigration from Canada during the second half of the 19th century, on infant mortality and environmental health and justice in Montreal, on the persistence of cultural differences in demographic behaviour, and on intermarriage and cultural diversity in Quebec. She is coauthor, with Sherry Olson, of *Peopling the North American City: Montreal 1840–1900* (McGill-Queen's University Press, 2011).

INDEX

Page numbers in italics refer to figures and tables.